Genghis Khan

France and the Jacobite Rising of 1745

The Jacobite Army in England

The Jacobites

Invasion: From the Armada to Hitler

Charles Edward Stuart

Crime and Punishment in Eighteenth-Century England

Stanley: The Making of an African Explorer

Snow Upon the Desert: The Life of Sir Richard Burton

From the Sierras to the Pampas:
Richard Burton's Travels in the Americas, 1860–69

Stanley: Sorcerer's Apprentice

Hearts of Darkness: The European Exploration of Africa

Fitzroy Maclean

Robert Louis Stevenson

C. G. Jung

Napoleon

1066: The Year of Three Battles

Villa and Zapata

Wagons West: The Epic Story of America's Overland Trails

1759: The Year Britain Became Master of the World

Lionheart and Lackland: King Richard, King John
and the Wars of Conquest

Heroes and Villains

Marcus Aurelius: Philosopher, Emperor

The Burma Campaign

The Road Not Taken: How Britain Narrowly Missed a Revolution

Genghis Khan

His Conquests, His Empire, His Legacy

FRANK McLYNN

DA CAPO PRESS

Cataloging-in-Publication data for this book is available from the Library of Congress.

First Da Capo Press edition 2015
First Da Capo Press paperback edition 2016
Reprinted by arrangement with Bodley Head, an imprint of Vintage Publishing
ISBN: 978-0-306-82395-4 (hardcover)
ISBN: 978-0-306-82517-0 (paperback)
ISBN: 978-0-306-82396-1 (e-book)
LCCN: 2015939688

Published by Da Capo Press
an imprint of Perseus Books,
a division of PBG Publishing, LLC, a subsidiary of Hachette Book Group, Inc.
www.dacapopress.com

Da Capo Press books are available at special discounts for bulk purchases in the U.S. by corporations, institutions, and other organizations. For more information, please contact the Special Markets Department at the Perseus Books Group, 2300 Chestnut Street, Suite 200, Philadelphia, PA 19103, or call (800) 810-4145, ext. 5000, or e-mail special.markets @perseusbooks.com.

LSC-C
10 9 8 7 6 5 4 3

To the four important
Ladies in my life:
Pauline, Julie, Lucy, Ellen.

Contents

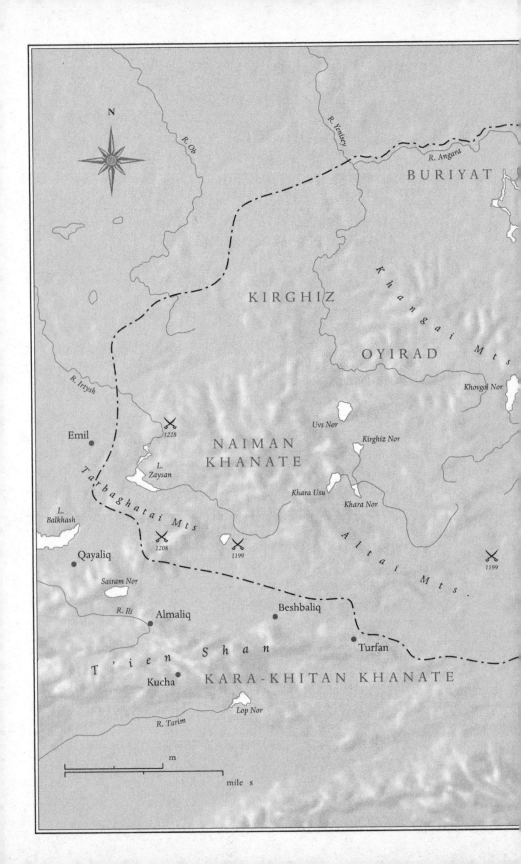

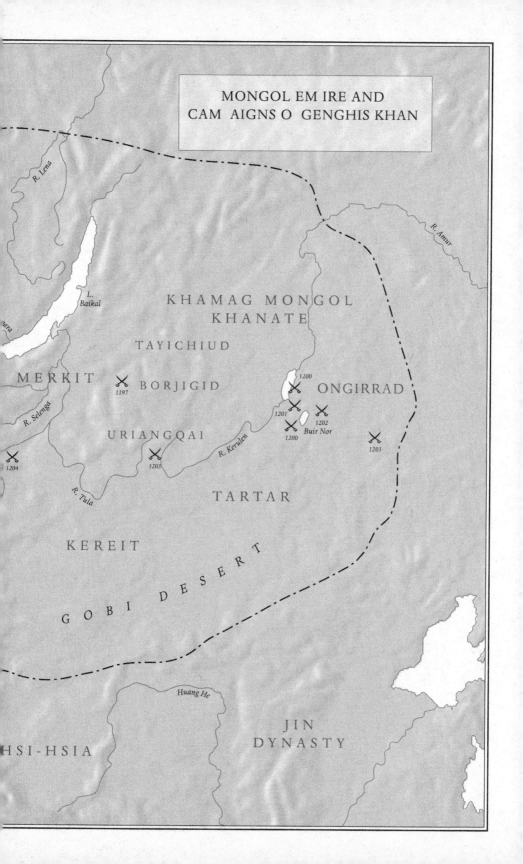

MONGOL EM IRE AND
CAM AIGNS O GENGHIS KHAN

R. Lena

R. Amur

L.
Baikal

KHAMAG MONGOL
KHANATE

TAYICHIUD

MERKIT   BORJIGID   ✗   ONGIRRAD
            ✗   1200
            1197
R. Selenga   ✗
                        1201   ✗
                             ✗   1202
URIANGQAI   1200   Buir Nor
✗   ✗   ✗
1204   1203   R. Kerulen   1203

R. Tula   TARTAR

KEREIT

        G O B I   D E S E R T

Huang He

HSI-HSIA   JIN
                  DYNASTY

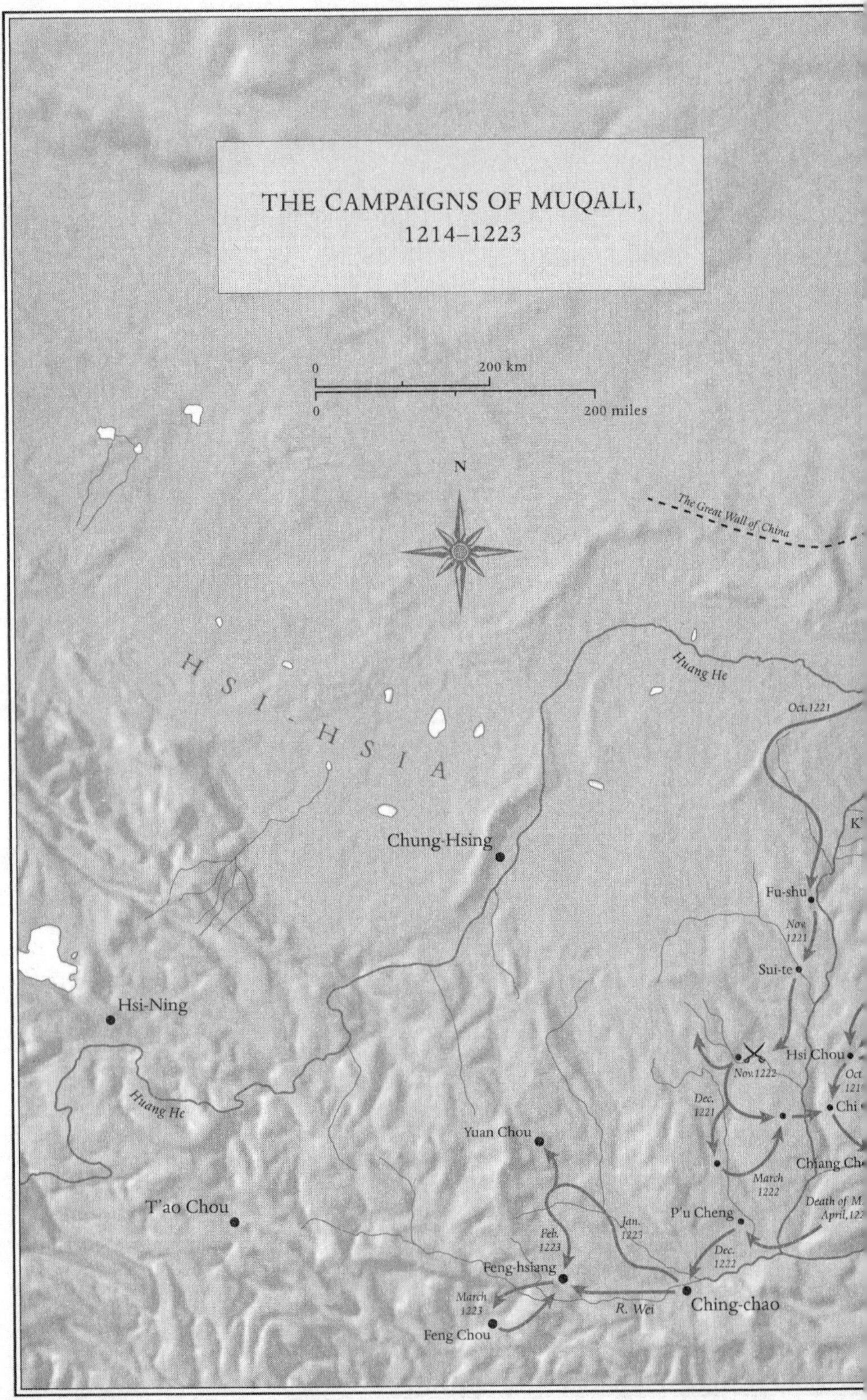

THE CAMPAIGNS OF MUQALI, 1214–1223

0 |——————| 200 km

0 |————————————————| 200 miles

N

The Great Wall of China

HSI-HSIA

Huang He

Oct. 1221

K'

Chung-Hsing

Fu-shu

Nov 1221

Sui-te

Hsi-Ning

Huang He

Hsi Chou

Oct
121

Nov.1222

Chi

Yuan Chou

Dec.
1221

T'ao Chou

Chiang Ch

March
1222

Death of M.
April,122

P'u Cheng

Feb.
1223

Jan.
1223

Dec.
1222

Feng-hsiang

March
1223

R. Wei

Ching-chao

Feng Chou

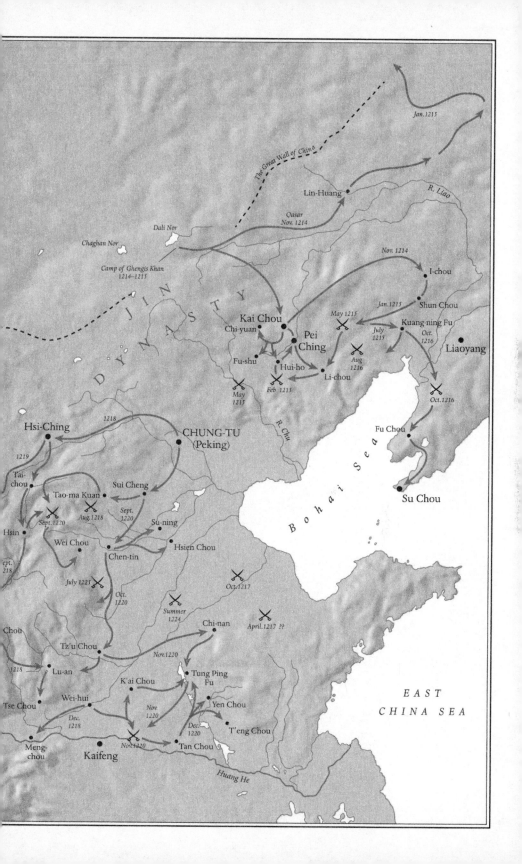

The Great Wall of China

Jan.1215

Lin-Huang

R. Liao

Qasar Nov. 1214

Dali Nor

Chaghan Nor

JIN

Camp of Ghengis Khan 1214–1215

Nov. 1214

I-chou

Jan.1215

Shun Chou

DYNASTY

Kai Chou

Chi-yuan

Pei Ching

May 1215

Kuang-ning Fu

July 1215

Oct. 1216

Liaoyang

Fu-shu

Hui-ho

Aug 1216

Li-chou

Feb 1215

May 1215

Oct.1216

R. Chu

Fu Chou

Su Chou

Hsi-Ching

1218

CHUNG-TU
(Peking)

B o h a i   S e a

1219

Tai-chou

Tao-ma Kuan

Sui Cheng

Sept. 1220

Aug.1218

Sept. 1220

Su-ning

Hsin

Wei Chou

Chen-tin

Hsien Chou

Oct. 1217

ept. 218

July 1221

Oct. 1220

Summer 1224

Chi-nan

April.1217 ??

Chou

Tz'u Chou

Nov.1220

EAST
CHINA SEA

1218

Lu-an

K'ai Chou

Tung Ping Fu

Tse Chou

Wei-hui

Nov. 1220

Yen Chou

Meng-chou

Dec. 1218

Nov.1220

Dec. 1220

T'eng Chou

Kaifeng

Tan Chou

Huang He

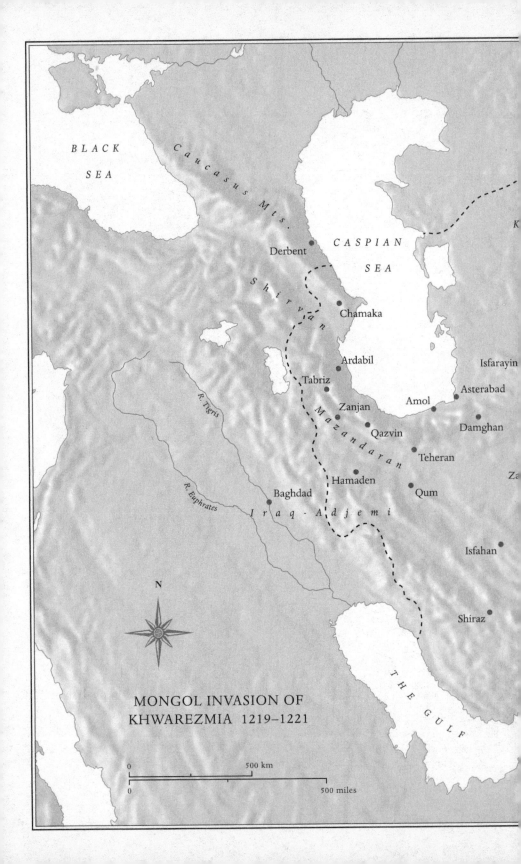

BLACK
SEA

Caucasus Mts.

CASPIAN
SEA

K

Derbent

Shirvan

Chamaka

Ardabil

Isfarayin

Tabriz

Asterabad

Zanjan

Amol

Mazandaran

Damghan

Qazvin

R. Tigris

Teheran

Za

Hamaden

R. Euphrates

Iraq - Adjemi

Qum

Baghdad

Isfahan

N

Shiraz

THE GULF

MONGOL INVASION OF
KHWAREZMIA 1219–1221

0   500 km

0   500 miles

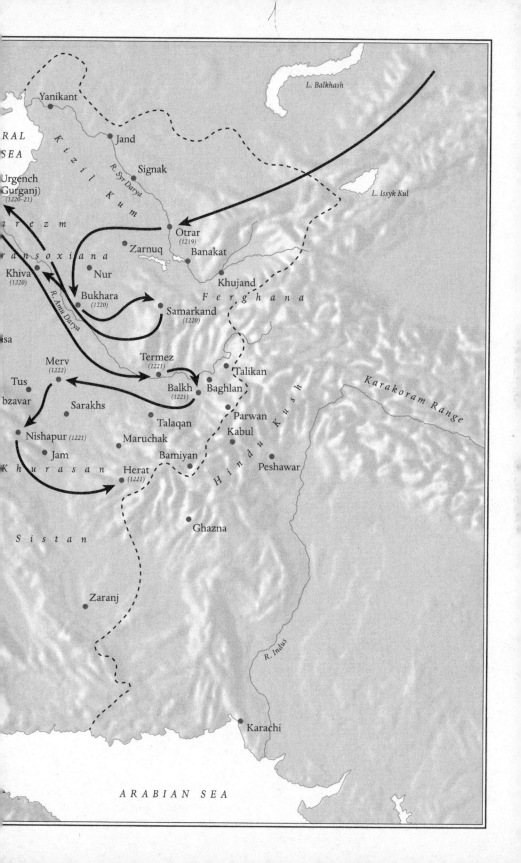

RAL
SEA

Yanikant

Jand

Signak

R. Syr Darya

Kizil Kum

Urgench
(Gurganj)
(1220–21)

arezm

ansoxiana

Khiva
(1220)

Nur

Bukhara
(1220)

Zarnuq

Otrar
(1219)

Banakat

Khujand

Samarkand
(1220)

Ferghana

L. Balkhash

L. Issyk Kul

R. Amu Darya

isa

Merv
(1222)

Termez
(1221)

Talikan

Karakoram Range

Tus

bzavar

Sarakhs

Balkh
(1221)

Baghlan

Hindu Kush

Nishapur (1221)

Talaqan

Parwan

Jam

Maruchak

Kabul

Bamiyan

Khurasan

Herat
(1221)

Peshawar

Sistan

Ghazna

Zaranj

R. Indus

Karachi

ARABIAN SEA

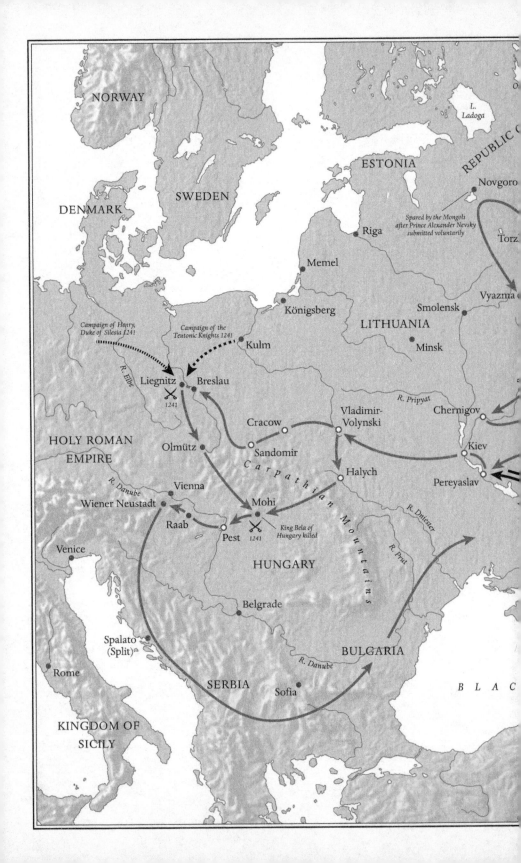

NORWAY

SWEDEN

DENMARK

ESTONIA

L. Ladoga

REPUBLIC O

Novgoro

Spared by the Mongols after Prince Alexander Nevsky submitted voluntarily

Torz.

Riga

Memel

Königsberg

Vyazma

Smolensk

LITHUANIA

Minsk

Campaign of Henry, Duke of Silesia 1241

Campaign of the Teutonic Knights 1241

Kulm

R. Elbe

Liegnitz

⚔ 1241

Breslau

R. Pripyat

Cracow

Vladimir-Volynski

Chernigov

Kiev

HOLY ROMAN EMPIRE

Olmütz

Sandomir

C a r p a t h i a n

Halych

Pereyaslav

R. Danube

Vienna

Mohi

R. Dniester

Wiener Neustadt

⚔ 1241

Raab

King Bela of Hungary killed

R. Prut

Pest

Venice

M o u n t a i n s

HUNGARY

Belgrade

Spalato (Split)

BULGARIA

R. Danube

Rome

SERBIA

Sofia

B L A C

KINGDOM OF SICILY

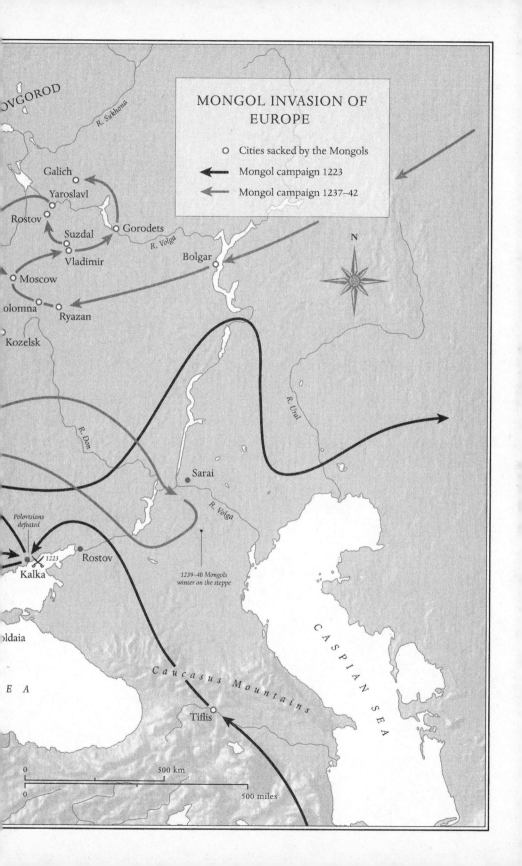

MONGOL INVASION OF
EUROPE

○ Cities sacked by the Mongols
← Mongol campaign 1223
← Mongol campaign 1237–42

NOVGOROD

R. Sukhona

Galich
Yaroslavl
Rostov
Suzdal   Gorodets
Vladimir   *R. Volga*
Moscow   Bolgar
olomna
Ryazan

Kozelsk

N

R. Don

R. Ural

Sarai

R. Volga

Polovtsians
defeated

Kalka ✕ 1223
Rostov

1239–40 Mongols
winter on the steppe

oldaia

E A

C A S P I A N   S E A

C a u c a s u s   M o u n t a i n s

Tiflis

0   500 km
0   500 miles

List of Illustrations

Glossary of Principal Personalities

N.B. almost all dates in early Mongol history are somewhat conjectural.

ALAQUSH (d. 1212). Chief of the Ongud. Revealed the Naiman plan of attack to Genghis in 1205. Assassinated by a rival faction in the Ongud while Genghis was in China.

ALTAN (dates unknown). Third son of Qutula. Pretender to the khanate. Jealous of Genghis, his cousin, and habitually and systematically treacherous. Said to have alienated Jamuga from Genghis.

AMBAGHAI (reigned 1149–1156), of the Tayichiud clan. Khan of the Mongol confederation. Crucified by the Jin Chinese.

ARSLAN (dates unknown). Chief of the Qarluqs, who lived in the region of the Black Irtysh. Formerly a vassal of Qara Khitai, he defected to Genghis in 1211.

ASA GAMBU (d. 1227). Anti-Mongol Tangut noble, appointed both prime minister and commander-in-chief by emperor Hsien-Tsung of Hsi-Hsia (reigned 1223–1226).

BARCHUQ (d. after 1227), the *idiqut* or ruler of the Uighurs. Switched allegiance from Qara Khitai to Genghis in 1209 and was given one of his daughters in marriage. One of Genghis's most trusted and valued allies. Fought in the Tangut campaign of 1227.

BATU (c. 1207–1255). Son of Jochi and founder of the Golden Horde dynasty. Commander-in-chief of the Mongol invasion of Europe in 1236–42. Loathed the great khan Guyuk and was close to civil war with him when Guyuk died. Allied with Sorqoqtani Beki to secure Mongke's election.

BEGTER (c. 1156–1180). Son of Yesugei and his (unknown) first wife. Genghis's half-brother but murdered by him.

BELGUTEI (c. 1158–c. 1252). Brother of Begter and Genghis's half-brother.

Remained scrupulously loyal to Genghis and performed well as a general, though was notably indiscreet and thus excluded from the Mongol council and top-level decision-making.

BO'ORCHU (c. 1162–1227). First and most loyal of Genghis's friends. One of the 'four steeds'. Saved Genghis's life and was a notable general. Particularly close to Ogodei. Died during the Tangut campaign of 1227, possibly of Parkinson's disease or maybe complications arising from epilepsy or Ménière's disease.

BOROQUL (c. 1162–1217). One of Hoelun's adoptees and one of the 'four steeds'. Second only to Bo'orchu in Genghis's personal esteem. Saved Ogodei's life at the battle of Qalqaljid Sands. Killed on campaign against the Forest Peoples.

BORTE (c. 1161–1230). Genghis's official wife and mother of four sons and five daughters begotten by Genghis. A woman of notable wisdom and one of Genghis's most trusted advisors.

BUJIR (c. 1200–c. 1264). Was with Jebe and Subedei on the 'great raid' of 1221–23. Later a senior Mongol administrator in China.

CARPINI, John of Plano (1182–1252). Franciscan friar, later archbishop. The first significant Western envoy to the Mongols in 1246–47 when he acted as the representative of Pope Innocent IV.

CHAGATAI (c. 1184–1242). Genghis's second son. Headstrong, quarrelsome and fanatically anti-Muslim, he was the least impressive of Genghis's sons and did a lot of harm by his vendetta against Jochi.

CHINQAI (c. 1169–1252). Of uncertain racial origin (among the Mongols 'Turk' was used as a catch-all term), he was the great peacetime administrator of the Mongol realms. Genghis's chief minister, he also served the great khans Ogodei and Guyuk in that capacity.

DAI SECHEN (dates unknown). Chief of the Bosqur clan of the Ongirrad tribe. Genghis Khan's father-in-law, he was honoured at the 1206 quriltai.

DARITAI (dates unknown). Genghis's paternal uncle. Made common cause with Altan and Quchar. Caught up in the disgrace of Belgutei.

DORBEI DOQSHIN (dates unknown). Chief of the Dorben clan. A general with a reputation for merciless ferocity.

ELJIGIDEI (?–d. 1251/52). Scholars dispute whether there was just one Mongol with this name, or two (probably two given the relevant dates). The Eljigidei extant at the beginning of the thirteenth century was the executioner of Jamuga. The one who died in 1251/52 was executed for disputing the election of Mongke. Chronology seems against a single Eljigidei, but see the career of Temuge.

HOELUN (c. 1142–c. 1216). Wife of Yesugei, who had five children with her, including Genghis. One of Genghis's most trusted advisors. Later married to Monglik.

HULAGU (1218–1265). Son of Tolui and Sorqoqtani Beki, grandson of Genghis, brother of Ariq Boke, Mongke and Qubilai Khan. Founded the Ilkhan dynasty in Persia in 1256. Sacked Baghdad in 1258.

JAMUGA (1161–1206), of the Jadarad clan. Childhood friend and blood-brother to Genghis and rival for leadership of the Mongols. May have been a double agent. His habitual ambivalence led to his eventual downfall and execution.

JEBE (c. 1180–1225), of the Besud sub-clan of the Tayichiud Mongols. Wounded Genghis with an arrow in battle in 1201, but was pardoned and became one of his star generals. Cooperated brilliantly with Subedei on the 'great raid' of 1221–24.

JELME (c. 1170–1207). Elder brother of Subedei. An important general. Saved Genghis's life by sucking the blood from his neck after he had been wounded by an arrow. Singled out for special favour at the 1206 quriltai. Died campaigning against the Naiman.

JOCHI (c. 1182–1227). Eldest 'son' of Genghis, though Genghis was almost certainly not his natural father. Accusations of illegitimacy dogged him throughout his life. Espousing a more liberal view of empire than his father, he became estranged from Genghis, was suspected of plotting against him, and eventually done away with on his orders.

JURCHEDEI (dates unknown). Chief of the Uru'ud tribe who switched sides from Jamuga to Genghis in 1201. Given the Kereit princess Ibaqa Beki as wife. Father of Ketei and Bujir.

KOKOCHOS (dates unknown). Of the Ba'arin clan and apparently named after a secret Mongol ritual. Was appointed 'minder' to Chagatai and tried in vain to keep the peace between him and Jochi.

LOUIS IX, St Louis (1214–1270). Reigned from 1226. The only canonised king of France. Went on the Seventh Crusade in 1248 and the Eighth Crusade in 1270.

MONGLIK (dates unknown). Close friend of Yesugei. Under Genghis granted the honorific title of 'spiritual father'. Disgraced after

Genghis had his son, chief shaman Teb Tengerri (a.k.a. Kokochu) killed for treason.

MUQALI (1170–1223). Genghis's only undefeated general. The master-mind behind Genghis's eventual conquest of Jin China. Appointed viceroy of China and de facto 'deputy khan' in 1217.

NAYA'A (dates unknown). Son of Shirkutu, chieftain of the Ba'arin clan. One of the important Mongol generals. Praised by Genghis for not breaking his oath to Targutai of the Tayichiud.

OGODEI (c. 1186–1241). Genghis's third son and his successor as Great Khan. Generous, charismatic but capriciously cruel, he expanded the Mongol empire to its greatest extent, with conquests in China, Korea, Central Asia, Russia and Eastern Europe. Scholars dispute whether he and his beloved brother Tolui died of alcoholism or were poisoned.

POLO, MARCO (1254–1324). Venetian merchant and traveller. The most important Western traveller to visit Qubilai Khan's China. Was absent from Venice, travelling in the Orient 1271–95, clocking up 15,000 miles.

QABUL (reigned 1130–1146), of the Borjigid clan. Khan of the original Mongol confederation. Genghis's great-grandfather.

QACI'UN (1166–?). Yesugei's third son with Hoelun. Little is known of him except that he was personally closest of all the brothers to Genghis. Father of Eljigidei (see above).

QASAR (1164–c. 1216). The most disloyal and treacherous of Genghis's brothers. A man of great physical strength and a superb archer. Frequently plotted against Genghis and enjoyed an up-and-down relation with the khan.

QUBILAI (dates unknown), of the Barulas tribe. A senior Mongol general. Not to be confused with the later Mongol khan and Chinese emperor Qubilai Khan.

QUCHAR (dates unknown). Nephew of Yesugei and pretender to the khanate. He and Altan habitually plotted against Genghis.

QUDUQA (dates unknown). Chief of the Oyirad, one of the Forest Peoples. Originally Jamuga's right-hand man but joined Genghis after the defeat of the Naiman. Performed unsuccessfully in the Tumed rebellion of 1217 and was taken prisoner by the dynamic Botoqui, the 'Boadicea' of the Tumed. After her defeat, he took her as one of his wives.

QUQLUQ (d. 1218). Son of the Tayang khan of the Naiman.

QUTULA (reigned 1156–1160), of the Borjigid clan. Khan of the Mongol confederation. Died fighting the Tartars.

RUBRUCK, WILLIAM OF (c. 1220–c. 1293). Flemish Franciscan. Served with Louis IX of France on the Seventh Crusade and was his envoy to the Mongols in 1254.

SHIGI QUTUQU (c. 1180–1250). A Tartar adopted when a boy by Hoelun. One of Genghis's special favourites. De facto Chief Justice of the Mongol empire under both Genghis and Ogodei. Literate and said to have been the first Mongol notable to master the Uighur script.

SORQAN SHIRA (dates unknown), of the Suldus tribe. A minor chieftain who helped the youth Genghis to escape from Targutai of the Tayichiud who had yoked him with a cangue. Rewarded at the 1206 quriltai by being appointed one of the *orloks*.

SORQOQTANI BEKI (c. 1187–1252). Daughter of Jaqa Gambu, brother of Toghril and thus a Kereit and Nestorian Christian. A master politician, one of the most influential and intelligent women of the age. Wife of Tolui, and mother of three Mongol khans (one also a Chinese emperor), Mongke, Hulagu and Qubilai. Mananged to secure the succession for Mongke in alliance with Batu. The Syriac scholar Bar Hebraeus said of her: 'If I were to see among the race of women another woman like this, I would say that the race of women was far superior to that of men.'

SUBEDEI (1175–1248). A member of the Uriangqai tribe. Allegedly the son of a blacksmith. Served Genghis and Ogodei brilliantly from 1192 to 1248. A superlative general, one of the greatest of the age, he was the Mongols' master strategist.

TATATONGA (dates unknown). Tangut administrator who introduced the Uighur script to the Mongol court. Appointed tutor to Genghis's sons and made Keeper of the Royal Seal.

TEB TENGERRI, a.k.a. Kokochu (?–c.1208). Chief shaman of the Mongols. Backed Genghis to the hilt until 1206 but after the 1206 quriltai tried to assert himself as the equal of Genghis. After the attempt to discredit Genghis's brothers, the khan had one of them break his back in a de facto execution.

TEMUGE a.k.a. Otchigin (1168–1246). Least warlike of Genghis's brothers and criticised by him for laziness. He was a skilled politician with intellectual and cultural interests. Executed after trying to seize the throne from Guyuk.

TEMULUN (1169/70–?). Genghis's sister. Little is known of her except that she made an exogamous marriage with Palchuk of the Onggirad.

TOGHRIL, a.k.a. Ong Khan (c. 1140–1203). Ruler of the Kereit. A Nestorian Christian. A turncoat and intriguer, involved in a complex three-way relationship with Genghis and Jamuga before his defeat and death.

TOLUI (1192–1232). Genghis's fourth son and the greatest general of the four. Genghis considered him too cautious to be an effective Great Khan. Extremely close to Ogodei and, like him, died either of alcoholism or poisoning. His sons Qubilai, Húlagu and Mongke were all distinguished Mongol rulers.

TOQTO'A BEKI (?–1208), ruler of the Merkit tribe and a doughty opponent of Genghis in the early days. Had a reputation for being excessively bloodthirsty.

TOQUCHAR (?–1221). Genghis's son-in-law. Sacked Tus contrary to Genghis's orders. Demoted, then killed during the siege of Nishapur.

WEI, SHAO, PRINCE OF (1168–1213). Seventh of the ten Jin emperors (under the name Wan-yen Yung-chi); third and last of them to be assassinated.

YELU CHU CAI (1190–1244). Khitan aristocrat. A superb administrator and a strong influence on both Genghis and Ogodei. Supervised the census and tax system in China in the 1230s.

YESUGEI (?–1171). Father of Genghis. A sub-chief, but never a Mongol khan.

Author's Note

I think it obvious that a definitive biography of Genghis Khan is impossible. The Platonic ideal of a Mongol scholar would have to master, at a minimum, Mongolian, Chinese, Persian, Arabic, Russian, Hindi, Urdu and Gujarati, and preferably also Japanese, Polish, Hungarian and the multitudinous dialects of the many worlds into which the Mongols penetrated: Vietnam, Burma, Indonesia, Siberia, Georgia, Azerbaijan, etc, etc. It would take a single human being several lifetimes to master all these tongues before he or she could begin to set pen to paper. This is why scholars of the Mongols tend to specialise in discrete areas and produce books on the Mongols and Russia, the Mongols and China, the Mongols in Iran, the Mongols in the West, and so on. I have not learned any of the difficult languages mentioned above and my modest, though still taxing, project has been to produce a synthesis of all the scholarship done in the major European languages in the past forty years relating to Genghis and his sons. There will doubtless be many things professional Mongolists will object to, but I hope I have covered Genghis's life in sufficient detail. I have not just concentrated on the 'blood and guts' of his notoriously bloody campaigns but also layered in, without, I hope, overwhelming the reader, enough discussion of Mongol society, culture, ideology and religion to make the narrative more than just 'one damn battle after another'. My debt to all scholars of the Mongols and their society will be obvious, but I am particularly indebted to Paul Pelliot (from the scholars of a previous generation) and the great Igor de Rachewiltz (from the current generation).

The principal sources for Genghis Khan are *The Secret History of the Mongols*, a court history by an unknown author, the *History of the World Conqueror* by the Persian historian Ata-Malik Juvaini (written in the

1250s), and two other key Persian works: Rashid al-Din's *Compendium of Chronicles* (completed in 1307) and the *Tabaqat-i Nasiri* by Minhaj al-Din Juzjani (completed in 1260). These Persian works contain much valuable information not available elsewhere, including eyewitness testimony. All three are excellent sources but, understandably, scholars differ as to their relative merits. Rashid al-Din is often preferred because of the scope of his work (the story of the Mongols is just part of a vast universal history) and his use of contemporary Mongolian and Chinese sources that have since vanished. Others opt for Juvaini, though the response to this author has been mixed. While acknowledging its wealth of information from sources no longer extant, academic critics fasten on his cavalier way with evidence, his opinionated intrusions, his absurd magnification of numbers and the inevitable tension between the deep dislike he felt for the Mongols and the need to disguise this because he was in their service (in Iran). Juzjani has the advantage over the other two that he was an eyewitness of the Mongol conquests in Central Asia in the 1220s, and that he did not live under the Mongol yoke and did not need therefore to choose his words carefully. From the safety of the Delhi sultanate he poured out his hatred and bile for the Mongols – Genghis is always 'the accursed one' – but this very distance in both senses gives his work a unique value.

The joker in the pack is the *Secret History*, written in Mongolian shortly after Genghis's death in 1227, an official record for the royal dynasty, secret in the sense that it was not divulged, disseminated or promulgated, and its readership was confined to court circles. It is a curious, enigmatic work, shot through with ambivalence and ambiguity, the mystery deepened by the riddle of its authorship. Although it has been suggested that Genghis's adopted son Shigi Qutuqu may have been the author, the critical tone of many of the passages makes this unlikely. It is also improbable that it was written by either Tatatonga, the influential Tangut pedagogue whom Genghis used as tutor for his sons, or by the great Turkic administrator of northern China, Chinqai, two of the other oft-cited candidates. The most plausible suggestion is that the writer was a close associate of Genghis's brother Temuge, who was positioning himself for a likely struggle for power after the death of the Great Khan Ogodei. Part sober history, part historical novel, part didactic allegory and part hagiography, the *Secret History* has to be used with extreme care as a source, for it quite clearly suppresses or distorts key episodes in the life of the young Temujin. As soon as Temujin was transmogrified into Genghis Khan in 1206, the author seems to go off the boil and lose interest. The career of Genghis proper, the world conqueror, and his great conquests are dispatched in short order. Nonetheless, it remains a fascinating work. It has been called the *Morte d'Arthur* of the steppes, but this is unhelpful. There never was a king Arthur in the true sense, but there certainly was a Genghis Khan; the clumsy analogy presumably refers to the didactic element in Malory. Others have hailed the *Secret History* as an *Iliad* without the genius of Homer, but much the same considerations apply as before. If there was a trade war between Mycenae and Troy, it was certainly nothing like the conflict depicted in Homer. The battles up to 1206 in the *Secret History*, on the other hand, were not only historical but also probably described by a participant.

A word on transliteration and the rendering of proper names. Anglicisation of the languages of Central Asia and the Far East presents notorious difficulties, and the fashions have changed over the years. Peiping became Pekin, then Peking and finally Beijing, with no guarantee that the latter will be the final linguistic resting place. One has a certain sympathy with the legendary newspaper editor who asked his Far East correspondent how long it would take to fly from Peking to Beijing. In the case of the anglicisation of the great conqueror's name, the most correct equivalent would be Chingis Khan, but as my subject has always been known traditionally in the English speaking world as Genghis Khan – and this volume is, after all, designed as popular history rather than an academic thesis – I have adopted the familiar spelling throughout. On the other onomatology I am sure I have not employed a level of consistency in every language to satisfy the purists, and in many cases my version of the relevant proper names has been guided above all by euphony. Nevertheless, it should always be clear which of the numerous *dramatis personae* I am referring to, and to this end I have also included a glossary of the principal personalities in my narrative. My editors and I are very grateful to Professor Timothy May of the University of North Georgia for at least putting us right on the best spelling of the names of many of the Mongol and steppe tribesmen.

No author can complete a book on his own, and accordingly I am very grateful to all the following: to Will Sulkin, who commissioned the volume, and his successors at Bodley Head, Stuart Williams, Will

Hammond and Emmie Francis who saw it through to fruition; to my daughter Julie for obtaining rare books about the Mongols; to Professor W.J.F. Jenner for providing me with a guide to Chinese place names, ancient and modern; and to the editorial, copy-editing and mapmaking team of Dr Henry Howard, Bill Donohue and Anthony Hippisley. My greatest debt, as ever, is to my wife Pauline, peerless editor, critic, friend and intellectual companion. God bless them all.

Frank McLynn
Farnham, Surrey, 2015

Note on pronunciation:
This is not the place for a full guide to the pronunciation of Mongol words and names but the reader may find it helpful to bear in mind the following:

CH is pronounced more or less as in English 'church'
J as in English 'jam'
KH and Q both as in Scottish 'loch' or German 'Achtung'

Introduction

Baghdad in 1257 was still regarded as one of the great centres of Islam. The seat of the Abbasid caliphate, it was to an extent living on past glories, for its halcyon days were in the late eighth and early ninth centuries. Al-Mansur, the second caliph (reigned 754–775) and the real founder of the Abbasid dynasty, had laid the groundwork, but the great wonders came under Harun al-Rashid (ruled 786–809), the fifth caliph. He made Baghdad a showpiece of the world, with mosques, palaces, hospitals and irrigation works that astonished visitors and won him eternal fame. Perhaps the most famous building of all was the House of Wisdom, the world's largest library – also a research institute and translation centre. The House of Wisdom contained volumes and professors particularly specialising in the sciences: astronomy, mathematics, medicine, alchemy, chemistry, zoology, geography, cartography. But this was no mere Los Alamos or MIT of its day; the rigour and erudition of the institute was counterpointed by the colourful city of bazaars and markets outside where snake-charmers, fortune-tellers and hucksters of all kinds throve. Harun al-Rashid's Baghdad, in short, was the one so unforgettably portrayed in the 1001 *Nights*. Under Harun and his immediate successors, Baghdad overtook Cordoba as the largest city in the world, but by the thirteenth century it had long since ceded the palm in the population stakes to Merv and the other great cities of Khorasan.[1] Even though Baghdad had declined since the glory days and had been on the wane since the late tenth century, an Islamic traveller around the time of the Norman Conquest could still marvel at it:

There is no city in the world equal to Baghdad in the abundance of its riches, the importance of its business, the number of its scholars

and important people, the extent of its districts, the width of its
boundaries, the great number of its palaces, inhabitants, streets,
avenues, alleys, mosques, baths, docks and caravanserais.[2]

Even those with jaundiced feelings about the Abbasid capital could
not deny the grandeur that remained in the eastern bank city, as Ibn
Jubayr, an Arab traveller from Moorish Spain reported in 1184:

> [It] has magnificent markets, is arranged on the grand scale and enfolds
> a population that none could count save God. It has three congrega-
> tional mosques . . . The full number of congregational mosques in
> Baghdad, where Friday prayers are said, is eleven . . . The baths in the
> city cannot be counted.[3]

City workshops produced superb silk and brocaded material, and in
Italy there was a special cloth brocaded with gold named for Baghdad
and the cloth of silk and cotton called *attabi* after one of the city's
quarters was known by name throughout Europe. Baghdad essentially
exported luxury goods: cloth, silk, crystal, glass, ointments and potions;
the city might have declined but its prosperity was the envy of most.

Yet there were always those, especially in an age when superstition
was rampant, who regarded it as an ill-starred city, beset by famine,
fire and flood. There was famine in 1057, attempts at social revolution
in 1077 and 1088, religious conflicts that led to violence and most of
all, the ravages of fire and water. Major fires were recorded in 1057,
1059, 1092, 1102, 1108, 1114, 1117, 1134, 1146 and 1154. There was an earthquake in 1117 and floods in 1106, 1174 and 1179. There were large-scale
riots in 1100, 1104, 1110 and 118, and in 1123 a confederation of Bedouin
tribes came close to capturing the city, which was saved only with the
help of reinforcements rushed in by the Seljuk Turks.[4] Inevitably
prophets and soothsayers interpreted all these bad omens as the
harbinger for an apocalyptic disaster that would finally destroy
Baghdad. The decline in calibre of the caliphs also seemed to point
in the same direction. Al-Mustasim, the caliph who had reigned since
his accession in 1242 at the age of 31, was a man of poor judgement
and little energy, a hedonist who spent his time in frivolous pursuits,
centred around women, music and the theatre. Like many such people,
he coupled these attributes with haughty arrogance, deeming himself

(on no evidence) to be a superior ruler. His attitudes exasperated his courtiers, especially the chief vizier, and there was much muttering in the corridors of power by malcontents who wanted to depose him. A particular concern was that he seemed heedless and insouciant about the growing threat from the Mongols, a mysterious people from the east, who on four different occasions (1236, 1238, 1243 and 1252) had made threatening forays in the direction of Baghdad only to veer off at the last moment when they spotted more promising prey.[5]

But now in 1257 such threats could no longer be ignored, and the caliphate faced what in the twentieth century would be called clear and present danger. The Mongols were coming and this time it was no drill, no bluff. Genghis Khan's grandson Hulagu, brother of the great khan Mongke, the future Chinese emperor Qubilai and a fourth ambitious sibling Arik Boqe, was on the warpath. Mongke had ordered Hulagu to annex those parts of Muslim Asia still not under Mongol control and had decided on a sweep through the western Islamic world as far as Egypt. The largest Mongol force ever assembled was put under Hulagu's command. Medieval sources speak of an army 150,000 strong, and by this date in Mongol history such a host was numerically feasible.[6] Hulagu struck first at the Ismaili Assassins, the most dreaded opponents in the Islamic world. The political and military arm of the Nizari Ismailis, a breakaway Islamic sect, the Assassins established their 'state' at the fortress of Alamut in north-west Persia. Under the Grand Master of the order, known as 'the Old Man of the Mountain', the Ismailis trained their adherents to become expert assassins, murderers of the great and powerful, whom they always dispatched in public places to intimidate everyone with the terror of their name. The great Saracen leader Saladin, was afraid of them, and notable crusaders had met their end from the Assassins' knives. But in December 1256 they encountered a force even more terrible. Under Hulagu the Mongols attacked Alamut, destroyed the supposedly impregnable fortress and ended the menace of the Assassins forever. The motive was said to have been an incautious threat made by the Master of the order to Hulagu.[7]

Flushed with this triumph, Hulagu sent a message to the caliph, requiring his surrender and personal obeisance and homage, the destruction of Baghdad's fortifications, and a huge sum in gold as tribute. Al-Mustasim treated this with the same lofty contempt the pope would have shown had he received a threat from one of the great temporal rulers of Europe. He told Hulagu's envoys that he was the head of Islam and as such superior to any mere temporal ruler, and that he had millions of the faithful from China to Spain to back him. 'Go home to Mongolia, young man,' was the gist of the patronising message he apparently sent Hulagu, just seven years his junior. Behind the caliph's back the Grand Vizier sent a secret message to Hulagu, encouraging him to attack and assuring him that he would experience a walkover, since Baghdad was honeycombed with conspirators and fifth columnists who wanted the caliph dead. Hulagu sent a final warning: 'The moon shines only when the fiery disc of the sun is hidden', meaning that the power al-Mustasim boasted of could be exercised only on Mongol sufferance.[8] This time the caliph sealed his fate by executing the Mongol emissaries – possibly the greatest crime of all in Mongol culture. Only when he had made war inevitable did al-Mustasim take fright at the precipice on which he was perched and summoned his council to ask if there was any way Baghdad could escape the Mongol whirlwind. The universal opinion was to buy Hulagu off with so much gold that he would have to agree a peaceful solution. But instead he heeded his chief astrologer, backed by a bevy of soothsayers, who claimed that 'it was written' that all who attacked the Abbasids were fated to perish miserably. The astrologer actually went into the details of the calamities that would attend Hulagu if he persisted in his sacrilegious folly: the sun would fail to rise, there would be no more rain, the soil would become sterile, a great earthquake would swallow up the invader's army, and finally Hulagu himself would die within a year. The astronomer made the fateful pledge that he was so sure of what he was saying that he would stake his life on it.[9] When the message was taken to Hulagu, his own astrologer confirmed the bad omens and said the caliph's seers were speaking the truth. For this 'treachery' Hulagu instantly executed him. When the caliph learned that Hulagu was unconcerned by the prophecies of doom awaiting him, once again he dithered and this time agreed to the massive tribute in gold demanded. Hulagu brusquely replied that the time for such negotiations was past; now he wanted to see the caliph's face.[10]

Hulagu advanced from his base camp towards Baghdad in November 1257 with great confidence. His huge army was supplemented by levies from conquered Armenians and Georgians, who had long since concluded that resistance to the Mongols was pointless and, more surprisingly, by Christian troops from Antioch. He also had a corps of elite Chinese siege engineers and sappers commanded by Guo Kan, at forty the same age as Hulagu, and already renowned as an example of the way Mongols promoted on merit rather than birth. Hulagu reached the suburbs of Baghdad on 18 January 1258 and began the encirclement of the city, probing its defences. The original circular fortifications built by caliph al-Mansur no longer existed but there was a ten-mile semi-circular kiln-burnt brick wall surrounding the inner city on the west bank of the Tigris, interspersed with powerful watch towers; the defensive brick-lined ditch was no longer effective, as it had been ruined by regular flood damage.[11] Additionally, al-Mustasim deployed his high-calibre Turkish troops in boats on the river, providing an extra layer of defence. The Mongols advanced down both banks of the Tigris. On the west bank the caliph made the mistake of sending out his 20,000-strong cavalry force to try to disperse the advancing marauders, but he reckoned without Mongol ingenuity. Their engineers broke the dykes of the dams along the Tigris and flooded the ground behind the cavalry, trapping them and then methodically destroying them. The Turkish soldiers on the river in front of the metropolis bore themselves much better and performed well. Hulagu was patient and methodical. He had his mangonels and catapults rain down missiles and naphtha at selected towers, particularly targeting the Persian Tower. Because the area around the Tigris and Euphrates was barren of stones, the Mongols transported them from the mountains and cut down palm trees which were then shaped into missiles. The Mongols dealt with the challenge of the Turks by crossing the Tigris at several points simultaneously and selecting the weak points they had identified around the semicircular wall. The Georgians were particularly to the fore in relentless sapping operations. Non-stop bombardment continued from 29 January to 10 February, when the Persian Tower collapsed and the way into the city was clear. At this point a formal surrender was arranged, but Hulagu refused to give terms. He waited for three days before ordering the final assault, to rest his men and, doubtless, to inveigle the gullible city notables into revealing where their treasures lay hidden. He demanded that the caliph's astrologer be given up to him, taunted the man about the threatened disasters and reminded him that he had sworn to the truth of the prophecy on his life. Then he had him executed.[12]

13 February was the start of a six-day sack of Baghdad. A Persian historian described the sequel with colourful poetic flourishes.

> In the morning, when the orange of the sun was placed at the rim of the dish of the horizon, and the light by sleight of hand had conjured away from the mercury blanket of the sky the imprint seals of the stars, Hulagu ordered the army to carry the torch of plunder and robbery into Baghdad . . . First of all they razed to the ground the walls . . . and filled the moat which was as deep as the contemplation of rational men. Then they swept through the city like hungry falcons attacking sheep, with loose rein and shameless faces, murdering and spreading fear . . . The massacre was so great that the blood of the slain flowed in a river like the Nile, red as the wood used in dyeing, and the verse of the Koran 'Both seed and stem perished' was recited about the goods and riches of Baghdad. With the broom of looting, they swept out the treasures from the harems of Baghdad, and with the hammer of fury they threw down the battlements headfirst as if disgraced . . . And a lament reached the ears . . . from roofs and gates . . . Beds and cushions made of gold and encrusted with jewels were cut to pieces with knives and torn to shreds. Those hidden behind the veils of the great harem . . . were dragged like the hair of idols through the streets and alleys; each of them became a plaything in the hands of a Tatar monster.[13]

For six days and nights the pillaging went on. Mosques were gutted, great buildings pulled down, people slaughtered. A sober estimate of the fatalities in the siege and sack of Baghdad provides a tally of 90,000 dead. Seven hundred odalisques and one thousand eunuchs were found in the caliph's seraglio. The worst act of vandalism was the destruction of the House of Wisdom – a literary loss to rank alongside the destruction of the great library at Alexandria. It was said that so many books were thrown into the Tigris that the river, previously red with blood, now turned black with ink and remained that way for several days.[14] There is a suspicion that Christians regarded the demise of the House of Wisdom as divine vengeance for the treatment allegedly meted out to the Alexandria library by Muhammad's companion and successor caliph Omar in 642 during the conquest of Egypt. According to Bar Hebraeus, the Syriac Orthodox divine, who was a contemporary of the destruction of Baghdad, Omar said of the Alexandria library: 'If these books are in agreement with the Koran, we have no need of them; and if they are opposed to the Koran, destroy them.'[15] The destruction of Islamic books in turn by the Mongols, who did not even have Omar's appreciation of the power of the written word, must have given smug satisfaction to anti-Islamic zealots in the West.

While all this went on, Hulagu beheaded some seven hundred members of the elite and their families. Al-Mustarim himself he kept in an agony of suspense for a while. First he starved the caliph, then ordered him brought before him. The famished man asked for food. Hulagu handed him a gold bar and said, 'Eat that.' 'No man can eat gold,' said the caliph, in a plaintive echo of King Midas. 'If you knew that,' said Hulagu, 'why did you not send gold to me at the beginning? Had you done so, you would still be eating and drinking peacefully in your palace.'[16] The caliph revealed the whereabouts of his public treasury, but Hulagu insisted that was not good enough: he also wanted to know where al-Mustarim kept his private hoard. The desperate caliph was forced to divulge the location of this also. Finally, Hulagu grew bored with toying with him and ordered his execution. On 21 February his personal servants were beheaded. The caliph and his son were put to death by a method the Mongols reserved for royal and princely personages; they were wrapped in rugs and then trampled to death by their own horses.[17] After this Hulagu grew tired of killing, announced that the survivors were his subjects and needed his protection, and called a halt to the massacre.

The destruction to the city was devastating. The canals and dykes of the irrigation system had been totally destroyed, making agriculture and subsistence next to impossible. Baghdad itself declined in all spheres: demographic, political, social, economic.[18] A garrison of 3,000 was left behind, what remained of the city was reduced to a provincial capital, and Iraq thenceforth was ruled from Tabriz. The survivors in Baghdad might well have wished they had perished in the holocaust, for the Ilkhanate imposed crippling taxes on them at the very time their ability to pay had diminished to perhaps one-third of its level in 1257. By the end of the thirteenth century many of Baghdad's suburbs were deserted, especially on the west bank. Its port Basra also went into decline, as the Mongols preferred to carry on trade with India from Hormuz. That was the end of the Abbasid caliphate, and some historians say Islam itself never really recovered from the trauma.[19] Throughout the Arab and western worlds people were stunned by the destruction of one of Islam's great centres. Baghdad joined the long roster of famous cities destroyed by the Mongols: Peking, Kaifeng, Samarkand, Bukhara, Kiev, Moscow, Cracow, Budapest. A new round of embassies and travellers set out from Europe to discover who exactly these ferocious people were. How could nomads from Mongolia have become the conquerors of most of the world? Who were Hulagu and his famous brothers? And who was their father Tolui? Most of all they wondered about a man who had already passed into history and legend, the man Temujin who had become Genghis Khan.

1

The Nomads of Mongolia

Central Asia is allegedly the cradle of so much – Neanderthal Man, nomadic pastoralism, warfare itself, even UFO sightings – but it is all but useless as an explanatory concept in history. We do better with the notion of the steppe, but even this is an umbrella term embracing a wide variety of terrains, differing in vegetation, altitude and climate. Some writers rather crudely envisage the steppe as a continuum, stretching from Hungary to Manchuria, the core or heartland of what the geographer Halford Mackinder termed the 'world island' comprising Europe, Asia and Africa.[1] On this model a mountain range blocks off the steppe at either end. In Europe the Carpathians divide the Russian steppe from the Hungarian plain, while in east Asia the Khingan Mountains separate the Mongolian steppe from its Manchurian epigone. Others prefer a dualistic model, with the 'low steppe' comprising western Turkestan, the north Caspian and the south Russian plains, and the 'high steppe' consisting of eastern Turkestan and Outer and Inner Mongolia. As the names suggest, the high steppe covers the lands at an altitude between 4,500 and 15,000 feet while the low steppe terrain is at sea level.[2] Yet others prefer a triad, with the steppe arranged in three rows or layers. The first contains all the lands from Hungary to southern Ukraine, the north of the Black Sea and the gap between the Caspian Sea and the Ural Mountains. The second or 'central steppe' runs from northern Kazakhstan to south-central Asia, where it merges with desert regions. The third is the great steppe-land of Mongolia and northern Sinkiang, running along the northern fringes of the Gobi Desert to the Khingan Mountains in Manchuria. The entrance to this is through the Dzungar gap between the Altai and T'ien Shan Mountains.[3] Still other geographers are unhappy with the whole idea of the steppe as the central organising concept and speak instead of a distinction between 'Outer Eurasia' (Turkey, Iraq, Arabia, Iran, Afghanistan, Pakistan, India, Thailand, Burma, Laos, Vietnam, Cambodia, Indonesia, China and Japan) and 'Inner Eurasia' (Ukraine, Russia, Mongolia and the modern 'stans' (Kazakhstan, etc).[4] It should be stated also that even those who cleave to a 'horizontal' explanation of Asia sometimes opt for the desert or for river systems as *the* important physical feature of the continent, rather than the steppe. On this view, attention should be directed to the continuous belt of desert south of the steppe, embracing the Gobi and Taklamakan Deserts, the Kizil-Kum south-east of the Aral Sea, the Kara-Kum east of the Caspian and the Great Salt Desert of Iran. Significantly, at these latitudes the spread of continuous desert extends through the deserts of the Middle East and Arabia to the Sahara, and is halted only by the Atlantic itself.[5] Similarly, a horizontal view of Asian river systems would reveal continuity running across from the Yellow River and the Yangtse, via the Indus and Ganges and finally to the Tigris and Euphrates.

The emphasis on the steppe provides in Mongolia's case a 'horizontal' west–east model. Some, however, say that the key to Mongolia is the 'vertical' north–south axis running from the tundra of northern Siberia and the Arctic Ocean through the forest or taiga directly north of Mongolia past the steppe proper to the Gobi Desert, through the mountainous regions of northern China down to the fertile valleys of the south. Accordingly, some experts prefer to differentiate the 'steppe-forest' of northern Mongolia from the 'steppe-desert' of the south.[6] This view stresses the importance of mountains rather than steppe-lands: the Alashan, Beishan and Kunlun ranges, the Pamirs with peaks up to 25,000 feet and canyon-like valleys, the T'ien Shan or Mountains of Heaven (with peaks up to 24,000 feet), the Khenti of northern Mongolia, the Altai of Western Mongolia (with peaks up to 14,000 feet) and their westerly handmaiden the Tarbaghatai range.[7] The Altai Mountains have always particularly attracted writers about Mongolia, possibly because the Sayan–Altai plateau correlates with the forest-steppe. The largely pine-wooded taiga is important in Mongolian history, as it is drained by four mighty rivers: the Ob–Irtysh, Lena, Yenisey and Amur.[8] The sub-Alpine valleys of the Altai provide exceptionally good grazing grounds, with rich grass overriding the gravel, salt and loam of the soil. Although there is no magical dividing line between the taiga and the steppes – nothing as clear as the abrupt transition from the Ituri forest to the open savannah in the old Belgian Congo (modern Zaire) or the Amazonian jungle and llanos of Colombia – some travellers claimed to discern a kind of no-man's land of black earth dividing the two. Between the forest and the Gobi Desert lies the Mongolian steppe proper – some even define it as the area between the northern edge of the T'ien Shan and the southern edge of the Altai. Much of it is a treeless pasture, with many areas below sea level, but there are high hills, often forested, such as Mount Burqan Qaldun, sacred to the Mongols, in the north-central part of the region.[9] These hills would have been very important, providing as they did both rich grazing in summer and abundant hunting resources. Crucially important to Mongolia are its rivers, though many are impermanent and evanescent. Water was always the most precious resource for the inhabitants. There are many wadis, some springs, in the south-west some salt lakes and marshes, but it is no exaggeration to say that the area's great reservoir is Lake Baikal in the north, surrounded by high hills – and noted for its plethora of seabirds, especially gulls.[10]

Mongolia is essentially a plateau occupying approximately a million square miles, set at a much higher altitude than the steppes in Turkestan and the west, ranging from 3,500 to 5,000 feet. Its central and ineluctable feature is the Gobi Desert which comprises one-third of the area of Mongolia (with steppe and meadow about fifty per cent, and forest fifteen per cent). The Gobi is not a desert in the same sense that the Sahara is, as its surface can be grassy, sandy, pitted with scree or boulders or striated with salt marshes. Some purists object to the very term 'desert' on the ground that the Gobi is primarily a dry steppe.[11] On the outer fringes a transparent veil of grass is apparent, and grassland is widespread and abundant, but as one penetrates deep into the interior vegetation tends to be limited to scrub and grassy reeds. Thereafter one confronts a melange of moving dunes, stable dunes, clayey plains, salt flats, isolated wells and desert trees such as the white saxaul (which can be used for firewood) and the ephedra. The Gobi stretches west–east for twelve hundred miles.[12] The south–north journey from the modern Chinese border to the Russian frontier is about eight hundred miles long and takes about a month of solid camel-riding. For about half the time the trek is over undulating grassy plains. Then comes a four days' march of about fifty miles through deep, sandy desert, punctuated by two high ridges of rock, colourfully described by one traveller: 'Adrift in the hot expanses were small rounded hills riding like whales in silver mirages of water.'[13] This sandy desert breaks up the monotony of the undulating plain but slows down progress. It is followed by a further week of gravelly plains, with the soil a deep red colour, distinguished by brightly coloured translucent stones and crystals. Nomadic peoples found the Gobi an eerie, unsettling, spirit-ridden place and even later European travellers were disconcerted by the mirages: 'The prevailing colour was a kind of misty, half-transparent white, exactly like arrowroot or cornflour prepared with water only.'[14] The desert was uncannily quiet at night, when, as one writer mused, 'the bright, unwavering lights of the Great Bear, and the soft glimmer of Cassiopeia and the Pleiades stood out with a distinctness rarely seen in other latitudes.'[15] Clearly for the traveller across the Gobi the primary problem was water. In normal circumstances wells ten feet deep had to be dug every thirty miles or so; only with heavy rainstorms in summer was aridity mitigated.[16] Dust storms were another hazard but travellers failed to agree on their frequency and severity in the Gobi. Some claimed that there were choking sandstorms in summer and icy ones in winter, yet others, even with direct experience of the phenomenon, claimed it as a rarity.[17]

Mongolia suffers from both a harsh climate and lack of water. With a lack of adequate rainfall (on average only 10–20 inches annually), the land is too dry to support agriculture without expensive irrigation schemes, and this fact alone restricted the population of the land (estimates range from a low of 700,000 to a high of two million, and the contrast with the population density of neighbouring China was especially marked).[18] The northerly latitude and remoteness from the sea mean colder average temperatures, less sunlight and greater extremes of temperature than elsewhere in Asia. The winters are especially harsh, with temperatures below freezing for as much as six months in the year. Even within a single month the entire gamut of weather conditions can be experienced. One meteorological study done in June 1942 testified to the wild variations. A calm and sunny early evening was interrupted by a 60 m.p.h. gale, bringing dust, fog and ninety per cent cloud cover. This storm lasted an hour, blew itself out and was succeeded by a clear sky, with the night stars especially brilliant. Then between 1 and 2 a.m. there were heavy showers of rain, and by dawn the sky was again clouded over. By 9 o'clock the next morning there was fog, driving snow and a temperature of 33 degrees Fahrenheit.[19] Mongolia's great distance from the sea does, however, bring some compensations. Even though the country is in general very cold, there is little air humidity and hence relatively little snow, with falls rarely exceeding three feet in depth. With so little air humidity to produce clouds, Mongolia enjoys five hundred hours more sunshine in summer than Switzerland or the Midwestern states of the U.S.A. at the same altitude. When the break in this weather pattern occurs, it tends to be violent; the Franciscan envoy Friar Carpini who wrote about the Mongols in the 1240s reported severe thunderstorms and snowstorms in midsummer (his diary for 29 June 1246 records heavy snow that day), together with hurricane-strength winds, hailstorms and duststorms.[20] And the summer which could be so violently disturbed lasts just three months, from June to August. September is already very cold, and in October the first snowstorms can be expected. By November the rivers are frozen, and then comes the six-month Niflheim lasting until May. Throughout the year the weather is both extreme and unpredictable, with temperatures ranging from 100 degrees F in summer to −43 in winter. Since there are no natural barriers to the wind, gales are always violent. One can be hit simultaneously by winds from the Siberian tundra and desert storms from the Gobi.[21]

Not surprisingly, the steppes look very different at different times of the year. Probably the most glorious month is May, for then the plains are covered with an immense green carpet, pullulating with flowers, especially red poppies, gentians, geraniums, eyelets, delphiniums, asters, rhododendrons, edelweiss, white convolvulus and forget-me-nots, that last until late summer. There is a huge diversity of plants in Central Asia, including 8,094 species of flora, of which some 1,600 species are desert flowers.[22] Naturally, some regions of Mongolia are more favoured than others. Some geographers distinguish two climatic zones, one in the west as far as the Altai and T'ien Shan Mountains, and another in eastern Mongolia. In the western zone there is little summer rain but the winter is affected by Atlantic cyclones, with deeper snowfalls than in the east. In compensation the mountain ranges of western Mongolia and the many rivers, mountain streams and springs created alpine meadows and ideal conditions for winter pasture. In the eastern zone monsoons bring moisture in summer and a prevailing anticyclone, lowering over the steppes, in winter. The winters often see clear, sunny days and quiet windless weather, with very little snow, so that livestock can pasture all year round.[23]

The eastern part of Mongolia is thus especially favoured, and within this favoured area most privileged of all is the area around the Onon and Kerulen Rivers – exactly where Genghis Khan was born. The Onon, about 500 miles long, rises in the eastern slopes of the Khenti Mountains (the highest peak of which is over 9,000 feet high), the watershed between the Pacific and Arctic Ocean basins, and which perhaps contained the sacred mountain of Burqan Qaldun. The Onon is a tributary of the Shilka which in turn feeds the Amur. (If the combination Onon–Shilka–Amur is treated as one river, at around 2,744 miles in length it counts as the world's ninth longest river.)[24] The Kerulen, which rises on the south slopes of the Khenti Mountains, flows through the eastern Mongolian steppes, enters China and empties into Lake Hulun. In years of high rainfall the normally exit-less Hulun may overflow at its northern shore and, after another twenty miles, flow into the Ergune River, the traditional border between Russia and China. Six hundred miles along the Ergune will again take one to the mighty Amur. (If, in contrast to the Onon–Shilka–Amur above, one computes the 'Amur' as the Kerulen–Ergune–Amur system and regards it as a continuous river, the resultant stream becomes the world's *sixth-longest* river, with a length of more than 3,000 miles.)[25] The Onon forest, four hundred square miles in extent, between the Rivers Onon and Kerulen, and in time the Mongols' heartland, is thus a kind of oasis in the midst of the steppes, and as such a sort of wonderland. Here can be found a plethora of trees unknown elsewhere in Mongolia: wild cherry, dogrose, currant, hawthorn, poplar, birch, elm, wild apple, Siberian apricot, willow, ash, buckthorn, Russian ash, juniper, walnut, acer, pistachio.[26]

The climate of Mongolia has always ruled out significant agriculture. The inadequate water supply, and the rapid disappearance of moisture because of evaporation and solar radiation are only the worst of the problems, to which should be added a short growing season, extensive swamps and marshes, cold and dry conditions and a salty, waterlogged or frozen soil. The people of Mongolia were (and are) mainly nomadic pastoralists. This simple phrase masks complexities, for there are pastoralists who are not nomadic and nomads who are not pastoralists. For example, the forest people of Siberia owned horses and were nomads, though not pastoral ones, while the gauchos and cowboys of the Americas were pastoralists but not nomads. Moreover, there is not even a necessary distinction between pastoralism and agriculture. Some peripheral peoples of Mongolia – the Ongud just to the north of the Great Wall of China and the tribes of the Yenisey – were partly pastoral and partly agricultural.[27] Even more nuances and fine distinctions can be introduced if we bring in the notion of transhumance and non-transhumance. The usual distinction is that transhumance involves journeys between winter and summer pastures but the pastoralists have a fixed abode, in a village, say. In nomadic pastoralism the drovers have no fixed abode, live in tents, and move with the animals from season to season.[28] Although animals were private property, pasture was held in common by extended kinship groups, where the strongest tribes and clans claimed the best pasturage at the optimum time of year. Water was always a paramount consideration on the steppe, so that different nomad groups exercised proprietary rights to the key wells, with the 'outsiders' having to pay for access.[29] Typically, winter camps and pastures would be in protected areas with reduced snow cover, in low-lying mountain valleys, river flood plains, the southern side of hills, or even depressions in the steppe. This was the grimmest time, with the animals very weak by spring. Once the drying of grass and the evaporation of water heralded the coming of spring, in late May or early June, the nomads moved to a higher altitude for the summer pasture and their animals rapidly gained weight. Moving swiftly out from winter camp, they made at once for large pools of melted snow to water the stock. The distances between winter and summer pasture could be as little as twenty miles, but were usually about fifty miles, up to a maximum of sixty in favoured locations such as the Onon–Kerulen valleys; for those having to eke out their existence on the fringes of the Gobi the journey might be seventy-five miles or even more. These journeys would be accomplished in leisurely tranches of between five and twenty miles a day, with the pace not pressed daily; rather, the nomads would travel on alternate days or have longer rest periods.[30]

The summer camps were pitched on high ground with cool breezes.

This was the season when yoghurt, cheese and the alcoholic drink koumiss, from fermented mares' milk, were produced. Wool from sheep and hair from goats and camels was used to make thread and thence rope, rugs, carpets and saddlebags. The Mongols were adept at making felt for tents. First they beat the wool, then poured boiling water on it and rolled it back and forth until the fibres locked to produce the fabric. Felt was a key aspect of the Mongol's tent, the ger (the more familiar word 'yurt' was a later Russian coinage), as it provided insulation and protection against high winds. Autumn was the time to breed sheep for a spring lambing but was otherwise a golden moment with the animals at their strongest.[31] When the cold weather began, the nomads started the trek back to winter quarters. They liked to graze the animals on the periphery of the winter pasture until the weather became too severe, only transferring them to the 'heartland' of the pasture when the temperature plummeted. The Mongols next made an educated estimate of how many animals would survive on the winter pasture and slaughtered the weakest and least hardy specimens. The meat would then be smoked as a winter food supply. The Mongols' diet was therefore also seasonal: dairy products in summer, meat in winter.[32] Naturally the nomads tried to retain as many live animals as possible, subject to the constraints of water and forage. Winter was always a worrying time, as its severity could never be accurately predicted; a small-scale drover could find his wealth wiped out overnight from a combination of frost, drought and disease. Since the animals were weak from the 'iron rations' of winter and spring was lambing time, seasonal regularity was crucial. If there were freak snowstorms in spring, much of the stock, especially the newborn young, would die; fortunately this did not happen on average more than once in a generation. The big battalions as always did best, as the herdowner with the most beasts would recover more quickly than one with a handful.[33]

The Mongolian pastoralist had a plethora of problems to solve and was never far from a knife-edge. Erosion – plant cover destroyed and dust storms blowing away the topsoil – and mineralisation due to the action of the wind and the workings of salt springs were serious problems. If these phenomena coincided with overgrazing, the result would be desert. In any case, salinity, alkaline soil and general aridity limited the amount of water and grass available. This meant that there could never be any real increase in herd numbers and, by the same token, in human numbers. This is another way of saying that pastoralism unaided is bound to produce a steady and constant population.[34] Moreover, even in such a steady state nomads had to make precise calculations about water supply and the distance between wells and waterholes, as the different animals they herded moved at different speeds and had different water needs.

In this context snow was a mixed blessing for the Mongols. On the one hand, it increased pasture resources, without which there would be overgrazing and, ultimately, desert. On the other hand, snow could be a deadly danger, as it covered up pasture grass and other plants, preventing livestock from grazing at all.[35] Particularly fearful was (and is) the phenomenon known as *zud*. This involved repeated and alternating thaws and freezes, creating thick, impenetrable sheets of ice under the snow. *Zud* was particularly feared since it could affect the whole of Mongolia, unlike drought, which never had such a universal impact.[36] The Mongol herdsmen had to balance all these climatic variables while maintaining five different types of domestic animal: sheep, goats, cattle, horses and camels – all with different needs and requiring different management techniques. Unlike the Bedouin of Arabia with the dromedary or the forest peoples of the taiga with their reindeer, the Mongols were not single-animal specialists. Their herding needed rotation of pastures just as much as agriculturalists needed rotation of crops.[37] Horses and cattle need wetter pasture than sheep and goats, so require streams and fertile land. In Mongolia this meant pasturing them separately from the other stock. Sheep and goats notoriously crop grass very closely, which means that larger livestock cannot graze the same land immediately after them. Overgrazing by sheep and goats was particularly serious, as their hooves cut the surface of the ground and exposed the soil, leading to wind erosion.[38] Proper husbandry of pasture meant that the grazing lands had at times to be rested altogether and then grazed by different stock – cattle and horses – to give it a rest from the remorseless sheep and goats. It was axiomatic that no pasture should ever be grazed by the same stock year in and year out. The technical reason, apart from erosion, is that a steady accumulation of dung and urine from the same kind of animal after a time ceases to have a fertilisng effect and instead becomes poisonous, not only providing less nourishment but also enhancing the danger of disease and epidemics.[39] All this meant either that special feeding grounds had to be set apart for cattle and horses, or that they had to be pastured before and ahead of sheep and goats.

A closer look at the five domestic animal types can help to point up the complex problems the herdsmen and drovers faced. There was a problem right at the heart of Mongol culture, what one might term a difference between the objective and the subjective. Objectively, the most economically valuable asset they possessed were their massive flocks of sheep, but subjectively it was the horse that was most prized. In their value system the Mongols rated their stock in descending order of importance as follows: horses, camels, cattle, sheep and goats.[40] Yet 50–60% of the animals they raised were sheep, which were the mainstay of their primitive economy. Since early twentieth-century Mongolia scarcely differed from its thirteenth-century counterpart, we can put flesh on the bones, as it were, by adducing some statistics. In 1918 Mongolia had a grazing area of some 300 million acres, supporting 1,150,000 horses, 1,080,000 cattle, 7,200,000 sheep and 230,000 camels. For 1924 the figures were 1,350,000 horses, 1,500,000 cattle, 10,650,000 sheep and goats and 275,000 camels. By 1935 these numbers were, respectively, 1,800,000, 2,350,000, 17,700,000 and 560,000.[41] Although there was a rapid increase in overall numbers because of special economic plans in the twentieth century, the basic ratios held good: and the centrality of sheep is obvious.

The Mongolian sheep is small, producing less meat than its European counterpart. Its wool was of little commercial value but was used to make felt and clothing. The most important sheep product was milk, used to make either butter and cheese or koumiss.[42] The sheep proved its value during the spring move from winter to summer pasture as it did not have to be watered, instead deriving the moisture it needed from dew and the grass wet from melted snowfalls. Spring was of course a risky time – both lambing and shearing took place before the move to mountain pastures. The pastoralist always had to be careful. Sheep numbers could decline alarmingly whenever pasture was poor – as it was at high altitudes, in deserts and on the margin of forests.[43] Most of the surplus animals slaughtered at the beginning of the winter season were sheep, but it seems that the Mongols were frugal in their consumption of mutton and lamb. The Franciscan Carpini reported that a single sheep could feed fifty men.[44] The traveller

Simon of St Quentin, in the course of a tirade on poor Mongol table manners, remarked: 'They eat so little meat that other peoples could scarcely live from it.'[45] An average family travelling in convoy with the seasonal migration would typically possess one hundred sheep, just a handful of oxen, five horses that could be used to ride into battle and three other ponies; it was conventional wisdom that the optimum size of an ovine herd was around one thousand. Sheep were herded together with goats, another important nomad resource, both for milk and wool. Their advantage was that they could survive on pasture other than grass, but their demerit was that they destroyed small bulbs as well as the trees the Mongols counted on for firewood or building materials.[46] Pigs were entirely absent from the nomad animal inventory, though not because of any religious taboo; the Mongols were happy to eat pork or 'black cattle.' The reason was simple. Pigs were not bred because they needed acorns, unavailable on the steppe, and because they could not migrate long distances.[47]

About nine per cent of the Mongols' livestock was cattle. The typical long-horned Mongolian cattle were used mainly as beasts of burden, drawing the carts on which the Mongols carried their mobile gers, though sometimes also for meat or hides; they were rarely used as herd animals. The ox was the most typical bovine among the Mongols; they saw the advantage of allowing bulls to develop their full musculature before castrating them. Possibly the most prized of all Mongolian cattle was the yak. It used to be thought that the yak was used only in high mountain regions, but this view seems to have been discarded. Weighing up to 2,200 pounds and standing 5–7 feet at the shoulder, the yak was prized both as a beast of burden and for its milk, meat and fibre; its dung was also thought to make the best fuel.[48] The well-known writer Vikram Seth has described the yak as a veritable machine for converting grass into butter, fuel, tent hide and clothing.[49] The most versatile variety is the *hainag* , a cross between a bull yak and a cow; this hybrid is particularly valuable as it can operate at both high and low altitudes, is docile and yields better milk. The Franciscan Rubruck and Marco Polo were also enthusiasts for the yak. This is Rubruck:

[They have] extremely strong cattle, with tails which are abundantly hairy like a horse's and with shaggy bellies and backs: they are shorter in the leg than other cattle, but stronger by far. They haul along the large dwellings of the Mo'als [Mongols], and have long, slender, twisted horns which are extremely sharp so that the points constantly require to be sawn off. The cow will not let itself be milked unless one sings to her. They have a bull's temper, moreover, in that if they see a person dressed in red they charge at him with a desire to kill him.[50]

However, yaks and cattle in general could not compare in utility with the camel, the Mongols' second most prized animal. The camel came close to the definition of an all-purpose beast, as it could work in almost all conditions and travel on any surface but was particularly valuable in areas where the Mongols' beloved horse would struggle, as in the Gobi, Ordos, Alashan and Taklamakan Deserts. Camels have always had a bad press, particularly from the Victorian explorers and adventurers like Sir Richard Burton and Fred Burnaby, who remarked scathingly that a camel galloped like a pig with its forelegs and a cow with its hind legs.[51] Yet those who know them well say that they are affectionate and drawn to humans; like dogs and horses, they instinctively ensured their survival by attaching themselves to Man, the protector against predators.[52] The Central Asian camel is the two-humped variety or Bactrian. Naturally, among the Mongols, a horse-loving people, it did not have the kudos or importance the dromedary possessed for the Bedouin, even though Mongolia was probably its aboriginal homeland, but it was better-tempered than its one-humped counterpart. Since in Central Asia it co-existed with the wheel, it could not aspire to the position of indispensable 'ship of the desert', but against this is the fact that the only study of the camel in literature is Mongolian.[53] The role of the Bactrian in Asian history is indisputable. In medieval times it was common in Anatolia, Iraq, Iran, Afghanistan, India, Mongolia and China and made the Silk Road possible.[54]

The Bactrian's advantages were manifold. It has a lifespan of 20–40 years. It can carry loads of between 320 and 370 pounds. It can go thirty days without water if there is decent grazing and can drink water with a higher salt content than seawater, though when water is available it will gulp down up to fifty-seven litres in one go. It is also a good swimmer. Its milk could be turned into camel *koumiss* and its hair was used as a staple in Mongol textiles. The Bactrian can travel at 4 m.p.h. unladen and 2½–3½ m.p.h. laden and can carry its 300-pound-plus load for thirty miles a day.[55] Yet it had several drawbacks as a would-be 'wonder animal'. It is a diurnal animal, and on military campaigns it was sometimes urgently necessary to travel at night. Bactrians tend to stray while grazing, which makes them much more labour-intensive than sheep or goats. They need eight hours grazing time each day. They hate to be left alone in the desert and, if they find themselves in such a predicament, are likely to trek on until they drop dead. If they slip on ice in winter, that spells death, for they cannot get up again. Even the very useful dung or 'chips' used as fuel produced a dense, pungent smoke, making their Mongol drivers bleary-eyed as they sat around the camp fire.[56]

The animal that allowed the Mongols ultimately to conquer the steppes was the horse, that indispensable adjunct of those centaurs of the plains; as has been well said, a Mongol without a horse is like a bird without a wing. The steppe horse as a species was similar to the wild or Przewalski's horse.[57] Horses were domesticated on the steppe as early as 3,200 BC, but early civilisations used them for chariot warfare rather than as cavalry. Probably first tamed as a ridden warhorse by the Mongol tribes between the fifth and third centuries BC (but on the western steppes not until the first century BC, by the Scythians), the horse became an even more formidable weapon of war with the invention of the stirrup in the fifth century AD.[58] Around 12–14 hands high, coarse, with a large head, straight neck, heavy coat, thick legs, heavy-boned, shorter, stockier and sturdier than the destriers of medieval Western Europe, the Mongol horse was an animal of incredible stamina, capable of galloping six miles without a break. Although in the West its height would classify the animal as a pony rather than a horse, zoologists concur in granting the Mongol steed the status of a true horse. It can survive in temperatures ranging from 30 degrees C in summer to −40 C in winter. Mongolian horses find a walk too slow for their short legs and a canter too exhausting, so their natural pace is a fast trot.[59] Their gait is ungainly and they provide an uncomfortable ride for the uninitiated. Their supreme talent is being able to use their hooves to scrape away snow from the steppe surface to reach grass or lichen below and to survive on leaves from trees; they do not need to be fed beans, grain or other fodder. In common with many other Asian equine breeds they can subsist wholly on grazing, unlike 'proper' horses which would quickly weaken if left outside in all weathers and given no supplementary feeding. It was this all-weather capability that so often allowed the Mongols to defeat their enemies, since they could campaign in winter.[60] When campaigning, each Mongol had three remounts and on forced marches rotated these every two hours to prevent exhaustion. Coupled with mobility – the Mongols could ride 600 miles in nine days, though obviously not on the same horse – this made the armed nomads almost unbeatable. Yet even the magnificently tough Mongol horse was vulnerable to freak weather. The real fear for the pastoralists was that a late blizzard in spring with thick snowfall would hit their horses at their weakest after months of semi-starvation.[61] Barring such acts of God, the Mongols could be confident that their horses would serve them well in every context. Such was the importance of the horse that the Mongols operated a kind of informal utilitarian calculus to estimate wealth and the value of their herds vis-à-vis other stock. They reckoned that each person needed five horses to live well, which meant that a family of five would need twenty-five riding horses and four to six pack horses. A ger containing five people that had more than ten horses was considered rich. A horse was valued as being equal to five head of cattle or six sheep or goats. A two-year-old counted as half a horse and a yearling as one-quarter.[62] The Mongols used mainly mares, as these were more docile and yielded the vital milk for making koumiss. If short of food, they had a technique for making an incision in the animal's vein, drinking the blood, and then sealing up the wound. The very strongest horses were kept as breeding stallions and each of these had 50–60 mares in his harem. The stallion, though troublesome, was very useful to a man on night watch, as he would not let his mares escape and was as alert in this regard as a herdsman against wolves.[63]

Men, women and children were all expected to be expert with horses. Children were mounted on horses at the age of 3 and strapped in even earlier so that they could get used to the motion of their mount; there are examples of infant horsemen who could ride before they could walk.[64] Mongols trained their horses to respond to calls and whistles, like dogs, to obviate the need for any special corps of wranglers. They broke their mounts early to inculcate obedience but did not push them to the limit until they were five-year-olds; one of the reasons for the early breaking was to train the horses not to kick or bite.[65] After breaking, the next stage was accustoming the animals to saddles and tack. Mongolian horses' tack comprised a simple bridle and a short-tread, deep-seated saddle with short stirrups. These saddles had a very thick felt pad; the bridle was an ordinary jointed ring snaffle. The noseband was linked to the cheek pieces, so that when the reins were pulled, the horse felt pressure over the nose as well as via the mouth, lips and tongue.[66] Mongols did not groom their horses but let the mane and tail grow so long that it almost trailed on the ground. They claimed that this kept the horses warm in winter and warded off flies in summer; moreover, if a bridle or stirrup broke, there was always a ready supply of horse-hair with which to do the mending.[67] Training then started with the horse at a standstill to get the animal used to noise, particularly the simulated din of battle. Next they set the steed in motion while shooting arrows from the saddle, so that it could get used to the different movements as the rider drew arrows from his quiver, moved the drawn bow from one flank to the other and shot from different angles. The horse had to learn to keep straight while receiving leg signals only, as the reins were not held but knotted. The rider had to keep the legs rigid so as not to confuse the horse; turning in the saddle was done with waist and hips. Other techniques involved getting the charger used to ropes and lassos being thrown, lances hurled and swords wielded, sometimes very close to the animal's head.[68] Strangely, the Mongols found that accurate shooting was easier at the gallop than at a canter; this was because when galloping on a free rein the horse lowered its whole topline, stretching and lowering its head and neck, giving the archer a free field of fire. To ensure that their horses could veer and turn rapidly the Mongols first turned them in a large circle, then gradually narrowed the range in ever diminishing circles until rapid turns became second nature. Marco Polo in the late twelfth century noted that Mongol horses were so well trained that they could turn as quickly as a dog.[69]

Then came the training in verbal commands. Noting the peculiarities of different kinds of horses, the Mongols preferred to use geldings if they were setting an ambush, as they did not neigh as much as stallions and mares.[70] The Mongols were fond of their horses, and those that survived the arduous campaigns were allowed to retire and graze into their dotage; only in extreme circumstances would they be killed for food. Since the horse was a precious resource, the Mongols were very solicitous for their welfare. They did not ride them in spring or summer but turned them out to grass, allowing complete rest and relaxation. When taken away from the grass, they were tethered around tents and their grazing rationed until all fat fell away and they were ready to go on campaign.[71] Always after riding their mounts, the Mongols unsaddled them and then held their heads up high to prevent their eating until their breathing was normal and they were cold; this controlled the eating process and prevented colic and laminitis.[72] Generally they left their horses unshod, since the hooves of animals raised in a dry climate like Mongolia were harder and resisted abrasions better than horses raised in a wet climate; but once they ventured outside Mongolia, the Mongols often found that their steeds needed to be shod.

The nomads' herds were of course not the only animal life in Mongolia. It has always been a paradise for wildlife, and in the thirteenth century not even the massive Mongol hunts put a dent in their numbers. Even today Central Asia as a whole contains over eight hundred species of vertebrates.[73] Most of these animal species are represented in Mongolia, and in the thirteenth century there were even more. Some of these were in competition with the Mongols' herds, and in two different ways. The nomads' livestock displaced many wild ungulates – red deer, fallow deer, gazelle, antelope, wild goats, the Siberian ibex, the wild boar – and it was notable that as soon as the Mongols drove their herds from winter pasture, the gazelle and antelope would congregate in thousands to graze there.[74] Naturally, as nomadic pastoralists, it was the carnivorous predators the Mongols most targeted, especially wolves, which they controlled with their own breed of ferocious dogs and specially trained eagles. There were also bears, leopards, lynxes and cheetahs to contend with. And when the Mongols later expanded into other parts of central Asia, they encountered still more big cats. In those days the Asian lion was plentiful and, like their imperial predecessors the Romans, the Mongols were fascinated by the inaptly named king of beasts, to the point where they sometimes accepted lions as part of a total package of tribute from conquered nations.[75] In the Mongol era, too, the even more formidable tiger was plentiful in Asia, especially along the River Oxus.[76] Yet the Mongols' most interesting feline relationship was with the snow leopard or ounce. Nowadays only found at altitudes between 11,000 and 22,000 feet, in the thirteenth century they were plentiful, could be tamed, and were used by the Mongols in their great dragnet hunts, sometimes amazingly being conveyed to the killing ground on horseback. They made very convenient pets for the Mongols, as they will eat large amounts of vegetation, grass and twigs as well as meat.[77]

There was also a plethora of small game that swam into the nomads' ken: wild camels, foxes, rabbits, squirrels, badgers, martens, wild cats, hares, the extremely fleet-of-foot onager or wild ass, and the Mongolian rat, described by one traveller as 'a soft, pretty little animal, with a feathery tail and . . . none of the disgusting attributes of the common Norwegian or English rat.'[78] Of the many rodents, including mice, gerbils, hamsters and lemmings, the Mongols had a special fascination for the marmot, which they ate as a rare delicacy. Extremely hard to hunt and catch, marmots taxed the ingenuity of nomadic hunters but, apart from their role in the pastoralists' diet, they were valued because of a peculiar superstition – though not so very different from that entertained in the contemporary U.S.A. about the groundhog (often classified in the marmot family) – that one could tell from examining marmots what the weather and the seasons would be like.[79]

The Mongols often came upon snakes, particularly the Mongolian viper but, though venomous, its bite is rarely fatal to humans. It was a different story when the Mongols later expanded in imperial form, for then truly dangerous serpents like cobras were encountered, especially in Iran and the Aral–Caspian basin. However, the Mongols always seemed to have an ambivalent relationship with snakes. Although they would kill vipers and 'milk' them for their venom – which they used to tip poisoned arrows – in general they had a superstitious regard for what the Roman naturalist Pliny the Elder called 'this detestable creature', on the grounds that they were related to dragons and had power over water.[80] In general it can safely be said that the more new frontiers the Mongols explored, the more exotic or previously unknown creatures they discovered, whether the striped hyena of Afghanistan, the seals of the Caspian, the ostrich of western Asia or the venomous spiders of Turkestan.[81]

The one surprising thing is that, their falcons and hunting eagles apart, they showed no interest whatever in Mongolia's teeming bird life. Although travellers' tales are full of descriptions of avian predators such as wild eagles, vultures, hawks, owls – as well as the innocuous partridges, grouse, swans, geese, cranes, spoonbills, egrets, pelicans and storks[82] – Mongol sources are silent. The same applies to Mongolia's seventy-six varieties of fish, which include trout, grayling, perch, roach, pike, sturgeon and the huge freshwater salmon or *taimen* – though here one can cite a deep cultural prejudice against fishing, which persists to this day. The consequence was that Mongolia's lakes were undisturbed by Mongol incursions into their fauna, and a great body of water like Lake Baikal could glisten undisturbed like a sea of sapphire picked out with white waves and snow-capped mountains round the coast.

The physical appearance of the Mongols always intrigued, and often shocked, Europeans and western Asians who met them. A Franciscan monk who accompanied Friar Carpini on his famous journey to the Mongol court in the mid-1240s described them as usually short of stature and slim, which he attributed both to their strenuous lifestyle and their diet of mare's milk. He described them as broad of face with prominent cheekbones and pointed up a hairstyle which seemed to be a melange of the Christian and the Saracen: on the one hand they had a tonsure on their heads like the Franciscans and other friars, and from this they shaved a strip three fingers wide from ear to ear; on the other hand, on their forehead they wore their hair in a crescent-shaped fringe reaching to the eyebrows and then gathered up the remaining hair and braided it like the Muslims.[83] A later Christian visitor, William of Rubruck, said that Mongol men had long hair behind the head, which they braided up in two plaits right up to the ears. While agreeing with Carpini that Mongol males tended to be short and slim, he found the women usually very fat. Females shaved their heads from the middle towards the forehead and had a particular fetish about noses. The smaller the nose, the more beautiful the woman was considered, to the point where they would even amputate the bridge of the nose, making the nose itself almost disappear.[84] Both these accounts were confirmed in a famous description by Carpini himself (he referred to the Mongols as 'Tartars'):

> In appearance the Tartars are quite different from other men, for they are broader than other people between the eyes and across the cheekbones. Their cheeks are also rather prominent above their jaws;

they have a flat and small nose, their eyes are little and their eyelids raised up to the eyebrows. For the most part, but with a few exceptions, they are slender about the waist; almost all are of medium height . . . On the top of the head they have a tonsure like clerics, and as a general rule all shaved from one ear to the other to the breadth of three fingers, and this shaving joins on to the aforesaid tonsure. Above the forehead also they all likewise shave to two fingers' breadth, but the hair between this shaving and the tonsure they allow to grow until it reaches their eyebrows, and, cutting more from each side of the forehead than in the middle, they make the hair in the middle long; the rest of it they allow to grow like women, and they make it into two braids which they bind, one behind each ear.[85]

Such descriptions from the Franciscans were calm and dispassionate, possibly because bitter experience had not soured them on the Mongols. Western Asian descriptions of the Mongols' appearance were vitiated by the perception of them as the scourge of God, so inevitably they were described in Persian and Arab sources as hideous or frightful to look at. Emphasis was placed on the lack of facial hair, the quick, glancing eyes, the shrill and piercing voices, the hardy bodies. Two witnesses may suffice. Here is a Christian Armenian of the thirteenth century:

They were terrible to look at and indescribable, with large heads like a buffalo's, narrow eyes like a fledgling's, a snub nose like a cat, projecting snouts like a dog's , narrow loins like an ant's, short legs like a hog's, and by nature no beards at all. With a lion's strength, they have voices more shrill than an eagle's.[86]

And this is a Persian poet:

Their eyes were so narrow and piercing that they might have bored a hole in a brazen vessel, and their stench was more horrible than their colour. Their heads were set on their bodies as if they had no necks, and their cheeks resembled leather bottles full of wrinkles and knots. Their noses extended from cheekbone to cheekbone. Their nostrils resembled rotting graves, and from them the hair descended as far as the lips. Their moustaches were of extravagant length, but the beards about their chins were very scanty. Their chests, in colour half white, half black, were covered with lice which looked like sesame growing on a bad soil. Their bodies indeed were covered with these insects, and their skins were as rough-grained as shagreen leather, fit only to be converted into shoes.[87]

Mongol women were a particular source of fascination to foreign observers. The accounts given of them ranged from arm's-length distaste – they were fat, they were ugly, they were indistinguishable from men – to grudging admiration – they endured great hardship uncomplainingly, they could ride horses as well as the men, they were expert drivers of carts, talented archers, and so on. Particular dislike was evinced for the garish colours in which they painted themselves, and particular admiration for the way they could give birth standing up and then carry on with their work as if nothing had happened. It was noted also that the Mongols respected women, as they were connected with the moon, and the moon was of great importance in Mongol religion.[88] Despite the complaints that the women were unisex, androgynous or epicene, the European chroniclers in effect contradicted themselves by drawing attention to the differential clothing of males and females. In the days before Genghis Khan and the luxury associated with world empire, the Mongols relied on clothes they could make from fur, leather, wool, felt and camel's hair. The standard garb was an ankle-length robe with loose trousers worn underneath. To combat the elements they had felt capes, fur hoods, leather boots and felt buskins; the fur clothes were double-layered so that the fur was on the inside as well as out.[89] Their favourite pelts came from foxes, lynxes and wolves. Although there were no great extremes of wealth and poverty on the steppes, there was inequality deriving from the different size of privately owned herds, and the most obvious sign of affluent status was the peculiar headdress worn by richer women known as the *boghtaq*. Described by one observer as a man's foot worn on a woman's head, the *boghtaq* was an iron wire frame between two and three feet tall, lined with bark and then adorned with red and blue brocade or pearls; sometimes the frames themselves were interwoven with red silk and gold brocade.[90]

This slightly meretricious aspect of the otherwise grim and stoical Mongol woman can perhaps be read as 'compensation' for the sparseness of her 'home'. Before the time of Genghis all Mongol tents were erected and dismantled at short notice. The domelike tent or ger was made from a latticework of willow lashed together with rawhide and covered with one or two layers of greased felt. The ger was thus a kind of hoop of interlaced branches and supports, converging at the top around a smaller hoop, from which projected a neck like a chimney. The outer layer was usually covered with white felt or a white mixture made from powdered bone, up to fourteen feet in diameter. The floor was covered with rugs of felt and hooks were fastened to the lattice work on which food, weapons and other items could be hung. The head of the household always faced the entrance which in turn always faced south; the men sat on the western side and the women on the east.[91]

Food and drink among the Mongols before the rise of Genghis Khan was largely a function of the narrow pastoral economy, that is to say, it was heavily dependent on milk and meat. In the summer, when mare's milk was plentiful, the Mongols actually preferred it to meat, but in winter this milk became a luxury item, available only to the more affluent. Only in an emergency was meat eaten raw; it was usually boiled or roasted. The staple diet in winter for the ordinary man and woman was a gruel made from multiply-boiled millet. Such was the knife-edge on which the Mongols subsisted in winter time that the nomads were not allowed to feed bones to their dogs unless the marrow had been extracted first.[92] Everyone ate with their fingers from a common pot, and there was careful sharing of the food. Yet all observers agreed that on the steppes one had to be a dietary opportunist, to be omnivorous and to devour anything that came one's way. The Mongols would eat any kind of flesh, including marmots (as we have seen), mice and other small animals. Some observers claimed that they would ingest any sort of protein except the taboo flesh of the she-mule: cats, dogs, rats, even lice and the afterbirth of mares. The English monk Matthew Paris, who was obsessed with the Mongols, claimed that they would eat frogs and snakes. The only general taboo was that one could never eat an animal that had been struck by lightning.[93] It was also alleged that the Mongols ate human flesh. Although there is only one authenticated case of cannibalism (during Tolui's campaign in China in 1231, in a dire emergency), the canard persisted in Western Europe that this was a commomplace practice in Mongolia. According to this version of events, the Mongols cannibalised for pleasure or to terrify their enemies. The most outlandish allegation, popular in the West, was that the nomads used the burnt bodies of their elderly and useless fathers as a kind of sauce to sprinkle over their food.[94]

On the Mongol fondness for alcoholic drink there was unanimity of opinion. Koumiss was a staple of nomadic life. This was churned in a large leather bag hung at the threshold of the ger during the three to five months of the summer when mare's milk was available; it could be made from the milk of sheep and goats but this produced an inferior brew. In the winter the Mongols also made a light wine from rice, wheat, millet and honey. Turbid and cloudy, koumiss had a sting on the tongue like sour wine but a very pleasant aftertaste like almonds.[95] There was also a superior clear mare's milk, known as 'black' koumiss, produced solely for khans, chieftains and high-ranking oligarchs. But since the alcohol content of koumiss was only 3.25 per cent at most, the nomads got used to drinking huge quantities of it. In the innocent days of koumiss alone, alcoholism was rare and hence fights also. Alcohol became a serious problem later when the Mongols became exposed to real wine, three or four times as powerful, but not even Genghis Khan could do much about it, as heavy drinking was so completely ingrained in Mongol culture.[96] Drunkenness was regarded as something to be proud of, an honourable estate and the ultimate expression of machismo. Sated on their brew the first time round, the topers liked to throw up and then settle in for a fresh alcoholic binge. Yet it was not the vomiting that disgusted foreign observers so much as the general filth and lack of hygiene among the Mongols – largely a result of the superstitious reverence with which they regarded water. William of Rubruck reported that a Mongol would stop in mid-conversation and urinate or, if defecation was called for, would simply move away, squat, shit and continue talking.[97]

The harshness of the Mongolian habitat and the complexities of nomadic pastoralism help to explain the many potentialities of Mongol society eventually actualised by Genghis Khan. Care of massive and variegated herds and flocks produced a number of consequences: adaptability and ingenuity of response and initiative; mobility and the capacity for rapid mobilisation; military virtuosity; low levels of wealth and of economic inequality; almost total absence of a division of labour; political instability. Migration meant constant alertness and readiness to fight, since wealth in livestock is almost by definition highly vulnerable to raiding, reiving and rustling. Managing large animals was inherently more strenuous and dangerous than tending crops, so the very nature of pastoral life produced a hardier breed than would be generated by the peasantry. Migration in peacetime also produced martial qualities via the surplus energy available for fighting, since in a pacific context warriors could leave the minutiae of herding and droving to women and children.[98] When the fighting came, it was less destructive than for sedentary societies that had to defend fields of crops, cities, temples and other fixed points.

There were other military 'spin-offs' from pastoralism. Moving huge herds of animals generated logistical skills and the capacity to navigate through uncertain terrain, coordinating with far-flung comrades while doing so.[99] The role of hunting was also very important. The Mongols began their hunting career with wolves and small animals, ruthlessly tracking down the former, and trading furs from the latter for clothes and other items. But they soon evolved into hunters of big game, and their gigantic battues (to be described in detail later) were an important form of military training.

Some scholars argue that, whereas a desert habitat is conducive to gradualism, the steppe habitat lends itself to rapid and violent solutions. Nomadic pastoralism on the steppe tends to isolate people and breed mutual incomprehension, so that raiding becomes an intrinsic part of life. Since raiding is a diversion from the primary purpose of pastoralism, there is an innate tendency for pastoralists to make their raids so savage and ferocious that sedentary agriculturalists, having once tasted the lash, will ever afterwards give in without a fight. One might simplify by saying that pastoral life engenders a kind of bully's charter.[100]

On the steppe, inequalities of wealth and rank were nothing like so great as in settled societies. In the Mongol world there was no agricultural land, no disarmed peasantry attached to the land, no lords defined by landholding, no castles, forts or defensive bulwarks, no stores of food or wealth (except for livestock). Possession of wealth and control of territory was therefore very volatile, and it was impossible for a strong sense of property in land (and still less money) to develop. One consequence was the lack of specialisation or division of labour in Mongol society; in particular, a distinction between herdsman and soldier did not exist, for every male Mongol was both.[101] And since both sexes tended flocks and drove wagons, the division of labour by gender was minimal. It is true that the men usually took charge of horses and camels, while women looked after cattle, sheep and goats, but Carpini's attempt to insinuate a division of labour by alleging that men were bone idle outside warfare while women did all the hard work in camp is refuted by better evidence, including that from his Franciscan successor at the Mongol court, William of Rubruck.[102] Rubruck's take was that both sexes were highly industrious but that they divided up chores according to rational preferences. Men made bows and arrows, stirrups, bits, saddles, built dwellings and carts, looked after the horses, milked the mares and churned their milk, tended and loaded the camels. Women made clothes, drove carts, loaded tents and gers onto them, milked cows, made butter and cheese, sewed skins, shoes, socks and clothes.[103] Carpini was misled because the Mongols disdained *regular* work, day after day, of the peasant kind. Idle sybarites such as Carpini describes would not have had their well-attested powers of endurance and ability to survive famines, nor would they have been tolerated in a culture where the leaders were supremely honourable about dividing food with their followers in times of dearth.[104]

The final aspect of pastoral society on the steppe to be noted is its gross political instability. Every tribal leader had to contend with the ineluctable fact that if he did not deliver considerable material success, his followers would simply melt away into the grasslands. No ties of kinship, real or fictional, clan loyalties, hereditary vassalage, territorial contiguity or tradition could prevent this. The steppe world was a treacherous one, where allegiance could never be assumed for any reason. In the absence of feud or vendetta, political alliances and coalitions were fluid and ephemeral, with a bewildering crossover of tribes, clans and even individual warriors. The only power a tribal leader had over his followers was the threat to appropriate animals and to massacre, enslave and 'adopt' women and children, but if a leader had such power, it is unlikely he would be deserted in the first place; and steppe tribesmen were brilliant at calling the bluff of blow-hards or posturers.[105]

2

Early Years

There had been powerful confederations, and even some empires, on the steppes before the thirteenth century – Scythians, Alans, Huns, Avars, Kirghiz and, especially, the Uighurs – but a historical punter, if such an animal existed, would hardly have bet on Mongolia as the birthplace of what would be by far the greatest of all. The Mongols began as an obscure tribe in one corner of Central Asia. Their foundation myth speaks of a mating between a male blue-grey wolf and a fallow deer who migrated to a high peak in the Khentei range nearer the headwaters of the Onon and Kerulen Rivers. From this union emerged a sole human male child named Batachikhan. A dozen generations later Dobun and his wife Ah-lan the Fair produced two sons. After Dobun's death she brought forth three more sons, whose father was supposed to be a mysterious being 'as yellow as the sun' who entered her tent by the light of moonbeams coming through the smoke-hole. Once inside the tent, he rubbed her belly with his hands and caused the light shining from him to enter her, then left much as he had come in, borne away by shafts of light from the smoke-hole. The five sons of Dobun – both the two he had actually begotten and the three born from a godlike source – each formed a clan once he had reached adulthood, and this was the origin of the massively complex clan system within the greater Mongol tribe.[1]

The youngest son, Bodonchar, founded the famous Borjigid clan from which the future Genghis Khan would spring. His great-grandson in turn was Qaidu, the first ruler of a fully united Mongol tribe. Again according to legend, the original Mongols were said to have been tall and bearded with light-coloured hair and blue eyes, but by systematic intermarriage they emerged as the people so well known for their short stature, black hair and black eyes.[2]

With Qaidu, who lived around AD 1050–1100, we finally emerge from the Stygian gloom of legend into the clear (well, fairly clear) light of history. The Mongols are first mentioned in texts of the Tang dynasty of China in the ninth century and during the succeeding Liao dynasty were reliable allies of the Chinese emperor. According to some accounts, they were originally forest peoples from the taiga who had migrated south. The Chinese traced their origins to the Mengwu tribe, part of the Shiwei confederation in the years of Tang dominance. By this time they had firmly established themselves in the Onon–Kerulen area of Mongolia.[3] Two things changed with the khanate (rulership) of Qaidu. First Qaidu began to intrigue with the Jurchen people of Manchuria, who would finally overthrow the Liao dynasty in the early twelfth century and establish the Jin dynasty. Then he decisively switched the Mongol economy from limited pastoralism and agriculture to full-blooded pastoralism, introducing new animals like sheep and camels; some historians claim that this was a backward step and that the Mongols had regressed from the Uighurs, who ran farms and homesteads.[4] Yet, despite his great abilities, Qaidu bequeathed to the Mongols a poisoned chalice in the shape of bitter feuding between the two principal clans in the Mongol tribe, the Borjigid and the Tayichiud (there were thirteen clans altogether but none as important as these). His eldest son Bai Shingqor Doqsin was made head of the Borjigid as the privilege of the senior sibling, but the younger (Charaqai Lingqu), formed his own lineage, the Tayichiud clan, as part of some obscure fraternal conflict. The desperate conflict between these two clans alone made it impossible for Qaidu or any of his successors to emerge as the khan of a united supertribe.[5]

The history of the turbulent twelfth century in Mongolia was dominated by relations with the new Jin empire in China. The atmosphere of chaos that emerges from the sources is partly explained by the fact that constant warfare between the Chinese and the nomads on the steppes went on at the same time as intra-steppe warfare between the five principal peoples of Mongolia – the Mongols, Merkit, Tartars, Kereit and Naiman – who were all at each other's throats, as well as the continuing feud within the Mongol tribe between the Borjigid and Tayichiud clans. Yet another factor is that the Mongol tribe did not simply consist of all the clans and sub-tribes whose native tongue was Mongolian, but that other tribes – Tartars, Naiman and

Kereit – also contained sub-tribes who were Mongols in an ethno-logical and linguistic sense. The only easy way to differentiate the Mongols from the other tribes is to say that they were the only purely pagan tribe – the others practising a mixture of Nestorian Christianity and shamanism.

Medieval Chinese historians made a rough-and-ready distinction between the various 'barbarians' on their frontier, dividing them into the 'civilised' or 'White' Tartars south of the Gobi and along the Great Wall, principally the Ongud; the Kereit or 'Black Tartars' who lived a non-luxurious and precarious existence on the steppes, sustaining them-selves with pride at their superiority over the cowardly 'White Tartars' who had sold their birthright for a mess of Chinese pottage; and what they called the 'Wild Tartars' of southern Siberia who eked out a living from hunting and fishing.[6] The Mongols, insofar as they were identified separately, were placed by Chinese historians as being somewhere between the White and Black Tartars; only with the rise of Qaidu did the Chinese realise they were something more formidable.

The reality of the power structure in Mongolia was more complex. The most powerful nation was the Naiman, a people of Turkic origins who lived on the southern slopes of the Altai Mountains and the upper Irtysh River and were gradually spreading over the Tarbaghatai and the upper reaches of the Selenga and Orkhon Rivers. They consid-ered themselves the heirs to the Uighur empire which had collapsed in the mid-ninth century. Politically cohesive until the early thirteenth century, they embraced a form of Nestorian Christianity mitigated by indigenous shamanism and were culturally more advanced than the tribes of northern and central Mongolia.[7] Next in importance were the Kereit, to the east of the Naiman with whom they were allied, also Nestorian Christians, who clustered around the upper reaches of the River Selenga and the Orkhon and Tula valleys.[8] The Tartars, comprising six different clans, who occupied the steppe region to the south of the Kerulen River, were the Chinese secret weapon in the twelfth century and have sometimes been called the gendarmerie of the Jin dynasty. All Chinese rulers sought to palliate the threat from their dangerous northern nomadic neighbours by a systematic policy of divide and rule, and the Tartars, until the end of the twelfth century, played the role admirably. As early as the tenth century Chinese historians identified the Tsu-pu (almost certainly the Tartars) as the dominant tribe in eastern Mongolia. They were the traditional enemies of the Kereit and were said to have annihilated a Kereit army 40,000 strong in the early twelfth century.[9] The Tartars were particularly dangerous to the Mongols as they lived just to the south of their territories, the Mongol homeland being around the Onon and Kerulen Rivers. To the northwest of the Mongols, on the lower River Selenga south of Lake Baikal and around Lake Khovsgol, was another warlike tribe, the Merkit, fortunately for the Mongols divided into three branches each with its own ruler; the Merkit were as fragmented as the Naiman were cohesive.[10]

The first half of the twelfth century brought a significant episode in the history of the Mongols with the khanate of Qabul, Qaidu's grandson, sometimes derided for his Pantagruel-like appetite but clearly a man of great ability. In 1125 he went to China to attend the coronation of the emperor Xi Zong and was said to have shocked his hosts by his gluttony. It was probably on a subsequent visit that he committed the ultimate social gaffe, getting horribly drunk at a banquet, tweaking the emperor's beard and generally scandalising his courtiers.[11] Yet the Jin did not make the mistake of treating him as a buffoon, for his able command of steppe politics had already made him a dangerous force on the frontier. So worried were the Jin by Qabul that, having allowed him to depart in disgrace from court, they had second thoughts and sent an armed party in pursuit to bring him back and force him to sign articles of vassalage. Alerted to the pursuit, Qabul lured the Jin posse into an ambush and slaughtered them to the last man. At this the gloves came off, and from 1135 to 1147 there was bitter warfare between the Jin and the Mongols. The Jin once again tried to use the Tartars as their secret weapon but Qabul defeated them on several occasions as well as doling out a serious check to a large Jin expedition that crossed the northern frontier into Mongolia in 1137.[12] He managed to form a temporary coalition of the principal Mongol tribes, but was very far from being a supreme ruler or khan of khans; he was a temporary military leader, not a permanent ruler, the coalition was shortlived and in no sense exhibited the permanent features of supertribalism.[13]

Despite having shown so much skill in steppe politics, Qabul left behind a shirt of Nessus by choosing a Tayichiud noble as his successor, passing over all his seven sons. In Tayichiud eyes this now made them, not the Borjigid, the senior Mongol clan. Recriminations and jealousies between the two septs were now raised to a new height. Some scholars think that this event, rather than Qaidu's misguided dividing of the realm between his sons generations earlier, was the truly significant event that weakened the Mongols and might have finished them off for all time as a serious political force.[14]

The Tayichiud chosen was Ambaghai. In 1143 he felt confident enough to take the war to the Jin and captured twenty of their forts near the Great Wall. Jin credibility was now at risk, and a large expedition was sent north in 1146. When this too failed – the Chinese could never defeat the Mongols in a pitched battle – the Jin were forced to accept a humiliating peace, in which the nomads for the first time gave terms to a Chinese emperor. The peace terms required the Jin to accept heavy reparations of sheep, cattle and grain, to abandon some of the frontier forts the Mongols perceived to be threatening and to pay a subsidy.[15] But the Jin had their revenge, and once again it was the Tartars who did the dirty work. To achieve this they were prepared to break the sacred customs of steppe hospitality. Ambaghai, thinking himself the equal as a politician of Qabul, went to the Tartar camp in the early 1150s to deliver his daughter as a bride, to seal what he thought would be a clever alliance with the Tartars. The Tartars played along but wanted none of Ambaghai's schemes. They handed him over to the Jin, who crucified him on a wooden donkey. At the moment of death he called on all Mongols to avenge him.[16] This was an atrocity that was never forgotten, and its memory would surface seventy years later with devastating consequences for the Jin.

Given the proviso that all dates in the early history of the Mongols are conjectural, we may tentatively place Ambaghai's death in 1156. He was succeeded by Qutula, a Borjigid, thus restoring that clan as the tribe's 'natural' rulers. Yet there is much that is obscure about Qutula's election. Some say that the Tayichiud broke away definitively from the Mongol confederation at this point and separated themselves physically from the Borjigid by finding themselves a new headquarters north and east of Lake Baikal.[17] Others claim that Qutula in desperation offered a fresh election in which he would stand but only the Tayichiud would vote. Yet another bizarre factor is that Qutula was Qabul's son yet had been expressly excluded from the succession when Qabul nominated Ambaghai.

Whatever the facts of his accession, the upshot was a further ratcheting of the tensions between Borjigid and Tayichiud. In Mongol lore there was a supposed difference between Nirun, 'the sons of light', and lesser tribesmen known as Durlukin – perhaps something like the distinction between the Guardians and the military class in Plato's *Republic*.[18] The problem was that both Borjigid and Tayichiud regarded themselves as Nirun and the rival clan as lesser beings. This caste difference was later strongly emphasised in the 'bible' of the Mongol empire – the *Secret History* – where only members of the Borjigid lineage are regarded as proper Mongols, with the Tayichiud as 'cousins' or poor relations, equivalent to other such minor appendages as the Besud, Oronar and Arulad clans.[19] All of this is properly Mongol esoterica, but the practical consequence of the feuding was that the Mongols were fatally weakened in the 1150s and no longer the force they were in Qabul's day. The Jin took full advantage of this, dug into their treasury to pay their gendarmes, and launched the Tartars again in a series of ferocious raids. Qutula fought thirteen pitched battles against them in this decade but could never achieve outright victory, probably through lack of numbers after the Tayichiud desertion.

He seems to have been an unlucky khan, for all the sources speak of his towering personal qualities. Said to have inherited his father's gargantuan appetite and to be immune to pain, he had powerful hands like a bear's paws and had a voice of a Boanerges worthy of history's other great bell-like declaimers, Danton and Pitt the Elder. According to one description, 'His voice resounded like thunder in the mountains . . . he could snap a man in two as you might snap an arrow. On winter nights he slept watched over by a fire built of great trees, and felt neither the sparks nor the brands that fell upon his body; at his awakening he took the burns for the stings of insects.'[20] Qutula could eat an entire sheep and drain a huge bowl of koumiss at a single sitting. Once, on the run from the Tartars, he hid among reeds, using one of them as a breathing tube while he lay submerged in water. The Tartars saw only his horse which appeared to be sinking in quicksands and concluded that the marsh had already claimed their quarry. Once they had gone, he pulled his horse out of the bog by its mane.[21] Yet for all his great qualities he lacked the numbers to deal decisively with the Tartars. After he had fought the thirteen indecisive battles, the Jin finally concluded he was sufficiently weakened to be easy pickings. They prepared a great joint expedition with the Tartars which achieved total victory over the Mongols at Lake Buir in 1161. It is unclear whether Qutula died in this battle but shortly afterwards he was no more, and the Borjigid clan was close to extinction.[22]

The next Borjigid to take up the reins was Yesugei. There is something of a mystery about Yesugei and his origins. The official version, in the *Secret History*, is that he was the third son of Bartan, Qabul's second son, and thus clearly a member of the ruling elite.[23] Yet Yesugei never ruled a Mongol confederation as Qabul, Ambaghai and Qutula had done. He had a camp on the River Onon near modern Gurvan Nuur, where he commanded a ragtag host of Borjigid, renegade Tayichiud and other clans, but he was never powerful enough to be elected khan.[24] His men were essentially guerrillas, a band formed of freelance operators and lawless 'wandering stars' who chafed against the duties and restrictions imposed by kinship and broke away from their original clans to be free spirits on the steppes. Since life as an individual in Mongolia was highly precarious, such men tended to gravitate around a charismatic leader, under pressure constantly to deliver booty.[25] As Yesugei was essentially a captain of *condottieri*, the suspicion has arisen that his inclusion in the genealogy of the Mongol ruling elite, as set out in the *Secret History*, is later propaganda, designed to enhance the glory and status of Genghis Khan. The probability is that Yesugei was the chieftain of a sub-clan, with no connection whatever with Bartan and Qabul and that he was in Mongol terms a mere *baghatur* or man of honour – the title habitually given to prominent nomads who were not of the royal line.[26]

In the 1150s Yesugei was in alliance with Qutula but he had his own goals and ambitions and for this reason often disobeyed his overlord. Yesugei's key idea was that to rise higher in the Mongol hierarchy he should ally himself with the Kereit leader Toghril (the name means 'gyrfalcon'), who needed allies since his position was under constant threat from his kinsmen. Toghril had had a difficult life. At the age of 7 he had been captured by the Merkit, enslaved, and made to grind millet with a mortar and pestle. He was rescued in a raid by his father but six years later was again enslaved, this time along with his mother, by the Tartars. This time his role in serfdom was to tend camels. Somehow he escaped, but the two incidents strongly suggest that Toghril was being 'set up' by treacherous relations.[27] Grown to adulthood, he was acclaimed as leader of the Kereit but immediately came under pressure from his two jealous brothers. Toghril decided to eliminate these pretenders to his position, but the two escaped and sought refuge with Toqto'a Beki, the principal Merkit khan. It says something about the almost routine treachery on the steppes in this era that Toqto'a immediately surrendered them to Toghril, who executed them. Toghril's uncle, disgusted by his nephew's cruelty and egomania, publicly condemned him as a murderer. The uncle, hugely popular among the Kereit because of his obvious concern for their welfare – Toghril cared only for himself – called on the people to eject this tyrant, and they responded. Toghril was lucky to escape with his life and fled south to China with just one hundred followers.[28]

This was the unprepossessing individual Yesugei chose to ally himself with, against the strong and vociferous opposition of Qutula, who rightly argued that the policy was dangerous folly. At the very time the Borjigid were struggling to fight the Tartars and the Jin and contending with opposition within Mongol ranks from the Tayichiud, it made no sense to become inveigled into the politics of the Kereit realm.[29] Yesugei was unmoved and even went through the ceremony of *anda* (roughly blood-brotherhood) with Toghril. For seven years Toghril was forced to roam the frontier lands as a minion of the Jin. Finally, when he and Yesugei were strong enough, they invaded Kereit territory and overthrew the regime there, forcing Toghril's uncle to flee west for sanctuary to the Tangut realm of Hsi-Hsia (the north-western corner of modern China).[30]

But Yesugei's foolish involvement in Kereit politics did not complete the tally of his idiocy. He displayed his complete lack of political nous by starting a feud with the Merkit too. Two issues are salient here. The Mongols practised exogamy and would travel long distances to find a suitable wife, but were not averse to stealing women, even other men's wives or betrothed, if the opportunity presented itself. Yesugei meanwhile was a notorious womaniser who already had one official wife and a harem of bedfellows. Sometime in 1159–60 he took a fancy to a fifteen-year old girl named Hoelun, who was then engaged to the Merkit leader Yehe Chiledu, Toqto'a's brother, and abducted her in circumstances not entirely clear.[31] This act of grotesque irresponsi-bility set off a fifty-year feud between Mongols and Merkits. Yesugei's sons would thus inherit a vendetta which was none of their making but which honour and culture compelled them to carry on.[32]

With Hoelun Yesugei begat five children, four sons and a daughter: Temujin, born in 1162 (for the date see below); Qasar, born 1164; Qaci'un, born 1166; Temuge, born 1168; and the girl Temulun, born in either 1169 or 1170.[33] Yesugei already had two children from an official wife, whose name is disputed. There are also hints in the sources that this earlier wife might have been unfaithful.[34] The two sons from the previous marriage were Begter and Belgutei. It is typical of all things connected with the early history of the Mongols that there is no agreement on Hoelun's tribal origin. The consensus view is that she was from the Buriyat tribe, one of the forest peoples, and even today the Buriyats trace their ancestry to Genghis Khan's mother. Others say that the Buriyat connection is bogus, even though there is the circumstantial touch that Genghis's wife Borte was buried in their territory. On this view she was a member of the Olqunu'ud clan of the Ongirrad tribe, situated in the most easterly part of Mongolia.[35] This would impart some rationality to Yesugei's abduction of Hoelun, since the Ongirrad were the Mongols' favourite target for intermarriage, so much so that the Mongols referred to them as the 'consort tribe'.

Temujin, the future Genghis Khan, was born in 1162. This is the only date that makes sense of the other events in the sources, though some historians, beginning with Rashid al-Din himself, have opted for 1155. At the other extreme is the eccentric view that he was born in 1167, which would require an entire recasting of all other elements in the traditional narrative.[36] Nor is there any agreement on where he was born. One suggestion is that he was born in a valley called Gurvan Nuur, while another goes for Delun Boldog in Dadal, 350 miles northeast of modern Ulan Bator, a small village in Khenti province in the middle of beautiful forests, mountains and lakes, though this hypothesis seems to resonate far more with Plato's idea that a beautiful environment produces greatness than on any documentary evidence. The commonsense view is that he was probably born somewhere on the upper reaches of the River Onon, or possibly the Orkhon region, which is rich in game; Baljun Island (actually a peninsula on the Onon) and Mount Duyiran have been mentioned.[37]

Inevitably legends grew up about his birth, including the story that he was conceived when a ray of heavenly light was beamed into his mother's womb – a story remarkably like the Virgin Birth in

Christianity, as well of course as closely recalling the legend of Ah-lan the Fair and the birth of Bodonchar. The legend preserved in the *Secret History* is that he emerged from the womb clutching a clot of blood the size of a knuckle in his fist, which was read as a sign that he would be a great conqueror; there is a similar story about the birth of Tamerlane.[38] The name Temujin has puzzled scholars as it means 'blacksmith'. If taken seriously, this would push Yesugei even farther down the social scale. The true explanation is that Yesugei named him after a Tartar chieftain, Temujin Uge, whom he had just captured. The idea was to transfer the chief's power to the child, but to make this effective the man would have to be slain; the inference then is that Temujin's birth was celebrated with slaughter – appropriately enough, cynics might say.[39]

The boy was brought up in the traditional way, learning to ride at an early age and honing his skill at archery by shooting at birds. In the winter he sped over the ice on skates made from bone or wood, learned to track and hunt squirrels and pine martens, then graduated to bigger game such as deer. A soon as practicable he began learning the art of falconry, considered an indispensable skill for a would-be future leader. There was no education in our sense. Temujin never learned to read and write, and the later great emperor Genghis Khan remained illiterate. Notably strong, enduring and physically resilient, even so he began to be overhauled by his brother Qasar who is reported as a veritable Samson. As an adult Qasar had shoulders and chest so broad and waist so narrow that when he lay on his side a dog could pass under him.[40] Like Qutula, he was said to be able to snap a man in two like a twig, and soon became the most famous archer in the Borjigid. Perhaps this was why there was always hostility and jealousy between him and Temujin, who far preferred the self-effacing Qaci'un and his favourite brother Temuge. But the relationship that was most important to Temujin at this time was with a young aristocrat from the Jadarad clan named Jamuga. He and Jamuga played knucklebones together and, though their paths later diverged, both would remember the happy days of their childhood. It was a sad day for Temujin when Jamuga was taken elsewhere; he did not see him for another eight years. But even at the age of 6 or 7 they had taken the oath of *anda*, which supposedly created a bond more powerful than any mere blood tie.[41] The *anda* relationship among the Mongols was meant to unite clans, sub-tribes and even different tribes and nations, and was thus a political affair, unlike blood-brotherhood among, say, the Scythians or Vikings, which was a personal bond between individual warriors.[42]

Shortly after Jamuga's departure, when Temujin was nine, Yesugei decided he needed to betroth him to a prestigious girl. Mongols married early, and the earliest possible engagement of a son added to the prestige of family and clan.[43] The traditional tribe for Mongol intermarriage was the Ongirrad of south-eastern Mongolia. Also known as Torolkin or The Nations, supposedly Mongolised Turks, the Ongirrad had a complicated origin myth, lineage and general mythology, all of which have had anthropologists scratching their heads. According to Mongol mythology, the close ties of Mongol and Ongirrad were because they had the same family names, with the Mongols as the 'black' family and the Ongirrad the 'white'. They first appear clearly in history in 1129 when they attended a meeting called by Yelu Dashi, the founder of the kingdom of Qara Khitai.[44]

To reach the Ongirrad country from the Mongol homeland meant travel over mountains and then across the south-eastern corner of the Gobi desert. This was an entirely new experience for Temujin, whose rovings hitherto had been confined to the movement between summer and winter pastures along the valley between the Rivers Onon and Kerulen. The first part of the journey was at high altitudes amongst black rocks, thorny scrub and heathland. Yesugei and his party trekked past Mount Darkhan, camping by night at the side of lakes, where there was more chance of finding game. Passing through a variety of terrain that intrigued the young Temujin, they began the crossing of the Gobi. Yesugei explained that the desert held no terrors for him, since it was autumn, the horses were in good shape, and the warriors were used to crossing the desert at this time of year to raid the Chinese border (in present-day Gansu). True, there were water shortages, but if you dug about thirty feet down into the earth you could find ground water. Once out of the desert, the Mongols entered fertile country with rich pastures, orchards, fields of corn and millet, elm trees and oases of willow and poplar.

The traditional meeting place of the Mongols and the Ongirrad was between Mount Chegcher and Mount Chiqurgu.[45] Yesugei had already explained to Temujin some of the complexities of the Ongirrad connection. The Ongirrad were divided into two main clans, the Nirgin and the Bosqur. Although the Nirgin were usually considered the more important branch of the Ongirrads, it was the Bosqur and their chief Dai Sechen with whom they would be dealing.[46] Dai Sechen greeted them cordially, but his mood darkened when he heard Yesugei's proposal for marriage. Nomads of the higher class were supposed to pay for their brides. Although he had prestige as a chieftain, Yesugei was cash-poor and all he could offer Dai Sechen was a single horse as a down payment.[47] On the other hand, Ongirrad women were by common consent the most beautiful on the steppes, and Yesugei had already identified Dai Sechen's 10-year-old daughter Borte as the girl he wanted his son to marry.[48] Secretly indignant at Yesugei's poor offer, Dai Sechen raised difficulty after difficulty, intending ultimately to reject the suit after face-saving formalities had been completed.

Here for the first time Temujin's personal charm made its mark. Alchi-Noyan, the Bosqur leader's favourite son, took to Temujin almost immediately and begged his father to accept the Mongol boy into his family. Dai Sechen finally agreed to the match, but only after setting a very high price on his daughter's favours.[49] He would accept the horse as down payment, but Yesugei would have to come up with the balance before the marriage could proceed. In the meantime, he would keep Temujin with him and use his labour as 'interest' on the outstanding debt. The 'live-in son-in-law' phenomenon was common practice on the steppes when the bride-price could not be paid at once, but was usually restricted to the poor.[50] Though not averse to staying in Alchi-Noyan's company, Temujin was shamed by his father's poverty and angry that he was being used as a mere pawn in a dynastic marriage. He remarked scathingly later about his father's behaviour: 'To decide a marriage based only on the amount of wealth is almost like merchant's conduct.'[51]

Before Yesugei left on the homeward journey, Dai Sechen announced one morning that he had had a dream about a white gyrfalcon clutching the sun and moon together with puzzling appearances by Temujin, which he interpreted as a sign that his prospective son-in-law would rule the entire world.[52] This seems to have reconciled him to the impecunious boy, who appears to have spent a pleasant three years or so with the Ongirrad. The inference is that he worked as a drover or herder, for the steppe peoples did not abide idle hands. The period with Dai Sechen was formative. By gaining a close knowledge of a people geographically far removed from his own, it may be that Temujin was unconsciously building a good foundation for a man who would later rule an empire.[53] He learned many valuable lessons from the Ongirrad, noting how often steppe feuds began with debts, how vengeance was a paramount motif, and how vendettas enforced narrow bonds of kinship, identity and solidarity and were thus inimical to the needs of supertribalism.[54] He noted the burgeoning trade between the Ongirrad and the Chinese south of the Wall, where furs, hides, horses, ewes, wethers, camels, yaks and salt were sent south in return for lacquer, textiles, ivory, ornaments and iron weapons. Dai Sechen spoke of the wealth and power of the Jin empire but Temujin reasonably asked, in that case why did they simply not conquer the tribes on the steppe and take what they wanted without having to trade it? Dai Sechen replied that the Chinese were not a warrior breed, which set Temujin thinking they could be conquered by those who were.

But soon enough the halcyon days came to an end. When Temujin was about twelve, word came that Yesugei was dead. It seemed that on one of his raids, he encountered a large party of Tartars. The sides were evenly matched, and the outcome of armed combat would have been uncertain. The Tartars, however, had recognised one of their old enemies and baited a trap. Since the two sides had met on Tartar territory, they invited the Mongol chieftain and his men to a great banquet, but put slow-acting poison in his food.[55] The possibility of being poisoned was ever-present in the nightmare world of the steppe, but this had to be balanced against the terrible insult that would have been offered the Tartars if Yesugei had refused their hospitality. Shortly after leaving the camp he suffered agonising pains in his stomach, lingered a while, then died. Essentially he was a martyr to the nomads' code of honour.[56] With his dying breath, he ordered his faithful retainer Monglik to bring Temujin back home. His followers deeply mourned his death, and it may have been Monglik himself who composed the famous epitaph: 'The deep waters have dried up, the sparkling stone is shattered.'[57]

Monglik rode hard to the Ongirrad country and brought the news to Dai Sechen. The Ongirrat leader was reluctant to let Temujin go, not least because it left his daughter Borte in marital limbo, but he

too was constrained by the mores of the steppe and had to allow the
lad to depart for the River Onon.

Yesugei had recalled Temujin hurriedly because he knew that on
his death the issue of succession would flare up again and, if his son
was not there, no one would speak for him; as the French say, *les
absents ont toujours tort*. But he could not have expected what took
place. The first sign of trouble came when the widows of Ambaghai
forbade Hoelun from attending the annual ceremonies to venerate
the distinguished Tayichiud ancestor.[58] Hoelun then tried in vain to
rally the Borjigid clan, asserting that she would lead them, but her
clansmen declined the offer. They were influenced not so much by
misogynistic contempt for a woman as by their unwillingness to have
a twelve- or thirteen-year old as the principal male in the clan, and
the rational calculation that, since Hoelun was not a *condottiere* like
her husband, the amount of booty and loot, and hence their shares
in it, would diminish alarmingly.

They also seem to have been displeased that Yesugei's youngest
brother claimed Hoelun as wife according to the law of levirate,
whereby a younger brother inherits his dead sibling's wife, but she
turned him down. This man, Daritai, Bartan's fourth son, took the
humiliation badly and began to conspire with the Tayichiud to destroy
the Borjigid once and for all.[59] Chieftain after chieftain, clan after clan
deserted Hoelun, and the first to go was the arrogant Targutai, leader
of the Tayichiud, who announced that his clan had now resumed the
leadership of the Mongols. The unkindest cut of all for Hoelun was
that Monglik, appointed by Yesugei on his deathbed to be his children's
guardian, also turned recreant. The rebels not only expelled the few
remaining Borjigid as virtual outlaws but took all their movable property too.

Reduced to a half dozen horses and a handful of serfs and retainers,
Hoelun and her family were now destitute.[60] They began to eke out
a sorry existence on berries, roots, edible plants and small mammals
like marmots and badgers. This enabled them to survive in summer
but in winter the animals disappeared and the diet was reduced to
plants, roots and boiled millet, fare which Hoelun and her family
would have despised while her husband was alive. The family relied
heavily on Qasar's skill with the bow and Temujin's expertise as a
tracker. Survival of the fittest was one thing, but soon Belgutei and

Begter, the bigger and stronger half-brothers from Yesugei's previous marriage, began to take the catches of Hoelun's sons, playing hyenas to their lions. Matters came to a head when Temujin and Qasar showed their versatility by catching a large fish (as we have seen, fishing was not a Mongol accomplishment and looked down on as the occupation of lesser beings).[61] Begter took the fish from them, cooked it and ate it. Coldly, Temujin plotted his half-brother's doom. He waited until Belgutei went fishing, then he and Qasar crept up on Begter and riddled him with arrows. In some accounts Begter is said to have known he was doomed, to have accepted the justice of his fate and faced death calmly.[62]

This murder, carried out when Temujin was thirteen or fourteen, shows both his supreme ruthlessness and his ability, even as an adolescent, to think through a long chain of causation. The homicide was justified by the unwritten code of the steppes which Begter had violated, but there was more to it than that. Temujin had identified Begter as a strong-willed rival whose claims to the Borjigid succession might be considered stronger than his, since he was Yesugei's eldest son.[63] He sensed no such threat from Belgutei, who seems always to have been a weak and submissive character, or possibly just a very clever survivor, as he lived into his nineties, an almost unheard-of old age for that era.[64]

Significantly Belgutei never sought to avenge his brother's death and became one of Temujin's most faithful followers. When he became khan of khans Temujin (as Genghis Khan) paid a graceful tribute to his comrades in those dark days with Hoelun: 'It is to Belgutei's strength and Qasar's prowess as an archer that I owe the conquest of the world empire.'[65] It was typical, too, of the Mongols that they always liked to use euphemisms for homicide; to murder and slay in battle thus became 'to abandon', 'to dismiss', 'to reject', 'to destroy the hearth'.[66]

But if Belgutei was meek and took the line of least resistance, Hoelun reacted with incandescent fury. She tore into Temujin and Qasar, making every disparaging comparison she could think of: dogs biting their afterbirth, panthers rushing over a cliff edge, angry lions, pythons with eyes bigger than their stomachs, gyrfalcons chasing their own shadows. How, she asked, could they ever hope to avenge themselves on the Tayichiud or the Tartars if they could not even make

common cause with their half-brothers? 'You are like wolves, like mad
dogs that tear their own flesh, like crazy young camels that attack
their mother from behind, like vultures that madly swoop to attack
rocks.'[67]

It may be that news of Begter's murder reached the Tayichiud, or
perhaps they simply wanted to check that Hoelun's family really had
pitchpoled into starvation and death. At all events they made a reconnaissance and found to their annoyance that the family was in fact
relatively thriving. Targutai, the self-appointed leader of the Mongols,
was shrewd enough to see that every day that passed made Temujin
more of a threat to his position. The simplest solution was to kill
him, but that would mean vendetta with his brothers, who would
surely raise the entire Borjigid clan against him. If he killed them too,
his credibility as a wise ruler of all the Mongols would be gone. The
best solution would be to take Temujin out of the power equation
altogether by enslaving him. The Tayichiud arrived at Hoelun's
encampment in force but Temujin was fortuitously absent, away on
a hunting trip. Targutai went out of his way to assure Qasar and his
brothers that he meant them no harm, he was interested only in
Temujin.[68] Again, for reasons of credibility, he had to justify the
capture, to assure the Mongols that Temujin had done something bad
enough to warrant punishment but not death. He hit on the murder
of Begter, for whom he cared nothing, as the obvious pretext.[69]

But first he had to capture Temujin, which was no easy task. He
threw a cordon around the woods into whose depths Temujin had
fled once his brothers warned him what was afoot. For six days Temujin
lay hidden, surviving on water alone. Finally, famished and desperate,
he tried to break through the cordon and was caught. Targutai bore
him in triumph to his headquarters then imprisoned him in a cangue.
This was a heavy, flat board with a hole in the centre large enough
for a man's head to be thrust through; the two pieces of the board
were closed around the neck, then fastened along the edges with locks,
and to make doubly sure the prisoner's hands were fastened to either
side of the yoke. The opening in the centre was large enough to allow
the captive to breathe and eat easily, though not large enough for the
head to squeeze through, unless the punishment was intended to be
severe, in which case the size and weight of the board made it impossible for the man to reach his mouth with his hands, leaving him at

the mercy of passers-by to decide whether he should be helped to eat and drink. The sources imply that the cangue was of the lighter type, and Targhutai felt confident his prisoner could not escape. But he reckoned without the resourcefulness of Temujin. The Tayichiud had foolishly left a single youth to guard their captive. When the youth started to doze off, Temujin crept up on him, clubbed him and made his escape.[70] He could not travel far but hid in a river with reeds up to his neck, the cangue giving him buoyancy and acting as a kind of lifejacket. Soon the hue and cry was raised and there was a frantic search.

Temujin was always lucky, and so it proved on this occasion. Of all the men looking for him, the only one who saw him in the reeds was a Suldus tribesman named Sorqan Shira, a secret Borjigid sympathiser; the Suldus had been compelled to become vassals of the Tayichiud. Daringly Sorqan removed the freezing and starving youth to his tent, where he hid him under a heap of fleeces; in one version of the story Tayichiud searchers actually prodded the fleeces with lances without making contact. A soon as the questing hullabaloo had died down, Sorqan removed the cangue, gave Temujin food and drink, and equipped him with bow and arrows. Around midnight, as soon as the moon set, Temujin stole a horse and made his getaway. The fearful Sorqan Shira tried to ensure that Temujin would go straight back to his family by providing just enough food and no saddle for the horse.[71] But Temujin never forgot what Sorqan Shira did for him, and later in his career would reward him handsomely.

Biographers have sometimes claimed that the captivity with the Tayichiud was a deeply traumatic incident in the life of Genghis Khan but, the cangue aspect apart, this kind of thing was relatively common on the steppes. As we have seen, Toghril endured two such episodes early in life, while his brother Jaqa Gambu was for a long time a prisoner of the Tangut; Jamuga too endured the perils of servitude, with the Merkit.[72] How much time elapsed from his initial capture on the Onon to the escape with the help of Sorqan Shira is uncertain, but it cannot have been longer than a few months unless, as some scholars allege, the *Secret History* has telescoped into a short time span events that in reality lasted many years. It seems that the Tayichiud did try to recapture him, but Temujin skulked on the mountain of Burqan Qaldun, whose defiles, byways and hidden tracks were known only to the Borjigid. Legend says that in this wilderness he was fed by a gyrfalcon, just as the biblical Elijah was said to have been fed by ravens. Once the coast was clear and the Tayichiud abandoned their search, Temujin sought out his family, only to find them in a worse plight than ever, existing mainly on marmots, having lost all possessions except nine horses.[73]

By this time Temujin was fourteen, physically precocious and almost an adult male. One day, when he, Qasar and Belgutei were out hunting, a party of Tayichiud raiders swept into their camp and ran off all the horses; the only mount left to them was the one Belgutei happened to be riding in the forest. Temujin commandeered the steed, and set off in pursuit on the very evening of the raid. He tracked the Tayichiud successfully but could never catch up with them, as he had to rest his mare for long stretches.

On the fourth day of pursuit, his horse was on her last legs and he was tired and hungry.[74] Suddenly he encountered a youth about his own age named Bo'orchu. Temujin had the same magnetic effect on him as he had had on Dai Sechen's son. The youth declared himself Temujin's friend for life, provided him with food and drink and fresh mounts, in return for which he craved only the boon of accompanying his new friend. Another three days of hard riding brought the pair in sight of the raiders. Under cover of night, the intrepid youths recovered all the stolen horses, but immediately the pursuers became the pursued.[75] Temujin told Bo'orchu they had nothing to fear as they both had reserve horses, but he grew gloomily thoughtful as the vanguard of the pursuing Tayichiud began to gain on them.

However the overconfident Tayichiud now made the mistake of getting strung out, with their leader, mounted on a splendid stallion, riding farther and farther ahead of his comrades. Temujin was already well aware of the principle of local superiority in battle, and he pointed out to Bo'orchu that for a brief time they had a two-to-one advantage. The Tayichiud leader came closer and closer and soon began to uncoil his lasso, ready to rope in the youths. Bo'orchu now revealed himself to be a talented archer. Drawing his bow, he took careful aim and shot; the arrow ran true, pierced the Tayichiud in the breast and severely wounded him. When his comrades came up, they stopped to tend his wound, breaking off the pursuit.[76] Bo'orchu meanwhile took Temujin back to his father, Naqu Bayan, who provided him with a bodyguard for the trip back to the Onon. Bo'orchu went with him, pledging his friendship for life.[77] From this tiny kernel would grow a mighty oak.

With Bo'orchu's men, along with recruits made up of freelance Borjigid, who sensed a leader in the making, and renegade Suldus warriors sent secretly by Dai Sechen, Temujin slowly built up his position as young warlord. It is from this period that many of his legendary exploits date, such as the time he was ambushed alone by six brigands and killed them all.[78] On these raids he must have picked up enough riches to be able to redeem the bride price with Dai Sechen, for the next significant event in his life was a journey with Bo'orchu across the Gobi to claim Borte as his bride. We may place this event in the year 1177 or 1178. The sources claim that Dai Sechen greeted him enthusiastically, and this may well be true for, considerations of the bride price apart, his daughter was now sixteen and in danger of becoming by Mongol standards an old maid. Since the engagement between Temujin and Borte had been formally ratified years before, no other suitor would have come forward, nor would Dai Sechen have risked abandoning the time-honoured exogamous tie between Mongols and Ongirrad and making an enemy of the Borjigid, until all other remedies had been exhausted. Perhaps it was relief that the marriage was finally to take place which made Dai Sechen provide a 'dowry' in the shape of a sumptuous brownish-black sable coat.[79] Strictly speaking the sable was not a dowry at all, but a gift from Dai Sechen's wife Chotan to Hoelun, the groom's mother; this practice was a deeply ingrained part of Mongol marriage procedures. But Dai Sechen was content. He was now not just *quda* to Temujin – a potential father-in-law – but the real thing, with a good-looking, red-haired, broad-shouldered warrior as his son-in-law.

The wedding feast was celebrated with the usual ocean of koumiss. Dai Sechen boasted about his tribe's complex genealogy, according to which the Ongirrad were descended from an entity known as the Golden Vessel, and pointed out the Ongirrad's prowess in iron smelting.[80] There seems also to have been some sort of distant kinship link between Temujin and Borte, though this aspect is obscure.[81]

Dai Sechen was a stickler for the niceties in Mongol marriage customs, and therefore regarded himself as obliged to accompany his daughter back to the groom's homeland; mindful however of Yesugei's fate when he traversed hostile territory and ended up drinking poison, not to mention the fate of others such as Ambaghai, he drew the line at travelling the whole way back to the Onon. He appears to have left the wedding party on the far side of the Gobi (or maybe at the great bend of the Kerulen River) and then returned to his base, leaving his wife Chotan to continue the journey and present the sable to Hoelun. The party had a tough time of it, crossing the Kerulen to reach the River Senggur and then proceeding upstream to Temujin's camp.[82]

About two years elapsed, during which Temujin continued to build up the strength of his band of raiders. It was in this period that he received another of his famous recruits, Boroqul, who was soon second in the hierarchy only to Bo'orchu.[83] There are hints in the sources that Borte found it difficult to conceive, became depressed about this, and was comforted only when Temujin allowed her to adopt a Tartar boy named Shigi Qutuqu, taken on one of his raids.

Then disaster struck. The Merkit had not forgiven or forgotten Yesugei's seizure of Hoelun, when she had been affianced to Toqto'a Beki's brother. Ever since they had yearned for revenge, and some time in 1179–80 the opportunity came. A very large raiding party, at least 300 strong, located Temujin's camp and attacked it. The Mongols, heavily outnumbered, were taken completely by surprise, panicked and after no more than token resistance broke and fled. Temujin and his four brothers got away together with Hoelun, but Borte was left behind.

This was a shameful episode in Temujin's career, and the *Secret History* remarks enigmatically: 'there was no horse for Borte.'[84] It is clear that Temujin abandoned her. The only thing unclear is whether he did so in a cowardly panic or whether, as so often with him, there was method in his badness, that he left her as bait so that his men could get away. If so, the plan worked, for as soon as the Merkit laid eyes on Borte they abandoned all thought of pursuit.[85] Temujin and his men fled to Burqan Qaldun and gave thanks for their survival; Temujin ritually removed his belt so as to make total submission to the spirit of the sacred mountain.[86]

When the Mongols finally returned to their camp, they found a wasteland: tents, carts, herds, horses, women – all were gone. Some sources say that among the captured was Chotan, then on a visit to her daughter. At first Temujin thought the raiders were Tartars but from various hints and pieces of evidence worked out that they were Merkit. He realised that if he had been taken it would have meant death or the most dreadful form of slavery.[87] Beyond that, he realised he was now involved in a struggle to the death, for just as the Merkit had never forgiven Hoelun's abduction, so he now would never rest until he had had revenge for Borte's seizure. A new phase of history had opened, what one commentator has called a 'Trojan war on the steppes'.[88] Temujin realised he could not fight the three large clans of the Merkit on his own, so looked around for allies. The obvious candidate was Toghril, his father's *anda*, but to win him over Temujin would need all his guile. He proved fully equal to the task.

It was typical of Temujin always to approach a problem from several angles. His overture to Toghril was therefore couched at a number of different levels, appealing to the Kereit leader's greed, pride and sense of realpolitik. He began by offering him the sable coat which Chotan had brought for Hoelun; this was accepted with avidity. Then he swallowed his own pride and claimed that he wanted to be Toghril's adopted son. Next he reminded Toghril that he was his father's *anda* and how much Yesugei had done for him. Quite apart from the unflinching support Yesugei had given the Kereit leader during his struggle with his uncle and his seven-year exile, there was a second incident when Toghril's half-brother Erke Qara had staged a a coup and dethroned him; again it was only with Yesugei's help that he was restored.[89]

Having listened to all these arguments, Toghril promised to throw all his resources behind Temujin's campaign against the Merkit. Some critics have accused Toghril of gullible stupidity for listening to flattery and emotional blackmail and for being bedazzled by a sable cloak, but Toghril was not quite so foolish as that. Hard, realistic calculations indicated that an alliance with Temujin made a lot of sense. The Naiman, traditional enemies of the Kereit, were emerging as the dominant political force in Mongolia, and had built an alliance embracing Oyirad, Ongud, Merkit, Tayichiud and, most ominously, the Tartars, who by this time had fallen out with the Jin and aggressively repudiated their former role as the strong right arm of the Chinese on the steppes. Toghril was in danger of being isolated and encircled and, in addition to this 'foreign levy', he had malice domestic in the form of his frighteningly ambitious son the Senggum and his

uncle, still waiting in the wings.[90] As an up-and-coming Mongol chieftain, who could attract many nomad warriors by his charisma, Temujin
was a plant worth cultivating.

Toghril mobilised all his forces for a massive campaign which aimed
to destroy the Merkit before their allies had time to help them. Some
estimates of Kereit strength claimed they could put 500,000 warriors
in the field but, although this is an absurd exaggeration, they were a
populous and powerful tribe. Temujin joined Toghril in a massive
sweep through Merkit territory. The 'coalition' crossed the Chikoy
River and for months – probably in 1180–81 – were engaged in hard
fighting.[91] The details are obscure, and the sources almost certainly
muddle a number of different campaigns fought by Temujin against
the Merkit, but the outcome was total victory for Toghril and Temujin.
Toqto'a Beki and his brothers sustained very serious, if not yet mortal,
losses and were forced to disperse as guerrilla bands. They would
probably have been exterminated had not Temujin, to the chagrin of
his allies, suddenly pulled out from the offensive, claiming his own
losses were too heavy.[92] The reality was that Temujin, already in his
mind revolving plans for the total domination of Mongolia, did not
want the Kereit to become too powerful.

Borte was recovered and found to be pregnant, having been pointedly given as a prize to Chilger-boko, younger brother of the deceased
Yehe Chiledu (from whom Yesugei stole Hoelun). Her mother had
also been humiliated, having been maliciously handed over as 'wife'
to a low-born Merkit; it was not the sexual defilement but the socially
degrading match she found most galling. By what are described as
'various means' (torture?), Temujin discovered the identities of every
last one of the original 300 raiders, executed them all and took their
wives and concubines into slavery.[93] Borte's pregnancy was deeply
embarrassing for Temujin, and he later ordered his court historians
to rewrite history. Rashid-al-din, the Arab historian, swallowed their
diaphanous propaganda, and produced a story that Borte was already
pregnant when the Merkit captured her. According to this fiction, the
Merkit immediately sent Borte to Toghril as a peace offering. When
Temujin pulled out of the campaign, Toghril's counsellors advised
him to rape Borte in revenge, but he simply sent her back to Temujin.
The whole tale was an elaborate mesh of nonsense to cover up Borte's
shame and the illegitimacy of the child she was carrying. Not even

the *Secret History* was prepared to swallow such a tall story.⁹⁴ Nevertheless Borte's child by Chilger-boko, born in about 1182, was accepted by Temujin as his own and named Jochi.

One of the unlooked-for consequences of the war against the Merkit was that Temujin was reunited with his childhood friend Jamuga. Jamuga had long since thrown in his lot with Toghril, out of much the same consideration that drew Temujin to the Kereit leader, and, hearing that Temujin had been taken under the Kereit's wing, suddenly seems to have remembered he was his *anda*.⁹⁵

Jamuga, now chieftain of the Jadarad, had had as tough an early life as his friend's. He had been captured and enslaved by the Merkit when very young, escaped, built up a band of warriors and then, calculating that the Merkit were much too strong to fight, offered fealty to Toqto'a Beki and was given amnesty for the earlier 'crime' of having escaped. It was a condition of the rapprochement that Jamuga could retain thirty men as a personal bodyguard. Supremely crafty, he wormed his way into Toqto'a's confidence, partly by insinuating (and it was probably true) that he was far more intelligent than his other counsellors.

A story told by Rashid-al-Din shows the young man in action. One day Jamuga spotted that a quail had made its nest in some long grass. He secretly marked the spot. Next day, when he was out riding with the officers of Toqto'a's inner circle, he suddenly pointed to the spot and said he remembered seeing a quail making a nest there a year ago, and wondered if any sign of it still survived. 'Let's see if it's still there and if the quail has produced any young,' he said with mock innocence. The Merkit officers approached the designated spot, at which the quail flew off, abandoning her young. The officers scratched their heads with astonishment. 'What kind of man can remember a patch of grass from one year to the next? He must be a supreme genius.'⁹⁶

The story, when reported to Toqto'a, lost nothing in the telling. But this kind of magician's sleight of hand was simply an overture to the main *coup de théâtre* Jamuga was preparing. Noticing that the guards outside Toqto'a's tent were very lax and sloppy, Jamuga primed his men and burst in on an astonished Toqto'a. Jamuga explained quietly that he had only done it to show how incompetent the bodyguards were.⁹⁷ Toqto'a, who realised how easily he could have been slain in his bed, was relieved and grateful, but demurred when Jamuga said that in return for this signal service to the chief he now required a signed and witnessed charter of release from all obligations and fealties. The mood inside the tent turned ugly. Finally Jamuga said that Toqto'a's choice was simple: he could do as requested or die at once. Toqto'a realised Jamuga was not bluffing and took the choice for life.[98] It was clear to all observers that Jamuga was both as able and as cunning as Temujin, and many wondered what their reunion would bring.

There was one drawback to Jamuga's character that Temujin did not possess: he was a proud and irascible prima donna. He made clear his contempt for Qasar and Belgutei right at the beginning of the Merkit campaign when Temujin sent them as his envoys to propose a joint expedition.[99] He soon reinforced the impression of being a loose cannon. When arrangements were made for Toghril's 20,000 troops to link up with Temujin's levies at a rendezvous on the eastern side of Burqan Qaldun in the Khenti area, Jamuga refused to join them but insisted his allies come to him instead at the source of the Onon River, which meant that Toghril had to make two long journeys, one to link up with Temujin and the other to reach the mustering point with Jamuga. To the amazement of Temujin and Toghril, Jamuga brought almost as many warriors to the rendezvous as they had, then showed his independence by publicly rebuking Toghril and Temujin and his brothers for arriving three days late.[100]

Jamuga clearly enjoyed Temujin's snubbing Toghril by pulling out of the campaign before they had finished off the Merkit, and went with his *anda* after the split. The two withdrew to Jamuga's camp on the Onon, while Toghril made his way to his base on the River Tula, proceeding via the Hokortu valley in the Great Khenti.[101] There followed a memorable eighteen-month period, during which the two young men were inseparable, a kind of Oriental David and Jonathan. They exchanged golden belts and beautiful horses. Jamuga spoke sentimentally about their childhood memories, the games of knucklebones, and much else. They hunted together, drank together, wenched together, and, as the *Secret History* relates, 'At night they slept together under one quilt.'[102]

The entente is odd and puzzling, and not just because Jamuga had been noticeably cool towards his *anda* during the Merkit campaign.

Different nomad groups very rarely cohabited like this. It has been suggested that, to further his ambitions, Temujin needed the support of his friend, whose followers were at this stage far superior numerically, but what was Jamuga's motivation?[103] Borte, who never liked or trusted Jamuga, warned her husband that he was being used as a pawn in his friend's ambition – and Hoelun backed her in this opinion – but Temujin at first dismissed this as female pessimism and overcaution.[104]

Suddenly, after eighteen months of harmony, sweetness and light, probably in the year 1183, Jamuga went out of his way to pick a quarrel, speaking in a Delphic and enigmatic manner but seeming to imply that the interests of his horse-breeders were being sacrificed to those of Temujin's sheep-breeders.[105] This reflected the fact that Temujin, even after the success against the Merkit, was still relatively horse-poor.

What can explain the outburst? Some have taken it at face value, as an obscure dispute about pasturage, with Jamuga possibly under pressure from his followers who felt Temujin was getting the better of the entente. Others claim that Jamuga was reprimanding his comrade for being too absorbed in the arts of peace when they should be considering war to fulfil their vaulting ambitions. The most bizarre suggestion, popular among Soviet historians in the early twentieth century, was that Temujin and Jamuga represented antagonistic elements in a primitive class war, with Temujin siding with the aristocrats and Jamuga as the people's champion.[106] The problem with this interpretation is that the exact opposite seems to have been the case. It was always a strength of Temujin's that he promoted his officers by meritocracy, whereas Jamuga stuck with the old oligarchic modalities. We are left then with only a few possibilities. Either Jamuga was expressing some esoteric, quasi-Gnostic sentiment, whose meaning was known only to a few at the time and is now lost to us. But in that case why would Temujin himself describe the outburst as a riddle?[107] The other is that Borte was right, Jamuga was biding his time until he felt confident enough to show his hand openly and that when he spoke he had finally decided that Temujin was no further use to him. On this view Jamuga was offering Temujin a choice of responses but, whatever he said, Jamuga intended to disagree with him.[108] A final possibility is that the two men were playing a very deep game. At the profoundest level the split was about which of them would be the man to reunite the entire Mongol nation.

Whatever the explanation, the differences were clearly irreconcilable. Temujin and his immediate family and supporters stole away at night and set up their base at the River Kimurkha. Shortly after the sudden and unexpected rupture, all the clans of the Mongol nation except the Tayichiud held a supreme council, where divided opinions were immediately apparent. The division was mainly by age: the tribal elders wanted to create a new federation of clans with Jamuga as the leader, but the younger warriors opposed this.

The attraction of Temujin was that he had created a haven for all who had broken away from the rigidities of the old kinship-based clan structure. The chaos on the steppes since the early 1160s, with the Tayichiud–Borjigid feud, Tartar incursions on behalf of the Jin, Merkit raiding and a power struggle between Kereit and Naiman, had created a kind of war of all against all, as in Hobbes's formulation, where life was cheap, herds were stolen or slaughtered and horses ridden to death by juvenile yahoos. Rebelling against the ties of kinship, ancestor worship, respect for elders and all traditional mores and folkways, young Mongols had welcomed Temujin as a breath of fresh air, a leader whose charisma depended on military victory and loot: one who, so to speak, delivered the goods instead of talking about them.[109] The downside was an increase in machismo and violence, with armed robbery and rape regarded as evidence of superior masculinity. For the young, talk of a new confederation meant simply the old wine in new bottles and they wanted none of it.

The upshot was a violent break between supporters of Jamuga and those who backed Temujin. Jamuga told anyone who would listen that the rift with Temujin was not of his doing, that the real behind-the-scenes villains were Temujin's uncles Altan and Quchar, who had always hated him. The sources speak of 13,000 warriors opting to take their chance with Temujin, though one must always beware of exact figures quoted in Mongol sources, which are notoriously unreliable.[110] Temujin, already showing the high flair for organisation and administration that was so marked a characteristic of his, divided his followers into thirteen units or 'camps'. He, his sons, bodyguards and intimates formed one of these; his brothers and their men another; and the rest of the warriors were temporarily assigned by clans – the Jurkin, the Baya'ud, the Jalayir, the Ba'arin and so on. What was notable was that some of Jamuga's previously loyal allies sided with Temujin, a sign

they thought he would eventually win the struggle.¹¹¹ All of these
thirteen units Temujin honed to a pitch of military readiness, soon
making them something far more than part-time soldiers. Temujin
encouraged the units to compete with each other and even staged
mock battles, some of which got out of hand and caused real bloodshed. Temujin also adumbrated some of his later famous reforms,
appointing trusted men as 'quiver bearers' and 'sword bearers' and
nominating stewards in charge of victuals, beverages, sheep, horses,
tents and wagons. Another of his innovations was to pitch camp not
in the old informal way with gers stretched out in a grid, but to form
a laager, circling the wagons and tents in a concentric pattern with
the chieftain and his family in the centre.¹¹²

Temujin's energy in this period contrasts with the somewhat inert
performance by his rivals. The Toghril of this era appears in the
sources as a treacherous, venal ingrate, flabby, dull if basically good-
natured, weak and temperamentally prone to compromise, which his
enemies invariably construed as weakness.¹¹³ Jamuga, unquestionably
a man of great ability and, within the limits of traditional steppe
codes, a stickler for probity and integrity, was an intriguer and a
short-termist, treacherous and volatile, notorious for jettisoning friends
suddenly and brutally. Although at one level he held all the cards, with
the support of the Tayichiud, Jeljud, Arulad and the Nirgin Ongirrad,
the long-term weakness in his position was that while Temujin was
trying to build a holistic *esprit de corps* in his, Jamuga maintained
traditional tribal divisions in his, assigned commands by social rank
not merit, and refused to do as Temujin did, recruiting shepherds into
the officer class, because he considered them *infra dig.*¹¹⁴

Another advantage Temujin had was the sheer quality of the
personnel he had attracted to his standard. Most of the senior members
of the Borjigid aristocracy had rallied to him, even his paternal uncle
Daritai who never liked him. There was Sacha Beki, the great-grandson
of Qabul and chief of the Jurkin clan (both the Jurkin and the Borjigid
claimed descent from Qabul Khan), his brother Taichu, Quchar Beki,
son of Yesugei's elder brother Negun Taishi, and Altan Otchigin, son
of Qutula – which meant Temujin had the support of the heirs of
the last two rulers of a united Mongol nation, even though it is likely
that at this juncture they supported him because they thought him
malleable and easier to handle than a loose cannon like Jamuga. There

was danger too in their adherence, for all the older men would have a better claim as khan of the Borjigid than Temujin.[115] One of them was the hugely ambitious Qorchi of the Ba'arin, who joined Temujin after claiming to have seen heavenly omens predicting him as the future great khan of the Mongol nation. Temujin was pleased both with his support and his eulogy and promised that, if victorious, he would grant Qorchi his own regiment. The lustful Qorchi replied that in addition to this he wanted thirty personally handpicked young women of superlative beauty; this too was granted.[116] Even the two-faced Monglik changed sides and came back to him.

Still more impressive were the meritocrats Temujin gathered around him. Bo'orchu's younger brother left the Arulad to join the cause, while from the Uriangqai tribe of the forest peoples came one of Temujin's star recruits, Jelme, son of Jarchigudai, a blacksmith.[117] The great future general Muqali, still in his late teens, joined up, praising Temujin as the great one promised by his people's legends.[118] Yet another future military genius was recruited through Jelme's good offices. He had a young brother, Subedei, who came to Temujin's camp when he was just ten years old, a starry-eyed boy who had spent all his life among the reindeer in the taiga and had never seen the steppe before. He had none of the riding, hunting and fighting experience of the usual Mongol boy; his only skill was ice-skating.[119] But he was highly intelligent and a 'quick study'. Employed as a factotum, with a special brief to guard Temujin's tent, he swiftly picked up all the necessary skills for a Mongol warrior. To an extent of course he rose on the coat-tails of his brother Jelme, whom Temujin always expressly mentioned as second in the hierarchy only to Bo'orchu.[120] Temujin was a notable talent-spotter and encouraged synergy among his followers, exhorting the most intelligent to get together and 'brainstorm' on particular issues; he liked to steer Belgutei towards Bo'orchu for this purpose.[121]

Such was the euphoria in Temujin's devoted band that in 1186 they elected him khan of the Borjigid, a signal honour. Sacha Beki, Altan and Quchar were the prime movers in this endeavour, in a classic recognition of necessity. Both Quchar and Altan were offered the khanate first and Temujin made it a point of understanding that he would put himself forward only if they declined the honour. Both did so, and the reasons were clear. They were irremediably tainted with the catastrophe at Lake Buir in 1161 and, in any case, realised that whoever held the formal leadership of the tribe, Temujin would certainly be the power behind the throne. They had switched from Jamuga, whom they deemed too powerful, thinking they could manipulate Temujin, and by now had realised their mistake.[122] Besides, Temujin had all the credentials for khan: he had proved his military talent in the campaign against the Merkit; he enjoyed the favour of Toghril and the Kereit, as no other claimant to the khanate did (Toghril formally endorsed it);[123] and he was very popular because he had enriched his followers with herds and other booty.

Nevertheless, the oath taken to the new khan by his followers bound them to be loyal to him only in war and on the hunt and to give him first pick of captive women; in no sense did they accept him as a feudal overlord – this would not come till twenty years later. The election as khan had great symbolic importance, however, despite the absence of the Tayichiud and other powerful clans. Temujin was the first khan to have 'gained the purple' by an unconventional route. He was neither a hereditary ruler nor one acclaimed by popular mandate, and he was always only a khan on probation; even those who swore limited fealty would desert at the first sign of trouble. He was an outsider who had risen to the top against all the odds and from an unconventional starting point. Lacking a secure base of tribal support, still clearly Toghril's junior partner, with no tradition or model of a steppe empire to build on (the last steppe empire, that of the Uighurs, had disappeared nearly four hundred years earlier), Temujin was very much launching into the unknown. To gain the solid political base he needed he would have to win more victories in the field, and this meant he would have to take great risks to do so.[124] It was this factor alone that nearly brought his career to a juddering halt.

3

The Rise and Rise of Temujin

The year 1186 was a joyous one for Temujin. Not only was he khan of the Borjigid but his wife presented him with a second son, Ogodei – the first one Temujin had truly sired with her. But he was not allowed to remain at peace for long. Jamuga had viewed his ascent with disquiet and may have been looking for a pretext to put his *anda* in his place. The *casus belli* came the following year. Jamuga's brother Taichar stole some valuable horses from Temujin's friend Jochi Darmala, who retaliated by shooting him dead with an arrow.[1] Jamuga took this as a declaration of war by the Borjigid, assembled his host and marched against them. The sources say that he had 30,000 men ranged against Temujin's 13,000. These numbers are exaggerated at least threefold, but it is easily credible that Jamuga outnumbered Temujin three to one. A terrible, murderous battle took place at Dalan Baljut ('seventy marshes'), an unknown location possibly on the Kerulen near the source of the Senggur.

Jamuga won the day, but it was a pyrrhic victory which gave him pause.[2] A lukewarm pursuit managed to bottle up Temujin in a defile near the Onon but Jamuga, displaying the half-heartedness always in evidence whenever he had Temujin on the ropes, did not press his advantage and allowed his rival to escape. He did, however, become notorious for an alleged atrocity immediately afterwards. Angry with the Jurkin clan for having joined Temujin, he is said to have boiled seventy of their senior members alive.[3] There have long been suspicions that the 'boiling' story was simply Borjigid propaganda; one suggestion is that Jamuga actually made a ritual sacrifice of seventy wolves.[4]

Whatever the truth of this incident, Dalan Baljut seems to have wrecked Temujin's position overnight. The tale in the sources that the boiling so alienated many of Jamuga's followers that they deserted and joined Temujin is probably the *Secret History*'s clumsy attempt to mask the fact that large numbers actually deserted Temujin. It is surely significant that after the battle the sources abandon the narrative trail and 'cut' cinematically to the year 1195.

This historical lacuna has been explained in various ways. Some say the entire account of Temujin's early life in the *Secret History* and the work of Rashid al-din is a jumble of incorrect dates and sequences, that the events recounted took place over a much longer time span, and this is the explanation for the blank space dealing with the years 1187–1195.[5] Others, more convincingly, argue that Temujin in effect returned to square one and had to begin the laborious process of building up military strength all over again. On this view he may have acted as a captain of guerrillas on behalf of the Jin, who had begun to grow disillusioned with their Tartar gendarmes, but this fact was suppressed because it tarnished his legend. Or, more plausibly, he may have actually gone to China as an exile, become a client of the Jin, and lived there for eight years, waiting for his hour to strike.[6]

Whatever interpretation we opt for, it is clear that in these years Temujin suffered a series of misfortunes which did not redound to his credit. Moreover, his eclipse dragged Toghril down as well. Without Temujin, he was not strong enough to contend against a legion of enemies, including the Naiman, the Tartars, the Merkit, the Tayichiud and his own uncle and brother. Soon after Temujin's departure south, he too was forced into exile. Some say he joined Temujin with the Jin for the entire period, but better evidence suggests a more complicated pattern of roving. Toghril's position as leader of the Kereit was always shaky because of the unregenerate hostility of his brother and his uncle Erke Qara, essentially an agent of the Naiman.[7] Shortly after Dalan Baljut he was ousted in a coup. He may have gone to Jin China initially, but his ultimate destination was the westerly kingdom of Qara Khitai. Once there he somehow raised an army of rebels against the ruler but was defeated and forced to flee. Moving eastwards with a band of desperadoes, he plundered the land of the Uighurs before coming to rest in the Tangut kingdom of Hsi-Hsia. Possibly using family contacts (one of his brothers had spent many years with the Tangut) he made a secure base there: some records in fact show him as having been in Hsi-Hsia twice, once on the way to Qara Khitai and again on his way back.[8] The Tangut initially received him hospitably but he outstayed his welcome when his famished followers started plundering the locals. Eventually expelled from Hsi-Hsia too, he wandered back to Mongolia where he eked out a living as a mountain bandit. The one aspect of Mongolian history in the years 1187–95 which no historian has ever explained is why, with his two principal rivals out of the reckoning, Jamuga did not establish an ironclad hegemony there. Perhaps Targutai and the Tayichiud, or more likely the Naiman, were simply too powerful.

Meanwhile in China Temujin bided his time. Almost the only witness we have for these years that the locusts ate is the biography of Subedei, who was eleven when the time of exile began and nineteen when it ended. During these years the youth evinced both self-effacement *and* ambition. It is likely that, as a protégé of Jelme, he was present at Mongol staff conferences and acquired a unparalleled insight into war planning and the human psychology involved.[9] That he went out of his way to make himself agreeable to Temujin is evident from the *Secret History*. This is how he offered his services to the exiled Borjigid khan:

> I'll be like a rat and gather up others. I'll be like a black crow and gather great flocks. Like the felt blanket that covers the horse, I'll gather up soldiers to cover you. Like the felt blanket that guards the tent from the wind, I'll assemble great armies and shelter your tent.[10]

Temujin's restoration to prominence in Mongolia owed much to the rift between the Jin and the Tartars. The relationship had always been an uneasy one, for the Tartars would sometimes turn on their over-lords and loot their property if they were disappointed with the outcome of a raid. In 1195 the Jin had earmarked the Ongirrad as a target for a pacification campaign, for unknown reasons but possibly because this tribe was uncomfortably close to the northern Chinese frontier and had been showing disturbing signs of wanting to jettison their status as Jin vassals. The Jin recruited the Tartars as their allies for this campaign. The Ongirrad were defeated but an overweening Tartar leader named Sechu complained bitterly about the Jin's sharing out of the spoils. The upshot was a pitched battle between the Jin and their auxiliaries. The Tartars were defeated and driven north, but the Jin had lost so many men in the fighting that the Ongirrad seized their chance and rose again. In February 1196 they defeated the Jin army.[11]

Temujin, who had his ear to the ground, proposed that he and his men take the place of the Tartars, pacify the Ongirrad and then take the war to Sechu and his rebels. It seemed that he requested that the Jin emperor formally recognise him as an ally, but the 'Son of Heaven' ignored this impertinent request from a mere barbarian. Temujin then repeated the offer to the Chinese frontier commander, who was not so squeamish and was actually in a desperate plight. A joint Jin-Mongol punitive expedition went north, caught up with the Tartars, and heavily defeated them in a series of running battles in the Uldza valley; the important Tartar princeling Meguzhin was killed in one of these engagements.[12]

At last Temujin could feel he had avenged his father. The amount of booty taken was staggering. As his personal treasure trove Temujin set aside a cradle made of silver and some sumptuous blankets decorated with large pearls.[13] Hearing of his adopted son's great triumph, Toghril saw the chance for restoration and sent a message asking for a meeting. The two men met at a secret location[14] to which Temujin had ridden hard from the source of the Kerulen. The fortunes of the two had changed radically: Temujin now had the power and Toghril was the suppliant and indeed almost destitute. But Temujin was magnanimous: he took Toghril into his camp, fed him lavishly and promised he would restore him. It seems there was still some hard fighting to come with the anti-Toghril faction among the Kereit, but by 1197 he was restored as their leader.[15]

The Jin commander on the frontier, Wan-yen Hsiang, after conferring with the emperor, announced that his allies were to be rewarded for their suppression of the Tartars with official Chinese titles. Far the grandest was that received by Toghril, who received the title of prince or Ong Khan; Temujin received a much lesser honour. Here was considerable irony, for Toghril ended up the beneficiary of events in which he took no part, while the real author of victory was given an honour equating to 'commander' in Chinese.[16] The question arises: why did the Jin, who presumably knew exactly what had transpired, confer such an honorific title while downgrading Temujin? One answer sometimes given is that Toghril was named as Ong Khan much later for some other service (but its nature is never specified). The most likely explanation is that the Jin had already noted Temujin's formidable abilities and did not trust him not to become a second Sechu, whereas they knew Toghril of old, he was considered reliable as their eyes and ears in Mongolia, and was a tried, tested and known quantity. Whatever the Jin thought and whatever snubs they gave Temujin, the fact remained that he was now a more important political player in Mongolia than Toghril and would prove himself far the intellectual, strategic and political superior to his nominal overlord in the land of the Kereit.[17]

Several important consequences flowed from the triumphant campaign against the Tartars. First, having vanquished one mortal enemy, Temujin felt strong enough to attack another, the Merkit, who had enjoyed a considerable revival during his absence with the Jin. In 1197 he decided to blood the 21-year-old Subedei in his first independent campaign. Subedei surpassed all expectations. He volunteered to go into the Merkit camp as a spy and carried off the deception so plausibly (it helped that he was not a Mongol) that he came back with the complete Merkit war plan.

The result was an easy victory.[18] As a young adult Subedei was already a total master of warfare, with a thorough grounding in staff work and a positive genius for tactics, strategy and, especially, grand strategy. Marrying a first-class mind with the soul of a gambler (rather like Napoleon), Subedei was also a specialist in dispersal, rapid mobilisation and concentration, ensuring that he would always have local superiority in numbers at any given time.

Temujin made a point of giving 90 per cent of the spoils from this campaign to Toghril, to set him on his feet again.[19] With both Tartars and Merkit cowed, Temujin took the opportunity to winkle out all traces of internal opposition. He had long experienced trouble with the Jurkin clan, led by Sacha Beki, who, he told his confidants, were 'fierce, arrogant, heartless and men of gall'.[20] There had been one spectacular instance of insubordination; the maddening vagueness of the Secret History over dates does not allow us to pin it down to a specific time, but it may have been during the years of exile in China. The incident took place at a banquet and was the consequence of a spat between women. Qorijin, Sacha Beki's mother and Qu'urcin, wife of the chieftain Sorqatu claimed there had been an egregious breach in the etiquette of precedence, in that the wife of Belgutei,

Temujin's half-brother, had been served ahead of them.[21] Since Sacha Beki and his entourage, which included their champion Buri-boko, were drunk, they got sucked into the dispute and started insulting and even physically pummelling members of Temujin's inner circle. Soon there was a genuine donnybrook, with pots, pans and kettles being hurled, fists flying, branches ripped from trees to serve as weapons and warriors wielding leather buckets of koumiss as if they were war-axes or maces. Buri-boko actually wounded Belgutei in the shoulder, sending Temujin into a rage. Belgutei, always the diplomat, assured his half-brother that it would be stupid to break up the alliance over a flesh wound, but Temujin refused to turn the other cheek; he called for his bodyguard who drove the Jurkin from the feast with tree branches.[22]

Temujin was particularly incensed by the behaviour of Buri-boko, who was, to make matters worse, a renegade Borjigid. Thinking himself superior to Temujin's entourage and even the khan himself, he had allied himself with Sacha Beki and Taichu, Numbers One and Two in the Jurkin hierarchy, and had been promptly promoted to Number Three. In Temujin's eyes he was already guilty of treason. By allying himself with the Jurkin, he had gone above Temujin's head and promoted himself from junior to senior rank. This was a much graver offence than the overweening self-belief that had drawn him to the supremely arrogant Sacha Beki and Taichu. And there was now the wounding of Belgutei and the melee at the banquet to enter into the ledger. Buri-boko was already a marked man.[23]

Temujin bided his time, waiting for an opportunity to settle accounts with the Jurkin. The chance came with the joint expedition with the Jin against the Tartars in 1196. Sacha Beki and his kin turned up late for the rendezvous and found that Temujin had already departed. Temujin proclaimed that the Jurkin were deserters and were to be arrested on sight. He ordered that Sacha Beki and Taichu be executed on the grounds that they had violated the oath taken when they elected him khan a dozen years earlier; part of the agreement was that they would never desert him in wartime on pain of death.[24] In vain did Sacha and Taichu protest that no one had ever been killed for being late before, and that Temujin himself had famously arrived late for a rendezvous with Jamuga and been merely berated by him for it.[25]

Charges and countercharges flew thick and fast. Temujin announced that Sacha Beki's non-participation in the Tartar war had created a gap in his line, through which the Tartars had penetrated, attacked his headquarters and killed ten guards. Sacha Beki replied that this was nonsense: it was actually Naiman who had attacked the camp. According to Sacha Beki, he himself saved the day, routed the enemy and displayed consummate loyalty (the ten slain men, he claimed, were actually Naiman, and he had sent another fifty or so prisoners on to Temujin, first stripping them of their clothes).[26] Temujin was not to be appeased. He made sure that Toghril was on his side, telling him that Sacha Beki and the Jurkin were disloyal to the point of secession. Then he sent out a powerful force to deal with them. Sacha Beki and the senior Jurkin fled, taking their families with them, but Mongol pursuits were known to be tireless and implacable. After several months on the run, the Jurkin were brought to bay (possibly near the confluence of the Rivers Kerulen and Senggur) and slaughtered. Temujin had decreed that since the oath taken by Sacha Beki when he (Temujin) was elected khan was no ordinary oath, the punishment had to be correspondingly severe. He expressly denied him and Taichu the usual aristocratic privilege of a bloodless death, and they were executed with the sword.[27]

Concealing the fate of his masters from Buri-boko, Temujin invited him to a wrestling match with Belgutei in his tent. Everyone knew that Buri-boko was unbeatable as a wrestler but, sensing danger from Temujin's black looks, Buri allowed himself to be thrown by Belgutei. At this Temujin bit his lip – a prearranged signal to Belgutei. He leapt upon Buri and broke his back.[28] Temujin evinced a savage vengefulness. He had not forgotten the insult at the feast when Buri wounded Belgutei and had set it up so that his half-brother was the executioner.

Quite apart from his long-running irritation at the ambivalence of Sacha Beki, the latter was a potential pretender as khan, so it made good political sense to take him out. Naturally Temujin did not reveal this motive but claimed he acted against the Jurkin unwillingly, at Toghril's urging; he was clearly a master of all the Machiavellian political arts.[29] Moreover, by acting so drastically against a man who was, after all, his cousin (Sacha Beki was the grandson of the eldest brother of Temujin's grandfather) Temujin showed that he was already moving beyond traditional Mongol modalities and introducing a new kind of militarised leadership. Nevertheless, the holocaust of the Jurkin was not popular in the ranks of the coalition. Many felt that Temujin had exhibited both cruelty and an unsure touch. It is clear that even fifty years later the Mongol court historians were uneasy about this incident and went into propaganda overdrive to attempt to point up Sacha Beki's unique treachery and wickedness.[30]

It was important to Temujin's long-term ambitions for the conquest of Mongolia that he should have Toghril as a reliable ally, but the latter's position as ruler of the Kereit was precarious. Temujin tried to consolidate Toghril's position by reconciling him with his second brother Jaqa Gambu; the other brother, Erke Qara, was a long-standing enemy who could never be won round. Jaqa Gambu had great prestige among the Naiman as head of the Tubegen and Dungkhait clans but had been dragged down when Toghril was ousted and, like so many nomad leaders, went into exile in China. Temujin sent an armed escort to bring him back, showed him every honour, and presided over a banquet where he felt he had achieved rapprochement between the two brothers.[31]

Toghril soon proved himself a deep-dyed ingrate for, feeling that his position was now secure, in 1198 he campaigned against the Merkit without informing Temujin and, what was worse, offered him none of the spoils – in contrast to Temujin's generosity in a similar position in 1196. This was a blatant insult as the campaign had been a great success; the Kereit killed Toqto'a Beki's son, captured his two brothers and daughters and the rest of the family and further diminished the Merkit's dwindling stock of warriors. Secretly enraged at this perfidy, Temujin kept his thoughts to himself; he still needed Toghril as a stepping stone to supreme power, so swallowed the insult.[32]

The obvious next target for Temujin and Toghril was the powerful Naiman people. In 1199 they persuaded Jamuga to join them in striking at the Naiman khan Buiruk. They all agreed this was an ideal time to make their move, for the once mighty Naiman were now divided. Their great ruler Inanch, who had kept the Kereit permanently off balance by his intrigues with Erke Qara and the successful coup against Toghril, had died recently but in his deathbed bequest divided his realm between his two sons Buiruk and Taibuqa (Tayang Khan), who were now at each other's throats. Steppe gossip said they were both in competition for the same woman, but the reality was that Buiruk felt that his father had insulted him by bequeathing him only the mountainous region of the Altai while his brother got the more desirable steppe area around the Black Irtysh.[33]

Jamuga, following his habitual practice, managed to absent himself from the expedition against Buiruk but Temujin and To'orghul achieved signal success, defeated Buiruk at Lake Kishil Bash on the northern slopes of the Altai and sent him scuttling across the mountains. It seems that this part of the campaign had had the tacit connivance of Tayang but, seeing his brother's rout, Tayang had second thoughts about his own judgement. Temujin and To'orghul were returning home after their victory when they were suddenly confronted by a fresh Naiman army under their best general, Koksu-Sabrak. This was at the Bayidaragh River in the southern foothills of the Khangai range. The two armies formed up, and a fierce battle began, but night supervened, so both sides prepared for renewal of the conflict next day.[34]

To his consternation, during the night Temujin learned that Toghril had pulled out and taken his forces with him. The rumour was that Jamuga had appeared and persuaded Toghril (quite falsely) that Temujin was secretly in league with the Naiman and intended to desert him.[35] Toghril thought he had left Temujin as an easy sacrifice for the Naiman but next morning Koksu-Sabrak, instead of pursuing the fleeing Mongols, turned, overtook Toghril and routed him in a pass in the Khangai. Toghril's son Ilkha (the Senggum) lost his wife, children and bodyguard, while at least half of the Kereit army was either slaughtered or enslaved and vast amounts of cattle and other supplies taken as booty.[36]

Ilkha went to his father and begged him for revenge. Toghril appealed to Jamuga, who predictably turned him down. He then turned to Temujin, the man he had seemingly abandoned to certain death by his desertion in the Khangai. Temujin responded, apparently magnanimously; in reality, having weighed up the consequences, he had decided that the extinction of Kereit power would make the Naiman too powerful. He sent out his best units with his best generals: Bo'orchu, Boroqul, the rising star Muqali, another leading warrior Chila'un, and Temujin's brother Qasar.[37] This expedition was notably successful. The Mongol reinforcements reached Ilkha just at the moment he was on the point of losing a second battle and saved him from annihilation. The Naiman were first driven off, then expelled from Kereit territory, most of the uplifted cattle were recovered and, to crown the achievement, Qasar won a great battle against the retreating enemy.[38]

This time Toghril appeared suitably grateful. He and Temujin held a council of war to decide their next move, and it was agreed that they should finish off what remained of the Merkit and settle accounts with the Tayichiud, still a major threat on the steppes and, ominously, allied to Jamuga. Any hesitation was ended when Temujin's spies brought word that the Tayichiud Angqu Huquchu had actually achieved a Merkit–Tayichiud alliance. In 1200 Temujin heavily defeated this coalition on the banks of the Onon and took thousands of women and children captive, even though the victory was not as complete as he would have liked. His old enemy Targutai, now fat and elderly, was captured and absurdly seemed to have expected amnesty; he, together with all the Tayichiud notables, was executed. He was sliced in two by one of Temujin's stars, Chila'un; Angqu Huquchu escaped.[39]

The run of unbroken success since 1196 was soon clouded by yet more internal turmoil among the Kereit. Toghril went on his travels again, this time ousted in a coup by Jaqa Gambu, whom Temujin, ironically, had brought back to guarantee stability. It seems that Jaqa Gambu was always uneasy and ambivalent about his brother's closeness to Temujin and his own role as underling to Toghril and intrigued against him behind his back. The Naiman saw a chance to retaliate for the humiliations of 1199 and provided all necessary backing. Toghril is next heard of in Manchuria, wandering there as disconsolately as he had previously prowled in Hsi-Hsia and Qara Khitai.[40]

Temujin's enemies seized their chance. By now it was clear to everyone that, not content with being the kingmaker on the steppes, he was aiming at supreme power in Mongolia. Alarmed at Temujin's ambitions and the way he was destroying the traditional way of life on the steppes, the old guard of the Mongol and wider nomadic aristocracy acted decisively. A conference was called on the Ergune River. The delegates convened, resolved their differences, then moved along the river to the confluence with the River Gan where, on a promontory, they elected Jamuga as gur-khan – supreme ruler or universal khan – and then swore a mighty oath of allegiance to him. They conferred the title of gur-khan as a deliberate snub to Temujin. It was pointed out that it was a grander title than his, that this one had true legitimacy, whereas Temujin's title of khan was a mere family affair.

What was novel about this meeting was that it brought together disparate nomadic elements and tribes hitherto hostile to each other. Apart from Jamuga himself and the Jaijirad, fifteen tribes were represented, including the Oyirad, Ongirrad, Merkit, Ikires, Saljiut, Qadagin, Qorolas, plus the three distinct factions of the Tayichiud, the three main clans of the Tartars and, significantly, the two sections of the divided Naiman kingdom.[41] This was the first time the three-way rivalry between Jamuga, Temujin and Toghril threatened to turn from tribal fighting into something altogether more serious: a Mongolian civil war. The other important aspect of the confederation was that it represented the last throw by the traditional oligarchy, and could thus be viewed – with a bit of licence – as a kind of class war.[42] All those who elected Jamuga stood for the old values, the old privileges, the old hierarchies, the old way of life. The electors at the Ergune River believed in loyalty and respect to a 'natural' lord, but those who wanted a life of qualified allegiance, greater freedom and self-interest would stand with Temujin, many of whose warriors were young men bitter and disillusioned by the way they had been treated by the elders or chiefs in their family or clan. The tide of history clearly favoured Temujin, for the old clan system was breaking down and, in a contest between traditional loyalties on one hand and meritocracy on the other, it seemed clear that the latter would win.

It should be stressed, though, that disaffection was by no means a one-way process, for some of Temujin's entourage, Altan, Quchar and Qasar, secretly sympathised with the coalition's social aims and were unhappy with the Borjigid khan's new bearings.[43] In general, however, dissatisfaction worked to Temujin's advantage rather than the contrary. Many of those formally committed by their clan and tribal leaders to fight Temujin were unhappy about the decision, which accounts for the sieve-like 'secrecy' of the war plans drawn up by the new coalition. At least three major leaks reached Temujin almost immediately, one from a spy he had planted at the conference, one from a Qorolas warrior disgruntled that his chieftain was deciding his future for him, and one from Temujin's old friend and father-in-law Dai Sechen.[44] The Ongirrad, despite their many ties with the Borjigid, had opted to oppose Temujin. Dai Sechen therefore had to make the difficult choice between clan loyalty and kinship; he chose kinship and at once defected to the Borjigid with his sons. Temujin later reproached Dai Sechen for taking a long time to join him, but the patriarch replied that he had had to wait for the right moment or else his entire family would have been slaughtered; as it was, Temujin's men had accidentally killed his daughter's husband after mistaking him for a Tayichiud. He also pointed out that it was only because of an unauthorised plundering raid on them earlier that year (by Temujin's brother Qasar) that the Ongirrad had joined Jamuga in the first place.[45]

Having learned of the coalition's plan to launch a surprise attack on him, Temujin urgently requested Toghril to come with all his power. Jamuga meanwhile was trying to reach Temujin before Toghril, which led him into a bad mistake: he did not wait until all the allies' levies had assembled but rushed off for glory with a force composed mainly of his own troops and the Tayichiud who had survived the defeat the year before. Temujin planned to intercept him halfway to the River Onon.[46] He drew up his men in carefully prepared positions and issued a strict order that there was to be no looting during the battle; after the victory was won there would be time enough for that. Needless to say, there was much grumbling at this, orchestrated by the almost predictably disloyal trio of Altan, Quchar and Daritai.

When Jamuga's forces came within sight of their enemy, Jamuga asked his sorcerers to conjure up a storm to assail Temujin. They obliged, using a rainstone or bezoar soaked in water – actually a hardcore concretion found in the intestine of ruminants.[47] But the magic went disastrously wrong. A storm – of snow – did arise but it blew into the faces of Jamuga and his men, causing the various detachments of his army to lose contact with each other. To add to Jamuga's discomfiture Toghril arrived on the battlefield with his reinforcements. With his foe in disarray Temujin was able to win an easy victory. Naiman, Oyirad, Merkit and Tayichiud streamed off the field in a panic, each detachment going its own way. The victors dispersed, Toghril to pursue Jamuga and his men, Temujin on the tail of the Tayichiud; for him revenge always trumped political expediency.[48]

There followed another rout of the Tayichiud, but only after a hard-fought running battle along the banks of the Onon, and mass slaughter, but the defeated came close to taking down the victorious general with them. Temujin was seriously wounded in the neck by a poisoned arrow. In Far Eastern warfare of this era arrows were usually poisoned, using vipers' venom, and they were deliberately notched, which meant they stayed longer in the wound, giving the poison a chance to spread.[49] Those wounded by arrows usually had the wound sucked clean and were then given milk to drink, but Temujin's wound was serious (his neck artery had been pierced) and he came close to death. Jelme proved the hero. Unable to stop the bleeding, he continuously sucked out the blood and spat it out while his master lay unconscious. As the blood was pumping out copiously, he was unable to spit it all out, and had to swallow much of it; in this way he estimated he ingested fully two pints of the khan's blood.

While all this was going on, the Tayichiud rallied and came close to defeating their demoralised oppressors, but in the end Mongol discipline won the day. When Temujin recovered consciousness around midnight, he asked for milk. There was none to hand, so the resourceful Jelme then performed a valiant and outrageous feat. Stripping to his trousers, he made his way to the nearby Tayichiud encampment, posing as a refugee from one of Jamuga's defeated bands. Having located a horn of milk, he then stole away with it and was able to bring it back to quench Temujin's thirst.[50]

That was the battle of Koyiten. It had a number of immediate and important consequences. Jamuga, infuriated by the early defection of the Naiman and others, attacked them once they were all out of Temujin's range and confiscated all the loot they had managed to take. It was a rash action, taken in hot blood, and it seriously affected his credibility. The Naiman pointed out, reasonably enough, that they had been in the vanguard, had taken the brunt of the short-lived battle and might even have prevailed had Jamuga not arrived late with the main army.[51] The coalition, begun with such high hopes, began to dissolve, as more and more disillusioned groups and clans broke away.

But Jamuga was not the only leader incensed by the behaviour of his colleagues. Despite Temujin's earlier express veto on plundering during the battle, Altan and Quchar broke off and did exactly that. Temujin also retaliated with confiscation, thus angering Altan and Quchar and nudging them closer to an open break.[52] Such was the fluidity of attachments and alliances on the steppe that it sometimes resembled a game of musical chairs.

One certain consequence of the battle was that the Tayichiud were now finished for good as a political force. They were never recruited for the later Mongol empire, and their fortunes revived only when the empire itself declined in the fourteenth century.[53]

Then there was the effect of the events of Koyiten on Temujin himself, his personality and psychology. Jelme's prompt action had saved his life. Sucking at the wound to remove the clot meant a continuous flow of blood which not only lessened the chances of dying of poison but also prevented an embolism. Temujin's initial attempts to self-doctor were disastrous, as he had attempted, by contrast, to staunch the blood. Moreover in his devotion to his leader Jelme had swallowed a large quantity of blood; both this and the spitting out were contrary to normal Mongol taboos.[54] Yet Temujin's response to this heroism was ingratitude and paranoia. With his morbid fear of treachery, he somehow formed the idea that when Jelme stole away half-naked, he was thinking of deserting. Why, he asked, did Jelme have to disrobe? Jelme explained that it was a brilliant circumstantial touch, so that his self-proclaimed status as refugee would not be queried; why else would a man fetch up at the Tayichiud camp half-naked? Jelme defended himself stoutly, pointing out that he had now saved his master's life on three occasions, once on Mount Burqan when Temujin was in danger from the Merkit, once by sucking out the blood, and once by going to the Tayichiud camp to get milk for him to drink. Temujin grudgingly conceded the truth of all this.[55]

But the dark side of Temujin, so openly on display in his reaction to Jelme's heroism, contrasted with the khan's wiser, more statesman-like behaviour in recruiting the man who had almost killed him. Among the haul of prisoners taken after the battle was a Besud clansman, identified by a number of witnesses as the one who had fired the near-fatal arrow at Temujin and clearly an archer of great skill. He was led before the khan expecting to be killed. Temujin asked if he had anything to say before he passed sentence. The clansman replied that he had nothing personal against the khan but he was a Besud, a sub-clan of the Tayichiud, and what the Tayichiud leader ordered he had to obey. This was the sort of loyalty that appealed to Temujin. The Besud warrior added that if his life was spared, he would become Temujin's greatest warrior. Something about the man struck a chord with Temujin, who announced that he was taking him into his inner circle and that henceforth he would be known as Jebe ('the arrow').[56] His judgement was sound. Appointed to command of a troop, Jebe soon proved his calibre and was promoted. Moving rapidly up the hierarchy, he was soon colonel of a division and went on to become one of the greatest Mongol generals.

Jamuga spent the year 1202 licking his wounds while he pondered his next step. His allies were now scattered all over Mongolia – the Naiman in the Uluq Taq area, the remnants of the Merkit along the River Selenga south of Lake Baikal, the Oyirad camped along the Sisgis River west of Lake Khovsgol. It was open season for the victors. Toghril spent the year hunting down the remaining Merkit – it was clear he had something of an obsession with this tribe – while Temujin prepared a self-avowed campaign of genocide against the Tartars.

At his war council he announced that he intended to kill all Tartar males taller than a wagon wheel.[57] This policy was supposed to be of the 'most secret' kind, but the foolish Belgutei, who was at the council, boasted about it to his friends, alleging that the idea was his, and word filtered back to the Tartars. Temujin's powerful army searched relentlessly for the Tartars and finally brought them to bay at Dalan Nemurges, near the Khalkha River in eastern Mongolia, probably on the western slopes of the Khingan Mountains. Once again Temujin decreed that there should be no looting during the battle, but there would be equitable distribution afterwards, and once again Altan and Quchar took the line that such a ruling did not apply to them. The battle was the usual slaughterous affair and ended in utter defeat for the Tartars.[58] Afterwards the Tartar males were lined up for execution, but suddenly there was a scrimmage followed by bloody resistance. It transpired that the Tartars, warned by Belgutei's loose talk, had prepared for a doomsday scenario, had concealed knives about their person, and were prepared to go down fighting. In carrying out the execution, the Borjigid took an unacceptable number of casualties.[59] An enraged Temujin could have executed Belgutei for divulging state secrets, but instead humiliated him by appointing him as judge in all cases involving commoners, in effect an arbiter of petty disputes. Temujin was always fond of Belgutei personally, but had no great opinion of his talents. Although he continued to be shown the usual courtesies customary for members of the khan's family, Temujin excluded him from his council of state and told him that he would never again be privy to important decisions.[60]

But Belgutei was not the only family member to cause trouble. Predictably Altan and Quchar had stopped fighting during the battle to pursue their own mania for loot. This time Temujin humiliated them publicly. Their booty was confiscated and distributed among the poorest members of his army. Furiously angry, Altan and Quchar stole away to join Jamuga and denounced Temujin as a tyrant.[61] The khan consoled himself by adding the Tartar princesses Yesui and Yesugen to his roster of wives.[62]

The winter of 1202–03 saw Temujin and Toghril facing yet another Naiman coalition. Buiruk put together a powerful army, stretching all his resources and recruiting the many diverse anti-Temujin elements in Mongolia: Toqto'a Beki and the surviving Merkit, the handful of Tartars left of military age and, potentially most important of all, Jamuga and his allies, who now included Altan, Quchar and Temujin's uncle and brother Daritai and Qasar. Altan, Quchar and Daritai were angry about Temujin's confiscation of their loot and considered themselves his superiors, as being more senior Borjigid. Qasar's was a more serious case. Systematically treacherous and disloyal to his elder brother, he pursued a zigzag pattern throughout his short life, always stopping just short of some action that would give Temujin no choice but to execute him. There had already been three major acts of disobedience which in a lesser Mongol oligarch could have been construed as treason. He had tried to hatch a conspiracy with Belgutei when Temujin slapped down his half-brother over the Tartar incident; he had disobeyed the khan's orders, refusing to kill one thousand Tartar prisoners because his wife was a Tartar; and it was he who had gratuitously attacked the Ongirrad and temporarily driven them into Jamuga's camp.[63]

Since Buiruk's estranged younger brother Tayang was also Jamuga's ally, the elder Naiman chief's golden dream was that his nation might finally be united and the past forgotten. This campaign was a major effort and ranged widely over Mongolia, from the Altai to the Khingan Mountains.[64] But at every point the Naiman and their allies seemed outthought and outwitted by Temujin who, in this campaign, began showing distinct signs that he was evolving from a journeyman steppe warrior into something more original. Where the Naiman acted conventionally and did everything by the book, Temujin proved versatile and protean, at one moment standing his ground to fight a pitched battle, the next switching to guerrilla warfare. The Naiman forces were ponderous and lumbering, but the Mongols seemed to have mastered the art of dispersing and reforming as if by magic. Temujin's strong personality and increasing confidence in his own abilities inspired his men, who were happy to follow puzzling or unusual orders. He seemed to produce an innovation a week, a feat of which his foe was quite incapable.

At some stage in late 1202 or early 1203 in the Black Forest on the banks of the River Tula, Toghril formally adopted Temujin as his son and, it was implied, his heir and successor to the Kereit kingdom; he told his adopted son that the heir presumptive, Ilkha was 'quite useless'.[65] The ceremony involved formal oath taking and entitled Temujin to call Toghril father; both parties agreed that, after all, this was the logical conclusion of the original *anda* relationship between Toghril and Temujin's father Yesugei.[66] The relationship got off to a happy start; some time that winter the Naiman were badly defeated at a place called Chegcher, possibly the mountain near Mount Chiqurgu. The engagement was fought in a heavy snowstorm, there were severe casualties on both sides, but the Naiman had the worse of the encounter, for many of their troops were said to have frozen to death when retreating, suffered severe frostbite and together with their animals, toppled over cliff edges to their death in the wind and darkness.[67] It was typical of Jamuga, nominally a Naiman ally, that he should have entered the fray at the eleventh hour, but only to harass and loot the stricken Naiman.

The year 1203 thus started promisingly but it was one of ill omen and bad fortune for Temujin. Testing the reality of his new bond with Toghril he asked for the hand of his daughter Chaur-beki for his son Jochi, but was curtly refused. Back at the Kereit court Ilkha had reacted with fury to the news that there was a new heir apparent. When Temujin's marriage proposal came in, coupled with the idea that the Senggum should take a Mongol bride, Ilkha protested bitterly to his father that this was a further insult. He pointed out the inequality of the proposed arrangement: if Temujin's daughter married one of the Ong Khan's sons, she would expect to sit at the back of the tent and be treated like a lady, but if Chaur-beki married Jochi, she would have to sit near the door of the tent like a servant.[68] Ilkha proposed that his father break decisively with Temujin and join a new coalition Jamuga was putting together. Toghril refused indignantly: it was one thing to turn down a marriage proposal – this might give offence but was not a declaration of war; but how could he forsake his *anda* to whom he had sworn a mighty oath to treat him as his son? Besides, Toghril never cared for Jamuga personally and told his son so in unequivocal words: 'Jamuga is a flatterer, of no consequence and untrustworthy.'[69] Ilkha, who was in secret correspondence with Jamuga, left it at that for the moment but stole away to confer with his fellow-conspirator.

Temujin's marriage proposal has divided commentators. Some think it was politically foolish, that Temujin was 'pushing his luck' and revealing his ambitions as overlord of Mongolia too openly, so that Toghril began to draw back and grow circumspect. Others, more convincingly, claim that Temujin was testing the waters, to see what value the entente with his 'father' really had. He suspected, and he was right, that both Toghril and his son were secretly snobs, who did not think him high-born enough for intermarriage with the illustrious ruling family of the Kereit, that Toghril would never actually accept him as his successor, and that in his opposition to Ilkha he was protesting too much, secretly pleased with the turn of events. He could now claim that he wanted to give Temujin all that he desired, but that his son and the Kereit people would not let him.[70]

By fuelling her husband's scepticism, Borte was the mastermind behind this episode, carefully advising her lord and rehearsing her points cogently and lucidly. Toghril, she argued, was systematically untrustworthy; what credence or dependence could you place on a man who had deserted an ally at the height of a battle (as Toghril had done with Temujin), and, having been restored by Temujin's good offices, offered him not a scintilla of the booty when he campaigned against the Merkit in 1198 – a campaign he could not have undertaken if Temujin had not restored him![71]

Meanwhile Jamuga, Ilkha, Qasar, Altan and Quchar met to discuss how to compass their ends. Jamuga advised that the best thing was to insinuate that they had clear proof that Temujin was in secret talks with the Naiman and that the Kereit people were on the brink of rebellion, and to present Toghril with an ultimatum – either Ilkha or

Temujin – so as to wear him down by a combination of *fait accompli* and cajolery. Jamuga knew his mark well: Toghril was old, tired and essentially weak and in the end would take the line of least resistance.[72]

The anti-Temujin conspirators rode to Toghril's encampment to confront him. Toghril's camp was in the Black Forest, only about two hours' ride away from Temujin's on the Sa'ari steppe; since the Ong Khan was now supposed to be Temujin's father and they were still allies, such proximity was not at all suspicious. Jamuga spoke eloquently about Temujin's fickleness and volatility, contrasting it with his own steadfastness. This may have been the occasion when he famously said 'I am the crested lark that stays put; Temujin is the skylark that breaks off and goes home,' contrasting his own steadfast reliability to the flightiness of the migratory skylark.[73]

Toghril was probably more impressed by the presence at the meeting of a deputation from a new confederation from the western steppes of Central Asia, with representatives present from Qara Khitai, the Uighurs and even (some say) the new power in Transoxiana, shah Muhammud II.[74] All of these were concerned about the rise of Temujin and badly needed the Kereit to win, for commercial reasons. Already the period of permanent warfare on the steppes, now some thirty years old, had escalated from petty tribal disputes to a grand conflict with two main deep structures. On the one hand was the social war, with Temujin and his host of have-nots ranged against the traditional aristocracies; it was Temujin's contempt for the old oligarchy that was the deep reason for the discontent of Altan, Quchar and Qasar. On the other was a concealed trade war for the control of commerce in Siberia and the Far East. The Uighurs and Nestorians of the West wanted Toghril to prevail so that the trade privileges in Mongolia would be theirs. Temujin, though, was favouring the rival Islamic merchants and, only recently, had received envoys from them asking for trade concessions in Siberia; one of them, Asan by name, bought up a huge quantity of squirrel and sable pelts from the Mongols.[75]

Gradually Toghril was worn down, and in the end ties of blood and kinship prevailed over his oaths to Temujin. But Toghril was aware that in battle there are no certainties, that even the most puny of Davids can defeat the mightiest Goliath in the press and confusion of battle. He insisted that subterfuge be used initially. An invitation was issued: Toghril announced that he had had second thoughts about the

Mongol proposal of marriage and now wanted to proceed; to celebrate the union he therefore invited Temujin to a great banquet he was preparing. The conspirators intended to assassinate Temujin as soon as he arrived at the camp.[76]

Temujin set off blithely unsuspecting, planning to make a leisurely journey to the banquet. First he visited 'father' Monglik, who had acquired the title by his recent marriage to Hoelun. Monglik warned him that there was an assassination plot afoot, and mentioned poison as the conspirators' preferred method. Temujin decided not to press on to the feast but sent two envoys in his place named Buqatai and Kiratai.[77] Shortly afterwards full details of the plot were revealed to Temujin by two herdsmen or horse wranglers, Kishiliq and Badai. As soon as Temujin was dead, Ilkha intended to swoop down on the Borjigid in a surprise attack that would surely annihilate them, demoralised as they would be by the death of their leader. This intelligence from two of the 'wretched of the earth' shows clearly that Temujin's 'coalition of the dispossessed' was paying important dividends. Temujin never forgot slights and favours; three years later he was able to reward Kishiliq and Badai when he promoted them from the ranks to generals of division.[78]

Temujin now had to prepare for an imminent assault from Toghril's coalition army, which was likely to outnumber his three to one. He sent out urgent appeals to his confederate clans to assemble with all speed. Some promised to bring their power but, alarmingly, others claimed that this was the Borjigid's khan's private war, that his actions had not been ratified at a full council, and therefore that they reserved the right to absent themselves from the muster. The plain truth is that many of them did not like the odds: they had joined Temujin on the promise of a cornucopia of spoils and booty but were now being asked to fight to the death; the plain subtext of their response was 'we didn't sign up for this.' Bitterly Temujin blamed the pernicious example of his brother and almost spat out to his confidants: 'I have had enough of my brother. Who can bear to see his retinue?'[79]

Alarmed by the perfidy of these recreant clans, Temujin led his forces on a dash to the Chinese border, hoping to acquire fresh allies and weapons and, maybe, help from the Jin. The enemy, in hot pursuit, caught up with him at Qalqaljid Sands, on the Manchurian frontier, near the River Khalkha. The battle that followed was one of the

bloodiest yet on the steppes and the most desperately fought.[80] Toghril
commanded the forces of the anti-Temujin coalition, having offered
the position to Jamuga and been refused. Jamuga's behaviour at this
juncture was nothing short of bizarre. In command of the vanguard,
he could easily have overhauled Temujin on the way to Manchuria,
but proceeded at a snail's pace on the pretext that he needed the Ong
Khan's main army to join him. After turning down the supreme
command, Jamuga proceeded to demoralise his allies by warning what
tough opponents the Mongols were, and capped it all by sending a
secret courier to Temujin with intelligence concerning the disposition
of the Kereit forces.[81] When Toghril was almost at striking distance,
Temujin struck camp, pulled his forces away and left camp fires burning
to make the enemy think they had located him. A wild Kereit charge
through the empty camp brought them up short, but at last Toghril
did locate the real forces and gave battle. Temujin delayed committing
his forces in hopes that reinforcements would arrive, and finally did
see one of his banners in the enemy rear. Unaware that only a small
number of clans had rallied to his cry, he badly overestimated the size
of his forces behind the enemy, and found himself sucked into a
general engagement where the Kereit held all the cards.[82]

It was fortunate for Temujin that two of the clans assaulting the
Kereit from the rear were first-class units led by doughty warriors.
Quyildar of the Mangqud clan performed prodigies of valour, vowed
to place his horse-tail standard on a hill on the far side of the enemy
and, amazingly, made good on his boast. He then charged the Kereit
centre and managed to break up their formation just as they were
preparing for a charge. Another chieftain in the Kereit rear, Jurchedei
of the Uru'ud clan, gradually forced the enemy to give ground and
capped his exploits by wounding Ilkha in the face with an arrow.[83]
The heroic fighting by these two prevented Temujin and his men from
being overwhelmed, and Temujin later testified that only the fortuitous
wounding of Ilkha saved his forces from annihilation. Finally, heavily
outnumbered, Temujin withdrew under cover of night and loitered
nearby, hoping for Mongol survivors to join him. His immediate circle
urged him to flee with all speed but he explained that he could not
abandon the force in Toghril's rear. He sent messages to them to break
off fighting and circle round for a rendezvous.[84]

That was the battle of Qalqaljid Sands. Although the Kereit did not score a knock-out blow, Temujin had been heavily defeated on points, but his propaganda machine managed to persuade posterity that he had won a pyrrhic victory; both Rashid-al-Din and the *Secret History* fell for this blatant lie.[85]

Once again Temujin, on the ropes, was given time to recover, courtesy of Jamuga. At first Toghril was minded to pursue the Mongols through the night, but Jamuga advised him that he would be better tending to his wounded son; the Mongols were weak, in disarray, had no refuge to fly to and could easily be mopped up later. The foolish Toghril not only accepted this advice but passed it off to his inner circle as his own original thought. After all, he reasoned, with Jamuga, Altan, Quchar and Qasar on his side and Temujin beaten, the future was his. 'If they do not come back we can go after them, collect them like horse droppings, and bring them back,' he boasted.[86]

Temujin needed the breathing space for, not only had his army taken a severe mauling, but Bo'orchu, Boroqul and, most importantly, his 17-year-old son Ogodei were all missing. Temujin spent an anxious night, sitting on his horse throughout the hours of darkness, with men stood to at the ready, awaiting the next assault from the Kereit. His army's discipline was superb: here was a defeated army, perhaps on the point of receiving the *coup de grâce*, but there was no panic. At daybreak Bo'orchu limped in. In the battle his horse had collapsed under him after being stricken with an arrow. On foot, he had been on the point of being captured when the fortuitous wounding of Ilkha led the Kereit to veer away to form a protective wall around their prince; after that he managed to steal a horse and found his way back to the Mongol force by a circuitous route.[87] Shortly afterwards, Boroqul came in accompanying a wounded Ogodei, strapped across a horse and unconscious. In an uncanny rerun of the incident at Koyiten he had sucked the blood from a wound in Ogodei's neck, and blood was still dripping from his mouth when he reported to Temujin, who burst into tears at sight of his bloody son. The Mongol medical staff cauterised the wound (the first time this process is described in the histories) and Temujin publicly thanked Heaven for his son's deliverance, but then boasted that even if the enemy had caught up with him, he could still have beaten them off.[88]

It was a moment of foolish vainglory, for having started the battle with some 4,600 men against Toghril's estimated 13,000, he was left

with just 2,600; the casualties had been horrific. With these tattered
remnants he retreated, initially to Dalan Nemurges, scene of his great
victory against the Tartars the year before, then along the Khalkha
River towards Lake Buir in Ongirrad territory.[89] Here, amazingly, given
that the man who was asking for help led a vanquished host, the
Ongirrad agreed to ally themselves with him and swell his ranks. This
was an early sign that the shrewdest brains among the nomads had
already concluded that in the long run Temujin would prevail in the
epic struggle for mastery of the steppes.[90]

There followed a period of sustained roving in the early summer
of 1203. Temujin's itinerary seems to have taken him initially south
to skulk in the forests of the Khinghan, then back north to the River
Khalkha, where he held a great hunt or battue and thoroughly revict-
ualled his army. One sadness was the death of Quyildar from the
wounds he had sustained at Qalqaljid Sands and news that another
commander, Borokhula of the Tumed (another hero of Qalqaljid) had
been ambushed and killed by enemy scouts. Then Temujin proceeded
north again to Lake Hulun, where he made summer camp. From
there he sent out a series of long letters of reproach to his principal
enemies. Altan and Quchar he berated for their treachery in very
harsh terms, his message to Ilkha was of the 'more in sorrow than
anger' type, while Jamuga was accused of envy and jealousy unbe-
coming in an *anda*. Temujin told Altan and Quchar that they were
getting one last chance – there was really no excuse for them as they
had not put themselves forward as candidates for khan of the Borjigid
despite still wanting the leadership, almost as if they expected to be
elevated by public acclamation. However – and this part of the message
was coded – if they were prepared to stay with Toghril for a year as
secret agents, when he settled accounts he would spare their lives.[91]

By far the longest screed went to Toghril, and it contained bitter
recriminations against the old man's treachery – inexcusable not just
because he broke the most sacred oaths sworn on the steppes but
because of the many favours Temujin had done him and the many
chestnuts he had pulled out of the fire, the restorations, the rescue
from penury, and so on. If Toghril had a grudge even so, he continued,
he should have settled it man to man and not involved Temujin's
family in the dispute: 'If a two-shafted cart has a broken shaft, the ox
cannot pull it. Am I not your second such shaft? If a two-wheeled cart

has a broken wheel, it can travel no farther. Am I not your second such wheel?'[92] Toghril seemed genuinely moved by Temujin's letter and proposed putting out an olive branch to the Borjigid, but his son Ilkha rejected the idea venomously and responded to his own letter with open contempt, saying that the only possible answer was *guerre à outrance*.[93]

Temujin cleverly made these missives read as if he were a desperate man, whose only remaining resource was repining and recrimination; in actual fact he was building up his strength, ready to strike back when least expected. Gradually he assembled a new coalition – Ongirrad, Ikires, Nirun, and – ominously for Toghril – the renegade Kereit clan of the Nunjin, including Chinqai, who would later be one of his most trusted advisors. As a skilled politician, he knew how to appeal to people's interests: to the Muslim merchants he promised a golden age of trade when he finally prevailed; to his men he held out the prospect of untold riches after victory; to the ousted Khitans, formerly the ruling dynasty of northern China, he promised restoration once he was ruler of Mongolia.[94]

Meanwhile he moved to his final camp of the summer, at Lake Baljuna, somewhere in south-eastern Mongolia near the border with Jin China.[95] Here, in swampland, he was safe from attack, but conditions were dire; the lake was almost dry and water had to be squeezed out of handfuls of mud.[96] But here too took place one of the most famous incidents in Temujin's life: the swearing of the Baljuna Covenant, when nineteen of his senior commanders took an oath that they would fight to the end at his side against the Kereit, come what might. To seal this mighty accord the Mongols slaughtered a horse, boiled it and ate it. The wording of the oath is variously reported, but one version reads: 'May any of our covenant who divulges this plan collapse like this riverbank and be felled like this forest.' Temujin himself then took a counter-oath while holding a handful of dried mud: 'If I finish the great work I shall share with you men the sweet and the bitter; if I break my word, then let me be as this water.'[97] This was the Mongols' equivalent of Henry V's speech before Agincourt, and those who pledged themselves were equally destined to become 'we few, we happy few'. Usually, Mongols would desert or drift away from a defeated leader, and this was the reason the later Genghis Khan so highly prized the veterans of Baljuna ever afterwards.

The band of brothers stayed a long time at Baljuna while Temujin digested the implications of the news that reached him from the Kereit country. As so often on the steppes, the victors had soon fallen out among themselves. The quincunx of Jamuga, Altan, Quchar, Qasar and Daritai conspired together to oust Toghril, finding him now surplus to requirements and needing a stronger leader for the final hunt to destruction of the Borjigid khan. Toghril, though, proved too nimble for them, and the conspirators were forced to flee. Altan, Quchar and Jamuga went to the Naiman; Daritai and Qasar, however, decided that their fortunes were best served by submission to Temujin.[98] Daritai asked to be readmitted to the fold and sent his nephew valuable intelligence, including the news that many Kereit had joined the rebels in their failed coup against Toghril, were on the run and thus capable of absorption into the Mongol host, and also that Toghril was not maintaining a standing army but relying on seasonal levies. Qasar demonstrated his newfound commitment to his brother by raising an army – mainly Kereit who had backed the losing side – but Toghril defeated this host and took Qasar's wife prisoner. Qasar narrowly escaped with some of his children and a handful of retainers and is said to have existed for a time almost entirely on bird's eggs.[99] He then had to make his way perilously to join Temujin at Lake Baljuna. He claimed to have sustained attacks by the Kereit and to have fought running fights all the way there, though there is no real evidence of this. Doubtless he was trying to exaggerate the hardships he had endured by switching back to his brother but, when he arrived at Baljuna, Temujin did not reproach him for his past treachery.[100]

Instead Temujin used Qasar as a pawn in an elaborate game of deception and disinformation. First he sent a message to Toghril, purporting to come from Qasar, saying that desperation, destitution and continued ill-usage by his brother meant he had no choice but to beg the Ong Khan for amnesty. Moreover, he added, Temujin's army had now dispersed in despair and the Borjigid khan was a fugitive. Since this intelligence was confirmed by his own spies, Toghril took the bait and arranged an envoy who would preside at a blood-brotherhood ceremony, at which Qasar was to swear to be Toghril's ally in perpetuity. The luckless representative sent out by Toghril was named Iturgen. Intercepted on the road by Temujin's men, he was brought back to Baljuna, where Temujin ordered Qasar to prove his loyalty by executing him. Qasar had no choice: it was kill or be killed.[101] Temujin was thus sealing off any possibility that Qasar could change his mind and return to Toghril, for killing an ambassador was not only perceived on the steppes as a war crime but went against Temujin's own deeply held principles. But to a Machiavellian the end always justified the means even if, in pagan terms, Temujin had to put his own soul in jeopardy.

Temujin had originally scheduled his final settling of accounts with Toghril for 1204, but now a great opportunity had presented itself. Thinking the danger from Temujin was past and Qasar was firmly in his net, the Ong Khan grew complacent. Besides, food shortages at Lake Baljuna meant that Temujin's army might diminish alarmingly over the gruelling months. Everything dictated a lightning campaign in the early autumn – an exact reversal of the strategy his enemies had used against him that very spring. The decision to use trickery shows that Temujin was still not strong enough to confront the Kereit in a pitched battle. Forced marches took the Mongols west from Lake Baljuna to the Kerulen, where they learned that Toghril was now based at his favourite camp on the River Tula in the Black Forest and a great banquet was being prepared, which meant that the Kereit soldiers would be drunk.[102] It seems, however, that the blitzkrieg was not a total surprise; at the last moment Toghril must have received warning, for the decisive battle was fought at Jer Gorge, usually located between the sources of the Tula and the Kerulen.[103]

Though caught off guard, the Kereit fought back ferociously. The battle raged for three days, and casualties were terrific. Finally, on the third day, Temujin's new star general, Muqali, stormed Toghril's armed camp and took it. Ilkha fought particularly well, but by nightfall of the third day he and Toghril were fugitives, their army utterly routed.[104] Though he got away under cover of darkness, Toghril was shortly afterwards murdered by a band of Naiman peasants or brigands near the Nekun River; allegedly they failed to recognise him. His head was cut off and taken to the Naiman ruler Tayang who had it plated in silver and kept above his throne as a mark of respect to a gallant ally.[105] Ilkha fled initially to north-eastern Tibet, where he was nearly murdered, then on to areas under the control of the Khitan and the city of Kashgar before ending in the territory of the Uighurs, in the region of Kucha, where he lived for a short time as a bandit before being killed by a local emir.[106]

Perhaps surpisingly, given his genocidal record with the Tartars and Merkit, Temujin did not order a general massacre of the Kereit aristocracy. He knew many of them personally, and both sides accepted that the conflict had been unnecessary, a product of Ilkha's pride and ambition and Toghril's weakness. This was a very different matter from Tartars and Merkit, whom Temujin loathed for reasons both personal and to do with tribal revenge. He incorporated all the most talented Kereit military officers into his army. An admirer of the general Qadag Baghatur, he spared his life on condition that he devote himself to the widow and children of the recently dead hero Quyildar.[107] Always well informed, Temujin knew which of Toghril's advisers had merely been doing their duty and which of them shared Ilkha's hatred and detestation of the Mongols. On this basis he pardoned Qadag, one of Toghril's inner circle, but executed Kokochu, officially the Ong-Khan's equerry but really more of a boon companion.[108] Temujin ascended the Kereit throne in a formal ceremony, announced that henceforth Kereit and Mongol would be one nation, and set in train an extensive system of compulsory intermarriage.

Why did Temujin defeat Toghril when on paper the Kereit ruler had greater numbers, greater resources and better political contacts? There can be many answers to this. Toghril was both weak and cruel, a treacherous fratricide who was indecisive and unable to think things through half a dozen moves ahead like a chessplayer – the ability Temujin possessed with a vast quantity to spare. Fitful, cowardly, vacillating, Toghril allowed himself to be made a fool of by Jamuga. His weakness particularly manifested itself towards his son whom he should have slapped down decisively for reasons of state. Instead he allowed a father's weakness to decide the future of the Kereit. It is unlikely there was much merit in his claim that he gave in to his son to prevent rebellion and civil war in his kingdom.[109] Temujin was far more intelligent than the Ong Khan, was a better politician, had a more disciplined army and a more efficient system of intelligence and espionage. One of the Kereit grandees he spared was Toghril's brother Jaqa Gambu, who later turned out to have been one of his reliable spies at the Kereit court.[110] Moreover, Toghril suffered heavily from desertions and defections both before the decisive battle and during the three-day encounter at Jer Gorge.[111]

Another important factor in Mongol superiority was the sheer brilliance of their commanders. No fewer than three of them – the 27-year old Subedei, the similarly-aged Jebe and the 34-year old Muqali – were authentic military geniuses, and this is to say nothing of the highly talented Jelme, Bo'orchu and Boroqul. Even the so-called 'lesser lights' would have been an adornment to a lesser army. One of Temujin's nine paladins was Chila'un who was unhorsed in battle with the Kereit yet seized a lance and routed a mounted opponent. Temujin expressed his stupefaction: 'How can a man who has fallen from his horse have the strength to get up and do battle? Even if he does get up, how can he charge a rider and defeat him? Have you ever seen a man on foot do battle to bring the heads of the unruly under his claw? I have never seen the likes of this champion.'[112] By contrast, the Kereit commanders, with the exception of Qadag Baghatur and Ilkha himself, emerge from the sources as boastful but effete, at once risk avoiders and irresponsible. It is difficult to improve on Rashid al-Din's sombre conclusion: 'This was the end of the rulers of the Kereit nation and the extinction of their tribe. God knows best.'[113]

The only obstacle now to Temujin's hegemony in Mongolia was the Naiman, but it was a formidable one. In great alarm after the unexpected defeat of Toghril and the overthrow of the Kereit state, Tayang assembled in the winter of 1203–04 the fourth and mightiest Naiman coalition, harnessing both the power of his own nation and the disparate and heterogeneous (though numerous) war bands of those tribes and clans who had suffered under the Mongols. To his standard flocked Jamuga, Altan, Quchar, Alin-Taishi, self-styled leader of the 'true' Kereit (those who refused to accept the rule of Temujin), Toqto'a Beki and the few remnants of the Merkit, Quduqa Beki of the Oyirad, and many others.[114] The sources are very clear that the war in 1204 was started by Tayang, but he had no choice, since coexistence with the new state that Temujin was founding was impossible.

Tayang's grand strategy rested on the idea of catching the Mongols between two fires, with the Ongud, a powerful tribe numbering more than 4,000 nomadic families, assaulting them from the south and the Naiman from the west. He hoped for solidarity from the Ongud because of their ethnicity (both Naiman and Ongud were Turkic tribes) and their religion (both were Nestorian Christians). But this idea very soon foundered; it was in fact always going to be a non-starter, as Tayang would have realised had he been less politically naïve. Alaqush Digid Quri, the Ongud chief, was already firmly in the Mongol camp, and his son had married an aristocratic Borjigid bride.[115] In terms of realpolitik the Ongud thought that Temujin's hegemony in Mongolia would stabilise the Chinese frontier, where they were uncomfortably ensconced, being involuntarily caught up in wars whenever nomads raided south into China or when the Jin in retaliation sent out punitive expeditions.

The Jin, meanwhile, anxious not to see a powerful empire solidified on their northern borders but afraid that the Naiman would win the coming encounter (until far too late they always underrated the Mongols) sent word of Tayang's intentions; it is said that their messenger arrived at the Mongol camp shortly after Alaqush's own envoy, bearing the identical message.[116]

But the failure of his two-pronged strategy was not Tayang's only problem; his own family provided even worse nightmares. To begin with, his brother Buiruk refused to collaborate or make common cause with him, thus halving the Naimans' military strength. Even worse, Tayang was completely under the thumb of his wife Gurbesu, an avid devotee of the war party, who was able to browbeat her husband into deferring to her wishes. Although still a young woman, Gurbesu had gained a psychological ascendancy over Tayang because she had been previously married to his elderly father; after his death Tayang inherited her. This is why the sources seem confusing about Gurbesu, at one time referring to her as Tayang's mother, at others as his wife. Gurbesu expressed open contempt for the Mongols and said their only use, 'once we have washed their dirty hands, will be as milkers of cows and sheep.'[117]

Temujin's preparations for war were more impressive. Even before joining battle with Tayang he had begun the radical reorganisation of the Mongol army that he would perfect after 1206, arranging his units in tens, hundreds and thousands, using the decimal system so beloved of the Manchurian Jurchens who ruled northern China but which actually went back as far as the Hsiung-nu nomads of the first centuries of the Christian era.[118] In addition to these decimalised contingents, there would be a personal bodyguard, eighty handpicked men for night duty, seventy to act as day guards; the *pièce de résistance* was the formation of an elite battle force like the Persian 'Immortals' of old or the Roman praetorian guard. Next he started on an inchoate imperial administration, trying to work out a system for pacifying all the peoples he had conquered recently. Opting for the magic number nine, he divided each non-Mongol territory into nine units, and built a hierarchy of local government based on faithful retainers with 'regulators' or governors at the apex, whose job was at all cost to keep the people pacified and avoid rebellion in the rear while Temujin advanced on the Naiman.

He sent out heralds to announce that, whereas all Mongolia was henceforth under his suzerainty, all tribes and clans would have de facto autonomy provided they made formal submission. Many of the tribes – Ongud, Ongirrad, Oyirad, and so on – were happy to do this; but not all. To the latter Temujin issued the warning for which he would bcome world-famous: surrender or die. He promised the recalcitrant that they could expect nothing except relentless, ruthless war, with no mercy when they finally surrendered.[119]

In strategic terms Temujin enjoyed several advantages. His conquest of the Kereit gave him access to the logistically crucial River Orkhon, providing a gateway to the Ordos Desert and western China, which in turn opened up key invasion routes through the Altai Mountains.[120] His leading generals war-gamed the various scenarios, taking into account that the Naiman were far superior numerically, and that the Mongols would have to march west to engage them and might therefore arrive tired, while the commissariat planned the numbers of animals to take with them on the trek and the location of the waterholes. Temujin, always a master of deceit, encouraged leaks from his army purporting to show that morale was low and that if the Naiman struck first, they would have a walkover victory.[121] One of his most famous bits of disinformation involved turning a horse loose close to the Naiman camp as if it had escaped from the Mongol army. The nag in question, a spavined, emaciated and sorry-looking specimen, duly limped into the midst of the Naiman, producing guffaws of overconfident laughter at the thought that this was an average example of a Mongol warhorse.[122]

Temujin's original intention was to attack the Naiman in the high summer of 1204, but he was determined that he should never be seen as a despot. He therefore declared that both the details and timing of all campaigns would henceforth by decided at a quriltai or grand council, attended by his senior generals and most trusted advisers. At the council, majority opinion at first backed the khan, on the grounds that before July the horses would be too thin for gruelling warfare. But then a troika consisting of Belgutei, Temuge and Temujin's uncle Daritai (newly restored to favour) argued strongly for the element of surprise. Belgutei was particularly eloquent, arguing that a pre-emptive strike would work, as the Naiman, bogged down with huge herds and flocks, were ill-equipped to deal with a mass raid.[123] Finally Temujin was convinced and, sending Jebe and Qubilai on ahead with the vanguard, he got under way on 17 May 1204.

Sadly, our sources, so detailed on some of the minutiae of the campaign, are a hopeless jumble right up to the final battle four months later.[124] It is clear that the Mongol army marched slowly west via the Rivers Kerulen and Tula and covered the 700 miles to the Naiman realm by the end of June. First contact with the Naiman appears to have come to the west of the River Kodasin. Battle was joined with a far superior Naiman force led by Tayang, with Jamuga and others in attendance as allies; some say the site of this first battle was in the Khangai near present-day Karakorum. This was probably the famous occasion when Tayang saw Temujin's 'four hounds' in action – Subedei, Jelme, Jebe and Qubilai – and asked Jamuga who they were; he, with perfect knowledge of all the notables, was able to identify them individually.[125] Marvelling at their prowess, Tayang might have got the first inkling of the immense task ahead of him, and his spirits cannot have been raised by Jamuga's panegyric on the brilliance of Mongol military talent. Someone with real political nous – which Tayang was not – might have been alarmed at the extent to which Temujin was already building up a pan-Mongolian confederation, for none of the 'four hounds' was a Borjigid; Qubilai was apparently from the Barulas, Jebe a Tayichiud and Jelme and Subedei hailed from the Uriangqai people. However, on this occasion Tayang enjoyed the bliss of ignorance for, finding himself hopelessly outnumbered and knowing how tired his men were after the long march west, Temujin withdrew at dusk.[126] He then issued a solemn order, to be disobeyed on penalty of death, that each man in his army should light five fires and set up dummies beside them which would be illuminated by the flames, so that the Naiman, seeing such a nocturnal inferno, would conclude that the Mongols had received massive reinforcements and would not pursue them.[127]

Perhaps doubting his ability to prevail against such opponents in a pitched battle in open country, Tayang announced a Fabian strategy: he would lure the Mongols into the Naiman heartland in the Altai Mountains, where the invader would be at a grievous disadvantage. This decision caused immediate uproar among his captains, who protested that it smacked of cowardice and would seriously affect morale in the army. Harsh words were uttered, with many opining that Tayang was no better than a woman; one of the generals is said to have remarked that the command should be turned over to Gurbesu immediately, as she showed far more steel than her husband.[128] Opposition to Tayang's strategy, which was undoubtedly the right one, was almost universal, with the 'antis' headed by Tayang's son Ququluq, who made much of the fact that they had Jamuga on their side. The Naiman ruler therefore had no choice but to accede reluctantly to the majority.

There followed, during the high summer of 1204, a game of hide-and-seek, with Temujin apparently trying to wear down the enemy before closing in for the kill. The sources are vague on the details of this cat-and-mouse period, but Mount Xanxar in the eastern Khangai, the Sa'ari steppe between the Tula River and the Dolon Uul and the region between the Dolon Uul and the Orkhon River are all mentioned: essentially the area between the Khangai to the south and Lake Khovsgol to the north.[129] Eventually, either Temujin brought the enemy to bay or Tayang decided to stand and fight. After crossing the Orkhon, Tayang drew up his forces at Chakirmaut at the foot of the eastern slopes of Mount Naqu, a small mountain between the Orkhon and the Burgut Mountains.[130]

The Mongols approached, primed for this moment: Qasar commanded the main force in the centre, the crack troops were on the wings, Temuge had the reserve and Temujin himself led the vanguard, ably supported by the 'four hounds', Subedei, Qubilai, Jebe and Jelme. Just before battle was joined, the issue was all but decided by the sudden defection of Jamuga and his host from the Naiman, at at a stroke depriving Tayang of his numerical superiority.[131] Of all the puzzling actions of this superfox over the years, this was the most enigmatic. Even more mysterious is the message said to have been sent by Jamuga to Temujin at this point, assuring him that Tayang was a paper tiger. This was the culmination of Jamuga's odd behaviour during the campaign; it is said that every time he spoke to Tayang about the martial prowess of the Mongols he depressed him further.[132] Others claim that the message itself was apocryphal, that Jamuga decided from the moment Tayang's Fabian strategy was rejected that the Naiman would lose and simply timed his exit to cause maximum damage to them. Yet another view is that the cultural divide between Jamuga's Mongols and the Naiman was a crevasse, that he feared that to order them into battle against Temujin would cause rebellion and desertion. At all events, no sooner had the first arrows been fired than Jamuga's men were streaming off the battlefield.[133]

What followed was the Borjigid khan's supreme achievement on a battlefield, and certainly the most crucial encounter he ever fought. With their backs to the wall, the Naiman fought superbly, winning astonished praise from Temujin, who had not expected them to be such doughty warriors. But the defection of Jamuga was a body blow, and the Naiman now faced the greatest warriors in Asia. Qasar, so often a disappointment to his brother, finally won his spurs with an outstanding performance directing the Mongol centre, yet the single most brilliant feat was the 'premature' attack by Temujin and the four hounds with the vanguard which surprised the Naiman before they were properly drawn up.[134] Pressure from the van and the wings gradually forced the Naiman back to the foothills; Tayang, fearing envelopment, formed a square and withdrew his men from the flanks of the mountain, which actually increased the danger of encirclement. It soon became clear that, whatever their valour, the Naiman were no match for the Mongols in either discipline or generalship. Tayang was forced to break up his square and begin withdrawing up the mountain to avoid being trapped. As dusk came on, the Naiman, taking terrible casualties, were forced farther and farther up Mount Naqu towards the summit. Struggling with horses and carts on the cliffs and narrow passes of Mout Naqu, Tayang's army lost hundreds more men as they plunged over cliffs and into ravines in the darkness; as the *Secret History* puts it, 'they died, packed close together like felled trees.'[135] Tayang himself, who had been mortally wounded during the battle and was losing blood rapidly, was in no state to rally his men, but his chieftains, once at the summit, decided they would go down fighting. In an amazing exploit that drew stupefied admiration from Temujin, they staged one final banzai charge down the hill before being surrounded and cut to pieces. The Mongols offered them terms as an honoured enemy if they would surrender, but the Naiman refused.[136]

By morning Temujin had won as complete a victory as it was possible to imagine. The Naiman army had been annihilated, Tayang died of his wounds after a few hours in captivity, and the great Turkic-Nestorian state was no more.[137] The campaign was officially wound up on 24 October 1204. Tayang's son Quqluq managed to escape with a handful of followers and fled, initially to the Irtysh River. At the news of the Naiman's disaster, all the tribal minorities, the Tayichiud and the rump of anti-Mongol Ongirrad, who had formed rebel or guerrilla bands against Temujin, concluded that the game was up and surrendered. Only the Merkit continued defiant.[138] As with the Kereit there was no general massacre, for Temujin's intention was to enrol all males of military age in his ever-victorious army.

Two consequences of his great victory gave Temujin particular personal pleasure. Gurbesu was brought in and, as punishment for her previous arrogance and insults, was taken as one of Temujin's concubines but assigned a very low position in his harem. Temujin taunted her cruelly when he first bedded her: 'Did you not say that the Mongols had a bad smell? Then why have you come to me?'[139] If this showed his savage side, his adoption of all useful aspects of Naiman culture showed his intelligence and penetration. Among those in the Naiman civil administration who were captured was one Tatatonga, keeper of Tayang's Great Seal. When the importance of writing was explained to him, Temujin was impressed and appointed him as the keeper of a new Mongol Seal, with the consequence that Uighur writing became the official script of the new Mongol empire. Grasping the importance of literacy, Temujin also made Tatatonga his sons' tutor, with special emphasis on teaching them to read and write in the new script.[140]

Next it was time to settle accounts with all who had aided the Naiman against their own kind. Altan and Quchar finally got their long-deserved comeuppance and were executed, as was Daritai, despite his final act of re-ratting at Lake Baljuna. However, the greatest prize was always going to be Jamuga. He was said to have been reduced to a following of just sixty men soon after the battle, since the majority of his followers, realising they would not be slaughtered but absorbed in Temujin's 'New Model Army', came in to surrender as soon as they realised the Naiman had been utterly defeated. Temujin sent out search parties all over Mongolia to find his childhood friend; he realised that Jamuga was the only serious threat still left to his total dominance. After a year on the run Jamuga was reduced to just five companions and was eking out a living as a bandit in the Tannu Mountains. Hearing there was a bounty on their leader's head, his companions suddenly surrounded him, trussed him up, slung him across a horse and took him to Temujin.

Jamuga, who knew very well how his *anda*'s mind worked, warned them they would not benefit from their betrayal, but they ignored him.[141] He was, however, allowed to write to the Mongol leader and sent one of those quasi-oracular messages that always seem to characterise the exchanges between him and Temujin: 'It has come to pass that black crows capture the mandarin duck.'[142] Jamuga proved a good prophet. His betrayers were executed immediately by Temujin, who always stuck rigidly to the principle that followers who betrayed their clan or tribal leaders merited death.[143] But now the question arose: what to do about Jamuga?

That this decision took a long time suggests that there was something very odd indeed about the lifelong on-off relationship between these two great Mongol chiefs. There are many things in the sources that make no sense. From the very first time Jamuga and Temujin faced each other across a battlefield – at Dalan Baljut in 1187 – Jamuga's attitude seems ambivalent. He broke off the battle and did not pursue Temujin, and the same thing happened on many subsequent occasions. He plundered the people who had chosen him as khan after Koyiten; he conferred with Toghril before their joint attack on Temujin and then broke off pursuit of the Borjigid; he refused to take command against Temujin when offered the leadership by Toghril; he abandoned the Naiman just as the battle of Mount Naqu began. What was Jamuga doing – at one moment with Toghril, the next sending messages to Temujin, then joining up with the Naiman? Why did he always plunge his putative allies into gloom by his estimate of the Mongols' prowess?[144]

Some of Toghril's advisers put it to him that Jamuga was mentally unbalanced. Did his pattern of abandonment of allies denote a neurotic compulsion to repeat history? Much depends on our analysis of Jamuga's psychology and personality. The sources show a man in a state of permanent motion and agitation, almost as though he had boundless energy but no clear aim in life. It is implied that he was less successful as a steppe leader than Temujin because he maintained traditional divisions between the different tribes in his army and did not try to create a new holistic ethos and ideology; there was no recruitment of shepherds for top positions in his host. Although a man of ability, Jamuga is shown as lacking vision, basically a Machiavellian intriguer, short-termist, treacherous and volatile, someone who had no code of honour and would cheerfully sacrifice a friend to attain his own ends.[145]

The problem is that this is a portrait painted by the Secret History, a tendentious, propagandist work dedicated to extolling the glories of the Mongol state created by Temujin. Moreover, it is a picture in terms of which other events shown in the Secret History become meaningless and even preposterous. The phrase 'letting the cat out of the bag' is often used by commentators who believe that, in putting together a farrago of the factual and the mythical, the compilers of the official record of the birth of the Mongol empire sometimes accidentally tell the truth at the wrong moments and thus alert us to the real state of affairs. The problem is compounded by the Delphic, almost Rosicrucian esoteric symbolism in which some of the key events involving Jamuga are recorded.[146] But some tentative – and perhaps even more than tentative – conclusions are possible by means of some historical sleuthing. To use Sherlock Holmes's famous formula, 'When you have eliminated the impossible, whatever remains, however improbable, must be the truth.'[147]

After eliminating the implausible thesis of mental illness, we are left with only two possibilities. Either Jamuga was an arch-Machiavellian, scheming always to make sure that none of his rivals on the steppes became too powerful, biding his time against the day when he would emerge as tertius gaudens, with all his competitors weakened, and scoop the pool. Or some other explanation is called for. However, the tertius gaudens hypothesis does not really explain his withdrawal at Mount Naqu, since his action then made it virtually certain that Temujin would win. Is it possible then that at some stage, most likely around 1196–98, Temujin and Jamuga made a secret pact to divide the empire they hoped to gain by cunning and trickery? This would be in line with the psychological profile of both men and would explain much that otherwise seems enigmatic, turbid or even meaningless.

The main objection to this hypothesis would be that it does not explain why, in that case, Jamuga fled to the Tannu Mountains. Why would he not have appeared at Temujin's side to collect his reward? It is of course possible that Temujin told him that he needed time to organise his new empire before he publicly 'forgave' his old 'enemy'. Certainly in the long conversation reported in the *Secret History*, Temujin as good as admits that Jamuga was a double agent.[148] It is time to look at this more closely.

According to the *Secret History*, Temujin offered to share his empire with his boyhood friend, but Jamuga refused and opted for death, saying that just as there could never be two suns in the sky, so there could not be two khans. Temujin's speech contains an encomium for all the services Jamuga did him, and it includes the many desertion episodes; why cannot we be two shafts on a cart, he asks. It is surely obvious that here the annalists have simply swapped the names of the speakers: Jamuga, aware that Temujin is thinking seriously of killing him, rehearses the many services he has done Temujin and how much the khan owes him. Temujin by contrast says that there cannot be two rulers at the top, that this would cause civil war.[149] The *Secret History* absurdly has Jamuga saying that once dead, his spirit can preside over the new Mongol nation and protect it: 'I will watch over you, your grandsons and their grandsons, into the distant future. I will be your eternal spiritual protector.' But a foolish secretary has also included what Jamuga almost certainly *did* say when Temujin pronounced his sentence of death: 'In the black night I will haunt your dreams.'[150]

If this hypothesis is correct, and Temujin was guilty of a massive double-cross of a faithful agent, we have to ask what the motive might be. In a modern context, killing your own agent, Gestapo-style, is meant to convince the opposition that he really was an enemy. No such consideration can apply in Jamuga's case, so we are left with the gruesome likelihood that Temujin executed his own agent to protect his own credibility. He claimed to be a universal ruler with a mandate from Heaven. What would posterity say if, instead of a peerless warrior who defeated the Kereit and Naiman by sheer military genius, it turned out that he had prevailed only by treachery and betrayal? But let us grant Temujin the optimum case, that Jamuga really was an enemy who had done his best to defeat him in a ten-year struggle for mastery on the steppes. How does that justify his subsequent conduct?

Even if we accept the propagandist nonsense spewed out by the *Secret History*, that Jamuga asked to be killed, this was always predicated on his being killed bloodlessly by crushing, as befitted his rank and status.[151] Yet Temujin not only devised the most hideously cruel death he could think of but in so doing offended against all the tenets of Mongol custom and morality. Careful not to have the blood of an *anda* on his own hands, he sought out a man whom he knew to hate Jamuga with a passionate hatred, his own nephew Eljigidei, son of his younger brother Qaci'un. Eljigidei, a shadowy figure, was one of those sinister personalities so often encountered in history who inveigle their way to the centres of power without having any discernible talent. We know that he was one of Temujin's favourites but that he considered himself above the law. On one occasion he had been arrested for trying to brush past Temujin's bodyguard without official leave or password.[152] Once his fate was in Eljigidei's hands, Jamuga must have guessed the worst. His last recorded words were supposed to have been to the effect that Temujin was a mediocrity, that he had beaten the Kereit only because of the valour of the Uru'ud and Mangqud troops and the Naiman only because of the brilliance of the 'four hounds'; the only complimentary thing he could say about Temujin was that he employed a good maker of armour. He was then led out and hacked to pieces by Eljigidei and his minions.[153]

This was cruel and unusual punishment, contrasting with the normal method of execution meted out to Altan, Quchar and Daritai. Jamuga's death was as much a hideous blot on the escutcheon of Genghis Khan as Napoleon's assassination of the duc d'Enghien would be six hundred years later.[154] Whether Jamuga's actions can be set down to his cunning as a double agent, miscalculation or simple stupidity, Temujin's debt to him was colossal. Without him there would have been no Genghis Khan and, as one Russian scholar has commented: 'the nine-tailed banner [the equivalent of the Mongol flag] would have been dragged in the grass along with the Khan's severed head.'[155]

4

Temujin Becomes Genghis Khan

The year 1205, when Temujin so brutally executed Jamuga, was an action-packed time and Temujin himself was on the move for most of it. In the spring of 1205 he crossed the Altai Mountains at the Alai pass and entered the valley of the Irtysh in preparation for a daring new exploit: an attack on the Tangut kingdom of Hsi-Hsia. His motive was twofold. He realised that his armies needed to be given constant activity to prevent the conjunction of the devil and idleness, and he wanted to test their calibre against a new kind of enemy, for the Tangut had the reputation of being militarily formidable. The official excuse was that the Tangut had sheltered Ilkha in 1203. He contented himself with a raid across the border and the siege of two cities, Ligi (Li-Chi-Li) and Kieng (Lo-Szu), pointedly avoiding the heavily fortified city of Qara Qoto (Heishuicheng). The Tangut, sensibly, did not send out an army to oppose the Mongols but waited to see whether this was to be a short-term incursion or a more prolonged threat. Satisfied with the results achieved, Temujin pulled his men out by the end of the year.[1]

While all this was going on, he had deployed other forces against the troublesome remnants of the Merkit, who seemed like the hydra's heads; however many times they were defeated, enough always seemed to survive to regroup. The Merkit gave Temujin far more trouble than the Tayichiud, the Tartars, the Kereit or the Naiman ever had. All these accepted absorption into the new Mongol empire, but not the Merkit. The army sent out against them brought Toqto'a Beki to bay in an unknown location by a river and he was killed. Many more Merkit and the 'no surrender' Naiman who had joined them were drowned when the Mongols pursued them across another river.[2] The sources say Toqto'a was killed in battle by a stray arrow, which presumably means an arrow not shot deliberately at him but one of the arrow-cloud the Mongols habitually discharged at the start of a battle to panic and disconcert the enemy and break up their formation.[3]

Unfortunately Toqto'a's sons, including Quqluq, the most troublesome, got away. Patiently Temujin assembled a new search-and-destroy force and gave the command to the 29-year old Subedei. His instructions to Subedei have become famous:

> If they (the Merkit) sprout wings and fly up to heaven, you, Subedei, become a falcon and seize them in mid-air. If they become marmots and claw into the earth with their nails, you become an iron rod and bore into the earth to catch them. If they become fish and dive into the depths of the sea, you, Subedei, become a net, casting yourself over them and dragging them back.[4]

A peculiarity of Temujin's instructions to Subedei was that he appended to his eloquent exhortation a somewhat pettifogging list of detailed advice on the day-to-day running of the army, which to an experienced commander like Subedei was a case of *sus Minervam docet* (or in English idiom, don't teach your grandmother to suck eggs). The only plausible explanation is that Temujin still had doubts about giving major independent commands to anyone not born and bred a Mongol.[5] (Another enigmatic *Secret History* footnote refers to Subedei's innovation of using iron carts with iron frames and iron wheels. This has seduced the unwary into positing that Subedei was a corpulent man who needed extra-strong carts to bear his weight, but the truth is probably that the annalists have confused a nickname for Subedei, meaning 'man of iron' with actual iron conveyances.)[6]

With 1205 a year of such signal success, there now remained no obstacle to the formal announcement of a new Mongol empire with a new emperor. In the year 1206 a great quriltai or general assembly of all Mongol nobles was held at the source of the Onon River. All oligarchs were bound to attend under pain of interdiction, and at these assemblies the most momentous issues were always decided: future military campaigns and strategies, the legal code, the succession, ranks and privileges granted to individuals. In a clearing a giant white marquee was erected, decked with brocades; wooden pillars supporting the roof were covered with gold plates. Foreign dignitaries were invited and many came, including an important envoy from the

Jin, the Prince of Wei, who would be a future Chinese emperor. As a reward for their attendance all such visitors received lavish gifts.[7]

The first part of the meeting was a formal request from the nobility that Temujin accept a new position as Supreme Ruler and the new title of Genghis Khan. This famous name has provoked many scholarly controversies, with some claiming that it means 'the khan of all who live in tents', others associating it with water by plumping for 'the khan of the oceans', yet others claiming that 'Chingis' was the name of a spirit of light worshipped by the Mongols, and the majority opting for 'universal or all-embracing ruler'. However, the best current scholarship suggests that the name really means 'fierce, hard or tough ruler' without any connotation of universal or the oceanic.[8] Temujin told the nobles that he would accept the new position and title solely on condition that all Mongols of whatever station would obey his orders without question, travel to the ends of the earth if asked to, and put to death anyone he ordered. All present accepted, paid homage and made obeisance. He was then sworn in as Genghis Khan. Then they lifted his white felt throne, put a golden sword in his hand, raised him high in the air three times and carried him all round the clearing in which the assembly was taking place, to the accompaniment of wild cheering. The emblem of the khan was displayed, crowned with yak horns and bearing four black horse-tails.[9]

There followed an opulent feast, with cauldrons brimming with meat and pitchers full of koumiss. In front of Genghis Khan lay heaps of gold and silver, furs, silks, brocade. Prominently displayed in front of the giant tent was his white banner with nine points, symbolising the nine Mongol tribes, and the combination of the number nine and the colour white signifying that Genghis was fortune's darling.[10] Over the next few days Genghis announced his rewards for his most faithful followers and began the massive programme of reorganisation and administration of his new empire. The quriltai of 1206 was a watershed, the beginning of a new state; nothing would ever be the same again. Thirty-one different tribes with a combined population of two million now obeyed Genghis's every word. His realm stretched 1,000 miles east–west, from the Khingan Mountains to the Altai range, and 600 miles north–south, from Lake Baikal to the southern limits of the Gobi.[11]

Genghis spent May 1206 issuing decrees rewarding his closest friends and followers and those who had done him special or memorable favours. Top of the list were Bo'orchu and Boroqul. Bo'orchu was his oldest friend and ally and Boroqul had earned special favour by saving Genghis's life when he was a young man, in an incident not recorded in the *Secret History*. Bo'orchu was given the title of commander of the right wing of the Mongol army – the title signified his importance, not his actual generalship on the right wing – and granted a pardon in the future for any nine crimes which would normally attract the death penalty under the new law code that Genghis proposed to publish shortly; the principle of the code and its general outlines had already been ratified at the quriltai. Boroqul was also granted the nine-crime exemption.[12] Genghis told these two that, whereas he would issue specific military orders to his top generals like Subedei, Jebe and Muqali, he would never do so to them. Why not, they queried in amazement. 'Your status is too high for me to give you a specific command,' he said, and informed them that henceforth they would occupy a unique position just lower than a khan but above a senior general.[13]

Muqali was given the titular command of the left wing of the army, rewarded not just for saving Gengis's life in an ambush and his consistent bravery and talent but because his father had ridden to his death to allow Genghis to escape capture by the Naiman.[14] Shigi Qutuqu, always inclined to be a peevish prima donna, was visibly jealous of the honours paid to Boroqul, Bo'orchu and Muqali; Genghis, who always spoiled him, appeased him by granting him the exemption from penalties for nine crimes and appointing him his Chief Justice.[15] Jurchedei was also rewarded, though at a lower level – marriage to a high-born woman – for three specific feats: wounding the Senggum Ilkha with an arrow, being a first-class spymaster and having been instrumental in defeating the Naiman and Kereit.[16] Jelme was another given the nine-crime exemption.[17] The talented Naya'a was given sub-command of the left wing, which sometimes became his own command of the 'centre left' of the army.[18]

Nor did Genghis forget the lesser folk. The herdsmen Kishiliq and Badai who had warned him of the murder plot hatched against him by Ilkha were made freedmen and given property, and Sorqan Shira, another great benefactor from the past, was allowed to choose his reward and opted for a huge grant of confiscated Merkit lands.[19] There were some prestigious promotions too. Usun, Degei, Qunan and Kokochos were all given the rank of Beki and assigned to Jochi as his immediate deputies, but Kokochos was detached by Genghis for immediate duty at the side of Chagatai, so he could keep tabs on him and warn the khan of any foolish or untoward actions by his intemperate second son.[20]

Finally, Genghis announced that his inner cabinet would consist of 'paladins' who would be seated just below the khan and higher than anyone else. Genghis had already nominated his four 'steeds' or warhorses – Bo'orchu, Boroqul, Muqali and Chila'un – and his four 'hounds' or dogs of war – Subedei, Jebe, Jelme and Qubilai. To make up the magic number nine Genghis appointed (inevitably) his favourite Shigi Qutuqu.[21] Even within the supposed equality of the nine paladins, however, there were anomalies and peculiarities. The special status of Boroqul and Bo'orchu above the other seven is one case in point. Another is that Jebe and Subedei were not granted the nine-penalty exemption, although they did later received the title of *orlok* (roughly field-marshal). Yet another is that Qubilai, although appointed head of military operations, had to share this function with Bedu'un, of whom nothing is otherwise known except that he annoyed Genghis by his stubbornness.[22]

Distributing rewards was the easy part of Genghis's task in 1206. The huge difficulty he faced was how to devise a social and administrative system that would break down all the old tribal, clan and regional loyalties so that everyone in the empire would perceive themselves to be Mongol. His aim, *mutatis mutandis*, was the one famously announced by St Paul: 'There is neither Jew nor Gentile, neither slave nor free, nor is there male or female, for you are all one in Jesus Christ.'[23] So: how to make people neither Kereit nor Naiman, neither Borjigid nor Tayichiud?

To appreciate the huge, almost insuperable, difficulties Genghis faced, we have to analyse the situation before he arrived on the scene. The overall Mongol tribe was riven by factionalism within the constituent clans, but the clans themselves were splintered and fragmented. In the early twelfth century there would be the khan's clan, the 'inner clans' associated with the khan's clan by intermarriage or unforced pacts of loyalty, and the 'outer clans': those who were hostile to the khan or forced into temporary loyalty by military defeat or economic marginalisation.[24] Within these different clans would be further subsections depending on whether one was a member of an *oboq* or an *uruq*. The *oboq* was a patrilineal descent group from a fictitious ancestor, whereas the *uruq* was a descent group from a relatively recent and known ancestor such as Qaidu or Yesugei; these groups were sometimes known as 'black bones' and 'white bones' respectively, the distinction being that intermarriage was allowed between the white and black bones but not within either group.[25]

The Borjigid clan members who were *oboq* would claim descent from the mythical Bodonchar, the Romulus of the piece, as it were, who was supposed to have been born after his father's death from a ray of divine light. But things became even more complicated because, according to another fictive genealogy, Bodonchar could also be traced back to the blue-grey wolf and the fallow doe, the ultimate ancestors of all Mongols.[26] Moreover, the *oboq* lineages tended to bifurcate and segment into sublineages that in turn produced entirely new lineages. Since everything was in a state of flux, it is peculiarly difficult to give a clear account of social structure on the steppes or the relations of clans, sub-clans and tribes with each other.[27] Paradoxically, though, fictive lineages rather than real ones were more expedient, for a chieftain's unrelated retainers were 'deemed' to be members of the same *oboq*.

Yet the confusions did not even end there. Some independent chiefs broke away from the rigid class structure and formed their own bands with retainers; these were the freebooters who had originally been attracted to Temujin. Clans split into subgroups and reassembled in ways that virtually amounted to new clans.[28] The result was chaos, with clans, sub-clans and individual bands all going in different directions. All noble members of any clan would have a claim to clan leadership, so that each man was everyone's actual or potential enemy. Even if a tribe managed to achieve political coherence, it would not possess a distinctive culture.[29] It is not surprising that many have referred to Mongol society in the twelfth century as an Alice-in-Wonderland world, complete with croquet matches, balls, hoops and mallets all with their own mind and moving around as they wished. Any political formation based on tribes, clans and lineages was bound to be inherently unstable, with no real social glue, and this explains why before Genghis nomadic empires had always been evanescent, nine-day wonders.[30]

It was the genius of Genghis to realise at once not only that this entire farrago had to be swept away and an entirely new system put in place *but also* that there was one element in the old system he could use as the basis of his brave new world. With his ability to knife through to essentials, Genghis saw that the really salient feature of Mongol society before his time was the institution of *nokor* – the trusted comrades of a war chief. *Nokor* is a difficult relationship to pin down exactly: it had some aspects of the *comites* of a Roman emperor, but probably more of the link between an Anglo-Saxon ruler and his housecarls.[31] If a powerful chief could provide the levels of booty and security from external threats the ordinary Mongols hungered for, they would soon enough forget the nuances of fictive and actual lineage.

With his deep knowledge of human nature, Genghis realised that at heart every man wanted either to be khan himself or to be an independent free spirit. Side by side with Mongol reverence of a great khan and the man on horseback was the Mongol's individualistic and even anarchic mentality. The only way to appeal to such a mentality was to palliate the thought that he could never become khan with huge and exponential amounts of booty.[32] The aim was to ensure loyalty to the khan, not to tribe or clan, and this loyalty could be secured if the rewards were big enough. Genghis had long realised that to build a political base on aristocrats alone was a dead end (such men would always consult the interests of their tribe rather than any super-polity); hence the meritocratic measures (promotions of shepherds and drovers) at the 1206 quriltai. At that time the gap in wealth between oligarchs and large herd-owning commoners was not as great as it was later to become. Genghis appointed as his *nokor* minor nobles, commoners and even ex-slaves promoted meritocratically; he fobbed off the senior nobility with positions elsewhere.[33]

With the nine paladins in harness and a majority of commoners on his Great Council he could be sure of getting his way for, though they might disagree with him on detailed policies, they were unlikely to dispute his political or strategic leadership, given that they owed everything to him in the first place. To keep his superstate in being, Genghis needed constant influxes of wealth, and that meant permanent conquest and war; too long a period of peace would encourage the powerful and frustrated custodians of his commonwealth to turn in on, and eventually against, themselves.

But Genghis was also a master of pacing. He realised that too rapid a rate of change disconcerts and alienates people, so went through the motions of pretending to believe in continuity with the old pre-1206 system.[34] He was determined to introduce a militarised society based on the decimal system, but it needed camouflage and obfuscation. He therefore invented entirely new lineages (actually simply a restatement of the decimal system in another guise), thus maintaining a link with the old ethos of fictional lineages. In effect by sleight of hand he produced a double fiction – engendering entirely notional and mythical lineages predicated on an original system that was itself fictive.[35]

The key to Genghis's post-1206 system was twofold: the tumen and the keshig. Tumen literally meant 10,000, akin to the Roman legion; keshig was Genghis' praetorian guard. Genghis began by decreeing compulsory military service for all males from fifteen to seventy. He organised his 95,000-strong army in units of ten (arban), one hundred (jaghun), one thousand (minqan) and ten thousand. Every man, woman and child in Mongolia's two million population was assigned to a minqan, and it was stressed that this was where their primary loyalty now lay.[36] The minqans functioned as political and social units as well as military ones and were the most important building block in Genghis's new state, even though the tumens were more famous. They were intended to replace the old clans, tribes and lineages and to form the basis of a monolithic Mongol people.

It was notable that Genghis appointed many ex-carpenters and shepherds to head these units. Perhaps about 20 per cent were Genghis's meritocratic promotions, 10 per cent new kin connected to him by marriage or adoption and 70 per cent traditional clan leaders. They had the right to keep war booty once the khan had declared 'open season' in this regard, along with any game they killed themselves.[37] All were there strictly on probation and could be dismissed at any time for failing to perform effectively or deliver what was required by the khan. But all leaders of the minqans were subject to the orders of the tumen commanders, who were all handpicked, trusted friends of the khan.

The relationship of the nine 'paladins' to the tumens is not entirely clear. The obvious thing would have been to make them all commanders of 10,000 but that is not what Genghis did.[38] Qorchi, whose only reward at the quriltai ceremony was to be given seven beautiful women, was given command of a tumen to deal with the forest tribes of Siberia. Qunan, elsewhere not mentioned as a major figure, was another given tumen command, as were Naya'a and Bujir, none of them paladins.[39] On the other hand, the *Secret History* states without any explanation that Subedei and Jebe were given only a minqan each, though they were paladins; even worse, Chila'un, another paladin, received nothing at all.[40] Of the paladins only Muqali, Bo'orchu and Qubilai received a tumen. Again, we are not told why Boroqul does not feature in these commands.

This decimal system did not immediately destroy tribalism but it allowed the khan to bypass the usual channels of tribal authority. Submitted Naiman, Kereit and others were broken up and dispersed to the four corners of Mongolia in different minqans to prevent their reforming as tribes. The leaders of the minqans decided where and how their subjects lived, subject to the orders of the khan. There were eighty-eight commanders of the 'thousands' rather than ninety-five because, as a huge and exceptional favour from the khan, the most loyal peoples – Ongirrad, Ongud and Ikires – were allowed to combine in their own units; there was thus a single commander for three Ongirrad units, the same for five Ongud units and also for two Ikires units.[41] For reasons of *esprit de corps* it was forbidden to leave one's unit or be reassigned to another, and any attempt at either was punished with the death penalty.[42]

From this embryo was born the administrative system of the Mongol empire. As conquests spread and it became necessary to govern far-flung territories, new refinements were added, particularly the expert civil servants, technocrats and financial specialists known as the semuren and the daruqachi, holding their appointments under imperial seal; but this was largely a phenomenon of the 1220s and 1230s.[43] For the moment Genghis could pride himself on having carried out a reorganization comparable to Cleisthenes's famous reforms at Athens at the beginning of the sixth century BC. The analogy is close, for Cleisthenes changed the political power base in Athens from four traditional tribes to ten new 'tribes' based on residence or deme, and replaced patronymics by demonymics. There was also the concentration of units of ten and the complication of mythical kinship groups or 'phratries', whose members were said to have a common ancestor in the mists of ancient mythology. The demes were combined to form

thirty 'trittyes' with each of the ten new tribes containing three trittyes of diverse origins, one from the city, one from the coastal region
and one from the inland region.[44]

And now at last the phenomenon of 'supertribalism', so often raised
as a possibility in Mongol history only to be dashed by factionalism
and the lack of imagination of the leaders, became a reality. To use
the rebarbative language of political science, this was 'state building'
at its finest. Earlier apparent attempts to construct a pan-Mongolian
polity had all had in reality the much humbler short-term aims of
maximising success in warfare.[45] Genghis brilliantly broke up the old
clan system with what one observer has called 'reformatted decimal
tribal structures'.[46] The new officer class could not bequeath privilege
to their children, for Genghis's meritocracy and 'reward for results'
system precluded any nepotism. The one possible problem about this
pattern of open recruitment, as some of the 'old Mongols' saw, was
that the day would come when personnel drawn from conquered
peoples would eventually form the majority in the minqans and
tumens.[47]

Genghis's critics have sometimes been grudging about his achievement, pedantically attributing the entire decimal system to the Khitans,
once dominant on the steppes. But the truth is that Genghis and the
Mongols cannot be contained by such a reductive analysis. They were
an original phenomenon in so many ways, not all of them pleasant.
They had a universalistic ideology, were capable of massive mobilisation, covered vast distances and caused enormous devastation. In their
thinking and practices they drew from many different cultures, Turkic,
Persian, Chinese and Khitan, among many others.[48] And Genghis's
new state was original too, not just an assemblage of a dozen or so
tribes but a unitary people that he had created by disbanding the clan
system, redistributing its individual elements, and melding and fusing
them in a novel polity.

It is worth re-emphasising just how far Genghis had gone in revo-
lutionising steppe society. The Mongols began as small parental groups
or extended families, evolved into camping groups of fifty to a hundred
people, then formed themselves into clans whose very culture be-
tokened factionalism and disunity. There was slavery – or at any rate
vassalage – whereby poor families presented their sons as retainers of
a clan leader in return for basic subsistence. Such young men (called

otogu bo'olod) could never leave their masters' service, unlike the free clansmen.[49] The two principal Mongol clans –Tayichiud and Borjigid – were at each other's throats on every conceivable issue, even disputing about who treated the serfs more charitably (historians would say it was the Borjigid).[50] Within each tribe there were supposed to be the traditional 'sons of light' (Nirun) and the lesser beings (Durlukin), but both Tayichiud and Borjigid regarded themselves as Nirun with the other clan as the Morlocks, so to speak.[51] Cooperation only ever took place in pursuit of booty or while on a great raid. When Genghis was born the Mongols were still paying tribute to the Jin, still a 'little people, a silly people, greedy, barbarous and cruel'. Whereas after the reforms of 1206 groups ranging from individuals to whole tribes found themselves fighting side by side with warriors they were recently trying to kill – for Genghis worked out with great skill the safe proportion of defeated Kereit, Naiman, and so on he could assign to each minqan.[52] Before Genghis the tribes of Mongolia had fought only for booty or in the civil wars of succession. After 1206, while there was booty beyond the previous dreams of avarice, there was also a new martial ethos where each man had the opportunity to win glory or kudos without the rankers' efforts automatically being attributed to the leader's brilliance, as happened before.

Naturally, there was a downside to all this. In throwing out the bathwater of lineages and other paraphernalia of clan culture, Genghis also threw out some valuable babies, including the previously all-important *anda* relationship, which shrivelled in importance after 1206. And, as large-scale mobilisation of the population led to the emergence of what could be recognised as a state, much steeper inequalities in wealth, rank and status manifested themselves; paradoxically, the new meritocracy led to the appearance of Mongol 'fat cats'.[53] Of course all these changes interpenetrated, for it was the new creed of unparalleled economic opportunity which diminished the importance of the *anda* relationship. As one historian has expressed it: 'After Genghis Khan's unification of the steppes, the *anda* relationship all but disappeared, for nomadic leaders became part of a new imperium and were no longer autonomous actors.'[54]

As a final touch to his system of government and to make totally certain that he had achieved lockdown, Genghis set up his own version of the praetorian guard, the keshig. The degree of militarisation in

Genghis Khan's new state becomes evident from a single statistic. Before 1206 he had employed 150 men as bodyguards, eighty as night guards and seventy for the day shift. As a result of the decrees following the 1206 quriltai, Genghis raised this number to 10,000 nominal day guards, 1,000 night guards and 1,000 'quiver bearers'.[55] This was the famous keshig. The sudden increase had nothing to do with security – if anything, after the successful conclusion of his Mongolian wars the threat to the khan was far less – but it was Genghis's way of maintaining an iron grip on the system he had created. To ensure the loyalty of the commanders of the minqans, and indeed of all powerful men in his realm, Genghis recruited at least one son from each of these men as a de facto hostage and guarantor of good behaviour.[56] Taking these sons at the age of 15 and socialising them in the norms of meritocracy and loyalty to the khan alone, Genghis ensured that he had a body of troops bound to the state with no hankering for the old clan values and folk customs or the traditional, chaotic freebooting ways. Here was a multi-tribal elite taking orders only from Genghis.

The key to the keshig's success was face-to-face acquaintance. Genghis knew each of the 10,000 by sight and, with his elephantine memory, knew the key names; the names of the others were whispered to him by his closest confidants, so that he could pretend to know everyone intimately, much as Napoleon did later.[57] As always with Genghis, he issued the most precise details setting out the respective duties of night guards, day guards and 'quiver bearers' – for example, the night guards were not allowed to sortie from the camp, no matter what the danger, unless the khan himself led the sally. Discipline was tough. For abandoning a shift the penalty for a first offence was three strokes of a rod, for the second seven and for a third thirty-seven strokes, followed by exile. The captains of the guards could not remove any individual guard without the khan's permission, beat them (except for abandoning shifts) or execute them. In return the guards enjoyed huge privileges in access to money, drink and women and, crucially, enjoyed superiority to all normal troops, even officers up to and including the commanders of the minqans.[58] The absurd situation was thus reached whereby Subedei and Jebe, who commanded minqans, were in theory inferior to everyone in the keshig even though they were officially in the inner cabinet as two of the nine paladins.

This is perhaps yet another example of the paranoid Genghis in action. The keshig was primarily a military force but it gradually took over administrative functions as well, becoming simultaneously a kind of military staff college and a training school for civil servants. It was eventually organised into ten groups or offices, each with a specific function, which could range from household, kitchen and camp duties and herding the camp's animals to acting as envoys on foreign missions.[59] As the years went by, Genghis increasingly used personnel from his bodyguard as administrators: in line with the many anomalies thrown up by Genghis's system, such people often had fairly low positions *within* the guard but very high ones outside, as imperial administrators.[60] The night guards were also allowed to sit as an advisory body alongside chief justice Shigi Qutuqu in his court.[61] The keshig was the nucleus from which the later imperial administration grew.[62]

Genghis's organisation and administration of his empire was so good that it survived the many years of extreme factionalism that followed his son and successor Ogodei's death in 1241 before eventually breaking up. But Genghis himself undermined his near-perfect system, ultimately fatally, by sheer human weakness, finally buckling under the relentless nagging of his sons who felt that their 'honour' had been impugned by the 1206 settlement. On paper this was an absurd claim. Tolui had been made commander-in-chief of the army, Jochi was appointed supremo of hunting and the chase, Chagatai was chosen to enforce Genghis's new law code, the 'Great Yasa', while Ogodei essentially ran the empire as chief civil administrator.[63] Yet, apart from Tolui, they had no military role beyond that of being commanders of minqans, and there were at least ninety other such souls in the empire. Besides, they grumbled, Genghis had used them like pawns, appeasing his conquered subjects by marrying them to alien princesses, Ogodei to the Naiman Toregene, a Naiman and widow of a Merkit, Tolui to the Kereit Sorgaghtani.[64] They could not even live where they liked, since the khan designated the residence of all his chiefs, who in turn designated the residence of the minqan commanders, and so on down along the line.[65]

Accordingly, in 1209 he announced a new division of the empire, assigning troops, lands and monies to his sons. There would be a system of appanages – which in medieval Europe meant gifts of land and money to the younger sons of kings but which in Mongolia, where a system of ultimogeniture obtained for passing on inherited homelands, had to be slightly different. There is a strong case that this was one of Genghis's greatest mistakes. Having created a central-ised bureaucracy which threw out all the traditional claims of kinship, he allowed them back in again under pressure from his sons.

First he announced a new distribution of troops. Of the army's strength 44,500 would now be distributed to his family. Jochi would receive 9,000 soldiers, Chagatai 8,000, Ogodei 5,000 and Tolui 5,000. Qasar would be given 4,000, Belgutei 1,500, the khan's favourite Eljigidei 2,000, while Hoelun and Temuge would share 10,000 – which Genghis's mother promptly denounced as insulting; why should she have to share with one of her sons?[66] New lands would also be assigned to his sons and brothers. Jochi received the Irtysh territory and all the lands to the west 'as far as our horses' hooves can reach', which in the end delivered Eurasia and Russia to his sons. Chagatai got the western T'ien Shan and the Tarim basin and later western Turkestan (eventually, after further conquests, his realm would stretch from Samarkand to Qara Khitai). Ogodei was given Dzungaria and the western slopes of the Altai, plus the territory east and north-east of Lake Balkhash – essentially the old Naiman realm. Tolui, as was trad-itional for the youngest son, inherited the Mongolian heartland. Qasar's descendants received lands near the Ergune and Hailar Rivers while Temuge, after 1219, would inherit the vassal state of Korea.[67] The appanages would be known as ulus, and with the land and troops went all the peoples as subjects, a vast stretch of grazing land to support this population, an *inju* that would give a revenue to keep up a court and high living standards. The ulus system alone would have made Genghis's realm an empire of permanent conquest, for the money for all this could come only from tribute.[68]

The ulus system was far more trouble than it was worth. Although the appanages given to his four sons were not intended to be the embryos from which future independent kingdoms would be born, that danger was always there and, inevitably, it was what eventually happened – yet another instance of unintended consequences in history. Genghis was blinded by paternal affection, meaning that his usual shrewdness and far-sightedness did not come into play.[69] Genghis granted the ulus to his sons on the strict understanding that they would expand and thus pay for themselves but, with the exception of

Jochi's khanate, this pious hope never fructified. They were also supposed to raise troops, contribute money to the treasury and be under severe central control, but naturally the sons chafed at these restrictions too.

Genghis tried to deal with the problems of disobedient sons or even (horror of horrors) the possibility of revolt by appointing political commissars (jarghuchi) to be his eyes and ears in the appanages. These men had to conduct censuses and estimate the available booty and wealth for distribution, so that the fruits of the ulus were shared between the sons and the central government.[70] The possibility of corruption and defalcation was also obvious. To try to arrest this possibility, Genghis appointed tax-collectors (daruqachi) whose task was to remit to the central treasury 70 per cent of the silk tax collected. Even to collect taxes in a settled and continuous way was alien to nomadic culture (as opposed to ad hoc levies for warfare or to relieve those in financial hardship), so the problem was how to gain consent and consensus concerning these imposts; the nomadic taxpayer usually 'solved' the problem by moving on.[71]

Another problem was that the frontiers of the various ulus had not been clearly defined, and this gave rise to endless disputes both among the brothers and between them and other local rulers. The ulus system worked against Genghis's own design, which was to rule indirectly, and to let the locals govern themselves so long as they paid tribute; the alternative was expensive and permanent military occupation.[72] And the arrogance of the sons was yet another problem, for Genghis's officials of all kinds found themselves in conflict with them over supposed infringements of their sovereignty and dignity. Genghis was obliged to appoint garrison commanders chosen from the keshig to remind his sons who was the ultimate boss.

At the limit, contumacious sons could be summoned to appear before the general Mongol assembly (jarghu), the one body given the power to examine misbehaving officials, rebellious vassals and fractious members of the royal family. At such royal trials Belgutei was supposed to lead the prosecution, Genghis himself would introduce experts in a kind of inquisitorial system, and the princes would have their own counsel.[73] Genghis was extraordinarily sensitive to slights (real or imagined) from his sons, and on a number of occasions had to be talked out of executing them for insubordinate behaviour, so for anyone to become embroiled with his officials was a dangerous path to tread.

But worst of all the problems with the ulus was that the freedoms granted to the appanages were in conflict with the general ethos that the empire was the common property of the entire extended royal family, and by implication, because of Genghis's identification of himself with the state, of the entire commonwealth.[74] It was a classic instance where the demands of private property were in conflict with the common good. For all these reasons, and because he feared the possibility of civil war after his death, in the last year of his life Genghis cut down the number of troops assigned to his family from 44,500 to 28,000. Tolui, as head of the army, was deemed not to need any, while the other three sons and their descendants were cut to 4,000 each. Eljigidei, Temuge and Genghis's son (by his favourite wife Qulan) Kolgen, who had all previously had smaller allocations, were the chief beneficiaries on this occasion.[75]

Some time in the years 1207–08 (the date cannot be pinned down with any certainty) Genghis faced a more immediate problem, nearer home. His chief shaman Teb Tengerri (given name Kokochu, the middlemost of Monglik's seven sons), had served Genghis faithfully for more than twenty years. He it was who originally proclaimed Temujin khan of the Borjigid clan and who, at the quriltai of 1206 had declared Genghis the promised one of Heaven. Teb Tengerri testified eloquently that before the coming of the saviour Genghis, the steppes had been riven by the war of all against all.[76] Perhaps Teb Tengerri considered that such services merited an outstanding reward but, whereas Bo'orchu, Muqali, Jelme and the paladins, not to mention a number of those he considered 'overpromoted' shepherds and 'low lifes' had been granted wondrous gifts and privileges, there had been nothing for Teb Tengerri.

At all events, he seems to have become seriously alienated after the 1206 quriltai and began plotting how he might displace Genghis – for was he not, after all, the high priest with unique access to the sky-god? His very title Teb Tengerri seems to have meant 'all-heavenly'.

In an evil hour he began forming secret cabals with his six brothers and stirring up discontent among the aristocratic 'old Mongols', some of whom could be heard to mutter that they had been thrown on the scrapheap while Genghis's new *nokor*, myriarchs and night guards scooped the pool.[77] Teb Tengerri pondered his options and concluded that Genghis's weak spot was his ambivalence about his brother Qasar; this might be the wedge he needed to prise apart Genghis's carefully-constructed new government. His opportunity came when Qasar returned from an unsuccessful attempt to put down a rebellion by the Qongqotad tribe. Genghis raged at his brother for his incompetence and Qasar, finding this public rebuke intolerable, stormed off in dudgeon.[78] Teb Tengerri moved in for the kill. When Qasar absented himself from the court for an unprecedented three days, Teb began to pour poison into the khan's ear, alleging that Qasar was even then hatching an insurrection.

Genghis did not need much persuading, as he had a long list of grievances against his brother. He had been two-faced during the long struggle with Toghril, and there was the memorable occasion when Genghis had had to order him to behead Toghril's envoy to prove his loyalty.[79] Besides, now that Sacha Beki, Jamuga, Altan and Quchar had all been executed, Qasar was the only credible candidate as pretender in the event of a palace coup. As a final incentive – one knows not whether this was a cunning 'set-up' – Teb Tengerri pointed out Qasar pressing the hand of the khan's favourite wife Qulan. Genghis therefore ordered his arrest and informed his intimates that he intended to execute him. Qasar was stripped of his cap and belt – the symbols of a free Mongol – and placed in chains.

There followed one of the most dramatic incidents in Genghis's family history. He had married off his mother to Monglik, thinking to nail down Monglik's difficult family thereby.[80] At Monglik's tent Hoelun heard his sons boasting that they had done for Qasar. Learning what was afoot, she mounted a white camel and rode all night to Genghis's headquarters. There she threw herself at her son's feet and begged for Qasar's life. Genghis at first toyed with her, at which Hoelun grew angry, got to her feet and roundly rebuked the khan for thinking to execute his brother, one, she pointed out, who had shared with him their mother's milk. Genghis raised her up and said he would grant the boon because of his love and deference for his mother.[81]

The truth was that the trio of Bo'orchu, Muqali and Boroqul – the three men he trusted most – had already urged him that the execution of Qasar was extremely unwise. Genghis took their advice, but sought around for some other way to punish Qasar. Eventually he decided public humiliation was the answer. The 4,000 troops he had assigned to Qasar at the 1206 quriltai were reduced to 1,400. It is said that when his mother Hoelun heard of this outcome, she died of shock.[82] The only certainty is that she died shortly after her epic camel ride. After a judicious interval, once his invasion of China began in 1211, Genghis ordered Qasar to the front, where he died in the fighting soon after.[83]

Teb Tengerri's arrogance and self-confidence increased after he had compassed the disgrace of Qasar. His next target was another of Genghis's brothers, Temuge. Because Temuge and Hoelun shared the 10,000 troops given to them in the 1206 distribution – an arrangement Hoelun regarded as an insult – and because she was married to Monglik, once she had died Teb Tengerri claimed that these 10,000 men should be given up to the house of Monglik as the rightful heirs, cutting out Temuge altogether.[84] Still Genghis did not react, assuring his confidants that Teb Tengerri was a hothead, this was all a storm in a teacup and it would soon blow over.

By now tempting nemesis with his hubris, Teb Tengerri announced unilaterally that the 10,000 were his. Temuge stormed down to Teb Tengerri's tent and demanded an immediate retraction and acceptance that he was the rightful heir. Teb Tengerri not only refused but had his brothers manhandle Temuge disgracefully, forcing him to kneel to Teb Tengerri; the house of Monglik had now publicly insulted a prince of the blood. Still Genghis seemed to dither about how to respond, but Borte, always a key adviser, warned him that unless he took decisive action, Teb Tengerri's next actions would be directed against him.[85] Genghis sent for Temuge and told him that he was summoning Teb Tengerri to explain himself but that he thereby authorised Temuge to deal with the matter in any way he saw fit.

The blustering Teb Tengerri arrived at Genghis's tent with his six brothers. Temuge immediately grabbed him by the throat and challenged him to a wrestling match. Genghis protested that the royal tent could not be defiled by such an unseemly display, and ordered the disputants to settle the matter outside; the brothers were to remain in his presence. Once outside, Temuge gave the nod to his bodyguard. They seized Teb Tengerri and broke his back, taking care not to shed blood as he was of the Mongol nobility. Temuge went back inside the royal tent and told Genghis that the deed was done. Teb Tengerri's brothers, initially stupefied, became enraged and blasphemously laid hands on the khan, meanwhile trying to barricade the threshold. Genghis called out for his guards, who rushed in and subdued the tempestuous sons of Monglik.[86] Genghis then publicly upbraided Monglik and, when the old man tried to defend himself, the khan brusquely cut him off. His sons' conduct merited instant execution, but Genghis decided family humiliation would be a better punishment. It was decreed that Monglik and his sons had been deprived of all titles, privileges and perquisites; henceforth they would have to live quietly in the country, under constant surveillance. Genghis then made a public announcement, informing his people of an attempted coup and declaring: 'Because Teb Tengerri laid hands on my younger brothers and spread tasteless slanders among my younger brothers, he was not loved by Heaven, and his life, together with his body, has been carried off.'[87] Genghis then subjected Monglik to a public dressing-down and rebuked him for not having controlled his sons, adding that if he could have foreseen the future, he would have exterminated the entire family at an early stage: 'When I realised your nature, I should have done for you what I did to Jamuga, Altan, Quchar and the rest.'[88]

The crisis with Teb Tengerri invites many comments. At one level it was a struggle for supremacy between the secular and the spiritual power, echoing a similar conflict that had taken place in England forty years before between Henry II and Thomas Becket. It is even possible that Genghis subtly encouraged the crisis, so that he could eliminate Teb Tengerri once and for all, since he was the only remaining barrier to absolute power.[89] The entire incident seems to have reinforced a growing contempt, albeit expressed only to his intimates, for priests and shamans as drones and parasites; they had to be conciliated as they had great influence but they were useless in war – the only true measure of a man's worth.[90] At another level it was a triumphant assertion of Genghis's new system against the claims of kinship and the clan ethos. According to the old rules of the steppe, Monglik and his family would have had a case for inheriting Hoelun's troops; Genghis made it very clear that under the new dispensation the only factor that would weigh was his own will, his commands, his decrees.

He then appointed the Ba'arin Usun beki as his new shaman, thus enhancing the prestige of the new title of beki but not before making it clear that henceforth all priests would be directly subservient to the khan.[91] He himself assumed many of the functions of a high priest and was soon reported to be going into trances in his role as shaman.[92] Yet the general religious impact of Teb Tengerri's downfall was to reduce the influence of shamanism in Mongolia and to increase that of the pagan cosmological sky-god and other religions. Shamanism related to the era when the Mongols were warring, disunited septs, but the worship of Tengerri the sky-god was altogether more appropriate for a world empire.[93] The Naiman, already largely conciliated by having been given so many state posts, were further overjoyed by the increased chances for the spread of Nestorian Christianity following Teb Tengerri's downfall. His death ushered in a golden period for the Nestorians, who were encouraged by Genghis as he needed a religion that would not challenge him.[94] It is, however, passing curious that even after the utter discrediting of Monglik and his family, Genghis and his successors should still think it important to remind the Mongols that Teb Tengerri had declared the khan the chosen one of God.[95] Perhaps Genghis's antennae were once again supersensitive, and he realised the Mongols could not be pushed too fast into a new era and that too rapid a rate of change would disconcert and demoralise them.

At the same time it made him more determined to push through his own legal code so that the secular would be seen to have clear superiority over the religious, the so-called profane over the so-called sacred. Hinting that Teb Tengerri had actually committed treason, Genghis promulgated a new law ordaining the death penalty for anyone who communicated with a foreign power without his knowledge.[96]

One final point to make about Teb Tengerri's death was how peculiarly similar it was to Jamuga's, except for the bloodless slaying. Both were talented figures, to whom Genghis owed much, but who were ruthlessly disposed of when they had outlived their usefulness or tried to threaten Genghis's hegemony. The two deaths, within a few years of each other, provided an awful warning of what would happen if anyone was foolish enough to challenge the will of the great khan or his laws.[97]

One of Genghis's great innovations at the 1206 quriltai was to devise a legal code or 'Great Yasa'. This was methodically revised at the quriltai of 1218 and at subsequent councils. There were many aspects to the Yasa. It was partly a 'King's Regulations' guide to military conduct, partly the systematisation of the traditional taboos of the steppes, partly a collection of the various ideas, jottings and aperçus of the great khan himself, and partly an original attempt to think through some of the problems the empire might face in the future.

Each of these aspects was important and ideally needs to be teased out into its separate strands. The easiest aspect to deal with are those norms, values, myths, ideas and shibboleths deriving from the Mongols' nomadic way of life itself. The killing of animals was a central concern. The Mongol way of slaughter was to lay an animal on its back and sedate or restrain it while the butcher cut its chest open and ripped out the aorta, causing deadly internal bleeding.[98] All the blood was thus kept inside the animal, to be drained out later and used to make sausages. The Mongols rarely killed animals in summer, but if one died, they cut the meat into strips and dried it. Even in winter sheep were the only animals killed for meat, unless a horse had to be sacrificed on a special ceremonial occasion.[99] All offences against horses merited severe punishment, whether merely striking a horse in anger with a bridle, maliciously wounding or, worst of all, stealing. Horse rustling made one an enemy of the people, as a horse could provide iron rations – as when the Mongols slit a vein in a horse's leg, drank the blood, then sealed up the wound again – and mean the difference between life and death. It was even forbidden to lean on the whips with which you lashed your horse (in the absence of spurs) or to touch arrows with a whip, as the implement with which you controlled a horse had to be treated with the same respect as the animal itself.

The general reverence for animal life extended to a veto on catching young birds; to destroy young life was of course self-destructive as species could become extinct.[100] Other taboos concerned the elements. Such was the reverence for fire that it was forbidden to stick a knife into a fire, touch a fire with a knife or to chop wood near a fire, as this would mean that the fire itself was 'beheaded'. The fire gods might then take revenge by sending forest fires.[101] The shibboleths about water were many, and most seem to have arisen because of the fear of thunderstorms – frequent in Mongolia and possibly disastrous if large herds were caught in a storm on the open steppe.[102] It was fear of lightning (thought by the Mongols to emanate from an animal like a dragon) that lay behind the prohibition on bathing or washing in running water in spring or summer. It was not, as Western visitors initially supposed, because of an innate Mongol disdain for hygiene but fear of offending the spirits of water, who could cause thunderstorms and floods; this also lay behind the ban on urinating in water or spilling any kind of liquid on the ground.[103]

Taboos about food also related to fears about offending spirits and demons. The penalty for spitting out food for any reason was very severe. The offender had a hole made in the side of his dwelling, was dragged out through it and then executed.[104] Yet another taboo was the ban on treading on the threshold of a chief's tent. The usual penalty was death, but when Carpini and his monks unknowingly breached this taboo in 1246, they were let off with a stern warning, as aliens could not be expected to know the ways of the steppes.[105] The frame of the door of a dwelling and the threshold itself had a numinous connotation for the Mongols, as images of the household gods were set up on both sides.[106]

Much of this Genghis felt necessary to incorporate in his new code, but his principal aim was to promote organic solidarity among his new Mongol nation, to break down the old cultures and ways of thinking and to inculcate a universal ideology by means of his Yasa. There was thus a contradiction at the heart of the code, for it had to provide continuity with the old ways while in another sense trying to destroy them.[107]

Unfortunately, nearly everything about the Yasa is a subject of impassioned scholarly debate. The core problem is that the code does not survive in a written form, with only fragments, some of dubious provenance, extant. This has allowed the extreme sceptics in the academic community to query whether the Yasa ever did exist in a written form, or even whether it had a reality that extended beyond Genghis's personal maxims, whims or *obiter dicta*.[108] The scepticism takes many forms. Some say the notion of such a written code would have been meaningless to the Mongols, as they were illiterate. Others say Genghis was concerned to promote the *belief* in such a code, even though it did not exist, as it gave him huge flexibility in issuing what might otherwise be considered arbitrary and even despotic orders and decrees.[109] The great Arab scholar Ibn Battuta, however, assures us that it did exist in its entirety in a written, systematic form in the

Uighur script.[110] The so-called 'Great Book of the Yasa' was probably the emperor's own handbook, an esoteric document for consultation by imperial lawyers, existing alongside a collection of public decrees known as the bilik, widely promulgated and generally known.[111] 'Little yasas' – collections of tribal and clan customs, mores and folkways – were permitted to exist alongside the greater version unless they collided, in which case, naturally, the 'Great Yasa' prevailed.

If the 'Great Yasa' really was an esoteric document and, like the *Secret History*, available for inspection only by the elite on the grounds that it was sacred or taboo, an obvious conundrum arises. Why would one devise a legal code, whose provisions were not known, if one wanted people to obey it?[112] Naturally this state of affairs would engender the well-known problems of quasi-biblical hermeneusis in interpreting the Yasa, but it was surely self-defeating; even though it is a well-known legal principle that ignorance of the law is no defence, it is also a well-sanctioned principle, going back to the ancients, that you cannot have secret laws: *lex non promulgata non obligat*. But it seems clear from many different strands of evidence that the 'secrecy' argument, however ingenious, has been overdone. Its proponents like to point out that the great Persian historian Rashid al-Din makes no mention of the Yasa, but by his time the code would have been generally assumed to be part of the furniture of the universe and therefore not in need of special explication. Moreover, another historian, nearly as important, Juvaini, devotes considerable attention to it; his evidence can be disposed of only by traducing him *ad hominem*.[113]

One way into the discussion of the 'Great Yasa' would be to compare it with the other famous legal codes of human history. There are interesting similarities between Genghis's system and the famous Babylonian Code of Hammurabi, usually dated to the eighteenth century BC, not just in the draconian penal codes both offer (basically 'an eye for an eye' in Hammurabi's) but also in the half of the Babylonian code that deals with the family, inheritance, paternity, divorce and sexual behaviour and commercial contracts. In the Code of Hammurabi one can even discern greater sympathy for the consumer – the statutes on wages for ox-drivers and surgeons and the penalties for 'cowboy' builders – than in the Yasa.[114]

The other great code from this early period is the Mosaic Law, containing purity laws concerning personal hygiene, clean and unclean food, sacrifices and offerings, and moral laws on murder, theft, marriage, divorce, adultery, property, inheritance and so on.[115] Such issues loom large in the Yasa and there are other Mosaic resonances. Working to pay off the bride-price, as an alternative to paying with cattle – the very experience Genghis had as a young man among the Ongirrad – seems to have an uncanny pre-echo in the biblical story of Jacob labouring for Laban, seven years for Leah and seven years for Rachel. Both codes, too, condemn bestialism and sodomy in vociferous terms.[116]

The other famous legal codes that we might turn to take us much farther from the world of Genghis Khan. The sixth-century Code of Justinian was largely a compendium of existing Roman law, containing public, private and customary law plus all the imperial rescripts since Hadrian and all the commentaries by learned jurists. This is a much more sophisticated universe than the world of Genghis Khan and the steppes, yet even here, in the harsh proscriptions of heresy and paganism, one can see the mentality of control at work.[117] There are even analysts who say that the famous Code Napoléon of 1804 is not entirely irrelevant to the Mongol case, for example in its preference for the inquisitorial system in criminal law, and the absence of case law which makes theoretical distinctions between executive and legislature hard to implement in the real world.[118] Naturally in Genghis's empire there was no question of a legislature being able to question one of his executive decisions, but there are conservative critics today who claim that in important instances the U.S. Supreme Court usurps what should properly be executive power. Cynics have even been heard to say that Genghis's code was more liberal than Napoleon's, as the French emperor abolished divorce for women.

All these similarities and divergencies become clearer on a close examination of the Yasa. Hardly surprisingly, in a militarised society like the Mongol empire, much of the code is concerned with military matters: mobilisation of the army, prosecution of campaigns, relations with foreign nations. Officers who failed in their duty or disobeyed the khan suffered the death penalty and even those who made genuine or understandable mistakes might be punished in this way if the khan's blood was up.[119] Captains of minqans could communicate only with the khan and not with each other and, if they committed an offence against his book of rules, they had to prostrate themselves before the emperor's messenger sent to summon them to explain themselves. In such cases, Genghis made a point of sending very low-class envoys, to increase the humiliation.[120] All commanders had to come to court for a personal briefing once a year, for Genghis decreed that those who did not hear his words were like 'a stone that falls into deep water or an arrow shot into the reeds – they disappear. It is not fit for such men to command.'[121] Military service was made attractive by the decree that anyone not employed as warrior must work unpaid for the state, but conditions of service were harsh. On mobilisation a soldier had to report with all his arms and armours in first-class condition or be fined; if you failed to present yourself at the muster, your wife or another woman in your household would be enrolled to replace you. If a soldier pillaged before his general gave permission, he was put to death. If he failed to pick up a weapon dropped by the soldier in front of him, likewise.[122] In a case where large numbers of Mongols had fallen in battle, the survivors were likely to be executed for not having given of their best. Genghis believed in enhancing the fighting calibre of his men by keeping them on short commons and at hard labour before a battle; the only way to escape this nightmare existence was to fight like a pack of wild dogs so that, victorious, you could enjoy ample food, booty, rest and relaxation.[123] As with the Spartans, the harsh military code was meant to inculcate supreme discipline and an ethos that said you should come back from a battle either victorious or dead on your shield.[124]

Since the hunt was one of the main methods of peacetime military training, rigorous rules also governed the conduct of the battue. All soldiers allowing animals to escape from the deadly closing circle of the great hunt were punished by running the gauntlet while they were beaten with sticks. There was a strict prohibition against killing deer, antelope, hares, wild asses and all game birds during the winter months from March to October.[125]

There is very little about private law in the Great Yasa, as such matters were usually dealt with by tribal custom. Apart from military matters, public law concerned issues to do with taxation, administration and the status of the khan and his families. On taxation the groups enjoying most immunity privileges were religious bodies and foreign merchants. Genghis's respect for all religions has often been noted; his motives were always pragmatic – religion could help with social control and it might lead the Mongol leaders in the directions of longevity or even immortality. Even so, the exemption of priests, lamas, imams, preachers and holy men of all kinds both from conscription and taxation was extraordinarily generous. Physicians and skilled artisans were also granted exemptions but never as total as those granted to the clergy.[126] Pragmatism was to the fore also in the exceptionally favourable terms granted to merchants and the deliberate bending of the law in their favour. Very tight regulations were in force concerning lost property or the appropriation of stray animals; Genghis was both concerned that the merchants should not suffer from 'inventory shrinkage' through pilfering or rustling and worried that unless he cracked down hard in this area, new feuds and vendettas would arise.[127] It has been speculated that many of the provisions of the Yasa favouring merchants were added after 1218, and probably around 1222 after Genghis conquered Khwarezmia, unleashing on his empire a pent-up tsunami of merchants and rich travellers; insofar as a *Pax Mongolica* did exist (which will be discussed later) this protection was an important part of it.[128]

A similar consideration applies to the death penalty incurred by anyone failing to pay fines or going bankrupt for a third time; again this is a relatively late accretion and may even be a clause added after the conquest of Jin China in 1234.[129] Most pre-modern codes ordained prison for bankruptcy, so capital punishment for something that would not normally be considered a criminal offence is noteworthy, but here again we see Genghis's determination that the ways should be made straight for the mercantile class. Slaves were an important part of the foreign traders' property portfolio, so it was decreed that everyone must return a runaway slave on pain of death. Even activities which under the traditional customs of the steppe would be classified as misdemeanours – banditry, highway robbery, intra-tribal feuds – attracted the death penalty under Genghis's code.[130]

A quasi-religious ordinance which sneaked in under the rubric of public law concerned the slaughter of animals, which had to be done strictly in the traditional Mongol way (no throat-cutting) or death would follow. Muslims in particular claimed that Genghis had ordained the harshest possible punishment for something which in their moral and legal system was not only no crime at all but actually prescribed as compulsory. Some scholars think that this clause in the Yasa was simply a hobby-horse of Genghis himself, that confederate tribes disregarded it, and his own commanders failed to enforce it; the Oyirad, for example, continued to kill their animals by bludgeoning them until they died. By the time of the election of the fourth great khan in 1251, when the western Mongol world was becoming Islamicised, it has been pointed out that, according to Genghis's Yasa, everyone present, including the royal family, should have been executed for slaughtering animals in the Muslim way.[131]

Another aspect of public law concerned the special respect due the khan and his family. Although Genghis espoused the principle of meritocracy in the army and a measure of communistic equality among the lower orders, and although he had appealed to the have-nots successfully in his steppe wars against Jamuga, the Kereit and the Naiman, he was emphatically no egalitarian when it came to his own prerogatives and those of his family. In all his decrees, his puta-tive audience was the aristocracy, not the people.[132] He claimed the right of 'micro-level intervention' in any matters in clan or family if he deemed that such disputes endangered the peace and order of the realm. In the case of the Yasa he showed the reality behind the code by appointing his own favourite Shigi Qutuqu as his imperial Chief Justice. Some have said that Genghis's concern for the masses was always bogus, and that earlier steppe leaders had been more genuinely concerned for them.[133]

The Great Yasa laid down that any successor to the post of great khan had to be a direct descendant of Genghis. No other titles except that of khan and beki were permitted; there was emphatically no honours system in the sense understood in the contemporary U.K. Not even vassal chiefs or allied rulers were allowed to bear honorary titles. If members of the royal family had to be put on trial, they would not appear before normal courts but a specially selected and convened Supreme Court.[134] If found guilty, the penalty was almost invariably deportation or imprisonment but, in the extreme case where the death penalty was called for, the guilty party had to be put to death bloodlessly, usually by strangulation or being smothered and asphyxiated in a pile of carpets. Genghis relished the Confucian precept 'physical punishment is not applicable to dignitaries' and in any case it was always open to him to grant his favourites further exemptions from criminal penalties.[135]

Although Genghis was himself bound by the principles of his own laws and had to go through legal forms, he could essentially do whatever he wished and some penal functions, e.g. the punishment of his own bodyguard, were expressly his own personal preserve.[136] To the question 'Was Mongol society under Genghis Khan a rule-governed system or a tyranny?' the answer can only be: both.[137] The only limit on the khan's despotism was that trials had to be held in public and that rank injustice might alienate his followers. Genghis would have answered the philosopher Hume's famous question – how does a man who rules by force coerce his own bodyguard and soldiers? – in a similar way to Hume himself: through opinion or a sense of legitimacy. In short, he claimed to have a mandate from Heaven and declared that if the grandees and aristocrats did not obey the Yasa, the state would fall: 'People will look eagerly for a Genghis Khan but will not find him.'[138]

One of the peculiarities of the Yasa was not just its draconian penal code but the way that so many issues ended up being subsumed under criminality. Of the thirty-six clear statutes that have come down to us, fourteen expressly ordain capital punishment, but the momentum of 'slippage' from other spheres added to the number.[139] Even though for a statement in court to be valid it had to be buttressed by three witnesses, acquittal rates were low. The death penalty was prescribed for murder, adultery, having sexual intercourse with another man's daughter or slave, sodomy, homosexuality, rape, bestialism, treason, desertion, lying, theft, embezzlement, taking food from another's mouth, failing to share food with a stranger, entering running water, polluting running water with water in which one had washed, urinating in running water, horse and cattle stealing, fraudulent bankruptcy (for such the third instance of insolvency was construed to be), interference with another's slave or captive, protecting slaves or fugitive prisoners, giving food to a prisoner without the say-so of his captor, interference with religious worship and freedom, polluting ashes, slaughter of animals except in the Mongol way, witchcraft, espionage, showing charity to captives, leaving one's post without permission, culpable negligence by soldiers or hunters, having no property out of which to pay fines or wives and children to be enslaved in lieu of debt, bearing false witness, want of respect for elders, gluttony or stepping on the threshold of a chief's tent, hurting a horse's eyes, and eating in front of another without offering that person food.[140] The death penalty was very widely inflicted, especially so as human life was considered to be no more valuable intrinsically than that of a domestic beast. Even more cruelly, a man's family was considered collectively responsible for his crime and wives and children could be put to death as 'accessories' as a consequence; the Mongols emphatically believed that the sins of the father should be visited on the sons.[141]

The element of 'slippage' was an inevitable concomitant of the peculiarity that the injured party had the right to decide the punishment once the sentence of 'guilty' was pronounced. In some cases, individuals guilty only of slandering or traducing another thereby suffered death.[142] Then there was the 'disguised death penalty'. In the case of aristocrats this might mean being sent to the front in a murderous war or sent on an embassy to an enemy known to butcher envoys as a matter of course. In the case of the common man it usually took the form of being beaten, for example for sheep-stealing. Since corporal punishment meant anywhere between seven and 107 lashes, it followed that those condemned to this penalty often died of it.[143] On the other hand, rich thieves and murderers (provided the victims were non-Mongols such as Chinese or Muslims) could often buy their way out of the death trap; in the case of theft, this was done by paying over nine times the value of the goods originally stolen.[144]

Genghis's version of the Bloody Code was undoubtedly cruel but no more so in general than contemporary laws in China, the world of Islam or medieval Europe. Needless to say, Mongol atrocities were always played up by hostile commentators. One form of execution was considered particularly barbarous. Denying the victim a quick death, the Mongols would often tie the condemned man to a post, then cover him with a dense layer of fat; when this gradually grew maggoty, the maggots would eat him alive.[145] There was always an arbitary element in the implementation of the Yasa, and sometimes flat contradictions. For example, the Mongols were tougher on rapists than any other people. Punishment for rape in the Middle Ages ranged from castration in Norman England to a fine or six months in jail in medieval Venice.[146] Yet Genghis issued a standing order that all pretty women captured on campaign must be paraded before him, his sons and his favourites so they could have first pick of bedfellows. A similar order was sent out to all Mongol families, who were supposed to take it as a great honour if their daughters were taken into concubinage.[147] What else was this but rape in another guise? Similarly, Genghis decreed the death penalty for adultery among the Mongols because it led to feuds but allowed adultery with foreign women as this did not endanger the harmony of the Mongol nation.[148] In general one can say that Mongol conquest made a lot of the sexual prescriptions of the Yasa otiose. There were no laws against the abduction of women, almost certainly because by the time the Yasa was being codified, there were hordes of captive women to satisfy the libido of the Mongol warriors, whereas in the period before Genghis, with lusts rampant and unsatisfied, female abduction was one of the great menaces of the steppes.[149]

Genghis did manage to avoid outright humbug by issuing no general prescriptions regarding manslaughter or blood-feud – just as well, as this had motivated so many of his own actions. As for international law and the Yasa, Genghis issued no general guidance except to say that peace could never be made with a foreign nation until that nation had submitted, but there was no overt threat of force. Genghis's posture was that God would decide but, since he regarded himself as the instrument of Heaven, it was clear what the outcome was supposed to be. The formula so often used by the Mongols in dealing with foreign powers – 'who knows what will happen, only God can decide' – was eventually widely understood as meaning 'surrender or die'.[150] The only other issue relating to international law – the inviolability of envoys – was a personal credo of Genghis and not incorporated in the Yasa proper.

Was the Great Yasa an instrument of arbitrary government, a device to ensure aristocratic hegemony or something that truly benefited all the people? This question in turn raises the issue of whether the Yasa was no more than Genghis's maxims enshrined in law or whether it involved a quantitative advance on these, evinced by the fact that the Yasa was far harsher than anything that could be extrapolated from the khan's sayings and apothegms.[151] And where was the popular element?

The answer to the latter point is that many of the most treasured tenets, taboos and predilections of Mongol popular culture and religion were consolidated in the code. Everything about food was of great concern to the Mongols, so it is above all in this area that we find the Yasa endorsing the usage of the steppes. For example, choking while eating food was thought to be a sign of demonic possession and as such it warranted death, for only by executing the person possessed could the demon be driven out.[152] Wasting food was another serious offence. The Mongols also had a pathological fear of poisoning, so the Yasa contained the warning that when offered food you should not eat it until the person offering it had tasted it first.[153] The water taboos were also catered for in Genghis's code. It was a grievous offence to spill any liquid on the ground, and there was a host of rules governing how one should behave around running water. We have already noted that the reason the Mongols seemed so filthy and unhygienic was because of the reverence for water and the many interdictions on bathing. It was even forbidden to wash clothes in running water, though some scholars claim that the Yasa forbade laundry only during thunderstorms – for thunderstorms were second only to poison on the Mongols' 'most feared' list.[154]

In these and many other cases the Yasa simply confirmed what was already the case. A very good example of this is the proscription against lying: mendacity was already taboo in Mongol culture (even though when dealing with foreign nations the Mongols proved expert and cunning liars). There is a famous story illustrating Mongol distaste for 'saying the thing that is not' (in Jonathan Swift's formulation). During the Afghan campaign of the early 1220s two sentries were caught asleep at their posts, brought before their commander and, when questioned, admitted they had dozed off, even though they knew the admission meant certain death. An Afghan observer expressed astonishment both at the truthfulness and the harsh sentence, to which the commander replied: 'Why are you astonished? You Afghans order such punishments *and* tell lies.'[155]

The case for the Great Yasa as a benefit to the people rests largely on its endorsement of traditional steppe custom, but there are one or two 'extras' that merit attention. As part of his general ideology of equality (at any rate in the army meritocracy) Genghis hit on the idea of having a 'complaints box' hung on a pole with a string in the middle of his camp. Anyone could write a complaint or petition anonymously, seal it and place it in the box; the khan would then open it every Friday and adjudicate on the matter.[156] Unfortunately, we possess no statistics on the percentage success of such written overtures. He also tried to incorporate elements of Nestorian Christianity (love your neighbour, swallow insults, turn the other cheek) into the ideology of the Yasa – always of course on the assumption that this was a prescription purely for Mongols when dealing with Mongols; for, as one scholar has wittily written: 'If the rule to love others as one's self, not to offer insults, etc, was a provision of the Yasa, whose violation was punishable by death, then the first person deserving death would have been Genghis Khan himself, who utterly wiped out such towns as Gazna, Balkh and others and put all their inhabitants to the sword.'[157] However, when all concessions to popular culture and interests have been made, it remains the case that the Great Yasa was essentially an instrument of aristocratic hegemony and hence a heavy burden for the ordinary people. The main defence would be that before Genghis murder, adultery, robbery and rape were common on the steppes, but after him they were very rare.[158]

A judicious conclusion on the Great Yasa might be that it was Janus-faced, looking backwards and codifying the important aspects of steppe culture but also looking to the future and the problems of world empire. Some have detected multifarious alien influences on Genghis's code. The Khitans duly make an appearance, as according to some Mongolists they were the prime influence on so many aspects of Genghis Khan.[159] This is debatable, whereas the salient influence of Chinese culture on the Yasa can scarcely be denied, especially after 1218. One item particularly merits attention. The Yasa speaks of beating by canes, which was the Chinese way; the Mongols by contrast, pre-Genghis, always used whips for their beatings. But besides this, the increasing use after Genghis's death of payment of ransoms and fines instead of the death penalty also shows clear Chinese influence.[160] The impact from south of the border, however, was not always in a liberal direction. Surprise has sometimes been expressed at the contrast between the Mongols' free-and-easy attitude to sexuality and the harsh provisions of the Yasa concerning adultery, and this is usually set down to the encroachment of Chinese culture.[161] Some say that the Great Yasa had barely come into fully fledged existence before it began to be phased out, and the principal culprit was the great khan Ogodei (Genghis's successor) and his partiality for Islam.[162] His ferocious brother Chagatai was the guardian of the flame of the Yasa's purity and was a notable anti-Muslim hardliner, but Ogodei, while avoiding open conflict with his brother, thought that religious tolerance was a more important consideration for the security of the empire than punctilious observance of the Yasa and that he would therefore take a relaxed attitude to infractions. Some of Ogodei's decrees granting privileges to his favourites in ad hoc decrees called *jarliqs* were in blatant contradiction to the spirit of his father's code.[163] Later Mongol khans tended to enact what laws they pleased and then claim that they were directly in line with the spirit of the Yasa even when this was palpably absurd. It was crucial for issues of legitimacy that no one ever repudiate the memory and legacy of Genghis, so a 'noble lie' or polite fiction was maintained.[164]

The later influence of the Yasa in the more settled parts of the Mongol empire seem to have been negligible. The Mongols allowed Chinese, Persian and Russian laws to remain in being provided they did not collide violently with the code of Genghis. The Yasa appears to have been a dead letter in Russia, as it was not consonant with Slavic culture or religion; this is a notable difficulty for historians who claim that Russia suffered under a 'Mongol yoke'.[165] In China we encounter the paradox that, whereas there was a huge impact of Chinese thought and culture on the Yasa, its later influence was slight (the influence on the legislation of Yuan China under the Mongols was minimal), except for the notion of a Universal Empire requiring a legal code – an idea which in any case may have been more influenced by the 'universal' Christian Church of the West.[166] The main impact of the Great Yasa in post-Genghis years was on the nomadic societies of Central Asia, which is much as we might expect. Here there was more reverence for the wishes of the founder of the empire. Inevitably, though, the changes and decline in the empire after 1241 dragged the Great Yasa down with it.[167] Genghis had partly anticipated this future development and may have accepted it stoically: *sic transit gloria mundi.*

After us the descendants of our clan will wear gold-embroidered garments, eat rich and sweet food, ride fine horses and embrace beautiful women, but they will not say that they owe all this to their fathers and elder brothers, and they will forget us and those great times.[168]

5

The Ever Victorious Army

Between 1206 and 1209 Genghis spent most of his time on administration and reorganisation while he made ready the Mongol nation for his great dream: the conquest of the Jin empire of northern China. To achieve this he required two things: a totally pacified Mongolia, so that there would be no revolts in the rear when he crossed into China, and an army of superb discipline and efficiency to deal with the formidable Jin. He needed to ensure that his army was a well-fed, well-armed and well-trained machine that could take on all comers, that the integration of all the different tribes was harmonious and effective and that his generals would have no thoughts or ambitions that would divert them from the conquest of the Jin.

He began by tweaking, honing and polishing his two great innovations: the tumens and the keshig. Theoretically the army was divided into three wings, though these did not denote the actual disposition and formation of troops in battle. The most powerful section was the left wing, with Muqali as its supremo and Naya'a as his deputy – though sometimes the left was split into a 'centre' under Naya'a and a 'real left' under Muqali; by the time of the invasion of China this was 62,000 strong.[1] The right wing under Bo'orchu and Boroqul was 38,000 strong. Qubilai was made chief of staff. The centre, effectively the reserve, was under Genghis's personal command. Having set up a bodyguard of 10,000 with the night guards who became the keshig, he proceeded to form an elite within the elite, analogous to Xerxes's 'Immortals' in the Persian Wars or Napoleon's later Old Guard. One thousand horsemen and four hundred dead-shot archers, originally recruited from the 'quiver bearers', formed a ring of steel around him during a battle; the commander of this unit was the Tangut Chaghan, Genghis's adopted son.[2]

The rules governing the tumens were also changed. It was decreed that a commander of a minqan (thousand) must have a son as a lieutenant, together with one other kinsman and ten trusted companions; the commander of a hundred had to recruit a kinsman and five comrades; and the leader of a troop of ten had to serve with a kinsman and three tried and tested followers.[3] Although Genghis accepted that for various reasons the numbers in a tumen might not reach the magical figure of 10,000 – in this regard it was much like the Roman legion with its theoretical complement of 6,000 – its commanders had to do their utmost to achieve this.[4] The myriarchs were now formally forbidden to associate with each other or mingle socially, to avoid the possibility of conspiracy; if Genghis had any doubts on this score, he liked to split the command of a tumen between two different generals. New death penalties were ordained for a range of offences, such as retreating in battle before being ordered to.[5] Looking to the future and foreseeing the situation when an array of conquered territories lay at his feet, the khan also trained the tumens in the intricacies of being an occupying force, so that they could form an efficient *tamma* or garrison – which Genghis envisaged as being formed partly from his own troops and partly from quislings and rebels against the previous government.[6]

The keshig was also reorganised on more rigid and formal lines. The 10,000-strong bodyguard was divided into four sections or shifts, each of which was responsible for the three day watches and the three night watches. It was decreed that the commander of the shift must himself stand night watch; that there would be severe punishments for anyone quarrelling with a guardsman; that the guard had the power to deal with anyone who was suspected of 'loitering' after dark; in the case of anyone approaching the imperial tent without authorisation the penalty was immediate execution. No one was allowed to mingle with or talk to guards on duty; watchwords and shift times would be changed every night for security reasons; to divulge the time of a particular shift change or the password constituted betrayal of an official secret and was punished by death. All audiences at night had to be cleared with the shift commander, and a new shift could take over only when the new commander revealed an official badge of authority, which was also changed every night to prevent forgery.[7]

Alongside the military functions, Genghis also tried to make the

Guard an embryonic civil service. Eleven senior staff oversaw specialist sections: a medical corps, a diplomatic corps, interpreters, surveyors, record keepers, map makers, quartermasters, field agents and intelligence analysts.[8] From the very earliest days Genghis had his own hand-picked espionage corps or secret service who not only reported on enemy strength and dispositions but spied on his own army, sniffing out the false accounting and payroll padding that were common in other medieval armies.[9] There was no snobbery about being a quartermaster, for overseeing herds of horses and camels was considered an important and prestigious job; the quartermasters also had to organise commissariat and communications, and to ensure that at the end of a day's march the encampment was correctly positioned, with Genghis's elite force facing south, the official left wing facing east and the right wing facing west.[10] Conditions of service in the keshig were tough, and the punishment for making a mistake severe and often terminal. So as to avoid a position in the keshig being considered a bed of nails, only partly compensated for by the superiority of its members to all other military personnel, Genghis was shrewd enough to introduce sweeteners. The members of the Guard wore black *kalats* (tunics) and armour trimmed in red, and rode black horses with red leather trappings and saddle. The greatest perk was the system of organised concubinage for all officers and guards; Genghis correctly sensed the power of this incentive.[11]

The principal way in which Genghis kept both guards and tumens at a pitch of readiness in peacetime was through the hunt or battue, which taught signalling, communication over vast distances, mobility and ruthless closing of the ring on a target. Hunts could last anywhere between a month and three months and usually began in early winter. The battue was a central event in the Mongol calendar and it had a threefold significance, as military training, an important source of food and as a great social event that inculcated the idea of the organic solidarity of the nation. Jochi was the proud organiser of this spectacular annual event. There were severe penalties, laid down by the Great Yasa, for infringing any part of the strict protocol associated with the hunt.[12]

The tumens lined up along a starting line that could be eighty miles long. The finishing line was about a hundred miles distant and the designated 'circle' was thousands of square miles in area. Each section was headed by a commander of a minqan, with the sub-commanders and sub-sub-commanders organised in the usual decimal system. The commander had a drum for sending orders to nearby contingents, and this could be beaten only at his orders. Each unit simulated a military operation, with scouts thrown far ahead and the position of the other units to right and left carefully charted. As the army advanced, the wings gradually stretched out to form a semicircle. Day by day the minqans drove animals before them and the semicircle narrowed until the finishing line was reached. Then part of them wheeled round and eventually closed the ring until the units formed a cordon; this was the most dangerous moment, for there were severe penalties for any commander allowing animals to escape the net or anyone killing an animal before the khan arrived.[13] Finally, the animals were contained within a narrow circumference, within which was a panicky melee of roaring lions, bleating stags, lowing wild oxen and all the ululation and cacophony of scores of different breeds.

Usually Genghis would choose a good viewpoint, then picnic with his family and concubines until informed by his commanders that the moment of truth had arrived. He and his entourage would then descend and begin the massacre.[14] The beasts to be killed for meat would be dispatched quickly, but more time was taken over the 'big game'. This was the time when those who had brought leopards, cheetahs and tigers unleashed them against the defenceless ungulates. The sources do not tell us whether the Mongols retrieved these valuable predators or whether they too were consumed in the general holocaust. When the khan and his inner circle had slaked their lust for killing, the commanders were given their head.[15] Finally it was the turn of the ordinary trooper. Here now was a great occasion for ambitious rankers to demonstrate to the watching khan their superior skills and thus perhaps win promotion. Like Roman gladiators, the more courageous would try to fight the beasts on foot or with a sword or knife alone; there were even some glory-hunters who tried to fight dangerous animals with techniques of unarmed combat.

Finally, when he had seen enough, the khan called a halt. A few animals were taken into captivity for breeding while the survivors were symbolically released after a curious ceremony in which a group of old men asked for 'amnesty' for the animals that were left.[16] This was granted, and the lucky few allowed to creep away to safety. When the hunt was over, there followed nine days of feasting and revelry. Any food left at the end was distributed to the troops.

The battue provides part of the secret of Mongol success. The hunt allowed the warriors to achieve perfection in flag waving, the use of torches and flambeaux, honed the system of post and couriers, provided invaluable training for battle and, not least, a valuable supply of high-protein food.[17] Some of his courtiers warned Genghis that the confusion of the hunt afforded the perfect opportunity for assassins to strike, but he always maintained this was a danger only on a small private hunt; no one would attempt homicide in the middle of mass killing when his warriors' blood was up.[18]

Genghis also made sure that arms, armour and equipment for his men were the best possible. Mongols wore fur coats stretching below the knee, felt boots and fur hats with ear flaps. In battle they wore helmets, with a steel cap, of which the upper part and that covering the neck and ears was made of leather. Armour, worn over a silk undershirt, consisted of strips of strong and supple leather several layers thick, lacquered to keep out humidity, or of overlapping iron scales laced together and polished brightly; there were also shoulder-plates and extra protection for arms and legs, and sometimes there would be a cuirass of leather-covered iron scales. Special armour for senior officers was bespoke: there would be six layers of leather tightly sewn and shaped to fit the body after softening by boiling.[19] Genghis claimed the silk undershirt as an innovation of his own, introduced after the very first campaign against the Tangut. This provided a measure of protection against arrow wounds, as the twisting motion of an arrow drove the silk into the wound, reducing the level of penetration and making it easier to extract the shaft, as rescuers could pull on the shirt. Armour was also used to protect horses, with the two heavy cavalry brigades swathed in lamellae, which covered every part of the steed; the three light cavalry brigades were not armoured, as they needed greater mobility and flexibility.[20]

Apart from his principal weapon, the bow, the Mongol heavy cavalryman carried a twelve-foot lance with a sickle-shaped hook behind the point, with which an enemy rider could be pulled off his horse; commanders additionally had a slightly curved sabre, honed and sharpened on one side.[21] Each rider also had an axe, a lasso of horsehair, a kettle, a whetstone and a whipstock for hitting horses on the legs.

There were also two leather bags in one of which was kept a reserve water supply; the other bag served to keep weapons and clothes dry during river crossings. During cold weather a sheepskin coat with the hide turned outwards might be worn. There was a standard issue of one tent for every ten men.[22]

The Mongols employed three kinds of shields. One, made of skin or willow wood, was a large artefact for use by guards on sentry duty. Another, much smaller, made of osier or wicker, was issued to the vanguard to ward off enemy arrows. Then there was a third kind, made of tortoise shell, used when scaling the walls of fortresses.[23] Light cavalry carried swords, maces and two or three javelins. When battle was about to be joined, the Mongols would switch hats, trading in the traditional brimmed felt and leather hats with earflaps worn on the march for the casque helmet of leather.

Yet the Mongols' chief weapons were always the bow and arrow and the ever-reliable warhorse; mounted archery is the very definition of nomad warfare. The Mongols used two bows, one short-range, one long, and every mounted warrior carried sixty arrows in two quivers of thirty each. The composite recurve bow was a complex artefact. It was constructed of layers of horn and sinew laminated over a wooden frame and lacquered to prevent moisture from delaminating the layers, and the result was a single, strong, flexible bow. The horseman carried the bow in a case strapped to the side of the horse and used a stone ring on the right thumb for grasping the bowstring The large long-range bow had a pull of 166 pounds – far greater than the English longbow – and was effective up to 300 yards.[24] Requiring enormous strength to pull and usable only by those who had been trained from an early age, the composite bow could remain strung for a long time without losing elasticity.

The brilliance of Mongol archers was legendary. Genghis's brother Qasar was famous for his skill with the bow, but his son Yisungge was even more talented: at an archery contest in 1225 he shot an arrow 550 yards.[25] The combination of archery and horsemanship that made the Mongols so formidable came from their being put on horseback almost before they could walk. This resulted in the *pièce de résistance* whereby juvenile archers were trained to release their arrows at the precise moment when all four of their horse's hooves were off the ground – so that the jolt of hooves hitting the ground would not throw off their aim. There were three kinds of arrows: short-range shafts for shooting tigers, bears and bucks; and two types of battle arrows, light ones with small, sharp points for long-range shooting and pursuit, and heavy ones with large, broad heads for close-quarter engagement; there were also whistling arrows used for signalling. The sixty arrows carried by the cavalryman contained both kinds, and he had to have the skill and expertise to decide in a trice which type to fit to his bow.[26] The arrows designed to kill outright, rather than break up the enemy formation by being loosed from afar, cut both ways like a sword and were specially designed to pierce armour by being hardened and then dipped into brine while red-hot. Arrowheads were usually made of bone (but there were some metallic ones) while the shafts were made of wood or (for greater accuracy) reed.[27] In Far Eastern warfare arrows were usually poisoned – in Mongolia with a poison made from the venom of the viper collected when it was at its most virulent.[28]

The Mongol's other great weapon was his horse. Each warrior had at least six mounts and some had up to eighteen; the official guideline was that each minqan had to provide 5,000 horses fully equipped and armed. The horse levy required owners to contribute one animal in every hundred from private herds over thirty animals, but by Ogodei's reign the demand for horses was such that the levy increased the requirement to one in every ten.[29] Fed on grass and water once a day, the Mongol horse was renowned for its stamina and could cover six hundred miles in nine days. They were not fitted with horseshoes until after Genghis's time, and observers noted that they could run around on rocky ground as if they were goats. The saddles were made of oiled wood and were tight-fitting, so that an archer could turn round in the saddle and fire backwards while the horse galloped forward.[30]

Mongol strategy was discussed at an annual quriltai in February–March, when targets, feasibility, commissariat, cattle, horses, logistics and the differential approach needed to overcome the enemy would all be thoroughly rehearsed. There were certain constants in Genghis's strategic thinking: march divided, attack united; always use the superior speed and mobility of Mongol horses; never allow the enemy to predict your movements; ensure that you do not fight on two fronts at once; bring the enemy to battle at the earliest possible moment;

annihilate the opposition or reduce his numbers by every possible means. Unpredictability was the key to his success: when marching against the Naiman in 1205 in April, he went against the received opinion that the horses had not put on enough weight for an early spring campaign; by crossing frozen winters in winter he threw out of the window the orthodoxy about needing to go into winter quarters.[31]

As a prelude to any campaign Genghis always collected as much information as possible about the enemy: their culture and religion, the personalities in the elite, the geography of the land, all the nuances of mores and folkways among the constituent tribes. He probed for the weak spots: was the elite divided, was there discontent in the regions, were there any pretenders to the throne, were any local rebellions currently in progress? Such information came from a variety of sources: his own spies and scouts, local malcontents and the Muslim merchants who liked to swap information for trade privileges.[32] His espionage system was outstanding, but he added to it by cunning use of a bureau of the black arts of disinformation.

A favourite device to confuse the enemy was somehow to get hold of official seals or parchments and then forge letters or documents purporting to give information about the Mongols' movements, or to claim that various army units had mutinied – anything to confuse, bamboozle or demoralise the foe.[33] And, since the Mongols invariably fought numerically superior opponents, Genghis was obsessed with concealing his real numbers and magnifying them in the eyes of the enemy. Various methods were used to achieve this. He mounted the camp-follower women on horses so that a distant sighting of the Mongol army would make the warrior complement seem much greater than it was; he mounted human dummies on horses; he tied branches to the tails of his horses so that they stirred up a dust cloud, suggesting the approach of a mighty host. Night-time deception was even easier, for he had each of his men carry three or four flambeaux and light several fires each.[34] Genghis's secret service arm gradually became more and more adventurous and intellectually audacious. Initially clueless about siege warfare, the Mongols soon learned the appropriate techniques including the use of catapults and siege engines.[35]

When invading enemy territory, the Mongols crossed the border in widely separated columns. A mobile detachment, anything from thirty-five to seventy miles ahead of these columns, notified the main army about good camping sites, towns with provisions, potential battlefields, any signs of hostile forces; there were similar detachments in the rear and on the flanks so that, as became generally recognised, it was impossible ever to take a Mongol army by surprise.[36] The Mongols achieved astonishingly great speed, mobility and daily rates of march while taking camp followers (and sometimes even their families, for nomads found no hardship in following armies) and huge herds of cattle and sheep with them.

Once deep into enemy country, the separated columns might even disperse further to find grazing for the horses, but there was always provision for a lightning reassembly if danger threatened. These smaller groups chose higher ground for their camps, maintained unceasing patrol and were in hour-by-hour communication with each other by means of couriers. In order further to guard against surprise attack, they liked to lay waste the ground around their encampment. Always there was the same rigid use of passwords, often the name of the officer on duty. The efficiency with which widely dispersed groups communicated with each other was one of the great secrets of Mongol military success.[37] It was one of Genghis's axioms that heavily fortified towns and cities should be avoided; once the enemy was defeated, these could always be 'mopped up' later. But he did believe in capturing and sacking smaller towns, for the refugees thus disgorged flocked to these very fortified cities, spread alarm and despondency, and increased the pressure on the food supply within. Meanwhile the loot taken in villages and smaller towns gave a fillip to the morale of his men, reinforcing a message he often dinned into them: in the old days nomadic leaders had distributed spoils to their aristocratic cronies but with him wealth was for *all* the people.[38]

This was very important, for Genghis's soldiers were not paid, but rewarded with booty and pillage. Even if baulked of fresh food supplies, a Mongol army on the march always had a supply of iron rations, notably two litres of koumiss, a quantity of cured meat and ten pounds per man of curdled milk dried in the sun; a meal would be half a pound of this dissolved in water and shaken in canteens to make a kind of syrup or loose yoghurt. The meat or 'jerky' was carried under the saddle where the movements of the horse tenderised it. In emergency the nomads opened their horses' veins, sucked out blood and then closed the wound.[39]

The advance during the strategic phase of a war was thus a marvel of discipline, speed, communications and first-rate staffwork. Warriors could sleep while armed and mounted on their horses and could do so even while the animals grazed. They could ride sixty-five miles a day – the highest-known aggregate was 600 miles in nine days (no army in history was able to match them until the era of Napoleon) – covering enormous distances without maps; they could link up with another army group with astonishing accuracy and understand all the various signals conveyed by flags, trumpets and lanterns. When crossing rivers they would stow their clothes and other impedimenta in a leather sack, which was then tied up tightly to resemble a cushion; the saddle was then placed on top and the rider used the whole apparatus as a flotation device, either paddling or hanging on to the horses' tails – while expert swimmers guided the horses to the far bank.[40]

Once the scouts had made contact with a hostile army and it was brought to battle, the Mongols employed an ingenious variety of tactics. The first thing was to concentrate the army by calling in the dispersed units. Then the scouts moved carefully forward to estimate enemy numbers and investigate the topography of the battlefield. While skirmishers went ahead to taunt the opposition, the Mongols spread out so as to overlap the enemy's flanks. The commander (usually not Genghis himself in the campaigns after 1206) then drew up the army in five divisions, each consisting of squadrons of about one hundred men. The front two ranks were composed of the heavy cavalry, in iron-scale armour and with long lances and heavy cuirasses. Behind them were the three divisions of light cavalry, armed with bows and in lacquered hide armour and light cuirasses.[41] Each rank would be about two hundred yards ahead of the next.

The usual procedure was for the light cavalry to ride through specially prepared gaps in the heavy cavalry to discharge a cloud of arrows at the enemy, hoping to break up their formation. It would be unusual for a breakthrough to occur at this stage, so the light cavalry would ride back through the ranks of the heavy cavalry, firing backwards as they went until they reached their own lines.[42] At this point the heavy cavalry would deliver a frontal charge. Sometimes this would be successful; if, on the other hand, the Mongol commander concluded that he had nearly broken through, he might employ what the Mongols called the 'chisel' method, whereby one heavy cavalry charge was followed by another and another until the opponents cracked and fled. The culmination of such a method would be the *coup de grâce* when all units which had already charged made a simultaneous onslaught from all directions, often criss-crossing each other as they charged.[43]

However, the more normal course of battle would involve a degree of attrition, where the enemy would be piqued like a bull by a matador, with constant arrow clouds being unleashed on them in unceasing probes by the light cavalry. At this stage the hostile force would either have to stand its ground and accept mounting casualties or charge the tormentors, which would mean an instant collision with the heavy cavalry. It has been claimed that the constant deluge of arrows by the light infantry represented the first time in history that firepower was used systematically to pave the way for a decisive assault.[44] With a particularly well disciplined army that would not rise to any of these baits, the Mongols sent the light cavalry to work round the flanks and rear, striking in several directions at once, confusing the enemy and weakening him prior to the decisive charge by the heavy cavalry.[45] A truly steadfast and determined foe might dig in and plant pointed stakes in the ground facing the Mongols, so that a charge risked eviscerating their horses. If this happened, the Mongols would keep their distance and continue to direct a fusillade of arrows, patiently waiting until the enemy's food or water ran out; when that happened and they moved out, they would be easy pickings for the Mongols who would have them surrounded.[46]

This sketch of Mongol tactics does not do justice to their infinite ingenuity, versatility and adaptability nor to the idiosyncrasies of the many brilliant Mongol commanders. For example, Genghis himself was fond of bringing a foe to bay at the foot of a mountain. He would then send out scouting parties to investigate the passes and defiles in the rear of the enemy and then suddenly appear behind them with a second force.[47] Sometimes he would have archers with shields dismount to tempt the enemy cavalry towards an apparently easy target. Protected by shields and screened by their horses, the archers would hold off the attack with a fusillade of arrows, daring the enemy to commit his reserves in order to achieve annihilation. At this point,

Genghis would send in his heavy cavalry for a full-scale attack, catching his opponents off balance. Occasionally he would confound expectations by stampeding horses and cattle into the enemy ranks.[48] In his victory over the Tayichiud in 1200 he stationed a wagon laager on one wing, defended by women and children, while concentrating the heavy cavalry on the other. He allowed a weak centre to appear to give way, while secretly masking the strength of his cavalry arm. The Tayichiud forces contained many allies who had joined them in hopes of easy pickings, and these then assaulted the wagon laager, expecting a walkover victory. The resistance from the laager was more stubborn than expected and, while the Tayichiud and their allies re-formed for a decisive charge, they were hit in the rear by Genghis's cavalry, whom they thought out of the reckoning.[49]

Catching an enemy at a river bank, so they could be surrounded on three sides with their backs to the river, was another favourite Mongol ploy. It was noteworthy that all these tactics were carried out silently, directed by flags, semaphore, battle banners and heliographs. Only when the final *coup de grâce* was ordered and the charge about to begin was the silence broken by the roaring and pounding of war drums and the ululation of the warriors. The Mongols also enjoyed the psychological advantage that they and their horses stank, subtly undermining those who faced them.[50] Some Mongol generals always tried to use the double envelopment method perfected in the battue, or to outflank the opposition by proceeding with the wings far in advance of the centre, in what later became known as the 'horns' method, made famous in the Zulu wars.[51] Another favoured ploy when the enemy was in desperate straits was for the Mongol army to appear suddenly to break up in confusion; large gaps appeared in their lines, through which the enemy could stream to escape and safety. Once a manageable number had been allowed through the gaps, the Mongols, with perfect discipline, would close them up; their rearguard would then pursue and pick off the fugitives at their leisure.[52]

If all these multifarious techniques failed, the Mongols would opt for one of their favourite ploys: the feigned retreat. They would simulate a defeated and demoralised host by suddenly making a precipitate departure from the battlefield, leaving piles of gold and silver behind to convince the opponent that this was no trick. The pursuers would then be led into a perfectly prepared ambush and slaughtered.[53]

Sometimes their feigned retreats could last for days and stretch over a distance of forty miles, when the superiority of their horses would tell. By the time the trap was sprung, the enemy's horses would be exhausted while the Mongol steeds would still be fresh.[54]

Two further points need to be underlined about Mongol tactics. As far as possible they liked to avoid hand-to-hand combat. Far from the cliché of Oriental hordes throwing manpower at an enemy with no regard for human life, the Mongols had something of a fetish about keeping casualties to a minimum, and became slaughterously angry if too many of their men fell in achieving victory.[55] Again, the modern notion that the victor is the one left in possession of the battlefield was meaningless to them. Victory meant annihilation of the enemy, and they were ruthless in achieving this aim. After a battle, the pursuit of the vanquished could go on for days. It was thought especially essential to run the defeated enemy leaders to ground, giving them no breathing space in which to retrench or reform or build a focus around which their scattered forces could rally.[56]

The campaigns of 1206–1218 are complex and confusing, and our understanding is not helped by the *Secret History*'s conflation (an abiding fault of this source) not only of two different campaigns against the Merkit *but also* two different campaigns against the Forest Peoples. For the purposes of clarity, it is better on this occasion to look at the campaigns thematically, rather than in strict chronological order. Simplifying, we can reduce the external events of 1206–18 (excluding the invasion of China) to five motifs: Genghis's final settling of accounts with the Naiman; the long process of disposing of the Merkit; the subjugation and subsequent revolt of the Forest Peoples; the accession to the empire of the all-important Uighurs; and the war against the Tangut. The quest for Ququluq, which turned out to be the most troublesome operation of all and which partially overlapped with these events, will be considered later, as it had wider geopolitical implications.

Between 1206 and 1209 Genghis took the field in person just once. At the end of 1206, learning from his spies that Buiruk, the undefeated prince of the divided Naiman, had grown complacent and was even then on a hunting trip in the Altai Mountains, he made a lightning dash across country and took the Naiman completely by surprise. The result was another total and stunning victory, in which Buiruk himself was slain.[57] The Merkit survivors of Subedei's great victory earlier that year, when Toqto'a Beki was killed, had fled to the Naiman, thinking themselves safe there. Enough of them got away from Buiruk's defeat to continue to be a menace, so Subedei was ordered after them once more. In 1208 Subedei caught up with them and routed them again, killing two of Toqto'a's sons, but still the multi-headed sept of the Merkit was not completely exterminated. Those who were left fled to the Uighur territory for protection, but the ruler feared the wrath of the Mongol khan and peremptorily ordered them out of his territory.[58]

The Merkits' next idea was to flee to the far north and ally themselves with the lords of the western steppes, the Cumans. Subedei, who had won two victories against the Merkits, was rewarded with ingratitude from Genghis, who considered he had botched the job by allowing even a single one of his most hated enemy to escape. The luckless paladin stayed away from the court in semi-disgrace until he was recalled in 1216[59] and told to pursue the remaining Merkit, however far west they fled. Some of the new Cuman allies were in the Merkit ranks when Subedei finally caught up with them some time in 1217–18, somewhere north of the Syr Darya (Jaxartes) River at a place known as Jam Muran and destroyed them, this time ending the nuisance from this defiant tribe for all time; Toqto'a's brother Qudu was the last of their princes to fall.[60] This campaign by Subedei took him all the way through the Tarbaghatai Mountains, through Almaliq and into the territory of the friendly Qarluqs south of Lake Balkhash. At various times he coordinated his massive sweep in search of the quarry with both Jebe and Jochi.[61]

Before invading China, Genghis had to be sure there would be no threat to his rear, and in 1207 sent Jochi and an army to secure the submission of the independent tribes of north-western Mongolia and southern Siberia. There was a whole host of these so-called 'Forest Peoples' – principally the Kirghiz, Oyirad, Buriyat, Tumed, Tuvans, Barqut, Ursut, Qabqanas, Shibir, Kesdiyim, Tuqas, Baya'ud, Kem Kemjiut, Tenleg, To'eles, Tas, Bajigid – of which the first six were far the most important. The Buriyat lived along the Angara River and its tributaries and on the eastern side of Lake Baikal, with the Barqut to the north of them, the Ursut and Qabqanas to the west of the lake, the Kirghiz and Kem-Kemjiuts in the Yenisey valley, the Tumed along the Iya and Angara Rivers, the Tuvans in the modern region of Tannu Tuva in southern Siberia and the others on the upper reaches of the River Irtysh.[62]

Much of this vast area was an immense forest of birch, poplar, cedar, larch and fir, with an interpenetrating undergrowth of rhodo-dendron, mosses and lichens. All four great rivers of northern Asia, the Lena, Yenisey, Ob and Irtysh crossed the region, which boasted a cornucopia of fauna: elk, forest deer, reindeer, wapiti deer, musk deer, wolves, bears, martens, ermines, otters, beavers and Siberian squirrels. Living mainly on hunting and fishing, the Forest Peoples are thought to have had a mentality very different from the Mongols. Nomadic herdsmen perforce had to adopt a collective, collaborative ethos and culture, whereas the forest hunters, relying mainly on individual skill, tended to be individualistic, and perhaps it was significant that shamanism had a much stronger hold on these northern regions than on the steppe proper.[63] This handed the Mongols an obvious advantage in war, and their attitude towards the Forest Peoples tended to be patronising, dismissive or contemptuous; in particular they guffawed at their habit of riding bareback on reindeer instead of horses. The allegedly benighted nature of the Forest Peoples was summed up in a well-known Mongol saying: 'A bird that knows nothing of limpid water will keep its beak in brackish water all year long.'[64] Another much-quoted item was attributed to the legendary Mongol leader Bodonchar: 'It's good for a body to have a head and a coat to have a collar . . . Those people . . . they have nothing big or small, good or bad, herds or hooves – everybody's equal. Let's go plunder them.'[65]

All of these tribes had tended to stay neutral in Mongolia's inces-sant wars, but a few of them had sided with Jamuga in the past. Quduqa Beki, chief of the Oyirad, had at various times allied himself against Genghis with the Merkit, Naiman *and* Jamuga.[66] For all these reasons and, because of the Forest Peoples' general unpredictability, Genghis decided he had to bring them all to heel before turning his attention southwards.

Jochi achieved great success on his mission. The Oyirad and Quduqa Beki offered no resistance and Jochi was able to make a leisurely inspection of his territory on the banks of a tributary of Lake Dood Tsagaan from which it stretched away for a vast distance to the south-west. Genghis followed his usual practice of cementing such alliances

with intermarriage and gave his second daughter Chechiyegen in
wedlock to Quduqa's son; his other children were also married into
Genghis's extended family.[67] In addition he incorporated Quduqa's
4,000 warriors in the Mongol army and honoured the chief by making
him commander of a minqan. Quduqa proved immediately useful by
having his alpinists guide the Mongols over the 9,000-foot-high Ulan
pass to the River Bukhtarma, a tributary of the Irtysh, where Subedei
scored his famous victory in 1208.[68]

The year 1207 also saw the peaceful submission of the Kirghiz in
the Yenisey valley, even more formidable militarily with 10,000
warriors, and an important source of grain. Taking their cue from
these two tribes, the other Forest Peoples also submitted. Genghis
allowed them formal independence provided they acknowledged his
suzerainty and paid tribute.[69] Jochi returned to his father triumphant,
and Genghis was delighted with his achievement. From the Oyirad,
Kirghiz and Tumed he received the most lavish gifts: black sables, a
treasured luxury item, furs, gyrfalcons (including the rare and much
prized white variety) and white geldings, which were the traditional
preserve of the bekis.[70] His northern frontier was secure, and Genghis
felt able to concentrate on his invasion of China.

But what Jochi had achieved by a show of military strength was
not easy to perpetuate in peacetime. Though there was no overt
trouble from the Forest Peoples during his five years in China (1211–
1216), Genghis found the performance of Qorchi, whom he had
appointed as supremo over that region, very disappointing. Mongol
authority over the regions around the Irtysh, Yenisey, Angara and
Selenga Rivers remained tenuous and shaky.[71] In fact it was Qorchi's
blundering insensitivity that set off a serious revolt of the Forest
Peoples in 1217 – fortunately for the Mongols just after Genghis had
returned from China. Always a rampant womaniser, Qorchi had been
rewarded with the gift of seven beautiful women at the quriltai in
1206 but that was not enough to satisfy his appetites. He asked Genghis
that, as a quid pro quo for the difficult role of governor of the Forest
Peoples, he should be allowed to pick out thirty of the most beautiful
Tumed women to add to his harem. Thinking nothing of the request,
Genghis granted it, but when Qorchi arrived at the Tumed village
with his demand, the Tumed felt insulted and humiliated. Outraged,
they seized Qorchi and made him prisoner.[72] Genghis then asked

Quduqa, leader of the Oyirad who were first to capitulate, to prove his loyalty by sorting out this imbroglio, for was not Quduqa an expert in all that related to the Forest Peoples? But when Quduqa arrived at the Tumed village, he too was taken prisoner. This was a declaration of war in all but name; the serious aspect was that once the Tumed raised the standard of revolt, the other Forest Peoples joined them. Genghis now had a major revolt on his hands. Even worse, when Genghis asked the supposedly loyal Kirghiz for troops with which to put down the rebellion, they refused.[73] The entire northern frontier seemed to be unravelling.

Genghis first asked Naya'a to command the punitive expedition to the Forest Peoples but he declined, pleading illness, in reality unwilling to accept the poisoned chalice. Genghis then turned to Boroqul who, likewise reluctant to accept such a gruelling mission and having a strong premonition that he would die if he went, nevertheless allowed his loyalty to the khan to prevail over his deeper misgivings. He achieved initial success against the Tumed but was killed in an ambush.[74] Furiously angry at the news, Genghis wanted to take the field against the Tumed in person, but was talked out of this by Muqali and Bo'orchu.[75] Instead he assembled a huge force and put Jochi in command. It was fortunate for Jochi that he had the assistance of the very able Dorbei Doqshin, chief of the Dorben Mongols of north-western Mongolia.

Jochi decided on an initial campaign against the 'lesser' Forest Peoples, following his father's advice that one should never attack the hardest target first. He detailed Dorbei to do his best against the Tumed, promising to join him later when he had wiped out the other rebel armies. Jochi marched north from the basin of Lake Uvs and over the Tannu Ula by a mountain pass to the valley of the upper Yenisey.[76] In the winter of 1217–18 Jochi crossed the frozen Selenga and Yenisey Rivers and defeated the lesser rebels before going on to mete out harsh punishment to the treacherous Kirghiz. He crossed the icy wastes of the Bii Khem to the Sayan range, pressed on into the Tuba valley and defeated the Tuvans and other neighbouring tribes.[77] He then split his army, sending one detachment north to the Abakan steppes (between the Abakan and the Yenisey), subdued all the vassals of the Kirghiz, then crossed the Kemchug River to the Kirghiz's 'breadbasket' and began laying waste to the territory. The hapless

Kirkhiz asked for terms, so Jochi, taking no chances, bore away with him the entire tribal nobility, so that there was no one left to head a revolt.[78]

Dorbei meanwhile pulled off one of those military tours de force in which Mongol history abounds. He outfoxed the Tumed by pretending to be laying an ambush on the road to the Tumed head-quarters (but in such a way that the Tumed easily learned of it), then branched off the road, following animal tracks through country supposedly made impenetrable by fallen trees, a tangled undergrowth of roots and high weeds, and a barrier of yellow acacia and wild currant trees. He then made his way around, above and to the rear of the Tumed and fell on them while they were feasting. He achieved total surprise and massacred the Tumed in droves.[79] Qorchi and Quduqa were released. It was typical of Qorchi that the first thing he did was to secure the prize for which he had come originally – the thirty beautiful maidens. Sending word of his success to Jochi, Dorbei stayed on in Tumed territory in case Jochi needed him.[80]

When he heard of the exploits of Jochi and Dorbei, Genghis was elated. He ordered that one hundred senior Tumed aristocrats be sacrificed to appease the shade of Boroqul, took personal charge of his fallen comrade's children and showered riches and favours on them. The entire surviving population of 44,000 Tumed was distrib-uted around the empire in slavery as condign punishment for their rebellion. Quduqa was rewarded for his ordeal in captivity by being given the Tumed princess Botoqui Tarqun as his concubine. Finally, in a calculated snub to Qorchi, Genghis appointed Jochi governor of all the conquered territories.[81]

Meanwhile, in 1209 Genghis had secured a great political coup when the ruler of the Uighurs submitted to him. The Uighurs, a Turkic people who dominated Mongolia in the eighth and ninth centuries, had fallen a long way from their previous greatness. From 745 to the middle of the ninth century they ruled an empire from Manchuria to the Caspian, but were then overthrown by the Kirghiz. The latter, however, had no imperial ambitions and returned to their homeland along the Yenisey.[82] It was the Liao dynasty in China which moved into the vacuum in Mongolia, displacing many Turkic peoples west-wards and thus, in the view of some historians, making room for the Mongols and facilitating their eventual rise.[83]

The Uighurs dispersed in two directions. The first segment of the diaspora settled in Gansu province in China and maintained a kingdom there from around 850 until 1036 when they were conquered by the Tangut of Hsi-Hsia. The second, more successful, Uighur remnant founded the Qocho kingdom, with its capitals at Qocho and Beshbaliq (modern Jimsar) in East Turkestan (Xinjiang), south-west of Mongolia.[84] The Uighurs, originally Manicheans, turned in the eleventh century to both Buddhism and Nestorian Christianity and maintained this religious dualism into the Mongol era. They were a highly cultured people, with an alphabet, a literate culture and a pronounced interest in trade and commerce, but the Qocho kingdom had eventually been forced to accept as suzerain the western state of Qara Khitai.[85]

By the beginning of the thirteenth century, Uighur discontent with their overlords was at white heat. There were two main sources of tension. The Uighur merchants' taxes alone made Qara Khitai viable, yet when they asked their nominal superiors to help them by eliminating Muslim commercial operations in Qara Khitai the request was refused. Secondly, the Qara Khitans began acting in an increasingly high-handed manner, seeming to go out of their way to send tyrannical and rebarbative individuals as 'residents' at Beshbaliq.[86] The latest envoy was a Buddhist monk who, against the precepts of his creed, acted despotically and arbitrarily on every occasion, suffused with the arrogance of his supposed invulnerability.

By 1209 the ruler of the Uighurs, *idiqut* ('sacred majesty') Barchuq Art-Tegin, had had enough. With key members of the Uighur aristocracy and bureaucracy he made the decision to switch his allegiance from Qara Khitai to the Mongols; his chief minister Bilge Buqa was perhaps his most important supporter. The monk fled for sancturary to a high tower; he was killed when the Uighurs simply demolished the tower around him.[87] The *idiqut* then made formal submission to Genghis, asking for his protection and to accept him as a 'servant and son'. Genghis sent envoys to investigate the situation, who reported favourably. Barchuq demonstrated a shrewd grasp of psychology by writing to his new protector in the most flattering terms: 'As when the clouds break and disclose the sun burning with renewed lustre, as the cracking ice displays the pure blue stream below, so did the arrival of your envoys change my grief into the most lively joy.'[88]

Genghis had already been impressed by the calibre of the Uighurs and relished the prospect of taking more talents into his service.[89] He therefore summoned Barchuq to appear before him in person. The *idiqut* took his own sweet time about it, and it was almost two years later, in 1211, that he finally presented himself at the Mongol court – actually Genghis's camp on the Kerulen River.[90] The reasons for the delay are obscure. Perhaps Barchuq asked for a binding guarantee of his personal safety, perhaps the merchant lobby among the Uighur elite wanted Genghis's assurance that he would cut out the Muslim traders, or maybe Genghis demanded prior proofs of loyalty, such as a token military attack on Qara Khitai. Some say it was simply that Genghis was away at the Tangut war of 1209–11 but Genghis often received visiting dignitaries mid-campaign. Whatever the reasons, in normal circumstances the delay meant that a happy outcome from the meeting could hardly have been predicted. Yet the outcome surpassed everyone's expectations. Genghis took to Barchuq hugely and announced that he would become his 'fifth son' – an honour shared with just a handful of others and have the supreme place of honour among the 'aliens' at the Mongol court.[91]

The Uighurs remained consistently and unfalteringly loyal, and the *idiqut* accompanied Genghis and his sons and generals on many of their most important campaigns, going with Jebe on his expedition in pursuit of Ququluq in 1216, and later serving with distinction in the Khwarezmia campaign of 1220–21 and the Tangut war of 1226–27. So fond of Barchuq was Genghis that he granted his request (in 1225) that all Uighurs scattered across the Mongol empire be allowed to return to their homeland. Not all took up the offer, of course, as many were by then serving in the army or the civil administration, but large numbers did, and this was a remarkable favour granted by Genghis, not only because it went against his fundamental tenet that non-Mongol peoples had to be dispersed to prevent possible revolts, but also because he had had to execute a number of Uighur nobles for unspecified crimes.[92]

Genghis also used his political ploy of intermarriage, giving his fifth and favourite daughter Qojin to the *idiqut* as his wife. When she died, Barchuq married her sister Altalun Beki – she who was later executed on suspicion of having poisoned Ogodei.[93]

The importance of the Uighur role in the Mongol empire can scarcely be overstated. It was the first state outside Mongolia to submit voluntarily, and disgorged a wealth of talent. Employed as generals, army officers, judges, scribes, secret agents, daruqachi, tax-collectors, and in many other important roles, they brought to Genghis's realm a host of skills that allowed the Mongols to administer sedentary populations without chaos.[94] Since their high skills, talents and culture had been placed at the service of the Mongols, and their script accepted as the first official language of the governing class, they helped to give the empire ideological and spiritual legitimacy; it could no longer be said that this was just a congeries of cruel, bloodthirsty savages. Part of the Mongols' success was that they used foreign personnel from defeated or submitted nations to rule different peoples, but ones who had a similar socio-economic base, so that the civil servants in charge knew intimately their problems of agriculture, sewage and drainage, urban development and taxation.[95]

Delighted with Barchuq's accession, Genghis proclaimed that any other rulers submitting peacefully would receive high honours and privileges. In 1211 Arslan, ruler of the Qarluqs, another of the Qara Khitai's vassals, took up the offer and journeyed from his capital in the Ili valley south of Lake Balkhash to Genghis's camp with lavish presents and one of his daughters to be put on the marriage market. He was well received, was given a Mongol princess in return as his bride, thus becoming a royal son-in-law, and was acknowledged as second only to the *idiqut*. He may not have been totally pleased with his position, however, as Genghis downgraded his title from Arslan Khan to Arslan Sartaqtai; no one but Genghis himself could bear the name of khan.[96]

The fifth item in his preparation for the invasion of China was Genghis's war with the Tangut. At the beginning of the thirteenth century what we know as modern China comprised four separate nation-states: the Song empire south of the Yangtse river; the Jin realm from the Great Wall on the borders of Mongolia south to the Yangtse; the kingdom of Qara Khitai in the far north-west; and the land of the Tangut or Hsi-Hsia in modern Gansu and Ningxia provinces of China.

Founded in 1038 by Tibetans, Hsi-Hsia (which called itself 'The Great State of White and High') was a society of more than three million inhabitants, multi-ethnic with Tangut, Tibetans and Chinese in the majority in its population and some Uighurs, Khitans and other

Turkic groups as the minority; it was, perhaps, an early example of multiculturalism.[97] It enjoyed a favourable climate and geographical position, with twenty inches of rainfall annually and being at the crossroads of long-distance trade between China and western Asia.[98] Hsi-Hsia depended on an economy which was a mixture of fixed agricultural settlements and nomadic pastoralism. The Tangut were famous for their livestock, falcons, camel-hair carpets, printed and illustrated books, high-quality salt and a range of herbal plants including rhubarb which, being in demand, could be used for barter. Their artisanship embraced weaving, leather, coinage, paper, astronomy, wines and liquors and a range of luxury goods that were the basis of a thriving international trade. Their public works and irrigation systems were much admired, and they had a lucrative business in the export of horses to the Jin empire – indeed, some said that horses and camels were the real bedrock of Tangut wealth.[99]

The Tangut were a highly sophisticated people with their own language and script (related to Tibetan and Burmese, with more distant affinities with Chinese), but there is much about their early history and genesis that is obscure.[100] Some scholars consider that Hsi-Hsia was always fundamentally unstable because agriculture and nomadism pulled in different directions, but probably a more potent reason for political entropy was the long series of wars with its neighbours waged by the realm in the eleventh centuries, when there were ferocious wars with the Song and the Liao empire of northern China (virtually non-stop in the years 1069–1099).[101] Many think that by 1100 Hsi-Hsia was exhausted and on the verge of collapse. What prevented the Tangut kingdom from becoming just another manifestation of the Central Asian 'here today gone tomorrow' phenomenon was threefold. The consolidation of Buddhism as the state religion provided an overarching homogeneous culture;[102] the economy reached new heights; and the state was centralised and strengthened by a long period of continuous rule by just two kings (or 'emperors', as the Tangut preferred to call them). Ch'ung-Tsung (1086–1139) and Jen-Tsung (1140–1193) ruled wisely and with statesmanship. Instead of lashing out in all directions, as their predecessors had done, they acted responsibly, first supporting the Liao dynasty against the uprising of the Jurchens of Manchuria, then, when the Jurchens overthrew the Liao dynasty in 1125, switching support to the new regime, the Jin empire. With new boundaries, Hsi-Hsia became cut off from the Song empire, and a long period of peace ensued; they remained neutral during the bloody wars between the Jin and Song in the mid-twelfth century. In 1185 the Song tried to tempt both Hsi-Hsia and Qara Khitai to join them in a campaign against the Jin, but the Tangut sensibly stayed out of the conflict, unwilling to jeopardise their splendid economic relations with the Jin.[103]

After Jen-Tsung, Hsi-Hsia experienced five short-lived rulers. Genghis's 1205 raid into the land resulted in a coup whereby Li An-Ch'uan murdered Huan-tsong (1193–1206) and installed himself as 'emperor' Hsiang-Tsung. In the 1205 raid the Mongols had not tarried long but carried off huge numbers of domestic animals, especially camels.[104] Two years later they returned, this time with more serious intent. Their principal aim was to raise revenue. Genghis's new militarised state was very expensive to maintain and, like the shark compelled ever to move forwards or expire, could maintain itself only by fresh conquests which brought in fresh tribute. There was not much wealth to be had from the pursuit of the Merkit or the subjugation of the Forest Peoples.

Accordingly, the need to raise tribute was primary among Genghis's motivations for ordering another invasion of Hsi-Hsia in 1207.[105] But it was far from the only actuating factor, and here we may see once again that Genghis's political motives were almost always overdetermined, illustrating how subtle and complex an operator he was. With the golden dream of an invasion of China uppermost in his mind, he needed a dry run for his reformed armies that would pit against them a foe fighting in the Chinese manner, with an effective military organisation that integrated cavalry, archery by the infantry, war chariots, artillery carried on the back of camels and amphibious units or marines.[106] Genghis was also aware that the constant battles he had fought up to 1206 (possibly exacerbated by a subtle change in the climate) had decimated his flocks and herds, which needed to be replenished from a fruitful source, and the land of the Tangut fitted the bill perfectly.[107] Hsi-Hsia was a locus for major trade routes so an invasion of that country, securing the trade routes west, made economic sense. At the same time, militarily, it would open up a western route into China to add to the direct northern one.

The motive of revenge was important too. Genghis had not

forgotten that in the past the Tangut had intervened on the side of his enemies and provided refuge for them, especially the Kereit and, in particular, the Senggum Ilkha, son of Toghril. Their meddling on the steppes could not necessarily be considered a thing of the past either; there was a danger that the Tangut would strike out at their powerful new neighbour and Genghis intended, so to speak, to get his retaliation in first.[108]

For all these reasons war with Hsi-Hsia seemed a political imperative. Genghis made his usual careful preparations, identifying all his enemy's weak points. Three seemed salient. Gradually over the second half of the twelfth century a rift had developed between the bureaucracy and the military, with unwelcome implications for the well-oiled Tangut military machine. Corrupt officialdom was sapping the state even before the Mongols introduced major instability after 1205. And, fundamentally, the Tangut were traders and scholars before they were soldiers, natural individualists and not team players like his own officers and troops.[109] Nevertheless, the military power of Hsi-Hsia was formidable, even if they could no longer put in the field the massive armies of more than 150,000 they had deployed in the past.[110]

In 1207 Genghis invaded Hsi-Hsia once more, quickly overran the countryside and announced that it would be returned only when the Tangut promised to pay an annual tribute.[111] In alarm the Tangut appealed to the Jin for help, pointing out their long history of loyalty and support for the Jurchen regime in China. The Jin declined to help, not only because they were preoccupied with their own war with the Song but also because they were becoming disillusioned with the sharp practice of the merchants of Hsi-Hsia: the Jin alleged that the Tangut traded worthless gems and jades for the high-quality Chinese silk and textiles and flooded the market with their valueless garbage.[112]

Left to themselves, the Tangut made a poor showing against the Mongol armies but were able to retire into heavily fortified towns which were impregnable to the Mongols, who had never yet had to deal with problems of siegecraft. Yet the devastation wrought by the Mongols was considerable, and in the end the Tangut concluded it was cheaper in the long run to pay the invaders off; they offered an annual tribute in return for the Mongols leaving them alone. Genghis was reluctant to call off his expedition, but his generals persuaded him, pointing out that their forces were making heavy weather of what was expected to be an easy conquest; it might be better if there was a period of calm while they studied the science of poliorcetics – how to take cities by siege.[113]

For two years all went well and the tribute was paid regularly. Then in 1209 the Tangut suspended payment. This time Genghis decided that only the toughest lesson would suffice to bring Hsi-Hsia into its rightful posture of submission. He gathered the largest invasion force yet. The expedition, its commissariat and itinerary were prepared meticulously. The Mongols spent the month from 6 April to 5 May 1209 trekking 650 miles along the eastern side of the salt lake Dabsun Nor, making for the city of Wu-La-Hai (Uruqai), which they had taken in 1207.[114] The first 450 miles of this journey were gruelling, as the terrain provided only limited grazing, and the last two hundred miles was desert, ranging from shrub-covered hillocks to the classic pyramidal sand dunes. For the first part of the trip Genghis had his men cache herds of sheep to feed the army, but when crossing the desert they had to take their own supplies. Once in the vicinity of Wu-La-Hai the invaders were in a land of plenty and could raid and gather large herds of sheep with ease.[115]

The Tangut ruler Hsiang-Tsung sent an army of 50,000 under his nephew Li-Tsun-Hsiang and his trusted general Kao Liang-Hui to hold up the Mongol advance at Wu-La-Hai. This force won an opening skirmish against the Mongols but had no idea how to exploit this initial advantage. Genghis then tempted the Tangut to try conclusions with him in a pitched battle, and won an overwhelming victory. The nephew managed to escape, but Kao Liang-Hui was captured and executed after he refused to bow to the Mongol khan. The Mongols then moved in on Wu-La-Hai and took it by storm after ferocious house-to-house street fighting.[116]

Genghis's next move was to advance on the Helan Mountains (Helan Shan) prior to an attack on the capital Chung-Hsing (modern Yinchuan). There was only one road to the capital, over the mountains past the fortress of Kei Men which was supposed to guard the approaches to Chung-Hsing. The Tangut general Wei-Ming was sent to intercept the Mongols on this route, and launched a heavy attack, winning a pyrrhic victory over the enemy vanguard but sustaining heavy losses himself.[117]

For two months Genghis patiently awaited another Tangut onslaught which he planned to defeat with the 'horns' formation, but the Tangut would not be drawn. Genghis dealt with the impasse by guile. It was imperative that the Tangut be lured into the open, so in August 1209 Genghis made elaborative, demonstrative and vociferous plans for retreat. He struck camp, began withdrawing and left behind a rearguard, seemingly leaving too large gap between it and the main force, while actually concealing an elite force in an ambush. Wei-Ming took the bait and descended from his strong position on the slopes of the hills into the plains, thirsting to win an easy victory which would win him glory. The Mongol rearguard appeared to bolt in panic and led the Tangut into a perfectly sprung trap, where they were 'eaten up' by the Mongols' finest.[118] After the crushing defeat Wei Ming was taken prisoner and the fortress of Kei Men surrendered. The way was now open to the capital.

Although the Mongols had learned enough in two years to be able to take smaller towns by siege, the big cities were still beyond them. The siege of Chung-Hsing began in August but by October there was little progress. Hsiang-Tsung conducted the defence with energy and skill, and the system of interlocking irrigation canals made the city impenetrable.[119] Frustrated that he had not been able to put a dent in the walls, Genghis turned to the weather for help. By the end of October the autumn rains began, and Genghis noticed that the nearby Yellow River was engorged. He hit on the idea of building a great dam and then flooding the city, but in January 1210 the dam burst and flooded the Mongol camp instead, forcing them onto higher ground and making the siege even more difficult.[120]

By now however the Tangut were already desperate and besought the Jin for help once more, promising the most lavish terms. Many of the ministers at the Jin court took the force of the Tangut arguments and put it to the emperor that if he did not intervene against the Mongol menace, it would soon be the turn of the Jin to face the fury of the dreaded nomads.[121] The former Prince of Wei, now emperor Wei Shao Wang, took the attitude of 'a curse on both your houses,' arguing that both the Mongols and the Tangut were powerful enemies of his realm; the best course therefore was to encourage them to eat each other up.[122] But just as Hsi-Hsia was at its last gasp and on the point of surrender, Genghis himself despaired of a successful outcome because of his inadequate siegecraft, and opened negotiations. A peace was quickly made. The Tangut were mightily relieved that the invader would soon be gone from their soil for, after nearly a year of warfare, they were close to financial ruin; virtually all agricultural and commercial life had ceased.

The Tangut agreed formal submission to the Mongol khan, promised to send military reinforcements to any expedition he might launch against a third party, pledged themselves to annual tribute and made a down payment of camels and woollen cloth, plus the daughter of the Tangut ruler as one of the khan's wives.[123] The Tangut salved their humiliation by declaring war on the Jin, crossing the Yellow River in 1210 and plundering Jin cities on the other side; the war thus begun would continue until 1225.[124] For Genghis, however, all was brilliant success. He knew that the Tangut could not possibly threaten his rear when he invaded China. It was time for his great dream to begin.

6

Character and Personality of the Khan

However unpleasant many aspects of Genghis's personality were, it must never be forgotten that he was a political genius. His genius was essentially fourfold: he was an incomparable master of military strategy, though less impressive as a tactician and battlefield commander; he had administrative talent of the highest order; he was an incomparable reader of men and human psychology; and he had a superb imagination, not just conceiving the idea of world empire but having the ability to think through and anticipate the myriad problems this would engender.

The private person was more complex and elusive. There are traces of a nervous, even neurasthenic personality possibly deriving from the three great traumas of his life: the Mongols' desertion of his family after his father died and the life of extreme privation thereafter; the desertion of the kinsmen (Qasar, Altan, Quchar, Daritai) who had elected him khan; and the many disputes with relatives after he became supreme ruler.[1] There are several pointers to the personality and deep character of Genghis in the sources but, unfortunately, the portrait of him in the *Secret History* is ambiguous and ambivalent. As described there he is at once far-sighted, shrewd, just, restrained, generous, talented, stoical, iron-willed, a natural ruler and at the same time cowardly, treacherous, devious, ruthless, ungrateful, vengeful, evil and even stupid. He is shown breaking down in tears when stoicism was called for.[2] His prayer on Mount Burqan after the Merkit raid which carried off Borte does not reveal nobility or greatness. 'I sought safety in flight with a heavy body on a clumsy horse . . . like a butterfly I felt great terror.'[3] Most of all, the abduction of Borte shows the young Temujin in a state of panicky cowardice. He abandoned his wife to the Merkit even though most of the women, including Hoelun, were able to get away. So far from fighting for her honour, it becomes clear from a close reading of the *Secret History* that she was probably captured because Temujin had taken her horse as a remount.[4] His own mother reproached him with cowardice when he slew Begter, calling him a beast and a demon.[5] Belgutei, Bo'orchu, Jelme and even Qasar are all shown as behaving more manfully than their khan.

However, on one point in the ledger of alleged cowardice we must acquit him. We are told, as if it were self-evidently the sign of a craven man, that he was afraid of dogs.[6] Yet a proper appreciation of this issue reveals that Temujin was displaying admirably good sense, since Mongol dogs were notoriously vicious and homicidal. Here are some assessments from travellers' tales: 'Mongol dogs are big, powerful and very dangerous to strangers; they will jump up at you even if you are on a horse or camel and they are sometimes too much to handle if you are on foot.'[7] And again: 'Big and bony brutes, long-haired and shaggy, loud-voiced and vicious, they are to be feared and avoided.'[8] It was part of steppe lore that only a fool approached a strange ger. As late as 1885 an unwary Cossack officer in Mongolia made this mistake and was torn to pieces by huge dogs, of the size and appearance of mastiffs.[9] The judicious conclusion on Genghis's courage is that he was *l'homme moyen*. Hypercautious and circumspect, he did not believe in exposing himself needlessly to risks and leading from the front, as a near-contemporary Richard the Lionheart did, ultimately with fatal consequences, or as Tamerlane did habitually. After all, it may well be the case that true courage is not the mad spur-of-the-moment quasi-suicidal impulse but a rational weighing of risks and dangers.[10]

Other negative personality traits included ingratitude, morbid suspicion and paranoia, deceitfulness, rage and jealousy. The most signal instance of ingratitude came after Genghis was wounded in the neck by Jebe's arrow in the battle with the Tayichiud in 1200. Jelme on this occasion saved the khan's life by sucking out the blood from the neck wound and spitting it out. Genghis's boorish reaction was to say: 'Could you not have spat farther off?' He then compounded his offence by suspecting Jelme of treachery when he went in disguise to the Tayichiud camp to fetch a pail of milk to quench the khan's burning thirst.[11]

That was probably Genghis's unfinest hour, but it was far from the only occasion when he revealed himself a hopeless, paranoid ingrate.

His attitude towards his own kin was suspicious at best and malevolent at worst; he was always sniffing out conspiracies, real or alleged, he put to death about a dozen potential pretenders and fell into a rage at the mere thought that a kinsman might be encroaching on his prerogatives. He was prepared to execute Qasar without trial and without any evidence merely on the insinuations and innuendos of Teb Tengerri.[12] Because of his propensity to rages, he escalated a drunken brawl with the Jurkin clan into a full-scale feud.[13] He had the talented and faithful Naya'a tortured and almost killed because of his unfounded suspicions that Naya'a had committed adultery with his queen Qulan.[14] Long before the final settling of accounts with Jamuga, it was clear that he envied his *anda* his many qualities and particularly resented his reputation for integrity, for being the knight *sans peur et sans reproche* who had a strict moral code and stuck to it.[15]

Genghis also had a fearsome reputation for being unpredictable in his rages. Some time in the 1220s, after he had conquered Transoxiana, he hired a linguist and scribe from that area to correspond with the Islamic princes of western Asia. Jebe had told him of a Persian prince of Mosul who was keen to attack Syria, so Genghis wrote to forbid him to do any such thing. The secretary, thinking himself a master diplomat, paraphrased and edited the letter in the Persian style, full of fustian and circumlocutions, employing the flattering form of address common in Islamic society. When Genghis had the letter translated into Mongolian and read back to him, he flew into a fury. 'You are a traitor,' he told the trembling secretary. 'The Prince of Mosul, reading this letter, will become even more arrogant.' He clapped his hands to summon the guard and ordered them to take the secretary out and execute him.[16]

The rages would not have been so bad if Genghis had not also been a humbug about displays of emotion. Though rage-filled himself, and never ashamed to exhibit his feelings, he issued a standing order that all others at court were to control their emotions, even extending this prescription to his son Chagatai, who wished to mourn effusively on the death of his son. The only time he himself was known to have controlled his own temper came when a Muslim cleric rebuked him for the colossal loss of life he had visited on Islamic territories. Genghis had been minded to make a favourite of the man on the strength of his earlier statements but at this manifestation of 'disloyalty' he became purple with rage and threw down his bow and arrows. All present thought he would certainly order the cleric executed. But he recovered and mastered himself sufficiently to storm out in the white heat of anger. The courtiers advised the unwise imam to depart at once and never show his face again.[17]

If we combine all these manifestations with Genghis's lacklustre performance on the battlefield, a very negative picture indeed begins to form. The *Secret History* almost seems to go out of its way to underline the fact that all Temujin's battles on the road to mastery in Mongolia were either won by his superb collection of talented generals or were achieved through luck and treachery. He lost Dalan Baljut, and won Koyiten by a fluke when the anti-Borjigid confederation suddenly and mysteriously broke up; the rout of the Merkit was mainly the work of Jamuga and Toghril, the defeat of the Kereit the work of one Cha'urqan, victory over the Naiman was due to the advice of Dodai Cherbi and the efforts of Jebe, Qubilai, Jelme and Subedei. The question arises: how could such an indifferent general, ungrateful, suspicious and paranoid, prone to uncontrollable rages and with no feeling even for his own kin, manage to found a world empire?[18]

The answer of course is that such an image depends on cherry-picking the most negative passages in the *Secret History*'s ambivalent portrait. It is time to redress the balance by bringing in the many positive virtues. Genghis was a good listener and a good judge of both men and opinions. He knew he had great generals and usually took their advice. He had considerable personal charm and charisma, as witness the many men who flocked to his banner after the most cursory acquaintance, most notably Bo'orchu, the Khitan Yelu Ahai, Sorqan Shira's children and Dai Sechen's sons. Though harsh to his kinfolk, he was extremely generous to his favourites and those who had helped him in time of adversity. The favours granted at the 1206 quriltai not just to the great ones like Bo'orchu and Muqali but to Badai and Kishiliq (the horse-herders who tipped him off about the murderous conspiracy of Toghril and Ilkha) largely speak for themselves.[19] He was also generous to the children of fallen heroes (an example was one Qildar) and to Narin To'oril, son of Chaqan-qo'a, killed by Jamuga at Dalan Baljut.[20]

He was partial to his young protégés, especially Sigi Qutuqu who nearly got the camp commander executed for dereliction when he slipped out at night, aged 15, to go hunting. His affection for his grandchildren was notable and when one was later killed at the siege of Bamiyan, he ordered every living thing in the stronghold exterminated, down to cats, dogs and poultry. He was also capable of sudden acts of generosity on a whim, as when he saw a peasant struggling with heavy burdens in the broiling sun and decided to free him thenceforth from all taxes and forced labour. On another occasion Chaghan, a Tangut boy, managed to save his home town from massacre during one of the numerous Tangut wars. He pleaded with Genghis and pointed out that the governor, his father, had wanted to surrender bloodlessly to the Mongols but had been overruled by a cabal of hardline officers in the citadel. Genghis subsequently adopted him.[21]

Nobody has ever claimed that Genghis Khan was a saint, and there is virtually universal agreement that he was cruel, vindictive, treacherous and duplicitous. Some have even claimed he was a genuine psychopath who masked his lust for killing under a barrage of rationalisations, whereby the executed ones were always disloyal, treacherous or recreant.[22] But how cruel was he? He was not perceived by contemporaries as being exceptional in this regard, since the atrocities he committed and the things we in the twenty-first century would perceive as war crimes were commonplace in the thirteenth century among all peoples of the time, including Christian crusaders. He did not have the kind of exceptional reputation for cruelty among his contemporaries that Henry VIII of England had in the sixteenth century, could not rival Tamerlane for slaughterous brutality, and can be documented as less bloodthirsty than contemporary Khitans, Persians and Jin Chinese.[23] Genghis appears to advantage beside his contemporary and dedicated adversary Jalal al-Din (see Chapters 9–10). Jalal looked on smilingly as his men drove pegs into the ears of Mongol captives, handed prisoners over to the mob to be torn to pieces or beaten to death in the streets, and then took a hand himself in beheading some of the others.

Some historians claim that the worst atrocities laid at Genghis's door – pouring molten lead into the mouth of the governor of Otrar (see also Chapter 9) or slitting an old woman open to get at the pearls she had swallowed – are apocryphal, the product of enemy propaganda.[24] Genghis maintained that his 'surrender or die' policy always gave the enemy a chance to save themselves. One of his advisers summed up his policy on massacre thus: 'The basis of the State is the people. If, when a country has been conquered, the population is then murdered, what advantage does the State have? Moreover, if the innocent are killed, this simply stiffens the enemy's will to resist. This is not in accord with the leader's wishes.'[25]

But the ultimate justification for any 'regrettable' massacre was that, according to Mongol ideology, anyone opposing the khan's wishes was *ipso facto* in rebellion, and all states recognised the right of a sovereign to execute rebels. Genghis, it was said, was literally the son of God, as he was conceived when a shaft of light entered his mother's tent and impregnated her; in the official creed the luckless Yesugei was reduced to the spear-carrying role of Joseph vis-à-vis Mary in the Bible. If you are God's representative, the Spanish conquistadores argued, you are justified in slaughtering the indigenous population if they refuse to be baptised and accept the word of God; how much more powerful the argument becomes if you, the conqueror, are the son of God, conceived by a mortal mother from an immortal father like all the greatest heroes of mythology.[26] The proof of Genghis's divinity was not just the visions vouchsafed to him by Tengerri but the many miraculous escapes he had had from death, most notably when ambushed at a ford by six assassins early in his career; you cannot kill a man whom God has marked down as the special agent of his providence.[27]

By the age of 44, Genghis had a commanding presence befitting the great khan. He was robustly healthy, tall, broad-browed, with a long beard and eyes like a cat. During his struggle for mastery of the steppes, his height, powerful build, unforgettable eyes and lack of grey hair made him appear calm, ruthless, calculating and self-controlled. In 1203, during the final campaign against Toghril and the Kereit, he noticed that his hair was turning white and immediately turned this to his advantage, announcing that since Heaven had designated him as his ruler on earth, it now wanted to bestow on him all the marks of *gravitas*. Observers said that the greying of his beard actually enhanced his charisma.[28]

Perhaps it was the extra confidence accruing to him by 1205, with all enemies defeated, that led him increasingly to pronounce maxims on a variety of subjects, which were written down by his scribes and broadcast publicly. Naturally, many of these relate to military matters. He tells us that an officer who cannot keep order in his own squad should be regarded as a criminal.[29] On the other hand, too much toughness in an officer is just as bad. He had a leading colonel named Yesun-Bey whom he described as the bravest of the brave, but he expected too much of his men and therefore was not fit to command. Only a man who felt the normal pangs of hunger and thirst would take care that his troops and animals did not starve or thirst.[30] On horses Genghis could sometimes sound like one of George Borrow's gypsies in his folk wisdom: 'Any horse that runs well when it is fat, when it is half-fleshed and when it is lean is a good horse; a horse that runs well in only one of these conditions is no good.'[31] Different behaviour was needed in peace and war: 'Amongst people one must be like a calf, small and silent; but in time of war one must be as a hungry falcon when it is hunting; he must go into battle shouting.'[32] There is plenty of advice on domestic matters. Genghis advises one never to generalise or argue abstractly unless one can quote chapter and verse in support from three accredited and acknowledged sages. Moreover, it is axiomatic that the truth, whether spoken seriously or in jest, can never be withdrawn or recanted.[33] He tells us that a man's good name is known by the good-ness of his wife and vice versa; in general it is wise to judge a man by his wife.[34] Some of the maxims sound cynical rather than earnest. 'Every man has his use, even if it is only to gather dried cow dung in the Gobi for fuel,' and 'everyone who is capable of cleaning out his own insides is capable of cleansing a kingdom of banditry.'[35]

By 1206, with the new Mongol empire gaining access to unheard-of new luxuries, including the fine wines of western Asia, which increas-ingly displaced koumiss, Genghis was becoming seriously concerned by the level of alcoholism among his subjects.[36] As a student of human nature, he knew that a ban or prohibition would be a pointless gesture which would not work, so he tried to moderate the problem by decreeing that none of his subjects should get drunk more than three times a month. Some of the sayings on this topic have an almost dithyrambic quality: 'If unable to abstain from drinking, a man may get drunk three times a month; if he does it more than three times a month he is culpable; if he gets drunk twice a month it is better; if once a month this is still more laudable, and if one does not drink at all, what can be better? But where can such a man be found? If such a man were found, he would be worthy of the highest esteem . . . the drunk is deaf, blind and devoid of reason . . . he is like a man who has received a blow on the head . . . the only thing he obtains by his state is shame. A sovereign addicted to drink is incapable of any great deed. An officer who likes drink is not fit to lead his men. The vice (of alcoholism) disables all it afflicts.'[37]

He also set out his goals and aims in life, which can best be described as militarised hedonism. He described his ambitions for his warriors as follows. 'My task and intention is to sweeten their mouths with gifts of sweet sugar, to decorate their breasts, backs and shoulders with garments of brocade, to seat them on good geldings, give them to drink from pure and sweet rivers, provide their beasts with good and abundant pastures, and to order that good roads and highways that serve as ways for the people be cleared of garbage, tree-stumps and all bad things; and not to allow dirt and thorns in the tent.'[38] And again: 'It is delightful and felicitous for a man to subdue rebels and conquer and extirpate his enemies, to take all they possess, to cause their servants to cry out, to make tears run down their faces and noses, to ride their pleasant-paced geldings, to make the bellies and navels of their wives his bed and bedding, to use the bodies of his women as a nightshirt, to admire their rosy cheeks, to gaze upon and kiss their rosy breasts, to kiss them and to suck their red lips.'[39]

The picture of Genghis that emerges consistently is a ruthless, practical and pragmatic man, obsessed with war and conquest, totally unscrupulous in his pursuit of power, energetic, discerning, shrewd, charismatic, awe-inspiring, just, resolute, intrepid, implacable, sanguinary, a cruel butcher, generous and affable with his trusted friends and chosen ones but peevish, suspicious, jealous and even malevolent to all outside the magic circle. He claimed to be above all conventional religions as he was his own shaman and could converse both with Tengerri and with demons – in a word, a genuine Nietzschean superman *avant la lettre*.[40]

His attitude to actual religion was, nonetheless, fascinating. As a pragmatist he was interested in what William James would later call the 'cash value' of different creeds: did they help to acquire food, win battles, enable one to live a long and happy life or even attain immortality? He was therefore tolerant of any ritual or belief-system that might enable him to attain these things.[41] There was also the consideration that, as a superstitious man, he could not be totally certain that there was nothing in the organised religions and that their priests, lamas and imams had no supernatural powers. Besides, wars of religion were dangerous, insidious and pernicious and threatened the stability of the realm. Because Genghis took a 'laid-back' attitude to the rival religions, and was content to allow traditional religious practices provided they did not conflict with his own laws – as when Muslims performed ablutions in running water[42] – the Mongols were often hailed as religious liberators. Islam, though, had the advantage that it was a warriors' religion. Buddhism, on the other hand, was unpopular in Mongolia and Genghis, at least initially, perceived it as an irrelevance. To see the world as a veil of illusion and to assert that complete inactivity was the only way for good to triumph over evil seemed to him a hideous lie. Although the Mongol empire would in due course essentially bifurcate into Buddhist and Islamic halves,[43] in the reign of Genghis and until the death of Ogodei in 1241, the great external religious influence on the empire was the creed of the Kereit and the Naiman – Nestorian Christianity, which had an influence out of all proportion to the number of its practitioners.[44]

Nestorianism was named after Nestorius, patriarch of Constantinople AD 428–431, who advanced the doctrine that the human and divine natures of Jesus Christ were distinct; there was no Virgin Birth, the idea of the Blessed Virgin Mary was a later accretion with no sanction in the Gospels. For Nestorius, Jesus Christ was not identical with the Son of God but he did partake of his nature. His essential nature was human but this somehow 'absorbed' the divine – a kind of possession, but by God, rather than the devil.[45] After his views had been condemned as heretical at the Council of Ephesus in 431 Nestorius relocated to Syria; many of his supporters went to Persia and it was in the East that his doctrine took flight, at first in tandem with Manichean dualism.

Manicheans distinguished between Jesus as bringer of gnosis and the historical Jesus of Nazareth, though with them the distinction was often blurred; Nestorius was more lucid and saw that there was a flat contradiction between God as *logos* or world-spirit ('the word' in the Gospel of St John) and the dogma of the Trinity. The only way to make sense of the various traditions and accretions was to postulate that Jesus had two natures – divine *logos* and human Jesus. It was only the latter that Mary, whoever she was, gave birth to, and therefore her correct title should be *Christotokos* (bearer of Christ) rather than, as in the orthodoxy, *Theotokos* (bearer of God).[46] To orthodox Christians the notion of two distinct natures in one person was absurd but, as Nestorius pointed out, it was much less so than the idea of three persons in one God.

Manicheism was a dead duck by the year 1000 but Nestorianism went from strength to strength and from the seventh century spread right across Asia; by around 635 it had reached China and was greeted benevolently by the government.[47] Nestorianism had a protected status under the caliphate, while in the China of the Tang dynasty (618–907) its missionaries had turned it into one of the principal minority religions in the Heavenly Kingdom.[48] In the eighth century the Tang emperors prohibited Buddhism but allowed the preaching of Christianity, at least until in a change of mind in 845 the Tang decreed Christianity to be illegal, alongside Buddhism and Manicheism. These two survived the onslaught better than Nestorianism, and in places there was a fusion or syncretism of Buddhism and Manicheism.[49] Christianity declined seriously in the Liao and Jin dynasties, only to enjoy a spectacular revival when the Mongols conquered China and established the Yuan dynasty; it proved a fragile flower, however, and wilted rapidly under the Ming dynasty after 1368.[50]

The importance of Nestorian Christianity for Genghis was that it was the principal ideology of the non-Muslim people he conquered in Asia, including Kereit, Naiman and Uighurs. Some of his most important officials and administrators were Nestorians, notably Chinqai, possibly the most influential of all.[51] Thanks to Genghis the Nestorians enjoyed a fifty-year heyday period on the steppes, and for this reason were cordially detested by the Franciscan missionaries from the West, Carpini and Rubruck, who made contact with the Mongols in the 1240s.[52] The sheer aplomb of Genghis the universal ruler can be appreciated when one reflects that he and the Mongols were an island of paganism and shamanism in an ocean of universal religions (especially Confucianism, Taoism, Buddhism, Islam and Nestorian Christianity) yet he never felt a scintilla of inferiority when contemplating his spiritual rivals.

Genghis's contempt for his kinfolk and generally low opinion of his brothers is notable. The many quarrels with Qasar have already been noted, and this was not a relationship destined to end happily. Qaci'un, close to Qasar but on bad terms with Temuge, is said to have had the best relationship with Genghis of all the brothers but as in the sources he is virtually 'the man who never was', this may not be saying much. Most of the time Genghis seems to have treated Temuge with amused contempt but occasionally he was prepared to pat him on the head, as happened during the war with the Naiman in 1204: 'Temuge,' Genghis declared, 'is the son of his mother Hoelun, he is famed as a daredevil. He is not late because of the weather, he will not lag behind because of a halt.'[53]

Born in 1168, Temuge was the longest-lived of Hoelun's sons (he was executed in 1246, aged 78, after a failed coup) and as the youngest son or *otchigin* ('hearth-prince') the most important of the male brood according to Mongol culture; he inherited his father's original dwelling-place and all his wives.[54] His mother's favourite son, he was a skilled politician and with Hoelun ruled the Mongol heartland while Genghis was away campaigning. Perhaps Genghis's slight distaste for him arose because he was lazy (allegedly), had intellectual interests, and was intensely interested in the culture of the Jin empire, Qara Khitai and Hsi-Hsia.[55]

But Genghis's lack of feeling for his extended family did not extend to his own sons, with whom he was (initially, at least) besotted. The oldest was Jochi, born in or around 1182, but there was always a cloud over his head because he was known to be illegimitate, the fruit of Borte's rape by the Merkit chieftain. To Genghis's credit this factor never weighed with him – and on several occasions he rebuked Chagatai, who hated Jochi, by asking him to reflect that they both came out of the same womb.[56] Jochi first came to the fore in 1203 when Genghis was trying to seal his alliance with a series of marriages to Ilkha (the Senggum, Toghril's son) and his sisters, but he emerges clearly into the limelight only at the 1206 quriltai when he received any number of glittering prizes.[57] Although Genghis treated him with every consideration, it is abundantly clear that he never liked his father, that Genghis thought him not tough enough as a military commander, and that there were frequent clashes between the two. Perhaps Jochi had not seen enough of his father during the formative years – Genghis was almost permanently on campaign – and this affected the relationship.

This was the view of Kokochos, one of Genghis's most intelligent courtiers, who was appointed as 'minder' to Chagatai in 1206. Genghis, he said, for many years was so busy that he never got off his horse, never slept in a proper bed, usually went hungry and was in constant fear of death: 'His black head was bound to the saddle, his black blood was poured into a huge leather bucket.'[58] Perhaps another factor was that Jochi, albeit boastful, may have been the most intelligent of Genghis's sons, and therefore more inclined to question his father's policy decisions and the direction in which he was taking the empire. Despite his father's reservations about his military talent, all the evidence shows him to have been warlike, energetic and intrepid, fond of hunting, shooting and fighting; some said that Genghis was secretly in awe of him.[59]

Jochi always opposed the indiscriminate 'surrender or die' posture taken up by Genghis, arguing that he wasted talent that way. On one occasion after a victory over the Merkit Jochi asked his father as a favour to let the great Merkit archer Qultuqan live, as he would be an adornment to the future empire. Genghis replied adamantly that no Merkit should ever be spared; they were the Mongols' mortal enemies, treacherous, backstabbing, a permanent fifth column in Mongolia for the Jin and others to exploit. 'I have stored up so many realms for you,' he declared indignantly. 'What good will he do you?'[60] This incident may have been the beginning of Jochi's serious disillusionment with his father. Jochi married Bek-Tutmish Fujin, a sister of Ibaqa Beki, one of his father's wives, and of Sorghaghtani Beki, Tolui's wife; with her he is said (how plausibly one cannot tell) to have had fourteen sons. Only the first three registered in history, the first Orda, something of a nonentity, then Batu and Berke, both of whom later won fame as khans of the Golden Horde (the renowned northwestern section of the later Mongol empire). Jochi also had a host of other wives and concubines, who are said to have given him nearly forty sons in total. Understandably the exact details of Jochi's wives and family are a matter of some confusion.[61]

Chagatai (c. 1184–1242), the second son, makes a very late entry in the Secret History and is not mentioned until we hear of him getting his share of the spoils at the 1206 quriltai. Since by this time both Jochi and Ogodei had played distinguished parts in Genghis's almost continual wars, this seems odd. Is it possible that because of his suspect temperament his father wanted to keep him out of the limelight until he had matured as an adult?[62] Another theory is that the education of Genghis's sons might have gone wrong when the seal-bearer Tatatonga, whom Genghis had appointed as their tutor, sloughed off the responsibility onto an Uighur pedagogue.[63] At all events, Chagatai emerged into adulthood as a stern, stolid, unimaginative, dogmatic, by-the-book pedant, euphemistically termed a 'soldier's soldier'. All the sources agree that he was a blinkered, irascible hothead.[64]

On two issues he was fanatically unbending. The first was that Jochi, as a Merkit bastard, was no brother of his. He frequently brought this matter up, disrupting council meetings and angering his father. So distressed was Genghis by this feud that he decided to cut both his elder sons out of the succession and to shortlist only Ogodei and Tolui. He frequently exhorted the two combatants to reconcile their differences but Chagatai refused angrily, even though Genghis urged his deeply-held belief that in the end, when one's back is to the wall, the only thing you can rely on is family, not courtiers, flatterers or 'friends'.[65]

The other fixed point of Chagatai's fanatical dogmatism was an almost visceral loathing of Islam; it may have been in the certain knowledge that Chagatai would never allow the slaughter of animals in the Muslim way that Genghis appointed him custodian of his 'Great Yasa' or code of law. Even after Genghis's death, the new khan Ogodei (Chagatai's younger brother), who favoured accommodation with Islam, had to tread warily on this subject. On one occasion Chagatai claimed that Genghis had appeared to him in a dream and revealed that all Muslims should be killed as a terrible danger to the Mongol empire.[66]

Another distinctive aspect of Chagatai was that he was the one true womaniser among Genghis's brood. All Mongol princes had access to hundreds of beautiful women, but only Chagatai seemed genuinely sex-obsessed (Tolui and Ogodei preferred alcohol). It was known throughout the empire that if Chagatai took a fancy to a woman she had to submit or face terrible consequences, and this requirement extended to married women, despite Genghis's formal ban on adultery.[67] To complete the plethora of unattractive qualities, Chagatai was also an arrogant, all-or-nothing personality. One of Genghis's distinguished concubines was Moga Khatun from the Bakrin (or Makrin) tribe. Genghis was very fond of her, but their liaison produced no children. When Genghis died, Ogodei, who was at hand, immediately took the beautiful Moga as one of his wives. Chagatai was on the frontier of Mongolia and, when he heard of his father's death, he immediately asked the new khan Ogodei for her. He replied that, alas, Chagatai's message had arrived too late since he had already married her, but invited his brother to choose any other woman in the kingdom.

Chagatai's response was typically boorish: 'She was what I wanted. If I can't have her, I don't want another.'[68] Chagatai had many wives, but the two most important were Yesulun Khatun from the Ongirrad tribe and her sister Togen, whom he married when Yesulun died. He had eight sons in wedlock, all famous drinkers, of whom the favourite was his second, Mogetugen, killed at Bamiyan during the Khwarezmia campaign in the early 1220s.[69]

Genghis's third son Ogodei (c. 1186–1241) has many claims to be his most distinguished scion, though his career was blighted by severe alcoholism. While perhaps not as intellectually gifted as Jochi, he surpassed him in wisdom and managed to enjoy cordial relations with all his brothers; he was especially close to Tolui, a fellow toper. Corpulent, genial, hedonistic, good-natured, easy-going, unkindly described by one historian as 'a clumsy, engaging, jovial sot',[70] he appealed to Genghis as the ideal ruler of a peacetime empire, the khan for retrenchment and consolidation. Flexible, with good judgement and gifts of diplomacy and statesmanship, placatory and with natural gifts of conciliation, Ogodei was steady, down-to-earth, commonsensical and generally affable, though capable of lurching into terrifying and murderous rages when under the influence of alcohol. He had four official wives including Boraqchin, Moga, a princess of the Bakrin tribe previously married to Genghis, Jachin, and Toregene, a widow of great intelligence and mother of five of his sons, including the future great khan Guyuk. He also had sixty concubines and two other favoured sons, Qadan and Malik.[71]

One of the qualities Genghis most liked about him was his quite extraordinary generosity, as the khan always considered avarice and love of money despicable qualities.[72] Moreover, he was not perceived as a potentially autocratic ruler by the senior Mongol military aristocracy so would be unlikely to cause rebellion or revolt. This was the main reason why, in the end, Genghis did not promote his beloved younger son Tolui to the khanate, for Genghis cherished him far above any of others.

Tolui (1192–1232) was needlessly cruel, even sadistic, some said, and was just the kind of despot who would spark off a conflagration that would drag the empire down. Genghis projected the period after his death as one of pacific consolidation, as by then he considered he would have vanquished all his major enemies. Tolui, as a brilliant general, was only credible as khan in a period of continual warfare. And there was another reason why Genghis did not want to promote Tolui to supreme power; he did not trust his wife Sorqoqtani, a Kereit and a Nestorian Christian (also niece of Toghril) but, more troublingly, a liberal and reformer who might not carry on the great Mongol traditions.[73]

Yet the decision to cut Tolui out of the succession caused Genghis much agonising. He was the single one of his sons most obviously like him in temperament, a born warrior and great general who had great martial exploits to his credit before he was out of his teens. Moreover, Genghis felt that Heaven had sent him many signs that Tolui was a special one, beloved of Tengerri. While he was still a boy and Genghis was away on campaign, the lad suddenly told his mother that the khan would return that day; she scoffed, thinking him hundreds of miles away, but it came to pass exactly as Tolui had prophesied, leading the Mongol elders to conclude that the boy was psychic.[74]

Again, it was said that when Tolui was five, a captured Tartar brigand suddenly broke free and held a knife to the boy's throat, intending to use him as a hostage. Boroqul and his wife Altani were at hand, Altani screamed, and while other Mongols came running to the rescue, Boroqul managed to creep up on the Tartar from behind and wrest the knife from him.[75] Such at any rate is the story in the *Secret History*. Rashid and others claim that the story was mythical, something invented by Genghis's courtiers so that the khan could grant his favourite Boroqul favours he had not really merited. The official version was that the incident had taken place in 1202, but at that date Tolui was ten or thereabouts, not five. Moreover, Rashid added, it was a Tayichiud, not a Tartar, who was wielding the knife (and that makes sense since that was the year of the great campaign against Targutai) and the actual saviours were Borte and Shigi Qutuqu; as a final flourish it was pointed out that Boroqul was married to Beki, not Altani. There is a host of other circumstantial implausibilities.[76]

Tolui (the name means 'mirror' in Mongolian) was always Genghis's pride and joy. It was important to him that he should have a son who was a brave and audacious commander, always dreaming of conquest. He also appreciated that Tolui was the only one of the three brothers who never taunted Jochi about the circumstances of his birth.[77] In some ways Tolui *was* the most important son, since his own four official sons (he had ten in all from numerous wives and concubines) in turn all made their mark in later Mongol history: Mongke as great khan, Hulagu as the first Mongol ruler of Persia, Qubilai as one of the most famous of all Chinese emperors, and Ariq Boke, who led a serious (albeit unsuccessful) revolt of Mongol traditionalists against Qubilai.[78] Genghis actually prophesied that this would be the case: 'In the end, when thou shalt have a large army, the children will be stronger and more powerful than all other princes.'[79]

Yet in addition to his four sons with Borte, Genghis also designated three other people as 'fifth son' – an honorary position conferring immense privilege. The three were men for whom Genghis for one reason or other conceived an extraordinary fondness or liking: Shigi Qutuqu, the Uighur ruler or *idiqut*, Barchuq, and a Tangut official named Uchaghan Noyan. He also had two other sons within wedlock by wives other than Borte, whose names were Urukhuchi and Kolgen, of whom little is known.[80] Shigi Qutuqu seems to have had some ability, though not enough to warrant his high position in the Mongol hierarchy; he was one of those royal favourites who appear in all eras. The legend was that he was a child adopted by Temujin and Borte in that initial period of their marriage when Borte, not yet pregnant, needed to have a child to care for. According to the story, he was a Tartar child, found crying in his cradle after the Mongols had decisively defeated his people, but chronology decisively refutes the story, for Genghis appointed Shigi as his chief justice at the 1206 quriltai when, according to the foundling tale, he would still have been in his teens. He was probably born around 1180; he probably *was* adopted by Borte and rose rapidly in Genghis's affection, receiving the appointment to the supreme court at the early age of 26; he went on to be one of the few really long-lived Mongols.[81]

With his sons, official and honorary, his greatest pleasure was to go hunting or to indulge in his favourite pastime: falconry. It is difficult to convey from this distance the mania for birds of prey that existed in elite circles in the Middle Ages; in that era it was undoubtedly the sport of kings.[82] Genghis's great contemporary, Holy Roman Emperor Frederick II, the so-called '*Stupor Mundi*', has the reputation in some circles as having been the greatest ever falconer, but his mania cannot have topped Genghis's, as the khan is said to have dreamed of the birds and to have remembered that they were the symbol of Attila, his great predecessor as steppe conqueror. Falcons were also deeply embedded in Mongol culture, since they were the favourite form for shamanistic 'shape-shifters' to adopt.[83] In Mongol culture these birds were revered, and to kill one was regarded as tantamount to murder. Falconry can also be regarded as a prime symbol of machismo, since to tame falcons was regarded in the medieval mind as analogous to seducing a woman.[84] Genghis kept eight hundred falcons and the same number of falconers, and had a standing order that fifty camel-loads of swans, the raptors' favourite prey, be delivered to his camp each week.[85]

Greatly as he valued his sons, Genghis took a largely functional attitude to his wives and daughters. At least five official daughters were born to Genghis: Qojin Beki, Chachayigan, Alaqai, Tumelun and Altalun, but Genghis always regarded his girls as pawns in the game of dynastic marriage.[86] He and his sons took two different kinds of women to wife: those married by formal agreement with allied tribes such as the Ongirrad and the Ikires; and oligarchic women taken from defeated tribes: Naiman, Kereit, Merkit, Tartar, Tangut and so on. It would be absurd to claim that his marriage to Borte, the chief wife, was a love match. Genghis probably never 'loved' any woman in a sense that would be recognisable to the twenty-first-century West, but he did have both a passion and distinct liking for wife Number Two, Qulan, whom he invariably took on campaign with him. Qulan (c. 1164–1215) was a Merkit, daughter of the chieftain Dayir Usan, who bore him a son Kolgen, later killed in Russia.[87]

Since this liaison began shortly after Genghis had married Borte, he was at first uneasy about wife Number One's reaction to Number Two. Muqali was designated as go-between. Patiently he explained that Genghis intended no slight but that the Mongols would not respect a khan who was monogamous and, besides, Genghis was marrying Qulan for reasons of state. Borte assured the envoy that she had no objections, that whatever her lord wanted was law. Although it was obvious that Qulan was the favourite wife, Genghis continued to show every respect to Borte, especially by having her at his side at his coronation in 1206.[88]

Yesugen, a Tartar, ranked as the third wife in the hierarchy, with Gungju, daughter of the Jin emperor, who was given as a peace offering, as Number Four and Yesui, sister of Yesugen, as Number

Five. We are told that Gungju was not good looking and that, as a consequence, Genghis begat no children on her (she played Anne of Cleves to his Henry VIII). Ibaqa Beki, daughter of Toghril's brother Jaqa Gambu, was Number Six. When Genghis married her he gave one of her sisters to Tolui as a wife and another to Jochi.[89] Altogether Genghis had twenty-three official wives, sixteen regular concubines and a harem of five hundred irregulars; among the concubines his favourite was the Naiman Gurbesu with whom he developed a rapport after their more than shaky beginning.[90] Additionally, there was a standing order that all pretty women captured had to be paraded before him to see if any of them took his fancy. The Persian historian Juzjani tells us that in the Khwarezmia campaign of 1220–21 twelve thousand specially selected virgins from among the prisoners followed his caravan.[91] He also had a seventeen-piece all-girl orchestra. And yet a biographer of Genghis can tell us with a straight face that the khan never went in for sexual excess![92]

Despite being lord of the steppes, Genghis encountered many problems arising from his wives, albeit indirectly. There was the abduction of Borte, and then his suspicion that Naya'a had delayed bringing Qulan to him for three days so that he could have sexual intercourse with her.[93] When he learned that Yesui had been engaged, that her fiancé was good-looking and that she still hankered after him, Genghis sought him out and had him executed as a spy.[94] What looks like sexual jealousy was probably really more that he felt his honour had been impugned or an insult offered, or that some insolent act constituted lèse-majesté to the head of state. But the problems continued. Yesugen made it plain that she found Genghis personally distasteful, so he took his revenge by demoting her in the hierarchy and elevating her sister Yesui to wife Number Three.[95] Marital problems even followed Genghis into dreamland. One night he had a nightmare and awoke trembling and in a sweat. The content of the bad dream can be readily inferred from the sequel. Genghis summoned the captain of the guard and informed him that he was divorcing wife Number Six, Ibaqa, with immediate effect; the officer was ordered to marry her and receive all her household, possessions and wealth – in effect a considerable promotion.[96]

It may seem anachronistic to project modern feelings onto thirteenth-century Mongol women, but Borte presents the curious spectacle of a woman to all appearances making up for her husband's coldness by a programme of mass adoption, which Genghis tolerated good-humouredly. Those adopted by her include the Tartar Shigi Qutuqu, the Besud Kokochu, the Husin Boroqul and the Tangut Uchagan Nayan, who became one of the three 'fifth sons' of the khan. Some claim that these adoptions are of doubtful historicity but, given the prevalence of adoption in medieval Mongol life, on the balance of probability we are justified in claiming them as fact.[97] And since there is a clear suspicion of broad-brush ecumenism in these adoptions, we may suspect that it was deliberate policy on Genghis's part.

His attitude to his daughters was certainly pragmatic and unsentimental. He might not have agreed with Napoleon that the best woman was the one who had most children but he certainly thought that the most useful were those who helped to cement his political alliances. All five of the daughters he had with Borte were married dynastically to important rulers or tribal chiefs. Chachayigan was given to the Oyirad chief Quduqa as wife for one of his sons; the sources are unclear on whether she married the eldest son Inachi or a younger one Torolchi. The youngest daughter Altalun (his favourite) was paired off with one of his top commanders, Taichu; Tumelun was married to the grandson of Dai Sechen, Chigu of the Ongirrad;[98] the eldest, Qojin, to Botu of the Ikires; while Alaqai, Genghis's third daughter, was married to the ruler of the Ongud, a tribe on the northern frontier of China and vital to Genghis's plans for conquering the Jin empire. Just before she left for the wedding with Alaqush Digid Quri, the Ongud chief, Genghis gave her his instructions:

> You should be determined to become one of my feet. When I am going on an expedition, you should be my helper; when I am galloping, you should be my steed. You have to remember: life is short, but fame is everlasting! No friend is better than your own wise heart. No ferocious enemy is worse than a resentful and wicked heart.[99]

In other words, Alaqai was to be his eyes and ears at the Ongud court, to influence policy there in the Mongols' favour and to alert Genghis to any untoward or unfavourable development. Such was his trust in her that he even made her nominal overlord of his great general Muqali. Alaqai proved most faithful. She ended up marrying four different Ongud princes, first Alaqush then, when he died, his son Alaqush, then Alaqush's nephew Jingue and finally Alaqush junior's younger brother Boyaoke – all done in a spirit of heroic self-sacrifice so that Genghis could maintain an iron grip on the Ongud.[100]

In his relentless quest for politically expedient exogamy, Genghis's favourite tribe was always the Ongirrads and more specifically Dai-Sechen's clan.[101] Only with the Ongirrad, the Ikires and the Oyirad would he permit intermarriage; with the Uighurs and the Ongud the marriage process was one-way – in other words, he did not permit his sons to marry into those tribes, though their men could marry Mongol princesses.[102]

The status of women among the Mongols was relatively high – that is, as judged by medieval, not modern standards. The main reason for this has already been given: that in nomadic and hunter-gatherer societies extreme specialisation of labour is not possible. In settled, sedentary, agricultural societies of the Middle Ages ownership of land was of paramount importance, so that women were compartmentalised, their main function being to produce male heirs to work the land.[103] In Mongol society, by contrast, women were expected to perform many tasks that in more advanced societies would be considered men's work, particularly when their menfolk were away on campaign.[104] One of Genghis's maxims was 'A man is not like the sun and cannot be everywhere before people; when the master is away hunting or at war, the wife must keep the household in good condition and order.'[105] The words 'good condition and order' and 'the household' covered a multitude of sins. In addition to all the household and pastoral tasks, women were expected to drive huge wagons, some of them pulled by twenty horses, as the fashion took hold after 1206 to transport the aristocrats' elaborate tents around the country. One woman would often be expected to drive as many as thirty interconnected wagons; seven women would often be needed to transport a single oligarch's possessions, for one of these elaborate dwellings, when transferred, could fill over two hundred wagons; moreover, a single noble with multiple wives might have several such portable palaces.[106] Women had to be expert teamsters, for if they were driving the lead wagon of a lashed-together 'train', they needed very nice judgement in apportioning the loads to the various horses and camels. And when camp was pitched, the selfsame women were expected to erect these tents and dwellings at the new stopover, making sure there was the space of a stone's throw between the dwellings of the different wives.[107]

At the limit, women could be warriors themselves. When Hoelun was deserted by the rest of the Mongols after Yesugei's death, she raised the war standard of the Borjigid clan in defiance of the Tayichiud and even fought in some of the skirmishes.[108] There were even more dramatic instances in later history. During the war in Transoxiana in 1220–21 a Mongol burst into a house and began slaughtering people. It was not until the residents finally realised it was 'only' a woman they had to deal with that they overpowered and killed her.[109] Qubilai Khan's nephew Qaidu had a daughter who was a champion wrestler and, like Atalanta of Calydon, refused to marry any man who could not best her in her chosen sport. When she beat a challenger, as she always did, he had to forfeit one hundred horses. In this way she beat over a hundred men and acquired more than 10,000 horses.[110]

The Mongols were both polygamous (taking many wives) and polygynous (many concubines), with the proviso that only the children of the chief wife could be considered for succession to leadership. They practised levirate – that is to say, when a man died, his son married his stepmother(s), while the dead man's younger brother or cousin married the widow who was the son's mother.[111] Marriage was not a private matter but a consideration for the entire clan or, in the most important cases, the entire tribe. It was not just for life but considered eternal, stretching on into the afterlife. The nomads thought exogamy crucial to prevent inbreeding and to this end they observed the first and second degrees of consanguinity but no degrees of affinity. A widow was not allowed to 'marry out' in case her husband needed her in the afterlife, which was why the youngest sons often married all his late father's wives except his own mother.[112] Members of the Borjigid clan did not take Tayichiud women as wives, as this would have been considered endogamous.

However, in the later years of the Mongol empire Genghis's sensible precautions about inbreeding were increasingly disregarded, and the barrier of consanguinity crossed, largely because so many thousands of intermarriages had been contracted with the Ongirrads. It has been noticed that the life spans of later khans declined rapidly in the years from the 1220s to 1350 – only Qubilai in China lived longer than Genghis – and some scholars correlate this with consanguineous marriages.[113]

In the marriage stakes women were undoubtedly treated as chattels, as they were in all medieval societies, though the lot of most non-oligarchic males – as arrow-fodder, hewers of wood and drawers of water, sometimes in actual slavery or serfdom – was not much better. But the lot of females improved under Genghis. In the first place, rape was now strictly outlawed, whereas previously for a woman to be ravished or abducted was accepted as an inevitable part of life. Moreover, before Genghis only women were executed for adultery but now both sexes suffered the same punishment, unless they were rich enough to buy their way out of the consequences.[114] Women could now decide whether or not to marry or, in the case of 'unimportant' non-oligarchic women, to remarry. The Mongols never set great store on virginity as a prerequisite for marriage, although intercourse with a virgin to whom one was not married theoretically merited the death penalty, and there was no stigma about previous marriages or previous children. This was why Chagatai's harping about the dubious circumstances of Jochi's birth was considered so eccentric and undignified.

Under Genghis's new legal code, the Yasa, divorce became possible by mutual consent, though the khan did not allow women the automatic right to dismiss their partners, as he did their husbands.[115] But a woman could do as she pleased with the family possessions, buying, selling, bartering, trading, subject always to Genghis's overriding prescription that women must at all times make sure their men were ready for war and must lay in stores of food for the winter. Women also benefited by the greater wealth and prosperity accruing from the Mongols' ascent to imperial status in Asia. The famous headdress or *boghtaq* became more elaborate as brocade and other materials became available.[116]

Subject to the provisos noted above, it is possible to risk the generalisation that women under Genghis Khan had a better time of it than their sisters anywhere else in the medieval world. There was no obvious misogyny in the Mongol world: the wise old woman was much prized for her wisdom, and the nomads valued the magical powers they thought certain women possessed.[117] Mongol women were not oppressed by Chinese footbinding, Persian chadors or Arabic burqas, and could move about freely in public; there was no seclusion as in Islam. The high status of women was attested to by foreign observers both Christian and Muslim who strongly disapproved of the fact that they could be shamans, advisers and even regents of the realm; Ibn Battuta thought the next step would be that ultimate horror: strict gender equality.[118] Significantly, the growing influence of Islam, Buddhism and Confucianism in the later empire saw more restrictions on women; the Golden Horde was notorious in this regard but the decline was noticeable also in Yuan China.[119]

It was due to Genghis that a hundred female flowers bloomed, for in the thirteenth century there was a galaxy of notable Mongol women. The first to make her mark was the Kereit Jagamba's daughter Sorqoqtani Beki, Tolui's wife. When Tolui died, Ogodei tried to marry her to his son Guyuk to unite the two houses, but she refused, as she was entitled to, as the obligations of levirate did not apply to queens and princesses. Biding her time through the short-lived khanate of Guyuk, she managed to secure the election for her son Mongke, in the teeth of very strong opposition from Batu.[120]

Another prominent princess was also a Kereit Nestorian, Doquz Khatun who married Hulagu, later emperor of the Ilkhan and had great influence on his religious policies.[121] Yet another was the woman married to Chagatai's grandson Qara-Hulegu, Orgina, who ruled the Chagatai khanate for ten years.[122] The most famous episode of female power was during the interregnum after Ogodei's death, when Toregene, his widow, intrigued to have her son Guyuk made great khan. The sources disagree on whether Toregene was highly intelligent, or merely a cunning woman full of domineering ignorance. The purge of Ogodei's governors, administrators and courtiers she conducted in the 1240s was legendary for its cruelty and bloodshed, and she was ably assisted in this sordid work by a female confidante Fatima, whose early career included a spell as a procuress in a bazaar. Toregene died mysteriously, probably poisoned, and in the counter-coup Fatima was tried for witchcraft and executed, by drowning it was said.[123]

But these were only the most prominent of the women who made their mark as rulers and regents. An exhaustive checklist would contain many other names: Kalmish Aqa, Qutlugh Terkhan Khatun, Padishah Khatun, Qutulun, Baghdad Khatun.[124] It is no exaggeration to say that none of these careers would have been possible without the initial philogyny of Genghis Khan.

7

The Invasion of the Jin Empire

From 1211 to 1216 Genghis Khan was absent from Mongolia, pursuing his golden dream of the conquest of northern China. When Genghis first dreamt of this ambition cannot be established with certainty. Some say that his contacts with the Ongirrad when he was a mere child opened his eyes to the astonishing wealth of the great empire to the south. Others, more plausibly, point to the war against the Tartars in 1196 as the turning point, and assert that the silver cradle and precious blanket decorated with pearls uplifted by the Mongols in that campaign had an irresistible attraction for him.[1] A conquest of China by a people with perhaps one-hundredth the population seems the very definition of the impossible dream, but the sequence of events after the 1206 quriltai permits no other conclusion: first the subjugation of all enemies on the western steppe, then the methodical neutralising of potential obstacles from the Tangut, Uighurs, Qarluqs and Onggud.[2]

Genghis's dream was made possible by a number of complex factors but primary was the simple circumstance that the mighty state we know as China did not exist. The ancient land, or at least that part of it comprising the eastern half of the modern nation, was at this time divided between three powerful and antagonistic military dynasties: the Tangut of Hsi-Hsia (dynasty lasted 1038–1227), the Song of southern China (960–1279) and the Jin of northern China (1115–1234). All three were successors to the last dynasty to rule a united China, the glorious Tang (618–907), the greatest period for Chinese poetry and usually considered to represent the golden age.[3]

Nomadic tribes had raided China's northern frontiers throughout history for loot, and the perception persists that Genghis's great invasion of northern China in 1211 was part of this tradition, but that he got sucked into permanent conquest by the sheer extent of his overwhelming victories.[4] On the contrary, Genghis's aims were never merely to extort loot from China. His thinking was original. Previous steppe rulers had made the mistake of simply invading northern China and then establishing a dynasty there. But that created a power vacuum on the steppes which other tribal confederations naturally moved in to fill. Genghis's grand strategy implied defeating China *and* maintaining his power base on the steppes, so that his dynasty could possess both China and Central Asia in a single empire.[5]

Genghis's originality thus makes irrelevant the scholarly dispute as to whether nomads would attack China when it was weak or when it was strong. The idea is that whereas commonsense suggests a weak China provided easy pickings, the reality was that China would normally buy off the 'barbarians' on its northern frontiers so there was no need for invasion; only when China was too strong to be browbeaten by bluster, threats and casual raids did the need for invasion arise.[6] In fact an examination of the Jin empire in 1211 reveals that it was both weak and strong; the idea of the Mongol invasion of 1211 as a great raid fails at two different levels of interpretation.

Meanwhile, an examination of Genghis's motives in 1211 reveals how complex and multidimensional his thinking about China was. With the Mongols one can never discount revenge, and Genghis explicitly stated that in campaigning against the Jin, he was taking revenge for the many humiliations and atrocities visited on the Mongols by the Jin during the twelfth century, particularly the crucifixion of Ambaghai; he also resented his own treatment as a Chinese hostage, even though he was held by their vassal rather than the Jin themselves. Moreover, in the thirty years after his birth (or more precisely, the years 1162–89) the Jin regularly raided the steppes and carried off Mongol children as slaves.[7] The arrogance of the Jin, and in particular their refusal to allow Mongol envoys passage to the territory of the Song, was another running sore.[8]

Furthermore – as so often Genghis' motivations were overdetermined – a Mongol assault on the Jin was a test of their credibility. If Genghis Khan claimed to be the Son of Heaven while the Jin emperor was simultaneously claiming that he had the celestial mandate, only war could vindicate Genghis's claim to be the true and authentic holder of that title; it was intrinsic to Mongol ideology that all other nations had to acknowledge their superiority.[9] Then there was the consideration that the Jin, having long neglected the northern frontier, were showing worrying signs of building up their strength in the region, rebuilding walls and fortresses on their north-western bound- aries, probably intending to strike at the Mongols; this information Genghis got from his reliable intelligence conduit, the Muslim merchants of Asia. Accordingly, Genghis had, as the saying goes, to get his retaliation in first.[10]

At a slightly deeper level Genghis was actuated by a range of social and economic considerations. He had to ensure that the empire he had created, based as it was on expansionist distribution of wealth, did not implode because of internal conflict. The Jin attracted hostility because of their embargoes or quotas on the sale of pastoral surpluses.[11] Warfare posed peculiar problems for the Mongol economy. The almost incessant conflict from 1196 to 1206 meant that, essentially, livestock was eaten not pastured. Genghis found himself in the position of having to order new conquests just to feed his army. This created a febrile atmosphere of 'permanent revolution' and meant that the Mongol state had to solve the tricky problem of an entire people permanently under arms – something no society in history had had to face. No government can survive without money and the obvious way to get money is through taxation – impossible if the only putative taxpayers are soldiers. Even if Genghis could somehow have levied such an impost and generated the surplus necessary to run his empire, this would inevitably have triggered internal rebellion. By enrolling all the tribes of the steppe in a war to the death against the Jin, however, he could divert all their rebellious energy and harness it against the Chinese.[12] This would have two advantages: on the one hand, if all the best fighting men were in China, the Mongol domain would suffer no disturbance. On the other, the necessary money could be raised from looting, ransoms, fines and, so to speak, Danegelds – precisely the financial rapacity that gained the Mongols the reputation of being ravening wolves.[13] Like a shark (to change the metaphor), the Mongol empire had to be in continuous forward motion.

There is also strong evidence that the Mongol state encountered severe economic turbulence at the precise moment Genghis rose to power. Some say that it was difficult to get all the booty taken on campaign back to the central coffers because of corruption, brigandage and other reasons for 'inventory shrinkage'.[14] Others incline to the view that the real problem was climate change – a dry period on the steppes – or overpopulation in a fragile pastoral economy.[15]

Fundamentally, however, the very needs of empire dictated an invasion of Jin China. There were now no more nomadic societies to prey on so as to accumulate wealth; they had all been conquered. This meant sedentary societies had to be the prey, but to organise such a predatory expedition, uniting the disparate and heterogeneous tribes of the empire, you needed 'supertribalism' or a 'superpolity', and the only way this could be financed was by attacking China.[16] Previously nomad tribes had refused to cede power to such a body, reasoning that they had no need for a central authority when they could trade peacefully with the agricultural societies. Genghis's conquests had created the political and administrative structure to plan and carry out the massive undertaking he dreamed of. By systematically invading Jin China Genghis transcended the limitations of previous nomads – what one historian has wittily called 'the Manchurian candidates'.[17]

The obvious question arises: why did the Jin not spot the danger earlier and take pre-emptive action? There are many possible answers to this. They had not been able to prevent the unification of the steppes because of their continuing war with the Song of southern China. They were confident that at the end of the long struggle in Mongolia the Naiman would emerge victorious and Genghis discomfited. They were complacent, since throughout history China had always been able to deal with the nomad threat in the north. They inferred too much from their success in 'making over' the tribes of inner Mongolia, who had to some extent been sinicised, underrating the ways in which the Mongols were totally unlike those tribes.[18] And in their intermittent attempts to deal with the frontier problem they had been extraordinarily ham-fisted. First they managed to alienate the *juyin*, the ethnically mixed peoples on the Jin-Tangut-Ongud borders. As a result their chief 'policeman' in the Gobi, the Ongud chief Alaqush Digid Quri, went over to Genghis. The Jin then compounded their folly by having Alaqush assassinated. This solved nothing, for his place was taken by his nephew, who formally acknowledged the Mongols as overlords.[19] Moreover, as we have seen, when Genghis attacked Hsi-Hsia and the Tangut appealed for help to the Jin, their attitude to the conflict was 'a plague on both your houses'.

As always when confronting a powerful enemy Genghis took an

almost intellectual and analytical approach to the grand strategy that would be involved, carefully researching every aspect of the target society and identifying its weak points. To appreciate the analysis he undertook we have to 'flash back' in Chinese history to understand how the Jin empire came into being.

When the great Tang dynasty collapsed like a house of cards in 907, China entered an era of almost four hundred years of disunification and an even longer period of 'alien' rule. First into the power vacuum were the Khitan people, one of the 'forest tribes' of Manchuria, whose existence as an organised tribe can be traced back to the fourth century AD but who were increasingly prominent in steppe affairs from the beginning of the seventh century.[20] The Khitans founded the Liao dynasty in 907 (incidentally passing on their name in the form of Cathay, the name by which northern China was known in North and Central Asia and the medieval West *Kitai* in Russian); the dynasty was the brainchild of their great ruler A-Pao-Chi (872–926), who from 907 to 926 styled himself the first Liao emperor.[21]

In 960 a new dynasty, the Song, was founded in southern China. At first the Song made feeble attempts to drive the Khitans out of China but the only real result of these wars was to increase the power of the Tangut, who had been allowed by the Tang to settle in the Ordos loop of the Yellow River.[22] The Song ended up paying tribute to both the Liao and the Tangut. In 1005 the Song accepted a humiliating peace treaty, virtually dictated by the Liao, in which they had their frontiers guaranteed in return for an annual tribute of 200,000 bolts of cloth and 100,000 ounces of silver.[23] Learning from their bitter lesson, the Song maintained cordial relations with the Liao for most of the eleventh century (there were short periods of warfare in 1042 and 1074–76). Yet the Liao knew few years of peace after 1050, and especially in the years 1069–99, when nomad tribes from Mongolia and Manchuria made frequent incursions into the empire, while the Liao, concerned about the rising power of the Tangut to their west, waged continual (though not continuous) war on the state of Hsi-Hsia.[24]

Protectionist and embattled, the Liao dynasty ruled an area from Korea to the Altai mountains, and their isolationist policies cut China off from western and central Asia. Suspicious and nationally paranoid, the Liao have been described as 'surrounded on four sides by militant peoples . . . crouched in their midst like a tiger whom no one dared to challenge'.[25] The reasons for the relative decline of the dynasty have been much debated. Some say the policy of sinicisation, integrating with Chinese culture and adopting traditional Chinese ways, fatally weakened the Liao, but others attribute the 'softening' to the embrace of Buddhism as a national religion.[26] A third view is that the Liao had foolishly allowed large numbers of Jurchen tribesmen from Manchuria to settle within the empire, thus creating a situation analogous to the influx of Anglos into the Mexican territory of Texas in 1821–36.[27]

The end of the Liao dynasty came suddenly. Its nemesis was the new Jurchen confederation. The Jurchens came from eastern Manchuria and were semi-agricultural forest dwellers dependent on hunting, fishing, farming and stockbreeding, and thus very different from steppe nomads. Their chief domestic animal was the ox rather than the horse, and they had the reputation of being industrious and prosperous, famous for their hawks and falcons, their gold, pearls, beeswax and ginseng.[28] By the end of the eleventh century they were beginning to diversify into horse breeding and pig rearing and to gain a reputation as formidable mounted archers. They had many of the skills of the Mongols but never abandoned their village-based agricultural life. There was always in Jurchen society a tendency towards bifurcation: one group stuck to the traditional tribal ways while a more progressive 'acculturated' group around modern Vladivostok tried to ape the Khitans and learn as much as they could from them, particularly about cavalry tactics.[29]

The secret aim of their chief Aguda (1068–1123) was to overthrow the Liao and displace them as China's ruling dynasty. His idea was that this ambitious project should be possible with the aid of the Song. It is difficult to establish exactly why Liao resistance was so weak when Aguda finally made his move, but a political crisis and divisions among the Khitans, alongside a peasant uprising, gave the Jurchen their chance; particularly important was the Court-versus-Country divorce between the Khitan aristocracy and their fellow tribesmen in the provinces doing all the hard work.[30] One historian describes the Liao collapse in these terms: 'The defection of the Khitans in their home territory, the collapse of impressive armies, and the surrender of imperial clansmen demonstrated that the dynasty had lost touch with its own people.'[31]

Even more astonishing was the speed of Jurchen conquest. In the words of the same historian, the invasion of Liao territories 'was so swift that it is almost better described as a coup than a conquest', and of another, 'the fierce rapidity of their emergence into history surpasses the rise of the Mongols a century later.'[32] In 1121 the alliance between the Jurchens and the Song was complete, and the conquest of northern China thereafter was rapid. In the years of the Khitan supremacy the borders of Liao China ended at the Yellow River. The agreement with Aguda stipulated that this frontier was to be guaranteed in perpetuity and that the Song would also have enclaves in the far north of China. Aguda proved in this respect most loyal and true. After he had taken four of the five Liao capitals in the years after 1116, as a prelude to all-out war, he took the last one (Zhongdu or Chung-Tu, later Peking) in 1122 and promptly handed it over to his allies the Song.[33] But he died soon afterwards and his successor, the Jin emperor T'ai-Tsung (1123–1135) promptly reversed this pro-Song policy and double-crossed the erstwhile ally. The Song were driven from northern China in 1125.

Next the Jin/Jurchen overran all the territory between the Yellow and Yangtse Rivers. Finally, in 1129 they crossed the Yangtse itself and invaded the Song heartland. For a while it looked as though they would sweep all before them, but they finally overreached themselves, hamstrung both by their overextended lines of communication and the Song skill at naval warfare. The war limped on until 1141 when a peace treaty recognised all land north of the River Huai (halfway between the Yellow and the Yangtse) as Jin territory. The Jin had thus expanded the frontiers of the old Liao empire. Their achievement in defeating both the Liao and the Song, the two most powerful nations in East Asia, was nothing short of fantastic.[34]

The Jin were tough opponents but Genghis identified a wide range of vulnerable points in their armour. The first related to their Chinese and other ethnic subjects. The Jin were always on thin ice numerically, as there were only four million Jurchens in northern China, about one-tenth of the population (most Jurchens had been settled in the conquered territories in the 'Great Migration' (c. 1125–45), when three million of them were moved into China and given land and oxen).[35] But whereas the native Chinese had settled down comfortably enough under the Liao, they never really accepted the Jin, and the consequence was frequent local rebellion.

Even worse, the Khitans never accepted their ousting. Only about half emigrated west to the new state of Qara Khitai and the rest remained as a sullen, disaffected nucleus under the Jin, biding their time and dreaming of a Liao restoration.[36] Ominously, many Khitans held key posts in the Jin army.[37] Again, whereas the Khitans had held Chinese culture at arm's length and obliged the natives to come to them ideologically, the Jin embraced, at least intermittently, wholesale sinicisation.[38]

Moreover, where the Liao had been bedevilled by a primitive Court-versus-Country split, the Jin experienced three-way factionalism, both between the Jurchens settled in China and the 'pure' Jurchens who remained in Manchuria, and between court and bureaucracy on one hand and the military on the other. Both the tribal leaders of Manchuria and the military were dissatisfied with the excessive centralisation practised by the early Jin emperors and their determination to impose 'one size fits all' policies, even to the extent of outlawing deviant religious sects, especially Taoism and all breakaway Buddhist movements.[39] The most successful Jin emperor, Shih-Tsung (1162–1189), was imposed on the court by a coalition of nobles in southern Manchuria, tribal aristocrats and local military leaders.[40]

Some of the more thoughtful souls in the Jin bureaucracy also queried the aggressive posture their emperors habitually took up against the external world. The Jin were deeply resentful of the success achieved by the new states of Hsi-Hsia and Qara Khitai, especially when the two collaborated, and it was anger about the close Qara Khitai-Tangut contacts that led them for a long time to seal off their western border markets.[41] Against the Tangut they sometimes resorted to actual warfare but against both they more usually used economic warfare, imposing trade embargoes as a trump card to bring these 'lesser' societies to heel.[42] The unintended consequence of this action was to align the Muslim merchants of Central Asia even more closely behind Genghis. They reasoned that only with a Mongol conquest of northern China could they ever gain access to the lucrative markets of Cathay.[43]

Yet the most self-destructive aspect of Jin foreign policy was their warfare with the Song. Whereas the Liao, apart from the very early conflicts, had lived in peaceful coexistence with the Song for most of their dynastic span, the Jin and Song were at each other's throats for much of the twelfth century. The fact that the Jurchen chief had previously double-crossed them scarcely helped, but the Jin were actuated by an abiding ambition to conquer all China, and the Song by a counter-vailing spirit of revanchism.[44] In a sense the two empires lived in different worlds, which partly accounts for their puzzling relationship. Northern

China was a dry land of wheat and millet, of cold winters and dry summers. China south of the Yangtse was an entirely different country – a region of lakes, rivers and flat fields with a warm, humid climate that supported the mass production of wet rice. Both empires were difficult for the other to win, for the north required skilled cavalrymen for its conquest – the precise military area in which the Song were most weak – while cavalry was useless south of the Yangtse; since the horses got stuck in the mud what was required was expertise in naval warfare.

For all that, relations between the Jin and Song were more complex than simply those of two mortal enemies, and in peacetime a thriving commerce went on. The principal Song export to the Jin was tea, followed by medicines, ginger, incense, luxury silks and brocades. From the Jin the Song imported gold, pearls, pine nuts, licorice root, furs and common silk. This was combined with the import trade through the harbours of southern China: furs, pelts, carpets, Persian and Indian cotton cloth, foreign silks, weapons, armour, saddles, perfumes, rare woods, pharmaceuticals, sharks' fins, betel, tortoise-shell, coral, gems, ivory and spices. The net profits of their trading easily covered the annual tribute the Song had to make to the Jin by the peace treaty of 1142.[45] The Song were economically formidable, knew how to encourage trade by reducing taxation and have even been acclaimed as 'world system' agents by some historians.[46]

But the regular, licit commerce did not exhaust Song–Jin economic links. A thriving smuggling trade went on in both directions. From the south came specie, cattle and rice – all three expressly forbidden as exports by the Song regime. From the north the main contraband trade was in horses, always in short supply in the Jin empire and therefore carefully hoarded. Nevertheless large-scale equine smuggling went on, and in this way the Song gradually learned some of the secrets of Jin cavalry warfare. Conversely, the desertion to the Jin of important generals and officers over time betrayed the secrets of Song shipbuilding and naval warfare.[47] In conventional warfare the Jin always had the upper hand – their cavalry arm was simply too strong for the Song – but Genghis realised that an empire with 100 million inhabitants could surely be mobilised to be a terrible threat to its northern neighbour with a population of just 40 million, especially given that only four million of those were Jurchens.[48] Genghis always kept the Song card up his sleeve, ready to play at the right moment.

Fiscally the Jin empire was strong and, on paper, Genghis should have been hard put to find weak spots. Agriculture, sericulture and cattle breeding were all prominent features of the economy. Salt production was very important in Shandong province, and wine was produced in large quantities, while elsewhere a mixed economy emerged. While foreign trade was a state monopoly, the mining of gold, silver, copper and iron was left to private enterprise. The Jin levied taxes on land, property and commercial transactions, and had received a windfall in the 1120s when they defeated the Song and seized their treasury at Kaifeng. This booty provided 54 million bolts of silk, 15 million bolts of brocade, 3 million ingots (150 million ounces) of gold, eight million ingots (400 million ounces) of silver and millions of bushels of grain, plus warehouses full of weapons, paintings and other artefacts and valuable manufactures.

However, by 1191 the reserves of the Jin state had been reduced to just 1,200 ingots of gold and 552,000 ingots of silver.[49] The explanation is partly cultural and partly due simply to corruption. Jurchen folkways emphasised the importance of gifts, and huge sums were disbursed in making sure the proper rules of etiquette, hospitality and rewards were observed. One victorious general received as his thank-you gift two thousand ounces of silver, two thousand bolts of cloth, one thousand slaves, one thousand horses and a million sheep.[50] Corruption was endemic in all the higher echelons of power. Bureaucrats tasked with land reform and equalisation of holdings seemed to go out of their way to achieve inequality and often simply seized land for themselves and their extended families. In the army morale was low, as it was known that all the officers were corrupt, well versed in all the familiar scams such as payroll padding and keeping their troops on short commons. Corrupt Jurchen nobles and officials seized government transport ships and exacted 'shakedown' levies from merchants. They refined and sold salt and brewed alcoholic liquor illegally.[51] No real care was taken to conserve the vital reserve stocks of rice and grain, even though this was how the army was mainly fed, and such perishables were vulnerable to drought and flooding as precious metals were not.

If the military was weakened by corruption, it was weakened even more by a serious shortage of horses. The Liao had been much cleverer in their husbanding of mounts than the Jin ever were.[52] The Jin, however, were hit from two different directions. Severe banditry in the east of their empire was a permanent problem, as the brigands were mainly horse rustlers. And a serious Khitan revolt in 1160–62 reduced the imperial herds to near extinction. Thanks to the efficiency and talent of the one 'good' Jin emperor Shih-Tsung, by the end of his reign, the herd figures had recovered to 470,000 horses, 130,000 oxen, 4,000 camels and 870,000 sheep – though significantly even this figure was less than the entire number of sheep given to the one victorious general already mentioned. This aggregate figure for horses made the Jin appear pitiful in comparison with the Mongols, and even the near half-million mounts was only half the amount the Liao had counted a century before in the census of 1086.[53]

Yet, as Genghis clearly saw, the worst defect of the Jin empire was the disastrous hand it had been dealt by nature in the form of the Yellow River. The sixth largest river in the world at 3,395 miles, the Huang He (Yellow River) flows through nine Chinese provinces and empties into the Bohai Sea. In its early stages it wound right round the Tangut kingdom of Hsi-Hsia, flowing north-east, then east, then south, forming three sides of an imperfect triangle, before finally turning east through the Hangu pass and onto the North China Plain on its final passage to the sea.[54] This triangular section of the river is the famous Ordos loop, a land of scant rainfall, mainly grassland and desert. To the north of the Wei valley is the Loess Plateau – it is the loess from the plateau that makes the river yellow. Flooding and the many changes of the river's course throughout history has led the Chinese to call the Huang He 'China's sorrow' and 'the scourge of the sons of Ham'.[55] In the 2,540 years until the end of the Second World War the river flooded 1,593 times and shifted its course significantly twenty-six times; both these manifestations produced famine and widespread disease. The floods of 1887 killed two million people; those of 1931 anywhere between one to four million, while the inundation of 1332–33 (in the Mongol era) is said to have killed seven million. The main cause of the flooding was the huge amount of fine-grained loess carried by the river from the Loess Plateau; the sedimentation produces natural dams. Building higher and higher levees coud be dangerous for, if the waters broke the levees, they could then no longer drain back to the river bed since the river was now higher than the surrounding countryside. Another cause of the flooding was the collapse of upstream ice dams in Inner Mongolia.[56]

The eleventh and twelfth centuries were a particularly bad era for

Yellow River floods. Flooding and changes in the river's course which took out the most fertile areas, causing famine and peasant revolt, occurred in 1166–68, 1171–77, 1180, 1182, 1186 and 1187. Emperor Shih-Tsung did his best with relief operations but in the political chaos after his death in 1189 the Jin administration simply could not deal with the Yellow River as well.[57] In 1194 the river burst its dykes, flooded Shandong province and then found a new route to the sea taking it south of the peninsula, bringing on widespread famine at the very moment the central government was hit by a financial crisis. Confidence in the financial system crashed when the Jin administration failed to redeem the paper money it had issued and circulated as cash. It followed that all relief operations would have to be conducted in gold and silver, but it was precisely the shortage of these precious metals that led the Jin to issue paper money in the first place.[58]

From the turn of the century, then, the Jin empire was beset by a number of simultaneous crises: flooding of the Yellow River, a financial collapse, weak emperors, a disputed succession, the dubious loyalty of Khitans and other key elements of the military, corrupt officialdom and increasing external threats, especially from the hitherto underrated Mongols. Genghis was always lucky in the timing of his wars with other external powers, and this time was no exception, especially as some historians speculate that all Asian societies dependent on agriculture were in decline at the very same time: the Jin, the Song, Khwarezmia, the Tangut, Qara Khitai.[59] It was boom time for nomadic warriors.

At this very juncture the Song chose to launch a war of revanchism. They crossed the Yellow River in 1204 but were heavily defeated. Jin emperor Chang-Tsung (reigned 1189–1208) proved conclusively that, for all their problems, the Jin were no paper tiger militarily. In 1206 145,000 Jin troops forced their way across the Yangtse, again defeated the Song and forced them to sue for peace. The Jin terms were harsh. First they demanded the head of Han T'o-Chou (c. 1151–1207), the minister who had led the Song party, and got it. Then they exacted an enormously increased tribute. The treaty of 1208 stipulated that the Song must pay annually 340,000 ounces of silver and 250,000 bolts of silk, as agreed in the original treaty of 1165, *plus* an indemnity of 390,000 ounces of silver. Additionally, they had to cede a number of towns in the Huai valley and recognise the suzerainty of the Jin emperor.[60]

But any advantage the Jin gained from this victory was soon wiped out by internal turmoil. In 1207 the Khitans engineered a great revolt in the north, in which the *juyin* joined. The Jin had hoped to build a new frontier wall in the north, to be garrisoned partly by their own troops and partly by the Tangut. But once the Khitan rising broke out, virtually all elements in the far north joined the insurrection: Tangut, *juyin*, and the Jin's own demobilised and dissatisfied troops.[61] Behind the scenes, stoking the fires, was Genghis Khan. The Mongols and the Khitans had developed a close rapport. They spoke related languages, had very similar cultures, maintained close political connections and were invaluable interpreters of events inside China. They also agreed that they faced a huge potential threat if, instead of their futile wars with the Song, the Jin decided to wage all-out war on the steppes.[62]

Khitans from China had begun to defect to the Mongols as early as the late 1190s. Yelu Ahai had been sent as Jin envoy to Genghis and was so impressed by what he saw that he immediately offered him his services. First he returned to China and brought back his brother Tuka as a hostage to guarantee his sincerity. Genghis waived this, took Tuka into his bodyguard and enrolled Yelu Ahai as one of his advisers. Yelu, forced to abandon his wife and children to the mercies of the Jin – who promptly imprisoned them – went on to a distinguished career with the Mongols. Both brothers were present at the Baljuna covenant, Ahai commanded troops in the campaigns against the Tangut and finally, in 1211, was given a senior position in the advance guard for the Chinese invasion under Jebe.[63] But these Khitan recruits were not the only renegades from the Jin. In 1208 four native Chinese, senior Jin officials, fled to the Mongols and endorsed Yelu Ahai's constantly rehearsed mantra that the Jin were highly vulnerable.[64]

Although Genghis had decided on a war of conquest with the Jin empire as early as 1206, he proceeded warily, where a lesser leader might have rushed his fences in the belief that the Jin were beset by so many different problems that they had already reached the end of the road. Even with all the considerable advantages the Khitan revolt and the internal turmoil in the Jin empire handed him, he waited until the famine of 1210–11 had bitten deeply before he crossed the Chinese frontier. Although it was true that he was 'a bold outsider, somebody who stood just on the fringe of power and was willing to take desperate chances to seize decisive power,'[65] Genghis was more chess player than gambler. Preconditions for a successful venture were the hobbling of the Tangut so that there would be no danger of a flank attack (achieved in the campaign of 1209–11), the submission of the Uighurs (achieved by the obeisance of his favourite, the *idiqut*) and the loyalty of the Ongud.

This last item was problematical, for after Alaqush's assassination, a power vacuum opened up and Genghis could not be sure his sons would follow in their father's political footsteps and support the Mongols. To hasten this end he used his favourite ploy of political matches and – as we have seen – married his daughter Alaqai Beki, Alaqush's widow, to the Ongud chief's successor (and his successor in turn).[66]

Having to his own satisfaction secured his power base on the steppes and ensured that no tribes in his rear would rebel while he was in China, at the beginning of 1211 he called a great quriltai on the banks of the river Kerulen to inform his inner circle and close allies of his general thinking, his grand strategy and the tactical details of the battles he expected them to win. Present were the *idiqut* Barshuq and Arslan, khan of the Qarluqs.[67]

It is unlikely that he confided to them his particular animus towards the new Jin emperor, but his closest associates would already have been aware of it. Prince Shao of Wei, a leading Jin oligarch, had attended the 1206 quriltai when Temujin was acclaimed Genghis Khan, but Genghis had found him stiff, overbearing and, from his viewpoint, insolent and insufficiently deferential. The next meeting with the Prince of Wei came two years later after Genghis announced he would no longer be paying tribute to the Jin. The prince again made the long journey north and did not enhance his credit with the khan by an overlegalistic insistence that the Mongols had a treaty obligation to pay, since they had conquered the Kereit, who originally owed the tribute. Genghis waved this away as the ravings of a man who did not understand power.[68] On his way home the prince learned that emperor Chang-Tsung had died and he had been chosen to succeed. He took the title of emperor Wan-yen Yung-chi with an official succession date of 27 December 1208.

When Genghis heard who the new emperor was, he guffawed with derision. Whereas previously his contempt had been implicit, he now sent a message which made it overt. 'How can the Jin choose a man like the Prince of Wei as their ruler? He is an imbecile.'[69] This open declaration, which Genghis hoped and expected would be relayed to the new emperor, crossed with a further fatuous 'demand' from the former Prince of Wei. Seemingly having learned nothing on his two visits to the Mongols, he capped his folly by sending an envoy to Genghis asking him to kowtow as a sign of fealty. The Mongols threw the luckless ambassador out, but not before sending a further insulting message to Wan-yen Yung-chi – which the envoy dared not repeat on his return to court.[70]

Addressing the quriltai, Genghis worked down from grand strategy to minute particulars. He explained that he intended to conquer China but at the same time maintain his power base on the steppes; not to do so was the great mistake previous invaders of China (including the Khitan Liao and the Jurchen Jin) had made. His ultimate aim was an empire that embraced both China and central Asia.[71] He emphasised the powerful support the Mongols enjoyed from Muslim and Uighur merchants, who wanted to see him as the superpower in the East. Sea trade had, since about the year 1200, become precarious, because of a war between the states of Kish and Ormuz, each trying to deny the Persian Gulf to any ship that traded with the other side. Meanwhile Chinese competition (both Song and Jin) was becoming increasingly strong on the eastern lanes of the sea route. Consequently trade routes had become a matter of considerable importance to the merchants.[72] The Islamic merchants of western Asia had also been won over to the Mongols by a simple stratagem: when Chinese merchants tried to rack their prices up, Genghis simply ordered their goods seized and confiscated. Taking his cue from this, a Muslim merchant made Genghis a present of the goods he was hoping to sell. On his departure he found his camels laden with gold and silver. From this arose a new definition of trade: travellers from the west of Asia gave the khan lavish gifts, and then waited to see how Genghis rewarded them when they left.[73] In addition to all this, the invaluable information Genghis gained from all sectors of the mercantile class meant Mongol intelligence was far in advance of anything the Jin could manage.

He then outlined all the Jin weaknesses adumbrated above. Yet he warned his listeners that the coming campaign would be no walkover. The Jin were formidable military opponents. Unlike many other enemies, they believed in *guerre à outrance* (they would fight to the bitter end), whereas intelligent people knew enough to submit, become client states and enjoy local autonomy. It is hard not to believe that Genghis nodded approvingly in the direction of his favourite, the *idiqut* at this point.[74]

He proceeded to military matters. It was true that the number of Jin subjects eligible for military service was above six million and that their standing army was 500,000 strong in infantry, with another 120,000 mounted bowmen; additionally they had several supposedly impregnable fortresses.[75] But these formidable statistics masked any number of enemy weaknesses. The disparity in numbers could be reduced to insignificance by the Mongols' greater mobility; could the Jin archers really fire five arrows accurately and then ride out of range, as the Mongols could? To match the talent of the Mongol archers it was not enough just to put men on horses and give them bows and arrows; it was something for which you had to be trained from birth. And the mobilisation of Mongol warriors did not harm the economic efficiency of nomadic peoples as it harmed that of agriculturalists; it was very expensive for the Jin state to train cavalry but for the Mongols it was a way of life.[76] The Mongols were naturally equipped for war. Their normal ponies could double as cavalry mounts. They did not have to buy warhorses separately and then have them ridden by specially trained cavalrymen. The Mongols' primary weapon, the bow, was used all the time for hunting. The cattle and sheep they drove would solve all commissariat problems, and meanwhile it was known that China was being devastated by severe famine. Nor was there any hardship for the Mongol women and children in being camp followers, whereas for sedentary societies this was impossible.[77] Finally, he urged his followers to be ruthless and have no sympathy for the Jin; it had to be remembered that these were the people who had tried to exterminate the Mongol nation, especially during the years 1135–47 and 1162–89.[78]

Genghis then sent an advance force south under Jebe to ensure that the Ongud were ready for his advent. The Jin emperor responded by sending an army north to intercept him, but his generals had no stomach for a march into the Gobi, and instead spent their time looting Ongud tribes near the Great Wall. Jebe came on this disorganised rabble and quickly routed it, prompting any ditherers among the Ongud and the *juyin* to throw their lot in definitively with the Mongols.[79] Wan-yen Yung-chi responded to these setbacks by clapping various generals and advisers in jail, but for the most part remained stupefied by the 'contumacy' of the Mongols and incredulous that they should be attempting such an impossible mission. He was hamstrung by cultural conditioning according to which the nomadic barbarians were beneath his dignity. He still thought he was easily strong enough to see off Genghis and his hordes but as yet had seen nothing of the speed, striking power, organisation, discipline and tactics of his opponent.[80]

Meanwhile Genghis ascended the sacred mountain of Burqan Qaldun to confer with Tengerri while all Mongol families endured a three-day fast below. He removed his cap and threw his belt over his shoulder in the traditional gesture of submission to the deity. He then genuflected nine times and offered the ritual libation of koumiss before virtually going into a cataleptic trance for seventy-two hours. On the fourth day he came down to announce that God had promised him victory.[81]

He knew very well that he was taking a great risk in invading China, for if he was badly defeated there, a kind of nuclear reaction would take place right through his empire, with all the recently conquered peoples rising up to throw off the Mongol yoke and his infant empire reduced to the insignificant tribe of his father's era.[82] Very careful preparations had been made to ensure the most efficient logistical and commissariat structures. Genghis probably set out for China with around 110,000 troops, to which he hoped to add anything from 10–20,000 Ongud auxiliaries, depending on his estimate of hostile risings in his rear.[83]

Such a force required at least 300,000 horses, all needing water and forage. Tens of thousands of sheep and cattle would accompany them to provide meat, and for transporting the effects and impedimenta of war they would use camels and ox-drawn two-wheeled carts. Even so, there would have to be careful rationing and husbanding of resources. Fortunately, the Mongols had long been inured to travelling vast distances on what for normal people would be inadequate food. Crossing the Gobi was the major obstacle, as there were limited wells and waterholes. Genghis therefore cleverly timed his offensive to avoid a shortage. He knew that during the early spring the normally exiguous water supply was greatly augmented by melting snow which collected in clay troughs and hillocks. He had already sent scouts to all parts of the Gobi and they had meticulously charted all the possible crossing routes, making special note of the best places for water and grazing.[84]

Genghis left Temuge in charge of the empire, with his Ongud son-in-law Toquchar as his second-in-command, in charge of a force of 20,000 men, with a roving brief to proceed at once to any trouble spots in the Mongol rear. He divided his army into western and eastern detachments and then subdivided the larger eastern unit so as to ease the pressure on water and food supplies. The two eastern units jumped off from the River Kerulen in March 1211. Genghis commanded the main force, with Tolui as his deputy and Muqali as his commander of the left wing. On his left and to the east was another force under Jebe, Subedei and Qasar. Muqali, a man of imposing mien and stature, an excellent archer and war planner, was already one of the 'four steeds' but was now emerging as Genghis's favourite general.[85] The westward detachment, commanded by the three princes Jochi, Chagatai and Ogodei, started from the River Tula and its target was the fortress of Chung-chou, about fifty miles north of the Yellow River at the point where it turns steeply south to complete the inverted horseshoe. This army struck due south before veering south-easterly to enter China at the extreme western edge of Ongud territory.

It must be stressed how vital was the Ongud role in the entire operation. A Turkic people, like the Kereit, Naiman and Merkit they were Nestorian Christians. Their vast territory stretched all the way from north of the Ordos loop along the line of the present-day Great Wall to the land of the Ongirrad in the east.[86] Their adherence gave Genghis easy access to the Jin empire, which would otherwise have been difficult to penetrate, protected as it was on its western side by Hsi-Hsia and the Yellow River, on the north-east by thick forests and on the east by the sea. During March and April the two armies marched along parallel lines in a south-easterly direction, about 230 miles apart, with the princes' force having to cover slightly more ground (about 530 miles as against the main force's 500). Despite the apparently huge gap between Genghis and his eldest sons, he was in constant touch with them via a relay of fast post horses; the two forces could reunite in a maximum of forty-eight hours.[87]

The princes struck into the western Gobi but encountered no opposition. At this time of the year the desert was at its most hospitable, and the spring season threw into sensuous relief the alternating habitat of yellow sand dunes, salt flats, clay ravines, saline lakes and low bushes. The princes reached Chung Chou in May and took it easily. While awaiting the expected Jin counter-attack but learning from Genghis that the enemy had as yet made no move westward, Jochi, Ogodei and Chagatai competed by sending out parties to chart the Ordos loop and the northern and eastern frontiers of Hsi-Hsia (it will be remembered that the Mongol campaign against the Tangut in 1209 had been launched from the Tula against the western part of their realm). These expeditions explored the western loess highlands directly north of the horse-shoe bend of the Huang He – an intricate landscape with 45-foot sand dunes and thin forest thickets along the water margins; the vegetation was scrub and grassland, broken up by sand dunes and belts of sand and clay, with occasional trees: wormwood, Siberian pear-trees, liquorice root plants.[88] In the Ordos Desert the Mongols were even able to supplement their food supply, for the alkaline soil allowed sheep and goats to thrive. It was also a great resource for Mongolian wild horses, wild asses, Bactrian camels and even snow leopards.[89]

Meanwhile in May the columns of Genghis and Jebe reached the Jin walls, marking the boundary of China. These fortifications have to be distinguished from the later Great Wall, which did not exist in its entirety as a continuous structure until the Ming era (i.e. after 1368). Completed around 1200, they were built to the north of Peking in two parallel lines. Since they were not linked up to form a continuous chain, the Mongols simply bypassed them. In any case, these fortifications were manned by the *juyin*, the very people who rebelled the second the Mongols invaded.[90]

Genghis began by raiding the land between these walls and the Gobi, hoping to tempt the Jin into giving battle on terrain favourable to the Mongols. But at first the much-maligned emperor Wan-yen Yung-chi boxed clever. He freed his imprisoned generals and put them in command of two large armies. He sent the army commander of the North-West to talk peace terms with Genghis, whether genuinely or simply as a stalling tactic it is difficult to tell; in any case the talks got nowhere. And he sent other commanders to strengthen the mountain fortifications leading to the most important cities in the eastern part of his realm.[91] The two Jin armies at first achieved some success and temporarily halted the threatened Mongol-Khitan alliance by discouraging major defections.

Seeing the enemy refuse to take the bait of pitched battle, Genghis decided to force the issue by penetrating deeper into Chinese territory, even if this meant fighting on the Jin's terms. His forces quickly overran the static Jin positions trying to hold a fixed line – always a chimerical project on the frontier.[92] Yet the two main Chinese armies remained intact. It quickly became clear that Jin strategy was to ignore the princes on the western frontier entirely. Their commanders' reasoning was that if the main force under Genghis himself was defeated, the princes would have to scuttle back to Mongolia immediately or risk disaster themselves. The Jin split their own forces and assigned one of the two armies to threaten the Mongol right flank; this force would also be in a position to intercept the princes in the valley of the upper Yang if they marched east.

To counter this, Genghis decided to take out the smaller army first so that there would be no menace on his flank when he engaged the larger force.[93] This task he gave to Jebe who, with Subedei, had already performed brilliantly by capturing their first two targets, the fortresses of Huan-chou and Ta-shui-luan. From the latter place Jebe marched due west, behind Genghis and cutting across his previous line of march, and came upon the smaller force, absurdly complacent and following the emperor's orders to reinforce the fortress at Wu-Sha Pao. Jebe swept down upon them like a whirlwind, took them by surprise and routed them, thus at a stroke removing the threat to Genghis's right flank. Jebe demolished the fortifications and moved on to Wei-Ning, where the governor panicked, left his post, shinned down the walls on a rope and came to offer his services to the Mongols. He was sent back to persuade the town to surrender, which it promptly did. Jebe rewarded him for this by making him a roving commissar, tasked with persuading other towns in the region to capitulate. Jebe then rejoined Genghis at Fu-chou in late August, just in time to take part in the storming of yet another fortress.[94]

Outwitted and with one army defeated, the Jin instead laid plans to lure Genghis deeper into Shanxi province. The traditional gateway from Mongolia to China was through two defiles, one the so-called Wild Fox Ridge (ten miles north-west of Chang-chia-k'ou and fifteen miles north-east of Wan-Chuan), the other called the Badger's Snout.[95] Here the general Chih-Chung, a veteran of the Song war in 1206–07, prepared his army, confident that vast numerical superiority would tell in locations where the Mongols did not have room to manoeuvre. It was true that his total forces outnumbered the Mongols almost ten to one, but the problem with Chinese armies was that non-combatants, workmen and camp followers outnumbered the actual fighting men by four to one.[96] Jurchens and Khitans largely provided the cavalry arm with Chinese peasants forming the infantry. The effective tally of the Jin host was therefore about 100,000. Chih-Chung sent an envoy to Genghis, ostensibly to parley but really to lull the Mongols by intimating a weakness he did not feel; as so often with Jin emissaries, the man instantly defected and revealed the Jin tactics.

The story goes that the details of the surprise attack planned by Chih-Chung were revealed to Genghis halfway through a meal break, and that he immediately ordered his men to stop eating and form up.[97] But Genghis was only pretending to be fooled. Advancing at dawn, he chose a spot where Jin numbers would not tell and they would have little room to manoeuvre. Chih-Chung took the bait and offered battle. Genghis relied on firepower, directing the most devastating fusillade of arrows on the Chinese ranks. Muqali then delivered a lightning attack in two waves, with Genghis's guard in the second.[98] Forced back by the sheer impetus of the charge, the Jin cavalry ended up trampling its own infantry. Soon the army dissolved into chaos, panic and rout. By noon Genghis had won a complete victory. Closely pursued by the Mongols, the Jin took terrible losses.[99] Finally, at Hui-ho Pao, thirty miles from the Badger's Snout battlefield, Chih-Chung made contact with his brother general, the one already defeated by Jebe. Together they rallied their forces and made a stand, hoping that since the Mongols had ridden so far from the Badger's Snout, they would be exhausted and thus easy pickings. Alas for their hopes, they were once again heavily defeated. Chih-Chiung fled with the survivors to the Sang-Kan River, where he was joined by a strong force of Jurchen horsemen. Next morning this combined force made another stand and gave a good account of themselves in a battle that lasted all day.[100] Finally the Jin cracked and fled, the Mongols once again hard on their heels. Chih-Chung, unaccustomed to this kind of warfare, where a victorious enemy did not stop to enjoy the spoils but pressed on with the goal of total annihilation, became both enraged and paranoid, convinced by now that the emperor had not given him enough support. When he reached Lai-Shui Hsien he had the town magistrate flogged in a fit of frustrated rage. Getting fresh horses, he rode on into the wilderness, with the Mongols still dogging him. By now he was convinced he was on his own, and decided that thenceforth he would take orders from no one and fight on as a guerrilla chief.[101]

The three pitched battles fought in September 1211 destroyed the Jin as a credible battlefield force; henceforth they would fight a war of attrition. It is difficult to convey the extent of the Chinese losses, but nine years later travellers reported the fields of carnage still covered with bleached bones.[102] The worst aspect of the triple defeat for the Jin was that it encouraged widespread revolt. In this respect the conduct of the Jin envoy sent to Genghis was typical. Held in the Mongol camp until after the first battle, he then confided to Genghis that he had always wanted to join the Mongols and volunteering for the dangerous task of emissary was the only way he could think of to achieve this end.[103]

At the imperial court Chih-Chung was widely blamed for the debacle. It was said that he was too timid, that he should have attacked the Mongols with cavalry alone much earlier while they were still pillaging, but that he insisted on fighting with both cavalry and infantry on the field. The victory at Hui-ho Pao delivered not just the eponymous town but a string of others: T'ien Ch'eng, Hsuan-Ping, Pai-teng Ch'eng, Te-Hsing Chou. Such was Mongol confidence that they even made an attack on Hsi-Ching (modern Datong) from the rear, though this was unsuccessful.[104] Even so, the Mongols were in possession of two of the three strongest cities in the north. Finally Genghis ordered Jebe to take Chu-yung chuan, a fortified pass at the southern end of which was Nankou, just twenty-five miles from Peking (then called Zhongdu or Chung-Tu).[105]

Jebe found the town much too strong to be taken by assault so played the time-honoured Mongol card: the feigned retreat. All along the fifteen-mile pass were fortresses perched on steep slopes. At news of Jebe's retreat they all sallied out, eager to be in at the kill. Jebe led them on a wild-goose chase for thirty-five miles, stretching them out so that the various detachments of pursuers lost touch with each other. Then he turned and demolished them piecemeal, spreading a contagious panic that in the end led the defenders of Chu-yung chuan to surrender meekly to the Mongols. As one unit was attacked, the

Jin would send reinforcements which in turn were eaten up. It was said that the corpses piled up like felled trees.[106]

Early in November Genghis and the main army marched down the pass and pitched camp twenty miles from Peking, accepting as he went the surrender of three other important fortresses (Wei Ch'uan, Chin-shan, Ch'ang-ping) which had all given up the ghost after the fall of Chu-yung chuan. He sent Jebe ahead to probe the defences of Peking itself. As a final cap to his great triumphs of 1211 he received word that Yelu Ahai had put the result of any future pitched battles beyond doubt. In a daring raid Yelu seized the imperial stud and its horses and pastures, hobbling the Jin cavalry arm beyond hope of recovery. The raid also provided the Mongols with tens of thousands of fresh mounts, used to Chinese conditions. This was particularly important as the soil of China largely lacked the selenium Mongol steeds needed.[107]

Meanwhile the emperor Wei Shao Wang was almost catatonic with mixed rage and depression as the litany of defeats was chanted to him daily. He put Peking under martial law and forbade all men of military age to leave the city under pain of death. His own inclination was to depart for the southern capital of Kaifeng, but the commander of the Imperial Guard persuaded him to stay, after promising that the Guard would fight to the last man. This was proved to be more than hot air when 5,000 of them repelled Jebe's vanguard when they appeared outside the city. The repulse earned the emperor a reprieve, for Genghis concluded that an attack on Peking would be premature and recalled Jebe.[108]

The emperor was right to be despondent, for 1211 was the only year in which the Jin could have defeated the Mongols, but he had himself to blame for the inept response to the threat from the north. So incredulous was he at the Mongol invasion that he did not even bother to call out the militia.[109] In little more than six months he had massively lost credibility. His advisers whispered behind his back, remembering how he had claimed the Mongols were so exhausted by their war against the Tangut that they could easily be rolled up. Another of his boasts that came back to haunt him was allegedly contained in a letter to Genghis: 'Our empire is like the sea; yours is but a handful of sand.'[110] His counsellors piled on the agony, reminding him of the physical hardihood of the Mongols, how they could cook without fires, go for days without food, mobilise and coordinate magically, as if they had just one brain like an ant colony.[111]

To make matters worse, the Tangut were so disgusted by Wei Shao Wang's rejection of their plea for help at the time of their own invasion by the Mongols that they raided Jin China in September 1210 and remained in a state of war with them until 1225. Moreover, no great military talent had emerged from the Jin, whereas the Mongols possessed at least three captains of genius – Muqali, Jebe and Subedei – and younger commanders were making a name for themselves: the Tangut Chaghan, Genghis's adopted son; and the two Khitan brothers, Yelu Ahai and Tuka.[112]

It soon became clear that the Jin reputation for military talent was largely built on their victories over the Song, not primarily a martial nation. And even apart from his prowess on the battlefield, Genghis had outpointed the Jin emperor at every level. His superior skill in exploiting the national, social and religious rifts in the enemy ranks was just one example, another being the generous treatment he gave defectors, unless they had broken a personal oath to a lord. On the other hand, although pitched battles were invariably lost, the war itself might still be won by the Jin. The Mongols lacked the manpower to garrison all the fortresses they took, they were anyway deficient in siegecraft, and even Genghis's usual policy of wholesale massacre – slaughtering everyone, soldiers, civilians, prisoners – made little impact as the population of China was so enormous.[113] When the Mongols withdrew for a winter break in December 1211, staggering back to Mongolia laden with booty, the Jin promptly regained most of the fallen fortresses.

If 1211 had been a year of unalloyed triumph for the Mongols, 1212 was anticlimactic. It began well. Liu Po-lin, the governor who had quit his post earlier by rope ladder, had by this time inveigled for himself a post as one of Genghis's key advisers. He cleverly suggested a campaign in the far north-east, in Manchuria, in hopes of igniting a general Khitan rebellion; the specific target would be the capture of the city of Liaoyang. This was more than two hundred miles farther east than the Mongols were currently operating. Although Genghis's favourite fighting general and battlefield tactician was Muqali, it was to Jebe that he always turned if he needed a daring long-distance raid. He issued the necessary orders. Jebe set off north of Peking in

December 1211, advanced north-east up the coast, crossed the Liao river on ice and arrived outside Liaoyang in January 1212.[114]

Finding the city heavily defended, he feigned panicky flight and left his baggage behind. Sensing a famous victory, the defenders of Liaoyang came out, initially to loot, then to pursue. Jebe left a deceptive trail, which led the Jin scouts to report back that the fleeing Mongols were about a hundred miles ahead (six days' march) heading for Peking. Liaoyang gave itself over to celebration but Jebe, taking advantage of the long winter nights, rode back in twenty-four hours, and swept into Liaoyang before any resistance could be organised.[115] There followed the usual slaughter and thoroughgoing sack of the city, after which Jebe and his men made a leisurely return to the environs of Peking.

As soon as he was safely back, Genghis ordered a withdrawal of all units around Peking and a general pullback to the Jin walls, leaving behind just enough men to guard the principal passes from Mongolia to China.[116] He needed to rest his cavalry and ponder the next step, yet still required an unceasing momentum in China. He therefore ordered the princes to open up their campaign in the west. The trio of Ogodei, Jochi and Chagatai sprang into action. Avoiding the dangerous passes south of the plain of Feng Chou, they swung south, then east to the Hung-ta River, where they divided. One detachment went south to besiege Ning-Pien while the main body went upriver and seized the pass of Sha-hu H'ou, from which they took the cities of Shuo-ping and Hsuan-ning, close to Datong. The princes then reunited for a march through Shaanxi province.[117]

For this enterprise Mongol versatility was needed, as this province was bewilderingly heterogeneous. In the north were portions of the Loess Plateau and the Ordos Desert, in the centre the Qin-ling Mountains bisected the province east–west, while in the south the climate was subtropical; with a large span in latitude Shaanxi accordingly boasted a wide range of microclimates. Here were plenty of the animals the Mongols knew well – deer, antelope, camels, snow leopards – and some that were new to them, such as the giant panda and the snub-nosed monkey.[118]

Genghis meanwhile withdrew to recuperate at Lake Hulun, on the extreme edge of Ongud territory. The Ongud alliance was proving shaky. In the short time Genghis had been in China, there had been

an anti-Mongol coup complete with the assassination of two key
Genghis supporters. When Genghis returned to the land of the Ongud
in early 1212, the putschists fled west to the Ordos. Untypically, he did
not choose to pursue them but the Jin did his work for him by appre-
hending the conspirators' ringleader and executing him. It seems
curious that they should have beheaded an anti-Mongol figure, and
scholars speculate that there must have been some idea of winning
over the pro-Mongol faction to their side. But the Jin spoiled their
case by insisting that their sovereignty over the Ongud be retained
and recognised; this annoyed the waverers and decided them to stick
with the Mongols.[119]

With just the princes now actively campaigning on Chinese soil,
this might have seemed the ideal time for the Jin to recoup their losses,
and they did indeed reoccupy most of the fortresses which had fallen
in 1211. Yet two prime factors prevented them from securing any real
advantage from Genghis's temporary withdrawal. In April 1212
northern China was ravaged by one of the worst famines yet – obviously a 'knock-on' effect of the previous year's devastation. The Tangut
chose this moment to launch another raid on the Jin. In the same
month a seismic revolt of the Khitans took place in Manchuria, headed
by Yelu Liuke, who proclaimed himself king of an independent Khitan
realm.

Scholars dispute the origins of this insurrection. Some say it was
a manifestation owing little to the Mongols, that the Jin provoked it
by sending an army of occupation to Manchuria to intimidate the
Khitans, and that the heavy-handedness of the Chinese general triggered a spontaneous uprising.[120] Others, more plausibly, claim that
Genghis's long game with the Khitans finally paid off, and that one
of the aims of Jebe's incursion into Manchuria was to encourage just
such a rebellion.[121]

Separated from Mongolia by the Khingan Mountains in the north
and the Jehol range in the south (in the gap between them the great
Asian steppe rolls on), thirteenth-century Manchuria was divided into
four distinct zones: the sinicised Lower Liao River, important for
agriculture; the gap between the two mountain ranges, home to
pastoral nomads; the dense forests bordering Korea and Siberia inhab-
ited by villagers running a mixed economy of agriculture and stockbreeding (including pigs – an animal never found among pastoral

nomads); and the community of fishermen and hunters in the far north. Despite the severe winters, it was a rich and populous, multi-cultural land.[122] The Khitan revolt opened the prospect of installing a Mongol vassal there who would relieve them of the need to conduct sustained campaigns of conquest against bitter resistance, as in Jin China. To rule such a land Genghis needed a strong man who could amalgamate the various cultures, and Yelu seemed to fit the bill. To detach this enormous territory from the Jurchens would be a lethal blow to the Jin empire. Its importance can be gauged by just one fact: immediately before Yelu's revolt the Jin brought a reinforcement of 20,000 cavalry from Manchuria to shore up the defences of Peking.[123]

Not surprisingly, the Jin were not prepared to take the loss of Manchuria lying down and immediately dispatched a strong army against Yelu. Encouraged by his earlier contacts with Jebe, Yelu appealed to Genghis for help. To show the importance of the alliance he contemplated, Genghis sent Shigi Qutuqu on an embassy, together with Anchar Noyan, the younger brother of Borte. The story goes that the two Mongol envoys virtually collided with Yelu on the road somewhere in the vicinity of modern Changchun in central Manchuria. Yelu pledged that he would be a loyal ally of the Mongols and largely kept his word. He told the envoys that the Jin had certainly received their last cavalry reinforcement from Manchuria but stressed the need for Mongol assistance, especially since Manchuria was so difficult to mobilise, with the northern hunting and fishing tribes such as the Solons largely apathetic.[124] Anchar secured from Genghis a small force of 3,000 but, together with the Khitans, this was easily enough to rout the Jin army. After the victory Yelu, a good politician, shrewdly sent the enemy's baggage and effects to Genghis who, delighted with the gesture, gave Yelu the title of Liao Wang (prince of Liao).[125]

In the early autumn Genghis returned to China and resumed his campaign, certain that the Jin would be weakened by the widespread famine, and especially that of June 1212 in the provinces of Shanxi and Shaanxi. This time his aim was twofold: to link with his three sons in the west and take Datong, and to achieve permanent occupation of the area in the extreme north of China just inside the Jin walls. Genghis had chafed at the 'waste' of manpower involved in this latter operation but it was, objectively, an advance in sophistication and probably owed much to the advice of clever renegades like Liu Po-lin.

The 'intramural' operation was to be directed by Tolui, assisted by Genghis's adopted son Chaghan.[126] Genghis himself, accompanied by Liu Po-lin and another wily defector named Kuo Pao-yu, turned west and, in coordination with the three older princes, converged on the still defiant Datong. This time Genghis was confident, for defectors had revealed to him many of the secrets of siegecraft, and his artillery park had all the latest mangonels and trebuchets. In October the siege began. A relieving force under a 'new blood' young general tried to take him in the flank but was lured into a narrow valley by a feigned retreat and slaughtered mercilessly.[127] Returning to the siege, Genghis was hit by an arrow shot from the walls and severely wounded. He broke off the siege and the army retreated north.[128]

Meanwhile Tolui had defeated a small force of 3,000 Jin and taken the city of Te-Hsing Chou with great difficulty, then abandoned it to join his father, whereupon the Jin reoccupied it. With both armies having failed to match the brilliant achievements of the year before, the campaign of 1212 was a disappointment, but the wounding of Genghis probably accounted for much of the failure. The only true positive for the Mongols was that they were slowly mastering siege-craft, and the Jin failure outside Datong meant that even the most sanguine among them largely abandoned the idea of confronting the Mongols in pitched battles.[129]

Even if the relatively dim showing of the Mongols that year gave the Jin some hope, at least three major factors militated against optim-ism. The realm continued to be racked by famine, with vast quantities of food having to be sent from Kaifeng and the lower Yellow River to the northern provinces; as a result of the Mongol incursion Shaanxi even suffered a second grievous famine. By now manpower shortages were becoming so acute that hardened criminals were being pardoned and released from jail on condition that they served in the army. There were more and more rebellions in the empire, and not just that of Yelu, who had so grown in confidence by the end of the year that he declared himself emperor Liao Wang; the Tangut had invaded both Gansu and Shaanxi provinces and captured a number of towns.[130]

After a long winter rest at the Dolon Nor oasis just north of the Jin walls, Genghis returned to China in 1213 for his third campaign. He invested the city of Te-Hsing and took it in less than a month. Muqali took the Jin's northern capital after a forty-day siege. The Jin seemed unable to accept the obvious, that they could never defeat the Mongols on a formal battlefield, for they once again tried their luck against the cream of the Mongol army. At Wei Chu'an they sustained another sanguinary defeat. The Jin drew up in their usual manner, infantry in the centre, cavalry on the wings. The Mongol mounted bowmen duly devastated the infantry with an arrow shower, which decimated the conscript army, formed of reluctant peasants. Finding the enemy centre still not inclined to buckle, Genghis ordered a massed charge. Forced to withdraw under the impact of this thunderbolt, the Jin reached more open ground where Tolui was able to take it in the flanks. On both sides the Mongol cavalry worked their way along ridges above the valley before descending on the rear and flanks, having 'appeared from nowhere'. It was said that the bones of the slain formed a white eminence which looked like a hill of snow, and that the ground was greasy and slippery with human fat.[131]

Yet even after this signal triumph Genghis was held up for a month by a stubborn defence at the Chu-yung chuan pass. He turned to his master of such situations, Jebe. A force under Jebe went up the Sang-Kan River and found another pass that would leave the Jin at the Chu-yung chuan high and dry. Genghis then left a solid force to bottle up the defenders of the latter while he hastened to join Jebe. The Jin commander tried to get an army between Jebe and Genghis, but in vain. He arrived to find Jebe and Genghis united, the new pass under their control, and the Mongol army drawn up ready for battle. At sight of this most of the Jin soldiers turned and fled without even making a token effort at hostilities. Genghis then proceeded to take the city of I-chou, and sent Jebe and Subedei by forced marches through the other entrance of the Chu-yung chuan so that they came upon the enemy from the southern end. Caught between those who were bottling them up and this new menace, the starving Jin defenders surrendered.[132]

All these battles and manoeuvres had taken time, so that it was the beginning of November 1213 before Genghis arrived before Cho-chou, some miles south of Peking. He sent a force of 5,000 men to guard all the approaches to Peking and left the siege to Muqali. Yet he was disappointed in the stubborn defiance of the Jin. He sent a Tangut envoy to the emperor outlining peace terms, but these were summarily rejected.

Many of the emperor's advisers thought his intransigence unwise, as it simply led more and more despairing generals and officials to defect to the Mongols. Already forty-six brigades of deserters had been enrolled in Genghis's army.[133] Jin China was rapidly descending into chaos. Countless bands of brigands, cut-throat bandits and self-defence groups arose from the maelstrom, setting themselves up as petty princelings, seizing grain, silk, gold, weapons, women and young boys (as slaves), expropriating houses and property and even taking over whole villages.[134]

While this was going on, dramatic events were taking place in Peking. The irrepressible Chih-Chung, tired of living on the scant pickings of a guerrilla leader, somehow got himself restored to favour with the emperor, was promoted to Vice-Commander of the Empire and given his own praetorian guard of 5,000 men. All this simply increased the arrogance of the never humble Chih, 'an irascible ruffian' in the words of one historian.[135] The emperor had given him these privileges on the strict understanding that he had to remain in the city, but Chih-Chung was determined to show that he and not the emperor was the real power in the land. When an angry emperor sent a messenger to summon him back and give an account of himself, the Vice-Commander simply ignored the summons. He followed this up by luring the city garrison commander for talks and murdering him, 'justifying' the atrocity by claiming that the dead commander had been planning a coup.[136]

His next exploit was breathtakingly audacious. He arrived with his cohorts outside the gates of Peking, claiming that the Mongols were close on his heels. When the guards opened the gates to admit him, his men slew them and proceeded to butcher the imperial guards. After seizing the emperor, on 11 September 1213 Chih-Chung proclaimed himself Regent of the Empire. The very same day he had the emperor murdered. Wei Shao Wang, former Prince of Wei, the seventh of ten Jin emperors and the third to be assassinated, was just forty-five.[137] In his place Chih-Chung appointed a figurehead emperor Hsuan Tsung (reigned 1213–1223) but treated him with contempt and pointedly remained seated in his presence.

At first Chih-Chung seemed to live up to his own propaganda as China's saviour. In November he defeated a Mongol force outside Peking – a feat all the more remarkable as, very ill, he directed operations from a bed placed on a cart. The Mongols returned to the fray next day and again Chih-Chung was victorious, this time very narrowly. He knew little of Genghis, for in such circumstances the khan was notorious for pressing on until he got the result he wanted. Presumably the first two encounters had not featured his best generals, for on the third day the Mongols won a total and overwhelming victory.[138] Chih-Chung, still ill, had sent out a deputy (general Kao Chi) to fight and had threatened him with death if he lost a battle. The menaced general thought quickly, hurried back to Peking before the news of his defeat reached the city, entered the imperial palace with a picked body of men and marked down his tormentor for destruction. Chih-Chung, surprised in his apartment, tried to escape by climbing over a wall, fell and was badly injured. He was scooped up and immediately beheaded. For a day or two civil war loomed, with Chih-Chung's praetorians angry at being ousted from supreme power. In a surprisingly Solomonic solution the emperor bought them off, pardoned Kao Chi and made him the new Vice-Commander.[139]

With defeats and desertions on all sides, emperor Hsuan Tsung petitioned for peace but included so many qualifications, caveats and escape clauses in his proposals that Genghis rejected the suit contemptuously. He was now convinced that the only way to bring the emperor to heel and face the reality of his situation was a campaign of destruction all the way down to the southern frontier and the lower Yellow River. Leaving 5,000 men to patrol the roads to Peking, he divided his army into four separate forces. Ogodei, Chagatai and Jochi, with Liu Po-lin as guide and political commissar, were to overrun Shanxi province and western Hebei.[140] Qasar, Anchar, with Jurchedei, Bukha of the Ongirrad and Tolub Cherbi as subsidiary commanders, would lay waste the territory between Peking and the Bohai Sea. To his three ace commanders – Muqali, Jebe, Subedei – was assigned the task of the conquest and destruction of eastern Hebei and Shandong provinces. He and Tolui intended to cut a swathe right through the Jin empire to the Yellow River.[141] The campaign of terror thus unleashed would make clear to everyone in north China that they should no longer hope for anything from the Jin emperor. Genghis (correctly) intuited that the Jin were so demoralised that they would remain on the defensive and not try to concentrate all their force against any one of these columns. The Jin had 36,000 armed men inside Peking but they suspected another of Genghis's famous traps – that if they ventured forth against one of these forces, at least one of the others would take them in the flank.

The simplest of these tasks fell to Qasar. After proceeding south-east to Yung-Ping (on the Bohai Sea), he then struck north-east to the Liao River, following Jebe's route a year earlier, and penetrated deep into Manchuria, following, first, the north-easterly course of the Sunggari (Songhua) River, the largest tributary of the mighty Amur. The Sunggari, a meandering stream with myriad oxbow lakes on either bank, was frozen at this time of year. Next he went down the River Nen, the principal tributary of the Sunggari, and followed it due north through the greater and lesser Khingan ranges.[142] Everywhere he went he destroyed Jin towns and fortifications and slaughtered all who remained loyal to the regime. The particular prizes they netted were Chi-chou (modern Ji Xian) east of Peking and I-chou, north-east of modern Jinzhou in southern Manchuria.[143]

The purpose of this epic ride was to show the flag and encourage Yelu and the Khitans to stand firm, but its curiosity was that Genghis had already assigned Manchuria to Qasar, so that he was in effect sending his brother to conquer his own appanage. In any case, this point remained academic, for Qasar died just after the expedition in circumstances not made clear in the sources.[144] There is, however, something of a mystery about Qasar's Manchurian exploits, for he made many claims for which the evidence is tenuous, to say the least. He was said to have plunged into the River Sunggari on his horse when it was in full flood, despite the fact that it was known to be frozen at this season.[145] He was also supposed to have reduced Ning-Chiang on the eastern bank of the river by asking for 10,000 swallows and one thousand cats, tying lighted wool to their tails and then catapulting them over the battlements where they set fire to the town. Unfortunately this is a very old story that goes back in history at least as far as the Vikings, for a similar story is told in the Icelandic saga the *Heimskringla*. The Moors in their wars in Spain were also said to have tied firebrands to the tails of bulls before stampeding them into the enemy. The ultimate source for all such fables seems to have been the biblical tale of Samson tying firebrands to foxes' tails.[146] Nevertheless, the submission of the Solon tribe to him in the Tao-Erh valley is solidly based in history.[147]

Muqali was given senior command over Jebe and Subedei in the laying waste of Shandong province, once again evincing Genghis's particular regard for him. A peninsula that juts out between the Bohai Sea to the north and the Yellow Sea to the south, 250 miles from north to south and 450 miles east–west, the province is geographically and climatically intricate, with plains, basins, hills, terraces, deltas and even a mountain increasing the complexity. The north and south of the province sinks down to the Yellow River delta, scarcely above sea level (the river has changed course often in history, sometimes debouching to the north of the peninsula, at other times to the south), but the central part of the province, including much of the peninsula, is hilly upland, rising to the 5,000-foot-high Mount Tai in the west. Well apprised as always of all relevant factors, Genghis had avoided the hot, rainy summer monsoon season and sent Muqali there during the long, cool winter, ideal for campaigning. He told him to concentrate on the northern part of the peninsula as he hoped himself to be campaigning in the Yellow River delta.[148] It was reported that Muqali destroyed all the fields of cotton, wheat, maize and sorghum he could find, obedient to the khan's orders. Genghis's attitude was that if the Chinese emperor was prepared to allow his own people to suffer simply to save his own face and assuage his pride, he would make it clear to the Chinese people just how high that price was.

Muqali also destroyed Teng-chou (modern Penglai), famous for its wine, and Cheng-Ching, known for its art treasures and in every respect a beautiful city, full of lakes, parks, silk factories and lotus flowers, also a notable centre of Buddhism.[149] It is also related that he was the first Mongol commander to see the Yellow Sea.

The princes enjoyed the second most spectacular campaign of 1213–14. They raided down the left bank of the Yellow River through Pao-ting and La-an, then turned west at Hua-Ching where the Huang He is joined by its second largest tributary the Fen (about 430 miles long) and almost immediately north into the valley of the Fen. Towns that fell included Ping-yang, Fen-chou and Taiyuan, the wealthy capital of Shanxi province and an important centre for wine-growing and metallurgy; it seems that the inhabitants were taken completely by surprise, since they had the fixed idea that any Mongol army would have to approach them from the north, not the south.[150] Reaching the head of the Fen they proceeded north and sacked the cities of Tai-Chou and Ta-t'ung (Datong). Other important towns

and strongholds that fell to the trio of Ogodei, Jochi and Chagatai
were Zhengding, Zhaoxian, Tung-ping and Shanqixian. Both Genghis
and the princes habitually used prisoners to form the front ranks of
their army and act as battering rams, so as to bear the brunt of the
casualties. Often the defenders would recognise their relatives among
the attackers, refuse to fight them and thus hand the Mongols an
easy victory. Groaning under a mountain of plunder, the princes'
army rejoined Muqali's host and Genghis and Tolui outside Peking
in March 1214.[151]

Genghis and Tolui, in the fourth and largest army, marched almost
due south through Hebei and Shanxi provinces directly to the Yellow
River and came within hailing distance of the southern Jin capital of
Kaifeng. They took Ho-chien but bypassed Chi-nan and Ta-ming on
the grounds that these were in Muqali's territory; Jin propaganda said
they were too strong for Genghis, but Muqali, as we have seen, had
no difficulty in taking Cheng-Ching. The overlapping of Muqali's and
Genghis's army in the Shandong peninsula, on the other hand, seems
odd and it may be, as some chroniclers have related, that Genghis
wanted to see the sea for the first time – which he accomplished by
riding down to the shore at Teng-chou at the north-western end of
the peninsula.[152]

Genghis's army then proceeded south to the Yellow River, sacking
and looting, destroying every village, town and unfortified city he
came to, wantonly destroying the crops of rice, millet, sorghum and
maize and all the vineyards, either through ignorance of the value of
agriculture or, more likely, as part of a scorched-earth policy. With
far fewer rivers on the great northern plain of China than elsewhere
in the country, travel by horse was easier. It was said that on this long
300-mile ride Genghis and his horsemen took eighty-six towns, sacked
them all and left only nine cities uncaptured in the entire area north
of the Yellow River. Seven major cities, each with a population of
more than 100,000 had been captured.[153] This – if nothing else – testi-
fies to their dramatically increasing sophistication as regards walled
cities and siegecraft.[154] On this epic adventure the Mongols also saw,
usually at a distance, a plethora of wildlife, including a number of
species new to them: the red-crowned crane, great bustard, the golden
eagle, the sea eagle, the white stork and black stork, yellow weasel
and sika deer, as well as the more familiar tigers, otters, martens,

civets, wild boar, foxes, badgers, hares, pheasants, partridges and vultures.[155]

The campaign was notable for lightning strikes and amazing Mongol mobility. Genghis shrewdly bypassed difficult targets like modern Linfen and Taiyuan in Shanxi and concentrated on easier objectives, thereby spreading a reputation for invincibility.[156] By the end of a complex campaign with four separate armies, Genghis and his horsemen had criss-crossed the entire Jin empire in three months. As one historian put it: 'Everywhere north of the Yellow River there could be seen dust and smoke, and the sound of drums rose to heaven.'[157] By the time Genghis reunited with Muqali and his sons north of Peking, they were using vast numbers of captured horses and oxen to drag enormous wagons laden with booty, especially bolts of silk, as well as thousands of young prisoners of both sexes.[158] While maintaining his grip on Peking, Genghis again withdrew for rest and recreation to the Dolon Nor oasis, but not before sending Muqali on another mission.

This time Muqali was sent to an entirely new region, the Liaodong peninsula between the Bohai Sea and Korea Bay, to reinforce the Mongol grip on Manchuria, to stiffen the revolt of Yelu and the Khitans and to build on the work done by Qasar, with whom he had collaborated successfully earlier. He had many talented lieutenants with him (Bukha, Uyer and Shih T'ien-hsiang) but, sadly for him, not his favourite Shih T'ien-ni, whose father had defected to Genghis in 1213 with several thousand men. Intensely loyal to Muqali, he had raised his own regiment of defectors to help his patron. Shih T'ien-ni fell foul of the inveterate plotter general Wu Hsien who, while outwardly submitting to the Mongols, was secretly plotting against them. Shih T'ien-ni snuffed out Wu Hsien's would-be coup and exposed his treachery. Determined on revenge, Wu Hsien actually went to the trouble of inviting his nemesis to a banquet, behaved with scrupulous politeness, then had him ambushed and murdered on his way home.[159]

Muqali swept through the hilly and forested region of the Liaodong peninsula (modern Liaoning province) as far as the Yalu River, the border with Korea. By this time Muqali was used to oceanic vistas, as the peninsula contains 1,300 miles of coastline (about 12 per cent of the Chinese total).[160] In November 1214 he sacked the principal town, Kao Chou, in the north of the province, noting for his report to Genghis that the Liao and the Jin had made his work easier by their massive programmes of deforestation over the previous two centuries.[161] Next he sent Shih T'ien-hsiang to strike due west at the important city of Pei Ching (modern Chifeng) and lay waste all the countryside in a fifty-mile radius; this task was completed by January 1215.

After completing his work on the Liaodong peninsula, Muqali marched north-east, then swung west to join Shih T'ien-hsiang, who had reported Pei Cheng as a very hard nut to crack. Muqali reconnoitred from the south and reunited with Shih, but was forced to agree that even with their combined forces they would waste too much time on a siege of that city. But their presence near Pei Cheng was timely, for the Jin had decided on one last effort in the north and sent an army of 20,000 under general Ing-Sing. Muqali defeated this host at Qoto in March 1215 with great slaughter; 8,000 Chinese troops were left dead on the battleground.[162] The Jin forthwith definitively abandoned their territories in the far north.

Muqali now considered catching up with Qasar, but the mounted relays that operated between them indicated that Qasar had already departed from the Nen River on his homeward journey to Mongolia. Qasar continued up the upper reaches of the Tao-Erh River, over the Khingan Mountains to Khalka Lake and thence to the Kerulen, completing his epic thousand-mile journey in January 1215.[163] Both Qasar and Muqali reported to Genghis that Yelu and the Khitans remained totally loyal, which gratified the khan immensely.[164]

Genghis, always sensitive to heat, withdrew to the Dolon Nor oasis for the summer of 1214 but left Peking tightly bottled up by his armies and to this end retained possession of the 'Chou towns' that encircled the capital (I-chou, Cho-chou, Pa-chou, Chi-chou) and of all important passes whereby the emperor could receive reinforcements. Genghis tried to encourage the emperor to make peace in April, stressing that though his generals were bloodthirsty he wanted a peaceful solution, but talks immediately foundered on the Mongol insistence that Hsuan Tsung relinquish the title of emperor and accept demotion to the level of king.[165] Genghis sent back the following message: 'The whole of Shandong and Hebei is my possession while you have only Peking. God has made you so weak that, were I to molest you further, I don't know what Heaven would say. I am willing to withdraw my army but you must give me something to quell the clamourings of my generals.'[166] He put a trusted counsellor Ja'afur in charge of further negotiations.

An agonised debate took place within the Heavenly City between 'hawks' and 'doves'. The doves' favourite idea was that the emperor should agree a peace and then move his court to Manchuria, where they could mobilise the old tribal loyalties of the Jurchens. It was a measure of the sinicisation of the Jin that this idea was dismissed out of hand. The hawks alleged that the Mongols were exhausted and weakened by disease, so that this was the perfect time to attack. The commander of the Peking garrison, however, tipped the scales by stressing that the morale of his troops was low and their loyalty uncertain: 'If defeated, they will fly like birds and animals; if victorious, they will at once return home to their families, and who will then guard the capital?'[167]

Even as the emperor and his courtiers dithered, word came in that the Song had announced they would no longer pay the tribute agreed in the 1208 treaty. The Song, as prevaricating as their old Jin enemies, could not quite decide whether to ally themselves with the Mongols or join the Jin in fighting Genghis Khan. They 'solved' the dilemma by simply opting out of their treaty commitments.[168]

After hearing this, the emperor reluctantly consented to agree peace terms. These were steep: his daughter was to be given in marriage to Genghis and she would have five hundred youths and maidens for her retinue; as war reparations the Jin would pay 3,000 horses, 100,000 gold bars and 300,000 yards of silk; moreover, the emperor must release a number of named political prisoners, relatives of the important Khitan officials who had defected to the Mongols.[169] It was a one-sided peace, for the Mongol princes were even then taking more towns in Shanxi province. But Genghis did at least end the tight investment of Peking by his armies, though he kept all routes in and out of the city blocked. Probably both sides regarded the peace as no more than a truce. The future was uncertain, but the Jin empire had been conclusively humbled, and by the military genius of a man who twenty years earlier was an obscure nomad.[170]

8

The Conquest of Northern China

The truce did not last long, as many on both sides had suspected would be the case. Scarcely had he ratified the paperwork than emperor Hsuan Tsung, tired of the vulnerability of Peking, decided to transfer his headquarters to Kaifeng in the south (June 1214). The members of his council in favour of the move argued that it was easier to defend than Peking, as its perimeter was said to stretch for 120 miles, with strong rampart walls and a series of moats interspersed with gardens and orchards.[1] This was the final stage in the process of Jurchen sinicisation, and it meant abandoning Inner Mongolia and Manchuria. It was said that the imperial counsellor Tu Chan'i, the most important representative of the 'old' Jurchens (and the man who had urged the emperor to relocate north to Liaoyang) died of a broken heart when he heard the news. With Hsuan Tsung went the supreme commander Kao Chi, but the prince imperial stayed behind in an attempt to rebut the canard that his father was simply running away; his military advisers were also left behind.[2]

Hsuan Tsung's motives may be variously identified; they include a hatred of the north, with its numerous Khitans; his fear that his power base was as insecure as his predecessor, the former Prince of Wei's had been (after all he had come to power by a coup and could be displaced by a coup); and a cynical analysis that the territory north of the Yellow River was more trouble than it was worth, whereas the Huang He delta, rich in crops and revenues, was the truly valuable heart of empire. As a pathetic sop to the people he was abandoning, the emperor announced an amnesty for all rebels.[3]

The two left behind did their best, made a heroic effort in the north and even recaptured Liaoyang only to lose it very shortly afterwards. In any case, the move south was attended by a number of bad omens.

An enormous convoy departed the Heavenly City in July on a two-month journey: 30,000 carts were filled with court documents and there were 3,000 camels in the cavalcade, all laden with treasure. About thirty miles south of Peking the emperor's paranoia finally got the better of him, and he peremptorily ordered the 2,000 Khitans in the imperial guard to return to Peking on foot, their horses confiscated by the Guard commander, as he could not rely on their loyalty. The Khitans promptly mutinied and, when the other Guard members were ordered to disarm them, trounced them in an impromptu battle. They then rode back to Peking, seized more horses outside the city gates and rode on north, meanwhile sending an offer of submission and service to Genghis Khan. Such was the result of the emperor's ham-fisted attempt to unhorse them.[4]

In Peking itself the emperor's flight was taken as desertion and simply increased the already river-like flow of defections to the Mongols. When Genghis heard of the move to Kaifeng, he was angry, claiming that Hsuan Tsung had deceived him and this was a breach of the truce conditions. He then resumed hostilities, to the joy of the hardliners in his council such as Subedei, who argued that without permanent warfare the Jin would gradually recover all the cities and territories they had lost. Officially Genghis used as his *casus belli* the continuing refusal of the Jin to allow his envoys to the Song free passage.[5] He sent Muqali to the north to keep the Khitan revolt there at white heat; Muqali performed brilliantly as usual and retook Liaoyang.[6]

The Jin position in Manchuria was very soon hopeless. A telling incident was the story of general Pu-hsien Wan-nu who was sent to the Jurchen homeland in 1214. When his expedition failed totally, Wan-nu decided he would not return to Peking – where there was a fondness for executing unsuccessful generals on the grounds that they 'must be' in league with Genghis Khan – but would set up his own kingdom. In spring 1215 he declared himself king of Ta-Chen and insisted that, since the emperor had fled south, he and only he was the legitimate heir of the crumbling Jin realm. He appointed as his vizier a semi-charlatan named Wang Kuei, a Taoist who doubled as fortune teller and interpreter of the *I Ching*.[7] The decay of the Jin empire was producing tragedy and farce simultaneously.

Genghis gave the command of the siege of Peking to Samuqa of the Saljiut tribe, yet another rising military star. Unusually combining flair with caution, Samuqa concluded that the assaults on Peking in the early months of 1214, when snow was thick on the ground, had smacked of overconfidence and underestimation of a very tough enemy. In those early assaults the Mongols had twice broken into Peking only to be beaten back. On the most disappointing occasion, the attackers had suffered heavy losses when they penetrated into the outer city but then found themselves cut off when the street they entered was set on fire behind them.[8]

Samuqa analysed the problems involved in a capture of Peking. Medieval Zhongdu (Chung-Tu) occupied the site of the southern section of modern Peking, but had a fortified perimeter of thirty miles, with twelve gates, forty-foot high walls of baked clay topped by crenelated brick battlements and 900 battle towers, three concentric moats and, most baffling of all, four smaller fortress cities outside the city walls but linked to the metropolis by a system of underground tunnels. Each of these was one mile square, had two gates, was fortified with towers and moats and contained a granary, arsenal and treasury of its own. One of the problems for a Mongol force penetrating the inner city, where they would then face another walled palace complex in its centre, was their vulnerability to attack from one or more of the forces in these four towns.[9]

The sheer size of China's population was another problem for, no matter how many the Mongols killed, there were always tens of thousands more to take their place, so that their task seemed like a Herculean endeavour against a myriad-headed beast. The population of the inner city had risen from 82,000 at the beginning of the Jin era in 1125 to an astonishing 400,000 by 1207, and that of Greater Peking and its environs from 340,000 to 1.6 million. There was a garrison of 20,000 battle-hardened veterans in the inner city and 4,000 in each of the fortress towns, but the rest of the male population was in arms, either willingly or under duress. Against this Samuqa had just 50,000 assailants (most of them Khitans).[10] The Mongols had still not reached the acme of siegecraft they would later acquire in their wars against the west, and to take the city by bombardment seemed a vain hope. Their main weapon was economic strangulation and slow starvation.

But all this assumed a Mongol army in a pitch-perfect state. The reality of the years 1214–15, however, was that both sides were severely ravaged by disease and food shortages. The Mongols were hit by what the chroniclers call 'plague', probably a combination of cholera and dysentery (the so-called 'campaign fever') exacerbated by the summer heat. It was noteworthy that the Mongols contracted these deadly diseases only when they occupied or besieged urban centres; there is no record of significant disease before that time.[11] As if that were not pestilence enough, they were simultaneously hit by epizootic animal disease, which may have been equine influenza (horse 'flu) or, more likely, bluetongue disease, which is viral and insect-borne, particularly associated with sudden changes of temperature.[12] Additionally, both sides were afflicted with severe food shortages. The dire position of the defenders of Peking is obvious enough, but by this time the Mongols themselves were experiencing short commons; their destructive, scorched-earth policies were now backfiring on them. Genghis was reduced to demanding food supplies from the Jin, on the pretext that this was the only way he could rein in his hawkish generals. The result was cannibalism on both sides. Mongol anthropophagy seems to have been non-existent in normal circumstances but these were not normal circumstances. Many unimpeachable sources confirm the reality of cannibalism among the Mongols when desperate, though we can perhaps discount Friar Carpini's highly coloured story that Genghis ordered a literal decimation of his troops besieging Peking, so that the remaining 90 per cent could gorge on their comrades' flesh.[13]

Samuqa took his time, relying on attrition and stranglehold, never making the mistakes of his predecessor by attempting to storm the city, waiting for disease and starvation to do his work for him, confident to the point of certainty that the emperor would not send a relief column north from Kaifeng. In January 1215 Genghis returned from his long layover in Dolon Nor. The collapse of the Jin position in Manchuria and the continuing torrent of desertions and defections convinced him that the time might be right for another major assault. By capturing the important town of Tong-Chou he put a further dent in the defenders' confidence, fading daily under the impact of starvation.[14]

In March Genghis sent a delegation to Kaifeng to discuss the terms on which the emperor might surrender, but this embassy was upstaged by another, from Peking, which somehow slipped through the Mongol line and arrived in the southern capital to exhort the emperor to do something before it was too late. Finally aroused from his torpor, Hsuan Tsung decided on a final effort to save his northern capital. Two separate armies were assembled in Hebei province, one in the west, the other in the south-east, and the plan was that both would converge on Peking. The south-eastern army was intercepted by a numerically smaller Mongol force and routed.[15] The western force fared even worse. Its commander, Li Ying, a drunkard, was attacked and defeated while in his cups and lost a thousand cartloads of food which were being conveyed to the starving inhabitants of Peking.

Hearing of these disasters, the commanders in Peking grew desperate. The two most senior advocated entirely different actions, one opting for a do-or-die final breakout assault, the other wishing to steal away surreptitiously to the south. Wan-yen Fu-hing, the 'do or die' commander, was so affected by the violent quarrel with his colleague on this point that he slipped into melancholy and committed suicide by drowning.[16] His successor and the crown prince then appealed to the emperor imploringly to surrender, but in vain. Chin-Chung, the man who had opposed Wan-yen and advocated stealing away at night, redoubled his efforts to break out, and the crown prince begged him to take him with him. Having promised to do so, he then stole away with his own family, slipped through Mongol lines under cover of darkness and made his way to Kaifeng where, after a characteristic period of dithering, the emperor had him executed.[17]

While Samuqa invested Peking more and more tightly, Genghis, at last coming to close grips with the enemy, took six other cities in early May. The Jin in Peking fought desperately, knowing what fate awaited them if the Mongols broke in. With no food whatever reaching the inner city, and the defenders famished and turning to cannibalism, the nerve of even the most valiant defenders began to crack. One of the crown prince's most important generals, the Khitan Shimo Mingan, managed to get out of the city and formally submit to Genghis. His defection may have been decisive, for he then arranged a mass sortie of men under his command, including China's greatest masters of the most modern siege engine technology – whose expertise he placed at the service of the Mongol khan.[18]

The Jin fought tenaciously to the end, and the defence was marked by one of the first clear uses of firearms in history. Pioneers in this area, the Chinese had made primitive cannons and muzzle loaders. When the shot for these weapons ran out, they used silver and finally gold, melted down as ammunition.[19] But all was in vain. Abandoned now by their most senior commanders, the defenders gave up and opened the gates to Shih-mo Mingan, now Samuqa's deputy while Samuqa himself was fortuitously some miles to the north conferring with Genghis.[20]

The ensuing sack of Peking, which lasted a month, was one of the most terrible incidents in the Mongols' scarcely peaceful career. The victorious troops tore down temples, destroyed massive gates, laid waste palaces and parks and raped and murdered by the tens of thousands. One of the imperial palaces was set on fire, and the inferno burned for a month. The human slaughter was terrific. According to one story, 60,000 virgins killed themselves by jumping from the city walls rather than become sexual prey of the 'barbarians'.[21] Reports spoke of a white hill of human bones outside the city, full of bleached skulls. Envoys from Western Asia witnessed another such mountain of the dead, and once again all around the ground was greasy with human fat.[22] Obviously some of this was exaggeration. There are two views. One is that atrocity stories lose nothing in the telling. The other is that they are mostly objectively true, but that the human mind cannot truly encompass the horror of what has happened and 'downsizes' the scale of human losses so as to remain sane. An exact estimate of the death toll is impossible. One estimate is that the population of the inner city of Peking shrank to 91,000 in 1216 and that of greater Peking declined to 285,000, which would imply a mortality count of 300,000 in the former and over a million in the latter.[23]

However one appraises it, there is no doubt that the sack of Peking in 1215 was one of the most seismic and traumatic events in Chinese history.[24] Only one factor can be urged in defence of the Mongols' destructive vandalism, which was clearly a reaction to a year's pent-up stress and the deaths of comrades from famine, disease and battle. This is that there was no attempt at gratuitous destruction outside the city itself. The Lugou Bridge, a stone bridge south-west of Peking and later described by Marco Polo as 'so fine that it has few equals in the world', was left untouched.

Another obvious target for mindless vandals and destroyers would have been the Grand Canal.[25] This was begun in the fifth century BC and almost completed in the seventh century AD. At 1,104 miles long, it ran from Peking through the provinces of Hebei, Shandong, Jiangsu and Zhejiang to the city of Hangzhou, the Song capital, said to be the largest city in the world, with a population of one million.[26] In the days of a united China (as in the Tang dynasty), the canal's main purpose was to link the Yellow River with the Yangtse. Thanks to the pound lock, invented in the tenth century by a Song engineer, it climbed to an elevation of 138 feet in the Shandong Mountains.[27] Beset by problems arising from the flooding of the Yellow River and by warfare (particularly the Jin–Song warfare of the twelfth century), the Grand Canal was unusable for long periods and gradually fell into disuse. The Liao notoriously put the canal out of action south of the Yellow River in 1128 to impede the Jurchen invaders by breaking the high dykes of the river. Ironically, it would fall to the Mongols to restore the canal to its former glory.[28]

All that autumn huge convoys of carts moiled their groaning way from Peking to Dolon Nor, bringing Genghis almost unbelievable riches, with carts almost collapsing under the weight of gold and silver. After spending the winter of 1215 at the Dolon Nor, supervising the Mongol occupation of Peking from afar, Genghis returned to Mongolia in the spring of 1216; he had been away from his homeland for five years. He rewarded most of his followers handsomely and there were significant winners among the Mongol inner circle (as well as a few losers). He appointed Muqali generalissimo in China and rewarded Shih-mo Mingan, who had supervised the final assault on Peking, by making him governor of the city.

He then sent an embassy to Hsuan Tsung in Kaifeng, suggesting that a permanent peace could be made if Hsuan accepted he was no longer emperor and instead took the title king of Henan. When the emperor angrily rejected this, Genghis decided to attack the Jin south of the Yellow River and appointed Samuqa to command a force of 20,000 for this task.[29] Confident of victory by 1214, Genghis had pulled Jebe and Subedei out of China. He rewarded Jebe with extensive demesnes, but there was no similar prize for Subedei; Genghis's ungrateful attitude, as indeed that of his successor Ogodei, remains puzzling.

Another major beneficiary was Chinqai, a veteran of Baljuna and later to be a key administrator in the Mongol empire. For his services against the Naiman Genghis had already given him an entire stable of the best horses. Chinqai had distinguished himself at the siege of Fu-chou in 1212, where he went on fighting despite an arrow wound in his left arm. On the capture of Peking in 1215 he climbed to the top of the Tower of the Great Compassionate One and shot arrows in the four main directions of the compass. Tickled by this exploit, Genghis gifted to him all the houses and properties within the range of the four arrows.[30] Another to receive a massive fief was a Muslim merchant named Ja'afur, who had been in close contact with Genghis ever since the Baljuna covenant. In 1213 Genghis had been held up on the march, unable to force the Chu-yung pass. Fortunately, Ja'afur had often traded in these parts and it was he who revealed to the Mongols the little-known path through forests and mountains which came down in the rear of the defenders; taken completely by surprise – they had not even posted sentries in their rear – the Jin were surrounded and slaughtered.[31]

The Khitan civil servant and top administrator Yelu Chucai was another who received promotion.[32] But probably the person to gain most kudos in the aftermath of the fall of Peking was Shigi Qutuqu. Genghis sent Shigi and two officers of the Guard, Onggur and Arqai, to make an inventory of the imperial treasure in the city. The Jin treasurer met Onggur and Arqai first, and proposed that they lop several millions off the count and share the skimmed-off money themselves. Onggur and Arqai readily agreed but when the same proposition was put to Shigi, he was appalled. He pointed out with some asperity that everything in Peking was now the khan's property and that the treasurer's proposal was treason. Shigi reported this to Genghis who, surprisingly, reprimanded them but did not execute them. But the khan was delighted with Shigi's behaviour and especially the words contained in his report: 'It is your property, so how could I steal it?'[33]

It is something of a miracle that the Jin did not collapse entirely in 1215–16. Their problems were legion. The province of Henan, south of the Yellow River, was so far the only one untouched by Mongol raids, but in the second half of 1215 it was hit by a disastrous famine, partly caused by the influx of a million new mouths – troops and their extended families – who followed the emperor south. Hsuan

Tsung tried to deal with this by the sale and redistribution of government land, but he placed the project in the hands of unscrupulous
landlords who, systematically corrupt, simply added the public lands
to their own portfolio or profiteered on their sale.[34] Particularly badly
affected was the province of Shandong which erupted into peasant
revolt in late 1215. This was another shock, as the Jin imagined most
discontented peasants had gone south to Song domains in the 1120s.[35]
Showing unwonted energy – or perhaps simply keen to appear in the
field against an enemy they had some hopes of defeating after their
constant humiliations at the hands of the Mongols – the Jin struck
back vigorously. They sent an army to Shandong to put down the
rebels and, in the guerrilla war that followed, 40,000 people died in
the last six months of 1215 alone. The peasant leaders were taken to
Kaifeng and executed, but the peasant movement proved protean and
soon even more able leaders emerged. Seizing their opportunity, the
Song entered the fray, forged an alliance with the Red Coats, as the
peasants were known, and by 1217 had wrested the province from Jin
control.[36]

The Jin were also attacked by Hsi-Hsia in 1214 and 1215, with the
Tangut taking the western city of Lintao. The Jin were now in serious
difficulties, cut off from all sources of fresh horses, in Manchuria,
along the Ongud frontier and now in the west.[37] Once again making
a supreme effort, Hsuan Tsung roused himself and sent a huge army,
which inflicted a devastating defeat on the Tangut outside the walls of
Lintao. Not easily daunted, the Tangut attacked again in the summer
of 1216 but were once more thrown back. It was perhaps something
of a relief to the Jin to reflect that though they could never defeat
the Mongols, they could see off Tangut, Red Coats and the Song easily
enough. As if to reinforce the point, one of their best generals, Shih
T'ien-ni, gave up the hopeless struggle against the Mongols in Hebei
and went over to Genghis Khan. A combined Mongol-Chinese force
then took the city of Ta-Ming Fu and advanced on Tung P'ing, which
proved a city too far. Stoutly defended on the eastern shore of a lake,
the fortress resisted all attacks. The Mongols were baulked as, lacking
naval know-how, they could not attack the place by lake or river but
had to attack along a narrow front which the defenders could deal
with.[38] Nevertheless, the Mongol campaign in Hebei in late 1215 essentially sealed off all Jin approaches to Shandong from the north, and

extended into Shanxi where many minor towns were also taken. For the Jin probably the worst aspect of 1215–16 was the feeling that a new crisis was arising almost daily. As one historian has put it: 'Between the Mongols on one hand and the Red Coats on the other, life north of the Yellow River was nothing short of a nightmare.'[39]

Faced now with four sets of enemies (Mongols, Song, Tangut, Red Coats), the Jin ordered universal conscription and (belatedly) a system of meritocracy for all promotions. They began by placing strong garrisons around Kaifeng to form a 'ring of steel', and constructed a system of blockhouses north of the Yellow River. A reward system was also proclaimed. Whoever retook Peking would become a field-marshal; whoever defeated the Mongol army in any engagement would become governor of a city; there were also financial rewards for the defeat of Mongol forces of 3,000, 2,000 or even 1,000.[40] All that made sense, but the other policy decisions of the Jin were unfathomable. The obvious course was to seek an alliance with the Song at any price to combat the Mongols, but Hsuan Tsung insisted on war with the Song even though he was hard pressed in the north. But if he thought he could win a propaganda triumph by boasting to his subjects about victories against the Song, to offset the almost predictably bad news from the Mongol front, he was soon disabused. While trying to cross the Yangtse in 1219, the Jin sustained a terrible rout.[41] The southern war with the Song was still dribbling on when Hsuan Tsung died in 1224.

Meanwhile, in March–July 1216 the Jin conducted a minor counter-offensive north of the Yellow River which managed to retake a few towns. But they were soon on the back foot again, for in 1216 Genghis launched his own fourfold offensive: in Shanxi, western Hebei, eastern Hebei and in southern Shaanxi. The last, and most ambitious, campaign was the one for which he had already earmarked Samuqa, and Genghis even went to the length of asking 'permission' from the Tangut to cross their territory in the Ordos. Not only did Hsi-Hsia grant this request, but they actually provided a large army to assist Samuqa.[42]

Before unleashing his hordes, however, Genghis made one final attempt at a negotiated peace. The terms were that all towns in Hebei, Shandong, Shanxi and Shaanxi were to submit immediately and the emperor must give up his title and accept that of king of Henan.

Once again Hsuan Tsung refused.[43] Wisely, Genghis kept out of Shandong for the time being, hoping that the Jin and the Red Coats would eat each other up, rather like the Kilkenny cats in the fable. It was fortunate that he did, for in 1217 another disastrous flood of the Yellow River prevented any serious campaigning by any army in that province. The loss of life in China in this era was terrific, but Shandong probably suffered more than any other region.[44]

Meanwhile the Mongols experienced a serious check to their ambitions in Manchuria. Their ally Yelu Liuke felt confident enough by 1214 to form a civil administration, and Genghis sent Anchar to him as a kind of ambassador and political commissar. After futilely trying to detach Yelu by bribery and diplomacy, the Jin reverted to main force, but the general they sent against him was quickly defeated with Mongol help. The Jin retreated to Liaoyang, licked their wounds, tried again and sustained yet another defeat; to add to their woes it was at this point that the defeated general Pu-hsien Wan-nu staged his own revolt, striking out on his own and declaring himself ruler of the new realm which he called Ta-Chen. Defeated a third time by a numerically inferior Mongol force, Wan-nu fled to Korea, whereupon Yelu made himself master of Liaoyang.[45]

At this juncture his lieutenants urged him to shake off Genghis's overlordship and declare himself emperor of Manchuria. Too shrewd for such a move – Yelu knew very well the consequences of treachery towards the Mongols – he moved in the opposite direction and in December 1215 set off on a visit to Genghis's base on the Kerulen.[46] Genghis was very well disposed to receive his visitor, as his agents had told him of Yelu's many laudatory references to him, but he was surprised and delighted by the lavish gifts Yelu brought – ninety cartloads of gold, silver and bolts of silk. A beaming Genghis gave his guest the title of senior ally in China and asked him to carry out a census of Manchuria. This was a laborious chore, especially in wartime, but Yelu eventually did it and reported a population of three millions.

But before any of this could come to pass, there was a rebellion in Manchuria against Yelu, on the grounds that he was a Mongol stooge.[47] The fuse was lit by an apparently trivial incident. While at the Kerulen, Yelu complained that one of the senior Mongol agents in Manchuria, Keteke by name, had disobeyed his orders and taken Wan-nu's deserted wife as his concubine; as Yelu explained, this would simply ensure that Wan-nu returned from Korea to disturb the peace. Angrily Genghis ordered Keteke arrested, bound hand and foot and brought to his presence. Learning of this dread sentence, a terrified Keteke, went to Yeh-ssu-pu, head of Yelu's civil administration, and asked for help, knowing that Yeh-ssu-pu was secretly enraged that Yelu had not declared an independent Khitan kingdom.[48] Together the two men opted for rebellion and were joined by Yelu's chief of staff Tung Kuyu. The conspirators spread the rumour that Yelu had died in Mongolia, treacherously massacred three hundred Mongols and started rounding up 3,000 prominent pro-Mongol Khitans. Three of these escaped and fled to the Kerulen to tell Genghis what had happened. More bad news followed them. Yeh-ssu-pu marched south, seized Yelu's wife and declared *himself* emperor Liao Wang. The seizure of a wife had a particular resonance for Genghis. Seeing Yelu cast down and depressed, he said to him: 'Be not discouraged, for if grazing is good and our horses in condition, I will give you an army.'[49]

Genghis sent out two armies, indulging his favourite ploy of aiming at two targets simultaneously. One was to position itself between China and Manchuria, to prevent any collaboration between the Jin in China and the rebels, the other under Muqali to put down the insurrection. Muqali decided that his principal objective was Pei Ching (modern Chifeng), about 150 miles west of Liaoyang, by now a huge city and unrecognisable from the time in the eleventh century when a Chinese traveller had described it as a glorified caravanserai.[50] His capture of this prime target was the result of an amazing exploit by Muqali's chief henchman Shih-mo Yeh-hsien. It so happened that the Jin sent a new governor to Pei Ching, who travelled by sea, landed on the coast of the Bohai Sea and began travelling overland to his post. Learning of this, Yeh-hsien intercepted the new governor and abducted him. Taking his credentials, he assumed the role of governor himself and presented himself at the gates of Pei Ching as the genuine article. Once inside, he persuaded the guards to go on leave as the Mongols had withdrawn. Having established his authority, he ordered all troops manning the city walls stood down and sent a message to Muqali, who entered the city unopposed that very night.[51]

This was a massive boost for the Mongols. At a stroke they gained a huge arsenal of arms and armour, war materiel, 108,000 taxable families, thirty-two towns under the jurisdiction of the city and 10,000 troops, whom Muqali saved from execution on condition they would fight for the Mongols. This intelligent restraint soon paid dividends, as a Jin general named Chang Ching murdered the Jin commander on the coastal corridor and submitted to Muqali.[52] When told of this, Genghis appointed Chang Ching commander of the 10,000 troops Muqali had spared.

Muqali followed up this great triumph by sending his lieutenants out to mop up in a wide radius around Pei Ching. They took twenty strongholds, at least 8,000 prisoners and suppressed a cleverly planned guerrilla war by two ingenious Jin junior officers. Muqali then routed a Jin army on the middle Liao River. The triumph was partly offset by a near-disaster when his two lieutenants Uyer and Shih T'ien-hsiang came close to defeat in another battle. Uyer was nearly killed by the Jin general in single combat during the battle, but his colleague Shih T'ien-hsiang saved both him and the battle.[53]

The Mongols now had a secure hold on the Liao valley, and Genghis ordered Muqali to march south into north-eastern Hebei. At this point Chang Ching showed his treacherous hand (he was another with aspirations to rule his own realm), refused to march, was court-martialled and then sealed his doom by escaping while in custody; Muqali had him executed. His brother Chang Chi raised the standard of rebellion, killed a Mongol envoy who summoned him to present himself at Genghis's court, and soon headed a formidable army. Instead of marching south, Muqali now had to suppress a major rebellion in Manchuria, and the rebels held the densely populated area just inland from the extreme north-west corner of the Bohai Sea. While Muqali reconquered this territory, Genghis summoned Shih T'ien-hsiang to his court to reward him for his heroism. He gave him Chang Ching's former command of the 10,000 Pei Ching troops and the much coveted golden tiger seal.[54]

In early summer 1216 Chang Chi launched a major offensive. Muqali waited until July before responding, to rest his horses who were suffering from equine distemper. Chang Chi barricaded himself behind the walls of Jinzhou, near the coast, not wanting to confront the Mongols in open battle.[55] Muqali tried to winkle him into the open by sending a weak force under Uyer to attack a strategically valuable fort nearby. Chang Chi took the bait and sent out a large force, where-upon Muqali quickly got his main army between that force and Jinzhou to cut off the retreat. Uyer's contingent then turned to face the enemy, trapping them between his men and Muqali's. The terrible slaughter that ensued left 12,600 dead on the battlefield. Muqali then returned to the siege of the seriously weakened Jinzhou. A disastrous sortie ordered by Chang Chi simply left another 3,000 dead, many of them drowned in the Hsiao-ling River.[56] Grimly defending, Chang Chi got it into his head that his commanders were not pulling their weight and executed twenty of them for the 'crime' of having been defeated by the Mongols. Another of his generals, fearing that he was next, seized Chang Chi, handed him over to Muqali and surrendered the city in exchange for his own safety. Muqali at once executed Chang Chi.[57] But once again, contrary to Mongol custom, he refrained from slaughter. Instead, following the precedent he had set at Pei Ching, he incorporated 12,000 troops into his ranks, taking care to write to Genghis to get his endorsement.

It soon became apparent why Chang Chi had been able to make such a good showing. He commanded an elite division, fortuitously the main survivors, known as the Black Army on account of their black uniforms. Because the towns of I-chou and Kuang-ning remained defiant, Muqali singled them out for an awful warning. After taking them by siege, he massacred every living soul there, except of course for the inevitable 'reserved occupations': masons, carpenters, craftsmen, artisans.[58] Manchuria was now, at least temporarily, pacified. As the last piece of the puzzle, Wan-nu sent his submission from Korea, guaranteed by the dispatch of his son as hostage at Muqali's side, and was allowed back into the mountainous region of Manchuria on the border with Korea, where he ruled as a local warlord until 1233.[59] Together with Muqali, he was the only clear beneficiary of the turmoil in Manchuria in 1215–16.[60]

Muqali's exploits in Manchuria were heroic. Unquestionably, though, the major event of 1216 was Samuqa's campaign in the south. Samuqa was not in Genghis's inner circle and had earned his advancement on pure merit. He was on particularly bad terms with Shigi Qutuqu who, for obscure reasons not divulged in the sources, hated him and spread the rumour that as a young man Samuqa had copulated with a goat.[61] Starting in September from Tung Sheng (near modern Baotou), where the Yellow River veers sharply south to complete the horseshoe bend, he marched south, keeping parallel to the river but further to the west, passing through the Ordos and Shaanxi on his way to the River Wei, where he sacked the town of Hsi-an (modern Weinan) on the south bank in November.[62] In marching the 375–400 miles further south to where the Wei meets the Yellow River, Samuqa passed through a variety of climatic regions, almost from the grasslands of Mongolia to the subtropical regions of the Yangtse basin.[63] At Yen-an he joined forces with 30,000 Tangut horsemen but rode fast with them to the Wei, bypassing the three 'Chou' towns (Fang-chou, Yao-chou and T'ung-chou), crossing the Wei and penetrating into Song territory.[64]

Since the Jin were already at war with the Song, they had no compunction about following Samuqa there. Emperor Hsuan Tsung was convinced that Genghis had finally made a major blunder in allowing this Mongol army to operate so far from its confreres, and assembled five separate armies that he sent in hot pursuit. Dodging, weaving, doubling back on his tracks and marching in circles, Samuqa managed to avoid them all, arriving eventually at a point only seven miles away from Kaifeng in December, and even capturing the town of Ju-chou before his pursuers could catch up.[65] Kaifeng was too strong to attack, but the unexpected presence of the Mongols so close to the southern capital caused a sensation; Samuqa made a point of laying waste the environs so as further to dent Jin credibility.[66]

His orders from Genghis were to reconnoitre the country south of the Yellow River and to keep the pressure on the Jin, and this he had done successfully. But Samuqa was aware that speed, mobility and voluntarism would carry him only so far; the five avenging armies were close on his tail. Stretching them out so that they became separated, he retreated at speed along an easier route on the south bank of the Yellow River and the valley of the Luo – a direct northward crossing was not possible because of the arc of fortified towns protecting Kaifeng on the north bank. At Mien-chou in January 1217 he turned and routed one of the pursuing forces, which through forced marches had lost touch with the other four. The Jin continued to be astounded at Mongol mobility: 'They come as though the sky were falling, and they disappear like a flash of lightning.'[67]

Next Samuqa crossed the Yellow River on the ice, and struck north towards Ping-yang on the western bank of the Fen River (modern Linfen). The Jin, now combined into a single huge army, continued to dog him. The Tangut, their contractual obligations completed, left him at the Ho-Ching ford at the confluence of the Fen and Yellow Rivers. Meanwhile emperor Hsuan Tsung had come up with the idea of declaring a general pardon for all Chinese personnel serving with the Mongols, on the grounds that they must have been forced. This ploy was remarkably successful; no fewer than 13,000 men deserted Samuqa's host.[68] Since his original force of 60,000 had contained 30,000 Tangut and there had been battle losses, Samuqa was reduced to an army smaller than 15,000 effectives. Forced to fight ferociously to avoid being caught between the Jin garrison at Ping-yang and the huge army in his rear, Samuqa fought his way past Ping-yang with losses which even he admitted were unacceptable. Still in deadly danger, Samuqa was essentially saved by the brilliant efficiency of the Mongol courier service. Alerted to his plight, the high command diverted the Jin pursuers in Shanxi by smokescreen raids on phantom targets, confusing the Jin and allowing Samuqa to get home safely. He at last reached the city of Ta-t'ung (Datong) in February to find that the Mongols had finally taken it by attrition after so many frontal attacks had failed.[69]

Samuqa's campaign was one of the great Mongol exploits. With just 30,000 men before the Tangut joined him, he penetrated to the heart of the Jin state, all the time moving through terrain alive with fortified towns and strongholds, and where vastly superior enemy forces were deployed against him. From mid-November 1216 to the third week of January 1217, besides the days when he was giving battle or besieging towns, he marched 700 miles in fifty days. The Jin were shaken by his great raid, and feared that it was simply the harbinger of further Mongol incursions, probably next time with at least two such armies, with maybe one of them following the same itinerary and the other cutting through Hebei; they thought it was likely the commanders would be Samuqa and Jebe (they were unaware he was no longer in China).[70]

They sent an embassy to Genghis to enquire what his revised peace terms might be but Genghis replied, after taking advice from Samuqa, that all places in Hebei and Shandong had to surrender as well as those in Shanxi and Shaanxi previously mentioned; moreover, the requirement that Hsuan Tsung drop the title of emperor and style himself king of Henan still stood. Once again talks collapsed and the war went on. Genghis increasingly saw little point in peace talks, for he now thought he could achieve all his ambitions without compromising. As he put it: 'The present situation is like a hunt. We have taken all the deer, only a rabbit is left, so why not let it go!'[71] Amazingly, no more was ever heard of Samuqa; he disappears from Mongol chronicles after 1217 as if he had never existed.

The immediate result of Samuqa's campaign and the intelligence he brought back was that Genghis summoned his generalissimo Muqali to his encampment on the Tula River for a summit conference to discuss grand strategy in China. When he arrived there in February 1217, Muqali received the greatest reception ever given a Mongol general. Lavished with gifts and publicly praised by Genghis, he was also given the hereditary title of Prince of the Realm and made the khan's viceroy and lieutenant-general in China. It was proclaimed throughout the empire that Mongol troops must obey Muqali's every command as though it came from Genghis himself. To reinforce this, before his departure Genghis paid him the unique compliment of giving him a seal of authority shaped like a golden tiger and a nine-tailed banner.[72]

The discussions were so protracted that it was not until September 1217 that Muqali returned to China. The two men agreed that the Jin must be eliminated from every last area north of the Yellow River before the final attack on Henan province. Although Genghis praised the strides Muqali had made in siegecraft, he told him that even more improvements would be necessary before they could hope to take Kaifeng. He should also begin administering conquered territory as if it was already a long-standing part of the Mongol empire, using Khitan and Chinese bureaucrats.[73] The force Muqali was given to achieve these objectives was perilously short on numbers: 10,000 elite Mongol troops, 10,000 Ongud, 3,000 Ongirrad, 20,000 troops from Manchuria, a mixed force of Khitans and *juyin* some 15,000 strong and 10,000 former Jin troops from Hebei, making 70,000 in all, with mounts. The danger was that many of the non-Mongol elements were deserters and defectors who followed the fortunes of war and embraced the winning side. If Muqali started losing battles in China it might be a different story, for these were men who had ratted and they could do so again.[74]

Muqali's idea was to divide these troops into three detachments, one to ravage western and southern Hebei, another to recover eastern

Hebei and invade Shandong, and the third to lay waste northern Shaanxi.[75] The last depended on Tangut assistance, but the new chief minister in Hsi-Hsia was anti-Mongol and persuaded the Tangut emperor to reverse the policy of aiding the Mongols – which had contributed so signally to Samuqa's success. In the light of this Genghis thought Muqali's tripartite strategy too ambitious and volunteered to handle the western campaign himself. In what was to be his final campaign in China, Genghis struck south once more in February 1218, crossed the northern Yellow River on the ice, besieged the Tangut capital of Chung-Hsing (Yinchuan) and forced the Tangut to think again. They quickly made peace on the old basis that they would supply troops as requested.[76]

In 1217–21 Muqali campaigned in Shanxi, Hebei and Shandong, initially dividing his forces into three and until January 1218 restricting himself to reducing minor towns, laying waste the countryside and generally waging a war of attrition, intending gradually to work round to the big cities that were very strongly defended.[77] Indeed one of the three forces, operating in Shanxi, mainly functioned as a diversion. But he was hampered by lack of numbers, and especially of the surplus needed to garrison towns, so that a Jin offensive in early 1218 retook most of the towns he had captured. The sheer number of Chinese constituted a headache in itself, and the task of winning hearts and minds was nearly impossible given the Mongols' reputation for being 'massacre-happy'; Muqali tried to lay this ghost by leniency and conciliation, but it was always an uphill struggle.[78] Moreover, Jin morale showed no real sign of cracking, despite the copious desertions, and every town he took cost him sorely in casualties. Muqali also could not be permanently on the warpath, since he had to fulfil Genghis's directive to find new methods of siegecraft, and this required study and research. Soon he was scaling down his Chinese ambitions. He decided to postpone the reconquest of Shandong and the occupation of eastern Hebei in favour of retaining his position in western Hebei and achieving the total conquest of Shanxi.

It may be queried why Muqali concentrated on the difficult and mountainous province of Shanxi, but in fact his thinking was sound. His reasons were threefold: whoever possessed it had a perfect defensive position; its occupation extinguished all hopes of reinforcement to the beleaguered Jin garrisons in the western provinces; and it was

crucial to depress morale in Hebei for, until that province was pacified, no campaign in Shandong could ever be successful.

Muqali acknowledged that he had initially miscalculated, thinking
the Jin would concentrate on their war with the Song and not counter-
attack north of the Yellow River.[79] But then he had two strokes of
luck. Genghis, by now concentrating on a different, far-distant war
with shah Muhammad of Khwarezmia, made a superhuman effort to
raise further manpower. By the end of 1218 Muqali had 100,000 troops,
including 23,000 Mongols.[80] And in Hebei he was able to do more than
the holding operation he had pessimistically envisaged, thanks to the
appearance of a new military talent.

Chang Jou had begun his martial career as leader of a militia unit
– almost a guerrilla band, but one officially recognised by the Jin; such
units were the principal way the Jin kept resistance alive after their
constant defeat in battle. Chang Jou surrendered to Muqali in 1217
and, if he had been dealing with a more traditional Mongol leader,
would certainly have been executed, for he refused to kowtow or
kneel to an image of Genghis when ordered to do so. The story ran
that Muqali took his parents hostage and thus forced him to serve
him loyally, but this appears to be apocryphal.[81] Chang Jou, though
cruel and treacherous, remained steadfastly loyal and proved to have
rare military flair. His duel with the Jin general Wu Hsien – reportedly
the most able of the emperor's captains and one of the nine 'dukes'
(field-marshals) appointed by him in the years 1218–20 – became
legendary. Aside from defeating Wu Hsien in four pitched battles and
taking thirty cities in Hebei, he came to Genghis's notice by his inspired
defence of the city of Man-ch'eng when, caught off balance by a Jin
attack with his main fighting force elsewhere, he improvised a
successful check on the attackers, using old men, women and soldiers
on sick call.[82]

With his flank more than secure as a result of Chang Jou's brilliance,
Muqali crashed into Shanxi in 1218, taking town after town until by
1219 only the southernmost tip of the province was in enemy hands.
His conquest was essentially a twofold affair: first the Fen River, the
principal food-growing area, then the highlands between the Fen and
the Yellow River. He then returned to Hebei to receive the formal
surrender in the summer of 1220 of the remaining Jin towns in that
province, including the key garrison at Ta-ming. By August 1220 he

felt confident enough to switch to the second part of his grand strategy: the total conquest of Hebei and the recovery of Shandong.[83]

Amazingly, in the light of the grim, slugging struggle he had endured in Shanxi, by the end of 1220 he was the complete master of Hebei. The surrender of the key city of Chi-nan (modern Jinan) marked a turning point in the Mongol conquest of north China, as for the first time the invaders were receiving the voluntary submission of vast areas. In part it was likely that Muqali's policy of conciliation and moderation had paid off, but most probably the major reason for the new attitude was that the Chinese people were finally losing confidence in the Jin and concluding that the future lay with the Mongols.[84] So confident was Muqali that he set up a court and a central administration in Ta-t'ung (Datong). In far-off Khwarezmia, Genghis heard that the Khitans referred to Muqali as *guyin* (ruler). Far from being jealous or peevish, Genghis sent a personal message to his favourite general: 'that title is a good omen.'[85]

Very tall, with curly whiskers, fond of conviviality and extremely generous, Muqali had earned the right to be considered a true viceroy. He had just one principal wife and eight secondary ones, and only one son, his beloved Bol. At ease with Chinese culture, Muqali was also something of a cosmopolitan, as he liked to wear turbans and other Islamic clothes imported from western Asia.[86] By now he was also massively wealthy, not just from the loot uplifted on campaign but more securely from the extensive lands deeded to him by Genghis for his sterling services.[87] Muqali's regime in north China was a complex mixture of Chinese, Khitan, Jurchen, Uighur and Mongol culture and folkways. He absorbed aspects of traditional China at his court but retained the Mongol custom of the public equality of the sexes. For his administration he recruited mainly from Khitan and Chinese bureaucrats, and integrated the Chinese approach to the civil service with the best of the Mongol socio-political system.[88] In religious matters he was as tolerant as his master. Where the lay Chinese population was on the sharp end of Mongol demands for military service, labour (*corvée*) and goods, and heavily mulcted in taxes on grain, clothing, horses, weapons, specie (the Mongols had a tax for practically everything), Buddhists and Taoists were exempt from all fiscal burdens.[89] The freedom Genghis gave to Muqali to run China as he saw fit was astonishing, bespeaking a rare rapport between autocrat and associate. It is sometimes alleged that Genghis was always paranoid, but the accusation seems hollow in the light of his relationship with Muqali.[90]

Meanwhile a final chapter was being written in Manchuria. The Jin made one last attempt to retrieve their situation in 1217, failed, and definitively abandoned the province. But Yelu Liuke's pro-Mongol grip on the country was always shaky, with a majority of Khitans yearning for independence, and in the very same year a powerful anti-Mongol alliance under Han-she plunged the country into civil war. Yelu managed to defeat him, but Han-she retreated into Korea with most of his army intact. Korea itself was already in turmoil, convulsed by the aftermath of an attempt at a *coup d'état* in which 800 Buddhist monks perished.[91] The Khitan invaders swept all before them and occupied the capital, Kaesong; the bewildered Koreans, at first not knowing what had hit them, initially appealed for help to the Song, who were uninterested.[92] Hard on the heels of the Khitans came Yelu and his Mongol allies with a powerful army. Yelu ran the rebel Khitans to earth, powering his way through terrible snowstorms to do so. He defeated the rebels, Han-she hanged himself, and his 10,000-strong force surrendered; the Mongols beheaded about a hundred of the officers.[93]

As a result of this incursion, Korea became part of the Mongol empire. The Korean king submitted but was ill requited: the first Mongol envoy sent to his court acted boorishly, making a point of wearing a bow and arrow to his first audience, seizing the monarch's hands and roughly thrusting Genghis's greetings into them. An annual tribute was fixed in 1221: Korea agreed to provide 10,000 pounds of cotton, 3,000 bolts of silk, 2,000 pieces of gauze and 100,000 enormous sheets of paper; in 1223 the tribute was consolidated into an annual quota of valuable sea-otter skins.[94] Yelu died in 1220, so the Mongols simply annexed both Manchuria and Korea.

There were several consequences of the Mongol absorption of Korea. They employed a policy of mass human transportation, moving any troublesome Koreans into north China.[95] They were bowled over by the beauty of Korean women, who became highly prized as wives and concubines. Genghis's favourite wife Qulan was considered so beautiful that it was commonly said that she was a Korean princess.[96] The Mongols also appropriated all the choicest agricultural land and earmarked it as part of Temuge's appanage. At a more general level the Mongols smashed the traditional balance of the three-way relationship between China, Korea and Manchuria, though this rhythm would reassert itself after the Mongol era.[97] Ironically, the Mongol invasion had the unintended effect of producing a true national consciousness in Korea. One result of all this was that, after Muqali's death in 1223, the Koreans rose in rebellion. Preoccupied elsewhere, the Mongols did not put down the insurrection until 1233. As a final irony the Koryo dynasty, founded in 918, managed to limp on until 1392, thus outliving the Liao, the Jin, the Song and even the Mongol Yuan dynasty in China.[98]

Muqali's ambition to achieve a definitive conquest of Shandong was complicated not just by the Red Coat rebels but by the entry of the Song into the war; the Song too wanted to annex Shandong. Song foreign policy in the twenty-three years that the Mongols fought the Jin has rightly been described as a disaster.[99] There was no attempt at an intelligent long-term geopolitical view, partly because of a mindset that said collaboration with a 'barbarian' ally always turned out disastrously. (The Song were thinking particularly of their alliance with the Jurchens to overthrow the Liao, which had ended with an even more formidable regime on their borders.) They were also blinded by their hatred for the Jin and the disastrous experience of the war of 1206–08, which led many of them to believe that, official rhetoric notwithstanding, they would never reconquer the north. The majority of Song decision-makers, though anti-Jin, thought it best to remain quietly behind 'fortress Yangtse'. They therefore greeted the Mongol invasion of north China in 1211 'with a mixture of caution and *Schadenfreude'*.[100] Only a handful of men in the upper echelons of Song government warned that the Mongols might be a more dangerous enemy in the future than the Jin had ever been.

Other factors too were at work in creating this Song apathy. Their achievements in science, technology, literature, poetry, philosophy, education and seamanship gave them the impression (probably rightly in the early thirteenth century) that they were the most advanced nation in the world, which bred a corresponding arrogance.[101] Nevertheless, there was an abiding feeling that the tribute they paid the Jin as a result of the war of 1206–08 was humiliating, as it undermined the Song claim to have the mandate of Heaven. Accordingly the 'hawks' gained the ascendancy and in 1214 announced the tribute would no longer be paid. Somewhat reluctantly, the Jin emperor declared war. Wiser heads at the Jin court argued that this was a bad mistake: north China was already groaning under a mountain of taxation, while the Mongols were winning the war and poised to take Peking. Morale would be seriously affected if, instead of concentrating on the Mongols, troops were pulled out of Shanxi and Hebei to deal with the Song. And surely it was stupid for the Jin to divide their forces, as any marginal gains they made from the Song could not compensate for the massive losses to the Mongols.[102]

The war began well for the Jin but all was undone by the disastrous defeat in 1219. The Song counter-attacked across the Yellow River and moved into Shandong, where they formed a partnership with the Red Coats, suggesting that they, not the Mongols, might become the masters of the province. (From 1218 to 1231 the governor originally appointed by the Jin emperor to rule Shandong in cohabitation with the Red Coats actually ruled as an independent warlord, changing sides whenever he thought he spotted a winner.)[103] But in 1220, while Muqali was campaigning in Shanxi, the Song lost a number of battles, and the Jin started to gain the upper hand.

Muqali had begun his campaign of 1220–21 cautiously, operating on the borders of Hebei and Shandong, capturing (as we have seen) the cities of Chi-nan and Ta-ming. An advance guard numbering 20,000 of the enormous 200,000-strong army the Jin were pouring into Shandong collided with him and was routed in short order. He followed this up with a major victory at Huang-ling kang, a ford on the south bank of the Yellow River, where he surrounded the Jin at the river bank, routed them and then pursued the fleeing survivors into the river, where thousands drowned. This defeat effectively doomed Jin attempts to recover Hebei and Shandong, though the full implications were not immediately apparent.[104] In both these victories, Muqali was immeasurably aided by the fact that, faced with a dire shortage of horses, the Jin was now almost entirely an infantry army, which could be devastated at long range by arrow showers.

Muqali next showed that he was the perfect versatile warrior by devising a stratagem to take a town (Chu Ch'iu) thought to be impregnable because of a wide moat which ran round the entire circuit of the walls. Muqali simply got his troops to collect huge quantities of wood, moss and grass and built an improvised causeway for his troops to ride across.[105] He then struck due south and by October 1220 was at the Ching-chang River, where he swung east as far as Chi-nan before again plunging south towards the Yellow River. By late November he was at the outskirts of Kaifeng. Concluding, like Samuqa before him, that this was too strong to be taken, he turned north-east to Tung-Ping. Despite heroic efforts he was unable to storm this city, so ordered a blockade. By May 1221 Tung-Ping was reduced to starvation and cannibalism. The governor achieved a breakout with 7,000 troops, but the Mongols followed them and picked them off ruthlessly. By the time the Jin reached the 'safety' of the town of Pei-chou to the south, they were down to just 700 men. When Tung-Ping surrendered, Muqali himself turned north, leaving mopping up operations to his deputies.[106]

The main problem that concerned him was that the more Jin armies he defeated, the more guerrilla bands formed from the rump of the defeated troops – and this continued to be a problem everywhere, even in the officially totally pacified Shanxi.[107] On the other hand, the more victories he won, the more opportunists would desert to him. A good example was the renegade Jin general Yen Shih, who defected to the Song and Red Coats in 1218 then, in 1220, concluding that the only likely long-term winners were the Mongols, defected to them. Muqali valued his talents and, preparing now to move west against Shaanxi and Gansu provinces, he left Yen Shih to deal with Jin, Song and the Red Coats in the east.[108]

Muqali's strategy now hinged on sealing off the western territories of Shaanxi and Gansu entirely from the rest of the Jin realm, thus effectively cutting it in half, prior to a further bisection of what remained. (It was essentially the strategy used more than six hundred years later by the North in the American Civil War, with Grant's victory at Vicksburg in 1863 cutting off the West prior to Sherman's bisection of what remained by the march through Georgia in 1864.) First, though, he had to clear this with Genghis, who was then entertaining a peace delegation from the Jin.[109] Worried that Genghis might heed these siren voices, Muqali made effective use of the new postal service or yam, making sure his own envoy got to the khan first with Muqali's negative message.[110]

Genghis scarcely needed this kind of nudging, as the Jin envoy was not able to offer him anything worthwhile. The emissary stated that the emperor was now prepared to be known as Genghis's younger brother provided he was allowed to keep the title of emperor. Genghis was dismissive. 'I asked you to cede the land north of the Yellow River on a previous occasion and you turned it down,' he said. 'Now Muqali has conquered it. So what am I getting out of this new peace?'[111] At this the envoy started to grovel, and asked what were Genghis's terms. He answered that the emperor would have to cede Shaanxi and Gansu. When the envoy rejected this, Genghis dismissed him contemptuously, saying there was nothing further to talk about. Genghis then summoned Muqali's man and told him that the plan to conquer Shaanxi and Gansu was approved, capping this with another paean to 'the greatest of his generals'.[112] The messenger returned to Muqali and told him the good news.

Muqali had been urging this strategy ever since 1217 but hitherto Genghis had vetoed it, on the grounds that his own absence at war in Khwarezmia gave the Jin heart. Muqali thus needed to concentrate on the east of China – the only place where real pressure could be applied to the Jin in the short term. When informed that the khan had bent his right thumb in a gesture of approval, Muqali was over-joyed and said: 'For this reason it is not in vain that I serve to the very death and demonstrate the greatest energy and eagerness.'[113]

He began serious preparations for his great adventure and asked the Tangut for permission to cross their territory in the Ordos; by now Genghis had totally defeated shah Muhammad in central Asia, so they were in no position to refuse. A total eclipse of the sun on 23 May 1221, which his soothsayers read as a bad omen, did not worry him for, as he pointed out to them, he was on a divine mission ordered by Genghis who had spoken to Tengerri in person. His departure was further delayed when Yen Shih asked how he was supposed to make progress in Shandong while Muqali was away, given that most of it was now in the hands of the Song, officially the Mongols' allies, and the Song's allies the Red Coats.[114]

Muqali requested an embassy from the Song. A large Song delega-tion waited on him, and their reception gives us an interesting and rare glimpse of Muqali the human being as opposed to the warrior.[115] The Mongols had put on one of their ball games (primitive baseball?) which they expected the Song to attend. When they failed to turn up, Muqali sent for the senior envoy and asked for an explanation of this unfriendly act. The envoy explained that they had not been invited. Muqali liked the calm, serene way the man spoke, took an immediate shine to him and declared that from the moment of their arrival the emissaries were de facto members of his household and, as such, were automatically invited to everything. He laughed at the ambassador's discomfiture and said the penalty was six glasses of wine. Evidently the glasses were large and the wine strong, for the man reeled away drunk to his quarters at dusk.[116]

Over the next few days Muqali gained valuable insights into the Song mentality and psychology. He learned that there was a powerful 'peace party' in southern China, advocating a resumption of tribute so as to avoid what they considered a pointless war with the Jin.[117] The war party on the other hand tried to blunt this by insisting that the top Song general, Chao Fang, be sent to the front.[118] It soon became clear that the Song were lamentably ignorant about the Mongols, and woefully underrated their power and potential largely because of Genghis's departure for the war in Khwarezmia.[119] What about the Red Coats, Muqali asked. The Song, it transpired, were ambivalent about all rebel groups fighting the Jin as they were outside their control; they were prepared to use them but did not want to give them safe haven south of the Yangtse or support them financially, as their own military budget was already sky-high. The Song came across as indifferent to the feelings of their allies and obviously did not know how to manipulate sympathetic groups, as Muqali and the Mongols had done with Yelu in Manchuria.[120] Nevertheless, they had a high opinion of two Jin apostates: the major warlord Li Chuan, whom they both feared and suspected of disloyalty; and the former Jin general Yeh Shih, who had defected to them the year before and suggested that the Song pay a bounty for each Jin soldier killed – a suggestion the Song had taken up.[121]

The talks were inconclusive, and perhaps both sides already realised that sooner or later they would have to confront each other in Shandong. But Muqali enjoyed himself hugely, insisting that the Song envoys participate fully in Mongol drinking binges. The Mongols loved it when the Song could not hold their alcohol, got drunk, shouted with excitement, vomited or passed out. Muqali rationalised this humiliating treatment of his guests: 'If they get drunk, they are of one heart with us and no longer different.'[122] He was effusively friendly and, when the Song deputation departed, told the leader of their escort: 'In all good towns you should stay several days. If there is good wine, give it to them to drink, and if there is good food, give it to them to eat. Good flutes and good drums should be played and be beaten.'[123]

Muqali then headed south-west and crossed the Yellow River at the traditional place, Tung-Sheng, where the river turns abruptly south to complete the horseshoe. He probably had a total force of around 50,000, half of them Mongols and Onguds, half Chinese and Khitans.[124] At the Ordos he was met by the Tangut, who brought a huge force of 50,000; they had had second thoughts about their folly in exciting Genghis's wrath by refusing to serve in Turkestan, and thought this gesture would make amends for their earlier lapse. Muqali also received good news from Shanxi and eastern Hebei where both a top Jin general and a leading Song commander had come over to the Mongols.[125] He was now supremely confident, commanding a huge allied army and with his position in the east secure. He began following Samuqa's route of 1216–17. The city of Chia-chou, about halfway down the north–south stretch of the Yellow River, surrendered without a fight. Muqali found this to be ideal as a base, left a garrison of 5,000 men there, and ordered a floating bridge to link both sides of the river.

Then the run of success was interrupted by a contretemps with the Tangut. Evidently Muqali was developing delusions of grandeur as a result of his talks with the Song envoy, for he suddenly demanded that the Tangut commander, General Taga Ganbo, pay the same homage to him as was paid to the Song emperor. Not surprisingly, Taga Ganbo stormed off in dudgeon and took his army with him. Muqali, enraged in turn, pursued him and, after a forced march through the night, fell on the Tangut at first light and routed them. Many were killed in a panic-stricken flight, and the survivors were herded miserably back to the Mongol camp, where Taga Ganbo finally performed the kowtowing ritual demanded.[126]

Advancing towards Henan, Muqali learned that a Jin army had taken up a strong position on a hillside. His deputy Mongka Bukha asked to be allowed to lure the enemy out of their prepared locations by pretending to have only a small force. The ruse worked perfectly, the Jin were crushed, and left 7,000 dead on the battlefield. Muqali proceeded to the siege of Yen-an but this proved a tough nut.[127] In mid-December 1221 he therefore began the conquest of the Lo River valley – the Lo runs due south to meet the Huang He exactly where the latter swings east towards Kaifeng. The towns of Fu-chou and Fang-chou were quickly taken. At the former there was a curious and unusual incident. Muqali was questioning a warrior with a great local reputation as to why he had fought so fiercely for the Jin. The man replied that he had done so for twenty years, and his honour required him to continue doing so, even though it meant that now he must pay with his life. Muqali, moved by his courage, arose from his throne to make the sign of pardon but before he could do so his impetuous officers killed the man for 'talking back' to the generalissimo. Muqali was angry, not just for his officers' pre-empting of his judgement, but for their rare display of insubordination, something almost unknown among the Mongols.[128]

While he was holding a celebratory feast at Fang-chou, word came in that Shanxi and Shaanxi were in revolt. At the end of February 1222 Muqali crossed the Yellow River eastwards on ice and soon put down the rebellion. He then made his way back across the Huang He and marched down the Fen River, reducing strongholds as he went, and making for Ching-chou (modern Xianyang), the former capital of the Qin dynasty, a powerful city almost at the confluence of the Ching and Wei Rivers, to the west of the final eastern turn of the Yellow River. He detached Mongka Bukha and sent him back to Shaanxi to ensure it did not rise in revolt again.

At Ching-chou he found a huge Jin army waiting for him but even though they greatly outnumbered him, they hesitated to give battle, given pause both by the number of raw, untrained levies in their army and by Muqali's reputation as an invincible captain. Realising that with this great force in the vicinity he lacked the manpower to reduce Ching-chou, Muqali tried to seal off all the routes by which the city could be provisioned. With the rest of his troops he marched north-west up the valley of the Ching and began methodically capturing towns and fortresses along its length.[129] Weariness was on Muqali now and he wrote to Genghis to ask to be relieved, pointing out that he had already taken seventy-two fortresses in his career in China, and that it was time for someone else to assume the burden. But he was the victim of his own success: Genghis had no confidence that anyone else could consolidate the Mongol position in China as Muqali had.

He therefore rejected the request and told Muqali's envoy: 'Let him not return until he has taken more fortresses.'[130] It was bad luck for Muqali that yet another peace overture from the Jin had been rejected because the emperor would not agree to drop his imperial title.[131]

Heroically Muqali stuck to his task, and by January 1223 Ching-chou and all significant cities in the south-west had fallen. He then marched to join Mongka Bukha at Feng-hsiang on the upper River Wei, marking the most westerly point of this campaign. Mongka, whose performances the previous year in Shanxi and Shaanxi had been lacklustre through a poor grasp of siegecraft, was once more struggling to reduce a town. Muqali again asked for help from the Tangut and, very unexpectedly, got it: Hsi-Hsia had already taken a policy decision to pull out of the war, but the Tangut probably feared the consequences of a refusal to help the fearsome Muqali, who was now on their doorstep. A large Tangut force marched to his aid – large, certainly, but clearly nothing like the 100,000 that Chinese sources speak of.[132] Unfortunately the Tangut commander was slain almost immediately by a chance arrow fired from the city walls. His subordinates were so depressed by this and by the failure of the legendary Muqali to put a dent in the walls of the city that they pulled out. Muqali broke off the siege and once again wrote despondently to Genghis: 'After a month's siege I have failed to take Feng-hsiang. Does this mean I have come to my end?'[133]

Raising the siege, Muqali retired down the River Wei to Shaanxi, leaving Mongka Bukha to cover his retreat by a number of diversions. The Tangut meanwhile announced that they were making peace with the Jin; Muqali's failure to take Feng-hsiang convinced them that the Mongol wave had crested and broken – a judgement apparently re-inforced when the Jin retook Ho-Chung at the junction of the Wei and Yellow Rivers.[134] The circumstances seemed particularly to reinforce the Tangut opinion. Shih T'ien-ying, who had the reputation of being Muqali's most talented officer, gave the key assignment of springing an ambush on the Jin coming to relieve the town to a drunkard; the man, in his cups, forgot to give the order to attack, and the Jin passed through the 'ambuscade' unscathed. The Jin were then able to surprise the Mongols and take the town. Mortified by this horrific loss of face, T'ien-ying refused to make his escape and went down fighting.[135]

Another defeat at Ho-Chung suggested that the Mongols were on the wane, even though a counter-attack from Anchar retrieved the situation. After repairing the bridges over the Yellow River broken down by Jin guerrillas, taking more forts betimes, Muqali crossed the river and marched north-east to Wen-hsi, intending to so position himself that he could deal with either a new Jin offensive across the Yellow River or a surprise thrust from the Song in Shandong. Suddenly, though, he fell ill and died. He was 53. His last words were that he had let his master down by failing to take Kaifeng.[136]

Muqali was unquestionably a captain of genius and he had performed wonders for Genghis in China while permanently short of manpower. It was Muqali who enabled Genghis to fight successfully on two fronts – something that would later elude Napoleon, the Kaiser and Hitler and is generally considered the most elementary mistake in the military textbook. He has the distinction of being the only Mongol general who was never defeated in battle.[137] But both he and Genghis singularly underestimated the sheer tenacity of the Jin – 'this truncated state in possession of astonishing resilience and determination'.[138] When the Jin concentrated on the Song instead of the Mongols this was thought consummate folly, but they not only held the Mongols in stalemate – Muqali was never able to land a knockout blow – but repelled the Song and eventually compelled them to sue for peace. The high talent of Muqali is clear from the way he fought successfully in terrain not suited to Mongol horses, in regions rife with disease and even in boats and on rivers – a form of warfare to which the Mongols were not at all accustomed.[139]

As to whether he was the *greatest* of Genghis Khan's generals, this is more doubtful. One may perhaps concede that Muqali certainly achieved the most *during Genghis's reign*, though many would still rate Jebe higher. Sceptics say that Muqali won all his victories against the demoralised and second-rate Jin, that he never defeated the best contemporary military opposition worldwide, as did Jebe, and even more so, Subedei.[140] Genghis always possessed what Napoleon considered the key to success – luck, and never more so than in his marshals. At least three of them – Muqali, Jebe and Subedei – were military geniuses who eclipsed anything that the lieutenants of Alexander the Great, Hannibal, Julius Caesar and Napoleon were able to achieve.

The death of Muqali gave new heart to the Jin and many others who had chafed under his dominance. The Tangut took no further part in the war, while in Korea a nationalist movement slew the Mongol commissar and his staff and declared independence.[141] More seriously, the Jin ended their war with the Song. Hsuan Tsung died on 24 January 1224 and was succeeded by Ai-Tsung, who saw the folly of simultaneous war with the Mongols and the Song; the latter, as well as being masters of Shandong, were by now beginning to make serious inroads into southern Hebei. They had already acted treacherously for, as soon as Muqali went west in 1222, they struck west and took Tung Ping, adding all of western Shandong and part of eastern Hebei to their conquests.

Losing sight of reality, the Song now aspired to the conquest of Hebei, but overstretched themselves and were fought to a standstill by the Mongols under general Shih T'ien-ni.[142] There was stalemate until 1225. Genghis appointed Muqali's son Bol to succeed him, with Muqali's brother Dayisun as his deputy. Bol was an impressive figure, not only a talented soldier but a gifted linguist and a Sinophile who was markedly more humane than most other Mongols.[143] He had his work cut out, for in May 1223 the Jin invaded southern Shanxi and made significant gains. Bol struck back and in a campaign in Shanxi accumulated much booty and pushed the Jin back across the Yellow River. In September 1224, mightily encouraged by the Song–Mongol war in Hebei, the Jin crossed the Huang He again. Bol once more campaigned against them but lacked the numbers to repel them decisively; the Jin held on to their gains as far as the lower reaches of the River Fen until 1231.

Frustrated by the situation, Bol went to Mongolia to seek Genghis's advice.[144] He received scant comfort: Genghis told him he was preparing a great expedition to crush the Tangut once and for all, so could spare no more troops for China. Even worse, the irrepressible Wu Hsien, specialist in multiple defections, reappeared as a rebel against the Mongols on behalf of the Song and assassinated Shih T'ien-ni. The rebellion under Wu Hsien was serious, and for a while it seemed that the Mongols might lose the whole of western Hebei; it did not help that Bol tarried in Mongolia and paid a second visit to Genghis on the banks of the Tula in spring 1225.[145] Another multiple defector was Yen Shih, who had been appointed governor of Tung-Ping, the key city within striking distance of Kaifeng. Tung-Ping was besieged in May–June 1225 by the rising Song military star P'eng I-ping, formerly a commander with the Red Coats. Finding that he could not be relieved by Bukha, Yen Shih negotiated his desertion and ended up back with the Song and Red Coats he had betrayed seven years earlier.[146]

The conjuncture was a grave one for the Mongols, but once again the fabled luck of Genghis held. A new military hero arose in the shape of the assassinated T'ien-ni's 20-year-old brother. Six foot six inches tall, with prodigious physical strength, a voice like a great bell, also a superb archer and horseman, Shih T'ien-tse made his name by collecting a small force, surprising Wu Hsien and scattering his army.[147] When the Song made a formal alliance with Wu Hsien and assembled a large army for the conquest of Hebei, T'ien-tse at once engaged them. Though superior in numbers to the Mongols, the Song were deficient in cavalry. To offset this, the Song set fire to the hills behind him so that he could not be taken in the rear. They reckoned without Mongol ingenuity for, almost incredibly, a large party of Mongol archers managed to penetrate the smoke and emerge in the Song rear. Attacked from both sides, the Song were then utterly routed; their commander was taken and executed.[148]

The Mongols immediately went over to the offensive and recovered not just the whole of western Hebei but western Shandong too. T'ien-tse was the hero of the hour, but perhaps he grew overconfident for in November 1226 the Song took him by surprise and attacked his camp on a dark evening. T'ien-tse got away in the chaos, but fumed at this affront to his credibility. He gathered a small army, returned to the spot and surprised the Song in turn.[149]

With their position in Hebei and western Shandong thus consolidated and led by Bol from January 1227 (the sources do not explain why he had been so long absent from the front), the Mongols next attempted the conquest of eastern Shandong, the heart of the Red Coat country. There followed an arduous siege of the city of I-tu, but the Song proved doughty defenders and refused to surrender. Finally in April, racked by starvation, they attempted a breakout, to which Bol responded with a fifteen-mile feigned retreat. Finally, having lured most of the enemy troops out of I-tu, he turned and gave battle. He quickly routed the Song; many who fled from the battle drowned in a river during the pursuit. Marching back to the city, Bol resumed the siege; this time the defenders could no longer stand the dreadful trinity of Mongols, starvation and forced cannibalism and surrendered in

May.[150] The sequel showed Bol at his most statesmanlike. He refused to execute the Song commander Li Chuan, on the grounds that he was a popular local figure and his death would simply harden resistance in Shandong. He covered himself by writing to Genghis for advice on what to do, giving his reasons for sparing the commander. Genghis replied that he must do whatever he thought best, at which Bol appointed the saved man as his governor in the province.[151] He then took the city of Teng Chou in the heat of the summer.

By now the opportunists were having second thoughts about Shandong and starting to put their bets on the Mongols. One such turncoat, general Chang-ling, a former Jin commander, who had defected to the Song (and now to the Mongols), suggested an attack on Huai'an, one of the most important places in China, as it lay at the northern end of the Grand Canal.[152] This too was achieved.

With the conquest of Hebei and Shandong more or less secure, Bol went north to Mongolia in November 1227. He returned to China the following year but died in 1229 aged 32. After 1227 the Song gave up their attempts to establish themselves north of the Yellow River. Their struggle with the Mongols was a taster of the fate that would befall them a couple of generations on.

The subjugation of Hebei and Shandong was a twofold father-and-son affair, first the expulsion of the Jin by Muqali, then the defeat of the Song by Bol. It is clear that Bol had an easier time of it, that the Jin in Muqali's time were more formidable than the Song in Bol's period. But the intervention of the Song was fatal for the Jin, albeit indirectly. Genghis now saw the strategy he needed for victory. In his deathbed instructions to his sons, he advised them that the key to taking Kaifeng was to encroach on Song territory and attack the Jin capital from the south.[153]

The desultory operations in 1228–1230 were initiatives by local Mongol commanders and formed no part of Genghis's grand strategy. In late 1227 the Mongols took various towns in the Wei valley and to the south of the Liu P'an and Qin-ling Mountains. In summer 1228 another Mongol force campaigned in Shanxi and Shaanxi but to no great effect. The final conquest of north China had to await the khanate of Genghis's successor Ogodei.[154]

The Mongols had learned a lot in the long war against the Jin, notably about siegecraft and gunpowder; some scholars even credit them with being the most important motor in the spread of firearms technology.[155] Their inchoate administrative policies were also important. Some authorities speak of the 'feudalisation' of north China – part of a process whereby the steppe aristocracy extended its privileges to their Chinese collaborators, so that the new lords received a portion of the taxes collected in their domains.[156] Genghis's military achievement in China was astonishing: it was not just the initial disparity of numbers and the idea of a mouse (on paper) swallowing a lion, but that he accomplished it while engaged elsewhere in what are generally considered his two greatest feats of arms; the defeat of the Khwarezmian empire and the conquest of Hsi-Hsia and the Tangut. The mystery deepens if we accept the view, popular in some quarters, that the Chinese crossbow at the time was a more accurate weapon than the Mongol longbow.[157]

The genius of Muqali provides part of the explanation. But Genghis was also lucky in that his enemies were hopelessly divided, with Red Coats, Song, Jin and Tangut all identifying one another as more important enemies than the invaders from the north. The rallying of Khitans (and later Chinese) in large numbers to the Mongol banner was also crucial. The Mongol–Khitan synergy was especially important, as both had machine-like organisation and high mobility.[158] Yet the genius of Genghis in spotting the potential for a conquest of China can never be denied. Although he was physically present for less than five of the twenty-three years of warfare with the Jin, it was his spirit that animated the whole enterprise.

9

Westward Diversions

The principal reason for Genghis's inability to complete the conquest of Jin China was that events to the west of his empire claimed his urgent attention. The expansion of the Mongol empire westwards was the result of both commercial pressures and geopolitics, but to show how it came about we have to 'flash back' to the twelfth century to examine the dual influence and impact of the realm of Khwarezmia and the kingdom of Qara Khitai (modern Xinjiang), their interpenetration and what Thomas Hardy would have called 'the convergence of the twain'.[1] Qara Khitai, the fourth of the twelfth-century states that make up what is now China, was founded by the Khitans after the overthrow of the Liao dynasty in China in 1125. Its rulers never entirely abandoned the dream of returning one day as the rulers of China. The Qara Khitans thus stood to the Jin empire in much the same relation as the Jacobites in Britain to the Hanoverians in the eighteenth century or, perhaps more relevantly, the displaced Kuomintang of Taiwan to the China of Mao Tse-tung. To put it another way, Qara Khitai was the continuation of the Liao dynasty by other means.[2]

The Liao dynasty was destroyed by a two-pronged attack from the Jurchens (who founded the Jin dynasty in 1125) and the Song. From the ruins of their empire one remarkable individual arose, a man of energy, resourcefulness and military talent that would have commended him to Genghis had they been contemporaries. Born in 1087, Yelu Dashi fled with the last Liao emperor Tianzuo north to Manchuria and then into Mongolia. Captured by the Jurchens, who seem not to have realised the importance of their catch, he managed to escape after five months and rejoined Tianzuo.[3] The emperor still hankered after a campaign of reconquest but Yelu, wisest of his advisers, warned that the Jurchens were far too strong and that the idea of a victorious return to China was a chimera. Unable to convince Tianzuo, Yelu parted company and started west with his companions. It was said that he joined the emperor with 7,000 men but when he left him he had just 5,000, along with 10,000 horses.[4] He was soon proved right in his prognostications when Tianzuo was taken prisoner, ending the dream of reconquest.

The subsequent history of Qara Khitai involved almost constant campaigning, including battles with the Qarakhanid people, the Seljuk Turks and, finally and most significantly, the kingdom of Khwarezmia and the shah of that kingdom, Muhammad II, who came to the throne in 1200. (See Appendix 2).

Into this turbid political bouillabaisse yet another element was dropped, this one the most important of all, for in 1208 the fleeing Quqluq, last hope of the Naiman, arrived in Qara Khitai after the Mongols' crushing defeat of the Naiman on the Irtysh. Appearing in the Qara Khitan capital with just a small band of loyalists, he was given a hero's welcome by the ruler, the gur-khan Zhilugu, partly because the Naiman and Qara Khitai had always been allies but, more importantly, because Zhilugu perceived Quqluq as a useful ally, beset as he was by the Mongols in the east and shah Muhammad in the West. He treated Quqluq as an honorary son, presented him with splendid robes and other raiment, conferred the title of khan on him, gave him one of his daughters in marriage and, more foolishly, allowed him to build up a private army with which, supposedly, Quqluq would one day strike back at the Mongols.[5] A magnet for fugitive and renegade Naiman, Merkit and all other enemies of Genghis Khan, Quqluq's 'praetorian guard' was soon 8,000 strong. It seems that Zhilugu was worried about the loyalty of his mainly Islamic subjects if it came to a showdown with Muhammad, and Quqluq was able to sell the idea of his second army as a non-Islamic 'ace in the hole' in case of hostilities. The foolish gur-khan saw clearly the threat from Khwarezmia and from the Mongols but ignored the dangerous cuckoo in his own nest.[6]

Once he was powerful enough to be a major player in his own right, the ingrate Quqluq, who owed everything to his father-in-law, began intriguing with shah Muhammad, proposing that they divide up Qara Khitai between them. Muhammad initially dithered, attracted by a counter-offer from Qara Khitai that involved intermarriage and a huge sum of money.[7] So confident was Zhilugu that his offer would be accepted that he departed on a hunt, during which Ququq tried to ambush him.[8] Baulked in this attempt, the dauntless Ququq found another partner in the form of Arslan of the Qarluqs. Together they launched a surprise attack on the Qara Khitan state treasury at Uzgand and emptied the vaults. Prompted by this, Muhammad finally agreed to support Ququq openly.

The war that followed was part external, part a civil conflict in Qara Khitai itself. At first Ququq did not fare well. Zhilugu made a forced march with his army, which was still formidable, with an especially proficient cavalry arm.[9] He caught up with his treacherous son-in-law and defeated him near the capital Balasaqun, regaining much of the money stolen from the treasury. At this Arslan took fright, abandoned Ququq and fled to Genghis to plead for protection on condition of becoming a Mongol vassal. Although badly defeated, Ququq and most of his troops escaped the battlefield. With Mohammed in the west and Ququq in the east, Qara Khitai was being raided from two different directions. Even worse, it seemed that Zhilugu's worst fears about the loyalty of his subjects were about to be realised, for when he returned to Balasaqun after his victory, the Islamic inhabitants of the town closed the gates against him. There followed a sixteen-day siege, at the end of which Zhilugu used war elephants to smash his way into the town. He then slaughtered every last inhabitant, to the number of 47,000.[10]

But in western Qara Khitai Muhammad was gaining the upper hand. Joined by Othman, lord of Samarkand and his mightiest subject, he crossed the River Jaxartes (Syr Darya), marched north up the valley of the Arys and over the pass to the Taraz valley. He then advanced against a huge army commanded by Qara Khitai's best general Tayangu and, after a ferocious battle in September 1210 near the Jaxartes, was lucky enough to gain the advantage.[11] The honours on the battlefield were even, with the left wing of both armies overcoming the opposing right, so that the outcome was indecisive. Then, in one of those flukes on which history pivots, Tayangu took the wrong turning, blundered into the enemy's ranks, was captured and immediately executed.[12] Nevertheless, at this stage the best military analysts thought that Zhilugu would win the war in the end, as he certainly would have done had Ququq not complicated the picture.[13]

In the years after 1211, however, the kingdom of Qara Khitai came to a sudden end. Continual warfare had drained the treasury, there was a dramatic and precipitous financial crisis, and Zhilugu was informed by his advisers that there was no money with which to pay the troops. Zhilugu hit on the 'solution' of confiscating the wealth his soldiers had seized back from Ququluq after the treasury raid – which of course was the money Ququluq had originally stolen but which Zhilugu had had to promise to his men as a reward for retrieving it; such was the Alice-through-the-Looking-Glass situation in Qara-Khitai. The inevitable consequence was an army mutiny. Ququluq put himself at the head of the mutineers, seized Zhilugu and held him under comfortable house arrest. For two years Zhilugu was the nominal head of state but Ququluq was the real power in the land. When Zhilugu died in 1213, Ququluq abandoned all pretence and had himself declared gur-khan.[14] His intentions for his new realm have divided scholars: some think he merely wanted to usurp the throne while others postulate a grandiose plan to extirpate the old traditions and build a new society.[15] He accepted a situation where the old boundaries of Qara Khitai were broken up, with Muhammad controlling the former western sector and himself lord of the eastern. This unsatisfactory compromise was unlikely to endure long, given the shah's vaulting imperial ambitions, but for a while Ququluq enjoyed a respite while Muhammad was occupied elsewhere.[16]

A profound problem for the shah, which would continue to dog him to the end of his life, was that he could not control his troops, who were almost the stereotypical licentious soldiery, alienating the shah's new subjects by rape and pillage. In 1212 Othman, lord of Samarkand, decided that the shah's tax-collectors were even more rapacious than the old Qara Khitan administration had been, and rose in revolt; or rather he tried to take control of a popular uprising that had already broken out. All the men of Khwarezmia in Samarkand were hunted down, butchered and their disjointed limbs hung as trophies in bazaars.[17] This massacre of Muhammad's men inside the city led to bloody reprisal. The shah besieged the city, took it, massacred 10,000 leading citizens *in terrorem* and beheaded Othman.[18] The great city of Samarkand, rich from commerce, industry and the great silver mines of the upper Zarafshan River, had now endured three sieges in as many years, and its travails were far from over.

Muhammad, though, was elated. This was the second time he had emerged as the victor after a three-cornered struggle. The first was in the early years of the century, when he, Zhilugu and the Ghurids fought for supremacy (see Appendix 2), and the second the contending troika of himself, Zhilugu and Quqluq. It is not surprising that he began to consider himself one of Allah's chosen ones. He moved his capital from Gurganj (Urgench) to Samarkand, took the title of sultan and styled himself 'the second Alexander the Great'.[19] Nonetheless it was objectively true that he was by now probably the greatest power in the Islamic world. Having conquered the western regions of the old Qara Khitai, sacked cities along the Syr Darya and in Ferghana, he controlled an area that extended from the Syr Darya to Iraq.[20] He was effectively lord of the Caspian, that great inland sea that had fascinated the ancients from Herodotus to Pliny the Elder.[21]

During his three-year reign from 1213 to 1216 Quqluq looked apprehensively westward at Muhammad's rising power but there were no overt hostilities: fortunately for him, as he had his hands full with internal revolts. In 1213 the people of Kashgar rose in revolt because of Quqluq's religious policies; this was a serious insurrection which failed the following year only because the people were reduced to starvation. The famine was no act of God but a deliberate policy of savagery by Quqluq, who not only burned the harvest but then billeted his troops on families who were already starving.[22]

The old saw states that those whom the gods wish to destroy they first make mad, and Quqluq fulfilled the precept to the last letter. For reasons that are obscure, he became a religious fanatic and an anti-Islamic zealot. Apostatising from Nestorian Christianity, he embraced an idiosyncratic faith that seems to have been part Buddhism, part shamanism.[23] He abandoned one wife for another more in sympathy with his new vision of salvation and announced that henceforth all his subjects would have to embrace either Buddhism or Nestorian Christianity. The Muslims, always the majority, were scandalised but when the imam of Khotan publicly denounced the policy, Quqluq had him crucified at the door of his own school.[24] The obvious consequence was that all Muslims now yearned for the day when a liberator would deliver them from Quqluq's tyranny.

It is worth emphasising Quqluq's arrant stupidity. Anyone wishing to build a new society on the foundations of the old Qara Khitai had to find some way of binding up the wounds of religious factionalism, and to dampen down the latent tension between Islam and Buddhism. Instead, the new gur-khan did the exact opposite.[25] He was absurdly confident of his position – absurdly, as he had a powerful nation on either frontier and had alienated the majority of his subjects through his despotism. Even worse, he had cut away at his own financial base as the powerful Muslim merchants wanted no further dealings with such an enemy of the faith.[26] Because Genghis had been absent in China for five years, Quqluq took his eye off the ball in the east and seems to have forgotten that he was still a marked man in Mongol eyes. In the west he continued to underestimate Muhammad, partly because of the shah's unaccountable diffidence about mounting a full-scale campaign against Qara Khitai, preferring periodic raids.[27] Quqluq, annoyed both by the devastation these caused and his inability to tempt Muhammad to a decisive battle, finally snapped and sent the shah a challenge to single combat. Muhammad, never personally courageous, became so petrified by the mere idea of a duel that he pulled out of the Khitan border towns he had occupied.[28] But his imperial arrogance did not diminish. In 1217 he made a triumphal progress through Persia, receiving the submission of any provinces that had hitherto held out. He quarrelled with the caliph once more and was on the point of marching on Baghdad when news came in that the balance of power on his eastern border had changed irrevocably. The Mongols had arrived in Qara Khitai.[29]

Genghis had never been particularly interested in Qara Khitai. It was true that Zhilugu had done himself no favours by welcoming Quqluq, but Genghis was wise enough to see that this was part of a continuing pattern whereby Qara Khitai tended to favour the losers on the steppes; in his dark days Toghril had been a frequent suppliant there but the gur-khan told him, reasonably enough, that Mongolia was too far away and the logistical problems too great for his army to be able to operate credibly there.

There were two main reasons why Genghis put the Qara Khitans in an entirely different class from the Tangut. Genghis's abiding ambition was to conquer the Jin empire of China. Hsi-Hsia was important strategically in the pursuit of such a goal; Qara Khitai was not. Again, Tangut meddling in the steppe wars had angered Genghis, but Qara Khitai played no part whatever in these conflicts, and was totally absent in the crucial years 1196–1205.[30] Therefore, Genghis had no particular animus towards its people and, in the second decade of the thirteenth century, no great interest in western Central Asia either. It was Quqluq's usurpation of power that changed everything. Angry that the Naiman prince was still at large and now, as ruler of Qara Khitai, seemingly thumbing his nose at him, Genghis needed little encouragement to send his well-oiled military machine west.

The occasion arose when Buzar, ruler of Almaliq on the River Ili (near modern Kuldja in Xinjiang), declared himself a vassal of Genghis's and asked for military help. Buzar was a former horse-thief who used the breakup of Qara Khitai to carve himself a fiefdom in a remote region. Never fastidious about the background of his allies, Genghis promised him one of Jochi's daughters as a bride. But before the Mongols could reach him, Quqluq launched a surprise attack on Buzar while he was out hunting, captured him and executed him. His son and widow appealed to Genghis to honour the ancient code of revenge, which he was happy to do.[31] He sent out Jebe at the head of 20,000 men with orders to occupy Qara Khitai and seek out Quqluq and kill him. Arslan was also sent ahead with a flying column, to reinforce Almaliq and stiffen its resistance until Jebe got there.[32]

As Jebe rode west, more and more cities opened their gates to him, the Muslim populations welcoming him as a deliverer from Quqluq's religious tyranny. Jebe scooped up the Uighurs, reached Almaliq, repelled the enemy and incorporated Arslan's Qarluqs into his host. At Balasagun Quqluq made a stand with an army of 30,000 but Jebe rolled it up contemptuously as if it had been a paper force and entered the Qara Khitan capital in triumph.

The whole of eastern Turkestan was now part of the Mongol empire.[33] More and more Muslim emirs went over to Jebe, convinced they had nothing more to fear from Quqluq. Qara Khitai was no more: the only (academic) question left was whether it ceased to exist in 1216 when Jebe entered the gates, or had already ceased to be after Quqluq's coup in 1213.[34] The leading Qara Khitan soldiers and bureaucrats were incorporated by the Mongols and went to work in the Mongol empire; they could be found later in positions from Russia to China as well as in important roles outside the empire, in India and the Baghdad caliphate. A handful of 'refuseniks' fled to the shah and a tiny remnant to the Cumans.[35]

After setting up a new government in Qara Khitai, Jebe turned south and pursued Quqluq into Kashgaria, proclaiming as he went that all who accepted Mongol suzerainty would have total freedom of worship. It had always been consummate folly for Quqluq to seek sanctuary in the region where he was most hated for his earlier scorched-earth campaigns, but at this concession from the Mongols Kashgaria simply erupted. All Muslim towns with Quqluq's troops billeted on them rose up and slaughtered them, and he was soon reduced to his personal bodyguard.[36]

Meanwhile Genghis proclaimed that 1217–18 would be the time when he finally swept aside all enemies. While Jebe and his host dealt with Quqluq, Jochi and Subedei were sent against the Merkit, who had found new allies north of the Aral Sea in the shape of the Cumans, a powerful confederacy of tribes destined to play a major part in Mongol history. The power of Genghis's streamlined militarised bureaucracy and his peerless army can be appreciated from one single fact: in 1217–18 he was able to commit major forces on three different fronts,[37] with Muqali in China, Jebe in pursuit of Quqluq, and Jochi and Subedei hounding the last of the Merkit north of the Syr Darya, where they inflicted a shattering defeat on them and their Cuman allies.[38]

Masterly though Jochi and Subedei's strategy and tactics were, they were matched by Jebe in Kashgaria. Pursuing his quarry relentlessly 'like a mad dog', he made sure that Quqluq was hemmed in on all sides, menaced by the shah in the west, Subedei and Jochi in the north, the Mongols in the east and continually harassed by a hostile population in all parts of the former Qara Khitai, who welcomed Jebe and his army as 'one of the mercies of the Lord'.[39] Jebe issued strict orders that there was to be no looting, since the locals hailed them as saviours but this favourable opinion could be altered by a single act of rapine. For 350 miles Jebe dogged the Naiman prince, through the Muztagh Ata mountain range and the Pamirs to the plateau of Badakhshan at 9,000 feet, climbing at one point to 12,600 feet to get through a pass, through a desolate, arid landscape of stark peaks, plunging ravines and massive glaciers.[40] He also sent a small detachment to northern Ferghana to receive the formal submission of the governor there.

At the border of Badakhshan and the mountainous Wakhan region (between today's north-east Afghanistan and south-eastern Tajikistan), near the headwaters of the Oxus (Amu Darya), Quqluq blundered into a box canyon where he and his small detachment were captured by a party of local hunters. Realising the value of their catch, they handed him over to Jebe, who had Ququluq beheaded; the severed head was placed on a pole and paraded all the way back to Almaliq.[41]

Jebe had achieved a complete triumph and once again displayed his brilliance, but his very success made Genghis uneasy. Always jealous and with more than a touch of paranoia, Genghis feared that Jebe might decide to set himself up as the new lord of Qara Khitai. But Jebe was far too intelligent to fall foul of a vengeful khan, whose wrath was like a typhoon. He sent Genghis a gift of one thousand chestnut horses with white muzzles, a reminder of a (single) identical horse he had received as a gift from the great khan many years before. A shrewd reader of human nature, Jebe had pressed exactly the right buttons; Genghis was delighted by the brilliant gesture and all his suspicions were allayed.[42]

Having finally quelled all insurrections among the Forest Peoples, destroyed the Merkit, mauled the Cumans, conquered Qara Khitai and executed Ququluq, Genghis naturally expected that he could return to the conquest of the Jin. But as it turned out he was overtaken by the sheer contingency of 'events' and forced instead to confront shah Muhammad. It has to be stressed that Genghis had at this stage no interest in conquest farther west than Qara Khitai and did his best to avoid conflict with the new empire of Khwarezmia. Geopolitical and economic considerations would certainly have made a clash inevitable by, say, the late 1220s, but that is very different from postulating bellicose intentions by the Mongols in 1218. It was essentially the stupidity and recklessness of Muhammad's policy of aggressive expansionism that must take most of the blame for bringing on the struggle with Genghis. It has been well said that Qara Khitai provided a wall or barrier between the Mongols and the world of Islam but that the shah mindlessly tore it down, with incalculably baneful consequences for his co-religionists.[43]

Genghis's remarkable restraint in the face of these different provocations arrogantly offered by Muhammad in the year 1218 was notable. First the shah offered battle to Jochi and Subedei. On many different occasions the shah had identical thoughts to Genghis but he arrived at his conclusions so slowly that when he finally acted he found himself pre-empted by the Mongols. Thus early in 1218 he became angry at the presence of the combined Merkit–Cuman host on the soil of his empire and set out with an army to chastise the interlopers, only to discover Jochi and Subedei had got there first. The sources are not totally reliable on the fine details of this campaign, but one account speaks of the shah reaching the River Irghiz, finding the ice on the river too weak to bear his cavalry and having to wait for it to melt.[44] We may take leave to doubt that he finally crossed it on the very day the Mongol army under Jochi and Subedei annihilated the Merkit, but at any rate at dawn the next day the two armies virtually collided with each other. Jochi requested peaceful passage, stressing in a message to the shah that his father had forbidden him to engage in battle with anyone but the Merkit or Cumans. Muhammad arrogantly sent back word that the Mongols were trespassers and must prepare to take the consequences.[45]

Reluctantly Jochi drew up his army, knowing he was heavily outnumbered, perhaps three to one (his own army of 20,000 facing possibly 60,000). His troops performed brilliantly and the cavalry charge from the Mongol right swept away the enemy left. However, the shah's right wing, led by his most talented general, his son Jalal al-Din, did likewise to the Mongol left. Both rights then wheeled around and in an all-day slugging encounter fought each other to a standstill until nightfall.[46] The shah confidently expected battle to be resumed next day, when he assumed his numbers would finally tell, but the Mongols performed their favourite trick of slipping away under cover of darkness, leaving campfires burning to make it appear they were still there.[47] Muhammad could claim a technical victory, but the truth was that he had been badly shaken by the ferocity and fighting spirit of the Mongols. Some historians go so far as to say that, with his tendency towards neurasthenia, from that day on Muhammad had a 'complex' about facing the Mongols on the battlefield – something that was to have dire consequences later.[48]

When the encounter was reported to Genghis, he was inclined to wave it aside as inconsequential, the result perhaps of a ruler's hyper-trophied territorial sensitivity. Khwarezmian propaganda to the effect that the shah was not personally present at the battle and had not authorised it made it easier for Genghis not to construe it as a personal insult, though he knew the truth full well. He decided on an exchange of embassies to agree a trade treaty and any boundary disputes. The shah sent a mission headed by Baha al-Din Razi, which Genghis received with full honours and even allowed to travel to China to see the extent of his conquests there. He told Baha that he wanted a comprehensive pact covering all possible contentious areas and that he should take a message to Muhammad that whereas he, Genghis, was the ruler of the East, the shah was the ruler of the West.[49] Whether by accident or design, Baha reported this to Muhammad in the following words: 'I am the sovereign of the sunrise and you are the sovereign of the sunset'[50] – with a subtext suggesting a waxing and waning power respectively.

Privately, Genghis was contemptuous of the gifts of silk and cotton Baha had brought from Muhammad, and said to his confidants: 'Does this man imagine we have never seen stuff like this?'[51] Nevertheless early in 1218 he sent an embassy to Bukhara under two of his top Islamic bureaucrats, Mahmud Yalavach and Yusuf Kanka, bearing lavish gifts including a huge nugget of gold found in China.[52] Genghis's oral message of peace and amity wound up by calling the shah 'my son', which sent Muhammad into a furious rage, as it was the way overlords usually addressed their vassals. He then accused Yalavach of being nothing more than a spy and threatened to execute him on the spot unless he turned informer and gave him every last secret detail about the Mongol empire. Yalavach proved a cool customer and talked his way out of a tight spot, shrewdly mixing circumstantial detail and general bromides in an olio that calmed and placated Muhammad.[53] He stressed that Genghis had no warlike intentions and wished only to return to complete his conquest of the Jin empire, that in any case the army of Khwarezmia was far stronger and more numerous than the Mongols' tumens and that in no way could the realm of the khan compare with the mighty empire Muhammad had created as the new superman of Islam. Flattered, cajoled and relieved, the shah relaxed and allowed Yalavach and Yusuf Kanka to go on their way.[54]

But secretly he still revolved bitter, angry and resentful thoughts. He had been slow about moving against Qara Khitai in 1216 and the Mongols had got there first; he had dreamed of the conquest of China only to learn that the Mongols had just sacked Peking;[55] and he had been intending to destroy the caliphate in Baghdad until the news of the Merkit and Cuman incursion – for which the Mongols were entirely responsible – had diverted his attention. It is not certain if he knew that his mortal enemy the caliph al-Nasir had been in touch with Genghis, encouraged by the glowing reports of Mongol religious tolerance in defeated Qara Khitai. It is unlikely that the caliph actually asked Genghis to attack Muhammad – this would have been a disaster for Islam, even if personally pleasing – but in any case Genghis never allowed himself to be influenced by the views of other potentates.[56] Such was Muhammad's ineptitude that in 1217 he finally did essay a march on Baghdad, which ended in disaster. The determined opposition of the Kurds on his itinerary and the fact of his army's getting trapped in a ferocious snowstorm in the Zagros Mountains put paid to that ill-advised endeavour.[57]

No sooner was Yalavach out of the shah's territory than a huge Mongol trade caravan arrived at the northern Khwarezmian city of Otrar. It comprised 450 Muslim merchants, five hundred camels and one hundred Mongol cavalrymen as escorts, along with a personal envoy from the Mongol khan. The arrival of this caravan at this juncture calls for further comment. It was sent under Genghis's personal aegis, and he had put up most of the operating capital for the venture.[58] By this time there was a firm commercial entente between Genghis and the influential and far-flung corpus of Islamic merchants. Long desirous of breaking into the lucrative Chinese market, they had been invited to do so by the victorious khan.[59] The relationship was mutually beneficial, as the Muslims were powerful middlemen, very important to the Mongols for two distinct reasons: by this time the Mongols bought their clothes internationally and needed agents for the transactions; and because they had devastated the agricultural lands of north China, they now needed to import grain. Common interests dictated a commercial alliance, and there was no real barrier, since the merchants of Islam were attracted by Genghis's well-known religious tolerance.[60] As icing on the cake, the Muslims were invaluable sources of intelligence.

The immediate aim of the trade mission to Otrar was to get Khwarezmia to lift a trade embargo resulting in a serious shortage of cloth in Mongolia. Once the shah seized Transoxiana from Qara Khitai he severed the trade routes between eastern Turkestan and Transoxiana; Genghis's personal envoy aimed to get this interdiction waived.[61] Some critics say that Genghis allowed himself to be inveigled into a trade war by unscrupulous and manipulative Islamic merchants, others that he was testing the waters of the shah's intent. Yet another view is that such a massive caravan, with bulging wealth, was meant to overawe the shah and impress him with the Mongols' enormous purchasing power.[62]

Whatever the truth of this, what happened at Otrar was an outrage that echoed round Asia. Inalchuq Qayir-Khan, governor of Otrar, flew into a rage and had all but one of his 550 guests massacred. He claimed his actions were necessary because the mission was one great espionage expedition.

This was absurd. All business and trade visits to foreign countries in all eras can be described as 'spying' if one takes the meaning of that word at its most elastic. It was natural that any caravan, anywhere, would routinely collect intelligence on the places it visited; not to do so would be unintelligent in the demotic sense.[63] He also claimed that a member of the caravan, an old acquaintance, had addressed him by his former name (Inalchuq) and not his new title as governor (the self-styled Qayir-Khan) – yet another absurdity. It is possible, as has been suggested, that he was angered by members of the visiting party boasting about their riches,[64] but the plain truth seems to be that he was actuated by greed pure and simple. It is inconceivable that he would have taken such an action, with tremendous international repercussions, if the shah had not already given the nod. Some say the governor sought Muhammad's permission first, others that the shah ordered him to do it.[65] So either Muhammad was unconscionably greedy himself and had hatched a plot to share the vast loot with the governor (perhaps aware of the extent of Genghis's investment) or he had already resolved on war with the Mongols and had decided to present them with an unavoidable *casus belli*.[66]

Only one man, a camel driver, escaped the slaughter. It so happened that he was taking a bath when the massacre began and managed to lie hidden by the fireplace of the hot bath as the governors' troops rushed by in their blood frenzy. He then hid for three days and nights on a mountain top before making his perilous way back to Genghis's court to report the atrocity.

Once again Genghis's restraint was extraordinary. The shah had offered him a gross personal insult, had offended against all the canons of the then rudimentary international law and was, even by medieval standards, guilty of a war crime. Besides all this, Genghis had taken a huge hit in the thirteenth-century equivalent of the pocketbook. Despite which, his response was to send yet another embassy to

Muhammad, this time a triumvirate consisting of a senior Muslim diplomat and two Mongol grandees. The envoys announced that Genghis was prepared to give the shah the benefit of the doubt and assume that the Otrar incident was a demented personal initiative by Inalchuq, provided Muhammad deliver up the governor to be tried by Mongol justice. An irate Muhammad declared this gross impertinence, slew the Muslim head of mission and sent the two Mongols back with their hair shaved and their beards singed off.[67]

Finally stirred to anger, Genghis remarked contemptuously of his enemy: 'He is no king, he is a bandit.'[68] He then went up into Mount Burqan Qaldun and prayed for three days to Tengerri to give him victory in the *guerre à outrance* he now intended to wage. Ironically, an embassy from Muhammad on its return journey – it may even have crossed with the two shaven Mongols on their disconsolate way home – brought sombre news to the shah about the enormous power and potential of the Mongol empire. When he heard their report, Muhammad was cast down and was heard to say that he wished he had never authorised the Otrar massacre.[69]

It was too late now. Genghis sent a final message to the shah: 'You kill my men and my merchants and you take from them my property. Prepare for war, for I am coming against you with a host you cannot withstand.'[70] A worried Muhammad called a grand council of war at which his advisers asserted confidently that they held all the cards. The Mongols would have to come to them over nigh-impossible terrain and, by the time they had crossed a series of mountain ranges and the River Jaxartes they would be easy meat.[71] The counsellors also pointed out that the Mongols liked to bring their foes to battle at the earliest possible moment, and that was how they had destroyed the armies of the Jin in the first year of the China campaign. The best thing, therefore, was to refuse to play by Genghis's rules, to shelter inside heavily fortified cities which the Mongols, with their primitive siegecraft, could not take and from which powerful garrisons could, at the right time, sortie and destroy the besiegers. What they advocated was essentially the strategy the Romans had used against Hannibal during the invasion of Italy in 219–202 BC and which the Russians would use against Napoleon in 1812.[72]

But they forgot two essential points. One was that the logical corollary of their argument that the Mongol armies would be exhausted when they reached Khwarezmia was surely that the shah had to engage them there and then, before they could rest and recover their strength. The second was that, although on paper Muhammad's armies outnumbered Genghis's by two to one, this advantage was simply thrown away if they merely retreated into fortified cities. In a word, they would never have local superiority of force. Their armies would be dispersed over huge distances, allowing a united Mongol army to pick them off piecemeal. This of course is the classical tenet of concentration of force.[73]

Genghis made his usual meticulous preparations for the following campaign. Maps were drawn, the accuracy of commissariat arrangements checked and rechecked, the geography of the vast area of Khwarezmia pored over. At the many war councils the Mongols rehearsed the several advantages they were likely to enjoy. The most important was the infancy and disorganisation of Muhammad's realm. The empire about which the shah boasted was less than two years old and riven by fissiparous tendencies of all kinds. The central weakness was the antagonism of the nomadic Turks Muhammad used as his military arm and the sedentary Iranians, between whom there was notoriously bad blood. The shah had never been able to control his troops, who rampaged at will through the empire, alienating the peasantry, who also suffered from the violence and lawlessness of tax-farmers. Even if he had been able to manage these foreign mercenaries, Muhammad would not do so, as he depended on them to keep himself in power.[74] Where Genghis's empire had been efficiently centralised and the old localist loyalties broken down by the new decimal system, there was no real patriotism or even *esprit de corps* in Khwarezmia. A victim of its own prosperity, the entire region always threatened to disintegrate into its constituent parts, with each area displaying a 'what's in it for me?' attitude towards the wider empire (in China prosperity had been limited to the elite, and a militarised peasantry offered stiffer resistance). Nor did the polyglot nature of the shah's realm help matters.[75]

The conflict between the shah's centralising policy and the traditional autonomy of the feudal lords produced a result where twenty-two of the mightiest regional oligarchs were even then languishing in Muhammad's jails; at the very first chance of liberation they and their levies would join the Mongols. Because of his disastrous relations with the caliphate Muhammad could not play the Muslim's usual trump card – declaration of holy war against the infidel. The shah's army itself was unreliable, too dependent on Cuman mercenaries who obeyed their own lords. No talented generals had emerged except for Jalal al-Din, who was eclipsed for other reasons.[76] The shah was personally unpopular in his land, being viewed as a capricious and arbitrary despot. There were serious divisions in his council, with some advocating abandoning Transoxiana and retreating to Khorasan or the Ghazni region of Afghanistan.

Above all there was the problem of the shah's family. His nepotism was notorious; particularly resented was the way he replaced tried and tested local rulers with useless cousins and nephews. Yet all this paled into insignificance beside the almost unbelievable problems posed by his own mother Terken Qatun, a cruel, violent, manipulative, wilful and opinionated woman, who dominated and browbeat the essentially weak Muhammad. Most government officials were from her tribe (the Qipchaq, close confederates of the Cumans), and a kind of dyarchy existed within the fragile empire, with the shah dominant in Samarkand and the matriarch ruling over Khorasan proper. The two competed with each other in issuing empire-wide decrees, often contradictory and sometimes expressly rescinding the ukases of the other. A bewildered and harassed officialdom usually solved the problem by obeying the decree bearing the latest date.[77] Terken Qatun forced Muhammad to pass over his talented eldest son Jalal al-Din in favour of Uzlaq-Shah the beloved youngest son of the family, born of a different woman, but one who was her protégé and servant. Her hatred for Jalal al-Din was notable, which was why he was given the unimportant post of governor of Afghanistan.[78]

Given the brilliance of his espionage and intelligence system, Genghis was able to make use of all these internal weaknesses even before the fighting started. The Mohammedan merchants and their own agents had penetrated the shah's inner councils, and 'moles' reported what went on there. Genghis even knew that the Iranian soothsayers had warned the shah that the omens for the coming war were not favourable.[79] Khwarezmia was a gift for masters of disinformation. It was the easiest thing in the world to issue bogus decrees, purporting to come from the shah or from Terken Qatun, snarling the military and bureaucracy up into a tangle of confusion. On this occasion Genghis surpassed himself by circulating rumours that

Terken Qatun intended to join the Mongols, that she would rather be their prisoner than submit to Muhammad and Jalal al-Din.[80]

Genghis and his generals also pored over maps, pondering the differential landscape of the shah's realm. Like the jungle, the difficult terrain of Khwarezmia was neutral, favouring neither the Mongols nor their enemy. The shah ruled over territory stretching from the Aral Sea to the Persian Gulf and from the Pamirs in the east to the Zagros Mountains in the west (including all of modern Afghanistan and part of modern Turkey), but his lands were wildly heterogeneous. There were many deserts and semi-deserts – of gravel and saline clay – as well as steppes. A possible approach was from the east across the vast Taklamakan Desert, 100,000 square miles of nothingness[81] punctuated here and there by the oases provided by the River Tarim and its tributaries, which flow eventually into the swamps of Lop Nor, a saline lake.[82] Even more formidable were the mountains surrounding the Taklamakan desert – the Altyn-Tagh ('Gold Mountain'), with its wooded slopes to the south, between the desert and the Tibetan plateau, the T'ien Shan to the north and the Pamirs to the west.

The runoff water from many of these mountains converges at Kashgar, a notable and fertile centre for agriculture and horticulture (maize, corn, orchards, vineyards). There were many oases along the Silk Route linking China, Persia and the Levant, and that would later be the main thoroughfare for armies, traders, pilgrims and western visitors like Carpini, Rubruck and Marco Polo. But that was a later development; in 1219 this seemed an unattractive line of approach for Genghis and his armies. Nevertheless all oases and cultivated areas would be targets for the Mongols, for Genghis realised one could bring an enemy to its knees by destroying its economic infrastructure. A more tempting target would be Transoxiana – the country between the Oxus and the Jaxartes – shaped something like the letter H lying on its side, with the populated area largely limited to the river banks and the broad crossbar of the H, that is to say the courses of the Oxus (Amu Darya), Jaxartes (Syr Darya) and Zarafshan. Today Transoxiana approximates to Uzbekistan, Tajikistan, southern Kyrgystan and south-west Kazakhstan. Later famous from Matthew Arnold's poem *Sohrab and Rustum*, in medieval times the region owed its fame to Alexander the Great's conquests there in the 320s BC.[83] Between this central densely populated area and the Aral Sea was the great desert or desert-steppe of the Kizil

Kum or Red Sands, 135,000 square miles in area. To the west of Transoxiana, with its western border on the Caspian Sea, was Khwarezm proper, and to the south of Transoxiana was Khorasan. East of the settled belt of agriculture rise huge mountains, the peaks getting higher the farther east one goes, with correspondingly difficult and precipitous passes. The only real means of communication between the upper Oxus and Jaxartes was the valley of the Vakhsh, itself almost impassable; at their lower end both rivers flowed into the Aral Sea.[84]

The geography of Khwarezmia alone was a tough nut for an invader to crack. But each separate area would throw up different problems relating to the horses, food supplies and logistics, and all would have to be carefully 'wargamed' beforehand. Genghis played his cards close to his chest as regards the itinerary he intended to take, as this was the most crucial piece of information an enemy spy could learn. As for the numbers in Muhammad's army, these were supposed to amount to 400,000 – probably a gross exaggeration, with 200,000 being a more credible estimate.[85] But Genghis knew from his spies that Muhammad did not intend to confront him in battle, so he realised that he would always have local superiority of numbers over the dispersed garrisons.

As for Muhammad's supposed prowess as a captain, Genghis largely discounted this. It was true that he had done well in the war of 1203–06 against Muhammad of Ghor and the Ghurids, but on that occasion he had been united with the then powerful Qara Khitai.[86] Even if, by some mischance, the Mongols had to confront the full host of Khwarezmia in battle, Genghis and his generals were confident. The shah might have great numerical superiority but his troops lacked the Mongols' iron discipline, their unswerving obedience to the khan, and their capacity for hardship; they had not been inured to the privations on the march and the suffering before and during battle that made the Mongol army so formidable. Besides, defending, the shah's troops could hope for little gain but, attacking, the Mongols would be spurred on by the thought of vast wealth and loot.[87] To offset all this, Muhammad would need to be superior in courage and military talent, but it was already clear he was far inferior in both. It was evident that he intended to lurk far from the fighting front, either on the bad advice of his generals or because he had been 'spooked' by the predictions of his astrologers. All in all, the omens for Genghis as he prepared another great endeavour were bright.

10

Downfall of the Shah

It is sometimes said that Genghis's reponse to the Otrar atrocity was tardy and that two years went by before he made his move.[1] In fact his riposte was remarkably rapid. While making elaborate plans for a grand rendezvous of the majority of his forces on the upper Irtysh, he ordered Jochi and Jebe, already in Qara Khitai, to take their 30,000 troops and begin the march west immediately. The idea was that when these two reached the Ferghana valley, 'arrow messengers' or fast-travelling couriers from the main force converging on Otrar would be in touch with the khan's latest orders. The orders to set out at once committed Jebe and Jochi to a gruelling trek in winter over high mountain passes, but there was no gainsaying the khan's commands. The barrier of the Altyn-Tagh range forced travellers to take a route either north of the T'ien Shan or south of the River Tarim through the fearsome Taklamakan Desert. The rule of thumb was that trade caravans took the southerly route to avoid the worst mountain passes, but large groups of migrants, needing more water than the desert could provide, went north.[2] With 30,000 men Jebe and Jochi had no choice but to go north, yet they do not seem to have followed the conventional route through Dzungaria; instead they veered slightly south-west and found a pass between the Pamirs and the T'ien Shan, most likely through the Altai range (the sources are anything but pellucid). It was probably the Terek-Dawan defile, an all-year pass at 13,000 feet, which later became the principal route from Qara Khitai and was used by Marco Polo.[3] On the way to this pass the Mongols rode through snowstorms and snow 5–6 feet deep, their horses wrapped in yak-hides and the riders wearing double sheepskin coats. Shortage of food meant they often had to open the veins of their mounts, drink the blood then close the veins up again. Not surprisingly, many horses dropped dead from the snow, ice and blood letting; any that did were devoured instantly.

Finally the Mongols reached the fertile valley of Ferghana in spring 1219 after an exploit that easily rivals Hannibal's crossing of the Alps.[4] Turkestan was then the name given to the entire area stretching from modern China to the Caspian, so it is a high commendation to say that the Ferghana valley was the commercial jewel of the entire region. It produced gold, silver, turquoise, quicksilver, iron, copper, naphtha, bitumen, millstones, perfume, cloth, weapons, needles, scissors, pots, bows, quivers, dyed hides, cloaks, flax, cotton, had a vast acreage of rice fields, extensive orchards and vineyards and a thriving pastoral sector concentrating on goats, horses and mules.[5] The Mongols could raid and seize all they needed in such a milk-and-honey land.

The news of a Mongol army in Ferghana seriously disconcerted the shah Muhammad II, who had thought that any army coming from the east would have to take a more northerly route, through the Dzungaria Gate. Here was confirmation of Jalal al-Din's opinion that the Mongols should be opposed on the eastern frontier. But already defeatism was evident at Muhammad's court. The majority wanted to abandon Transoxiana and retreat to Khorasan or the Ghazni area of Afghanistan and build an invincible stronghold against which the Mongol hordes would fling themselves in vain until fatally weakened. The shah provided no proper leadership but instead declared that Allah had told him to attack the Mongols; he ranted against Genghis as an idolater and complained to his entourage that the Mongols had 'unfairly' beaten him to the punch by invading China.[6] Yet the provocation of learning that the Mongols were laying waste Ferghana was too much to bear. Muhammad assembled a large army and marched against them.

Jochi's orders from his father were not to allow himself to be sucked into pitched battles with the shah; his role was as a diversion, to keep the Khwarezmians occupied while Genghis came through the Dzungaria Gate.[7] The headstrong Jochi never liked obeying his father's orders, and this occasion was no different. Jebe strongly urged that the Mongols should retreat, if necessary up into the foothills of the mountains, so as to lure the shah further away from Otrar, where Genghis intended to strike. Jochi took a perverse pleasure in overruling a superior general (Jebe), exercising his prerogative as a prince of the blood, saying that such a course of action would be arrant cowardice.

The sources differ in their accounts of the battle. One version is that the Mongols were in a poor state to receive the enemy after their exertions on the long trek and, instead of their usual guileful manoeuvres, simply charged the shah head on. Another is that the Mongols gave a textbook demonstration of their tactics – the light cavalry appearing to discharge their usual arrow cloud, with the heavy cavalry waiting to deliver the killer blow. It is even suggested that Muhammad came within an ace of being captured.[8] At all events, night came down on a battle that was still indecisive, but with the heavily outnumbered Mongols (perhaps 25,000 to twice that number) having outpointed the enemy in every area: speed, mobility, imagination.

This was the second time Muhammad had taken a mauling, and it reinforced what was becoming an *idée fixe* with him – that it was always folly to engage the Mongols in open battle.[9] Jebe and Jochi meanwhile followed the time-honoured tactic of withdrawing under cover of darkness, managing to take most of their cattle and horses with them. Muhammad's failure to pursue has puzzled some analysts, but at least three major factors were responsible. He was unsure of the true strength of the Mongols and could not know for certain that the army he had fought was not just a vanguard, with the main army lying in ambush, waiting for him to pursue. Then, in order to campaign effectively, the shah had to raise taxes and this in turn led to open rebellion among some already disaffected towns; to deal with these insurrections Muhammad had to divert his army from pursuit of the Mongols. Thirdly, by late summer he learned that the vanguard of another Mongol army was already pouring through the Dzungaria Gate in the north. He now had his answer. The Jebe–Jochi force had been a classic diversion.[10]

Genghis set off with the main army in May 1219, following the Orkhon and Tula Rivers.[11] Angling south-west, he crossed the Khangai Mountains through passes ranging from 8,000 to 10,000 feet and reached the Altai Mountains by mid-July. There is much scholarly wrangling about the exact route he took thereafter (geography was not the medieval chroniclers' strong point); he may have used the Dabistan-Daban Pass, though at least two other defiles in this area are open from May to September.[12] He made camp on the upper Irtysh in summer 1219, to give his men and horses rest and recreation and await the advent of his allies to this rendezvous. While encamped there, the Mongols experienced a freak summer snowstorm.[13]

To confuse the shah still further Genghis sent a small detachment (maybe 5,000 strong) on a circuitous route south to enter Turkestan by the famous Dzungaria Gate. This (on the modern China–Kazakhstan border) was already known in ancient times to Herodotus and Ptolemy and thought to be the home of Boreas, the North Wind, on account of the fierce and constant winds encountered there. Basically a small rift valley, the Dzungaria Gate is a six-mile-wide, 46-mile-long gap between the lakes Alakol and Ebi Nur, the most important mountain pass between China and Central Asia and the one gateway in a mountain wall that otherwise stretches 3,000 miles from Afghanistan to Manchuria.[14] This is the route Muhammad would have expected Genghis to take, on the expectation that he would be marching west from a base in Qara Khitai.

Meanwhile on the upper Irtysh Genghis took stock of his position and reviewed his strategy. In his retinue were Qulan, his favourite wife, his sons Tolui, Chagatai and Ogodei, and all his important generals and advisers except for Jebe and Jochi, already engaged on the western front, and Muqali in China; the most important personality of all may have been Subedei, who acted as Genghis's chief of staff and is usually credited with the brilliant strategy used against the shah.[15] (The government of Mongolia had been left to Genghis's brother Temuge.)

Quite how many troops Genghis led is a vexed question, as are all issues relating to numbers in Mongol history. Estimates range from the grotesquely impossible 800,000 to the absurdly low 80,000. The lunatic figure of 800,000 mentioned by some popular writers is implausible on a number of grounds, chiefly that this would imply also herds of 800,000 horses and 24 million sheep and goats all on the march.[16] Much depends on what figure we assign to the total population of Mongolia, and here again estimates range from 700,000 to two million. Given that the pastoral economy of Mongolia is inelastic and therefore can support only a constant population, and given also that the population of Mongolia in 1967 was three million, there is every justification for accepting the higher figure of two million in the thirteenth century.[17] This might give us a total military strength of 200,000 and take us close to some of the higher estimates.[18] Yet we must remember that large numbers of troops were still waging war in China, and that some of the newly conquered regions in Genghis's rear could not be totally counted on and needed garrisons to keep them loyal. All in all, counting allied contingents, Chinese sappers, engineers and siege experts, we might settle for a total force of 120,000 effectives, including the 30,000 under Jochi and Jebe.[19]

The most alarming news that reached Genghis at his summer camp on the upper Irtysh was that the expected Tangut contingent would not be coming. At first the campaign of 1209–10 seemed to have borne ripe fruit, for to start with Hsi-Hsia stayed loyal. There was an open usurpation of the crown in 1211 when a new ruler, Shen-Tsung, a man in his late forties, secured the throne by a coup, but he confirmed the Mongol alliance and remained steadfast until 1217. But then he repudiated all his commitments, under the influence of the virulently anti-Mongol general Asa Gambu.[20] Together ruler and general offered the Jin an anti-Mongol alliance to take advantage of Genghis's absence in the west; Asa Gambu, moreover, was convinced the Mongols would lose the war against Khwarezmia.[21]

The Jin refused, on the basis that both the Mongols and the Tangut were their sworn enemies. The Tangut had better luck with the Song, but the latter told Shenzong they could not formally commit to an alliance until 1220 at the earliest. When the Mongols officially protested at Hsi-Hsia's perfidy, Asa Gambu replied with heavy irony that since Genghis Khan styled himself the Khan of Khans (though actually he never took this title), he scarcely needed the help of the Tangut, as Heaven was already on his side.[22] When this reply was conveyed to Genghis, he is said by some sources to have become apoplectic with rage. He asked one of his secretaries to remind him at noon and dusk every day thenceforth that the treacherous Tangut realm still existed.

Soon it was time to move on, to the first target, Otrar. Genghis ordered his commissariat to make the most careful and meticulous preparations for the march ahead, factoring in all known wells, water-holes and oases. Every ten horsemen had to carry three dried sheep, with the mutton salted and dried in the sun, and an iron cauldron in which to cook the meat; similar 'slide-rule' projections were formulated for all other food. Genghis's itinerary next took him across the Irtysh, past Lake Zaysan, then, by way of the River Emil and the Tarbaghatai Mountains, and passing the eastern shore of Lake Balkhash, one of the world's great inland seas, he came to an autumn rendezvous on the plain of Qayaliq south of the lake; here he was joined by Arslan of of the Qarluqs, Suqnaq-tigin the new ruler of Almaliq, and his great friend the *idiqut* Barchuq.[23]

Ten thousand Uighurs, 6,000 Qarluqs and a contingent from Almaliq made a hefty reinforcement; Ongud, Khitans, Solons, Kirghiz and Kem Kemjiut are also mentioned among the recruits. The allies were all much impressed with the Chinese engineers and the heavy equipment they brought for siegecraft.[24] At Qayaliq Genghis sent Chagatai ahead with the vanguard to build bridges to take them across the remaining rivers, making sure they could bear the weight of heavy transport wagons. Chagatai had many faults but he completed this task with supreme efficiency, building forty-eight timber bridges wide enough for two heavy carts to drive across side by side.[25]

The army proceeded south-west, reached the Ili River and followed it down to Almaliq, the final significant stop before their destination.[26] Passing to the north of the Lake Issyk Kul, they reached the River Chu (in today's northern Kyrgyzstan and southern Kazakhstan), the last significant obstacle before Otrar itself. Genghis gave strict orders that from now on there should be no hunting, so as not to tire the horses; he made sure food supplies were adequate, then struck due west for Otrar. Once across the Chu they were in the realms of the shah.[27]

In October 1219 the Mongols finally arrived outside Otrar on the banks of the Syr Darya, the mighty river known to the ancients as the Jaxartes. (Alexander the Great fought a famous battle on the Jaxartes in 329 BC and proclaimed it the northern limit of his empire.) Genghis had spent three months on the march, excluding stopovers on the Irtysh and elsewhere, and had covered over 2,500 miles.[28] Now he decided to leave the siege of Otrar to Ogodei and Chagatai while he waited with a large reserve force in a pass at the top of the Arys valley, in the foothills of a nearby mountain range.

As always, his strategy was masterly. Knowing that the shah was based at Samarkand, he sent 5,000 men upstream along the Syr Darya to seize Banakat (near Tashkent), where the road from Samarkand reached the river and where any army coming from that direction would have to approach.[29] He hoped to lure Muhammad into an expedition to relieve Otrar. If that happened, the 5,000 Mongols at Banakat were to leave and link up with Ogodei and Chagatai outside Otrar. Genghis's plan was to tempt the shah to imagine that the besieging army at Otrar could be caught between two fires, between his army advancing from Samarkand and the powerful garrison in Otrar, which would then sortie and assail the Mongols in the rear as they turned round to face the new army. If that happened, Genghis hoped to destroy the Khwarezmian military power in one go, using his expertise in uniting far-flung detachments of his army with lightning speed. The shah was unaware that there was a second army in the north, lurking in the foothills, and had lost sight of Jochi. With Genghis appearing unexpectedly on the flank of the sallying garrison and Jochi in the rear of Muhammad's army, the stage would be set for a victory that would echo down the centuries.[30] It would be more complete than Gaugamela, Cannae, Zama or any of the great battles of history.

But the shah would not take the bait. He was confident that the huge force of defenders at Otrar could hold out, and he wanted to be able to locate Jochi and Jebe accurately before committing himself to a clear course of action. He dithered and procrastinated, a true martial Hamlet, while his son Jalal tore his hair out that his earlier advice – to oppose the Mongols at the Syr Darya – had been rejected. In fact merely by abandoning the Syr Darya to Genghis, Muhammad had lost the first round of the struggle.[31]

There was some rationality in his decision not to endorse Jalal's plan. Since all the cities on that river (including Otrar) were on the north bank, any army defending them would have the river at its back and nowhere to escape to if defeated. On the other hand, if he used the river as a defence, defying the Mongols to cross it in the face of strong forces on the south bank, he would have to abandon all his northern cities. Moreover, even if he was victorious on the north bank, the Mongols would retreat into the mountains, and it was too dangerous to follow such a foe into that kind of terrain.[32] Muhammad's strategy therefore was to place such an enormous garrison in Otrar that the Mongols, already weary after a long march, would tire themselves out trying to take it. When he deemed that the besiegers were sufficiently exhausted, Muhammad told his advisers that he would indeed order the march from Samarkand to Banakat. This, too, was not entirely irrational. The garrison at Otrar contained no fewer than 60,000 fighting men, with the cavalry and infantry stationed all round the walls.[33]

Genghis waited patiently for two months while the siege of Otrar dragged on, but finally concluded that the shah would never be tempted into battle. He therefore left express instructions with Ogodei and Chagatai to press the siege with all their might, assisted by Barchuq and the Uighurs, and sent orders to Jochi to advance from Ferghana and conquer all cities along the north bank of the Syr Darya.[34] Sadly for his own ambitions, Muhammad had imbibed the myth that the Mongols were hopeless at siegecraft, which his agents based on the lacklustre performance in the campaign against Hsi-Hsia in 1209–11. He had no idea that as a result of their war with the Jin the Mongols' expertise had proceeded almost exponentially, and the well-defended fortress of Otrar held no terrors for them. Inalchuq, the governor responsible for the original atrocity, and general Qaracha, sent by the shah with 50,000 men to bolster the governor's original 10,000 garrison, are said to have been caught completely off guard by the Mongol host appearing outside the walls, with the neighing of armoured horses and the braying of chain-armoured mules.[35] Naturally, the Mongols used all kinds of tricks to exaggerate their numbers. Gradually they pounded the walls and cut off all supplies of food and water. By their fierce discipline the numerically inferior nomad army triumphed over an enemy who should have been able to resist.[36]

Nonetheless, it took five bitter months of fighting before Otrar finally cracked, in February 1220. In January, Qaracha, foreseeing the inevitable end, tried to make his escape with a bodyguard but was captured and executed; Ogodei fully shared his father's belief that a general should never abandon his master.[37] After this debacle large numbers of the shah's dreaded mercenaries deserted. Some civilians, tired of the privations of a five-month siege, opened a side gate and let the attackers in, but Inalchuq, after abandoning the city to the Mongols, withdrew into the citadel with 20,000 of his crack troops; many of them soon deserted and in the end he was left with just 6,000.[38] It took another month for the Mongols to winkle them out. When the citadel fell Inalchuq and his diehard loyalists retreated into a central tower. The defenders fought bitterly and in the end, desperately short of firearms, were reduced to showering the attackers with tiles. The Mongols mined the tower and, when it collapsed, dug a still living Inalchuq out of the ruins.[39] All the Turkish deserters and any other soldiers left alive were instantly slaughtered. Ogodei and Chagatai ordered the city razed to the ground; it was never rebuilt, and its ghostly ruins attested to the folly of opposing the greatest power on earth. Inalchuq was taken and held for Genghis's pleasure whenever he should appear. He was of course executed, but the story that Genghis first tortured him by having molten silver poured into his eyes is apocryphal.[40]

With the fall of Otrar there was now no obstacle to the systematic reduction of all the cities and towns along the Syr Darya. Jochi and Jebe decided they should split up, with Jebe striking south, intending to cross the River Zerafshan and bar any southern escape route from Samarkand whenever Genghis decided to assault it. Jebe had with him somewhere between 10,000 and 20,000 men, scarcely enough to engage a large army; nevertheless when he encountered a larger Khwarezmian force, he attacked it and put it to flight. It was a great exploit but Genghis was none too happy when he heard of it. He always tried to avoid heavy casualties and to win by mobility and other indirect means.[41]

Jochi, after parting from Jebe, proceeded with the task of subjugating the Syr Darya. The first target chosen was Signak. Jochi called on the town to surrender, but the burghers responded by killing his envoy. After a tough seven-day siege, he took the town and killed all its inhabitants.[42] He pressed on to Jend, reached on 20 April 1220, but this time the citizens had the good sense to surrender; they nonetheless had to evacuate the town to allow the Mongols to plunder in peace; the sack took three days. Yanikant, just short of the point where the Syr Darya debouches into the Aral Sea, was next to fall, and there are also mentions in the sources of the seizure of smaller places named Ozkend and Asanas.[43]

Another commander, Alaq Noyan, was meanwhile operating upstream from Otrar. With 5,000 men and ably backed by his deputies Sogetu and Taqai, he invested Banakat, which held out for three days, with the defenders sortieing for a pitched battle every day, but capitulated on the fourth morning, the Turkish units having been assured that they could join the Mongol army; once disarmed they were executed en masse by showers of arrows. All civilians were drafted into the army unless they had the good fortune to be artisans or skilled craftsmen.[44]

While Alaq proceeded to take the towns of Kulab and Talikan, Chagatai and Ogodei moved down from the ruins of Otrar to besiege the great fortress of Khujand where the Syr Darya, having till then flowed due south, turns sharply east.[45] The governor of Khujand, Temur Melik, one of the most able commanders in Khwarezmia, realised he was too weak to do anything but postpone the inevitable, so fled Ferghana's capital with a thousand-strong elite corps and ensconced himself on an island in the Syr Darya, far from both shores. There he held off Mongol attempts at amphibious warfare by using twelve fireships laden with Greek fire (an early equivalent of napalm), which inflicted heavy damage on Mongol shipping. Finally, when the food on the island ran out, Temur and his men made a break for it and tried to escape downriver. The Mongols had strung a chain across the Syr Darya at Banakat but the dauntless Temur managed to crash his way through the chain. Next he learned that the Mongols were lining the shores and that a huge army under Jochi was waiting to intercept him at Jend, having barricaded the river with an impassable barrier of boats. Quickly disembarking, he managed to find horses and with a small company set off into the wilds of the Kizil Kum.[46] Without question Temur Melik and Jalal al-Din were the most distinguished captains the shah possessed.[47] But Temur's valour availed him nothing. The Mongol conquest of the Syr Darya valley was now complete.

Genghis meanwhile seemed to have vanished into the unknown. He and Tolui took the bold decision to march across Transoxiana via the Kizil Kum, a vast desert with pyramidal sand dunes. Despite the absurd hypothesis of some writers that he went north from Otrar, looped round the top of the Aral Sea and descended on the western side of the Aral through the Kara-Kum,[48] – such an itinerary made no sense at all, does not fit the time-frame and would have been an act of utter madness – it is very clear from the sources that he struck south-west, trusting that the intelligence from his agents and local spies was good and that sufficient wells and waterholes could be located to water a large army (Genghis had perhaps 40,000 riders with him). He reached the fortress of Zarnuq, overwhelmed it, and pressed on to Nurata, still bearing south-west. Nurata had been founded as the city of Nur by Alexander the Great in 327 BC and was renowned as a Muslim place of pilgrimage. When Nurata opened its gates to him, Genghis treated it with remarkable leniency, and the explanation is almost certainly his desire not to offend Islam by desecrating one of its holy places, which would cost him the covert support of the imams of Khwarezmia and allow Muhammad to claim that he was fighting a holy war. The people and buildings were left unscathed and a merely nominal tribute exacted.[49]

Next, to the consternation of the enemy, he suddenly appeared outside the gates of Bukhara at the beginning of February 1220. The news stupefied Muhammad and he repeatedly queried whether Genghis Khan was really to the west of him, and how this could have happened. With Jochi, Ogodei and Chagatai to the north and east and Jebe to the south, he was virtually surrounded, his line turned and his communications with his western provinces all but severed. All his hopes now rested on the strong garrison he had left in Bukhara. Without question Genghis's march through the Kizil Kum to outflank the shah is one of the greatest exploits in all military history, revealing him once again as a strategist of genius. He was at the height of his powers in this war against Khwarezmia, brilliant, original, innovative, creative, richly endowed with improvisatory genius and an unparalleled instinct for reading maps and understanding spaces.[50] To quote the words of one of his most distinguished admirers, Basil Liddell Hart: 'In strategy the longest way round is often the shortest way there; a direct approach to the object exhausts the attacker and hardens the resistance by compression, whereas an indirect approach loosens the defender's hold by upsetting his balance . . . the profoundest truth of war is that the issue of battle is decided in the minds of the opposing commanders, not in the bodies of their men.'[51]

Bukhara was one of the largest cities in the Islamic world, renowned for learning and scholarship, especially Sufism; it was the sister city to Samarkand, 150 miles away to the south-east, with Samarkand the shah's political capital and Bukhara the religious one. A walled city, thirty-six square miles in area and enclosed by a great wall which the credulous claimed was one hundred miles in circuit, it was a tripartite affair. There was a citadel, one mile in circumference, an inner town, the shahristan, and outer suburbs called the rabad; the citadel was on the outside of the inner town.[52] The inner town was built on a platform and had a wall with seven gates – the Bazaar Gate, the Gate of the Spice Merchants and the Iron Gate being the most famous. As befitted the religious capital of the Khwarezmian empire, it boasted many ornate mosques, such as the Great Mosque (built in 1121), the

Friday Mosque and the Mosque of the Syrians.[53] The rabad was also enclosed within a wall, this time with eleven gates. Bukhara had a brilliantly devised irrigation system with sluices, reservoirs and canals, supplying both inner and outer towns; the main canal was known as the Roud-i-zar ('the river that brings gold'), showing how important it was. The water supply was used to irrigate the many sumptuous gardens and detached houses in the wealthy suburbs, abounding with large trees that hid these residences from anyone viewing the wealthy quarter from the main minaret. Outside the great wall that enclosed Bukhara and its suburbs still more canals spiralled out, providing irrigation for land both inside and outside the city; these canals were big enough to allow boats to sail on them.[54] Less commonly remarked on were the extensive and overcrowded slums containing the urban poor, and from the feculent miasma of the narrow streets there arose the bad air and water that diminished the city's lustre.[55] The city was legendarily wealthy, deriving riches from both trade and industry; its carpets, textiles and copper work (especially beautiful copper lamps) were famous in the Islamic world, not to mention its melons. Between the citadel and the inner town, hard by the Friday Mosque a large textile factory turned out superior goods that were exported to Asia Minor, Syria and Egypt.[56]

All this, known to him from his spies within the city, Genghis pondered as he rode around the city walls, probing for the weak spots. The shah had poured troops into the city and was even then sending a relief column. Theoretically, Bukhara should have been impenetrable, but Genghis thought the acute class conflict within the city might be his entering wedge. In 1207 an artisan-led popular revolt was on the point of overthrowing the old feudal-clerical-patrician elite when Muhammad came to their aid and annexed the city.[57] Genghis hoped to use the slum dwellers as a fifth column; in any case they would be useful when it came to getting the elite to disgorge their wealth. His particular animus against the Bukhara wealthy was that in his eyes they had stolen his money, for they had bought up all the silver and jewels that Inalchuq had put up for sale after his plunder and massacre of the Mongol caravan at Otrar.[58]

There ensued a twelve-day siege. Genghis followed the usual pattern of putting his prisoners in the front rank as arrow fodder, always mindful of the casualty roster of his own men. For two days the attackers battered away without major success, but then the nerve of the Turkish commander cracked. He led his 20,000 men out in a night sortie and almost got clean away, but they were detected and pursued to the banks of the Amu Darya (Oxus), where they were massacred.[59] At this the city surrendered, all but four hundred loyalists in the citadel. Genghis ordered the citizens to fill up the moat around the citadel, then brought up heavy catapults which breached the walls. Even so, the defenders managed to fight on for an amazing eleven days before they were finally taken and massacred. The date was variously given as 11 or 15 February, but a day-by-day count makes the 13th more likely.[60]

Genghis decided to make an example of Bukhara that would cause the rest of the shah's empire to tremble. He decreed that all merchants who bought goods from the plundered caravan at Otrar had to return them without compensation on pain of death. Moreover, all rich men, whatever their source of wealth, were to be taxed heavily. With the help of informers inside the city, Genghis identified 280 such persons (190 residents and ninety foreign traders) and mulcted them accordingly.[61] Then an order went out that all people of all ranks had to leave the city in just the clothes they stood up in, with the exception of the nubile women, who were then sacrificed to his licentious soldiery in an orgy of mass rape.[62] Young males were corralled for use as human shields in the next battle or siege, while artisans and craftsmen of note were sent to Mongolia.

Particular controversy has always attended Genghis's attitude to the religion of Islam. It is true that he executed all clerics and imams who preached against him, but the wilder canards about his behaviour are pure myth.[63] One says that he got up in the pulpit of the Great Mosque and announced that he was 'the scourge of God', another that he destroyed mosques and desecrated holy places and sacred books. Genghis would never have done anything so signally stupid as to hand the shah such an obvious propaganda weapon.[64] Better grounded is the story that he listened to a sermon on Islamic teaching in the Great Mosque, said he agreed with most of the doctrines but could not understand why pilgrims had to go to Mecca since God is everywhere.[65]

The sufferings of the people of Bukhara were nonetheless grievous; they were bullied, molested, casually murdered and, if rich, tortured to reveal the whereabouts of hidden wealth. At least 30,000 of them died in the siege and its aftermath though, in contrast to the experience of some other cities later in the war, there was no systematic massacre or genocide.[66] As a crowning touch, a great fire swept over the city and gutted it. Hostile propagandists said that Genghis had started it deliberately, but the overwhelming probability is that it was accidental and spontaneous, since the tightly-packed wooden houses in the slums were an obvious firetrap.[67] At any rate the destruction was terrific. The great Arab historian and traveller Ibn Battuta, visiting the city a century later, found it still devastated, almost as if the Mongols had swept through the year before.[68]

Genghis now had a plentiful supply of human shields and, more importantly, the psychological upper hand. The next, and inevitable, objective was Muhammad's capital, Samarkand, where the people were severely demoralised by the fall of their sister city. For some people Samarkand had always been considered the jewel of Islamic culture, and its very geographical situation alone made it seem an oasis of civilisation. Another walled city, set on high ground, with a civilian population of 100,000, it attracted admiration, even more so than Bukhara, for its irrigation schemes and fertility. Canals striated the city, almost as though mocking the arid hills round about; as in Bukhara, there were wealthy residential suburbs and fecund orchards. Where the river left the mountains, several dams diverted its waters to irrigate the lands around the city and the districts on the north bank of the river; two of the canals flowing to Samarkand were big enough to carry boats and indeed there was a network of canals between Bukhara and Samarkand irrigating the many large towns between them. There was an enormous wall with four gates, including the China Gate to the east and, to the south, the Major Gate, the most densely populated area, where all the bazaars, caravanserais, warehouses and factories were located. Like Bukhara it was a three-stage conurbation, with citadel, inner city and outer city.[69] Oozing wealth with its plethora of artificial lakes and ponds, parks, botanical gardens and detached houses, Samarkand delighted the eye with the visual counterpoint of mosques with flowers, canals with cypress trees. It had thriving industries that turned out paper, silver and red cloth, brocade, jars and goblets, as well as more utilitarian objects like hides, stirrups and all kinds of oil and grease, including tallow.[70]

The walls were thought to be impregnable, and the shah, in residence together with his mother, had brought in his crack troops to defend it; the Arab historian Juvaini may or may not be exaggerating when he says that Muhammad had 60,000 Turks under the city's governor Tughai Khan and 50,000 Tajiks, loyal to the shah's mother Terken Qatun (Turghai's sister), in arms behind the walls.[71]

But behind the superficial confidence he exuded, or pretended to, the shah was deeply worried. The impregnability of Samarkand had been predicated on a Mongol attack *from the east* – which would have allowed it to be massively reinforced from Bukhara – but now there was no backup. He had also assumed that the Mongol army was still in its infancy as regards siegecraft, but they had battered down Bukhara as if it had been a sandcastle. Moreover, although he had a huge force of defenders at his command, Muhammad must have known that the overwhelming majority of influential oligarchs and merchants had no appetite for a fight to the death with Genghis Khan; the fall of Bukhara had made manifest the various latent and fissiparous weaknesses in the Khwarezmian empire.[72] Virtually the entire civilian population of Samarkand had been alienated from their 'emperor' a year earlier when he strengthened the wall around Samarkand but levied three years' taxes in advance to pay for the work.[73] The presence of his mother in frontal areas of the empire was another headache, especially since the Mongol campaign of disinformation and the issuing of bogus commands in her name had been spectacularly successful.[74] And the Mongol host converging on Samarkand seemed enormous. Genghis and Tolui had been joined by Ogodei and Chagatai, fresh from their triumph at Otrar; moreover, Genghis had recalled the 5,000 troops previously sent to Banakat, determined to leave nothing to chance. Additionally, the Mongols made their number seem even larger by propping up unmanned shields on the plains and placing dummies skilfully among the real soldiers.[75]

Genghis approached Samarkand slowly and cautiously, marching along both banks of the River Zerafshan, invested the city, then made a leisurely inspection of the great walls and their fortifications. The first thing to consider was that it was likely the shah had already got off a message requesting a relief column to take the Mongols in the rear. Genghis was right. Two different sets of reinforcements did appear, one an undersized force of 10,000 horsemen which took one look at the size of the Mongol army and promptly decamped, and another, 20,000 strong, which rashly gave battle and was routed in short order.[76]

All these abortive measures took time, so it was only on the third day that the Mongols began the siege in earnest. As always, the front ranks were filled with prisoners, mostly from Bukhara, who were cut down in hundreds by their compatriots. Finally Genghis ordered a mass charge at the defenders, throwing all his prisoners into the assault; they had the choice of being scythed down by the Mongols from behind or destroyed by arrows from in front. Taking massive casualties, the luckless 'volunteers' broke and fled. Sensing an easy victory over what looked like a demoralised foe, the Turkish defenders broke cover and sortied. With them went two dozen war elephants, which Tughai had claimed were his secret weapon, but which turned out to be the dampest of damp squibs. The Turks ran straight into an elaborately planned ambush conducted by the battle-fresh true Mongols, and were slaughtered in their thousands.[77] There is no need to credit the historical hyperbole of some chroniclers, whereby 50,000 perished in a single day, but it is clear that the death toll was terrific and unacceptable.

Samarkand could no longer be effectively defended. Tughai Khan and the half of the defending force that was unscathed withdrew into the inner city while the Mongols poured into the suburbs and the outer areas. The defenders' numbers were whittled down still further when the shah, reportedly accompanied by 30,000 horsemen, broke through the Mongols' ring of steel and escaped into the countryside.[78] Wretched, panicky and psychologically crushed, he admitted to his confidants that the war was already effectively over and that Genghis had won.[79]

After the great ambush and the flight of the notables, a delegation of clerics and burghers went to see Genghis, saying they were surrendering forthwith, had never wanted to fight and were always secretly on his side. They identified 50,000 members of the pro-Mongol fifth column in the city, whom Genghis promised to spare on payment of a huge fine of 200,000 gold dinars.[80] After another five days of futile resistance, the Turks and Qanglis in the inner city led by Tughai Khan asked for terms. Genghis promised they would be spared, then, once they were disarmed, slaughtered them almost to a man.[81] About a thousand doubters, who had never trusted the Mongols' word, retreated to the citadel for a last-ditch stand, but Genghis cut their water supply and then scythed them to pieces in a final assault. The date was late March 1220.[82]

Apart from those he identified as being particularly wealthy, Genghis paid no attention to the 50,000 alleged quislings unless they could pay for an 'exit visa' to leave the city. The sequel was otherwise usual and predictable. Artisans and craftsmen were sent to Mongolia; young males drafted to act as human shields in the next siege; and all nubile women raped, with the choicest specimens being reserved for the khan and his generals.[83] Genghis evinced the nomads' unsentimental attitude to animals by turning loose twenty of the war elephants (miraculously most of the pachyderms had survived the ambush) into the arid wilds around Samarkand, where they very soon perished from lack of suitable vegetation.[84]

Once all the humans he had permitted to survive had left or been taken aside, Genghis gave his men leave to kill, rape and plunder at will, and after a ten-day siege their blood was up. The devastation was enormous, as was the loss of life. Military casualties aside, of the 100,000 civilian inhabitants of Sarmarkand, only 25,000 survived to pick up the pieces in their ruined paradise once the Mongols moved on.[85] As with Bukhara, a hundred years later Ibn Battuta noticed that Samarkand had not yet recovered and still bore the marks of the conqueror. But Samarkand was lucky. Tamerlane chose it as his capital, restored the city to its former glory and even enhanced it – a particular irony, given that he fancied himself as Genghis Khan *redivivus*.[86] Meanwhile Genghis appointed a very able Khitan bureaucrat named Yelu Ahai as the new governor, with Chinese civil servants as his underlings. This turned out to be a happy choice. Whether raising taxation, maintaining postal relay stations or dispatching tribute to Mongolia, Yelu proved an inspired appointment.[87]

Genghis remained in the neighbourhood of Samarkand until May, then took his army to summer camp in the mountains to the south of the city. The court of the khan was located in Nakhshab (Qarshi) sheltered by the Hissar Mountains, the most pleasant part of Transoxiana. Genghis felt it necessary to give an extended period of rest and recreation to an army that had been at maximum exertion for almost a year since leaving Mongolia – and indeed the original corps commanded by Jebe and Jochi had been in the field far longer than that. Now that Samarkand had fallen and Muhammad was on the run, Genghis did not expect any serious opposition in the field – the fortified cities might be another matter – but he saw that it would be a mistake not to keep up the momentum.

The first of his two major initiatives at this time was an invasion of the Amu Darya basin to secure the river ready for a major offensive the next year. Curiously, the enemy seems to have thought that the Amu Darya, a wide river 1,500 miles long (an almost exact parallel of the Syr Darya) would be a major barrier to the Mongols, but they crossed it with ease, floating on wooden rafts, with themselves and their effects lashed to their horses.[88] Then began a major reconnoitre of the Amu Darya, which veterans of the China campaign thought looked remarkably like the Yellow River.[89] Traditionally the boundary between the Turks and the Persians, the Amu Darya was famous for the precious stones that abounded in its environs – rubies, lapis lazuli, rock crystals – and was navigable for the whole of its lower course in summer, though like its twin the Syr Darya, it froze over in winter. The Mongols absorbed a multitude of knowledge about the river – how it formerly used to flow into the Caspian rather than the Aral Sea, how the Transoxianians regarded it and the Syr Darya as their own (and superior) version of the Tigris and Euphrates, where the best bridging points were (with Nawidah on the right bank being the point where travellers to and from Balkh and Samarkand made the crossing).[90]

Using the elements of speed, mobility and surprise, they quickly destroyed Muhammad's fleet on the Oxus, using fireships. Then Genghis, properly briefed by his reconnaissance patrols, sent a large force under Jochi and Chagatai to besiege Termez on the north bank.[91] His two sons, who hated each other, predictably quarrelled and made a mess of the operation, which dragged on for eleven days instead of the forty-eight hours Genghis expected. The trouble began when the Mongols, overconfident, tried to seize the nearby bridge over the Amu Darya, but were repulsed, taking heavy casualties (3,000 according to some reports). Nothing enraged Genghis more than heavy loss of Mongol life and, hearing of the wrangling between his two eldest sons, in exasperation he sent Ogodei down to sort out the mess, bearing a commission as supreme commander.[92]

With the army united by Ogodei's presence, the siege was begun in earnest. The most ferocious street fighting ensued, with virtually every house becoming a defender's blockhouse – which the Mongols overcame with jars of burning oil. The attackers cut their way through the mounting rubble, the night sky lit by fire, with scenes redolent of Hieronymus Bosch's hell, complete with the stench of burning and rotting cadavers. After seven days of fighting inch by inch, the Mongols finally pinned down the defenders in the only section of town now left standing. Seeing that the struggle was hopeless, the Termezians asked for terms, but Jochi made it a point of honour that Ogodei should not grant them, so incensed was he by the mounting Mongol death toll.[93] The outcome was the usual tripartite one: enemy fighters massacred, artisans sent to Mongolia and women and children sold into slavery. The slaughter was notable for one incident that lived on in Mongol annals. A foolish old woman begged for her life and said she would give the Mongols a massive pearl if spared. When they asked where it was, she said she had swallowed it. She was cut open where she stood, disembowelled, and the pearl recovered.[94] Unfortunately, the Mongols now conceived the idea that all siege survivors might have adopted a similar strategy, so henceforth they tended to eviscerate first and ask questions later so as not to miss any swallowed treasure.

The shah meanwhile was fleeing from place to place in total panic, announcing *sauve qui peut*, telling everyone that the war was over and they should look to their own salvation. All was confusion and anarchy, and matters were not helped by a division of opinion among his counsellors. His best generals advised him to consider Transoxiana lost but recommended regrouping to defend Khorasan in the south and Iraq-Adjemi (the northern part of modern Iraq) in the west; in either of these places he could call a general muster, and maybe even patch up his differences with the caliph and proclaim a holy war against 'the Accursed One'.[95] Others advised him to make his stand at Ghazni in Afghanistan for, if defeated there, he could always retreat into India.

Muhammad initially opted for the latter course and got as far as Balkh, but there he was joined by his vizier, who talked him round to a change of plan. The vizier had his own agenda which he did not reveal. In Iraq-Adjemi, where he wanted to be based, he was under severe pressure from one of Muhammad's sons, Rukn al-Din, who had ordered him east to help his father (but really to be rid of him). Realising that his only true protection was under the shah's banner, the vizier strenuously argued for a withdrawal to the west, until Muhammad agreed.[96]

His son, Jalal al-Din, the only first-class captain the Khwarezmian empire possessed, angrily rounded on his father when he learned of his decision and described the Iraq plan as the worst possible scenario. Stop looking for redoubts, fastnesses and 'wolf's lairs', Jalal urged, muster your army, stand and fight. It was imperative, Jalal said, that the shah's people should not be able to say: 'They have collected taxes and tribute from us for so long, and now at a time like this they renounce our affairs and abandon us to be captives to infidels.'[97] The shah paid no heed whatever to this; Jalal became more and more angry and denounced him as a coward. The reality was that Muhammad did not trust either his feudal lords or his generals, and did not want to give anyone his head, lest he defeat the Mongols and then feel strong enough to turn on the shah. Thus he never committed all his troops in a once-and-for-all battle but spread them throughout his realm, enabling the Mongols to destroy them piecemeal.

His attitude so disgusted and infuriated some of his senior people in Afghanistan that they actually laid a plot to seize him and hand him over to Genghis in return for a negotiated peace. One of his ministers, Badr al-Din, forged a correspondence purportedly between Genghis and senior Khwarezmian commanders, asking for Mongol aid if they overthrew the shah, and then arranged to have copies fall into the hands of the most trusted members of Muhammad's coterie. Forewarned in the evening, Muhammad decamped quickly westwards overnight but his panic and paranoia simply grew. In the morning the pavilion where he was to have slept was found riddled with arrow holes.[98] Again Jalal begged his father to reconsider, but his case was badly weakened by the assassination attempt. Muhammad patronised his son and called his advice youthful folly, adding the supremely unhelpful observation that everything was in any case fixed by the stars and that the wise man's course was to await a favourable conjunction of the planets.[99] By now the empire was beginning to disintegrate into its erstwhile principalities, with a series of warlords trying to carve out territory for themselves, hoping to come to an accommodation with the Mongols. Most of Khorasan and Khwarezmia proper (between the Aral and the Caspian Seas) still remained astonishingly loyal to the shah, so it was to Khorasan that he fled first.[100]

Seeking to drive a wedge between Muhammad and his mother, Genghis wrote to her to say that his quarrel was only with the shah, that he disliked making war on women and that she could have a negotiated peace if she surrendered her army. Genghis realised that this force could still be extremely troublesome if it took the field against him when he invaded Khorasan. Terken Qatun was then based in Khiva in the north but proved unreceptive to the Mongol overtures. Thinking that Genghis and his armies would withdraw once they were sated with looting Transoxiana, she spurned the feelers put out to her and showed her contempt for Genghis by executing (by mass drowning) all the political prisoners she held in captivity – in other words, all the known pro-Mongol grandees in her realm.[101]

But she was soon on the run, a marked woman, as Muhammad informed her that the north, expecially Gurganj and Khiva, were the next Mongol targets. There were to be no negotiations and no mercy for the shah. Genghis assigned a force of 20,000 men to seek out and destroy him. The command of these three tumens was given to Jebe, with Subedei, his favourite collaborator, as his deputy and Genghis's favourite son-in-law Toquchar as the Number Three.[102] Their orders were plain and uncompromising. They were not to come back until Muhammad was dead or a prisoner and must pursue him relentlessly 'even if he has climbed to the sky'.[103] As for the towns and cities through which they passed on their pursuit, they were not to waste time trying to besiege the heavily fortified ones. If there was defiance from the smaller towns, they were to be sacked, but the hope was that most places would surrender. If the large cities did not acknowledge Mongol suzerainty, they were to be marked down for future destruction.[104]

Meanwhile the shah had reached Balkh on his headlong flight. He seems to have tried to anticipate Kutuzov's strategy against Napoleon in Russia in 1812 by ordering a scorched-earth policy, and exhorting his people to destroy all their crops and animals so as to deprive the enemy of sustenance. But there is no evidence in the sources that this command was ever heeded. Deserted by more and more of his troops and, for reasons of speed, accompanied only by a small bodyguard, Muhammad did not have the power to compel obedience and, besides, most of his subjects were disgusted by his cowardice and incompetence. The shah also foolishly thought that the Amu Darya would pose an insuperable obstacle to any pursuing force or that it would at least have to spend weeks building a suitable bridge for the passage of an army. Subedei and Jebe, though, found a crossing place north of Balkh where the river narrowed from a mile wide to a width of only 450 yards. This time they used a variation on the tried and tested method of so many campaigns. Instead of individual riders using horses and bladders, they constructed a gigantic flotation raft by lashing together their leather bags, and tied this to the tails of hundreds of horses, who swam across the river towing the raft.[105]

From Balkh the shah headed west through a gap in the Elburz range to Nishapur, which he reached in April 1220.[106] He sent Jalal al-Din back to Balkh to discover what he could about the Mongols' movements, but to his alarm Jalal learned that the Mongols were already at Balkh. When Jebe and Subedei approached, the city surrendered without resistance and paid the requested tribute; they simply appointed a governor to rule in Genghis's name and sped on. Jalal rode back to Nishapur to warn his father that the enemy was hot on his trail. The panic-stricken Muhammad managed to flee Nishapur just in time, lighting out for Iraq-Adjemi. He was already in a poor mental state, so paranoid and fearful of execution that he slept in a different tent each night. He left the city with a small retinue on the pretext that he was going hunting, but when the truth was learned, morale in Nishapur plummeted alarmingly.[107] Little more than twenty-four hours after his departure, Jebe and Subedei appeared outside the gates.

In contrast to the shah's dithering and lethargy, the Mongols were clocking up astonishing mileages. Riding up to eighty miles a day, they did not proceed straight to Nishapur but from Balkh went south-west to Herat then due north to Merv, to receive the surrender of these important cities.[108] Contrary to the shah's decrees, both these localities provided abundant food for the Mongol army. Faithful to Genghis's orders, Jebe and Subedei ignored any heavily defended fortresses and bypassed them. The one exception was at Zaveh (modern Turbat-i-Haidari) where the inhabitants did not just close the gates against them but stood on the walls and jeered and insulted the Mongols as they rode past. This was too much for Subedei to stomach, so he returned and besieged the fortress. After three days it fell, and Subedei took his usual grim pleasure in slaughtering the defenders to the last man.[109]

Jebe meanwhile pressed on to Nishapur, which he reached after covering 450 miles in five days. He issued Genghis's official proclamation that the city would be spared if it surrendered and paid tribute. The people of Nishapur called his bluff, replying that they were prepared to accept a Mongol governor but would not pay tribute.[110] Shrugging his shoulders, Jebe moved on, at a slower pace, allowing time for Subedei to catch up. The next target was Tus to the north-east, one of the most famous and revered of the cities of ancient Persia, celebrated as the burial place of the great caliph Harun al-Rashid (d. AD 809) and the one-time home of Ferdowsi, the author of Iran's national epic the *Shahnameh*.[111] Prosperous and affluent, making prized striped cloth and boasting extensive orchards, turquoise mines and a sophisticated irrigation system, Tus had often been a target for invaders, and had been captured by Alexander the Great in 330 BC. Perhaps the wealth had bred arrogance and hubris, for when Subedei sent in the usual formulaic demand for surrender, it was rejected in the most insolent terms. Subedei was the wrong man to cross in this way. He burst into the city with his horde and gave in to his usual habit of mass execution and slaughter.[112]

Again Jebe and Subedei split up and again Subedei indulged his passion for sacking cities. From Tus he proceeded north-west to Esfarayen and then south-west to Damghan, looting and pillaging both places. It turned out that this was the exact route Muhammad had taken when fleeing from Nishapur (when he had temporarily given the Mongols the slip).[113] Jebe struck west through Mazandaran province just to the south of the Caspian and sacked the towns of Amol and Asterabad (Gorgan) on the southern coast of the Caspian. The province contained the most diverse habitat: arid plains, prairies, rainforests, sandy beaches on the shore of the Caspian and the snow-capped Alborz sierras.

The shah had fled to Rayy with Jalal al-Din but, hearing that the Mongols were closing in on him, divided his family, sending one section to the fortress of Qarun and other to the fastness of Ilal. At Ilal was the formidable Terken Qatun, the shah's mother.[114] Ilal should have been a safe haven, as it was at high altitude with a plentiful water supply. But it so happened that the Mongol incursion into Mazandaran coincided with a freak drought. Parched with thirst, the defenders surrendered to Jebe after a fifteen-day siege. Jebe sent Terken Qatun and the rest of Muhammad's harem to Genghis at his winter base in Talaqan. He ordered all male children of the shah, no matter how young, to be put to death. Chagatai took two of the most attractive daughters of the shah as his concubines, and the rest of the harem was distributed to senior officers. Terken herself was sent as a captive to Karakorum in Mongolia, where she lived miserably until her death in around 1233.[115] But before that Genghis had a final humiliation in store for her. She and the captive women from the family of the shah and Jalal were forced to walk ahead of the Mongol troops bareheaded, lamenting publicly the downfall of Muhammad's empire, so that all viewing the spectacle should heed the folly of opposing God's will and thus absorb the awful message.[116]

Subedei and Jebe then reunited at Rayy, 450 miles from Nishapur and the largest city in Iraq-Adjemi, famous throughout the Orient for the export of silk fabrics and 'beautiful polychrome ceramics, decorated with exquisite miniatures'.[117] Rayy was taken completely by surprise. The Mongols suddenly appeared in the suburbs and came sweeping into the city, avid for killing and plunder, long before the inhabitants could muster any kind of defence. After a thorough sack of Rayy, the women and children were enslaved.[118] Jebe and Subedei then cut a swathe of destruction south-west to Hamadan before being brought up short by news that the shah was to be found to the north-west, at Rasht in the province of Gilan (another littoral region of the Caspian). Near Hamadan occurred the one and only real pitched battle between the Mongols and the shah's troops. Jebe's forces won easily and brushed aside the last obstacle between them and their quarry.

The defeat hammered another nail into Muhammad's coffin, for the vanquished forces dispersed in anarchy. Hungry and desperate, they rampaged and marauded throughout the countryside, making themselves even more feared and unpopular than the Mongols. Muhammad fled from Rasht at the Mongols' approach and reached the province of Qazvin, where Jalal had assembled an army of 30,000. On paper this should have given him the strength to turn around and face Jebe and Subedei with some confidence, but by this time rationality had long been conquered in the shah's psyche by panic and paranoia; a broken man, he had just one instinct – to flee.

In desperation he opted to try to escape to the caliph in Baghdad and got as far as Hamadan to the west. On the way there he was overtaken by the Mongols, who, incredibly, failed to recognise him. Spotting a column of stragglers, whom Jebe took to be refugees, he allowed his men cynically to loose a shower of arrows in their direction, one of which struck and wounded Muhammad's horse.[119] The valiant steed limped on and managed to convey its useless master to the gates of Qarun.

The shah's vizier suggested that he retreat farther north into the Caucasus, where he could raise tens of thousands of Kurdish mercenaries. Muhammad suspected this this advice was really about using him as a pawn so that the vizier could knock out the political opposition in his own province. Besides, he objected, if he raised taxes to finance fresh troops, new rebellions would break out; to deal with these he would have to disperse his troops, so he would be back to square one. Yet another reason for the impossibility of confronting the Mongols with a single powerful army was that all the component tribes in his empire hated each other and had only been prevented from being at each other's throats before 1219 by his own record of victories; even in the garrisons in the fortified cities, the battalions had to be of equal tribal strength to prevent bloodshed.[120]

With his men now deserting him in ever greater numbers, Muhammad did not stay long in Qarun but gained a day on his pursuers by having it bruited around that he was still there when in reality he had long departed.[121] Once alerted by a spy that they were on a fool's siege, the Mongols sped on. To slow them down, the shah sacrificed his rearguard, who perished heroically. Pursuing an erratic track through the province of Gilan and the town of Amol, he finally took advice from his emirs who urged him to find a refuge on one of the islands of the Caspian. For once Muhammad took a snap decision and embarked; it was well for him that he did, for he just managed to push off from the shore when his craft was pinpricked with a shower of Mongol arrows.[122]

Even when he was on the open sea and free (for the moment) from pursuit, the miserable Muhammad could not relax. He insisted on moving from island to island. At first he was on Ab-i-Sugun but moved on to Ashuradeh and later an island near Abaskun. This was a smart move, for a few days later the Mongols launched an amphibious attack on Ab-i-Sugun only to find the bird flown.[123] Half out of his mind with anxiety, paranoid, suspicious, jumpy, by now dressed in rags,

Muhammad additionally suffered from pleurisy and diarrhoea. He began to rant and rave and told the faithful few followers who still remained to him that he wanted to return to Khwarezmia 'to begin again'. He paid for his sustenance and the costs of his men by issuing land deeds to the islanders which, almost a decade later, they presented to Jalal for payment; amazingly he honoured the IOUs.[124]

In a lucid moment he revoked the gift of succession he had made to his son Uzlaq-Shah and announced that Jalal al-Din was now his heir. This angered his courtiers, for Uzlaq was a paper tiger they could dominate easily, but Jalal was an entirely different proposition, a natural autocrat, talented general and shrewd politician. He said to Jalal: 'When men become distracted about their own affairs . . . it will be better that the thread of life be severed.'[125] Finally seized by pneumonia, he died on 10 January 1221 and was buried on the island.[126] So great was his destitution that Jalal could not even find a winding sheet to bury him in, so he was interred in his day clothes. Some time later Jalal removed his father's remains to an island fortress, but the Mongols learned of this, exhumed the bones and burned them.[127]

By his incompetence and cowardice during the Mongol invasion Muhammad lost all the kudos he had obtained as ruler of Khwarezmia. The Arab historian Ibn al-Athir was, however, prepared to praise him. He said that he was brave, stoical, learned and educated, well versed in law and theology and respectful to imams.[128] His total failure contrasted with the glittering success achieved by Jebe and Subedei, which drew Genghis's appreciative praise. The one blemish on the great Mongol raid was the disgraceful performance of Toquchar. Warned by Genghis before he set out not to loot and pillage on his own account, Toquchar disregarded his father-in-law's words. For this egregious offence, Genghis reduced him to the ranks and ordered him into the thick of fighting as a common soldier.[129] Yet, though the shah was dead, the Mongols had merely scotched the Khwarezmian snake, not killed it. There remained much more hard fighting and many more hundreds of thousands of deaths before Genghis could declare the war at an end.

11

The Khwarezmian Empire Destroyed

While Jebe and Subedei relentlessly harried the doomed shah, Genghis, in ignorance of the rapid sequence of events, targeted the realm of Khwarezm, the heartland of Muhammad's domains, as his next objective. Whereas Samarkand and Bukhara were late additions to the shah's infant empire, Khwarezm – the Amu Darya delta region, the area bounded on the north by the Aral Sea, to the east the Kizil Qum Desert, the south by the Kara Qum Desert and the west by the Ustyurt Plateau (and today at the crossroads of Uzbekistan, Kazakhstan and Turkmenistan) – was its heartland. Intensely loyal to Muhammad and his family, it was where his mother had had her power base.[1]

Determined to complete the 'blooding' of his sons in difficult campaigns, Genghis intended to remain aloof from the actual fighting and in the autumn of 1220 sent Jochi north instead, telling him that Khwarezm was to be part of his ulus. He himself remained at Qarshi (Nasaf), with headquarters at the Nakhshab oasis, moving slightly upstream to Sali Sarai in the winter of 1220–21. Always inclined to forgive a favourite, he decided to blot out Toquchar's earlier disobedience when he looted and pillaged, took him out of his humiliating position in the ranks and raised him to command once more. Toquchar's task was to ensure that no enemy troops escaped south from Khwarezm to Khorasan.[2] But the attack on Khwarezm itself and its great capital Gurganj he assigned to Jochi.

As a prelude he sent one Taynal Noyan with 20,000 men to advance towards Gurganj and take out the city of Khiva en route. This force proved much more successful than Jochi's main army that followed in its wake. First, in early December 1220, it took Khiva after a bloody and strenuous seven-day siege followed by savage street fighting.[3] Then the Mongols rode the hundred or so miles north-west of Khiva to Gurganj itself, where they almost managed to end the campaign before Jochi had even arrived. Using one of their favourite ruses, they sent a small body of horsemen to drive off cattle under the very gates of the city. Naturally the men of Gurganj at once sallied in strength and pursued. The Mongols cunningly drew the pursuers away from the city, feigning a panic-stricken flight, and led them into an ambush. The ensuing battle was grimly fought from early morning to noon, but ended in complete victory for the Mongols. The pursuers became the pursued and fled back to the city, entering by a side gate. The Mongols followed them into the suburbs, but were not in sufficient strength to overcome the numerous defenders or gain a decisive advantage, so withdrew.

Two days later Jochi arrived with the main army.[4] He was anxious to spare both the city and the province massive destruction, since this was his own ulus, but a letter explaining this and counselling peaceful submission was returned with an insulting reply by the burghers of Gurganj.[5]

Gurganj was an immensely wealthy city and its beauty was praised by the famous Arab geographer and biographer Yakut al-Hamawi (1179–1229). The wealth derived from many sources: its position as a nodal point on the caravan routes; a thriving slave trade, an agricultural sector producing cotton, cereals, fruit, grapes, currants, sesame, honey, hazelnuts and other foodstuffs, a manufacturing base turning out bows, arrows, swords, cuirasses and other armaments, a luxury trade in amber, falcons, carpets and brocades of silk and cotton and, perhaps most of all, its famous commerce in Russian furs (marten, sable, fox, squirrel, stoat, ermine and weasel) as well as domestic pelts of horses, goats and wild asses.[6] Quite apart from the personal loyalty to Muhammad's family, the inhabitants had assets worth fighting for. From the Mongol point of view the city was the most difficult of nuts to crack, for all the approaches were plashy, marshy and foetid – one consequence of the fact that the Amu Darya, which formerly flowed into the Caspian Sea, by the thirteenth century emptied instead into the Aral.[7] Attackers not only had to approach over mudflats and marshlands but faced the serious problem that the terrain was void of all large stones necessary for siege engines; the Mongols solved that one by chopping down mulberry trees and hewing the wood into circular 'stones' for use in their catapults. However, this proved a temporary expedient only. The wooden missiles turned out to be ineffective against the thick and massive walls of Gurganj, so Jochi had to order real stones from distant areas to be laboriously transported there in carts.[8]

Jochi rode all round the walls, taking careful note of the landscape and any weaknesses in the defence. He also had good intelligence about the state of affairs inside the city. Once again the endemic factionalism of the Khwarezmian empire was playing into the Mongols' hands. Temur Melik, after his earlier daring escape from the enemy, made his way to Gurganj and tried to rally the people but soon gave up, discouraged and depressed by the incessant intrigues in the military high command.[9] Then, after the shah's death in January 1221, Jalal al-Din and his followers crossed the Caspian to the Mangishlaq peninsula and cut east to Gurganj. Jalal fared no better than Temur Melik and beat his head in vain against the intense – and insane in the light of the threat from the Mongols – factionalism. Jalal found himself unable to rally the powerful coterie centered around Uzlaq-Shah the former crown prince, notably the emirs of the north, who had always hated Jalal. When Uzlaq and his men tried to assassinate Jalal – and failed narrowly only because the plot was betrayed at the last minute – Jalal abandoned Gurganj as a hopeless case. He and his brothers took off east across the Kara-Kum Desert.[10] Jolted into sense by Jalal's departure, the feuding cliques finally made common cause and appointed a general named Khumar Tegin as their sultan.

Jochi pressed the siege hard, using prisoners in the front line to soak up the casualties, and employing siege engineers brought from China. He also tried to divert the river and cut off the water supply but the first 3,000 men he sent on this task were ambushed by a sortie from the defenders and badly mauled. At this reverse the defenders took heart and morale rose.[11]

Meanwhile Genghis was fretting and fuming about the continued lack of good news from Jochi. In an evil hour he decided to send Chagatai to the siege with a considerable reinforcement; predictably, Jochi was enraged both by the implication that he was incompetent and at the salt-rubbing implicit in the dispatch of the hated Chagatai. Equally predictably, Genghis's two eldest sons clashed violently from the moment of their first encounter. Chagatai accused Jochi of a 'softly-softly' approach dictated solely by the fact that Gurganj was his appanage, and that he was sacrificing wider Mongol interests to his own ambition.[12] The two soon exemplified the old adage that the only fun in war is to be had from fighting your own side. Bo'orchu, who had been sent by Genghis to be his eyes and ears and a steadying influence on Jochi and whose record at Gurganj was most distinguished, reported to Genghis that instead of concentrating on the siege, his two sons were battling each other.

One canard was that Jochi challenged Chagatai to a wrestling match and that the bout had actually started when Bo'orchu heard of it. He rushed to the spot to intervene, and was able to part the combatants only when he revealed a plenipotentiary 'to whom it may concern' note from Genghis, ordering all who heard it to obey Bo'orchu as they would the great khan himself. But it was certain that the slanging match between the brothers did escalate to the point where their supporters clashed violently and there were deaths on both sides.[13]

When he learned this, Genghis's anger was seismic. On this campaign he had already had to endure open quarrels between the two in his own presence. Qulan urged him to cut through and settle the succession then and there, in case any accident should befall him. Genghis took her advice and nominated Ogodei as his successor. He then sent Ogodei to Gurganj as commander-in-chief, with strict orders to his two elder sons to accept the succession and to obey Ogodei in all things; Ogodei brought with him a further 20,000 men.[14] Chagatai seems to have been well content that the detested Jochi would not inherit the empire and anyway he liked and admired Ogodei. Jochi, though, was secretly furiously angry. In his mind he had been insulted twice over: he had been replaced as commander at Gurganj and now had been deprived of his birthright. His secret hatred of Genghis grew. Yet Ogodei was a good choice as supremo. Cast down both by their inability to put a dent in the walls of Gurganj and by the feuding and altercation of Jochi and Chagatai, the Mongols began to droop in morale and commitment: Ogodei put the steel back into them.[15]

His first move was to renew the attempt to divert the Amu Darya and deprive the defenders of water, though spies told him such a strategy would be hugely protracted, since the people of Gurganj had already dug wells and laid in a huge water reserve. But Khumar Tegin was by now beginning to quail at the enormous, and continually augmented, number of besiegers and by Ogodei's new artillery tactics that involved hurling naphtha at the city walls. He put out feelers asking for terms, but the enraged burghers learned of this, repudiated the overtures and deposed Khumar.[16]

Although the burghers of Gurganj were determined to fight on, slowly but surely the initiative passed to the Mongols, as every day that passed made the besiegers seem stronger and stronger. Ogodei ordered his prisoners forward to fill in the moats. It took them ten days to do so, taking terrible casualties all the time, but Ogodei was now able to get close up and sap and mine all along the walls. Finally, he sensed a weakening in the pulse of the defenders and ordered an all-out attack. While naphtha rained down on the city in an unceasing barrage, a Mongol commando unit managed to establish a toehold on the walls and planted their standards triumphantly there.[17] Using this bridgehead as a wedge, the Mongols gradually fought their way into the city, but the desperate defenders disputed every step. It took seven days of the most brutal, slugging streetfighting, hand to hand and house to house, before Ogodei's men broke the Gurganjians' will.

Finally in April 1221, exhausted, they asked for terms, their envoy adding that his people had now had enough of the Mongol lash. A furious Jochi, remembering the heavy losses taken by his 3,000-strong river-diverting party, replied that on the contrary up till now it was the Mongols who had tasted the lash, but that Gurganj was now about to get a taste of it.[18] Surrender terms were agreed. Every last person was ordered out of the city. Artisans were taken off to stand on one side, but all others were corralled into a killing ground, women and children included, except for a few comely wenches who were taken into concubinage or slavery. The massacre then began. There is no need to believe the hyperbole of some medieval chroniclers who said that each Mongol was given the task of killing twenty-four people, but there is also no reason to doubt that the slaughter was terrific. As a further refinement, the Mongols first made the women strip naked and fight each other with fists for the amusement of their troops. When they tired of the spectacle, they moved in and killed them all.[19]

The victors then thoroughly sacked the city, gutted it and, as a *pièce de résistance*, flooded it by opening the dykes inside the city that controlled the waters of the Amu Darya – though some claimed that the dykes spontaneously (and very conveniently) burst. A veritable tsunami engulfed the town. All buildings were destroyed and the hapless refugees who had tried their luck by hiding in them were drowned. It was said that, whereas in Mongol sacking of cities there were usually a handful of escapees, in Gurganj not a single soul escaped destruction.[20]

Ogodei and his brothers followed up the massacre at Gurganj with a wholesale laying waste of all Khwarezm. The total devastation of the province certainly made it impossible for Jalal or any of the shah's erstwhile followers to use the region as a rallying point, but in the process most economic life there ceased also; it was only later that the Mongols realised that it was more sensible to keep people alive so that they could work and be taxed rather than slaughter them.[21] Meanwhile the holocaust at Gurganj seemed to observers to have inaugurated an entirely new era and dimension of horror – an impression that would only be strengthened by the other mass killings to come, which would make 1221 a year to live in infamy. In the Arab world Genghis was beginning to be known by what would become a familiar piece of nomenclature: 'the Accursed One'. As Ibn al-Athir said of the destruction of Khwarezm: 'Nothing like this had ever been heard of in ancient or modern times.'[22]

Genghis of course cared nothing for his reputation. What concerned him was that his sons had made such heavy weather of the siege of Gurganj, had taken five months to accomplish it, and then only after two lots of pump-priming with reinforcements.

Meanwhile his favourite Toquchar had once again disappointed him. He began well by taking the town of Nisa but was then outwitted by Jalal al-Din, who emerged from the desert of Kara-Kum, fell on the garrison of seven hundred warriors Toquchar had left at Nisa, and cut his way through; Toquchar's two brothers were killed in the fighting.[23] By forced marches Jalal reached Nishapur and pressed on to Ghazni in eastern Afghanistan. To try to save face Toquchar made a rash attempt to take Nishapur, but his troops were driven off and he himself was killed in the fighting. His deputy, Borkei, tried to pick up the baton but he too was checked at Nishapur and had to console himself with the much lesser target of Sabzawar after a three-day siege.[24] At news of Toquchar's death, Genghis forgot the long litany of his failures and grieved excessively, telling his confidants that Nishapur would pay dearly for that day's work.

He was jolted out of his angry mourning by further bad news from Gurganj. It turned out that, after looting the city, Ogodei, Chagatai and Jochi had simply divided the immense loot between them, omitting to send the khan his customary tithe. From anyone else but his sons such an action would be high treason and, in the immediacy of his wrath, Genghis actually toyed with the idea of executing the three reprobates, as he termed them.[25] When they returned to court, he refused to receive them in audience for three days and kept them dangling in a limbo of uncertainty. It fell to Bo'orchu and Shigi Qutuqu, in concert with the three 'quiver bearers', to talk Genghis down from his homicidal rage. They argued that he was being much too harsh on them, for they were simply rash and headstrong young men, 'like young falcons about to enter training'. Gradually Genghis was won round. When he finally calmed down, he acknowledged the wisdom of his counsellors' advice and promoted all of them to even higher offices in gratitude for their efforts.[26]

After resting his horses and reserves for most of 1220, Genghis decided that the priority for 1221 was the pursuit of Jalal al-Din into Afghanistan. He intended to cross the River Vakhsh into the Hindu Kush near Baghlan, with the fortress of Talikan as his next major objective, and it therefore made sense for him to accompany Tolui as far as Balkh, the Mongols' first target in Khorasan. In January 1221 he crossed the Amu Darya at Termez, which had already fallen, but was wrong-footed when a deputation arrived from Balkh to say that the citizens would submit and offer no resistance.[27]

Genghis advanced and surveyed the city. Its houses of sun-dried bricks were watered by an intricate irrigation system, which also fed the rich vineyards, orchards and fields of sugar-cane in the environs. An important religious centre – some called it the Mecca of Persia – Balkh boasted three concentric walls and thirteen gates and its wealth made it a constant target for marauders; apart from the Mongols there were the Turkish nomads who sacked it in 1155, while Tamerlane would destroy it once more in 1389.[28] It seemed to Genghis that he could not leave such a rich and populous city in his rear when he turned east to deal with Jalal, so he decided to break his own rules and ignore the peaceful submission.

It is important to realise that Genghis was permanently obsessed with the Mongols' paucity in numbers and hence with casualty lists.

In his mind it was the merest realism to reduce the numerical odds against himself by the massacre of all who would not surrender; this was the method he had employed against Tayichiud, Tartars, Merkit, Kereit, the Jin and all other enemies; there were never to be any prisoners unless they could be used as arrow-fodder.[29] Genghis always allowed pragmatism to trump concerns of humanity, so the luckless people of Balkh paid the price. He ordered all citizens of property to emerge from the city, ostensibly to assess the taxes they should pay to their conquerors, then massacred them all, thereby, in his mind, destroying any possible focus for future rebellion.[30] He salved what passed in Genghis for a conscience by not ordering the killing of every single soul, which was his normal practice when a city refused to surrender, and contented himself with a 'routine' sack of the city.

He and Tolui then parted, he to Afghanistan, Tolui to complete the conquest of Khorasan. Before he left, Genghis gave explicit and chilling orders for his youngest son. If there was the slightest resistance in the major cities, Tolui was to kill everyone without exception. If the burghers surrendered, Tolui was to use his best judgement about how to proceed, always bearing in mind the crucial factor of numbers.[31] The task Genghis gave Tolui was no easy one. Khorasan was a long series of steppes where only the occasional grove of elms or poplars grew, punctuated by fertile oases, ending in a desert at the heart of the Persian plateau. Life was hard and, outside the major conurbations and oases, almost impossible, for it was only the complex irrigation systems that sustained the orchards, vineyards, and fields of rice and millet, to say nothing of the ornate gardens in the big cities.

Exulting in his unfettered command, Tolui decided to strike northwest and invest Merv, which his spies had reported on to his fascination. Allegedly one of the largest cities in the world at the time, an architectural showpiece, with an estimated population of around 200,000, and reckoned second in importance in the shah's empire only to Bukhara, Merv was another of those urban centres with over-determined sources of wealth.[32] The city of the *Arabian Nights*, an important oasis on the lower River Murghab and situated on a fertile plain, it was famed for its exports of silk, cotton and cloth, for its ceramics, fine fabrics and carpet-making. It stood at the nodal point of the Silk Route, with roads striking north-west to Nisa (near modern Ashgabat), due west to Asterabad (Gorgan) on the Caspian Sea, due

north to Khiva (Khwarezm), south through Herat to the Persian Gulf
and south-west via Nishapur to Iraq-Adjemi and Mesopotamia. The
Silk Route itself was already the conduit for goods from Byzantium,
India and the Arab caliphate (under the later Mongol empire Russia
and Europe would be added).[33] With its plethora of weavers, potters
and brass-makers, Merv was a magnet for all the caravans of the
Orient and the Middle East, and it was famous too for containing the
tomb of the sultan Sanjar, whose turquoise-blue dome could be seen
from a great distance.

Yet what most bedazzled Tolui was its altogether miraculous irrigation system.[34] South of the city the River Murghab was prevented
from changing course by dykes and embankments faced with wood-
work. Three miles south of Merv the river's waters were impounded
in a great round pool, whence four canals radiated to the various
quarters of the city and the suburbs, with the height of water in the
pool controlled by sluices. At high flood time the dams were cut and
the waters divided according to set rules, and this was the occasion
for a festival of thanksgiving.[35] Tolui was particularly intrigued that
the irrigation system was under the control of a special official, the
mir-ab, said to have more power than the city prefect. He employed
12,000 men in the maintenance of dykes and the regulation of the
water supply, and even had a team of three hundred divers, each of
whom had to keep a supply of timber to repair the dykes. On the
embankment was a gauge which regulated the flood height. In a year
of abundance this rose to 'sixty barleycorns' above low level, but in a
year of drought only six. The mir-ab was at the apex of an entire
hydraulic hierarchy. He was responsible for the main canals, officials
known as bandbans (aka varkbans) for the dams and divers, juybans
(supervising the offtake canals) and ab-andazs (water measurers), in
charge of the release of water from the upper reaches of the river.[36]
The collective labour carrying out the irrigation work was known as
the hashar.[37] The Mongols, and especially Tolui, were far from mindless; they learned from this system and later, as imperial overlords,
themselves built many huge dams and irrigation works in Iran and
Central Asia.[38]

Nonetheless, greatly as he admired the ingenuity of the people of
Merv, it was Tolui's duty to destroy the entire intricate edifice unless
Merv surrendered promptly. It did not. When Subedei and Jebe

appeared before the city during their pursuit of the shah, the citizens seemed divided in their response to the Mongols. Muhammad had ordered all the troops inside the walls to retreat to the nearby fortress of Maragha and advised the burghers to submit. But the generals felt insecure in Maragha, and they and their men drifted back to Merv, strengthening the anti-Mongol faction. The peace party, also powerful, was led by the mufti but he was discovered to be a fifth columnist for the Mongols and executed.[39] Subedei and Jebe tried to lure Merv into submission by lavish promises and cajolery but the war party tortured their envoys, who revealed the Mongols' intended treachery before being executed. When Jebe and Subedei, obedient to their orders, did not tarry but pressed on in pursuit of the shah, the citizens grew complacent and overconfident; they were thrown into consternation by the approach of Tolui with a large army. Contemporary chroniclers estimated the Mongols at 70,000 strong – an absurd exaggeration – but Tolui's host was large enough to be frightening, especially as there was a large number of drafted prisoners in the ranks.[40]

Tolui began briskly by luring 10,000 crack Turkish troops into an ambush and demolishing them. Next day he made a tour of Merv's defences and thought the city vulnerable. But the war party still had the upper hand within and staged two sorties, easily swatted away.[41] After a week the defenders asked for terms and sent a deputation to Tolui. He promised that no one would be killed and there would be no looting if the citizens surrendered promptly. Cunningly he asked to see a second deputation composed of all the leading citizens and, once he had them in his power, had them garrotted, but not before they had revealed the names of the two hundred richest men.[42] Tolui issued a decree declaring that all who wished to surrender must leave the city with their effects; all artisans and the two hundred identified plutocrats were to received special treatment. After an exodus which is said to have taken four days, Tolui surveyed the masses dolefully gathered with their possesions, mounted a golden chair and ordered mass execution to commence.[43] Every last person who had come out onto the plain was slain. The soldiers from the garrison were beheaded, and each Mongol allegedly had a quota of four killings to complete. One report said the massacre went on for four days and nights. The two hundred plutocrats were then tortured to reveal the whereabouts of their wealth.

Next Merv was sacked and gutted and the irrigation system eviscerated. The mausoleum of sultan Sanjar was demolished in hopes of finding treasure there, and the city walls and citadel razed to the ground.[44] From the beginning of the siege to Tolui's departure three terrible weeks had elapsed. Thinking the Mongols had departed, some 5,000 survivors who had gone into hiding crawled out of cellars and secret passages and emerged onto the rubble, only to be cut to pieces by returning Mongol squadrons. Some said that Tolui had a shrewd suspicion that not all the Mervians had perished; others that the survivors were just plain unlucky, in that a rear detachment, slow to quit the city, just happened to see them as they emerged from their underground bolt-holes.[45]

One unintended consequence of the destruction of Merv was that a clan of Turkish Oghuz pastoralists, who had sacked Balkh in 1155 and liked to graze their herds near Merv, were so terrified of the Mongols' advent that they decamped west in panic, made their way to Asia Minor and eventually founded Turkey's Ottoman dynasty.[46] Yet another was that those people who had managed to escape Merv before the Mongols' final onslaught and had fled to nearby villages or the desert now swore revenge, formed themselves into guerrilla groups and harassed Tolui severely on his line of march.[47]

Before turning south to Nishapur, Tolui detached a sizeable corps of his army and sent it to attack ten-gated Nisa, the most northerly city of Khorasan on the southern edge of the Kara-Kum Desert and the northern slopes of the Kopet Dagh Mountains, where the green vegetation around the town contrasted sharply with the black sandy desert of nearby Turkmenistan. It will be remembered that Nisa had fallen to Toquchar in 1220 but that the garrison he had left there had then been overwhelmed by Jalal al-Din and his army. In the course of the fighting one of Tolui's close friends, Borke, had been killed by an arrow. Tolui was determined to avenge his old comrade.

The Mongols adopted their usual formation: prisoners in front to absorb the missiles of the defenders and twenty catapults raining missiles above their heads against the walls. After fifteen days the trebuchets made a large breach in the walls, the Mongols poured in during a night attack and became masters of the city within hours. All the inhabitants were driven out onto the plain and ordered to tie the hands of the next person to them behind their backs. Then they were all – men, women and children – dispatched with arrows. The figure of 70,000 slain in Nisa and the northern provinces given in some contemporary chronicles may not be too far from the truth.[48]

The route from Nisa to Nishapur ran almost directly south, and the victorious Mongols hastened to catch up with Tolui who proceeded in leisurely fashion from Merv to Nishapur, taking twelve days.[49] Tolui was under orders from Genghis to wreak a terrible vengeance for the death of Toquchar, but Mongol credibility in general was also at stake, as Nishapur had repelled Toquchar's powerful army in November 1220 and attitudes there seemed to have hardened since the city behaved politely to Jebe and Subedei on their way past earlier in pursuit of the shah.[50]

Whereas Tolui, ever the practical man of action, could see the importance of Merv's irrigation scheme, the glories of Nishapur largely left him cold. Famous as the city of the great poet and polymath Omar Khayyam, renowned for its religious scholars and as a centre of Sufism, Nishapur was another wealthy city, with its fields of rice and cereals, its carpet-making and distinctive ceramics, its cotton factories, glass-blowing, manufacture of metal and stone vessels and musical instruments, the turquoise mines in the suburbs, its sumptuous houses, exquisite gardens and general opulence. Possibly the most beautiful city in all Iran and certainly in Muhammad's empire, Nishapur was a watery delight, with twelve canals and seventy watermills bringing the precious liquid to a population of some 170,000.[51] It had been destroyed twice in historical memory, once by the Oghuz Turks in 1153 and more recently, in 1208, by a calamitous earthquake, but poor Nishapur can have had little conception of the hell that was now to descend on it. Once the citizens saw the size of Tolui's army, they sent envoys, both imams and oligarchs, to ask for terms, but Tolui was constrained by Genghis's rage over Toquchar and his code of vengeance, so could offer them nothing. In any case the Nishapurians had done themselves no favours since, before Tolui's arrival, they had been attacking Mongol outriders and scouting parties. The ferocity of the Mongol onslaught was such that, though better defended than Merv, it lasted just three days, as against Merv's three weeks.[52]

The battle for Nishapur (April 1221) began with a furious cannonade from both sides. Nishapur's defences included 3,000 javelin-throwing ballistae and 500 catapults, against which the Mongols brought to bear the same number of ballistae, 300 catapults and 700 naphtha-hurling trebuchets, plus 4,000 scaling ladders, 250,000 large stones and 2,500 sacks of earth for filling up moats.[53] An all-out assault ordered by Tolui on all four quarters of the city lasted an entire day and night and ended with sixty-six breaches in the city walls. In just over twenty-four hours, a bridgehead of 10,000 Mongols was inside the city. The inevitable result was ferocious street fighting where every house was contested and every block involved bloody hand-to-hand combat.[54]

The battle inside the city began on a Wednesday and was finally completed by Friday night. Since more and more Mongols continued to pour through the breach there could be only one ending. By Saturday morning Mongol death squads were roaming the streets, including a special corps of killers led in person by Toquchar's widow, more bloodthirsty than the warriors, screaming for vengeance. The resulting massacre lasted a full four days. As at Merv, survivors tried to hide among the bodies and in the rubble, but most were winkled out and executed (Tolui, alert to enemy survival tactics after the experience at Merv, left behind a squad of killers to deal with anyone who emerged; all killings were to be by beheading).[55] The others died of starvation and thirst in their caverns and subterranean hideouts.[56] The Mongols piled up three pyramids of skulls from men, women and children respectively. Obedient to Genghis's orders that no living thing was to be spared the killers even wiped out dogs, cats and rats. Out of a population of 170,000 only four hundred hand-picked artisans survived.

Their blood up, the Mongols diverted to nearby Tus and sacked that town as well. Amidst the general devastation they managed also to destroy and plunder the mausoleum of Harun al-Rashid, famous from the *Arabian Nights* and most celebrated of all the caliphs. This act of vandalism fittingly epitomised the way the Mongols had destroyed so many of the jewels of Persian civilisation in a mere three months in Khorasan, for this was its heartland: Tus boasted Ferdowsi the poet and al-Ghazali the philosopher among its famous sons, while Nishapur basked in the glories of Omar Khayyam.[57]

Only one act of humanity emerges from this terrible period. The ruler of Tabriz, to the west of the Caspian, and thus more in the orbit of Jebe and Subedei than of Tolui, placated the Mongols by sending some samples of a special ointment to palliate the effects of insect bites. Tolui was so impressed by this that he issued a general order that Tabriz was not to be harmed provided it submitted peacefully.[58]

Nishapur was as far west as Tolui proceeded on his whirlwind tour of terror. He made next for Herat to the south-east, an oasis set amid a 125-mile stretch of steppe and desert along the Hari Rud valley and a five-day march from Nishapur. This was a delightful spot, famous for its carpet-making, with Aleppo pines and poplars along the river bank, set in a fertile plain surrounded by mountains and a cluster of nearby mountainside villages with fecund cornfields, vineyards, orchards and gardens.[59] Tolui sent an envoy to demand surrender, but the governor of Herat killed him and sent a message of defiance. There followed a ten-day siege, with the Mongols assaulting from all sides and bitter fighting daily. During one of these encounters the governor was killed, and the peace party in Herat gained the ascendancy.[60] Another peace overture was made, and Tolui promised clemency if the city surrendered at once. Mongol promises to this effect usually meant nothing but during the course of the siege Tolui, always a creature of caprice, had begun to take a distinct liking to the city, its situation and its climate.[61] When Herat duly surrendered, he contented himself with slaying only the 12,000 troops in the garrison and all known supporters of Jalal al-Din. He then installed a Mongol prefect and military commander and swung north-east for a rendez-vous with Genghis and his brothers at Talikan in Afghanistan.[62]

In contrast to the glowing successes gained by the Mongols in Ferghana, Transoxiana, Khwarezm and Khorasan, the campaign in the Hindu Kush did not go well and slumped into a series of slugging encounters, protracted sieges and battles of attrition. Part of this was due to the very different nature of Middle Eastern fortresses as compared with Chinese ones. Unlike their equivalent in China, the cities of the shah's empire were heavily fortified with separate citadels. Such cities, if simply bypassed, could seriously limit the Mongols' control of territory and freedom of movement, and in the Hindu Kush, unlike Khorasan, these fastnesses were relatively close to each other and could impair an invader's progress by simple synergy.[63]

Another factor was the talent (and luck) of Jalal al-Din. For a long time fortune seemed to smile on him. He left the suburb of Shadyakh in Nishapur just one hour before the besieging Mongols arrived, then threw off his pursuers by cleverly placing his crack troops at a fork in the road east. While they fought a holding action and diverted the enemy down the wrong turning, he made his escape down the other fork.[64] The Mongols quickly realised their mistake, reformed and soon were hard on Jalal's heels again. Unable to halt at Zozan as planned, since the enemy was so close, Jalal pressed on through Mabarnabad and Yazdawiah, seventy-five miles south-west of Herat. Here the Mongols broke off the pursuit, either because they lost his tracks or because Genghis recalled them.[65] When he arrived at Ghazni, Jalal found 50,000 loyalists awaiting him, and more recruits began to flock in once they realised the shah's son was heading the resistance. The most significant accession was Temur Malik with 30,000 veterans. Altogether Jalal soon had an army of 70–80,000, easily large enough to face the Mongols.[66]

Knowing nothing of this, Genghis yet made careful preparations for the Afghanistan campaign. Young Persians and Turks were cynically and remorselessly drilled in the techniques of besieging vanguards for use against their own fortresses, knowing that they faced death from the arrows of their own side if they advanced and death from the Mongols behind if they did not. And Genghis did not make the mistake Napoleon later made with his Old Guard of never using them, so that when they were finally called into action at Waterloo they let him down. Fearful that his reserves, strung out along the parks and orchards between Bukhara and Samarkand, had not seen action for a long time and were rusty, going soft and reportedly turning to bodily pleasure in great numbers, Genghis ordered a great hunt to exterminate all game within a huge cordon and personally took part in the battue, held in the mountainous country near Termez.[67] It seems that Jochi, still in disgrace after the fiasco at Gurganj, took no part in this, but afterwards he joined his father and made ample amends by going down on bended knee, craving forgiveness and giving his father the staggeringly generous present of 100,000 horses; there were 20,000 each of carefully selected greys, piebalds, bay, black and chestnut. Genghis, particularly delighted with the gift as he was short of mounts, raised Jochi up and formally pardoned him for all offences. Yet there appears to have been some residual mistrust between the two, for Genghis announced that his eldest son would not be joining him on the Afghanistan campaign. Jochi, secretly brooding about all his real and imaginary wrongs, departed for his ulus.[68]

Genghis's Afghan strategy was to reduce the numerous fortresses, besieging three or four at a time, with his armies seemingly strung out, tempting Jalal to attack, at which point the Mongols would perform another of their miracles of rapid concentration. His first target was Talikan in the northern Hindu Kush, to the south of the Amu Darya; Tolui was to join him there once he had finished his sweep of the great cities of Khorasan. Talikan held out for six months. The Mongols, using captive labour, painstakingly erected a rampart to the same height as the defenders' walls, then used their powerful siege engines to batter the fortress into submission. Sensing the inevitable end, the garrison staged a mass sortie; most of the cavalry got away but the infantry were cut to pieces. Enraged by the defence of a place that had made him lose face, Genghis ordered every living thing there put to death.[69]

But Talikan was to be only the first in a series of protracted sieges, many of which lasted six months or more.[70] Another fortress to put up a spirited resistance, this time for just a month, was Kerdnan, and this too was punished by annihilation. Then word came in that his beloved grandson Mogetugen, son of Chagatai, had been killed by an arrow at the siege of Bamiyan far to the south-west. Leaving his deputies to proceed with the conquest of Talikan, the grief-maddened Genghis crossed the Hindu Kush to conduct the siege of Bamiyan in person. It soon fell and in revenge Genghis once again issued his dread order that not a single living creature be left alive. Even reptiles were killed, and foetuses ripped from their mothers' wombs. Bamiyan came to be known as 'the accursed town' and remained long uninhabited.[71]

The death of Mogetugen led Genghis into another of his excursions into abnormal psychology, which can be read as a kind of transmogrified sadism or simply the exercise of power by an unbalanced potentate. When Chagatai arrived at Bamiyan and found no Mogetugen there, he inquired about his son. Genghis fobbed him off with an excuse. A few days later, when Genghis sat at table with Tolui, Ogodei and Chagatai, he spoke enigmatically of disloyalty and gave Chagatai a hard stare. Chagatai, knowing how easy it was to offend his father unintentionally, began to protest vociferously that he would rather die than disobey the great khan, sank to his knees and asked forgiveness for any offence he had unwittingly given. Genghis then told him coldly and cruelly that Mogetugen was dead, adding quickly: 'But I forbid you to weep, grieve or in any way to complain about it.'[72] This was particular humbug from a man who was known to wail and lament piteously at the demise of any of his favourites, but Chagatai accepted the directive unquestioningly. Though thunderstruck and wanting to know more, he forced himself to suppress his tears until the banquet was over, at which point he rushed out and allowed himself to grieve in private.[73]

Suddenly Jalal al-Din showed his hand by moving north from Ghazni and engaging the Mongol vanguard of about seven hundred men on the banks of the River Panjshir, killing a number and putting the rest to flight. The Mongol van fled back across the river and tried to lure Jalal towards the main force with the time-honoured ploy of the feigned retreat, but Jalal refused to take the bait and pointedly destroyed the bridge the Mongols had built across the river. The two sides ended the conflict by a pointless exchange of arrow fire across the river.[74]

When this defeat was reported to Genghis, he was angry at the slight to his martial prowess and ordered Shigi Qutuqu to take four tumens and seek out and destroy Jalal. The two hosts clashed outside the town of Parwan. Shigi was said to have had 45–50,000 men in his army as against 60–70,000 in Jalal's; these numbers are exaggerated, but the ratio of Jalal's numerical advantage is probably accurate.[75]

Shigi was overconfident, thinking that the terror of the Mongol name alone would do the trick. A terrible two-day battle resulted. Jalal used unusual tactics and had his men dismount and hold their horses' bridles in their hands to form a laager; the probability is that the bridles were fastened at the saddle and then round the horses' girths, leaving their riders free to fight. Clouds of arrows were discharged in both directions. The Mongols charged repeatedly but were always beaten back by Jalal's men, who performed prodigies of valour.[76] Ferocious fighting went on until nightfall, at which point Shigi employed the old Mongol trick of mounting tens of thousands of dummies on the spare horses. It nearly worked, for in the morning Jalal's officers noticed a vastly increased Mongol host and concluded that the enemy must have been reinforced overnight. They advised immediate retreat but Jalal opted to stand and fight. Shigi tried one last mass assault on his left, which was commanded by Saif al-Din Ighrak. The first attack was beaten off by a hail of arrows, but Shigi tried again and came close to success after the Mongols managed to trap five hundred of Ighrak's men and slaughtered them all.[77] Jalal then ordered his improvised infantry back on their horses and managed to blunt and crumple Shigi's right. The battle seemed in danger of ending in stalemate.

Next, timing his movements perfectly, Jalal waited until the struggle in the centre was poised on a knife-edge, then released his cavalry in a mass charge. Surprised and shaken, Shigi could muster no answer to this. Seeing himself in danger of encirclement, he cut his way out with his bodyguard and rode to Genghis with news of his own defeat.[78] Abandoned by their leader, his surrounded men fought to the end or were taken prisoner, only to be tortured to death in horrible ways which revolted even the case-hardened Genghis when he heard about it.

Yet Jalal's great victory turned out to be pyrrhic. A violent dispute arose between Ighrak and Temur Melik over the distribution of the booty and, in particular, over possession of a treasured white horse; Temur actually struck Ighrak.[79] Jalal was in an impossible position, for if he decided in favour of one, the other would storm off with his men, yet he was subjected to taunts from both sides about dithering and indecisive leadership, so in the end reluctantly plumped for Temur, as being his oldest ally. At this Ighrak taunted him bitterly with ingratitude, pointing out that his repulse of Shigi's right had been the turning point. Ighrak commanded 30,000 Qanglis, who rode sullenly and silently out of camp. Some said this happened at first light, others that the Qanglis stole away at night, leaving their campfires burning.[80] Seriously weakened by this defection and thus unable to go on to confront Genghis in battle, Jalal decided to cross the Indus and retire into the Punjab or Sind, leaving a holding force to delay the inevitable Mongol pursuit.

Volcanically angry at the news of the first serious reverse to Mongol arms, Genghis ordered his army into the most strenuous forced marching mode, abandoning all baggage and stopping to eat only every forty-eight hours. Fifteen days behind Jalal when he started, Genghis made up the ground with astonishing speed, brushed aside Jalal's masking force with contemptuous ease, bypassed Ghazni and, late in September 1221, caught up with his quarry at the exact spot on the banks of the Indus where Tamerlane would cross in 1399 during the campaign when he sacked Delhi (at Dinkot near present-day

Kalabagh).[81] He had made only one significant stop en route, at Parwan, where he inspected the battlefield together with Ogodei, Tolui and Chagatai. For a lesser commander, the penalty for failure might have been death, but Shigi was one of Genghis's favourites and the khan thought humiliation the more suitable punishment. He rubbed salt in the wounds by having Shigi point out all the relevant topographical details.

After surveying the scene of his favourite's defeat, Genghis publicly criticised Shigi for his tactics and for having allowed Jalal to choose the time and place of battle; he added that both commanders had been ham-fisted and amateurish in their choice of battleground. 'You didn't know the terrain adequately and you were both at fault,' he remarked waspishly.[82] To his confidant Bo'orchu he said he thought Shigi had been spoiled, having known only victories hitherto, had learned a bitter lesson and would benefit from his mistakes, adding that any one of his top generals (Muqali, Subedei, Jebe) would certainly have defeated Jalal on such a field.[83]

At the Indus Genghis caught Jalal totally by surprise at dawn as he was organising his army to cross the river. Jalal had been delayed by the throngs of refugees who joined his army – extra mouths to feed but of little use to him militarily. He also had the few remaining members of his family with him, including his sons. Genghis was lusting for combat, dearly wishing to lay hands on the man who had not just humiliated Shigi but compounded his sins by the hideous tortures inflicted on Mongol prisoners, for example by driving nails into their brains through their ears.[84]

Very soon he had Jalal surrounded in a semicircle, with the river at his back. Jalal considered his limited options. He began by destroying all his boats so that his men could not escape, but would have to stand and fight. He threw his wings forward, and remained in the rear with his crack personal force of about 5,000, while the refugees straggled along the shore. He was outnumbered, since for the first time in his military career Genghis had a clear numerical advantage over an enemy. Jalal was hopeful that the Mongols would be exhausted after their long, forced marches and that they would spend themselves in vain against his powerful left, dug in under the cliffs.[85] At first his hopes rose, for the the first Mongol attack was beaten back. One of Genghis's problems was that there were too many fighting men crammed into a small area, so that archery was difficult and the fighting had to be mainly at close quarters, with swords.

With the daylight becoming more and more evident, Genghis ordered another attack, concentrating on the right wing where Temur Melik was in command; Melik was very soon forced to retreat and was killed in the melee.[86] Meanwhile Genghis sent a commando squad to scale the cliffs behind the enemy's left wing and take them in the rear. Many lives were lost on the perilous ascent of the precipitous ridges, but at last the deed was done and a force descended on the Turkish warriors of the enemy left. Soon this wing was also crumpling.[87] Jalal was just congratulating himself that he could see daylight in the Mongol centre and it might be time to order a charge by his 'Immortals' when news of the cliffside disaster came in. Ignoring the threat to his centre, Genghis now drove his troops forward on both wings. The sultan himself, a curious mixture of despicable cruelty and outstanding bravery, fought on until noon, but it was soon evident that his cause was hopeless. As Ibn al-Athir remarked (referring to a now lost proverb): 'Like the sorrel horse, if he hangs back, he will be killed, and if he advances, he will be hamstrung.'[88]

With superb discipline, the Mongol troops on either wing resisted the temptation to pursue the fleeing enemy but wheeled round and closed in on Jalal in the centre.[89] At this point Jalal and his 700-strong bodyguard made a dash for freedom, abandoning the refugees to their fate. They charged the Mongol centre, forced their way through and made for the river. Jalal coaxed his horse up a cliff. Weeping with frustration but still dodging a hail of arrows from the Mongols, Jalal and his horse then plunged sixty feet into the Indus, surfaced and began swimming away from the shore. He was quickly carried downstream by the current, running at 9–10 m.p.h. in a river 180 feet deep at this point. Carried diagonally across the 250 yards width of the Indus, Jalal reached the far bank safely.[90] Genghis, who had ridden after him in pursuit, saw all this and forbade his archers to continue shooting once he saw Jalal's head bobbing in the water. Full of reluctant admiration, he exclaimed loudly: 'Such sons should have a proper father!'[91]

No such courtesies were extended to his men who, following his example, plunged into the Indus. Most of them were dispatched by accurate arrow fire from the bank, so that the Indus soon ran red with blood and its waters were churned by the death struggles of the mortally wounded. All Jalal's warriors who did not make it to the Indus were killed, mainly by Mongol parties waiting in ambush at roadblocks Genghis had set up on all tracks leading from the Indus.[92] Unsentimental and driven by realpolitik, Genghis had Jalal's sons and all his male relatives executed.

Once he reached the far bank Jalal rode back upstream until he was directly across from where he had plunged into the river, and dolefully watched as the Mongols plundered his camp. He had had all his gold, silver and jewels thrown into the Indus but Genghis's divers recovered a lot of it. Ever afterwards Jalal treasured the horse that saved him that day and cosseted the steed until its death near Tiflis in 1226, never mounting him again as a token of his gratitude.[93]

Alone at first on the far bank, he was gradually joined by a handful of survivors who trickled in. His powers of recovery were remarkable. Very soon he procured horses, arms and clothes and had 400 men under his command and within a matter of weeks this number had swollen tenfold. The local princeling, alarmed at this cuckoo in his nest, attacked him with 6,000 men against Jalal's makeshift and tatterdemalion force but was soundly beaten. Learning that the Mongols intended to track him as they had dogged his father, Jalal set out for Delhi. The sultan there refused him official protection, not wanting to precipitate an invasion of India by the Mongols. He seems in any case not to have taken to the arrogant Jalal; perhaps he had heard the stories of the Senggum Ilkha in Hsi-Hsia and did not want a repeat performance.[94] Another factor was that the sultan Iltutmish (reigned 1211–1236) was loyal to the caliph and alienated by the hostile and arrogant attitude displayed towards his spiritual leader in Baghdad both by Muhammad II and Jalal himself.[95] The story that Jalal browbeat Iltutmish is apocryphal – simply more of Jalal's lying bravado – but he does seem to have given him one of his daughters in marriage, doubtless to keep him quiet.

Jalal remained in India until he was sure the Mongols had abandoned pursuit, defeating a number of attacks by local tribesmen and continuing to attract recruits.[96] For two years he skulked in Lahore and its environs. News came in that one of his brothers had established a power base in Iraq but that the people there wanted Jalal to lead them, which made Jalal keen to leave India. Yet only when he heard definitively that the coast was clear and Genghis had returned to Mongolia did he take ship at the mouth of the Indus and return to Iran by sea (together with his 4,000 men), where he was next heard of stirring up anti-Mongol sentiment in Shiraz and Isfahan.[97]

It may seem surprising given the Mongols' normal ruthless pursuit of their enemies that Genghis did not order his armies into India. In fact he did send two tumens, under Bala and Dorbei Doqshin, who traversed Sind, devastated the provinces of Lahore and Multan and were on the point of taking the city of Multan after pounding it with catapults and mangonels when they were halted in their tracks by the excessive summer heat.[98]

Whenever the Mongols did not penetrate farther into a region, absurd stories arose that the might of the local rulers frightened them and turned them back, and so it was with the short-lived Indian campaign; the particular spin given to the story this time was that Iltutmish's heavy cavalry were superior to the Mongol horsemen. One is tempted to ask how many times this canard had been used of enemy cavalry before, only to be refuted on the battlefield.

The reality was altogether more rational, a product of Genghis's unblinking pragmatism. It is quite clear from the sources that Genghis originally intended to return to Mongolia via Bengal, Assam, the Himalayas and Hsi-Hsia.[99] A number of different factors made him change his mind. Sultan Iltutmish declined to allow the passage of Mongol armies, just as he had kept Jalal al-Din at arm's length. Very apprehensive about the Mongols, he did not anger Genghis by making a flat refusal, but dithered, procrastinated and prevaricated, refusing either to confirm or deny that he would allow passage.[100] Genghis read his mind. He knew that the Sultan did not want a full-scale war over an issue as trivial as Jalal, but neither did he. He knew that such a campaign would be hard fought and costly in lives and, though he had no doubts about its eventual outcome – how could Iltutmish prevail when Muhammad and the Jin emperors had failed? – there were peculiar problems about a march on Delhi that he was well aware of. In the first place, the summer heat in India was almost unbearable. Whereas temperatures in Lahore and Delhi were between 60 and 65 degrees F in winter, this rose to over 90 degrees in summer. Bala and Dorbei Doqshin turned back for precisely this reason.[101] Secondly, there were particular problems concerning horses. The great

Arab historian and traveller Ibn Battuta put his finger on two of them. Even a single tumen of the Mongol army required 250 tons of hay or other forage for its horses and 250,000 gallons of water. The water was available in Sind and Multan but not the forage.[102] Moreover, spare mounts were extremely scarce in the Hindu Kush, as huge profits could be made from trading steppe horses in India, so that any potential surplus had already been eaten up by the desire for profit.[103] Apart from all this, Genghis feared both imperial 'overstretch' – he barely had the troops to contain the regions he had already conquered and had not yet recruited enough domestic collaborators or quislings – and manpower shortages. As a result all Mongol forays into India were made with inadequate manpower (never more than 20,000 men).[104]

Then there was the troops' health to consider. Large numbers of troops were already on the sick list as a result of fevers and other tropical diseases. Fearing the possible consequences of dwindling Mongol numbers, Genghis ordered the huge mass of Indian slaves and captives that he had acquired to gather rice in vast quantities and store it in warehouses, then massacred them all so as not to have feed 'useless' mouths.[105] Furthermore, Genghis could obtain no accurate information about the forests, mountains and jungles he would have to traverse on his original itinerary.[106] His advisers, too, counselled him that he should next concentrate on chastising the Tangut, whom he had vowed to exterminate for their treachery, and there were worrying signs that the latter intended to anticipate his attack.[107] Finally, and for a superstitious man, importantly, all the omens and auguries his soothsayers sought to find for a successful Indian venture turned out adverse. An examination of the shoulder-blades of sheep produced discouraging results and, additionally, reports came in that the invading Mongols had seen a 'unicorn' (obviously an Indian rhino), which was construed as an evil portent.[108] The weight of all this evidence, real and imaginary, decided Genghis to return home by a tried and tested route.

Before he turned north, Genghis gave orders to settle the two outstanding military issues remaining: the pacification of the Hindu Kush and the reconquest of rebellious Khorasan. The news of the defeat of Shigi at Parwan caused a sensation throughout the Khwarezmian empire and encouraged many a benighted city to think it could throw off Genghis's yoke. When the great khan heard that even some of the provinces in greater Mongolia were contemplating rebellion because of his long absence in the west, he sent Chagatai back to the homeland with a large army, with orders to proceed by forced marches and spread fire, sword and terror all the way to the borders of Jin China. Ogodei was ordered to lay waste the entire territory from the Indus to Ghazni, so that Jalal would never have an incentive to return to that region.[109]

Ogodei's task was a hard one, for many of the fortresses in the Hindu Kush and Gharjistan were more like galleries on the face of the mountains; as heavy rain fell it tended to create a further obstacle in the shape of a natural moat in front of these galleries.[110] The Mongols were constantly menaced by sorties from these strongholds, one of which, a daring raid on the Mongol base camp, carried off many horses and wagons and freed a number of prisoners. Ogodei determined never to rest until the perpetrators were punished, but the task of destroying the fortress took fifteen months, and the defenders were overwhelmed finally only after they had turned to mass cannibalism.[111]

The usual method of reducing these strongholds was by cutting the water supply and interdicting food supplies. The attacks on cities were an easier proposition. Although Ghazni had previously surrendered without resistance, Genghis for obscure reasons blamed the people there for Shigi's defeat at Parwan and ordered Ogodei to destroy it. Ogodei obeyed his orders efficiently, sacked the town in spring 1222 and massacred most of the population, and then did the same to the city of Ghur.[112]

After these exploits Ogodei asked his father's permission to march west into the extreme southerly Iranian province of Sistan but Genghis refused, on the grounds that the summer heat was too excessive to make success in that area likely. Ogodei then went on to fix his winter quarters on the upper Hari Rud, having completed what one commentator, perhaps overimpressed by the reduction of the mountain fortesses, has termed the Mongols' most brilliant military campaign.[113] Yet Ogodei had certainly reinforced the image of the Mongols as irresistible and resistance as useless. A story from Nisa is indicative. There a handful of Mongols ordered the citizens out onto the plain and ordered them to tie each other's hands behind their backs. Even though they could easily have overpowered the Mongols and fled to the hills, they obeyed meekly and then stood helpless and listless while they were slaughtered by arrows.[114]

Genghis was very pleased with the results of Ogodei's campaign, but his real anger and hence his real interest was focused on the reconquest of recreant Khorasan. Incredibly, Merv and Balkh had somehow revived, sent messages of defiance and killed their governors, thinking the Mongols bogged down in the Hindu Kush. Displaying what Genghis considered monstrous ingratitude, Herat, largely spared by Tolui, had joined the insurrection. Genghis summoned Tolui and berated him for leniency, preaching the lesson that people will always construe mercy, compassion and leniency as weakness; Herat could not have revolted if the people had all been killed the first time around. Dripping sarcasm, he remarked grimly: 'It seems the dead have come to life again and the people I ordered killed are still extant. This time I want to see heads severed from trunks.'[115]

So as not to humiliate the beloved Tolui further, he did not press the point but gave command of the expedition to punish Herat to his most sinister enforcer, Eljigidei, the man who had put Jamuga to death with such cruelty. The reduction of Balkh and Merv was entrusted to Shigi Qutuqu and Dorbei. Both armies contained contingents drawn from the survivors of Shigi's defeat at Parwan, who were now given the chance to rehabilitate themselves with deeds of valour.[116] After the battering they had taken the year before, neither Balkh nor Merv was in any condition to put up much resistance when the Mongols reappeared. Both cities were taken with ease and every last inhabitant slaughtered; Merv remained an utter ruin until the fifteenth century.[117] In Balkh it was said that the heads of the slain were piled outside the city walls, while the trunks were devoured by wolves, eagles, vultures and, finally, flies. As the Persian historian Juvaini put it: 'For a long time the wild beasts feasted on their flesh, and lions consorted without contention with wolves, and vultures ate without quarrelling from the same table as eagles.'[118] Once again, following Genghis's explicit orders, Shigi and Dorbei meticulously sifted through the rubble to find any survivors, dragged them out and executed them.

Herat, though, having been spared the massacres visited on the other cities of Khorasan, was in a position to give a good account of itself, and did so. Eljigidei had to press a six-month siege (December 1221–June 1222) before he could take the city. Loss of life on both sides was enormous, with the defenders claiming they would fight on to the last drop of blood, but the Mongols had the advantage that Genghis had specifically earmarked 50,000 captured 'auxiliaries' to soak up the inevitable casualties.[119] In the campaign against the shah Genghis perfected his 'leapfrogging' method whereby the survivors of Bukhara were used against Samarkand, the survivors there against Balkh, Merv and Nishapur and so on. The consequence was that, even though tens of thousands of pressed prisoners died, many survived and, once he had closed accounts with Jalal, Genghis used this surplus for the costly reconquest of Khorasan.

After months of ferocious combat and with no signs of slackening in the Mongols' resolve, the people of Herat began to despair. As always in such circumstances a peace party appeared in the city, but they must have known that their hopes of mercy from the Mongols were very slender. Eljigidei cunningly exploited the divisions in the city and at last his patience was rewarded. A section of the walls, pounded continually by catapults and trebuchets, collapsed and killed a few hundred of the attackers.[120] Enraged, the Mongols burst in and the terror began. Apart from about a thousand young women that he sent back to Genghis, Eljigidei massacred every living soul. The slaughter took a week to complete. Even when it was over, the Mongol commander was not satisfied and held back a 2,000-strong corps, who were to conceal themselves outside the city until the inevitable survivors emerged from the rubble on the third day. When they did so, they too were taken and beheaded. When the Mongols did finally move on, no more than forty Heratians remained alive – those who had had provisions and water for weeks and were hidden in the most elaborate and intricate hideouts.[121]

Ighrak, Jalal al-Din's general whom he had left behind in Khorasan, tried to organise local resistance under tribal chieftains, and the result was that even after the retaking of the major cities, there were still many fortresses that had to be reduced. The siege of the fortress of Kalyun dragged on for sixteen months. The Mongols began by blockading the place, but a relieving force broke through the blockading cordon, so they had to begin again. There was the usual ferocious close-combat fighting. The Mongols were said to have bottled Kalyun up so tightly that a fox was trapped at the foot of the rock on which the fortress stood; surviving on scraps, the fox took seven months to break out, so tightly invested was the stronghold. At the end of the sixteen months most of the defenders were dead from disease – some said a pestilence caused by a diet of dried meat, pistachios and butter. By this time only fifty defenders were left, twenty of them suffering from trench foot. After throwing all their gold and silver down a well, the fifty then ended their torment with a suicide charge at the Mongols, banzai-style.[122]

Another cliff-castle to put up heroic resistance was Fiwar; here most of the garrison died of starvation and when the Mongols stormed the place only seven defenders remained alive.[123] Another saga-like siege took place at Saif-fud. Here the defenders' spirits were high, as they had laid in a forty-day supply of water and a huge number of domestic animals which were progressively slaughtered for meat. Even with rationing, after fifty days the people of Saif-fud were down to their last day's supply of water. It was decided to kill all the women and children and then sortie to a glorious martyrdom. At the very last moment before this planned holocaust there was a violent rainstorm which replenished the town's reservoirs. So much water was left on tent coverings and roofs that the people gorged themselves on water for a week. With a months' water supply in hand they were now jubilant, thinking the Mongols would not be able to complete the siege before the winter snows came. The Mongols duly lifted the siege but in the new year (1223) they returned and announced that the siege would go on, if necessary for years, until the defenders surrendered.[124]

Wearying of the impossible struggle, a peace party emerged, which was quickly suborned by the Mongols. Soon in the majority, the peacemakers overpowered their commanders and arranged a three-day truce. The Mongols began friendly trading, telling the people that they would depart in peace on the third day, before the truce ended. Having gulled the people of Saif-fud, the Mongols adopted a variant of the Trojan horse strategy. They made as if to depart with a great hullabaloo and much panoply, having hidden a crack regiment in the rocks nearby, but suggested a goodbye bout of trading as a sign of goodwill. The people came out to trade. A signal was given, and the hidden Mongol warriors rushed out and slaughtered them, all but the richest three hundred (the chronicler Juzjani gives an exact count of 280), who were held for ransom. When townspeople refused to ransom them, the Mongols publicly beheaded them. Next day the Mongols attacked in force, but they had overestimated the numbers they had killed during the bogus trading session. To their surprise they found

Paradox: the conquerors of the world had no fixed abode. A Mongol yurt.

Mongol ponies could deal with any terrain, including snow and ice.

Infinitely adaptable and resourceful, the Mongols could switch from horse to camel when crossing the Gobi desert to close with their enemies.

Genghis Khan. The greatest conqueror in the history of the world.

Ogodei. A wise ruler but a glutton and drunkard.

Mongolia still looks back to the golden age when it shook the world.
This statue, erected in 2008, stands 40 metres tall.

اودرعمد اوكتا بحان حنايج دودطاستان او بشروح كنه بندا اورا بابادران دد کربغزاد کان رونعوزان بشین بنغردیان شمایی وحوم

Batu Khan, Genghis's grandson and founder of the Golden Horde.

Badger Pass. The decisive clash in the invasion of Jin China, after which the Chinese never dared to meet the Mongols in pitched battle.

The Mongol siege of Peking in 1215, rather than Magna Carta, was *the* decisive event of that year.

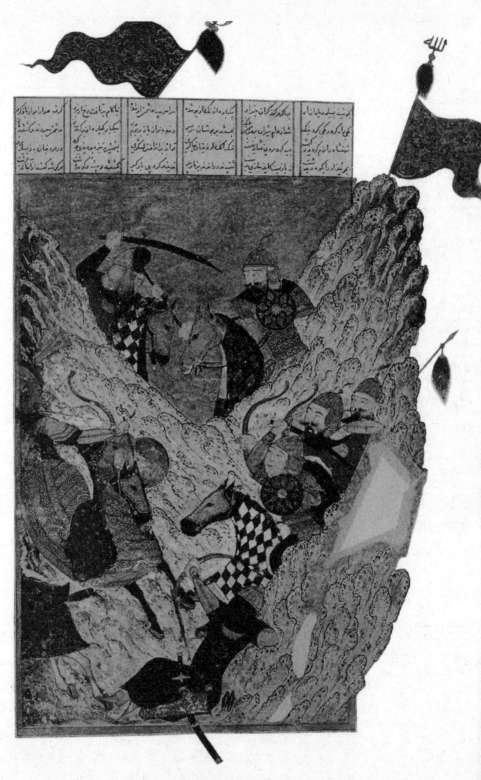

It took Genghis and his sons 23 years of gruelling
warfare to conquer Jin China.

Initially deficient in siegecraft, the Mongols were fast learners.

The fall of the Caliphate in 1258 sent shockwaves through the world.

Michael of Chernikov, one of the petty princelings of medieval Russia,
decisively outclassed by the Mongols.

Divided but arrogant, benighted but confident, Russia stood
no chance against the world conquerors.

Vladimir joined the long list of Russian cities devastated by the Mongols.

Henry II of Poland,
victim of the Mongols' wrath.

Even today Legnica (Liegnitz) is recalled as one of the blackest days in Poland's history.

The battle of Mohi, 1241. One of the most decisive defeats for Christian arms in the entire Middle Ages.

Hopeless as a military commander, King Bela of Hungary proved a resourceful
fugitive from the Mongols, who never caught up with him.

il por auoir barbues et la
tius z aces gadges um t
orét. ij. latis q orét de la
lumware q fu de lille de
cyppre z lautre auoit nó
boniface de molins qui
fu de la cite deuenise. Qint
le soldac certurche ot asse
ble son ost de toutes purs
il uint z se combati auec
les tartres en um leue q
est nomes cosacuch. Grát
fu la bataille z assez i furét
mors z oune partie z lau
tre. Et ala fin les tartres
orét la uictoire z entre
rent en la tarre de turquie
z la conquistrét en lan nře
seignor. m. cc. xl iiij.

Apres ce por ce téps octotá
l emperor des tartres mo
rut z fut fait seignor aprs
luy un sien filz qui ot nó
guiotá cestui guiotan
uesqui por ce temps et
apres luy fu fait emper
or un sien cosin q auoit
nó mágoca qui mlt fu
uaillant z sage z assez a
quist de tres z de seignio
ries. Ala fin si cóme soritz
de grát cuer entra par in
eu roiaume de cathay.
Et cóme il asseignast une
ille la qle il uoloit prendre
par mer la gét de cele tře q
sont mlt engignors ma
ceret homes qui sauoiet
noer z ceaux entrerent

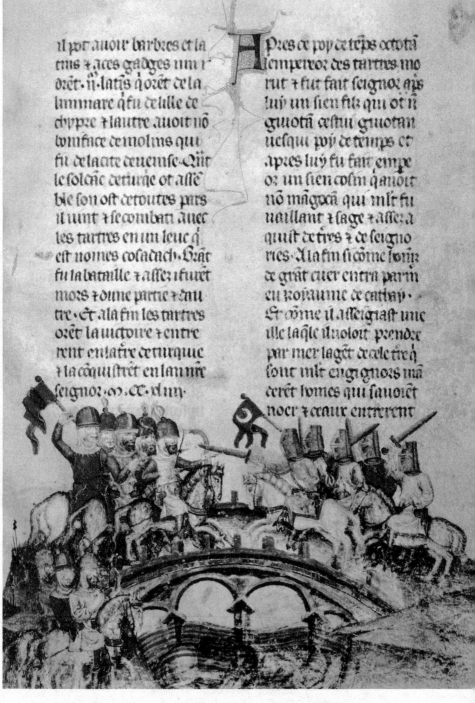

The Mongols finally reached the Danube around Christmas 1241.

plenty of defenders prepared to resist them, and were driven back by a fusillade of huge rocks and boulders. Thus repulsed, the Mongols finally gave up in earnest; the fortress had held out for over a year. However, the victory on points still went to them. Even when they withdrew, the people of Saif-fud concluded that this was merely to gather reinforcements and that they would soon be back. In despair they abandoned Saif-fud; informed of this, the Mongols entered the deserted fortress and reported a great victory to Genghis.[125]

Finally, all worthwhile cities, fortresses and military targets were under the Mongol heel, and the once mighty Khwarezmian empire was at last definitively vanquished. Genghis Khan now ruled an empire that stretched from the Pacific to the Caspian, from Korea to the Caucasus, and from Siberia to the Yellow River. After initially contemplating a campaign in Tibet, he abandoned the idea when his scouts told him the passes into Tibet were impenetrable.[126] In the opinion of many, if not most, his conquest of the shah's empire was his greatest military achievement.

The comparative ease of this accomplishment prompts the question of why Genghis was so much more successful here than against Jin China. Some of the answers are obvious. The Jin had struck deep roots in Chinese society, whereas Muhammad ruled merely an empire in embryonic state, no more than a few years old. By the time of the invasion of Khwarezmia the Mongols had mastered siegecraft and acquired some knowledge of primitive firearms – a skill virtually unknown to them when they crossed the frontier into China in 1211.[127] In the campaigns in Central Asia Genghis could afford to be wasteful of manpower since he had tens of thousands of captives to put in the front line. Moreover, by this time the Mongols had acquired a reputation for savagery, ruthlessness and invincibility they had not had in China.

The shah, on the other hand, started with almost every conceivable disadvantage except brute numbers. His realm was fatally split between prosperous Iranian cities and the Turks who made up the bulk of his army; his army consisted of mercenaries who were bound by no ties of loyalty such as prevailed among the Mongols and indeed were ready to desert to Genghis at the first opportunity.[128] The shah had no proper military structure, was not backed by a clan or feudal system and his own family was split by hatreds, especially that between him and his mother. Since he had picked a fight with the caliph, he could not invoke the nations of Islam in a holy war – indeed caliph al-Nasir considered him a worse menace than the Mongols – and even within the boundaries of his empire, and especially in Transoxiana, he had gravely alienated the Muslim clergy. But most of all the shah was personally eclipsed by Genghis. Where he was an irresponsible fire-eater who went to pieces as soon as things went wrong, Genghis exhibited all his best gifts: he was cool, methodical, prudent, tenacious.[129] Yet it is possible to imagine an alternative scenario where things might have gone much harder for the Mongols. If Jalal al-Din had been given supreme command and could muster the fighting spirit shown by the fortress tribesmen in Khorasan in 1222–23, even the great Mongol military machine might have run out of steam.[130] As it was, the campaign was a glorious testament to Genghis's genius. And now he received a wholly unexpected bonus. His armies had also reached Europe and defeated everything in their path, in one of the greatest exploits in military history.

12

The Great Raid

Once he received news of the death of the shah, Genghis summoned Subedei to Samarkand for a conference. Subedei is said to have ridden 1,200 miles in a week to attend his master's bidding, sometimes lashing himself to the saddle so that he could sleep while the horse jogged on. Genghis needed to hear from a man with a first-hand knowledge of the terrain what the chances were for a military revival in the west of Muhammad's empire. Subedei expressed scepticism. The heat and drought in summer were prohibitive and, in winter, cavalry could not move quickly because of the lack of forage; unlike Mongol ponies, the Iranian horses could not paw their way to the grass beneath the snow.[1] Finding the khan in a good mood at this welcome news, Subedei suggested that he and Jebe be permitted to ride all round the Caspian and penetrate the land of the Cumans, the shah's mysterious allies from the Russian steppe. To his delight, Genghis approved the idea, making the sole proviso that the 20,000 troops he released for the task must be back in Mongolia within three years.[2]

Subedei returned to western Persia in the same hard-riding way he had come. While Subedei was away conferring with Genghis, Jebe had not been idle. The Sunni inhabitants of Rayy, only partially plundered when Jebe and Subedei passed by hot on the trail of the shah, now approached Jebe with a proposal that he attack the Shi'ite holy city of Qom, setting out a mouth-watering menu of the treasures he would find there. Jebe took the bait and sacked Qom, then reflected that the Machiavellian Sunnis of Rayy were unreliable as putative allies. If they could look on calmly while their co-religionists were slaughtered in Qom, what other treachery might they not dream up once the Mongols' backs were turned? Jebe therefore followed his destruction of Qom with a wholesale sack of Rayy.[3]

As soon as Subedei rejoined him, the two Mongol commanders decided that Hamadan, a green, fertile city in the foothills of the Elburz Mountains (known to Alexander the Great's Macedonians as Ecbatana) would be their next target. On the approach of the Mongols Hamadan surrendered, preferring to pay a massive ransom or *Danegeld* rather than suffer the fate of Qom and Rayy.[4] The Mongols targeted the city of Qazvin instead, an important commercial and strategic centre (ninety miles north of modern Teheran) at the crossroads of routes from Turkey, the Caspian and the Persian Gulf, and noted for its carpet manufactures and gigantic silk storage houses. But Qazvin was made of sterner stuff and sent a message of defiance to the invaders. Early February 1221 saw bloody and ferocious fighting, with the Mongols hacking their way into the city block by block and street by street. There could be only one end to such an encounter, and the Mongols visited their usual penalty of pitiless massacre on the defenders who had been rash enough to hold them up and inflict heavy casualties. The entire population of 40,000 Qazvinians perished. The Mongols completed their punishment of northern Persia by sacking the city of Zanjan.[5]

Already the two Mongol commanders were exhibiting both individual brilliance and (notably for Subedei, whose relations with his peers were usually fractious) a unique ability to cooperate and work in harness. They evolved a method of working whereby Jebe's would always be the strike force (or 'forehead') and Subedei's corps the reserve or mirror army.[6] Even more impressively, while half the army dealt with Qom, Rayy, Qazvin and Zanjan, the other half was resting in winter quarters, ready for a proposed expedition against the kingdom of Georgia. Most of northern Persia and the Caspian environs were blanketed with snow and beset by snowdrifts but the Mongols found a spot on the shores of the Caspian near the mouths of the Kura and Aras (Araxes) Rivers where pasturage was good, the winter climate was mild and vegetation began to renew as early as January. Here a good portion of the army practised manoeuvres and rested their horses prior to the attack on Georgia.[7]

The idea was to enter Azerbaijan first, seize its capital Tabriz, and use it as a base for the assault on the neighbouring kingdom of the Georgians. By this time the fame of the Mongols and the stories of their martial deeds had reached the Caucasus, sucking in masses of irregulars, guerrillas and freebooters among the Kurdish and Turcoman tribesmen who sensed that the newcomers were winners and wanted to share in the spoils of victory. The tribesmen descended from the mountains to offer their services. Jebe and Subedei used these levies as their advance guard and moved out into the Mugan plain in mid-February, aiming for Tabriz. Using their usual methods, the Mongols aimed to sap Tabriz's will to fight and to this end had already suborned a warlord pretender to Tabriz, Aqush by name.[8] They were halted in their tracks, however, by the news that Tabriz had suddenly surrendered without a fight. Uzbeg, atabeg (prince) and governor of Tabriz, was a hopeless drunk who lacked the stomach for a fight and panicked when he heard of the Mongol advance. He asked for terms. Jebe and Subedei, itching for action, named an impossibly high figure as ransom but, to their surprise, Uzbeg accepted the sum without demur. The Mongols received a huge influx of warhorses and tons of rich clothing in addition to a money payment.[9]

Uzbeg's decision was really the only realistic one. Now in the eleventh year of his reign (1210–1225), Uzbeg had inherited a state weakened by separatist movements and Georgian incursions. The state of Azerbaijan had once been strong. Founded by the atabeg Ildeniz, the principality had won its freedom from the Seljuk Turks and at one time held sway over the entire South Caucasus area, but after the death of Ildeniz in around 1176 it declined rapidly. Uzbeg, the fifth ruler, was no more than a paper tiger.[10] The problem with his act of 'statesmanship' was that the Mongols now regarded Tabriz as their cash cow, a kind of Bank of the Caspian as it were, so they made repeated demands on the stricken city. For a few days they lingered in its environs, enjoying the idyllic situation amid forest and grasslands (probably unaware that it was notoriously prone to earthquakes)[11] and marvelling at its intricate irrigation system.

Then it was time to march on Georgia, a powerful Christian kingdom, reputedly with the finest cavalry in the world west of the Urals. Subedei and Jebe would have preferred it if their path through the Caucasus had been uncontested; they did not want to fight unnecessary battles around the southern Caspian, but free passage was not granted them. The Georgian monarch was George IV Lasha (reigned 1213–1223), an attractive character who had married a commoner and was drawn to mysticism and Sufism.[12] Jebe and Subedei cleverly kept their shock troops in the rear and sent ahead a vanguard consisting of the Turcoman and Kurdish volunteers, the Azerbaijani levies under the pretender Aqush and an auxiliary corps of mercenaries led by a Mameluke commander. This force entered Georgia by the Kura River, a mighty stream nearly 1,000 miles long which flows from Turkey through Georgia and Azerbaijan to the Caspian. Having begun in terrain known to Alexander the Great and his myrmidons, they were now in territory within the ambit of western Europe, since this region had been described by all the great Roman geographers.[13]

Subedei's plan was to wear the Georgians out through attrition before delivering the *coup de grâce*. First he had the vanguard split up into raiding parties that spread fear and havoc, then he united them for a pitched battle with George, who won the encounter, giving him a false sense of security. George took heavy casualties while slicing through the Kurds and Turcomans and was not prepared for another battle immediately after. He was disconcerted to find a second army – the main Mongol force – confronting him. Subedei's tactics were textbook. His light cavalry swept along the Georgian front, just out of range, unleashing clouds of armour-piercing arrows which took a deadly toll on the flower of Georgian chivalry. Undaunted by the heavy losses George Lasha pushed forward relentlessly and finally seemed to have the Mongols on the run but the effort produced a skewed effect on the Georgians, with their cavalry strewn right across the plain. Then Subedei played his master card. In a wood to the rear of his army, he had stationed a reserve of fresh horses. These the Mongols mounted and launched a devastating counter-attack. Caught between a fresh fusillade of arrows from the Mongol reserve and a head-on charge from the heavy nomad cavalry, the Georgians, their formation now hopelessly tangled up, broke and ran. Subedei's forces quickly cut the Georgians to ribbons. A last Georgian stand on the road to Tiflis simply increased the casualties.[14]

It was a catastrophic defeat for King George, but it was not the Mongols' intention to tarry in Georgia this time. They needed fresh men and horses after this martial effort on the Kura plain. Moreover, Subedei and Jebe were under orders to return to northern Iran in the early spring to ensure that there would be no flank attack from the north when Genghis's armies marched on Nishapur and the cities of western Khwarezmia. By early March they were once more outside

Tabriz, where another huge ransom was levied. The Georgians meanwhile rationalised their disastrous failure by crying foul. The Mongols,
they alleged, had duped them by carrying crosses in front of their
host, leading George to conclude that an army of Christian allies was
marching towards him.[15]

Subedei and Jebe sent scouting parties out to Rayy and Khorasan
to make sure there had been no armed revival in that quarter, and
next highlighted the city of Maragha on the Iran–Azerbaijan border
as their prey. The Arab historian Ibn al-Athir sneered that this was an
easy target because it was ruled by a woman ('No people will prosper
who appoint a woman to rule over them') but the city resisted as
doughtily as any other, inevitably suffering the same fate. Following
their usual pattern the Mongols slaughtered the citizens as punishment
for resistance and perfected the cruel techniques learned in the war
against the shah. Having sacked the city on 31 March 1221, they
pretended to have departed, waiting until the survivors crawled out
of the rubble, then returning suddenly to massacre them also. The
Arab contempt for women seemed particularly inappropriate as this
was the occasion on which a female Mongol warrior killed an entire
family in a single house.[16]

The city of Erbil appeared an appropriate objective for the next
push, but after an initial probe the Mongol leaders concluded that the
mountains were too difficult to negotiate and changed tack towards
Iraq. Their aim was not so much permanent conquest of the caliphate
(that lay more than thirty years in the future) but another huge Tabriz-
style ransom. This was the moment when the Mongols most clearly
impacted on the world of Islam, complicating also the already turbid
bouillabaisse that was the Fifth Crusade. The prince of Erbil tried to
rally the Islamic world against the threat from the steppes but his
co-religionists were already preoccupied with the Crusader threat at
Damietta.[17] The defeat of Georgia added another dimension to the
Crusade as the crusaders had been expecting King George to open a
second front in the north; some historians think this hope accounts
for their curious complacency. The caliph at Baghdad had to take the
Mongol threat seriously and assembled an army at Mosul to guard its
northern front but this soon disintegrated, partly because the Muslims
could not rid themselves of the idea that their main danger was at
Damietta.[18]

Jebe and Subedei switched their attention to Hamadan, which had submitted peacefully first time around and seemed likely to prove another cash cow like Tabriz. Yet this time Hamadan treated the Mongol demand for money with contempt and, to reinforce the point, murdered the prefect or political commissar the Mongols had left in the city. This was the sort of defiance that could not be ignored. In August 1221 a bloody siege began. For three days the Hamadanis put up a defence that astounded the Mongols by its vigour; they sortied on several occasions and inflicted heavy casualties.[19] But the city was short of food and nearly destitute – which was why they had rebuffed the Mongol demand for money in the first place. By the third day Hamadan had done all it could. Alid, the governor of the city, added to the diapason of despair by abandoning the city with his family via an underground tunnel. His desertion was crucial, as the Mongols were by now despairing of taking the city and considering withdrawal. He left a note telling his unfortunate subjects there was nothing more he could do and suggesting they write to the caliph for reinforcements. Amazingly, the Hamadanis took the advice and composed the message. The last nail in their coffin was hammered in when a Mongol herald appeared outside the city gates a few hours later waving the message, which they had intercepted.[20]

Finally, on the fourth day, observing that no sorties had been attempted, the Mongols put two and two together and ordered a massive assault which succeeded in breaking into the city. Ferocious street fighting ensued, but the attackers' blood was up, their anger boiling over because of the heavy casualties they had taken. Inevitably in such circumstances the inhabitants were slaughtered to the last man, woman and child.[21] Elated by their eleventh-hour triumph, Jebe and Subedei used the euphoria to urge their men on to Erbil, which this time was taken easily and again given over to fire and massacre.

Messages from Genghis assured Jebe and Subedei that Khwarezmia was now pacified and there was no longer any need for them to remain around the southern edge of the Caspian. It was autumn, and time for a thorough destruction of the Georgian state and their allies in neighbouring Armenia. First the Mongols made a third demand on the resources of Tabriz but this time the governor's nerve cracked, he left the city secretly and made for the town of Nakhchivan. The Mongols accepted a huge ransom from Tabriz, which must have brought the city near financial collapse as it was the third such requisition. But at least the citizens thereby escaped massacre – a fate visited instead on the luckless inhabitants of Nakhchivan.[22]

Proceeding methodically, the Mongols then sacked Saran, another Islamic settlement on the Georgian marches. Thinking to spare themselves further casualties, they next sent a demand for surrender to the important city of Baylaqan, but the burghers made the foolish mistake of killing the envoy. This was the great mortal sin in Mongol eyes, so an elaborate revenge was planned. Early in November 1221 the Mongols smashed their way through the city's defences; an express order had been issued that no one was to be left alive. The licentious troops took the leaders at their word and indulged in an orgy of rape and murder that shocked even a medieval world hardened to atrocities. Apart from the favourite pastime of gang-rape, the Mongols delighted in slitting open the bellies of pregnant women, extracting the foetuses and slicing them in half.[23] Such was their fury that scarcely a stone was left on a stone.

Terrified by this spectacular manifestation of the wrath of God, the city of Ganja, capital of Arran province, bought the invaders off with a hefty payment. It is worth remembering that all these terrible deeds were performed by an army no greater than 20,000 in number. The Mongols were living off the land, and indeed a larger force would scarcely have survived even if it had been able to solve the problem of mobility in the plethora of narrow passes, deep valleys and bad roads. With astonishing versatility the invaders were able to discard full kit and all unnecessary baggage so as to act as light cavalry, leaving their pioneer corps to bring up the heavy armour in case of a pitched battle.[24]

Now it was time for settling accounts with the Georgians and Armenians prior to the perilous crossing of the Caucasus. The Mongols did not intend a systematic conquest of Georgia – they lacked the numbers for that – but wanted to destroy the kingdom as a credible military threat. They therefore avoided the capital, Tiflis, and spent most of their plundering energies in southern Georgia, Armenia and the Islamic vassal state of Shirvan, making sure they avoided the tricky passes and defiles where the Georgians would have a clear advantage.[25] Their route into Armenia from the south-east was into the western province of Nakhchivan and thence north to the Aghstev region.

There they looted and sacked almost without hindrance, making their base in Utik.[26]

The Armenians responded to the savage newcomers with a mixture of terror, awe and admiration. Wonderment was expressed at the strange religious beliefs – the Mongols believed Genghis Khan, not Jesus Christ, was the Son of God. The invaders could switch from indulgence to discipline almost within hours; they ate and drank prodigiously when there was plenty but could endure hardship when there was not. There seemed to be no rigid social stratification in their ranks, for lords and servants lived and ate together; they disdained prostitutes, preferring rape. Most astonishing to the Armenians was the Mongol loathing of theft; they would visit horrible tortures on any Armenians they found guilty of it.[27] The Mongols were regarded as supermen, and the story of a Mongol warrior trapped by the Georgians lost nothing in the telling. The Georgians surrounded a man and were about to take him prisoner but he dismounted and beat his brains out on a rock rather than be taken.[28] Above all, the Armenians concluded that this plague of human locusts was being visited on them for their sinfulness: 'Worship was blocked, and Mass ceased to be offered at altars; the singing of songs was no longer heard. The whole country was plunged into darkness and the people preferred night to day.'[29]

The Georgians semed to be made of sterner stuff. Subedei decided that the way to tempt the Georgian army to fight on terrain favourable to the Mongols was to stage a massacre in a Georgian city. Credibility would then require that the Georgians appear in force to protect their subjects. It was essentially the stratagem Duke William of Normandy used to tempt King Harold II to battle at Hastings in 1066. The town of Shemakha was chosen as the bait.[30] Here the Mongols employed a novel method, again underlining their inexhaustible versatility. They heaped up the bodies of dead and slaughtered animals to make a pyramidal mound overlooking the town's walls, whence they rained down an incessant deluge of missiles. Shemakha capitulated after a three-day siege.[31] A fearsome massacre did indeed oblige the Georgian ruler to appear in the field. Mustering all resources, King George and his queen assembled a force of 30,000 men. They confronted Subedei who had perhaps 20,000, with the addition of forces from some renegade khans on the Caspian periphery.

This second battle was fought near the location of the first, but on a much more restricted arena, with a range of steep hills running along the eastern edge of the battlefield. Subedei had found a concealed defile along this ridge, and there he stationed Jebe with a reserve of 5,000 men.[32] King George for his part had learned from the earlier defeat and had issued strict orders that his horsemen were to advance slowly in a massed formation and on no account to be tempted to break rank. Subedei appeared to be terrified and the Mongols retreated. As an added refinement, he issued orders that the Mongol archers should appear to be off form that day. They shot their arrows deliberately short of their targets. Foolishly the Georgians pursued the enemy with more and more confidence, finally breaking into a gallop. Sadly for them, it was the veteran stratagem of the feigned retreat that was being employed. Subedei led the enemy into the mouth of the defile, where the waiting Jebe sprang the perfect ambush. The Georgians wheeled round to confront this fresh menace, confident that they had Subedei on the run. At this point Subedei turned round, ordered the charge and struck the Georgians like a mighty wave, rolling them up into Jebe's maw. Caught between the two forces, the Georgians were mewed up as terribly as they had been in the first battle. It was a textbook illustration of the Mongol way of war. According to the chroniclers, most of the Georgian army of 30,000 perished in a single day.[33]

The terrified survivors fled to Tabriz, where they cowered behind the city walls. George escaped from the battlefield, but may have been badly wounded as he died the next year. He was succeeded by his sister, Queen Rusudan. She sent letters of appeal to anyone she could think of, from the crusaders to the Pope. The missive to the pontiff, complete with its ludicrous exaggerations, is justly famous. She wrote: 'A savage people of Tartars, hellish of aspect, as voracious as wolves in their hunger for spoils as they are brave as lions, have invaded my country . . . The brave knighthood of Georgia has hunted them down out of the country, killing 25,000 of the invaders. But, alas, we are no longer in a position to take up the Cross as we had promised your Holiness to do.'[34] She even raised another army, but this proved too terrified to take the field against the Mongols and was soon disbanded.

The Mongols next reached the city of Derbent (in modern Dagestan), still on the shores of the Caspian but at the foot of the

Caucasus, a place often identified with the legendary Gates of Alexander. Derbent was initially defiant but Subedei offered the citizens a deal: he would spare the city so long as ten of its leading oligarchs volunteered to guide the Mongol army over the Caucasus. The ten duly arrived at Subedei's tent, whereupon he had one of them beheaded on the spot, to show that he meant business – *pour encourager les autres*, as Voltaire would say. Suitably cowed, the nine survivors guided the Mongols over the difficult passes with no tricks or treachery. Yet the bland statement that the Mongols crossed the Caucasus conceals a nightmare journey comparable to Hannibal's passage of the Alps. Subedei and Jebe were forced to abandon their siege engines and all heavy baggage and lost hundreds of men to frostbite and hypothermia during a mountain crossing in dead of winter. The route seems to have been through the Derbent pass, between Dagestan and the Caspian and then along the Terek valley.[35]

Then they began to descend into the great steppe that stretches from the Caucasus to the northern shores of the Black Sea, whence it follows the Kuban basin to the Danube estuary. No sooner safe from one ordeal, the Mongols encountered another, for on the plains on the far side of the Caucasus they ran into a formidable array of steppe tribes: Alans, Lezgians, Circassians and, most fearsome of all, the Cumans. The Alans had been a menace to sedentary peoples ever since Roman times, but the Huns had wiped out their western septs in the fifth century, leaving the eastern Alans or Ossetians as the guardians of the Caucasus since the eighth century.[36] The Circassians were ethnically related to the Mamelukes, who had just seized power in Egypt.[37] Most numerous and dangerous were the Cumans, a massive tribal confederacy that dominated the southern steppes of European Russia from about 1060 to the advent of the Mongols. They were closely – almost indistinguishably – confederated with the Qipchaqs, while to the Christian princes of Russia they featured as the dreaded menace and nemesis known as the Polovtsians.[38]

These tribal nomads proved doughtier opponents than the Persians and Georgians had been. Subedei and Jebe were forced to assemble their warriors immediately after the exhausting crossing of the Caucasus when the tribes offered battle and – a source of anxiety for the Mongols – the first encounter was bloody and inconclusive.[39] Where force of arms failed, the Mongols would always turn to subterfuge, and so it proved on this occasion. Subedei sent a deputation to the Cuman camp, complaining, more in sorrow than anger, that he was saddened to see the Cumans fighting their steppe brothers the Mongols – were they not both Turkic peoples, unlike the Alans and Circassians? To reinforce his appeal to ethnic solidarity, Subedei promised that if the Cumans made common cause with them against their erstwhile allies, they should share any booty fifty-fifty.[40] The Cumans took the bait, joined the Mongols, and achieved a devastating rout of the Ossetians and Circassians.

Predictably for anyone who knew the Mongols, they then turned on the Cumans. Having detached the Cumans from the other peoples of the Russian steppe, Subedei and Jebe used their financial clout and talent for espionage to weaken the Cumans still further. Subedei suborned a slave of the Cuman khan, who betrayed his master's secrets and revealed that there was dissension in the Cuman camp; they had already in effect split into two separate armies. Subedei had none of Genghis's scruples; as a result, when he told his master what had happened, the great khan ordered the slave's execution for violating the code of loyalty between a servant and his master.[41] Nonetheless, the intelligence proved valuable; the Mongols routed both Cuman forces with ease. The terrified survivors fled west to the princes of Rus, gabbling in fright about this terrible apparition from the East and warning that Russia must surely be next.[42]

The next development was wholly unexpected. After the rout of the Cumans, the Mongols were approached by a mission from the Venetians, who had been trying to establish themselves on the north coast of the Black Sea against determined opposition from the Genoese. Although the high tide of the famous Genoa–Venice rivalry was in the years 1256–1381, involving four major naval campaigns (in which the Venetians always had the edge), early signs of this deadly duel were apparent on the Black Sea, where Genoa attempted to spike the ambitions of its rival by establishing their own colony at Soldaia in the Crimea.[43]

The envoys of Venice evidently made the Mongols a very attractive commercial offer – the followers of Genghis were becoming increasingly money-minded as the empire expanded – for a treaty was signed granting the Venetians very great privileges in terms of access to Central Asia and the Mongol Empire. The treaty of late 1221 or early

1222 can be seen as the acorn from which would grow the oak of Marco Polo's famous journey later in the century.[44] For their part the Mongols always liked dealing with the Venetians and, although Genoa later made strenuous attempts to detach the descendants of Genghis Khan from their Venetian sympathies, the Mongols remained unimpressed. Venice gave cast-iron promises that it would confine its commercial hegemony to the Black Sea, and not compromise the fruitful relations between Genghis and the Islamic merchants. The Mongols could rely on these because the Venetian settlements on the Black Sea were tightly controlled by the doge and his council in La Serenissima. The Genoese on the Black Sea, on the other hand, acted independently from the mother city so could not be relied on, and their aggressive approach to territorial expansion both irritated and angered the Mongols.[45]

The Venice–Mongol accord would prove a fruitful one. As a 'down payment' Subedei and Jebe raided and destroyed the Genoese colony of Soldaia. Mournfully, the Genoese joined the Cumans in their assessment, reminiscent of Tacitus, of the whirlwind from the East: 'They came, they sapped, they burnt, they slew, they plundered and they departed.'[46]

From the Venetians too the Mongols learned of the parlous political condition of Russia, then a collection of petty principalities, mainly centered in forested regions but highly urbanised by the standards of contemporary Europe, with 13–15 per cent of its population in towns and at least 300 urban centres by the early 1200s.[47] Politically medieval Russia was a world of chaos, forever throwing up vicious autocrats and bloodthirsty despots which, some say, were ever afterwards internalised in the collective memory as the need for rule by a strong man. The land was characterised by 'internecine wars of faint-hearted princes who, oblivious to the glory or good of the fatherland, slaughtered each other and ravaged the people'.[48]

It was not ever thus. In the late ninth century Vikings from Sweden founded a colony in the Ukraine which became the great city of Kiev. The titanic figure in early Russian history was Yaroslav the Wise (978–1054), grand prince of Kiev from 1019 (and father-in-law of Harald Hardrada), a man powerful enough to threaten and attack Byzantium, as he did in the 1040s. But Kiev was always fragile, as not only did Yaroslav prove an impossible act to follow, but there were other, structural factors, at play also. The Crusades shifted European trade routes away from Kiev, which had formerly stood at the crossroads of commerce from Byzantium, the Islamic East and Western Europe.[49] From the beginning of the twelfth century Russia subdivided into breakaway principalities that grew ever stronger as the century progressed. At the same time the volume of Polovtsian raids increased in intensity. Kiev was sacked on several occasions, and the loss of manpower from all these disasters saw its population plummeting from an estimated 100,000 in the time of Yaroslav to no more than half that by the year 1200.[50] Unquestionably, in the hundred years before the appearance of Jebe and Subedei Kiev had been losing out to the principalities of Vladimir and Suzdalia in the north-east and Galicia and Volynia in the west. Nevertheless, the political and commercial decline of Kiev was only relative. In spite of the many Polovtsian raids the city was still wealthy, still a major trading and religious centre, still with the reputation of the mother of all the Russias and hailed as the fount and origin by all the major states in what is now Russia, Ukraine and Belarus.[51]

In the second half of the twelfth century the south of this region became the scene of a three-cornered struggle for power between Smolensk, Chernigov and Volynia – all three of which were by that time larger in area than Kiev, albeit not so populous (Chernigov boasted 30,000 inhabitants). What prevented any of these three from inheriting Kiev's mantle as the major Russian city was the endemic fighting among themselves; a good example was the ferocious Chernigov–Smolensk conflict of 1196. When these southern and central states did put aside their mutual enmities, they posed a clear threat to Kiev, as proven by the occupation of the 'mother of Russia' by the armies of Galicia and Volynia in 1200, which in turn was dwarfed by the sack of Kiev three years later by the Polovtsians, acting in concert with Chernigov and Smolensk.[52]

Yet the clearest beneficiaries of the decline of Kiev lay in the far north (Novgorod) and the north-east (Suzdalia). Located north-east of Kiev, between the Rivers Volga and Oka, Suzdalia asserted its independence from Kiev as early as 1125 and demonstrated that it had the upper hand over its founder by a nasty sack of Kiev in 1169.[53] Suzdalia was blessed with many advantages. It profited from a number of rivers flowing east and west, with the main ones linking easily with the

Volga. The Oka River and its tributaries provided waterways to Smolensk in the south-west, Novgorod in the north-west and to the Baltic and the Black Sea. It was geographically well placed to interdict the trade of its great northern rival, Novgorod, and consequently controlled the trade of the entire Volga basin before the coming of the Mongols, at first in alliance with the Volga Bulgars, then, as Suzdalia's military might increased, with the Bulgars as very much the junior partner.[54] Agriculturally, it enjoyed fertile soil and farmlands, especially around the cities of Suzdal and Vladimir. Politically, it bene-fited from the happy accident that just three strong rulers reigned there for almost one hundred years (Yuri, Andrei and Vsevolod, 1120s–1212) – in contrast to Kiev which suffered from almost continual strife over the dynastic succession. By the beginning of the thirteenth century Suzdalia was the strong man of Russia. The only conceivable challenge, from Roman, prince of Volynia (1170–1205) was ably blunted by Vsevolod.[55]

Yet at the very moment of its greatest political power Suzdalia imploded and fell victim to the horrors of civil war. When Vsevolod died in 1212 his realm was torn apart by civil war as his sons fought over the succession. Konstantin, the eldest son, claimed the throne but was challenged by his younger brother Yuri. The battle they fought in 1216 was the biggest and bloodiest seen in Russia until that date. At first Konstantin had the edge in the fratricidal conflict, making clever use of the political and economic power of the merchant classes. But when Yuri lost the battle, he took a cruel revenge. He rounded up every last merchant he could find, even sending raiding parties to Novgorod and Smolensk to swell the number of captives, then impris-oned 150 of them in a cellar in his own version of the later Black Hole of Calcutta. All the luckless traders died there of suffocation or asphyx-iation. Konstantin opportunely died in 1218, so Yuri succeeded to a state considerably weakened militarily and financially. He tried to restore his fortunes by four years of peace, fighting 'only' with the Volga Bulgars, but by 1222 the Mongols were upon him.[56]

If Suzdalia had come down a notch from its glory days, its great northern rival Novgorod had ascended correspondingly. Famous as a cultural and literary centre, for its icons and its state-of-the-art sewage system, Novgorod was the second city of Russia after Kiev in terms of population (around 35,000) and second in political importance only to Suzdal.[57] Extremely wealthy from its commerce, handicrafts and tribute collection, it governed vast northern provinces stretching into the Arctic Circle and as far east as the Urals, and was connected by rivers, lakes and portages to the Baltic, the Volga and the Dnieper. But its disadvantages were threefold: its agricultural land was poor and infertile, it had too many enemies on its western frontier (principally Swedes and Germans), and it suffered continual interference in the election of its rulers from the princes of Suzdalia, Smolensk and Chernigov.[58] The ruling elite was forever ejecting princes and electing new ones – there was a new one every year from 1154 to 1159 – and a major succession crisis in 1167–1169 when Suzdalia strongarmed her northern rival.[59]

The poor and dispossessed of the Russian principalities, regarded as no more than arrow fodder in wartime and slave labour in peacetime, were too weak for the history of the nation at this era to be characterised in terms of class warfare. What there was in abundance, apart from dynastic conflict within the princely families, was a four-way struggle between the rulers, the nobility (boyars), merchants and the Church and, within these categories, between conservatives and reformists and revisionists.[60] In the more advanced cities merchants would tend to make common cause with artisans and craftsmen against the Church and the boyars, with the princes as uneasy referees. Indeed in many instances the furious dynastic struggles were disguised versions of the conflict between liberals and traditionalists.[61] In some localities, such as Novgorod, the common people were relatively powerful vis-à-vis their rulers, partly because of alliances with external interests.

All this strife weakened the military potential of the Russian states. The princes usually had about one hundred personal retainers (like the old Anglo-Saxon housecarls), and thereafter had to recruit from among ordinary citizens, from mercenaries or, reluctantly, the Polovtsians. The major cities could usually scrape together a force of 2–3,000 men, usually of poor quality – a major decline since the days when Yaroslav the Wise attacked Byzantium with a crack force of 10,000 first-class troops.[62] Yet all the military activity in the Rus states – whether against the Polovtsians or as part of the civil wars that plagued the land for eighty of the 170 years between the death of Yaroslav the Wise and the final Mongol invasion of 1237 – was of the kind described by the historians of Ancient Greece as 'stasis', a kind of meaningless strife which engendered no advances in military technology and simply mired Russia deeper in a realm of chaos.[63]

What interested Jebe and Subedei much more than this recital of native Russian strength – which did not seem to make them out to be formidable foes – was the information they could glean about the Polovtsians or Cumans, their old enemies, whom Subedei had long identified as the principal threat to Mongol expansion on the steppe.[64] The Polovtsians/Cumans controlled a huge swathe of territory from Central Asia into eastern Europe, from Lakes Balkhash and Zaysan through modern Kazakhstan, the Aral Sea, the northern Caspian, northern Caucasus, Ukraine and Russia, including the whole north coast of the Black Sea. The Cumans, whose homeland was south-west Siberia, were originally a distinct tribe from the Qipchaqs but gradually merged and intermarried. It was their most westerly sept operating in Russia that was invariably called the Polovtsians; all the names for this vast tribe in German, Russian and Turkic languages approximate to 'blond' or 'yellow'.[65]

They first appeared as a major factor in international politics in the middle of the eleventh century and influenced the history and affairs of Khwarezmia, Georgia, Ukraine, southern Rus, Bulgaria, Hungary, Moldavia, Wallachia and even Byzantium. In the 1030s they dominated the Volga–Urals area while the Pechenegs held sway from the Volga west to the lower Danube, including Ukraine, Moldavia and Wallachia. They were used by Byzantium to crush the Pecheneg hegemony in the Balkans and were instrumental in establishing the Bulgarian empire in 1185–86.[66] They even played a significant role in the Fourth Crusade. Sometimes they were used by sedentary societies as mercenaries, as when the king of Hungary recruited them to help his ally the king of Swabia in his bid for the German crown.[67] They maintained informal alliances with other nomadic tribes, such as the Qanglis, who lived north of the Caspian and were a tribal confederacy related to the Cumans. One estimate of the total population of the Cumans is 600,000. If we assume one-eighth as a rough and ready guide to the number of fighting men available, this would make a putative Cuman army of 75,000 men, easily powerful enough to sweep away all the principalities of Kievan Rus. Yet the Cumans never did unite to form an empire and were forever riven by factionalism and ruled by a wide variety of independent khans – exactly what allowed the Mongols to defeat them so easily and supplant them on the steppes.[68]

For two centuries the Polovtsians were a reliable menace to the southern Rus states (Suzdalia and Novgorod, further north, were largely immune), partly because medieval Russia was always more oriented towards Byzantium and Baghdad than to the Catholic world of western Europe. For about 150 years the pressure was unrelenting, and from 1068 to 1210 there were at least fifty major raids on Russian territory, with the rate of incursion increasing after 1125. They blocked both land and riverine trade routes to Byzantium, sacked cities (including Chernigov), burned down granaries, destroyed crops, killed peasants and carried off women and children into slavery.[69] They were notably cruel. To prevent prisoners from escaping, they would often cripple all males by slitting their heels and placing chopped horsehair on the wounds so that they kept chafing.[70] The plight of the conquered was fearful, as described in one account:

> The Polovtsians, after seizing the town, burned it. They divided up the people and led them to their dwelling places, to their own relations and kin. Many Christians suffered: miserable, tormented, numb from cold, from hunger, from thirst, their cheeks sunken, their bodies blackened; in an unknown land, their tongues swollen, naked and barefooted, their legs torn by thorns that spoke to each other in tears, saying 'I was from such a town' and 'I was from such a village,' and so they spoke of their homelands with tears and sighs.[71]

The ferocious treatment meted out to their captives was of a piece with the Polovtsians' general cruelty, even to their own kind who fell by the wayside. The Franciscan William of Rubruck later related that, while fleeing from the Mongols after their disastrous defeat, the Cumans/Polovtsians would cannibalise their own men who were dying or dead.[72]

Occasionally, the Rus felt pushed too far and unable to take any more depredations from the nomads, at which point they would shelve their differences and unite for a great campaign against the Polovtsians. Such a moment came in 1113 when the Kievan prince Vladimir II Monomakh led a coalition army against them and inflicted a grievous defeat.[73] Coalitions like this usually suffered from the non-participation of the most powerful military state, Suzdalia, whose efforts against raiders were invariably directed east against the Volga Bulgars – such as the major offensive of 1183-84 – rather than south against the Polovtsians.[74]

So important were the Polovtsians in this era of Russian history that they were involved in the most celebrated event in the country's annals before the coming of the Mongols. The 1180s were a decade of general crisis. While Vsevolod of Suzdalia chastised the Bulgars, Prince Igor of Chernigov was inspired to win his own share of martial glory against the Polovtsians.[75] He joined forces with his brother Vsevolod, prince of Trubchevsk and Kursk, to seek out a major concentration of the Cuman enemy along the Donets River. An eclipse of the sun on 1 May 1185 seemed to the superstitious a bad omen, but Igor scouted this as priestly nonsense and pressed on.[76] He found and engaged the Polovtsians on 10 May. A grim three-day battle ensued, where at first Igor had the advantage, but it soon transpired he had not committed sufficiently numerous forces for the task. Victorious on the first day, he saw to his alarm on the 11th that the enemy host had been massively reinforced.[77] Igor's council of boyars advised an immediate retreat but he allowed himself to be swayed by his 19-year old nephew Sviatoslav, who objected that his men were tired and would be cut to pieces if they withdrew at this juncture. Vsevolod then weighed in on Sviatoslav's side, and the foolish Igor allowed himself to be overruled. Next day a terrible battle continued long after dusk, but finally Igor's Turkic mercenaries, on whom he had relied heavily, panicked and fled. The Polovtsians emerged completely victorious, and netted Igor, his son Vladimir and brother Vsevolod as prisoners.[78]

Buoyed by their success, the Polovtsians at once planned a surprise raid on southern Rus. Igor meanwhile was urged by his comrades to escape captivity but declined, saying such conduct was not honourable. Soon two of his advisers who had remained at large crept into the camp with word that the Polovtsian raid had been heavily defeated and that, in retaliation, the Polovtsians intended to kill all prisoners. A Polovtsian guard was bribed to assist Igor to escape. He provided two swift horses, only just in time, for the returning Polovtsians saw the bird in the act of flying and gave chase. Igor threw off his pursuers, crossed the Donets River, rested in the town of Donetsk, then went on to Kiev, where he was received with joy.[79] This adventure provided the subject matter for medieval Russia's most famous epic poem, *The Lay of Igor* and its later musical immortalisation by Borodin.

However, the struggle between the Rus princes and the Cumans/ Polovtsians could never be brought to a proper conclusion by either side. The Russians lacked the sheer numbers needed to deal decisively with the Cumans, and the latter realised that the Russian cities and forests could be garrisoned only if they abandoned the very nomadic way of life that gave them the military edge over the sedentary societies.[80] Gradually the stand-off was resolved as the Polovtsians began trading for the goods they so coveted – furs, wax, honey, slaves – instead of seizing them in raiding expeditions. More significantly they began to intermarry with the Rus and even live among them. Polovtsian khans and their children became kin with Christian princes and princesses.[81] This factor was all-important in 1222. The most important of all Cuman khans, Koten, had been in the army that was defeated and devastated by Jebe and Subedei. Because of such intermarrying, though, Koten was also the father-in-law of Prince Mstislav the Bold of Galicia. At that time Koten had appealed to Mstislav, adding prophetically: 'It will be your turn tomorrow.'[82] But the Galician council of state had been initially reluctant to get involved. Many of them, mindful of the incubus that the Polovtsians had been for 150 years, were secretly pleased at the turn of events. Others were angry that Koten seemed to have involved them in a quarrel that was not theirs. Still others called for greater clarification, since they did not know anything about the Mongols or their intentions. The *Chronicle of Novgorod* summed up their uncertainty well: 'The same year [1222], for our sins, tribes came, whom no one exactly knows who they are nor whence they came, nor what their language is, nor of what race they are, nor what their faith is, but they call them Tartars.'[83] The anti-Koten faction on the council was right. Jebe and Subedei would probably have swung back eastwards soon after their defeat of the Cumans had Koten not appealed to Mstislav and had he not, in the end, acceded.

After destroying the Genoese port of Soldaia the Mongols once again split up, this time to probe the Russians' intentions. Jebe began moving west towards the Don while Subedei methodically sacked all towns along the coast of the Sea of Azov, making sure that a unified

Mongol army could not be taken in the rear. He also convinced the chief of the Brodnik tribe to enlist with him and thus acquired another 5,000 troops. The deciding factor for both the Russians and the Mongols turned out to be Koten. The Polovtsian chief's powerful rhetoric – 'Today the Tartars have taken our land, tomorrow they will take yours' – had already begun to convince some waverers, who had intitially been glad Koten had been taught a lesson, that they needed to unite against the invaders. The turning point was a council of war convened at Kiev by Mstislav of Galicia, where eighteen Rus princes formed an anti-Mongol coalition. The leading lights were 'the three Mstislavs' – Mstislav Mstislavich of Galicia, Mstislav Romanovich of Kiev and Mstislav Sviatoslavich of Chernigov. They convinced the others not to wait for the Mongol onslaught but to march east and intercept them at once.[84]

The army eventually assembled by this coalition was a powerful one, at least 30,000 strong, and the vanguard made an impressive showing as it moved east to Zarub on the west bank of the Dnieper. The river Dnieper, the fourth largest in Europe at over 1,400 miles long, was a major obstacle to invaders at this point, as it was in the final stages of its journey through Belarus and Ukraine to the Black Sea. Here the Russians were met by ten Mongol envoys who brought a message from Subedei, demanding to know why the Russians were advancing on him, since he had not attacked them. After pointing out that anyone fighting the Polovtsians should logically be embraced as a friend after all the depredations the Rus princes had suffered from these raiders, Subedei wound up his protocol by demanding the surrender of Koten and his fellow refugees.

Many societies in the thirteenth century believed in shooting the messenger; the three Mstislavs accordingly put the envoys to death.[85] Like so many before them they thus unwittingly ensured war to the knife. Blithely confident, the three Mstislavs waited for reinforcements to arrive from Smolensk, Galicia and Chernigov, bringing the army up to its full strength, before advancing to the easternmost bend of the Dnieper at Protolochi. The host led by the Mstislavs now also included contingents from Kiev, Kursk, Halych and Volynia, plus the Polovtsians under Koten. Apart from the trio of leaders, other notables present included Vladimir Rurikovich of Smolensk, Daniel Romanovich of Volynia, Mstislav Yaroslavich of Lutsk, Oleg of Kursk and Mstislav of Kiev's son Vsevolod; in other words, all the southern and western principalities took part.

Yet there were already problems. The three Mstislavs, all men of overweening pride, could not agree among themselves on the assignment of commands and precedences, and a virtual three-way feud resulted. More seriously, although the prince of Suzdalia had agreed to take part in the campaign, there was as yet no sign of his levies.[86]

Jebe and Subedei had meanwhile united their forces, crossed the Dnieper, and concentrated at the Dniester River, another large stream that runs through the modern Ukraine and Moldova before emptying into the Black Sea. The Mongols devastated settlements on both sides of the river (the west bank is high and hilly, the east low and flat), seemingly content to take their time and in no hurry to engage the enemy. According to some accounts, they were still hoping that the promised third army under Jochi would join them, but at some stage a message arrived making it clear they should look for nothing from Genghis's eldest son. The dauntless Subedei sent another embassy to the Russians, this time just two men, who delivered the following message at Protolochi: 'You have hearkened to the Polovtsians and have killed our envoys and are marching against us. March on, then. But we have not attacked you. May God be judge of all men.'[87] The Rus princes were so astonished at this display of Mongol aplomb that this time they let the envoys live.

Finally the two armies came in sight of each other across the Dnieper. It was part of Subedei's master plan that the Russians should think the Mongols were afraid. He had primed the envoys to 'let slip' that Subedei and Jebe were seriously cast down by Jochi's non-appearance and to pretend to ask for terms in a fawning manner. Mstislav the Bold answered that only a humiliating admission of Russian superiority followed by headlong flight would suffice. Subedei played along with the pretence that he was terrified and let the Rus princes see that he was retreating, leaving behind a force on the river bank to buy him time.[88]

The reality was that Subedei was sacrificing 1,000 of his men as a de facto suicide squad. Leaving this cohort behind under a notable captain named Hamabek, the Mongols commenced a slow, ostentatious retreat. The Mstislavs needed no second bidding. An amphibious assault was prepared across the Dnieper. The Russians took terrible casualties as Hamabek and his men fought like lions in a kind of replay of Thermopylae. Eventually, inevitably, they were overwhelmed and Hamabek led out to execution.[89] Subedei and Jebe meanwhile retreated slowly over the terrain north of the Sea of Azov they now knew so well, using Fabian tactics, refusing to make a stand but forever tempting the Russians with the promise of an overwhelming victory.

The original Russian strategy had been admirable and highly competent. The idea was that as the main army advanced down the Dnieper under Mstislav the Bold, the princes of Kiev and Chernigov would patrol farther along the western bank to make sure the Mongols could not simply cross back across the Dnieper lower down at a ford or on a pontoon bridge. Meanwhile a flotilla of boats would float down the Dniester to block the Mongols' escape that way, and the Polovtsians under Koten would attempt to loop round behind the Mongols and cut off their retreat to the east.[90] These well-laid plans were abandoned in the euphoria of the victory over Hamabek. With Mstislav of Kiev now on the opposite bank, Mstislav the Bold saw a chance to win a unique, unilateral victory over the invaders, covering himself with glory, cutting out the rival princes and establishing himself in the glorious pantheon of great Russian heroes. He cancelled the encirclement order to the Polovtsians and ordered Koten and his levies to join him on a forced march to catch up with the Mongols. The prince of Galicia thus played into Subedei's hands, for he split his forces and managed to string them out over the steppe.[91] The Mongols held their course along the north of the Sea of Azov, which they had already discovered was a virtual reservoir but was only 46 feet deep at its greatest depth, as it was forever disgorging its waters into the Black Sea.

For nine days Subedei managed to sustain the gap between his forces and their pursuers. Finally, near Mariupol, on the west bank of the Kalka River, a tributary of the River Kalmius, one of the many that discharge into the Sea of Azov, he turned to face Mstislav. The date was 31 May 1222. Seeing the Mongols drawn up in battle formation, the reckless Mstislav gave no thought to waiting for the rest of the army to come up, but ordered his Galicians and the Polovtsians into an immediate charge; this took place slightly before the contingents from Kursk and Volynia arrived on the field. Subedei had all his favourite officers in his line-up, including his veteran comrade Bujir, originally a chiliarch in Genghis's left wing of 1206.[92]

The battle began in the traditional Mongol fashion, with showers of arrows being loosed on the advancing Russians. As a further refinement Subedei released black smoke from carefully prepared firepots, which drifted across the battlefield, increasing the chaos. This fusillade created a gap between the Galicians and the Polovtsians, but Koten continued his cavalcade. The Mongols easily repelled the Polovtsian charge, at which point Koten's men panicked.[93] They fled back to the Russian ranks, where the newly arriving contingents from Kursk and Volynia quickly parted to let them through. Hard on their heels came the Mongol heavy cavalry, who charged through the gap, detaching the men of Kursk and Volynia and attacking them with great ferocity. Meanwhile the Polovtsians added to their baneful contribution to the battle by colliding with the cohorts from Chernigov, who seem to have blundered into the Kalka valley unaware that a battle had already begun.[94] Reeling from the impact of the Polovtsians, the Chernigovians had no time to recover before the Mongols were upon them.

At this point Subedei's choice of battleground showed his quality as a general. On the marshy ground the Russians found it impossible to regroup or manoeuvre. Soon the whole of the coalition army was surrounded, and the Mongols could take their time over the slaughter. Following their usual pattern, they alternated showers of arrows with charges from the heavy cavalry. The mayhem was terrific. Mstislav the Bold and his bodyguard managed to cut their way out of the maelstrom, but there was no escape for Mstislav of Chernigov, who was killed in the fighting along with his son. Probably 20,000 Russians were engaged that day, of which at most only 2,000 survived.[95]

Vainly trying to make up ground on his namesake, Mstislav of Kiev reached the far side of the Kalka River to watch helplessly as the battle entered its final, bloody stages. But now he had his own safety to think of, for the Galician's prince's folly had left his ally dangerously exposed. Quickly he tried to retreat and managed to reach the Dnieper before being overhauled by the Mongols. On a hill by the side of the river he and his 10,000 troops made a stand in a stockade camp, ringed by a wagon laager. The Mongols surrounded the camp and guarded all approaches so that the prince of Kiev could not be reinforced. There followed a three-day blockade, with Subedei waiting for hunger and thirst to do their work.

The defenders ran out of drinking water on the third day and asked for terms. A man named Polskinia, a quisling *voivode* (nobleman) was chosen as the go-between. The Mongols promised to allow the Kievans to march out, disarmed, and return to Kiev under articles of war; Polskinia kissed a crucifix to make the deal binding.[96] Once the Russians were disarmed and helpless, the Mongols cynically slaughtered them, explaining that this was punishment for the killing of their envoys. Since the prince of Kiev was a royal personage, and the Mongols never shed blood in such cases, a novel end was prepared for him. He was placed under a 'wooden bridge' – stretched out under boards above which hundreds of Mongols caroused in a victory feast – and suffocated.[97] For the Mongols this was an honourable death, but to the Russians it was the ultimate humiliation.

The fate of Mstislav of Kiev and his followers was just one of many calamities to rain down on the Russians in the aftermath of Kalka. The army of Chernigov had been virtually wiped out, so the prince of Smolensk and his one thousand men seemed to have fared better. Koten escaped but his brother Yuri and son Daniel were slain on the field.

Yet the refugees of Kalka had not tasted the last dregs from the cup of bitterness. On the retreat the disgruntled and soured Polovtsians attacked the Russian refugees and killed a number of them.[98] Some of the Rus loaded their goods on ships on the Black Sea coast and tried to escape to the Islamic world; one of the ships foundered and sank in a storm with the loss of all on board.[99] The riverine refugees had a better experience. The men of Galicia and Volynia got back to the Dnieper, where their fleet of boats was still intact. They crowded into the best boats, then smashed and stove in the others so that the Mongols could not follow before launching out onto the Dnieper and safety.[100]

Much of this panic was unnecessary. The Mongols had achieved their purpose and were not inclined to follow, especially as Genghis had set them a strict three-year timetable. They sacked a number of towns along the Dnieper, sometimes allegedly using the old trick of displaying Christian crosses to trick the burghers into leaving their defences.[101] Then they turned eastward for home. The Russians were overjoyed to see them go. The general feeling in Rus was that this visitation by steppe demons was God's punishment for terrible sin. As the Novgorod Chronicle put it, 'For our sins, God put misunderstanding into us, and a countless number of the people perished, and there was lamentation and weeping and grief throughout towns and villages . . . And the Tartars turned back from the River Dnieper, and we know not whence they came, nor where they hid themselves. God knows whence he fetched them against us for our sins.'[102] The trauma for Rus can hardly be exaggerated. In a few months at least 60,000 Russians had perished (about 1 per cent of the total population) including nine of the eighteen princes (three in battle and six on the retreat). Only Mstislav the Bold, who died in 1228, and Daniel of Volynia, wounded, are explicitly mentioned in the sources as survivors. The real winner in the Kalka campaign was the prince of Suzdalia who, either through tardiness, incompetence or Machiavellianism (almost certainly the latter) got no farther than Chernigov in his march to join his supposed allies.[103]

Jebe and Subedei set a course eastwards and crossed the Volga near present-day Volgograd (more famous in history under its former name, Stalingrad). The forested lands died out and treeless steppes began. The Mongols then struck north-east towards Samara and the territory of the Volga Bulgars. Once clear of the Rus principalities, the raiders found there were few towns or settlements of any kind except for a few straggling villages on the banks of rivers. Here cultivated land was scarce and oasis-like. Only skylarks, turtle doves, swarms of insects and a huge variety of wildflowers disturbed the barren monotony.[104] Jebe and Subedei followed the course of the Volga north-east into Bulgar territory.

The Volga Bulgars (who were Muslims as contrasted with the shamanistic Cumans) at one time commanded the entire trade of the Volga and thus much of the overland commerce between Europe and Asia, but had been in relative decline since the start of the Crusades and had gradually been pushed eastwards by pressure from the Rus principalities. Though on the wane, the Bulgars were still dangerous. At the Samara bend, where the Volga makes a sharp turn east followed by an immediate U-turn to the west, they proved it by ambushing the Mongol vanguard and badly mauling it.[105] Subedei and Jebe then came up with the main force and chastised the Bulgars in a battle further north at the Kama River (the Kama, at over 1,100 miles in length is the largest tributary joining the Volga from the east). The Bulgar commander at Samara Bend was Ilgam Khan, but if the Bulgars did finally lose in their clash with the Mongols, they won a final propaganda victory by 'talking up' their victory over the vanguard and

suppressing the later defeat on the Kama. Even expert modern historians have been seduced by the legend of a major Mongol defeat which,
if it had really happened, would have made Ilgam one of the great
unsung military geniuses of the ages. The truth was that Samara Bend
was not even a setback as serious as the annihilation of Hamabek on
the Dnieper.[106]

Pressing on towards the Urals, the Mongols again defeated the
Qipchaqs or eastern Cumans and followed with another triumph in
a battle with the Qanglis. Both peoples were obliged to pay tribute
and pledge fealty. From the land of the Bulgars Jebe and Subedei
headed south-east to the Ural River, then passed north of the Caspian
and the Aral Sea, finally rejoining Genghis in the steppes east of the
Syr Darya.[107]

It was a delighted Genghis who received the reports from his two
star commanders, especially as they brought back 10,000 horses as a
gift to their master. Genghis singled out Jebe for excessive praise,
unfairly attributing the bulk of the success to him. The great khan
also lauded Subedei but not at the same level. For some obscure reason
he always seemed to underrate him – an oddity in a person usually
so shrewd about the worth and capability of the men who served
him. One is almost tempted to think he might have been jealous of
Subedei's brilliance. Subedei did, however, have his main request
granted. Out of the defeated Polovtsians, Bulgars, Qanglis and others
some had elected for service with the Mongols. Subedei proposed
using these and supplementing the most trustworthy Naiman, Merkit
and others to form an entirely new unit for permanent service on the
steppe as far west as the Volga. Genghis granted the boon without
demur, and some scholars see the new force as the pilot version of
what would later be the *tamma* or nomadic garrison force overseeing
conquered territories.[108] Subedei's steppe army was charged with
gradual but permanent conquest of the eastern steppe, with particular
emphasis on the Volga Bulgars.

Genghis had in mind to load Jebe with new honours, but before
he could do so Jebe was dead, stricken with an unidentified fever.
Some foolishly asserted that he died of wounds sustained at the Bulgar
ambush at Samara Bend but, in the first place, it is most unlikely that
Jebe was with the vanguard that day and, secondly, he would scarcely
have lingered so long if he had received a mortal wound. The place

of Jebe's death is confidently asserted to be the Tarbaghatai, west of the Altai Mountains, on the border between modern Kazakhstan and Mongolia – at least five hundred miles east of Samara.[109] His demise was a great loss for Genghis, who lamented his passing. Subedei may have been the master strategist but there is no reason to dissent from the view that Jebe was 'probably the greatest cavalry general in the history of the world'.[110] Eight hundred years later the scale of his achievement with Subedei on their great raid is still astonishing. In three years the two captains and their men rode 5,500 miles – history's longest cavalry raid – won seven major battles (always against superior numbers) and several minor engagements and skirmishes, sacked scores of cities and revealed the world of Russia and eastern Europe to Genghis. Subedei made sure that this would be no evanescent achievement by leaving behind him a whole cadre of spies and secret agents who would keep the Mongols informed of all future developments in the West.

To be sure, the feat had been costly. Jebe and Subedei left 10,000 Mongol dead behind them, and the scale of destruction they wreaked was considered egregious even by Mongol standards.[111] The speed, mobility and military prowess of the nomads created a legend of the Mongols as numerous, ubiquitous and invincible. As the Arab historian Ibn al-Athir noted, what Jebe and Subedei achieved in the years 1220–23 was so incredible that the future generations of Islam would be sure to refuse to credit it as sober historical fact.[112] The two great generals may not have been the wolves of God, but for the Mongols they were the hounds that harrowed Hell for their very own Son of God, Genghis Khan.

13

The Twilight Years

The history of Genghis Khan and the Mongols can sometimes seem no more than an endless recital of massacres with pyramids of skulls. Yet Genghis and the Mongols were more than that. Even before Genghis there existed among the Mongols a 'steppe intelligentsia' of men interested in long-distance trade, the modalities of the sedentary world, literacy and even abstract thought.[1] One sign of this was the care with which the Mongols preserved the caravanserais or oases, intended to provide shelter for caravans that had been travelling for days and useful for billeting troops on the march. There were two main types. In one a central courtyard had a covered area for the quartering of pack animals with separate living quarters for travellers, plus refectories and areas set aside for religious devotions. In the other model the caravanserai was more clearly divided into two, with one courtyard in front with general living quarters and a separate courtyard at the back around which were set more elaborate bedrooms.[2] So far from wrecking or pillaging these caravanserais, the Mongols took particular care of them and ensured they were up to date in all respects.

So much for practicalities. At the level of abstract thought there was a surprising mutual sympathy between the Sufis of Iran and the Mongols. The Sufis, roughly speaking the practitioners of the mystical side of Islam, accepted to an amazing extent Genghis's claim that he had been divinely appointed to rule the world. They thought that God guided the Mongols and provided them with a dazzling array of military talents and gifted collaborators; some Sufis even claimed that Genghis had the divine protection accorded a dervish.[3] In particular, they asserted that he was wholly in the right in his conflict with Muhammad and the empire of Khwarezmia. The spirits were said to have been so angry at the luxury and decadence of the shah and his people that they cried out to the Mongols: 'O infidels, kill the evil-doers.' For them the sole cause of the calamity that overtook Iran and Islam was that Muhammad had lusted after Genghis's riches and had stolen them at Otrar, and the devastation of the Khwarezmian empire was essentially divine punishment for wickedness.[4]

It was true that some leading Sufis such as Najm al-Din Kubra and his disciple Majd al-Din did not go over to the Mongols. Najm was offered safe passage out of Khiva when the Mongols besieged it but he preferred to stay and go down fighting with his compatriots; the story goes that he was struck down in the main square when the enemy burst in, in the very act of throwing stones at them.[5] Majd al-Din got away to Anatolia, but the orthodox Sufi position was that he had been punished with exile for boasting about his spiritual powers.[6] For his part, Genghis was always fascinated by holy men and their alleged powers, and this fascination led him to one of the oddest encounters of his career.

As a result of his partial conquest of China Genghis became aware of a new religious cult which had sprung up there and which attracted him for two reasons: it held out the promise of a 'universal' religion in which his subjects might stop doctrinal bickering and learn to live together harmoniously; and, much more significantly for him, it seemed to be concerned with longevity and even, conceivably, immortality. The Mongols were always bedazzled by this notion, and were interested in the Pope at Rome purely because he was rumoured to be 250 years old. The story begins in 1159 when the Taoist monk Wang Chongyang founded a radical breakaway sect known as Quanzhen ('All True' or 'Way of Complete Perfection'), as strict and austere an interpretation of the Tao as the Franciscan order was of Christianity. Traditional Taoism had degenerated into a kind of organised religion, with its own hierarchy and even a kind of 'pope'; catholic in more senses than one, it found room for spells, charms, talismans and provincial witch doctors.[7] Wang wished to purge it of all these accretions. To an extent Quanzhen can be construed as Taoism leavened by Buddhism, complete with asceticism and celibacy – the exact model of religion the rulers of the Tang dynasty had long wanted to see in China.[8]

Originally based in a hermitage in the Zhongnan Mountains north of Shanxi, Wang Chongyang changed his name to Zhe and relocated to Shandong province where, by his charismatic personality and

powerful preaching, he made many converts. Soon he had instituted a
hierarchy among his true believers, at the apex of which stood his
'magnificent seven' – the most talented of his disciples – and then made
a division into the inner and outer circles of the seven. The four most
favoured ones, Ma Yu, Tan Chuduan, Liu Chuxuan and Qiu Chuji,
accompanied him on a mission to western China in 1169, where he died.
They brought his body back to the Zhongnan Mountains for solemn
burial, then dispersed, each one preaching a variant of the basic
Quanzhen doctrine, as did the 'outer' three: Hao Datong, Wang Chuyi
and Sun Bu'er. Some experts in Taoism aver that Wang's choice of
disciples was poor and identify Sun Bu'er, a woman who emphasised
good works in the here and now, as the most talented of all.[9] Like some
of the famous female saints in the Christian hagiography, Sun Bu'er,
by all accounts a beautiful woman, rejected her femininity, in her case
by splashing boiling water on her face to disfigure her good looks. The
sects founded by the seven may be briefly noted: Ma Yu founded Meeting
the Immortals, Tan Chuduan the Southern Void, Liu Chuxuan founded
Mount Suio, Qiu Chuji the Dragon Gate, Wang Chuyi established Mount
Yu, Hao Datong Mount Hua while Sun Bu'er herself set up the appropriately named Charity and Stillness. Of the seven it was Qiu Chuji
who made the biggest impact, with his sect of the Dragon Gate, though
his rise to supremacy within Quanzhen would not have pleased Wang,
who had earmarked Ma Yu as his successor and would not have approved
of the direction in which Qiu Chuji took the cult.[10]

Like so many Taoists, Qiu Chuji changed his name, to Chang Chun,
the name by which he became famous. Born into a middle-class family,
he was orphaned as a child but the sources cannot agree about his
education. Some say he was illiterate until his teens but, if so, he
made up for it and was soon devouring books at enormous speed.
Despite his pretence of unworldliness, Chang Chun was a clever politician who knew how to network and cosy up to the powerful, getting
official backing for his White Cloud temple in Peking.[11] In 1187 the Jin
emperor Shih-Tsung summoned him to preach at his court and
demanded his presence at his deathbed two years later.[12]

Chang's main selling point was an allegedly superior syncretism of
Taoism, Confucianism and Buddhism, but there was a profound intellectual dishonesty in his claim to be original and to be far in advance
of Buddhism in point of wisdom. His dogma of the 'Three Doctrines'

drew from the Confucian Tzu Tsu, from the Zen Buddhism of Bodidharma and from Lao Tzu himself. His main tenet was that Taoism was the true source of both Buddhism and Confucianism, but this was a very old idea. Directly insulting to Buddhism, however, was the claim that Buddha himself was simply one of many incarnations of Lao Tzu. In any case, Buddhism, drawing in ideas from India as well as China, was theologically far more sophisticated than Taoism.[13]

The 'Three Doctrines' would certainly not have carried Chang Chun very far but, a notable eclectic, he fused this idea with several others of more widespread appeal. First, he stressed the contrast between innocent Man in the State of Nature and his corruption by society (ideas which would become of worldwide importance in the Enlightenment when propounded by Rousseau and Alexander Herzen). Then he emphasised the salient role of alchemy, a spiritual quest sometimes allegorically described in terms of laboratories or, as with the Taoists, the life-giving power of jade, cinnabar, pearl and mother of pearl. This notion, something of a fetish in the Middle Ages, had three main facets. The aspect emphasised in western alchemy was the attempt to produce gold from base metals such as lead. In the East the other two facets predominated: the attempt to produce a liquid gold that would prolong life; and the idea that if you produced the allegedly life-prolonging cinnabar, that in turn would generate more life-prolonging gold.[14] Chang Chun argued for 'internal alchemy' (neidan) as against 'external alchemy' (waidan) which emphasised homoeopathy and the ingestion of herbs and minerals. In other words, notions involving blowpipes, furnaces and chemicals gave way to ideas of mental, physical and spiritual re-education and regeneration. Chang Chun always talked about longevity and when the rumour arose that he could secure immortality, he did little to disabuse the credulous.

When the Mongols swept into northern China, they soon made contact with Quanzhen and its practitioners. Liu Wen, Chinese physician and arrowmaker in Mongol service, shrewdly intuited that Chang Chun would appeal to Genghis and wrote a letter recommending him. Genghis's trusted bureaucrat and adviser on Chinese matters, Yelu Chu Cai, also recommended Chang, to his later bitter regret.[15] The descriptions of Chang written by his disciple (and later biographer) Sun Hsi, describing his master in Peking in 1219, sharpened the khan's interest.

He sat with the rigidity of a corpse, stood with the stiffness of a tree, moved swift as lightning and walked like a whirlwind . . . there seemed to be no book he had not read . . . To him life and death seemed a succession as inevitable as cold and heat, and neither of them occupied in his heart so much as the space of a mustard-seed or spike of grass.[16]

Intrigued by all he had heard about the sage, in May 1219 Genghis issued a 'request' that Chang Chun should visit him and impart his wisdom. The long letter contained the following:

Heaven has grown weary of the excessive pride and extravagant luxury in China and has abandoned her . . . But I, living in the barbaric north in the wilderness, have no inordinate passions . . . I wear the same clothes and eat the same food as the cowherds and horseherders. We make the same sacrifices and we share the same riches. I look upon the nation as a newborn child and I care for my soldiers as if they were my brothers . . . Do not think of the extent of the sandy desert . . . Have pity upon me and communicate to me the means of preserving life.[17]

Since Chang was in Shandong province, then controlled by the Mongols, refusal was not really an option but, always a complainer and a prima donna, he protested at the length of time – at least three years – he would have to be absent from his disciples and showed his refusal (in his own mind at least) to truckle by insisting on lengthy breaks and stopovers on his journey. He agreed initially to visit Genghis on the assumption he was in Mongolia but became alarmed when he realised he was committed to an arduous journey all the way to the Hindu Kush. He salved his wounded pride and *amour propre* by a typically self-regarding letter in April 1220, grudgingly accepting the necessity for extensive travelling but underlining the message that he was paying Genghis a very special favour; he pointed out that he had had an invitation from the Song emperor but had declined to go and was obeying the Mongol khan's summons only because it was obvious that he was Heaven's chosen one.[18]

Chang started the way he meant to go on, taking from February to May to complete the journey to Peking (including lengthy stops in Chi-yang and Peking itself); this was the beginning of a four-year odyssey that would last from February 1220 to January 1224. When Liu Wen finally prised him out of the Heavenly City, Chang was surly, continually complaining about the length of the journey that lay ahead and looking around for excuses to halt. Finally, he found what he thought was the perfect excuse. Accompanying his caravan was a bevy of harem girls bound for Genghis's seraglio. Chung protested vociferously to Liu Wen that this was an insult, that having such girls in his party would besmirch the sanctity of his office.[19] The plan worked. Once the party reached the city of Te-Hsing in midwinter, Chang refused to go on until Liu Wen had clarified the situation with Genghis. Naturally the dispatch of messages between northern China and north-west India took time, so that in the end Chang was able to parlay his stay until March 1221. Some despots would have been angry at such obvious stalling, but Genghis bent over backwards to be accommodating. The odalisques were sent on by separate caravan so as not to 'pollute' the sage, and Genghis sent a most flattering letter, almost as though Chang were the powerful one and he the suppliant. Insisting that Chang must proceed, Genghis laid it on with a trowel, praising Chang as a perfect master superior in wisdom even to the founders of Taoism:

> Now that your cloud-girt chariot has issued from Fairyland, the cranes that draw it will carry you pleasantly through the realms of India. Bodidharma, when he came to the East, by spiritual communication revealed the imprint in his heart: Lao Tzu, when he travelled in the West, perfected his Tao by converting Central Asia. The way before you, both by land and water, is indeed long; but I trust the comforts I shall provide will not make it seem long.[20]

The journey turned out even longer than Genghis had expected. It was recorded in detail by Chang's disciple Sun Hsi and remains a treasure trove for social historians of the Mongol empire.

Once word spread about Genghis's besotment with the Chinese sage, all influential Mongols wanted to get in on the act. His brother Temuge sent a message demanding that Chang visit him too in the Mongolian heartland, and this would necessitate a massive diversion north into Mongolia before striking south-west for India. Chang protested about this as well, and Liu Wen tried to intercede with Temuge, but Genghis's brother was adamant. There was nothing for it then but a gruelling trek north across the Gobi in winter, when the desert was an arctic landscape with thick snow and ice.[21]

It was 24 April 1221 before Chang's party reached Temuge's encampment on the River Kerulen. Temuge tried to show who was boss by refusing to receive Chang until six days of a wedding feast had elapsed, then on the seventh interviewed him and brusquely demanded to know the secrets of immortality. Chang stalled, saying he needed a period of meditation first but, when Temuge persisted, came up with the novel argument that it would be improper to reveal his secrets to anyone before he had divulged them to the khan himself. Temuge was forced to acquiesce and, thinking forward to the report Chang was likely to make to Genghis, provided the sage with a lavish farewell gift of ten wagons and hundreds more horses and oxen.[22]

On 10 May Chang moved on again, striking south-west along the Kerulen, past Lake Buir and the scene of a great victory over the Merkit. Chang was delighted to record an eclipse of the sun on 23 May and soon they began to see the looming peaks of the great mountains ahead. There followed a series of mountainous ascents and river crossings with some of the streams in stormy spate. The next stop was at the *ordo* (palace) of one of Genghis's wives, where they were royally entertained.[23] Setting out again on 29 July, they endured many gruelling days in snow-capped mountains before passing close to the famous city of craftsmen that Chinqai had built. This was Chinqai Balasaqun, a.k.a. the 'Black City', situated halfway between Genghis's base camp in Mongolia and the area of later operations in Turkestan (north of modern Zhanjiakou/Kalgan). Primarily an agricultural colony, it was composed of artisans, farmers and captured foreign craftsmen. The Chinese artisans, who knew all about Chang, went out to meet him and crowned him with garlands of flowers.[24]

Chang saw the chance for another long stopover and suggested it, but Liu Wen impressed on him that he had explicit instructions from Genghis Khan to allow no further delays. Chinqai, who was there in person, confirmed these instructions but, to show goodwill, offered to accompany Chang on the rest of his journey; the charmless sage simply shrugged and said that whatever happened was *karma*. To save face he left behind his chief disciple and eight monks to spend the winter there and build a monastery. Chinqai, an administrative genius, was a valuable addition to the party. He cut down on the baggage and impedimenta weighing down the wagons, explaining that there were many high mountains and treacherous swamps ahead.[25]

On 26 August the party set out again – Chang, ten monks, Liu Wen, Chinqai and about one hundred Mongol cavalrymen. As Chinqai had predicted the going was strenuous and gruelling, and they had a hard time threading through defiles in the Altai Mountains. On good days they followed a crude military road that Ogodei had built, but on bad days they had to drag wagons up the slopes of mountains with ropes tied to the wagon shafts, then lock the wheels and lower them gingerly down the far side. In this way they negotiated five mountain ranges and emerged on the River Ulungur on the southern side.[26] Although they had reached the other side of the mountains, Chinqai informed them that the worst was yet to come, as they had to cross salt flats and deserts, the first of them with abundant grass and water, but then an arid stretch whose extent was unknown. By now the heat was so intense that they travelled by night and rested by day. They were wearied by crossing innumerable sandhills: 'our progress was like that of a ship climbing continually over the crest of huge waves.'[27] Oxen proved useless in the desert, so Chinqai hitched them to the wagons and used horses. Chang was amused by the fearful demeanour of the Mongols as they travelled by night, forever looking over their shoulders for demons; contemptuously he informed them that demons always fled from honest men.

Finally, on 15 September the party reached the foot of the T'ien Shan, where towns started to appear. After a four day stay at Beshbaliq, they pressed on through Chambaliq, west along the T'ien Shan, now travelling from dawn to dusk in intense cold but mercifully downhill, past Lake Sayram (with snow-capped peaks reflected in its waters) and finally to Almaliq, which had the distinction of having a Muslim governor who was formerly a highwayman.[28] They were now in fertile country, abounding in orchards and fields of cotton and watermelons. On 18 October they endured a perilous crossing of the deep, wide and swift-flowing River Ili, trekked for twelve days through heavy snow south of Lake Issyk and came at last to Balasagun, once the capital of the now defunct Qara Khitai. On the way they were able to admire the road Chagatai had built with its forty-eight timber bridges, wide enough to take two heavy carts abreast.[29]

Next they followed the lines of the mountains west for eight days, passed through red-stoned Taraz and Sayram in heavy rainfall and reached Tashkent on 22 November. Then it was on to Banakat and the crossing of the Syr Darya on a floating bridge, through the last range of mountains and then the Zarafshan valley and at last to Samarkand on 3 December, where they were greeted by enthusiastic crowds. Hearing that the roads to the Hindu Kush were impassable because of roadblocks set up by bandits and guerrillas, Liu Wen suggested to a mightily relieved Chang Chun that the meeting with Genghis be deferred to spring.[30]

Following its sack by Genghis two years before, Samarkand had declined from its former glory to a little town of some 25,000 inhabitants. Chang was lodged in the shah's palace over the protests of the governor, who warned him that this location was not safe because of local brigandage. Chang's reply was typically arrogant: 'No man can defy Fate. Moreover Good and Evil go their own way without harming one another.'[31] Ignoring the ingratitude, governor Yelu Ahai (older brother of Yelu Tuka, the distinguished general who had served under Muqali in China) took the prickly sage under his wing. Yelu Ahai, now a man aged around 70, had plenty of experience of prima donnas and disregarded Chang's behaviour.[32] Instead, he sent him ten pieces of brocade which, predictably, Chang sent back on the grounds that he was not interested in luxury. Yelu tried again and sent one hundred pounds of grapes. The charmless Chang declared that he was not interested in the fruit for himself but would keep them for his guests. Nevertheless, he did accept a monthly allowance of rice, corn, salt and oil. The governor, a Khitan born to an oligarchic Chinese family, probably plumbed the depths of Chang's secret insecurity but knew only too well that favour and advancement depended on keeping sweet this suprising object of the khan's affection. As a Nestorian Christian, he would have had little time for Chang's nostrums.

Another Khitan seriously alienated by Chang Chun during his long stay in Samarkand was the top bureaucrat Yelu Chu Cai, later to be Ogodei's key government official in China and a relative of the governor.[33] Yelu had known Chang only by hearsay but recommended him on the basis of his promising advocacy of religious syncretism. He was disposed to be friendly towards him as he was starved of intellectual company in Samarkand, but the first meetings with him brought severe disillusionment. It transpired that Chang had no interest in using his influence to bring Genghis round to a less savage way of governing his empire, but was concerned only to convert the khan to his own narrow and blinkered version of alchemical Taoism. Conversation with Chang moreover revealed the sage's utter and total ignorance of Buddhism, which did not prevent him from uttering *ex cathedra* remarks about that religion. Moreover, Yelu, who knew Chinese history backwards, caught Chang out in an elementary lie. Chang claimed that the Jin emperor Shih-Tsung, whom he had met in 1188, had followed his advice and prescriptions and completely recovered his physical strength, but Yelu knew very well that, far from recovering, the emperor had died in the same year. It did not take Yelu long to conclude that Chang was an unregenerate charlatan, but he had to tread carefully because of Genghis's intellectual love affair with him. Therefore, Yelu commented, 'I behaved politely in his presence, but in my mind I thought little of him.'[34] When asked if he would compose a verse eulogy on Chang, Yelu maintained a scornful silence, but those who knew his secret thoughts were convulsed with amusement at such an idea. To add insult to injury, Chang's disciples suggested that he become a lay disciple of their master. Relaying this to Yelu Ahai the governor, Yelu Chu Cai remarked with some bitterness: 'In my youth I practised Confucianism; when I grew older I embraced Buddhism. Why should I descend from lofty trees to enter into a dark valley?'[35]

Chang Chun passed the winter of 1221–22 in Samarkand in the kind of eremitic solitude he so prized. His only recorded activity was a discussion with a local astrologer about the eclipse of the sun he had seen on the Kerulen River. Liu Wen and his horsemen had meanwhile been reconnoitring the roads to the Hindu Kush, and returned in mid-February 1222 with the news that Chagatai and his cohorts had repaired all the damaged roads, boats and bridges ahead of them. But it was the end of March before a definite missive arrived from Genghis to say that he was ready to see Chang; a subsidiary message was sent to Liu Wen to tell him that his reward for getting the Chinese master all the way to the Hindu Kush would be a gift of ultra-fertile lands.[36] Chagatai also requested that Chang pay him a call but the sage declined, on the eccentric grounds that there were no vegetables or rice south of the Amu Darya.

The almond trees for which Samarkand was famous were already

blooming when the party set out anew. Chinqai was in the party, as
was governor Yelu Ahai, who was to act as interpreter at the interview.
The importance Genghis attached to this became clear when he
dispatched his favourite Bo'orchu with an elite bodyguard to escort
Chang's cavalcade through the difficult pass between Qarshi and
Termez. Departing on 28 April, they met Bo'orchu at Karshi, spent
two days negotiating a high pass in the mountains, then followed a
river south to the Amu Darya, which they crossed seven days later.
Bo'orchu was forced to divert in the final stages to deal with bandits
but Chang and his acolytes finally reached Genghis's camp at Parwan,
north of Kabul, on 15 May 1222.[37]

Chang presented himself at once to Genghis, who showered him
with praise; he knew that other rulers such as the Song emperor had
been turned down (he said), so he took the epic journey Chang had
made to see him as the highest possible compliment.[38] Chang's reply
– that it was the will of Heaven – delighted the khan. Overeager,
Genghis at once asked for the elixir of life. Chang replied that he had
some ways of ensuring longevity but no elixir for that purpose, and
still less one that could secure immortality or the life span of a
Methuselah. Pleased – or so he said – by this frankness, Genghis
ordered a special tent to be erected for Chang to the east of his own.
He then consulted with Chinqai on the best way to address his guest
and finally settled on 'Holy Spirit', the Mongol equivalent of the
Christian Holy Ghost, conceived as an ethereal being destined to
ascend to Heaven, either as a bird or on a bird's back.[39]

Genghis ringed 24 June on his calendar as the day he would question Chang about 'the Way'.

However, hot weather soon pushed Genghis and his guests farther
up the mountains, and a serious outbreak of guerrilla activity forced
Genghis into the field, which meant he had to postpone the interview
until 5 November.[40]

Since there was now a four-month gap until the meeting, Chang
asked if he could return to the greater comfort of Samarkand. Genghis
pointed out that the round trip would be strenuous but in the end
reluctantly agreed. Chang departed on 27 May and was back in
Samarkand on 15 June, where he was finally obliged to grant an interview to Chagatai. Three months later, on 13 September, he left on the
return journey, this time following a slightly different route past the

ruins of Balkh.[41] He arrived at Genghis's camp on 28 September, complained about food shortages in Samarkand, was at once invited to take all his meals with the khan but declined, saying 'I am a mountain man and am only at my ease in quiet places.' It is doubtful if Genghis would have taken such impertinence from any other person in the world, but he acceded and sent his guest gifts of wine, grapes, fruit and vegetables. However, he decided that the original date of 5 November was too far in the future and brought the interview forward to 1 October.[42]

When the day came, six people were present: Genghis, Chinqai, Liu Wen, Chang, Yelu Ahai (who transcribed the sage's words into Mongolian) and an official interpreter. The meeting was considered a great success, with Genghis loud and affirmative in his praise of Chang, so further 'seminars' were arranged on 25 and 29 October.[43]

Chang's formal lecture contained six main themes. First, the Tao is the origin of all things – the Earth, Sun, Moon, even Heaven; but to know the greatness of Heaven is not to know the greatness of Tao.[44] Secondly, Man is a secondary manifestation – a product of Heaven and Earth, which were in themselves a product of the Tao. Thirdly, he introduced the somewhat confusing quasi-Manichean idea that primitive man had lost the 'holy Light'[45] – confusing in that he elsewhere extolled primitive man. Fourthly, in a clear echo of Stoic philosophy, he declared that all sensuous and sensual pleasure must be rejected. Fifthly, he preached that the two elements of Yang (fire, male) and Yin (water, female) interpenetrated in a greater Whole. Finally, there was the message that perfection consisted in nurturing that part of human nature which belonged to Heaven and rejecting the part that belongs to Earth, including sexual activity, hunting, drinking, gambling, et cetera, et cetera. For this 'wisdom' Genghis gave Chang the title Spirit Immortal and appointed him religious supremo in the entire Mongol empire.[46]

Yet one wonders what Genghis secretly made of all of this. If Chang was preaching that a pauper with just one wife could ruin himself by sexual indulgence, what then must be the fate of a great khan with access to thousands of women and whose palaces were filled with nubile females? Chang urged Genghis to sleep alone for a month: 'To take medicine for a thousand days does less good than to lie alone for a single night.' But Genghis protested that he was too old a dog to learn new tricks. Similarly, when Genghis was out hunting boar soon afterwards and was injured when his horse slipped, Chang advised him to give up hunting and to take more care since life was a precious gift. Genghis replied that he could not abandon a traditional pursuit so embedded in Mongol culture and, were he to do so, he would lose credibility with his men. But, out of deference to Chang, he did not go hunting again for another two months.[47]

On 5 November Genghis accompanied Chang back to Samarkand, where he was lodged in his own quarters. Genghis wanted to keep Chang at his side indefinitely, but Chang was desperate to get back to China. A tug-of-war developed, with Chang nagging to be allowed to depart, and Genghis stalling, always promising to let him go soon. Soon Genghis moved on north from Samarkand and insisted that Chang accompany him. Chang began his war of attrition by claiming that the noise and bustle of the caravan was too much for him, and asked permission to travel with a small escort well in the rear of the main convoy. Whether out of genuine concern or because he was determined to win the battle of wills, Genghis agreed.

On the journey, Chang availed himself of the chance to see fauna very different from that in China, including the Central Asian tiger, common in these parts right through to the nineteenth century.[48] But he was put through an elemental wringer. The party left Samarkand on 30 December but in January they were assailed by horrendous snowstorms. They just managed the crossing of the Syr Darya before a terrible storm destroyed the bridge of boats.[49] Genghis made the mistake of asking his unwilling guest what caused natural calamities like storms and earthquakes. Chang, aiming straight at the jugular of traditional folkways, replied that the way to avoid the wrath of heaven was to give up silly taboos about water and forbidding bathing. Warming to his theme, he told Genghis that of 3,000 different sins the worst was the ill-treatment of parents, and he had seen too much of this among the Mongols. He seemed almost to be provoking Genghis to dismiss him, but the khan would not rise to the bait. Cleverly, he turned Chang's flank by saying he completely agreed, ordered this wisdom recorded in Uighur script and told him he would add the recommendation to the Yasa. Meanwhile Genghis continually dinned it into his sons' ears that Chang was a being sent from Heaven and they should revere him accordingly.[50] The battle of wills continued.

On 9 March 1223 Chang told Genghis that he *must* now depart as he had promised his disciples he would be back in China within three years. Genghis turned this by saying he also was travelling east so why should they not go together? Chang protested that he wanted to go at his own pace and begged to be released. Genghis insisted that Chang stay with him until all his sons, legitimate and natural, were gathered in one place so that they could learn the wisdom of the Tao.

At last, in mid-April, Genghis finally tired of the game of cat and mouse and told Chang he could leave.[51] As a parting gift Genghis made the unwise decision to exempt Chang and his sect from all taxes and compulsory labour and to appoint him director of religious affairs in China.[52] He offered Chang and his monks extra oxen for the homeward journey but the faux-ascetic Chang replied that the only animals he required were posthorses. Genghis sent a senior Mongol official with him to make straight the ways. In contrast to his sluggish, snail-like outward progress, when he claimed he needed frequent and lengthy rests and stopovers, the unleashed Chang moved like a swift arrow. Travelling rapidly via the Ili River, Lake Sayram and Almaliq, thence across snowy mountains and arid deserts to the Tangut territory, he and his party shot across country during the summer to the borders of Shanxi province, greeted everywhere by enthusiastic crowds, making hundreds of converts and generally enjoying a triumphal passage. Whenever he was asked to pause on the journey to preach or visit communities to provide pastoral or spiritual guidance, he declined, on the grounds that his rapid onward passage was *karma* and that Fate would not allow him to tarry.[53] He arrived at Peking in January 1224.

The sequel shows how one-sided the relationship had always been. On 3 July 1224 another message issued from Genghis that comes close to meriting the epithet 'pathetic': 'Since you went away, I have not once forgotten you for a single day. I hope you do not forget me . . . I wish your disciples to recite the scriptures continually on my behalf and to pray for my longevity.' The rest of the letter was full of pious hopes that on his return journey Chang had been working hard to reconcile the people he met to Mongol rule. He ended by telling the sage he was welcome to live anywhere he liked in the Mongol empire, with all bills to be sent to the khan.[54] The reality is that in his headlong race back to Peking Chang did not lift a finger on Genghis's behalf. Nor is there any record that he ever replied to this letter.

Naturally Genghis's confidants put a favourable 'spin' on the entire affair. Liu Wen wrote: 'From the moment the Adept came into the Khan's presence, it was clear that as sovereign and subject they fitted one another perfectly. After they parted, the khan felt the greatest affection for him and never showed any signs of forgetting him.'[55] Chang was concerned not to promote the Mongol empire but to secure privileges for China and, in particular, for his own sect. He actually had the effrontery to suggest that the whole of Jin China be exempt from taxation for three years but this was a bridge too far even for the besotted Genghis.[56]

He did, however, make the generous provision that all religions be exempt from taxes and *corvée* – this to apply only to existing monasteries so as to prevent the emergence of tax-dodgers masquerading as converts. Foolishly he allowed Chang to write the manifesto and affixed the imperial seal to the document without reading it. Yelu Chu Cai, who was away at the time, and would otherwise have examined the decree searchingly, was very angry when he realised that Chang, instead of writing that *all* religions should be so exempt, wrote that only *his* followers should enjoy the exemption.[57] Chang and his acolytes then used the decree they had essentially forged to appropriate Buddhist and Confucian temples in lieu of tax and began persecuting rival sects under the pretext of 'pacifying' them on Genghis's behalf. When Yelu eventually returned to China in 1227 (the year of Chang's death) he found that there had been a mass 'conversion' to Quanzhen Taoism by people wishing to avoid taxation and that this provision, which Genghis had specifically excluded in the decree issued to Chang, had been waived by Chang in his capacity as director of spiritual affairs for the empire. Genghis's noble attempt to introduce religious toleration throughout his realm had ended in fiasco.[58]

There was in fact no real rapport between the khan and the 'Adept'. As the French say, in every affair there is always '*celui qui baise et l'autre qui tend la joue*' and Genghis in this case was definitely the one doing the kissing. At another level one can see the Genghis–Chang story as yet another unwise attempt at convergence between a thinker and a temporal ruler, alongside Plato and Dionysius of Syracuse, or Voltaire and Frederick the Great.

After parting from Chang, Genghis spent some time in Tashkent, then headed north and spent the summer of 1223 on the Qulan Bashi steppe north of the Kirghiz Mountains.[59] By the spring of 1224 he had reached the Emil River, where he was met by his grandsons, the sons of Tolui: Qubilai (later emperor of China but then an 8-year-old boy) and Hulagu, his younger brother, aged 6. Qubilai had just killed his first big game and, following Mongol custom, his middle fingers were pricked so as to mix their blood with the meat – a kind of baptism of the chase.[60]

By summer 1224 Genghis arrived at Lake Zaysan and the Black Irtysh (Kara Irtysh), where he met Muqali's son Bol and his mother. Bol was one of the khan's favourites for, like Shigi Qutuqu, he was unusually receptive to new ideas. But on this occasion it was the mother, Yao-li Shih, that drew Genghis's attention. Having been previously married to the Khitan Yelu Liuke, who in turn had a son by a previous marriage, Yao-li Shih petitioned the khan that her stepson Hsieh-he be allowed to take up the post left vacant by his father.

Three things about this request appealed to Genghis. He was touched by the spectacle of a woman entering a plea for another woman's son; he had received a strong recommendation from Temuge for Hsieh; and he remembered that this was the man who had saved Jochi's life in 1216 at the battle of Kimach. Genghis expressed astonishment that the woman had travelled all the way from China on this sentimental quest and said to her: 'Not even an eagle or a sparrowhawk could reach here but you, a woman, have made it.'[61] He granted her petition with alacrity.

Meanwhile, hearing that even after Eljigidei's pacification campaign Khorasan and areas west were still in ferment, he sent Ogodei and Chagatai back there to deal harshly with the rebels. By this time Khwarezm proper and Transoxiana had bowed to the inevitability of Mongol rule but Afghanistan and especially Khorasan, with access to Iraq-Adjemi and the West, still seemed unreconciled. The son he would have chosen for this task, Tolui, was currently unavailable, having gone down with smallpox.[62] Jochi was still in a sulk in his northern eyrie but he did send a conciliatory gift of 20,000 horses and a huge herd of wild donkeys. To show his disapproval of Jochi's wayward behaviour, Genghis used the donkeys for target practice then, when he tired of his archers' slaughter, released the survivors into the wild; the horses he retained, for chargers were always much too valuable to be squandered in this mindless way.[63]

On his way home, Genghis made deliberately slow progress, holding many feasts and hunts to celebrate his great triumph in the war against the Khwarezmian empire. There was much to be pleased about, for his great favourite the *idiqut* Barchuq had distinguished himself at the siege of Nishapur, while every single objective in the war except for the pursuit of the shah had been achieved by Genghis himself or his sons. It was true that he had been very displeased with the lacklustre military performance of Jochi and Chagatai at Gurganj (Urgench), but all had turned out well in the end. He told his confidants that he was particularly pleased that he and his sons had managed everything so well, without having to turn to their three ace generals, Muqali, Jebe and Subedei.[64]

He arrived back in Mongolia in February 1225, having been absent at the war against the shah for six years. When his great friend Bo'orchu died later that year, he showered his family with gifts, favours and promotions, and he did the same for Muqali, who had died in 1223, but whose kin he had been unable to reward adequately because of his absence at the war.[65]

The year 1225 was spent taking stock. Genghis often reflected on the mixed legacy of his empire and his own ambivalence towards it. On the one hand he had given the Mongols wealth, power and luxury beyond their wildest dreams, and had turned an obscure tribe of nomads into the virtual rulers of the world; the people who had dressed in rags and eaten dogs and mice when he was a boy now took the most sumptuous luxury for granted. Genghis had authorised the use of paper money, backed by precious metals and silk, and used silver ingots to assess the amount of paper money issued so as to prevent runaway inflation.[66] Because of the vast numbers of artisans and craftsmen deported from China and Persia the Mongol empire had become a powerhouse of trade and technology.[67] (So unstoppable was this economic and commercial momentum that, for example, Gurganj, seemingly destroyed beyond any possibility of revival in 1221, had recovered in the 1230s to the point where it once again became an important trade centre.)[68]

Genghis took justifiable pride in the wealth his empire had accumulated, but he appreciated there were associated costs, the most important of which seemed to be the loss of the old Mongol ethos and culture. Integration with conquered, sedentary peoples, and especially the sinicisation of the Mongols in China threatened the old way of life in exactly the ways the far-sighted Genghis had predicted. Genghis had wanted to 'mongolise' the rest of the world, but his policy of cohabitation produced the opposite effect, whereby it was the Mongols who were absorbed, thus proving that the cultures of a pastoral life and of urban, sedentary peoples were ultimately irreconcilable.[69]

But the very success of his imperial project brought other dangers too. The greatly improved Mongol diet, with such items as chickpeas, fenugreek seeds and spices such as cardamom added to the menu, brought undoubted benefits, but this was easily outweighed by the deleterious impact of new and more powerful alcoholic beverages.[70] Koumiss, the traditional recreational and festive drink, was no stronger than a very weak beer, but now the Mongols had access to much more powerful wines and other brews, whose alcohol content might be four times as much. The craze for strong drink became a really grave social problem in the last few years of Genghis's reign.[71] The worst offenders were the high Mongol aristocrats themselves. Ogodei and Tolui were serious topers while Jochi's son Batu had a permanent supply of fine wines provided by thirty riders stationed one day's ride from his camp. Even before he switched to European wines, Batu was a devotee of the superior, clear black koumiss, and it was calculated that it took the milking of 3,000 mares daily to satisfy Batu's household's needs.[72] Like the Romans, Mongols gloried in their ability to vomit up an excess of wine and spirits and start again. Severe alcoholism was the major reason for the short lifespans of the great Mongol khans and aristocrats. They rarely lived beyond fifty; only Genghis, who died at 65 and was a moderate drinker, and Qubilai Khan (who died at 78) bucked this trend.[73]

Increasingly Mongol society, previously relatively egalitarian, began to display the crevasses between richest and poorest which are commonplace in affluent societies. The inequality even extended into burial practices. When a rich man died, he was buried secretly in open country, being placed in a ger with a basket full of meat and a jar of koumiss. With him were buried a mare, a foal, a colt with bridle and saddle and a bow with quiver and arrows, along with gold and silver. His friends then ate the flesh of a horse, stuffed its hide with hay, and set it up on a wooden scaffold. A variant on these practices was to impale a horse on poles over the graves of the wealthy. A man was thought to need all these things on the Mongol 'ship of death' that took him to the afterlife.[74] Alternatively, the survivors pretended to bury the dead man openly and publicly near his ger but in reality interred him in a secret pit with a square opening in open country. The deceased's favourite slave was placed under the corpse in this open grave for three days. If the slave survived, he was immediately made a free man and treated forever as an honoured guest in the family. After this the open grave was covered, earthed over and trampled by horses and cattle so that no trace of the burial place remained.[75] The ordinary Mongol, however, did not even enjoy the 'luxury' of a mass grave. The corpses of such people were simply dumped in remote, uninhabited parts of the steppes, in a kind of macabre human landfill. The practice continued until the nineteenth century, and one traveller from that era describes it thus:

> It would be impossible to imagine a more horrible spectacle than met our eyes on arriving at Golgotha, an open space or cleft between two green hillocks . . . a valley literally crammed with corpses in every stage of decomposition, from the bleached bones of skeletons that had lain there for years, to the disfigured, shapeless masses of flesh that had been living beings but a few days or hours ago. The moon shed a pale, unearthly light over the grinning skulls and grey upturned faces of the dead, some of whom lay stark and stiff, just as they had been left by their friends, others with their blue shrouds ragged and torn, with disfigured faces and twisted limbs, lying in the horribly grotesque positions in which the dogs or wolves had dragged them . . . The Mongol is, at any rate, free from an evil which always more or less threatens us of superior civilization – that of being buried alive.[76]

Amid the most indescribable stench wolves, dogs, vultures and other carrion birds fought each other for the human remains. But the Mongols rationalised all this through their beliefs in shamanism and animism. They reckoned that to deposit a corpse in the steppes enabled the deceased to perform a last virtuous act, since animals too were important in the world order. They argued that the prolonging of all life was a desirable goal, and that if vultures and wild dogs feasted off cadavers they would therefore not prey on other animals, which in turn would live longer.[77]

Genghis's thoughts on his own death in the last two years of his life were not, however, focused on burial practices but on the likely fate of the Mongol empire when he was no more. By 1226 the alienation of Jochi had reached the point of acute crisis. Genghis had frequently batted away Chagatai's violent remonstrances about his hated elder brother, usually employing his favourite argument that, even if Jochi had been sired by a Merkit, he, Chagatai, Ogodei and Tolui had all emerged from the same womb. But Jochi's behaviour since Gurganj and, in particular, his potentially disastrous failure to protect the flank of Subedei and Jebe adequately on their perilous journey home in 1222–23, raised his behaviour to a different dimension. Juvaini additionaly claims that Genghis was obscurely jealous of Jochi for his leadership abilities, his wisdom and his abilities as a field commander (whatever his deficiency at sieges).[78]

Chagatai, eaten up with his insensate hatred of Jochi, seems to have sensed his father's change of mood and began a drip-drip of insinuation, propaganda and downright lies designed to compass the destruction of the detested one. His chance came when Genghis, tired of his son's insubordination, expressly summoned him to court. Jochi replied that he could not obey the summons as he was gravely ill – which turned out to be true.[79] But Chagatai saw a golden opportunity. He employed an agent provocateur to inform the khan that, far from being ill, Jochi had been seen out hunting, hale and healthy. Again Genghis sent the summons and again came the answer: Jochi was ill. This time Genghis sent out his most trusted envoys to ascertain the truth.[80] Meanwhile Chagatai played his trump card. He seems to have obtained a document, either genuine or forged, in which Jochi condemned his father in the most forthright terms. The letter claimed that it would have been easy for a real statesman to make a lasting peace with the shah and thus avoid millions of deaths. It also hinted at a desire to rebel against his father. The plain truth, it said, was that Genghis did not want this peace. He was a man who believed only in slaughter and, in Jochi's view, was mad, since what was the point of governing an empire if you had killed off all its inhabitants?[81]

Enraged by this filial treachery, Genghis became alarmed the more he pondered the implications of Jochi's posture. He was already known to be sulking in his tent like a latter-day Achilles because the succession had been given to Ogodei. The overwhelming probability was that when Genghis died, Jochi would raise the standard of revolt against Ogodei. The result would be civil war and the implosion of all that Genghis had spent his life working for.[82] As for the policy of pacific reconciliation with the conquered, that seemed to Genghis simply the rationalisation of a disappointed man and wholly unrealistic for, after all, to quote the words of a later worshipper of power, covenants without swords are but words.[83]

It was clear, then, that Jochi had to disappear from the scene before the khan himself did. Genghis therefore sent one of his secret assassination squads to his son's ulus. It is a moral certainty that Jochi died of poison, either late in 1226 or the first two months of 1227. Ironically, his other envoys crossed with the assassins and brought back word that Jochi's illness had been authentic, but by that time Genghis's fury had moved him on way beyond that (now) somewhat academic point.[84]

The year 1225 and the return to Mongolia also signalled the beginning of the final settling of accounts with the Tangut. Genghis had never forgotten for a single day the treachery of Hsi-Hsia in refusing to send troops for the Khwarezmian campaign and the insulting message that accompanied the refusal (see above, Chapter 10). According to the treaty of 1210 this was an ironclad condition of the peace.[85] With the death of Hsi-Hsia's ruler Li An-Ch'uan in 1211 and the accession in a coup of Shenzong, continuity and peaceful relations with the Mongols seemed assured, but the evil genius of general Asa Gambu, a virulent anti-Mongolist, soon wove its spell.[86] While continuing to profess friendship, Shenzong, by 1220 completely under the influence of Asa Gambu, made the refusal that so infuriated Genghis and began intriguing with the Jin for a military alliance. This backfired, with the result that Hsi-Hsia and Jin China were soon at war. Overconfident of their superiority, the Tangut menaced the north-western region of the Jin state and refused all peace offers. The Jin surprised them with a forced march and badly defeated them. To make matters worse, in 1221 Muqali took an army across Hsi-Hsia, plundering and looting as he went, alienating the locals with their savagery and rapine and the demands for levies of troops.[87] Shenzong's policy of simultaneous war with the Mongols and Jin became massively unpopular, and in 1223 he was forced from the throne and died the same year (some say in battle). The new emperor Hsien-Tsung, one of Asa Gambu's creatures, threw aside all his predecessor's ambiguous posturing, announced an alliance with the Jin and defied the Mongols.

Still on his way back from Khwarezmia, Genghis was not yet ready for full-scale war with the Tangut but sent an army from eastern Shanxi under the Tangut renegade Shih T'ien-hsiang to sack cities in the southern Ordos; this army was soon forced to retire by the appearance of a Jin host in its rear.[88] Uncomfortably aware that he had roused the sleeping giant to his west and north, Hsien-Tsung tried to conciliate the Mongols by a bizarre volte-face when, in January 1224, he sent an army to attack the Jin; this too was defeated. Finally, under pressure from Asa Gambu, he was forced to reveal his true colours, and began fomenting anti-Mongol feeling among the people of western Hsi-Hsia, encouraging them to raid across the border into Mongol territory.[89] Continuing the poor Tangut military showing, these forces too were heavily defeated by Mongol outposts, and this at a time when Genghis and his main army were absent and major operations (conducted by Bol) continued in northern China.

Genghis appointed Bol as his commander and sent him with a force of perhaps 20,000 men to attack key cities in eastern Hsi-Hsia. Nearing the town of Yin Chou, Bol collided with a far superior Tangut force, routed it and then took the town.[90] Genghis decided to recall Bol, in readiness for the all-out campaign he was planning, but left his army besieging Sha-chou. At this point Hsien-Tsung decided he had had enough and sued for peace. Genghis, his own preparations not quite complete, consented, provided the Tangut ruler sent one of his sons as hostage. This was agreed, the siege of Sha-chou was then lifted and the Mongols went home. But Asa Gambu was angry with Hsien-Tsung and his peace policy and insisted on yet another about-turn. Soon the Tangut were intriguing with the Jin once more for an anti-Mongol alliance.[91]

Genghis meanwhile assembled a huge army, maybe 70–80,000 strong on the banks of the Tula River in southern Mongolia (between the Selenga and Kerulen Rivers). For the khan the campaign against the Tangut was so important that he insisted on conducting it himself, despite his age and failing health. As his deputy commanders Genghis took Tolui, Ogodei and the great Subedei; Chagatai was left behind to govern Mongolia. This time, instead of Qulan, Genghis opted to take Yesui as his consort and bedmate.[92] Before departing on another major war of conquest, he took the unusual step of publishing his reasons for going to war with Hsi-Hsia. These were that the Tangut

had broken faith by breaching the treaty of 1210 in which they promised to provide troops for the Mongols' future campaigns and by
intriguing with the Jin for a military alliance.[93] Furthermore, he had
halted Bol's campaign the year before on a Tangut pledge that their
king would send one of his sons as a hostage and there was no sign
of him. He was now giving them one last chance to send the hostage
and make massive financial reparations for their other sins.[94]

Genghis did not really expect the Tangut to accept his terms and
indeed he wanted war with them, both to avenge the previous 'insults'
and because, if he was to complete the conquest of the Jin empire,
he needed to have the Ordos, Shanxi and Gansu firmly in his grip so
that the Tangut could not stab him in the back. But he hardly expected
the virulence and contempt with which Hsien-Tsung and Asa Gambu
rejected his overtures. Asa Gambu sent back a defiant message: fight
or look for your 'reparations' among the Jin. Genghis exploded: 'Is it
possible to go back now? I may die but I shall bring him to account.
This I swear by the Everlasting Sky!'[95]

The issue of the hostage is one of those on which the sources (and
modern scholars) are divided. The Tangut were adamant that they
had sent the king's son, a lad of about five or six, but that the Mongols
had murdered him, and had compounded the crime by leaving his
body on the steppe for vultures to pick clean instead of burying him.
To show their horror at the Mongol action and as a kind of ritual and
symbolic act of substitution for the murdered son, the Tangut osten-
tatiously took under their protection the son of Quqluq, Genghis's
old enemy, who had been petitioning without success for sanctuary
in Hsi-Hsia since his father's death in 1218. The Mongols claimed that
since no hostage had arrived at their camp, they now wanted both
the promised king's son and the son of Quqluq.[96] It is hard to know
what to make of all this. To kill an envoy or hostage was acknowledged among the Mongols as a heinous crime, and the atrocity would
have been enhanced in the eyes of all Asia by the boy's tender years.[97]
At one level, the entire story sounds like black propaganda by the
Tangut. But it may be that Genghis, determined to destroy Hsi-Hsia
and to give the Tangut no loophole for escape, engineered it so that
no pacific resolution was possible.

Once the charges and countercharges had petered out in mutual
acrimony, Genghis got his host under way. His first target was Qara

Qoto on the other side of the Gobi. His strategy was to conquer western Hsi-Hsia and thus in effect cut the kingdom in half, before swinging east to assault the Tangut heartland in the Ordos loop, an area of 8,000 square miles; other forces would be deployed on the northern border of Hsi-Hsia to prevent the Jin from intervening. His ultimate aim was to devastate the irrigated areas of the realm, just as he had done in the Khwarezmian campaign. He knew that the Yellow River was Hsi-Hsia's vital artery and that within the Ordos loop the Tangut had created an irrigated area complete with canals of some two million acres, feeding a population of 3–4 million people. If he severed that lifeline, Hsien-Tsung and Asa Gambu would be finished.[98]

For his part Hsien-Tsung knew he was in a fight to the death, as he had been refused sanctuary in the Jin empire in the event of a defeat, but he was reasonably confident. His army was large, powerful and well equipped, while the Mongols, he hoped, would be worn out after their exertions against the Khwarezmian empire, heavily outnumbered when the Jin allies finally took a hand and also in danger from Song intervention – for he knew of the Song–Mongol clashes in China.[99]

But Genghis aimed to strike hard and fast before the Tangut's putative allies could mobilise. He considered it most unlikely that Asa Gambu would send his huge, unwieldy army across three hundred miles of desert to confront the Mongols in the west, so in the first part of the campaign he expected sieges rather than battles. In February 1226 he left the Tula River and struck due south for Qara Qoto. The Gobi posed no problems for the mounted cavalry, as the gravel, sand and clay provided a firm surface to ride on, and the Mongols knew the location of all the waterholes. As it was not yet summer, even the thin vegetation of July – artemisia, nitraria and dwarf iris – had not yet appeared and the only thing to break the monotony of the pale yellows and ochres, the duststorms and the deep red sunsets and dawns, were the intermittent caravans of nomads, or the occasional herd of antelope or wild horses.[100] By March they were at Qara Qoto and the Ejin River basin. Qara Qoto was an important stronghold in the extreme west of Hsi-Hsia, but it yielded easily.[101]

Moving farther south to where the upper Ejin bifurcated, the Mongols next struck at Su-chou (modern Jiuquan) and Kan-chou, confident that their sophisticated Chinese siege engineers and modern trebuchets would accomplish the job swiftly. But Su-chou held out for five weeks and Kan-chou a wholly unexpected five months.

At Su-chou there was huge loss of life. Genghis had set great store by the renegade Tangut commanders who were serving him, but when one of them, Hsi-li Chi'en-pu, promised he could deliver the city without bloodshed as his brother commanded the garrison there, Genghis was delighted. But the recalcitrant brother refused to surrender; when the city fell, Genghis ordered everyone put to the sword, and it was with great difficulty that Hsi-li managed to secure the survival of his immediate family.[102] At Kan-chou another Tangut renegade in the khan's service, Chaghan, likewise tried to persuade his father and younger brother to come over to the Mongols, but this time the plan was aborted when the loyalist second-in-command in the city got wind of the scheme and executed them both. To compensate for this, and in appreciation of a service that went back nearly twenty years, Genghis spared 106 specially earmarked civilian families (for whom Chaghan had interceded) but massacred the garrison.

By this time the summer heat was upon the combatants, so Genghis wisely retreated to cooler summer quarters in the Qin-ling Mountains to the east.[103] He always became impatient, frustrated and angry when sieges dragged on in this way, so issued the first of his draconian decrees dealing with the Tangut; from now on if there was resistance, every living creature should be killed. The Tangut campaign soon turned into the nastiest, most vicious quasi-genocidal campaign yet waged by the Mongols.[104]

His armies took Ganzhou (modern Zhangye) in Gansu, a classic frontier town for much of China's history, the scene of many battles between Chinese and Hsiung-nu in the first two centuries AD, and later famous for Marco Polo's spending an entire year there.[105] Determined that there should be no let-up in which the Tangut could draw breath, Genghis switched his headquarters to the far north, involving a 300-mile journey to Uraqai (Wu-La-Hai) north of the Yellow River, a location well known to him since it had been captured by the Mongols in raids in 1207 and 1209. The most northerly Tangut stronghold, close to the Yellow River, probably along the outer loop of its northwestern bend, it was situated at the precise place where any Jin reinforcements might enter Hsi-Hsia.[106] He left Subedei to mop up in the west and south.

The ever-efficient Subedei soon defeated the recalcitrant Sa-li Uighur prince, a Tangut ally, and brought to heel all hostile tribes operating in the Nan Shan (Qilian) Mountains south of Su-chou and Kan-chou.[107] Next he proceeded up the valley of the River Tao, a tributary of the Yellow River on its right bank. The sources mention a number of towns and regions through which his armies marched: Ho-chou, Tao-chou (taken easily) and Min-chou, which put up such a frenzied resistance, lasting into 1227, that when it fell Subedei ordered every living thing destroyed; the military governor killed all his family and then committed suicide to escape the Mongols' wrath.[108] Subedei reported to Genghis that resistance in the west was no more, except for Min-chou and Sha-chou in the far west, both under siege and strategically unimportant.

This meant that the Mongols were now masters of the commercially important Gansu corridor, the narrow sliver of territory, part of the northern Silk Route, which ran north-west from the Yellow River along the northern edge of the Tibetan plateau, full of the oases that had just fallen to Subedei. The Tangut seemed to have no answer to the Mongols, and it gradually became clear that they had seriously exhausted their strength in the long wars with the Jin. Their only successes came from trickery, as when the Mongols were lured into an ambush at Sha-chou by a mendacious offer to surrender.[109]

Pursuing his policy of permanent mobility that had so often confounded his enemies, Genghis next ordered Subedei east from Gansu to the west of Shaanxi, taking in the arid areas of Ningxia en route.[110] Ogodei and Chaghan meanwhile were ordered to invade Jin territory along the valley of the River Wei and pin the Jin down in southern Shaanxi. As a further refinement he sent units over the Qin-ling Mountains to debouch into Song territory, swing north to the lower Yellow River and raid the Jin capital Kaifeng from the south. The Jin were so disconcerted by all this that they negotiated an armistice and promised to pay tribute pending the final outcome of the Mongol war with Hsi-Hsia.

By September 1226 Genghis was well rested, the heat had abated and he was ready to take personal charge of his armies once more. He struck east, made his way along the foot of the Nan Shan Mountains on the border between modern Qinghai and Gansu provinces, and crossed the Alashan Desert (which extends all the way from the Tibetan plateau northwards to the Gobi), passing sand dunes up to 900 feet in height and marvelling at the fauna that could survive in such an arid land, especially as temperatures fluctuated wildly both between seasons and from daytime to night-time; brown bear, snow leopards, wolves, wild asses, antelope and ibex were all reported by scouts.[111] Genghis was in good heart, for the news came in that the Tangut's second city, Liang-zhou (modern Wuwei), a key place on the northern silk road at the junction of the Loess, Tibetan and Mongolian plateaux, had surrendered without a fight to avoid destruction.[112]

With most of the territory in the northern Ordos loop already in Mongol hands, Genghis was slowly closing the circle on the Tangut. He now approached the Yellow River itself and sent parties to reconnoitre the famous 'Nine Fords' so that he had an intimate knowledge of the mighty stream and all its quirks.[113] But on the left bank of the river he was embarrassed by the furious resistance of the town of Ying-li. This put up such a doughty fight that it was early December before Genghis was able to cross to the right bank to invest his primary target, Ling-chou, a fortress which guarded the approaches to the Tangut capital, little more than twenty miles away. Before assaulting Ling-chou, he took Yen Chu'an Chou with great slaughter and set up his headquarters there on 16 December.[114]

Suddenly word came in that the Tangut ruler Hsien-Tsung had died and been succeeded by the emperor Modi (a.k.a. Li Hsien). Genghis pondered the implications. It took him another two weeks to break down the defences of Ling-chou (which the Mongols called Dormegei) and this too was achieved only with great loss of life and with great difficulty, because the area around the fortress was striated by a complex system of irrigation canals; the Mongols used captives in the front line as usual.[115]

Modi proved far more energetic than his predecessor and by heroic efforts assembled a huge army; the chroniclers as usual leapt into the realms of fantasy and produced figures of anything between 100,000 and 500,000 men.[116] For all that it was clearly a formidable host. Now Genghis pulled off his last victory, and it was one of his most spectacular. Modi and his army advanced down the western bank of the Yellow River, presumably hoping to sever the Mongol lines of communication. By this time the river's flood plain was frozen and the overspill had turned the terrain around the banks into a frozen lake.

Genghis ordered his army across this 'lake' and it was said that he sustained significant losses on the trek over it, but he caught the enemy unawares and inflicted a crushing defeat on them.[117]

So decisive was the victory that Genghis decided to leave the final stage, the siege of the Tangut capital, to subordinates while he went in search of the Jin. Such was his confidence that he divided his army into three: one to conduct the siege, another to block all approaches so that no reinforcements could arrive from any conceivable allies, whether Song or Jin, and the third to accompany him on another raid into Jin China. A combined operation with Subedei was devised, with the two armies operating at great distances from each other but always in touch via a relay of couriers. Subedei's raid netted a number of smaller towns but failed to budge the large cities. Genghis meanwhile struck east along the Wei valley, causing havoc and consternation along China's western frontier, but he was not strong enough to do more than score token victories. Then, feeling the summer heat once more approaching, he made his way back to the Liu-pan Mountains for the summer, reducing a few more Tangut strongholds as he went.[118]

The faithful Chaghan was put in charge of the siege of the Tangut capital, Chung-Hsing (modern Yinchuan) and the forces north of the city at Uraqai were also brought in to hasten its downfall. Modi made one last desperate attempt at breakout and managed to get away with a sizeable force, which he took across the Helan Mountains to Uraqai. Hearing of this, the troops at Uraqai made no attempt to intercept him in the mountains but waited until his tired soldiers came down the other side. Then they dealt with them bloodily, killed most of Modi's men and chased him back to his capital.[119] Even after this reverse Modi was at first defiant, rejecting every call for surrender the Mongols made. Gradually, though, he grew more despondent as more and more disasters, military and natural, piled up. Caught between the pincers of the Mongol army, the Tangut's hopes were very slender. Next the city was convulsed by an earthquake, then plague and pestilence broke out, spreading even to the Mongol attackers.[120] Finally, by July, food supplies started to run out. Modi realised the game was up and agreed to surrender, on condition that he was given a month with which to assemble suitable gifts when he made obeisance to his conqueror. He sent a pathetic message to Genghis, saying: 'I was afraid. Accept me as a son.'[121] Genghis was in no mood for mercy and, knowing he himself was near death, ordered his generals to kill emperor Modi and all his family when they came to surrender.

When the city finally admitted the Mongols, there was the usual sack and massacre. Asa Gambu was killed but Modi and family were held over at the khan's pleasure and not told of their ultimate fate.[122] The victors made a point of systematically desecrating the royal tombs of Hsi-Hsia to destroy the reputation, status and credibility of the Tangut rulers.[123] Genghis had repeatedly called for thoroughgoing genocide, but there seems to have been a significant number of survivors. Some resettled in Sichuan, some found refuge in north-east India, and a considerable colony established itself along the Yalong River in eastern Tibet. Others found a refuge in Henan and Hebei in China where they continued to exist into the middle of the Ming dynasty.[124]

Since it is often claimed that Genghis's treatment of Hsi-Hsia amounted to genocide, it is worth asking why he did not persist with his oft-announced policy.[125] There can be many answers. Chaghan had already secured the safety of some Tangut oligarchs and was even more merciful to Chung-Hsing once Genghis was dead and the Mongol leadership had other concerns. Some say the typhus epidemic which ravaged both the attackers and the defenders led to a dissipation of the killing impulse. Others claim that Genghis himself waived his 'slaughter on sight' order when five constellations appeared in the night sky to the south-west and his soothsayers told him it was a bad omen.[126] Even without a deliberately murderous policy, however, the Mongols had ensured that Hsi-Hsia and the Tangut would never rise again.

The conquest of Hsi-Hsia was a remarkable feat – some claim it was Genghis's most brilliant campaign – and seems even more remarkable when one considers that he achieved it while very far from his physical best. Just before he set out across the Gobi, probably in January 1226, he held a great hunt, in the course of which he was badly thrown from his horse and may have suffered severe internal injuries. At all events, he never afterwards returned to full health.[127] Perhaps realising that the clock was ticking in earnest, sometime in the Tangut campaign, probably during one of his sojourns in the Liu-pan Mountains, he called a great quriltai to decide formally on the succession and the disposition of the empire after his death. Once again one can marvel at his confidence; deep in conflict with the

Tangut, he was so sure of ultimate success that he felt able to turn to matters of imperial administration.

First, he confirmed the ulus system. The empire was to be divided between his four sons and their successors. Ogodei was to receive the Altai region and all the lands around the headwaters of the Ob, Irtysh and Yenisey Rivers stretching from Lakes Zaysan and Uvs into Siberia; as the youngest son Tolui was to inherit the Mongol heartland around the Selenga, Orkhon, Tula, Kerulen, Khalka and Onon Rivers together with Lake Baikal; Chagatai was to have Lake Balkhash, the Ili River valley and Transoxiana.[128] Potentially the richest ulus was given to Batu, son of Jochi – it is interesting that Genghis did not visit the 'sins' of the father on the son. His territory was to extend west from the Aral Sea 'as far as the hooves of Mongol horses can take him', which theoretically allowed him to establish a realm as far west as the Atlantic.[129]

Genghis gave each son and descendant just 4,000 families each as their quasi-feudal followers, which he calculated was not enough for any of them to set up as an independent power. Although the four subdivisons were never supposed to be independent khanates, that possibility was there from the beginning. From an administrative point of view, Genghis took the correct decision, as his empire was too vast and unwieldy for a strongly centralised ruler to control; but humanly and politically it was a very great mistake and, not surprisingly, it was precisely along the fault lines of the ulus settlement that the empire would eventually break up – and the problem was compounded by the Mongols' integration with other cultures instead of sticking with the traditional tribal ways.[130]

Next, Genghis formally confirmed, and the quriltai ratified, his earlier informal announcement of Ogodei as his heir. He was never convinced that any of his sons was a truly worthy successor, for a great khan needed military skill, tenacity, willpower, energy, deep knowledge of human nature and political genius. Each of his sons had some of his qualities: Jochi had had the generosity, liberality and imagination, Chagatai the stern, unbending ruthlessness and ability to go at once for the jugular, Tolui had great military talent, while Ogodei was shrewd, good natured, a good politician and a clever reader of human beings. There was no perfect choice, but Ogodei was the best option.[131]

At the quriltai Ogodei said he would do his father's will but was sceptical that his own sons had the ability to carry on the empire. Genghis replied that in that case, there would be no future hereditary rulers; all would be chosen on merit by a quriltai. But it could be argued that Genghis's touch deserted him at this stage. Basically there were four conflicting possibilities of succession in contention in Mongolia. There was lateral succession, where a younger brother inherited from an elder brother – this would have put Temuge in the driving seat. There was primogeniture, whereby Jochi or his heirs would have succeeded. In direct collision with this was the Mongol tradition of ultimogeniture, whereby the youngest son inherited the realm, which would have made Tolui the next khan. Finally, as a new and original kind of despotic ruler, Genghis could simply nominate the successor himself and establish this as the dynastic precedent.[132] It is worth pointing out that Genghis took none of these options and gave no clear guide for the future. He simply chose Ogodei as the most satisfactory lineal descendant, provided no satisfactory logical or 'philosophical' guide for the future, left it to future quriltais, whose composition and membership he did not discuss, and virtually guaranteed a future of factionalism and near-civil war. If ever there was a poisoned chalice, it was here.[133]

By the end of July 1227, with the surrender of Chung-Hsing all but negotiated and only the massacre of its population still to come, Genghis was laid up; he summoned his sons and most trusted generals and confidants to his bedside. Yesui and Tolui announced to the Mongols in general that the khan had a fever but the assembled elite knew he was near death. The military high command wanted to pull out of Hsi-Hsia temporarily as a mark of respect, but Genghis drew himself up in his bed and vehemently countermanded any such idea, on the (surely correct) grounds that it would give the Tangut new hope. To his sons he reiterated the arrangements about the succession and the division of the empire, remarking sadly: 'Life is short. I could not conquer all the world. You will have to do it.'[134]

Turning to religious affairs, he told the company he wanted his new capital, Karakorum, located not in the holy land of the Burqan Qaldun, which would emphasise Mongol parochialism, but in that of the Otuken-Yish Mountain near the Orkhon valley, to underline his divinely appointed status as ruler of the world, as a corollary of which anyone not submitting to the Mongols was a blasphemer and deserved to die.[135] On the theme of the punishment of the Tangut, he said he wanted his previous 'kill them all' order to be limited to the royal family, the Tangut elite and all military personnel; mass extermination might send the signal to the world that Genghis had some special animus against Buddhism (the Tangut were Buddhists) and he was keen to promote the image of the Mongols as religiously tolerant.[136]

Next, he gave Tolui and the generals his instructions for the final conquest of the Jin empire. It was clear to him, he said, that the Jin had their best troops in heavily fortified cities at the western entrance to Henan province, where they were protected by the Yellow River to the north and the Qin-ling Mountains to the south. The attack against the Jin should therefore be launched from the south, starting from the headwaters of the Tang River in Henan province. It was true that this was Song territory and the action might mean war with the Song but, if his strategy was followed, Kaifeng would already have fallen by the time the Song mobilised. And since their enemies the Jin would have been annihilated by that time, the Song might even shrug the whole thing off.[137]

His final instruction was a detailed prescription for the death of Modi and the Tangut royal family. The Tangut ruler was to be given an honorific title before he was executed, partly to assuage Buddhist hostility and partly because, according to Mongol belief, the 'virtue' and kudos of a defeated enemy could increases one's power in the afterlife; moreover, the executed person thus honoured will switch in the hereafter from being an enemy to being a protective genius or spirit. One of the motives for the original order for mass extermin-ation, excessive even by Genghis's standards, was as an insurance policy; the more Tangut massacred, the more deferential escorts he would have in the next life.[138] When Modi and his family were brought to Genghis's camp, the khan was already dead, but they did not know this. A black farce was played out whereby the Tangut were suppos-edly not allowed into the imperial presence but had to stand outside the tent and speak through a kind of veiled grill.[139] Sentenced and condemned, they were then executed, reputedly by being chopped to pieces on a spit.

Needless to say, the death of a man already revered as the conqueror of the world caused a sensation and, since human nature requires that the demise of a great man can never come about for any normal or banal reason, the wildest rumours began to circulate. One said that he succumbed to the typhus epidemic that had been ravaging the Mongol army, but this had faded by August 1227 and the time lapse between the typhus's virulent phase and the khan's death effectively rules that out as a cause.[140] Others claimed that he died of malaria; Mongol shamans pointed to 'witchcraft' as the cause, while Friar Carpini, who visited the Mongol court in the 1240s, stated that he had been killed by lightning, making an unwarranted extrapolation from the Mongols' morbid fear of that phenomenon.[141] The Tangut were keen to claim the scalp of the great Mongol khan and declared that he died of septicaemia after an arrow wound in the leg; it has been convincingly demonstrated that this was a wilful mutation of an actual occasion when Genghis was wounded with an arrow – while campaigning against the Jin in 1212.[142]

The most blatant of the Tangut's consoling myths has it that Genghis took Kurbelzhin, wife of the Tangut ruler to bed, where she mortally wounded him in the genitals. Unfortunately for the myth makers, this is a direct copy of the (better-based) rumour that Attila the Hun was murdered in this way and that, to cover up the 'shame', the Huns gave out that he had expired after an unstoppable nosebleed.[143] In any case, the sources tell us that the Tangut queen was executed alongside her husband, and that the two of them arrived in Genghis's camp only after he had died. Not to be baulked, the operators of the rumour mill changed the story somewhat. In the revised version it was an unknown Tangut patriot and beauty who martyred herself, having placed a piece of glass or a steel blade in her vagina which ripped Genghis open, causing him to bleed to death; needless to say, the physiological details of this complex procedure are lacking.[144]

Yet when all the tall stories have been sifted, the overwhelming probability is that Genghis died from some delayed effects from his earlier fall from a horse. Severe falls and the resulting internal injuries are known to trigger carcinoma, and the deathbed scenes in the sources suggest a death by cancer. Certainty is impossible in this area. As the wise and scholarly Igor de Rachewiltz comments: 'The real cause of Cinggis' death is unknown, and was certainly unknown also to most people at the time (except of course to the *qan*'s inner circle) judging by the conflicting reports of our sources.'[145]

It is typical of the fog that surrounds many of the crucial incidents in Genghis's life that neither the sources nor subsequent scholars have been able to agree on the exact date of his death, with 16, 18, 25 and 28 August 1227 all being offered as candidates.[146] Even more controversy attends the sequel, for Genghis's burial place is likewise unknown. If Rashid can be believed, it seems clear that the Mongol elite disregarded the khan's last wishes, for it was said that one day, shortly before his death, he was out hunting and took a fancy to a lone tree somewhere in the Liu-pan Mountains, giving express instructions that this was to be his burial place.[147] Instead, the Mongols tried to take his body back to Mount Burqan in Mongolia. There is a very strong tradition that the corpse never reached Mongolia, that the burial party got bogged down in the Muna Mountains north of the Ordos and panicked, and that prayers were said to Heaven to allow the cortege to proceed, one of which has been preserved.[148]

The overwhelming probability is that Genghis was buried not in Mongolia but in or near the Ordos, as in the great heat of August decomposition of the body was setting in fast and the Mongols had no knowledge of embalming.[149] From the fact that no early thirteenth-century artefacts looted from the cities of Persia and China have survived, it is inferred that they were all buried with the khan. Probable rather than certain is the enduring legend that all fifty members of the burial party were taken to another location and then executed by an assassination squad, who in turn were then executed, so that the secret of the khan's final resting place would die with him. We cannot be certain that this happened on this occasion, but we do know this was Mongol practice after the burial of later khans.[150]

This grisly coda to Genghis's career was not quite the last slaughterous occasion with which his memory was 'honoured'. The Mongol elite preserved the fiction that the great khan was buried on Burqan Qaldun, declared it a prohibited zone and posted guards there. At Ogodei's accession, forty aristocratic virgins were sacrificed there to his father's spirit.[151] Genghis departed this life much as he had lived in it, in a tourbillion of death and bloodshed.

14
Ogodei

For nearly two years after the death of Genghis the Mongol empire was in limbo, with Tolui, the youngest son, acting as regent. It seems clear that a majority of the Mongol nobility wanted him as their next khan, chiefly because of his reputation as a great warrior. They faced the difficulty that Genghis had explicitly nominated his second surviving son Ogodei as his successor. To the conflicting claims of primogeniture, ultimogeniture (the traditional Mongol way) and lateral succession, the choice of the great khan himself became an additional element in the turgid political broth the Mongol nation would have to sup at the next great quriltai, to choose the new emperor. In theory the quriltai was an assembly that merely ratified by public acclamation choices that had already been hammered out in the thirteenth century's equivalent of 'smoke-filled rooms', but it seems that the succession issue was fought all the way to the great assembly in 1229.[1]

The delay was unconscionable as well as being politically inexpedient, since the Jin used the power vacuum to recover some of their position in China. The only plausible explanation is that Tolui was lobbying hard to be the next khan, but two factors work against this interpretation. First, Tolui was Genghis's favourite son, and he of all people would never have opposed his father's wishes. Secondly, Tolui loved and admired Ogodei – Juvaini indeed speaks of a fondness 'beyond the degree of brotherhood'[2] – and there was none of the hatred that disfigured the relationship between Chagatai and Jochi. Another reading of the years 1227–29 is that the Mongol aristocracy pressed very hard for Tolui and it took a long time to convince them that the wishes of Genghis were paramount.

One version of this story makes Genghis's close adviser and court astrologer Yelu Chu Cai the key figure in the drama, with Yelu arguing persuasively for a Chinese model of hierarchy: a khan of khans (khaghan) at the top, princes of the blood second, a wider imperial family third and a host of courtiers and nobles beneath it. This is usually considered a myth both because it overstates Yelu's influence and because Yelu could have spoken out thus only if he had been the official executor of Genghis's written will – but Genghis left no such will.[3]

Ogodei was reluctant to accept the succession and proceeded cautiously, even with his father's nomination and his brothers' written acceptance of him. Playing devil's advocate, he exhorted the Mongols to consider his brother's great qualities, stressed that Mongol tradition favoured Tolui and even brought Genghis's brothers and uncles into the picture.[4] The Mongol nobility were won round to Ogodei as the next khan – and he did indeed take the title of khaghan – because his succession was upheld in such a way as to foreshadow the eventual replacement of his line by Tolui's. He was elected khan on either 11 or 13 of September 1229.[5] The assembled oligarchs at the quriltai were bound by a mighty oath, whose wording was used to endorse future Mongol khans:

> So long as there exists a piece of flesh from the children of Ogodei Khan, and even if you roll it in grass and this grass the cow won't eat, and if you roll it in fat, and this fat the dog won't eat, yet we shall elect him to the khanate and nobody else will sit on the throne.[6]

For Genghis the critical consideration was that his conquests should continue and that there should be no struggle for power between his sons. Genghis was fortunate in having sons who carried his work forward; by contrast, the work of most of the great conquerors and rulers of history was undone by their lack of successors or by disastrous ones: Alexander the Great, Marcus Aurelius, Tamerlane, Napoleon, the list goes on and on.

Ogodei's elevation to supreme power was as unlikely as that of Richard the Lionheart, his near-contemporary, to the kingship of England, for both were third sons. What had cleared his path was the implacable enmity between the first and second sons, Jochi and Chagatai, which meant the choice of either would have plunged the Mongol empire into civil war. Jochi's devastating riposte when Chagatai taunted him with being a bastard and therefore unworthy of the succession was well known: 'only in point of stupidity are you perhaps superior.'[7] This deadly hatred was why Genghis announced ten years before his death that Ogodei was to succeed him – the command repeated on his deathbed. He also made it clear that Chagatai was out of the reckoning by not consulting him in his final days in August 1227, closeting himself only with Ogodei and Tolui to discuss the succession.[8]

Ogodei's first actions showed his strict obedience to his father's parting instructions. He granted an amnesty for all crimes and misdemeanours committed between Genghis's death and his own accession, while making it clear that thereafter he intended to be very tough and come down hard on corrupt administrators, defalcating governors and other forms of official corruption.[9] Crucially, he confirmed the system of appanages and the division of the empire into spheres of influence – the sensitive balance of power between his sons that Genghis had aimed at. Ogodei got all the territories in the far north: the Tarbaghatai Mountains, the Kara Irtysh valley and the region from the Altai Mountains to Lake Baikal. Tolui inherited his father's military forces and was lord of the Mongolian homeland, in accordance with Mongolian tradition.[10] Chagatai got the richest and most fertile lands: both the former Qara Khitai and parts of Transoxiana (but not Samarkand and Bukhara, which were administered directly from Ogodei's central chancellery).[11] Jochi had originally received the lands between the Urals and the Irtysh, including Khwarezmia proper, the Syr Darya and both sides of the Aral Sea. On his death his realm was further subdivided. Orda, his eldest son, received Syr Darya while Batu, the second son, received the north coast of the Caspian as far as the Ural River (and as we have seen, all the lands west of the Caspian 'as far as the hooves of Mongol horses can reach'); the third son, Shiban, received an area from the upper reaches of the Ural to the Irtysh, including the Tourgai and Irghiz Rivers.[12] North China, unconquered as yet but in Genghis's opinion surely doomed, had been earmarked initially for Genghis' brothers, with the proviso that it would eventually be divided among his grandchildren.[13]

Aged 43 when he ascended the throne, Ogodei (his name means 'uphill') was a physically huge man with a distinct liking for women. His two principal wives were Boraqchin and Toregene (sometimes known as Tura-Khinah) and he had two others (Moga and Jachin) as well as sixty concubines, one of whom, a particular favourite whose name is not given in the sources, bore him two sons, Qadan and Malik. Moga had been previously a concubine of Genghis himself. Toregene, a Naiman previously married to a Merkit chieftain, was no beauty but intelligent, able, domineering, wilful and determined. She bore Ogodei five sons, including his successor Guyuk.[14]

Ogodei in person was a mixture of the wholly admirable and the despicable. Intelligent, shrewd, conscientious, tolerant, open-minded, usually calm, laid back, dignified, firm, reasonable, a master politician and conciliator, he could suddenly switch to a capricious mode of harsh and despotic cruelty, especially if he was in his cups, which happened nightly. The Persian historian Juzjani, who had an implacable hatred of him for reasons that are not entirely clear, called him 'a butcher and a tyrant'.[15] The *Secret History* is not much kinder, presenting him as a drunkard, womaniser and miser (the latter is certainly false), who fenced his hunting reserves in case any animals escaped onto his brothers' lands.

Taking the negative attributes first, on at least three occasions he behaved like the stereotypical oriental autocrat. We have already noted the ritual killing, immediately after his election as khan, of forty beautiful girls chosen from the best families, who were adorned in jewels and sumptuous raiment and then sacrificed on his father's grave along with the same number of horses – this despite there having already been two years of official mourning for Genghis.[16] On another occasion he had a senior Mongol named Doqolqu killed out of pure jealousy – he resented the way his father had elevated him as a favourite.[17] Yet his worst atrocity occurred when the Oyirad tribe opposed his will. In 1237 Ogodei decreed that all nubile women in the empire were to be married to husbands of his choosing. The Oyirad tried to pre-empt this by marrying off all virgins and spinsters to men in their own tribe. Foaming with rage at this thwarting of the imperial will, Ogodei ordered all 4,000 Oyirad young women, other than wives of long standing, to parade in front of him. He then had the most aristocratic of them gang-raped by his men in the sight of their fathers, brothers and husbands. After this the girls were divided into three categories. The most beautiful ones were kept for his own seraglio; those ranked of average looks were kept to service foreign diplomats and foreign dignitaries; the homely ones were distributed to men the Mongols considered 'low lifes': servants, falconers and animal

keepers (for some reason keepers of leopards and cheetahs are particularly mentioned in the sources).[18]

On the credit side, Ogodei was both sentimental and excessively
generous. Always open-handed, he was widely regarded as a 'soft
touch', and his largesse often had his officials tearing their hair out.
An old man asked for money to start a company, and Ogodei gave
him the required funds without any form of security; when asked
why, he shrugged and said the old man had not long to live. When
someone else approached him with the begging bowl, his financial
advisers tried to kill the request stone dead by pointing out that the
man already had massive debts. Ogodei asked how much was the
debt, then paid it off, in addition to giving the man the sum originally requested.[19] Seemingly indifferent to money, he allowed himself
to be routinely swindled by profiteering merchants and entrepre-
neurs; he was expert at rationalising in his own mind money-making
schemes that to any disinterested third party were obvious scams.
He became irritated by the waste of troops needed to guard his
treasury at Karakorum, ordered the guard removed and let it be
known that anyone who needed money could enter the treasury and
take it.[20]

Once, observing a craftsman of obvious incompetence vainly trying
to sell his wares, he felt sorry for the man and bought his entire stock
of files, awls and other tools. When he heard that his officials had
deferred some of the payments he ordered out of his excessive and
absurd generosity, on the grounds that the khan must have been drunk,
he fell into a rage and threatened to execute them. With a weakness
for anyone poor, in debt or who made a personal appeal to him,
Ogodei was even munificent to people coming from nominally hostile
countries, claiming that this was the way to disarm them and win
them over, so that there would never be any appetite in their native
land for making war on the Mongols.[21]

This sentimental generosity extended even to the animal kingdom.
A wolf which had been killing sheep was brought into his presence
prior to execution. Ogodei ordered the wolf released on condition it
spoke to its fellow lupines and got them all to move away to another
area. He then solemnly conjured the wolf to agree to this deal. On
this occasion, his officials managed to hoodwink him, for as soon as
the wolf was released they set the massive Mongolian hunting dogs

on it and it was torn to pieces. Ogodei was so angry that his will had been thwarted that he ordered all the dogs killed.[22]

Some said Ogodei's excessive generosity came about because he was an inveterate gambler, with a particular relish for betting on his favourite sport, wrestling. He himself declared that the generous impulse was the only way to secure immortality. Having been told that the only proposition true in all circumstances is 'All this too will pass away', he decided that he could refute the dictum by gaining such a reputation that his fame would last forever. Others, more shrewdly, claimed that Ogodei despised the pure financial power of merchants and financiers who had never fought in battle, that he valued only political power and martial valour, and took his cavalier way with money simply to show his contempt for non-warriors.[23]

Usually a circumspect and wise ruler, Ogodei always took particular care to keep Chagatai loyal and satisfied, habitually consulting him on important matters and treating him with the utmost consideration. In response, Chagatai was almost exaggeratedly deferential and respectful to the great khan. On one occasion, when the two brothers were out riding, Chagatai challenged Ogodei to a race, which Chagatai's horse won. That night Chagatai reflected that it might have been lèse-majesté to act thus with his khan. Next morning he insisted on going before Ogodei to be punished. Ogodei was at first alarmed by the sudden appearance of Chagatai at his palace, thinking that he was staging a coup. When he heard of the purpose of the visit, he was massively reassuring and showered Chagatai with compliments. Nevertheless Chagatai, a stickler for etiquette, insisted that a proclamation be issued that the khaghan had spared his life and that, in compensation for his grievous error, Chagatai had given him nine fine horses. This overt show of support helped Ogodei, as it encouraged all those who had been lukewarm supporters of Ogodei's accession to accept that he really was the khan and that Chagatai would never challenge him.[24]

Nevertheless, there were occasions when Ogodei had to rap his brother over the knuckles. Once Chagatai assigned some provinces in Transoxiana that were under the direct rule of Ogodei's governor Yalavach to someone else. Yalavach complained to Ogodei, who ordered Chagatai to reverse his order. Chagatai complied immediately and sent an abject apology to the khan: 'I acted from ignorance and without guidance. I have no answer that I can write but since the khan has ordered me to reply I am emboldened to write this much.'[25] Ogodei was so pleased with the reply that he said Chagatai could have the disputed provinces anyway. In private Chagatai fumed at Yalavach's 'impertinence' and made it clear to the governor that he was seriously displeased. Yalavach, a highly talented individual with great powers of improvisation, saw at once that he needed to conciliate a dangerous enemy and enlisted the help of Chagatai's vizier Vazir, who ran the palace at Beshbaliq in the north that was Chagatai's pride and joy.[26] Vazir was a fascinating individual in his own right. A Khitan, he had come up the hard way, having been a herdsman for a Jalayir chief and then a servant to Chagatai's personal physician. Chagatai once said he wanted to learn everything possible about his father's life and achievements. Possessing an encyclopedic memory, Vazir conducted his own research through interviews, then made it known to Chagatai that he was the man to consult. At first put off by the physical appearance of the short and ugly Vazir, Chagatai soon grew to be astonished by the man's memory, intelligence, quick wit, eloquence and courage. He promoted him to vizier and allowed him extraordinary indulgence. Once at council Chagatai's wife intervened and Vazir, in Chagatai's presence, told her to shut up as she was just a woman. Chagatai did not reprimand him and later even allowed him to put his own daughter-in-law to death for adultery without consulting him, as he was supposed to. Here was the obvious man to help Yalavach to patch up his fractured relationship with Chagatai. Yalavach wrote to Vazir to say that he was just as influential with Ogodei as Vazir was with Chagatai; it followed that he could persuade Ogodei to put Vazir to death. By contrast, he could do him untold favours if Vazir could mend the breach with Chagatai. Vazir recognised a fellow *éminence grise* of supreme cunning and restored Yalavach to Chagatai's favour.[27]

The historian Juzjani's partiality for Chagatai is just as puzzling as his hostility to Ogodei. He calls Chagatai dignified, open-hearted, opulent of temperament, valiant and hospitable – no other chronicler or commentator was able to discern those qualities – and compares his 'noble' love of hunting favourably with Ogodei's 'banausic' mania for wrestling and gambling.[28] This partiality is all the more puzzling as Juzjani was a Muslim, and Chagatai's most marked characteristic was a hypertrophied hatred for Islam; Ogodei, by contrast, was spectactularly pro-Muslim.[29]

It will be recalled that the Mongols had certain strict taboos about water – no bathing or washing in streams in spring or summer; water scooped up in vessels of gold and silver was believed to cause thunderstorms, and so on – whereas Islam was equally strict about aspects of washing and hygiene. One day Ogodei and Chagatai came upon a Muslim washing in a stream during the forbidden season. Chagatai, as the keeper of the flame of the Yasa, wanted to kill the man on the spot but Ogodei spoke up: 'Let's consider the matter tomorrow.' He reserved judgement but took the Muslim in chains back to his headquarters. That night Ogodei had the prisoner brought to him and coached him in his responses for the morrow: he was to say that, conscious of his blasphemy, he had thrown his last coin into the water even though he was very poor. Next morning in Chagatai's presence the man repeated the story. Chagatai at once sent his men to search for the alleged coin and there in the stream, sure enough, was a silver coin, surreptitiously planted by Ogodei. The khan then used the 'discovery' as an excuse to wax eloquent on the evils of poverty. He not only pardoned the man who had blasphemed but gave him ten extra silver coins.[30]

On another occasion Ogodei pardoned a Muslim who killed a sheep by slitting its throat in the Muslim way instead of slaughtering it in the manner ordained in the Mongol Yasa.[31] He also rebuked a troop of strolling players for putting on a puppet show which burlesqued Islam and said that the satire must never be performed again.[32] Ogodei clearly had no great opinion of Genghis's legal code but dared not dismantle it. Not only would he have lost all credibility by outraging his father's memory, but such a flagrant action might well have precipitated a coup or civil war.

Chagatai might have been vaguely aware that Ogodei was condoning the Islamic practices of the Muslims he (Chagatai) so detested, and possibly this explains an otherwise absurd incident. Chagatai prevailed on a Buddhist priest to tell Ogodei that Genghis had appeared to him in a dream and said that Islam spelt doom and destruction for the Mongol empire, and therefore that all Muslims should be exterminated. Ogodei saw at once that this was pure intrigue brought about by Chagatai. He asked the priest what language Genghis spoke in and was told: Turkish. Ogodei smirked and asked the priest if he understood Mongolian. No, said the Buddhist. 'Then you are a charlatan,' said Ogodei, 'for Mongolian was the only language my father knew.' Ogodei announced that he would not punish the man as he was Chagatai's protégé but ordered him to return to his master with a message not to bear false witness against Islam.[33] According to Juzjani, Ogodei was being disingenuous when he said he would not punish the priest, for he later had one of his death squads abduct and execute him.

In the excessive regard Ogodei showed for Islam, he may not have been so much naturally pro-Muslim as circumspect. He remembered clearly the time Ququluq had ordered the Kashgar Muslims to convert en masse to either Buddhism or Christianity, as a result of which they deserted to Genghis in their thousands.[34]

Ogodei was an inspired choice as khan in one respect: he had inherited from Genghis a deep understanding of the dynamics of the Mongol empire, and realised that everlasting conquest was the only way to preserve the realm, given how many aspirations by greedy and power-hungry nobles had been aroused.[35] In some ways he marked an advance on his father. Genhis liked to eliminate his enemies patiently and systematically, one by one. Ogodei, knowing he could recruit troops in all corners of his huge empire, favoured simultaneous attacks on a number of fronts. Using Turks, Tangut, Khitans, Jurchens and Tajiks as well as renegade Alans, Cumans and Circassians he was able to campaign at one and the same time in China, Korea, Persia, Iraq, the western steppes, Russia and, eventually, eastern Europe.

The first target was western Iran, only partially conquered during Genghis's great defeat of the Khwarezmian empire. While Genghis was concentrating on the final destruction of Hsi-Hsia in 1225–27, his old enemy Jalal al-Din had reappeared, taking advantage of the chaotic state in which the Mongols had left the western regions of the shah's one-time empire. After being banished by the sultan of Delhi, Jalal had returned secretly to Iraq-Adjemi in 1224 and set about making himself the regional overlord.[36] He was recognised as the legitimate ruler by many Turkish governors. Basing himself initially at Isfahan, he tried first to overthrow the caliph of Baghdad, hoping to succeed where his father had failed, but was repulsed.[37] He then based himself at Hamadan and set out to take Tabriz. His capture of Azerbaijan's capital showed all his old ferocity. The atabeg Uzbeg of Tabriz had bought off the wrath of Jebe and Subedei in 1221 with a huge payment of tribute, but the tactic did not work with Jalal. Uzbeg fled the city, leaving the defence to his wife, who at once communicated to Jalal that she would surrender the city if he promised to marry her.[38]

Master of Tabriz and Azerbaijan by 1225, Jalal next turned his attention to the Georgians, posing as the champion of all Islamic states on the borders of the infidel kingdom. Almost eviscerated by Jebe and Subedei in 1221–22, the Georgians had revived sufficiently to be able to defeat the Cumans in 1223.[39] They were hobbled to an extent by queen Rusudan (1223–1245), sister and heiress of George IV, who badly affected the loyalty and morale of her subjects by her blatantly open affair with a Mameluke lover.[40] The Georgians had already battled neighbouring Muslim states in 1223–24 and come off worse; the advent of Jalal further tipped the balance and they once again emerged second best.[41] Jalal fought the Georgians almost constantly in 1225–28, but never concentrated wholly on them, taking time off to consolidate his gains in Khwarezmia and Azerbaijan.

His movements in 1225 were typical of his butterfly-like trajectory. He returned to Tabriz and occupied it peacefully after marrying the atabeg's wife.[42] In August 1225 he defeated the Georgians with great slaughter at Garni in Armenia – a victory he owed to betrayal and treachery among the Georgians, not to mention arrant stupidity. Jalal had sent a letter to queen Rusudan, demanding that she submit to him, but her advisers discounted the threat and sent back an insulting reply, reminding Jalal how badly beaten he had been by Genghis at the Indus. Advancing to meet him near Garni, the Georgian vanguard took up a very favourable position on high ground. As Jalal began to surround them, the vanguard commanders called up the expected reinforcements, but none came. The failure to support their gallant knights was purely due to the endemic feuds and factionalism among the Georgian nobility. The result was disaster. A heavily outnumbered Georgian army was pulverised, and barely a man in the vanguard escaped alive.[43]

Jalal continued his relentless drive into Georgia and took Tiflis on 9 March 1226 after ferocious combats in which 100,000 Georgians are said to have perished. The survivors were ordered to convert to Islam; when they refused they were massacred.[44] Jalal pressed on and in late 1226 began the siege of the cities of Ani and Kars (just inside modern Turkey). By now poised for a definitive conquest of Georgia, Jalal had to suspend operations when urgent business in Iran drew him eastwards.

There were two main problems. The southern province of Kirman had escaped devastation during the Mongol invasion of 1219–22, was prosperous and peaceful, and had been assigned to Jalal's lieutenant

Balaq Hajib, who ruled as governor. Secretly loathing Jalal, as so many of his 'comrades' did, Balaq contacted the Mongols to warn them of Jalal's spectacular revival, and declared his independence. Jalal tried to trick him into surrender but Balaq was wise to all his former overlord's treacherous and duplicitous ways, and did not take the bait.[45] Forced to accept for the moment the fait accompli of Kirman's independence, Jalal turned to the more serious problem of the loss of Isfahan. This had been given to his younger brother (some say half-brother) Ghiyath al-Din, who also hated Jalal; Ghiyath sent a secret message to the Mongols saying that he wished to defect to them.[46]

Now we come to one of the most mysterious episodes in Mongol history, which the sources do nothing to clear up. It seems that one of the Mongol commanders left behind in eastern Iran after the conquest of Khwarezmia went rogue and tried to turn himself into a local warlord.[47] Ghiyath sent his plea to him, thinking he was still in good standing with Genghis. Together they hatched a plot for the overthrow of Jalal, knowing he was always for battles, whatever the circumstances. The Mongol general drew up his forces to make it look as though they were outnumbered and easy pickings. Eager for glory, Jalal gave battle, only to have his flank turned when Ghiyath deserted him and went over to the Mongols.[48] Only with great difficulty did Jalal make his escape. But the victors underrated him. He always had the ability to raise new armies at great speed and this time was no exception; quickly gathering a fresh force, he struck back at the victors while they were still celebrating and routed them. He took four hundred prisoners and beheaded them, acting as axeman himself until he grew tired.[49]

Jalal had a 'complex' about the Mongols after his defeat by Genghis at the Indus, and now trumpeted his victory all over Asia. Ogodei, not yet confirmed as khan, was not prepared to allow Jalal this propaganda victory, and sent him an open letter, denying that he had defeated Mongols: 'These are not our followers. We banished them from our presence.'[50] Ghiyath fled westwards and found refuge with the Assassins. As previously mentioned, these were Nizari Ismailis who broke away from the Fatimid empire around 1080 and operated out of mountain fastnesses in north-west Iran, with their headquarters at Alamut. The legend was that their leader, the 'Old Man of the Mountains', controlled his followers by inducing hashish-inspired dreams of paradise – though this has been shown to be a Western myth. Nevertheless, the Nizari

Ismailis, like the Japanese ninja, became adept as professional assassins, and had several notable scalps to their credit, including Crusader leaders.[51] Every government in the Middle East feared them, and Jalal was no exception. To demonstrate overt contempt for the Assassins (though critics said it was more like whistling in the dark), Jalal himself put out a contract for Ghiyath's assassination.[52]

Having restored his position in Iran and recaptured Isfahan, Jalal turned back to Georgia, where he discovered that two salient events had occurred in his absence. In February 1227 the Georgians took advantage of his problems in the east to retake Tiflis but soon abandoned it when a great conflagration swept over the city. The cause is disputed: some say the fire was pure accident, others that the Georgians, lacking the numbers to garrison it effectively, burnt the city down so as to deny its use to the enemy.[53]

The second development was more serious. Queen Rusudan had forged an alliance with the sultans of Rum and Ahlat, creating a powerful anti-Jalal bloc and boasting the name of the 'Caucasian Federation'. Once again Jalal used speed and cunning to prevail. First he formed his own alliance with the Cumans, to threaten Georgia from the north, then proposed a truce to the Confederation which he claimed would lead to a permanent treaty. Then he assembled an army and attacked the Georgians before they had linked up with their allies' forces. Even though the Georgians were led by their best general, Ivane Mkhargrdzeli, Jalal defeated them at the battle of Bolnisi (1228).[54] Then he moved against Rum and Ahlat. After systematically plundering Armenia in the winter of 1228–29, he moved on Ahlat on the northwestern shore of Lake Van (eastern Turkey today) and besieged it. The siege dragged on from August 1229 to April 1230, and in the end was successful only through the treachery of one of the defending chieftains.[55] The pillaging and slaughter were as ferocious as anything the Mongols had done. Ibn al-Athir, always inclined to give more benefits of the doubt to Jalal than to the Mongols, was disgusted, commenting 'No wonder that God Almighty did not spare him for long.'[56]

The atrocities at Ahlat indeed marked Jalal's high-water mark. On paper he had gone a fair way towards restoring his father's empire, as he controlled Fars, Kirman, Iraq-Adjemi, Azerbaijan and Mazandaran, as well as being the hegemon in Armenia and Georgia. Yet this apparently favourable position masked a host of problems. The rapacity of his tax-collectors and the brutality of his licentious soldiery alienated many who had originally supported him; his men eventually achieved a more sordid reputation than the Mongols.[57] And it was gradually borne in on his counsellors and advisers that he was ultimately a very stupid man, needlessly cruel, heedless of consequences, an impatient short-termist with no political nous. Despite the pretence that he was fighting for 'Persian independence', it was very clear to all that he was a selfish adventurer and a glory-hunter. His worst fault was taking on a plethora of enemies simultaneously. By 1230 he had on his roster of foes not just the Georgians, Mongols, the Assassins, but also the caliph at Baghdad, the sultans of Rum and Damascus, the Ayyubids of Syria and the Seljuks of Turkey.[58] He refused to listen to any advice and snubbed his vizier when he suggested Fabian tactics against the sultanate of Rum: 'They are a flock of sheep,' he said contemptuously. 'Does the lion complain of the size of the flock?'[59] The selfsame vizier foolishly thought that Jalal had overreached himself as the siege of Ahlat dragged on and, when no news came in, concluded that he was free to do as he liked with his master's treasury and harem. After returning from Ahlat, Jalal threw the vizier into a dungeon, where he died.[60]

Meanwhile Jalal was becoming daily more unpopular with his own troops, who were scandalised by his homosexual love for a eunuch called Qilij; when the man died Jalal went almost berserk with grief, further disgusting his associates. For weeks he toted the corpse around with him, refusing to bury it and even offering it food and drink. His emirs became exasperated and muttered among themselves that he was mad.[61] In the circumstances Ibn al-Athir's judgement seems mild: 'Jalal-al-din was a bad ruler who administered his realm abominably.'[62]

The year 1230 saw Jalal's overdetermined downfall. The Seljuk Turks and the sultans of Rum and Damascus brought him to bay near Erzincan in August 1230 in a bloody three-day battle. Jalal fought well on the first day and came close to winning before the battle was interrupted by a sandstorm. In the end, though, Seljuk discipline, morale and efficiency won the day, and Jalal was overwhelmingly defeated, losing tens of thousands in casualties that this time he could not replace.[63] Almost simultaneously with this defeat, a huge Mongol army under a newly promoted general named Chormaqan moved west, obedient to Ogodei's urgent directive that he must defeat Jalal once and for all; a letter had even arrived from the Assassins to the Mongols (their future nemesis) urging joint action against this common menace.[64]

Chormaqan was one of the three 'quiver bearers' in the imperial guard who had spoken out in favour of the three Mongol princes when Genghis was angry with their performance at the siege of Gurganj (Urgench) (see Chapter 11). He had waited ten years for his first major command, and now his hour had struck. Chormaqan knew of Jalal's methods and his reliance on speed, so concluded he could outsmart him by moving with even greater velocity. Once across the Amu Darya and with intelligence from the Assassins on Jalal's where-abouts, he acted decisively. A blitzkrieg series of forced marches took Chormaqan through Khorasan to Rayy and thence to the outskirts of Tabriz, where he took the defenders completely by surprise. Other Mongol forces took Qom, Hamadan, Fars and Kirman.[65]

Jalal at once patched up a peace with the Seljuks and the Ayyubids, appealed in vain to the caliph for help against the Mongols, told both sides that he was their bulwark and without him they would not be able to resist the Mongols, and frantically rushed around trying to organise a defence against the invaders, only to realise that no one wanted to lift a finger to help him. There followed a chase, reminiscent of that of Subedei and Jebe in pursuit of his father ten years earlier, through the plains of Mugan and Arran to the region of Diyar Bakr, with Jalal losing more and more men all the time.[66] The Mongols took Maragha in Azerbaijan, routed Jalal's forces at Amid (Diyarbakir) and took a succes-sion of towns: Amid itself, Tanza, Mardin, Nisibis (Nusaybin), Sinjar, Badlis (Bitlis), Khilat; Chormaqan himself wintered at Rayy.[67]

But Chormaqan was angry and impatient that his troops had not managed to catch Jalal. Accordingly, he sent out a fresh army in pursuit. The original Mongol force had withdrawn from outside Tabriz in its deviously circling search for Jalal, at which the foolish prince concluded the Mongols had retreated. He ordered a three-day banquet to cele-brate. The Mongols came upon the reeling carousers at midnight on the first day; Jalal was comatose in a drunken sleep. His general Orkhan managed with great difficulty to arouse him and warn him of the imminent peril. Jalal begged Orkhan to buy him time while he got away, and Orkhan did so, raising aloft Jalal's standard to make the Mongols think he intended to go out in a blaze of glory. Confident

that they had secured their quarry, Chormaqan's men closed in, whereupon Orkhan took a picked corps of men and fled. The Mongols
pursued, cornered him and, once they realised they had been duped,
slew every last man in their rage and frustration.[68]

But Jalal did not survive long. Near Amid, on his way to the land
of the Kurds, he fell asleep, exhausted somewhere in the mountains.
Kurdish bandits saw his campfire and came upon him. Not recognising
him, they killed him and took his clothes and money.[69] Doubling back
to Amid with their spoils, they were apprehended and executed when
Jalal's distinctive clothes were recognised. That was not quite the end
of the story, for a number of false Jalals arose over the next decade,
trying to claim his patrimony.[70] But this particular thorn in the
Mongols' side was no more, giving particular satisfaction to Chormaqan
because of his unheroic death. Nonetheless one of his few admirers
eulogised: 'It seems to have been preordained by Fate that this bravest
of lions should be slain by foxes.'[71]

From 1231 to 1237 Chormaqan was busy bringing the whole of Persia
under Mongol rule, subduing risings among the tribes of the Caucasus
and generally enjoying his position as military governor of Iran, basing
himself on the fertile plains of Mugan that he found so congenial. He
appointed notable civil governors in Khorasan and Mazandaran,
respectively a Qara Khitan named Chin Temur, who had a distinguished administrative career until his death in 1235, and a Nestorian
Uighur recommended to him by Chinqai.[72] In 1231 Chormaqan's troops
sacked Maragha on the eastern side of Lake Urmia and massacred
the inhabitants because they had resisted. Ibn al-Athir relates that the
Mongols laughed and mimicked prayers to Allah as they slaughtered.
From Maragha too came another of those stories about one Mongol
being able single-handedly to massacre dozens of people because they
were so terrified they simply lay down and awaited the dolorous stroke.

The Mongols then moved against Erbil but withdrew when that
city agreed to pay an annual tribute to Ogodei; Tabriz soon followed
suit.[73] Amid, the target of the 1233 campaign, suffered as grievously as
the cities of Khorasan and Transoxiana had in 1221–22. Chormaqan
destroyed Ganja in Caucasia in 1236 and by 1237 had achieved the final
and definitive conquest of the whole of Iran and Azerbaijan.[74] Though
never with the rabid hatred of Chagatai, Chormaqan seemed permanently hostile to Islam and seemed to favour Christianity, except in the

cases of Georgia and Armenia.[75] The supremely astute king Hethum I of Cilicia (1226–1269) cleverly submitted to the Mongols very early on and made a point of stressing the congruent interests of Ogodei and Christianity, especially vis-à-vis Islam.

As for Chormaqan, he followed the traditional policy of religious tolerance laid down by Genghis – not so much out of open-mindedness per se as a cynical realisation that one could divide and rule by playing up religious differences.[76] It was not until late 1236 that he proceeded to his final objective: a definitive conquest of Georgia and Armenia, realms so resilient that they had already survived two defeats by Jebe and Subedei and three by Jalal. Chormaqan was under orders from Ogodei not to complete this task until the army of Batu was on the Bulgar steppes en route to the conquest of Russia, so as to seal off any Russian retreat into the Caucasus or any reinforcement from there.[77] He quickly overran Georgia, forcing queen Rusudan to flee. Before she did so, she left orders with her governor in Tiflis that on the approach of the Mongols he should burn the working-class quarters of the city but leave the palace and affluent suburbs intact; the man panicked and set fire to everything. The Mongols accepted the surrender of many feudal lords disillusioned with Rusudan but forced them to serve in their ranks.[78]

More ferocious than the easy conquest of Georgia was the campaign in Armenia which opened in 1239. The siege and sack of the cities of Ani and Kars were especially sanguinary affairs. But by 1240 Chormaqan was able to report to Ogodei that all Mongol objectives in Georgia and Armenia had been secured.[79] By a curious kind of pre-established harmony his health gave out in the very moment of final victory. In 1240 he mysteriously lost the power of speech and resigned; his wife Altan Khatun became the acting governor until a replacement arrived. Chormaqan died the following year, yet another in the seemingly unending roster of highly talented Mongol generals.[80]

An even more important campaign for Ogodei was the renewal of the war against the Jin, which had gone into limbo during the inter-regnum of 1227–29. The few engagements that had been fought had gone in the Jin's favour, including a victory (albeit in a minor battle) by the Jin general Wan-yen Ho-ta – the first ever triumph on a battle-field against the Mongols by a Jin commander – and another success by the Jin Ila Pu'a, who lifted the siege of Ching-yang in southern

Shaanxi and discomfited the Mongol commander Doqolqu.[81] The Jin emperor Ai-Tsung had tried to appease the Mongols by sending gifts to honour the shade of the departed Genghis, but Ogodei refused to accept them unless they were accompanied by a declaration of submission. When they sent envoys south with this message, Ai-Tsung had them killed, thus making a renewal of the war certain.[82]

The Jin were irrationally sanguine about their position, buoyed up as they were by the recovery of most of the Wei basin in central Shaanxi in 1227–30, including the key fortress of Tung-kuan just south of the junction of the Wei and Yellow Rivers, which commanded the entrances to Henan province, plus the fortress of Ho-Chung, north of the Yellow River in the south-west corner of Shaanxi.[83] Moreover, the current crop of Mongol generals in China seemed to have produced no one anywhere near the stature of Muqali; the limp effort by Mongol forces in these years also caused many former allies to desert and join the Jin or to waver in their allegiance.

Ogodei raised a huge army – said to be at least 100,000 strong[84] – and, with Tolui crossed into China. Ai-Tsung, swallowing whole the hyperbole from Ho-ta and Ila Pu'a that they were the conquerors of the Mongols, put them in charge of the resistance, much to their trepidation; they knew the reality of what they had won and what they were now likely to face.[85] They were right to be worried, for Ogodei's strategy was not to try to conquer fresh territories but to seek out and destroy the Jin armies. The Mongols began by marching through Shanxi and Shaanxi, extinguishing the Jin presence there and destroying sixty forts.[86] For a while they were bogged down in the siege of the strongly defended Fung-Chang-fu, where Aizong ordered the reluctant Ho-ta and Ila Pu'a to intercept them. The result was what the Chinese duo had feared; total defeat by a far superior enemy. Aizong sent out no more relief forces, and the Mongols proceeded with a methodical reduction of Fung-Chang-fu, cutting off all food supplies and interdicting all towns from which the beleaguered garrison could possibly be provisioned. Slowly throttled, Fung-Chang-fu surrendered.[87]

By May 1230 the Mongols had recovered all towns in the Wei basin lost in the 'phoney war' years of 1227–29. Ogodei confided to Tolui that 1231 would be the year they invaded Henan and forced the Jin to a definitive encounter. He planned to bamboozle them by retreating north while Tolui went south, following the strategy recommended by Genghis, which involved entering Song territory and then swinging in an arc to come at Kaifeng from the south.[88]

Ogodei's strategy involved the coordination of three separate Mongol armies: Tolui's force operating in Song territory, his own advancing south through Shanxi, and a third under Subedei (the left wing) also moving south along the Shanxi-Shandong border and protecting Ogodei's left flank.[89] Each of these operations calls for further analysis, but by far the most important part of the strategy was Tolui's high adventure. He was to approach the Jin capital at Kaifeng from the south-east, thus obviating the need for a long and difficult siege of Tung-kuan, the key fortress whose possession made the Jin confident and complacent.

In mid-1231 Ogodei sent envoys to get the Song to agree to free passage of Tolui's army across their territory, but a local Song commander killed them: a bizarre twist given that the Song had previously asked the Mongols for an anti-Jin alliance.[90] Ogodei sent another mission, demanding an explanation, and this one reached the Song capital. Not wishing for a war with the Mongols, the Song apologised for the atrocity committed by its commander but were non-committal on the subject of crossing their territory; nonetheless, they made it clear by winks and nods that they would not oppose Tolui.

He accordingly prepared for another of the famous Mongol long rides, taking with him as his principal aides Shigi Qutuqu and Doqolqu Cherbi, brother of Bo'orchu. With 30,000 horsemen Tolui made a wide flanking movement far to the west of Jin territory, violating Song sovereignty by his deep penetration into their territory. He crossed the upper Wei then ascended into the Qin-ling Mountains, where his men suffered terribly from frostbite and starvation.[91] He crossed the upper Han River, and, basing himself in the mountainous area between the upper Han and the Tao River, proceeded to take the Song city of Hang-chung with great slaughter.

The massacre was essentially the result of the Song mastery of maritime and riverine transport and Tolui's consequent frustration. After a 40-day siege, about 12,000 troops from the garrison escaped on rafts. To punish this Tolui killed all who were left behind, apart from some of the women and children whom he took into slavery.[92] He then struck even farther south, down the Chia-ling River. Deep in

Sichuan province, travelling over mountains and 'plains like oceans', his men could descry the distant peaks of Tibet. Then, in November 1231, having allegedly taken 140 towns and fortresses on his great ride, he began to angle north-east. In December he camped on the banks of the Han and, after a period for rest and recreation, crossed the river into Jin territory at the end of January 1232.[93]

His appearance in Henan caused a sensation in the Jin capital. The imperial councillors advocated a mass withdrawal of the population into fortified towns, arguing that the Mongols would be so exhausted after their epic ride that they would probably lay siege to just one or two of these. But Ai-Tsung took the view that his people had suffered too much already and could not be asked to do more. With great moral fibre, he ordered the muster of another army to defend the western and southern borders of Henan against the Mongols.[94]

Concerned about the depletion in his numbers after the rigours of his odyssey, Tolui decided to postpone a battlefield struggle with the Jin and elected for a war of attrition. He was influenced in this by the long talks he had previously held with Subedei, who was a great believer in wearing down 'soft' peoples like the Chinese in this way.[95] The Jin commander wanted to wait until Tolui attempted the crossing of the Yellow River before attacking him, but he was being pressed from Kaifeng for quick results. A scrappy engagement with Tolui's vanguard was meant to lure the Jin into an ambush, but they did not take the bait. Thinking himself safe, the Jin commander ordered his men to stand down, whereupon Tolui mounted a cleverly staged ambush in a wood and stole the enemy's baggage. To cover up this fiasco, the Jin reported that the earlier skirmish had been a great battle which they had won; the gullible Ai-Tsung was overjoyed.[96]

But in the field the Jin hankered after revenge for the latest humiliation. Goading them further with more ambushes and long-range archery blizzards, the Mongols retreated into the mountains where Tolui had prepared camps for his men in caves on the mountainside. Bit by bit they lured the Jin ever upwards, past the snowline. Unprepared for snow, the Jin lost large numbers of their men to cold and exposure.[97] The Mongols' victory, however, was pyrrhic. Both in this manoeuvre and in the earlier operations in Sichuan they had been desperately short of food, unable to live off the land and with game scarce in winter. Starvation threatened, avoided at times only by cannibalism – one of the few clear and irrefutable instances of the practice in Mongol history.[98]

After dispersing his Jin pursuers, Tolui advanced again, to the great fortress of Tung-kuan near the junction of the Yellow and Wei Rivers. Anyone coming from the south had to go through a pass, which the Jin had blocked with a huge army. Heavily outnumbered, Tolui thought of evening the odds with yet another feigned retreat, and sent Shigi Qutuqu with the vanguard to try to tempt the enemy to pursuit; the tactic proved unavailing.[99] Tolui was thus in a quandary: retreat would seriously affect his men's morale as they had endured myriad hardships already; but an all-out attack on such strong defensive positions would be dangerous folly.

First he tried tempting the Jin by a semi-suicidal movement that involved Doqolqu Cherbi riding with just 1,000 men almost within arrow range, but the Jin reacted faster than he expected, and there was heavy loss of life as Doqolqu scrambled to withdraw.[100] Forced back onto the desperate expedient of magic, Tolui besought his Qangli sorcerers to come up with something. They suggested a rain magic ceremony carried out with stones. Amazingly, the hocus-pocus worked, a deluge came down, and Tolui ordered his men to don their heavy raingear. Screened by the stair-rod-like precipitation, Tolui's army passed across the front of the Jin army and on into a region where food and clothing was plentiful, much of it left behind by the peasantry fleeing from yet another war visited on them by their social 'betters'.[101]

For three days and nights Tolui's men rode on, with Tolui taking care to billet them in villages, 1,000 men apiece, to escape the pelting of the pitiless storm. Meanwhile the Jin army realised what had happened and set off in pursuit. Unfortunately for them, on the fourth day the heavy rain turned to snow, and they found themselves in the open, exposed to the full fury of the snow and ice; and in every village where they sought shelter, they found it destitute, the Mongols having swept the place clean.[102] For another three days the blizzard beat mercilessly on the Jin while the Mongols were comfortably ensconced in villages. On the fourth day, it was still snowing but Tolui judged his men well-fed and rested and in a high state of morale. He doubled back on his tracks and found the Jin huddled 'like a flock of sheep with their heads tucked into one another's tails'. The result was another massacre: the Mongols fell on the stricken Chinese and tore them apart like lions preying on antelopes. Some Jin remnants managed to get away in the heavy snowdrifts, but 5,000 lay dead in the white silence.[103]

Tolui's final exploit showed Mongol ingenuity at its best. They reached the Yellow River near modern Luoyang only to find it engorged with the recent heavy rains and floods. Fortunately, a huge quantity of large stones had been washed down to the river bank by the floods. Tolui set his men the Herculean task of taking these stones, wading into the river, building primitive breakwaters and diverting the mighty stream into a number of channels, which reduced its depth at the crucial crossing point. After a week of these labours, Tolui and his men rode across by their improvised causeway; it was allegedly the first time anyone had succeeded in fording the lower Yellow River.[104] The Mongols had solved the problem that had so long baffled the Jurchens, both before and after their incarnation as the Jin dynasty – how to get horses across deep rivers.[105]

Once on the other side, Tolui was able to send couriers to Ogodei to tell him of his whereabouts. Ogodei had been seriously worried about the fate of his beloved brother's risky expedition and was over-joyed at the news. He himself had advanced to the extreme south of Shanxi and then turned east along the Yellow River in the direction of Kaifeng. He was held up only by the siege of Ho-Chung, which took thirty-five days; it was taken eventually with the aid of a 200-foot tall pyramidal tower.[106] Angry that the civilian governor had held him up so long, Ogodei immediately executed him but was then further enraged to discover that the military commander and 3,000 troops had escaped in boats. The exploit did not help the Jin commander because when he reached safety, he was accused of cowardice and immediately beheaded.[107]

In some ways Subedei, commanding the third army, had the toughest assignment, as he faced the Jin's best general Wan-yen Yi, the man who had been responsible for most of the Jin successes in the Wei valley and Gansu in the 1227–29 interregnum. Early in 1231, before being assigned to Tolui, Doqolqu Cherbi had been defeated by Yi – a defeat he blamed on Subedei's not having supported him. Because Ogodei did not want to besmirch the reputation of a man who was the brother of Bo'orchu (who as Genghis's oldest comrade,

had virtually been canonised in the Mongol pantheon), he accepted
Doqolqu's transparent excuses and decided to pin the blame on
Subedei, a man he had never cared for. Ogodei's dismissal of Doqolqu's
defeat as a mere flea bite was a masterpiece of rationalisation:

> Since the reign of Genghis Khan we have fought many times with the
> army of Khitai [China] and always defeated them; and we have taken
> the greater part of their lands. Now that they have beaten us, it is a
> sign of their misfortune, a lamp which, at the time of going out, flares
> up and burns brightly and then goes out.[108]

When Subedei lost a minor engagement afterwards to Wan-yen Yi,
Ogodei's judgement seemed confirmed.[109] Yet Subedei soon regained
any lost face by a brilliant campaign in eastern Shanxi and western
Liadong, helped in the latter location by the multiple defector Yen
Shih. Always an enigma – curiously in Chinese communist historiography he is a leader of 'landlord forces' as against the 'Peasant force'
of the Red Coats – Yen Shih was really nothing so elevated. Only by
legerdemain can his origins be considered different from those of the
Red Coat leaders while the man himself was the grossest opportunist
or, as has been well said: 'like a chameleon, he not only changed
colour as required to survive all vicissitudes, but actually came out
better off each time.'[110]

This time Ogodei seemed pleased with Subedei and his acolytes.
To their consternation the Jin suddenly realised that Tolui's army, on
which they had concentrated their efforts, was not the main force
after all, that if anything it was a feint, with the juggernauts of Ogodei
and Subedei now coming into play. Somehow they scraped together
an army, said to be 110,000 strong, under Wan-yen Yi. The three Mongol
armies came together in euphoria near modern Yuzhou. They celebrated their triumph by an overwhelming victory over the Jin, in which
Subedei managed to get between the Jin army and Kaifeng. Caught
in a trap on an open plain, the Jin army of last resort was systematically destroyed. It was the last time a full-sized Jin army ever faced the
Mongols on a battlefield.[111]

After the battle Wan-yen Yi was offered his life if he would enter
Mongol service but he refused, saying his honour would not allow it.
He made one last request: that he should be able to set eyes on the

great Subedei. The veteran warrior, now in his fifties, was sought out, and Wan-yen was presented to him. Busy supervising executions, Subedei listened, bored, while Wan-yen paid him a handsome compliment: it was not chance, but destiny, that produced great conquerors like him, said Wan-yen. Subedei, never a man known for his charm, seemed uninterested, and ordered him away to his own decapitation.[112]

The Jin were now in a desperate plight. After Tolui's campaign in the west, all hope of reinforcement from that area was gone. Even if their troops were not utterly demoralised, they could no longer fight the Mongols, as they possessed at most 20,000 horses.[113] The Mongols had blocked all avenues of escape. When Ai-Tsung finally realised that three separate Mongol armies were converging on him, he sent men to open the dykes on the Yellow River and flood the terrain round the city, but they found that the Mongols had anticipated this move and were already heavily entrenched on the dykes. Since all their troops had been hurriedly recalled to Kaifeng when the gravity of the crisis dawned, the emperor could hope for no relief and no reinforcement; indeed the great families who had remained in the truncated Jin empire after 1227 had by now migrated deep into the security of the Song realm.[114]

Only desperate remedies remained. One forlorn hope was that the Song might intervene. Ai-Tsung wrote to the Song court, pointing out what was indeed obvious, that once victorious, the Mongols would soon turn their attention south of the Yangtse. But the Song turned this appeal down mercilessly, even taunting the Jin about their supposed status as the Song's feudal superiors.[115] The only thing left to cling to was the possibility of disease striking the Mongols. The task of the besiegers was very difficult, for Kaifeng was a city of nearly one million inhabitants.[116] The people had clean water and febrifuges, which the Mongols did not, and it was well known that Henan province was a hotbed for plague, dysentery, cholera and, especially, smallpox.[117] Perhaps Nature would do what the Jin themselves could not. As the heat of the summer approached, Ogodei and Tolui withdrew to the north, leaving Subedei in charge of the final phase of the extinction of the Jin: the reduction of Kaifeng.[118]

If the Jin had actually wished that Fate would strike at the Mongols, their prayers were answered though, unfortunately for them, it was not Subedei or the besiegers who succumbed, but the original architect of their doom, Tolui. Ogodei and Tolui were on their way back to the Mongolian border when the khan fell seriously ill and seemed to hover near death. His shamans 'explained' that he was possessed by water spirits and could not recover unless an expiatory subject presented himself as the substitute victim. Tolui, who loved Ogodei with a deep fraternal love, proposed himself as the victim; he then drank a bowl of water over which the shamans had pronounced incantations, fell sick shortly afterwards and died.

Thus, at least, the *Secret History*.[119] Juvaini tells a very different story – that Tolui, a notorious toper, overindulged in a massive drinking session, contracted alcoholic poisoning and died painfully after three days in agony, at the age of 40.[120] But there is a yet a third theory, powerfully advocated by some of the best scholars. This is that the endemic factionalism that would later destroy Genghis's united empire was already at work, and that an anti-Tolui cabal, possibly the descendants of Jochi, had him poisoned.[121] All the steppe nomads were especially adept at the secret administering of slow-acting poisons. They obtained venom from the Mongolian viper, particularly abundant in the Lake Baikal area, by squeezing it out of the snake's fangs onto a plate; the dried venom was then left for later use. The poison was usually prepared in autumn, as the viper's venom, varying in virulence with the seasons, was most dangerous in autumn.[122]

Whatever the reason for Tolui's death, Ogodei was devastated by it. He found it very hard to forget his beloved brother and whenever he was in his cups, would weep and lament over Tolui. To show his esteem for the departed one, he appointed Tolui's wife Sorqoqtani as senior administrative overlord of the empire, and from this power base she promoted her sons Mongke, Hulagu, Arik Boke and Qubilai (later the famous emperor of China).[123]

Subedei meanwhile tightened his grip on Kaifeng. Formal siege operations began there on 8 April 1232. The peace party inside the city put out feelers to the Mongols but on 24 July the war party stymied the approach by killing the Mongol ambassador and his entourage, who had arrived to discuss terms; that meant war to the knife, with no quarter. In any case, with Ogodei far away and Subedei on the spot, the chain of command was confused. Ogodei had originally proposed surrender terms, without the original sticking point that the emperor be stripped of his title, but specifying a financial indemnity, hostages from all leading Jin families and bevies of beautiful girls. Since he was allowed to keep his title, Ai-Tsung accepted with alacrity. Subedei, however, refused to relax his grip on the city: he said his orders from the khan were to take the city by siege and he had received no countermanding orders.[124] Ai-Tsung had already written to Ogodei to accept the peace terms and foolishly told his men not to fire on the Mongols in case that jeopardised his delicate negotiations. His troops were disillusioned by the order, and became even more so when Subedei made it clear he was not interested in peace; in the peace of his palace Ai-Tsung raged at Mongol duplicity.[125]

The Mongols pressed on with the siege. Their task was not easy, for Kaifeng had twelve supposedly impregnable towers defended by 60,000 troops (40,000 veterans of the garrison and 20,000 young 'national servicemen' drafted in to bear arms). Subedei countered by building ramparts to the height of the walls, using prisoners as the builders, so that they took the brunt of fatalities from the defenders' arrows. A sixteen-day bombardment with enormous loss of life failed to crack the Jin spirit, so Subedei ordered a cooling-off period while he considered his options. He was lucky, for he pulled the Mongol troops back just as an outbreak of plague swept over the city; for fifty days the pestilence raged, causing huge loss of life.[126] More and more Jin generals who had been lurking in the Chinese outback came forward to surrender, but spoiled their chance of survival by refusing to kneel before Subedei or images of Genghis. One of them, Cheng Ho-shong, said he could not kneel as he did not want anyone to say he had been treacherous to his emperor. The Mongols cut off his feet to punish him for the refusal to genuflect, then cut his mouth open to the ears. Courageous and defiant to the last, he won the admiration of his persecutors. One of the Mongol commanders said to him, 'Illustrious warrior, if ever you are reborn, make sure you are reborn as one of us.'[127]

Subedei resumed the siege in September 1232, using mangonels, trebuchets and gunpowder; this was said to be the first clear occasion in history when firearms were used in a major engagement. Flame-throwers and rockets were especially prominent during the siege. The Chinese had invented a 'fire lance'. Sixteen layers of strong yellow paper were pasted together and formed into a long pipe, which was then filled with a mixture of charcoal (made from willow wood), iron

filings, powdered porcelain, sulphur and nitre; the pipe was then fitted
to a lance. The soldiers handling the pipes carried a small iron box
containing glowing embers with which they ignited the fire lances,
which then spewed out a flame nine feet long.[128] The Mongols for
their part fought back ferociously, using similar technology. They had
catapults and mangonels and also a primitive cannon made of bamboo
tubes which fired after being ignited by a slow-burning fuse.[129] The
difference between the two sides was that whereas the Jin were
constantly losing numbers through battle casualties and (especially)
starvation, the Mongols preserved their numbers by using prisoners
in the front ranks and sacrificing them without compunction.

They showed at Kaifeng how much they had learned about siegecraft in the twenty years since they started fighting the Jin. In addition
to the 54-mile wall Subedei built right round the city to seal off all
escape routes, he constantly experimented with new technology, using
the skill and know-how of Muslim engineers recruited during and
after the war with the shah. These engineers had constructed a trebuchet that hurled 166-pound projectiles with such force that they dented
beaten clay walls to a depth of seven to eight feet.[130] They built
mangonels with a range of 400 yards. Additionally, the Mongols had
light catapults for use on a battlefield and a range of crude mortars
and bombs. Whether the newest siege weapon, the counterweight
trebuchet, was used at Kaifeng is disputed, but they were certainly
commonplace in the later Mongol campaign against the Song.[131]

It seems that Subedei would sometimes permit a lull in the siege
to enhance his men's morale and would allow some of his troops into
the countryside for easy rapine. The sources speak of throngs of
refugees, including children and old people, trying to escape to the
mountains, being caught in snowdrifts and then being mercilessly
massacred by these roving parties of Mongols.[132]

The long-drawn-out struggle for Kaifeng was extinguishing whatever residual humanity there was in the invaders, for increasingly there
was a tendency to execute generals and commanders even if they
surrendered. Incredibly, at this late stage, some Jin divisions were still
at large and resisting. Within Kaifeng conditions were almost inde-
scribably piteous, with all the phenomena associated with long sieges
– famine, disease, cannibalism, civil murder – raised to a new power of
horror. With heat in the summer fuelling disease and food desperately

short, the Jin ate, first horseflesh, then the bones mixed with green weeds and finally a soup made of leather from saddles and military drums. The danger from plague was so great that Subedei often had to break off the siege and withdraw his own army for long periods, while never relaxing the blockade.[133]

The siege of Kaifeng was also an opportunity for the great and good in Mongol society to impress Ogodei with their deeds (real, imaginary, contrived, self-assigned or mendacious). Chinqai, the nearest Ogodei had to a chancellor or chief minister, was prominent, while Subedei, for once playing the politician, and knowing that he himself was not one of Ogodei's favourites, made a point of presenting him with a nine-dragon banner and the right to use a sedan chair.[134] Inside Kaifeng all was desperation, and finally the emperor's nerve cracked. Leaving behind his empress and all members of the royal family, he slipped out of the city one night in February 1233 with a small escort, made his way through the Mongol lines and set off for Henan to raise a new army. Before he went he bribed his senior officers with lavish gratuities from the imperial treasury to persuade them to continue the fight until he could return with a relief force and appointed general Cui Li as his supreme commander.[135]

It seems that he very soon fell in with one of those roving Jin armies still at large and put himself at the head of it. Ai Tsong resolved to cross the Yellow River to attract more men to his banner but, searching for a ford, he was held up by a terrible storm. While stranded there, he was discovered by the Mongol force sent by Subedei in pursuit. The result of the ensuing battle was almost a foregone conclusion, but the loss of life was terrific, both in slaughterous fighting and by drowning after the battle when the Jin survivors tried to swim their way to safety. More than 8,000 corpses were counted, many of them washed up by the Yellow River.[136] Ai-Tsung got away with some troops but any idea of rallying the countryside was ruled out when the defeated ones went on a rampage through the countryside, further diminishing support for the Jin regime. Soon reduced once more to his original entourage, Ai-Tsung sent a courier to summon his queen and princesses to join him. An exodus was planned but was unsuccessful, as by this time the Mongols had the city bottled up so tightly that it was said a flamingo would have had trouble escaping.

While all this was going on, Subedei had opened the second phase of his siege, once again assailing the city on all fronts.[137] The plight of the Jin defenders was so desperate that it was reported some of the soldiers had eaten their wives and children and had destroyed their own houses to provide combustible material for the cannons and rockets. Particular demoralisation was caused by the news that Ai-Tsung had sent for his family, which was construed (rightly) as a tacit admission from him that there was no hope.[138]

Realising that he and everyone else in Kaifeng would be massacred if the dithering Ai-Tsung was allowed to continue negotiating with Subedei, general Cui Li staged a coup, executed the civilian governor and all high officials loyal to the emperor. The exiled Wan-yen Tsung-ko was proclaimed as the new regent and invited to return; he did so, was proclaimed regent and Cui Li became his prime minister. The new regime then asked Subedei for his latest surrender terms. Subedei seemed amenable to the overture and replied that all defences of the city must be demolished and a huge war indemnity paid.[139] Cui Li, aware that his best chance of survival lay in being Subedei's creature, immediately sent a cache of jewels and a seraglio of beautiful girls to Subedei as an earnest of his good faith and instituted a reign of terror to force the wealthy of Kaifeng to disgorge their treasure. He then arrested the entire royal family and sent them under guard to Subedei, who at once put to death all the princes of the blood; the princesses were sent to Karakorum and were brutally treated en route.[140]

After this Subedei made his triumphal entry into Kaifeng, where he was greeted deferentially by Cui Li. His troops then went on the rampage, looting, pillaging and raping in defiance of the pledges Subdudei had given to Cui Li. Subedei always hated the Chinese and considered them subhuman, and this breach of an undertaking was his cynical way of showing his contempt.[141]

But he was baulked of his ultimate prey. He sent an express letter to Ogodei to tell him that Kaifeng was his and asked permission to sack the city, arguing that the high loss of Mongol life during the siege made this a fitting punishment. Yelu Chu Cai, then at the height of his influence with Ogodei, made a dramatic intervention, pleading for the lives of the Chinese and arguing that what Subedei proposed was mindless: Kaifeng had surrendered, its inhabitants were now Ogodei's subjects and, if he killed them, he would simply lose tens of thousands of taxpayers, to say nothing of a host of artisans and other skilled people who would be swept away in the holocaust of blood Subedei proposed. Ogodei listened, was convinced, and sent an urgent message to Subedei that only members of the royal family were to be killed.[142]

Five hundred members of the extended dynasty (especially the dominant Wan-yen clan) tasted the headman's axe. Cui Li now expected to be rewarded but was assassinated, not by an imperial loyalist angry at his treachery but by a Jin officer whose wife he had allegedly raped.[143] Subedei was furious at the implicit rebuke from Ogodei but knew well enough what would happen if he disobeyed, so simply moved on to his next target, the city of Caizhou, where Ai-Tsung had taken refuge in August 1233.

By this time Ai-Tsung was beside himself with frustration and rage. He could think of nothing better to do than execute all those generals who had failed or betrayed him (i.e. been defeated by the Mongols). He still clung to the outside hope that the Song, finally alarmed at the advent of the new Mongol superpower on their doorstep, would intervene on his side. But so far from doing this, the Song signed a treaty of alliance with the Mongols, which provided 20,000 troops for the attack on Caizhou and huge stores of grain to provision the Mongol army.[144] Together the allies advanced on Caizhou, which finally fell on 9 February 1234. For some time it had been obvious that the city was doomed but Ai-Tsung's generals dared not tell him the truth – either because the emperor still had a powerful bodyguard who could seize them and execute them or, more likely, because they had run out of options and feared the truth would induce an imperial heart attack; they left the useless Ai-Tsung in dalliance in his harem and simply tried to do their best in an impossible situation.

Finally alerted to reality by the weeping of his wives and concubines, Ai-Tsung learned of the danger and tried to escape by fleeing along a canal, only to find that the Mongols had securely blocked all exits.[145] Returning to the city, he saw the first flames leaping up and licking over the suburbs. Knowing the end was near, he hanged himself rather than face an ignominious captivity or worse. At first Subedei did not believe he was dead but was finally convinced when the Jin leaders dug up his body and brought his severed head before him.[146]

So perished the last Jin emperor and with him the entire Jurchen/ Jin dynasty which had lasted just short of one hundred and twenty years. The Jin had fought bitterly and courageously for twenty-three years and had provided the Mongols with their toughest military task to date. But the Mongols themselves had shown their calibre. As one historian has written, 'No steppe power had ever fought so tenaciously against a dynasty so firmly entrenched and capable of self-defence.'[147]

Almost inevitably, the victorious allies soon fell out. In gratitude for Song assistance, Ogodei allowed them to retain a foothold in south-east Henan, but the Song emperor immediately became greedy for more and attacked the Mongols, even managing to occupy Kaifeng and Luoyang briefly in July–August 1234 before being driven out.[148] At the great quriltai of 1235 Ogodei announced a huge campaign of conquest against the Song. At first this was a brilliant success. Three armies converged on the Song, one under Ogodei's son Koden, another under another son, Kochu and a third led by Chaghan.

When the Mongols pulled out of Henan in 1234, the Song foolishly thought they dared not face their own mighty armies. In fact they had withdrawn because of a great famine. Invading in force, the Song blundered into Henan only to find themselves starving; in their weakened state they were no match for the Mongols when they counterattacked and were driven out of Henan with heavy losses.[149] The Mongol armies reached Huangzhou (near modern Wuhan on the Yangtse) but were unable to hold on to their gains. By 1239 the war had petered out because Ogodei's attention was elsewhere. The precivil war situation in Mongolia in the 1240s precluded serious campaigning in the Song empire and it was not until 1279, after a further twenty years of constant campaigning, that emperor Qubilai was able to rule over a united China.[150]

Alongside the titanic Mongol efforts in China and Iran, Ogodei finally brought the troublesome Koreans to heel. It will be remembered that when Muqali died in 1223, Korea used the occasion to try to throw off the Mongol yoke. Busy with other, more important, concerns, Genghis paid little attention to events on the far side of the Yalu. Not even the murder of his envoys in 1224 – officially by bandits, who however were really Korean troops in disguise – stirred him to send a fresh expedition. Simultaneously, the revolt in Manchuria by Pu-hsien Wan-nu was allowed to dribble on until 1233.

Korea was not able to take full advantage of Genghis's distraction elsewhere, for in 1223, the very year of Muqali's death, its coasts began to be ravaged by large-scale raids from Japanese freebooters, who had been inactive for the previous hundred years. The devastation wrought by these pirates severely taxed the power of the Korean state and led it in turn to be distracted from the Mongol problem.[151] However, on Ogodei's accession he ordered a full conquest of Korea, with a large army sent to the peninsula under the general Sartaq (not to be confused with the more famous Sartaq, son of Batu).

In 1231 the Mongols swept into Korea, laying waste the land mercilessly, killing all males over the age of ten, and distributing the women and children as slaves among the soldiers; their onslaught caused further trouble for the Korean elite by triggering a slave rebellion.[152] The Koreans were used to the Mongols' deadly archery but were taken aback by the new weapons since perfected, including a new kind of flame-thrower in which fat was used to make the belched flame rage inextinguishably.[153] The reign of terror was spread from Pyongyang to Kaesong. King Gojong of Korea fled to the island of Ganghwa west of Seoul and remained there for the next thirty years. Meanwhile huge reparation payments were agreed to persuade the Mongols to withdraw: the tribute included a vast amount of gold, silver and pearls, otter pelts, 20,000 horses and hostages as surety for future good behaviour by the Koreans.[154] The Mongols then trekked back across the Yalu into Manchuria to deal with the rebels there, leaving behind governors and political commissars to make sure Ogodei's writ ran. But Sartaq suddenly died, and this seems to have encouraged a revival of the resistance movement. Guerrilla bands arose, the Mongol officials in post were killed, and a ferocious anti-Mongol propaganda campaign was set in motion by Buddhist monks.[155] Further instability was caused by the annual withdrawal of the small Mongol army of occupation, on which the commissars could theoretically call for help, for the winter hunt in Manchuria.[156]

Angered by the inability of his subordinates to subjugate Korea properly, at the great quriltai of 1235 Ogodei announced a new expedition to pacify Korea once and for all. A large army was prepared, under the command of the Tangut general Baghatur, with the Korean traitor Hong Bok-won as his second-in-command; they were instructed to destroy all vestiges of opposition but not to waste time or resources on a seaborne assault on the island of Ganghwa. The Mongols crossed the Yalu and rolled up the Koreans in a devastating campaign in spring 1236 which took them south of the Han River via Anju and Kaeju.

The Koreans switched to guerrilla warfare, but in response the Mongols instituted full-scale genocide.[157] Every time the country seemed finally tamed, there would be a fresh guerrilla outbreak, triggering a fresh Mongol atrocity in response. Finally, from his eyrie on Ganghwa king Gojong decided he could bear the sufferings of his people no more. In 1238 he signed a binding truce and sent a team of negotiators to Ogodei's new capital at Karakorum to agree a permanent treaty. Although the Mongols demanded his personal presence at Karakorum he refused, but satisfied face and Mongol honour by sending all his closest relatives as hostages.

Peace came finally in 1241, but the fearful Gojong spent the rest of his life on his island. Nonetheless, in Korea the Mongols gained useful experience of amphibious operations, which they would later use in their conquest of the Song. When Gojong died in 1259 after a reign of some 46 years, they moved in on the island and demolished all walls and fortifications. Korea was then annexed by Qubilai Khan, though the Koryo dynasty limped on till 1392.[158]

But by the end of his reign Ogodei could truthfully say that he had completed his father's work and now ruled an empire from the Pacific to the Caspian. Only one small piece in the transasiatic jigsaw puzzle remained: Tibet. Genghis himself had often expressed interest in this mysterious mountainous realm, and Ogodei inherited this trait. He sent two expeditions into Tibet, the first in 1236 under Koden and another in 1240 – this one was said to have caused great devastation.[159] The proper conquest was finally achieved under Mongke's khanate in the 1250s.

One story – disputed by some scholars – is that Genghis's grandson met Sa-pan, the abbot of the Sa-skya sect of Tibetan Buddhism to urge peaceful submission to the Mongols. Sa-pan agreed that this was a wise course and sent a 'pastoral letter' to the various spiritual and secular leaders in the country recommending this. In return, Qubilai Khan made the Sa-skya sect the most favoured religion in Tibet.[160]

The result of all these endeavours – in Tibet, Korea, China and Iran – was that Ogodei succeeded brilliantly in completing his father's work in warfare and foreign relations. Yet in many ways the peacetime tasks he faced proved more onerous and more difficult.

15

Administering the Mongol Empire

Ogodei has been severely underrated by historians, perhaps because no one has published a laudatory account of his life. Genghis, Qubilai and even Mongke have had their admirers, even uncritical ones just this side of hagiography, but Ogodei's brilliant successes in foreign policy have rarely been pointed up, nor the way he consolidated Genghis's work and put the empire on a sound financial footing.

It has been insufficiently stressed that Genghis bequeathed to him a poisoned chalice in three ways. Ogodei inherited a financial crisis; he had to assert the power of the khaghan against proud, unruly, anarchic, greedy and aggressive local oligarchs, including his brother Chagatai; and he was a second-generation ruler whose elevation was controversial. Lacking Genghis's personal prestige, massive reputation and imperial charisma as world conqueror, Ogodei had to shore up his position by building an institutional power base.

His power overwhelmingly depended on the imperial bodyguard, the keshig, whose role was particularly important as the centrifugal process which would break up the empire after 1241. He began implicitly reversing Genghis's great imperial work immediately after his death. There were two elements powering this break-up: the tumens and their mini-realms based on actual and fictive kinship; and the imperial clan with its control over the patrimony or ulus. To counteract all this Ogodei depended on the power of his night guards and a strong central administration run by trusted aides.

The key military personality was Eljigidei.[1] Ogodei aimed to dovetail military control with civilian administration by setting up a central secretariat: within this Eljigidei commanded the night guards while Chinqai was chamberlain, keeper of the imperial seal, and decision-maker on the distribution of booty and ultimate civil authority, though

Ogodei never gave him the title of chief minister. Another important official was Nianhe Zhongshan, a Khitan, who was in charge of all written texts relating to the empire – in effect the keeper of archives.[2] As against the military practice of having, say, Chinese troops serve in Khwarezmia and Turkish soldiers in China to prevent collusion and possible revolt in league with local elites, Ogodei opted for a 'horses for courses' approach in civil administration, relying on local experts. Three different major administrative figures thus emerged, representing different cultures: Mahmud Yalavach and fellow Islamists in the old Khwarezmian empire; Yelu Chu Cai, a Khitan, in China, represesenting the Khitan–Chinese–Jurchen constellation; and Chinqai himself, a Nestorian Christian, who was a symbol of the eastern Turks, Kereit, Uighurs and others who embraced Nestorianism.[3]

Chinqai (c. 1169–1252) was of uncertain origin – Naiman, Uighur and Ongud ancestry have variously been attributed to him – but his primary culture seems to have been Chinese, and he spoke the language fluently. He was Genghis's de facto first minister as early as 1206, when he had sixty bureaucrats under him. One of the 'band of few' of the Baljuna Covenant, he accompanied the troublesome Chang Chun on his journey to see Genghis in 1222–23. Chinqai encouraged the commercial alliance between the Mongols and Muslim merchants and even employed some of them as financial experts and tax officials. In Genghis's time Chinqai did not have quite the eminence he was to have under Ogodei, for Genghis appointed the Tangut Tatatonga as his keeper of the seals, and from this appointment came the emphasis on Uighur scripts and Uighur secretaries. When he became Ogodei's chancellor, Chinqai had all imperial decrees and top-level discussions recorded in Mongolian, Turkish, Persian and Chinese as well, on the grounds that the narrow Tatatonga system had allowed members of the secretariat to enrich themselves; corruption was always a problem for the Mongols, largely because the khans thought principally in terms of conquest and glory, not money.[4]

Genghis had spotted early on one of the problems in his empire: the Mongols were heavily dependent on native administrators in the conquered territories, but could they be trusted? He and Chinqai came up with the idea of daruqachi – political commissars – in key cities, law-courts or military commands; the first appointment of such an official mentioned in the sources was at Peking just after its fall in 1215, though later writers have picked up stray indirect references going back to 1211.[5] Similar to the system known as *hsing-sheng* under the Jin in China, these commissars – nearly all Mongols – were personal representatives of the khan, his plenipotentiaries in conquered territories. They collected taxes, levied troops from the local populace, conducted censuses and sent off tribute to the khan's court. They also supervised and controlled local feudal lords, regional elites and the native bureaucracy.[6] There were also officials called basqaqs, lower in the pecking order precisely because they were not Mongols. These were primarily military figures sent to protect the daruqachi in their tax-collecting role. In time the distinction between basqaq and daruqachi became eroded, to the point where it became customary to use the terms as shorthand tags for military and civilian rulers respectively. But the whole business of basqaqs was essentially an ad hoc mess – some had viceregal powers and some did not; to add to the confusion, khans sometimes sent out quite separate plenipotentiaries extraordinary.[7]

Chinqai's administrative genius was twofold. First, he had to solve problems caused by the Mongols' ignorance of sedentary populations. The Mongols were nomads and warriors and had no one trained for the task of administration. Nor were they linguists, and in their raw state they knew nothing of a money economy. They therefore had to depend on literate, multilingual members of the very nations they had conquered. Like the British in the nineteenth century, they had to rule vast numbers with a tiny bureaucratic force and like them depended on quislings and converts to the Mongol vision of global conquest. Genghis and Ogodei always had the trump card of religious toleration, which tended to make the local clergy their loyal supporters.[8] Secondly, Chinqai had to assert the khan's claim to the wealth of the empire and to ensure that local Mongol aristocrats did not siphon it off surreptitiously. To sugar the pill, Ogodei reorganised his secretariat system across the empire and then allowed powerful local elites representation on the local bodies.[9] In 1229 he created branch secretariats in eastern and western Turkestan and a third in northern China; he later added a fourth, for northern Iran. The purpose of these bodies was to adjudicate on disputes between the khan and the regional rulers and this meant, in this reign, especially, between Ogodei and Chagatai.

This was the context in which Chinqai's protégé Mahmud Yalavach (d. 1254) first made his mark. He was the son of a Turkish-speaking Muslim, a merchant from Khwarezmia. Yalavach senior entered Mongol service as a diplomat in 1218 and his first assignment was a dangerous embassy to shah Muhammad, who liked to kill Mongol envoys. He then disappeared from history until his re-emergence in 1229 when Ogodei appointed him governor-general of northern China. At the same time his more famous son became governor-general of Central Asia.[10]

The task of Yalavach junior was to restore the shattered economy and infrastructure of Khwarezmia and reform taxation. He hit on the idea of simplifying taxes, reducing them to just two, a poll tax (*qubchir*) and a land tax (*qalan*), with no extraordinary imposts or levies. His system was so successful that a later khan, Mongke, introduced it on an empire-wide basis.[11] But in fulfilling Ogodei's wishes so faithfully, Yalavach fell foul of Chagatai, as we have seen (see above, Chapter 14). Chagatai always loathed Yalavach's close supervision, and the scandal in 1239, when he highhandedly made a land grant not in his gift to a favourite, could have led to civil war had Ogodei not handled it so skilfully.

This crisis had no sooner subsided than an even more serious one followed. In 1238–39 an early proletarian rebellion in Bukhara became so serious that for a time the Mongols were driven out of the city. Ogodei sent a huge army which suppressed the insurrection, but Chagatai argued that only large-scale massacre would inculcate the lesson that it was folly to defy the Mongols. Yalavach appealed to Ogodei and, to Chagatai's fury, Bukhara was spared total destruction. Knowing that a vengeful Chagatai would now throw all his resources into intriguing and manoeuvring to compass Yalavach's downfall, Ogodei transferred his favourite to north China in 1241.[12]

Yet the administrator in Ogodei's reign who has attracted most attention is Yelu Chu Cai (1190–1243), largely because he was not just an able civil servant but a multitalented polymath of the kind that bedazzles intellectuals and historians. He is a controversial figure and much about his career is disputed, especially as he is mentioned neither in the *Secret History* nor in the history by Rashid al-Din. It is not even known for certain whether he was a Confucian or a Buddhist, partly because his attitude to religion was so eclectic.[13] He was born in Peking, the son of a chief minister under the Jin and related by marriage to the founder of the Liao dynasty. It was said that he graduated top of the class in the Chinese civil service examination around the time of the Mongol invasion. He was present in Peking during the terrible siege of 1214–15 and the month-long sack, and found the experience so traumatic that

he suffered a nervous breakdown. Seeking a way out of his dark labyrinth, he studied Buddhism at the feet of the renowned sage Wan-sung
(a.k.a. Hsing-hsiu, 1166–1246), who was well known as a syncretist who
sought a middle way between Confucianism and Buddhism.[14]

After three years of this (1215–18), he was identified by the Mongols
as 'one to note' and recruited into their service. He often amazed his
masters with his versatility: he played the lute, was a talented linguist,
had a mastery of mathematics and the sacred texts of Confucius, was
a lover of fine art and collector of books and musical instruments and
wrote interesting travelogues.[15] He was interviewed personally by
Genghis, who expressed sympathy for the nervous breakdown but told
him he had taken revenge on the Jin on behalf of the Liao and that
was something Yelu, as a Khitan, ought to understand.[16] Yelu replied:
'My father and grandfather both served the Jin. How can I, as a subject
and a son, be so insincere at heart as to consider my sovereign and my
father as enemies?'[17] This was just the sort of thing to impress Genghis,
who always placed a high value on self-denying loyalty. Moreover, Yelu
appealed to him personally, as he seemed to discern in the tall, long-
bearded young man with the sonorous voice a younger version of
himself. Yelu was at once recruited into the khan's inner circle.

He was attached to Chagatai's army during the invasion of
Turkestan, was present at the siege of Samarkand and was at Genghis's
side almost continually until 1226. During those years he combined
the offices of scribe-secretary with that of court astrologer. The superstitious Genghis often consulted him, and Yelu accurately predicted
the fall of the Khwarezmian empire, the death of shah Muhammad
and later of the Jin emperor. He it was who interpreted the sighting
of a rhinoceros in India as a bad omen and persuaded Genghis to
withdraw from the subcontinent.[18] One of his least palatable tasks was
to be deferential towards Chang Chun, the Chinese sage and favourite
of Genghis whom Yelu secretly considered a charlatan.

In 1229 Ogodei appointed Yelu as a senior administrator in China
with a special brief to investigate methods of taxation. This appointment has been widely misunderstood. One Russian historian, in a
moment of hyperbole, remarked that the absence of mention of Yelu
in the two principal Mongol sources was 'as strange as if a historian
of Louis XIII forgot to mention Richelieu'.[19] But Yelu was never a
Richelieu – not even a Mazarin. Quite apart from the consideration

that Ogodei never appointed a chief minister, Yelu's remit was restricted to China and every memorandum he sent Ogodei had to be endorsed by his superior, Chinqai, who translated his reports into Uighur.

Nevertheless, the baby should not be thrown out with the bathwater: there is no doubt that on Chinese affairs Yelu's opinion was hugely influential. Yelu persuaded the khan to issue a paper currency backed by silver; this was highly successful and won the admiration of all later European travellers.[20] Influenced by the bloodthirsty Belgutei, prime representative of the 'old Mongols', Ogodei at first inclined to the view that the proper fate for the defeated Jin was genocide, but Yelu quoted the old saw 'a nation conquered from horseback cannot be governed from horseback' and urged on Ogodei the massive wealth that could accrue from taxing a hardworking sedentary population; just as there are no pockets in a shroud, he argued, one cannot generate revenues from people who are dead.[21] Ogodei took the point but challenged Yelu to offer concrete proof of his proposition. Yelu estimated that he could generate a tax yield of 500,000 ounces of silver, 80,000 pieces of silk and 400,000 sacks of grain. He then cunningly asked for plenipotentiary fiscal powers, which were granted.

His immediate aim was rooting out corruption among 'monks' in religious houses. When Genghis foolishly granted sweeping tax exemptions to Chang Chun, the number of religious vocations, not surprisingly, increased dramatically. Yelu ended all the exemptions and decreed that all religious persons under fifty had to pass a stiff theological examination to prove their *bona fides*. Moreover, all monasteries which had used the Chang Chun laws to acquire land and engage in commerce were expressly forbidden to do so in future or to expand existing activities, while being heavily taxed on their current assets.[22]

Yelu then issued a manifesto, taking care to get Ogodei's immediate endorsement, which contained eighteen points relating to law and order, strong central government, clamping down on corruption and a strict division between military and civilian jurisdiction. He divided the country into ten administrative units, each one with a tax collection centre run by two mandarins recruited from enthusiastic ex-Jin personnel; these twenty tax officials answered directly to Ogodei so that they could not be overawed or browbeaten by greedy military officials. Yelu levied his main taxes on land, estimated by a household rating, and also collected impost on commerce, liquor, salt, vinegar, iron smelting and iron products.

Every adult had to pay a fixed tribute in silk yarn, with the rural population mulcted more highly than city-dwellers. A set amount of grain was
levied for each household, regardless of the quality of land, with city-
dwellers paying a supplementary levy in silk yarn; taxes in silk yarn were
usually commuted into silver for payment to the government.

By September 1231 he was able to tell a delighted Ogodei that he had
raised the exact amount (10,000 ingots of silver) he had promised in his
original estimate. As a reward Ogodei gave him the title of chief of the
Chinese secretariat, responsible for drafting rescripts, decrees and official
documents plus the keeping of records. The secretariat also provided
interpreters, envoys, astronomer-astrologers, economists and supervi-
sors of military colonies. Yelu recruited a staff of officials writing in six
languages: Mongolian, Chinese, Uighur, Jurchen, Persian and Tangut.[23]

The Chinese hailed Yelu as their saviour. Yet his initial 'miracle-
working' in China soon went sour. There were a number of reasons.
Until 1234 and the final defeat of the Jin, the requirements of war
meant that extra taxes were raised, over and above the 'official' ones.
But the war itself produced famines, epidemics and displacement of
population at the very time the Mongols were seeking these extra
taxes. A kind of financial version of 'mission creep' meant that Yelu's
initial 'reasonable' taxes increased anyway. By 1234 the land tax had
been raised from two bushels of grain to four while the annual quota
of silver was doubled.[24] And as if to confirm the old maxim that no
good deed goes unpunished, there was grumbling that Yelu had not
extended any of his much-vaunted reforms to the non-Chinese, especially those from Central Asia, living in China.

By the time of Ogodei's great quriltai in 1235, Yelu's problems had
expanded to the point where he seemed a perfect Ishmael, with every
man's hand turned against him. The Confucians and Buddhists, and
the disciples of Chang Chun, had not taken his measures directed
against monasteries and bogus monks lying down. The Confucian
backlash was mild, as Yelu favoured them over rival religions and
thought them more useful socially. (One of his maxims was 'Buddhism
for the substance, Confucianism for the functions' – by which he
meant that both religions on their own were inadequate: Confucianism
because it did not pay enough attention to self-cultivation and the
inner man, Buddhism because it ignored the everyday world and the
practical concerns of here and now.)[25]

The Buddhists were most vociferous in their defiance. They rejected Yelu's idea of canonical tests for all monks, arguing that their religion was based on virtue not knowledge and that virtue could not be tested in an examination. This patently self-serving and disingenuous argument was sustained when the Buddhists got the support of the powerful Shigi Qutuqu, who agreed to reduce their theological examinations to a mere formality, with no provision for failure; because Shigi had enjoyed such favour with Genghis, Ogodei would never overrule him in favour of Yelu.[26]

In any case, Yelu had not really thought through the implications of his anti-monk policy, even if he had been given a free hand. Enforcement of his religious laws conflicted with his fundamental drive towards centralisation, as it would require a local bureaucracy. Now not only did such a body not exist but, if created and trained, it would be in competition with the khan's 'normal' officials.[27] Besides, religious commisars could come only from the native Chinese, and the Mongols were adamant that they should never be given unnecessary powers. The programme of sinicisation that Yelu liked to plug as his gift to China was largely an illusion, a congeries of ad hoc concessions granted by Ogodei cynically and pragmatically as a way to buy time.

Nevertheless, in 1235–36 Yelu was still hopeful. At the 1235 quriltai Ogodei accepted his proposal that a census be held in China to identify the missing taxpayers. Yelu had long argued that because of corruption which he could not control, there had been a massive flight from the land by the Chinese peasantry to avoid the burden of the household tax; some say as many as 50 per cent of the population of Jin China were tax evaders in this way.[28] Moreover, at this stage Chinqai was on Yelu's side and argued for more rigour and regularity in taxation throughout the empire and for sanctions to make people accept the new paper currency. Small traders still preferred to deal in coin and said that they did not trust a paper currency that had no expiry date. Chinqai wanted a new law to make refusal to accept the paper currency a capital offence, at the same level of gravity as forgery and counterfeiting; this was granted.[29]

Although Shigi Qutuqu had backed the Buddhists against Yelu, on the issue of the census, which Ogodei appointed him to conduct, he was at one with Yelu and considered erratic taxation a sign of Mongol backwardness.[30] Yelu wanted to keep his old household tax – somewhat paradoxically in the light of his stress on the flight from the land – but Ogodei, Chinqai and the senior Mongols wanted a capitation tax so that no one could escape the fiscal net simply by absconding or migrating. The compromise reached resulted in both a poll tax – Yelu had argued against this, saying that having been registered on the census and forced to pay his year's taxes, the average adult male would simply abscond before the next annual payment came round – and a modified household tax. The new household tax, previously levied at an inelastic flat rate, was now assessed on the quality and quantity of land, roughly 10 per cent of income or harvest; nomads were taxed one animal in every hundred.[31] Yelu maintained that he had been right, as the new household tax raised only 10 per cent of the previous one, but Shigi and others hit back with the argument that the other 90 per cent was made up by the revenues collected from those who were 'invisible' before the census.

Yelu lost another argument when he asked Ogodei to stop his officials receiving 'gifts' (i.e. bribes), but Ogodei said the practice should remain as long as the officials did not ask for them or extort them.[32]

Thus far the arguments conducted after the census concerned the minutiae of taxation. But Yelu now learned to his horror that Ogodei's motive for the census had been to discover how much land he could distribute as further appanages to family and favourites. In other words, whereas Yelu's motives for the census had been for tax and administrative purposes, the Mongols simply wanted to know how many people would be on the land they intended to earmark for themselves.[33] Put technically, Ogodei aimed at the feudalisation of north China while Yelu aimed at its centralisation; the two principles were on a head-on collision course.

Realising that his officials would not be able to control these quasi-independent fiefdoms, in some desperation Yelu suggested a compromise: that his tax-collectors should be allowed to enter the appanages, collect taxes, compute them centrally and then redistribute a portion to the fief-holder. Ogodei gave formal approval for this, but never implemented it; his system of appanages in China therefore effectively destroyed Yelu's centralisation programme.[34]

This programme had never functioned perfectly anyway, if only because of the number of Jin renegades who had been rewarded for their services to the Mongols in the war. One such was Yen Shih who, in defiance of Yelu's separation of civil and military powers in 1231–32, had been appointed both myriarch and chief administrator in his enclave of Tung-Ping. But if Yen Shih had survived Yelu's thrust for centralisation, he faced a real and imminent threat after 1236 because of the new appanages, which would have reduced him to a cipher. Ogodei's proposal for Tung-Ping was that it should be divided into ten sections and given to ten of his favourites. Yelu and Yen Shih were unlikely bedfellows but they came together in alliance in 1237 to oppose this move. Yelu wrote to Ogodei to remind him that he had received Yen Shih in audience in 1230 and held a great banquet in his honour; would not the present proposal be seen as treacherous ingratitude? Ogodei therefore decided not to proceed in this case, but warned that his generosity should not be read as a precedent.[35]

Perhaps to soothe Yelu's ruffled feathers, in the same year he agreed to his proposal for a meritocratic and competitive civil service examination, reviving the custom of the old Tang dynasty which was also currently practised among the Song. The astonishing aspect of this was that all literate denizens of China, even including slaves and prisoners of war, were allowed to take part; Yelu ordained severe penalties for the owners of enslaved scholars who tried to stop them sitting the exam.[36] There were 4,030 successful candidates, including more than 1,000 slaves, who thereby earned their freedom. Yelu found them jobs as councillors, where they were exempt from tax and *corvée*. Few of them, however, were given the really top positions their qualifications merited; the Mongols had no intention of allowing the Chinese to administer China and made sure all key positions went to Uighurs or personnel from the old Khwarezmian empire. In any case, having thrown this sop to Yelu, Ogodei changed tack; no competitive examinations were held thereafter.[37] Both the principle of promotion on merit and that of evaluating the authenticity of monks by formal tests perished together.

By the late 1230s Yelu was losing ground on all fronts. Four major opponents can be identified: the 'old Mongols', the military high command and local warlords; Muslim merchants; individuals within China and the administration who had the ear of the khan; and, to a certain extent, Ogodei himself in the latter part of his reign. The 'Old Mongols' were headed by Genghis's brothers Temuge and Belgutei in alliance with Subedei, who had not forgotten that Yelu talked Ogodei out of the wholesale sack of Kaifeng in 1233. All of these men loathed

Yelu and went out of their way to discredit him.[38] They alleged that China needed to be taxed more heavily to provide the surplus for financing the projected campaign in Europe; was a mere Khitan official and his parsimony to stand in the way of Mongol martial glory? Besides, it was not appropriate for a mere man of letters to hold high office in a military society; he knew nothing of the art of war and was a meddling fool who should be confined to the academy.[39] (This was one of the first recorded laments in history concerning the vexed question of 'the professor in politics' which so engaged twentieth-century analysts.) Most of all, they insinuated that he was 'soft on China', that he granted the Chinese taxation and other privileges contrary to the interests of the Mongol empire. Sometimes Yelu fell into this trap himself and alienated even the khan by his 'bleeding heart' pleas for the Chinese people. On one occasion an exasperated Ogodei asked him: 'Are you going to shed tears for the people again?'[40] Military commanders and Mongol oligarchs swelled the chorus of anti-Yelu propaganda, incensed that he stood between them and the acquisition of vast lands there. Some of the opposition of these groups to Yelu had a basis in military actuality, but most of it was simply frustrated greed.[41]

Yelu hit back in his dispatches to Ogodei by claiming that if the military were given their head in China, tax yields would plummet, not only because their rapacious demands would cause the peasants to flee the land but because the commanders, interested primarily in forage for their horses and cattle, would turn over huge tracts of agricultural land to grazing.[42] As for his supposed status as an obstacle to the European campaign, this issue arose solely because the Mongols were so poor at preparing estimates; they were always seeking to increase taxation simply to make up the shortfall in their budgets produced by incompetent accounting.[43]

Unable to defeat Yelu's arguments by logic and reason, in their frustration Genghis's brothers hatched a plot to assassinate him. Belgutei and Temuge were implicated, but the ringleader seems to have been Temuge. Ogodei's efficient intelligence service uncovered the plot. It was a huge embarrassment for Ogodei to have to punish his uncles, so he asked Yelu for his opinion on suitable retribution. He replied that he was not interested in revenge. Ogodei managed to avoid a family scandal by hushing up the incident but for a time it swayed him to Yelu's way of thinking. As a compromise on the vexed appanage issue, he decreed that central government officials could enter these territories to secure the empire's rightful share of the taxes; any attempt to dissuade or turn them aside by bribery would be punished by death.[44]

The Muslim merchants were the proximate cause of Yelu's ultimate downfall. Throughout the 1230s their influence in China increased. They were organised via the *ortaq* (a Turkish word meaning 'partner') – an association of officially licensed merchants in partnership with the Mongol elite for the purposes of personal enrichment.[45] Hugely unpopular in China on a number of counts – they were foreigners, alien in culture and language, they were corrupt and exploitative and ruthless when used as tax-collectors by the government – these Islamic plutocrats were the enemy of a peaceful, organised, well-administered China. Taxes made to the Mongol court in silver were typically invested with these merchants who lent it out at usurious rates.[46] Often they would borrow from the Mongols and then reloan the money at an interest rate of 100 per cent, and they found takers because of the high cost of living in north China in an era of war, famine and natural disasters and the steep level of taxation. The Muslims converted the 100 per cent interest payments into capital each year, so that after ten years the principal and compound interest amounted to 1,000 times the original loan.[47] The *ortaq* repaid this original loan at an interest rate high enough to satisfy Ogodei, so that, when they proposed raising additional revenue through tax farming, he was receptive.

In vain did Yelu warn the khan that tax farming would weaken central government and geld the secretariat. By 1238 the annual tax quota for China was already 22,000 ingots of silver, and he warned that if this was doubled, as proposed by the merchants, peasants would turn to violent crime, murder of government officials, highway robbery and banditry.[48] Ogodei paid no attention to the warning. Though not interested in money per se, he derived the gambler's pleasure from winning and the associated feeling of power. He had dabbled in the speculative market from the early 1230s and, when the entire annual tax yield from China was a lowly 10,000 ingots of silver, invested 500 ingots of his own. As a modern historian has said, 'with monies leaving the treasury at this rate, it was not surprising that there was always pressure to readjust the tax quotas upward.'[49]

Finally, in 1239, Ogodei sold the pass completely, approved tax farming and doubled the tax quota from 22,000 ingots to 44,000. While all this was making his life a nightmare, Yelu faced continuing opposition from Mongol oligarchs, other officials appointed by Ogodei and even from within his own secretariat. Shigi Qutuqu and Chinqai, much better politicians than Yelu, had originally tried to hold the ring, with Chinqai protecting Yelu from the merchants and Shigi from the wrath of the old Mongols. Once they sensed that Yelu was losing favour with Ogodei, they jumped on the bandwagon and began to sabotage him.[50] Three of Chinqai's protégés, Qadaq, who had done most of the work on the census under the nominal direction of Shigi, Mahmud Yalavach and the tax-farmer Abd al-Rahman, would all be instrumental in his anti-Yelu campaign in 1239.

Other powerful opponents of Yelu inside China included his fellow Khitan Shih-mo Hsien-te-pu, who had defected from the Jin as early as 1212 and was a particular favourite with Ogodei and Chinqai (Shih-mo was a senior figure under Yelu in the secretariat) and Buyruq Qaya, an Uighur who had originally been one of Genghis's bodyguards but in the 1230s performed important functions in China as Ogodei's extraordinary envoy.[51]

Finally, Ogodei himself lost confidence in Yelu. The khan was always personally fond of him but, particularly after 1235, when Ogodei's alcoholism became dominant, he seems to have lost interest in protecting him. Yet in the early years there was a powerful rapport. Hearing that Yelu (in an uncanny echo of Pliny the Elder of whom he had certainly never heard) had declared that the daytime was for government service and the evening for study, Ogodei insisted that when Yelu came to court he had to take part in drinking sessions. Once Yelu got badly drunk at a palace reception and crept into a carriage to sleep it off. Ogodei noticed him there and shook him awake. Bleary-eyed and half asleep, Yelu did not recognise the khan and responded with some angry imprecations. Finally he realised who he was dealing with, jumped up in fright and apologised. Ogodei laughed heartily, said: 'Oh, so you prefer to imbibe in secret and get drunk alone rather than enjoy yourself with us,' and went away chortling.[52]

As the decade wore on, Ogodei began to have second thoughts. We can only guess at his motivation. It may be that Ogodei came to despise his minister after Yelu said he wanted no vengeance for the assassination plot against him, for with the Mongols revenge was a sacred duty. It may be that as Ogodei progressively withdrew from politics and national affairs, becoming a kind of Tiberius with Karakorum as his Capri, he began to find Yelu tiresome. Or perhaps, like Napoleon with the failed candidates for the marshalate, he simply concluded that Yelu was unlucky and had made too many enemies. The simplest explanation is that Yelu got in the way of the khan's enjoyment at making a killing with the Muslim merchants.[53] Attracted by Abd al-Rahman's plan to double the tax quota, in 1239 Ogodei gave him a contract for tax farming and sacked Yelu, who was allowed to retain his titles and his position as court astrologer but was no longer consulted on affairs of state. At the same time Ogodei transferred Mahmud Yalavach from Turkestan to China as his senior administrator there.

The years 1239–41 were nightmare years for the Chinese peasantry, as al-Rahman and his minions ran amok. A popular scam was to borrow money from Ogodei, buy up merchandise and then claim it had been stolen so that the locality in which the 'theft' occurred had to make good the losses (in some cases this led to an effective quadrupling of taxation, as happened between 1238 and 1239).[54] By 1241 even Ogodei had had enough of the rampant corruption, so he got rid of al-Rahman, abolished tax farming and returned to Yelu's system, without restoring the man himself.[55]

Chinqai meanwhile had brought charges of defalcation against Yelu, supported by the circumstantial evidence of corruption among some of his tax-collectors.[56] All this was subsumed in the power struggle at the top after Ogodei's death in December 1241. Once again Yelu backed the wrong horse at court, was disgraced and died in 1244, worn out and saddened by the death of his wife earlier the same year – some say, just in time, before his enemies murdered him.[57]

The regent Toregene brought back Abd al-Rahman for another reign of extortion in 1243–46. In a sense, though, Yelu had the last laugh. Chinqai came to regret bitterly his alliance with the Muslim merchants. Mahmud Yalavach and Chinqai were disgraced and had to flee for protection to Ogodei's second son Koden to escape the regent's wrath. And in a final irony most of Yelu's programme for China was carried out in the reign of Qubilai Khan.[58] A highly talented individual who could transcend petty limitations and provide a

Solomonic view of empire, Yelu was a genuine man for all seasons;
his tragedy was that his one fatal flaw was his lack of ability as a
politician.

Despite his profligacy on falconry, hunting, gambling and the generosity of his arbitrary handouts, Ogodei still had a huge surplus to
spend from the income from his investments. Some of it he devoted
to building a permanent Mongol capital, which he felt the empire
required, even though he himself, like his father, preferred to live in
a ger. Genghis, on his return from the Khwarezmian campaign, had
set up a permanent headquarters on the banks of the River Orkhon,
comprising thousands of tents and carts, and instructed his brother
Temuge to plan a proper capital. The upper Orkhon was considered
a significant area for a number of reasons: commercial, strategic,
ideological. The site of Karakorum had been a summer pasture for
the Kereit, and there had been a Buddhist temple there in the era of
the Liao dynasty.[59]

Genghis died before this could be achieved, but Ogodei took up
the baton and built the town of Karakorum, completed in 1235. Here
at last the huge number of artisans and craftsmen made prisoner on
the various campaigns came into their own, as hitherto the Mongols
had used them mainly for the routine shoring up of their own primitive technology. Craftsmen made stirrups and sighting devices for
their crossbows, blacksmiths shod horses, tanners cured furs and made
leather goods, saddles and harnesses, carpenters fashioned bows and
arrows, saddle frames, wagons and gers, plus the staves that held up
the nomads' felt tents.[60]

Some of these captives with special skills were female. A woman
from Metz (in what is now France), unlucky enough to be in Hungary
when the Mongols invaded, knew how to build luxury tents, so she
was taken back to Mongolia to ply her skills instead of being butchered – her most likely fate if she had been unskilled.[61] For these
prisoners the construction of Karakorum, and especially the palaces
therein, opened new vistas. The best of them were summoned from
the four corners of the realm, and especially from Chagatai's seat at
Beshbaliq and from the 'city of craftsmen' called Kemkemjek on the
north-west of the Mongolian plateau, patronised by Tolui's wife.
Several thousand captive families lived here, mainly Chinese and

Muslims from Turkestan, specialising in metalwork, producing weapons and agricultural implements.[62] The Mongol prince Buri (son of Mogetugen and grandson of Chagatai) also brought back from Europe a number of German goldminers and ensconced them at his court near Talas (Taraz), 170 miles north-east of modern Tashkent.[63]

The significance of the location of Karakorum was that it was situated on the shortest route from Mongolia to Transoxiana and Persia – on the east–west line of communication that ran along the northern slopes of the Tien Shan Mountains.[64] There were two distinct quarters in the town, a Muslim ghetto and a Chinatown where merchants and craftsmen lived. Ogodei wanted his capital to symbolise 'inclusiveness', pointing up the way the Mongols drew inspiration from both China and Islam. Everyone who wrote about the Mongols had something to say about Karakorum, though most agreed it was no more than a glorified village; Rubruck indeed remarked that the Parisian suburb of St Denis was more impressive.[65]

Karakorum was nevertheless a thriving town with four gates, though it was not completed until the reign of Mongke. The town walls were four miles in extent and the main streets were arranged north–south and east–west in a grid pattern, with a total absence of rich and poor areas, since official residences could be found next to mean houses and temples next to workshops. It had the peculiarity that the four gates were assigned to four different kinds of trade: at the east gate millet and grain were sold, at the west gate sheep and goats, at the north horses and at the south oxen and carts.[66]

Far the most striking thing about the town and its environs were the twelve temples, each representing a different denomination, and the palaces built for Ogodei and his immediate family. On the eastern bank of the Orkhon Ogodei ordered a Chinese bureaucrat named Liu Ming to oversee the building of his own palace, to be called Wanangong ('Ten Thousand Tranquillities').[67] Completed in a year, Wanangong palace had walls nine feet high, 240 feet long and 150 feet wide. There were nine lines of pillars from south to north and eight lines from east to west (seventy-two in all). According to Rubruck it had three great doors on the southern side. At the northern end was the seat of the great khan, with two stairways leading up to the throne. On the right side of the emperor were the seats of the princes and on the left those of the queens and imperial concubines. Outside the palace, in front of the middle door, stood a large silver 'beverage tree' (said to have been built for Ogodei by a goldsmith from the West) at the foot of which were four silver lions, each with a pipe dispensing drinks.[68] Inside the trunk of the tree four pipes, connected to different vats of liquid, led up to the top, and the ends of the pipes were bent over and downwards in the shape of a gilded serpent whose tail twisted around the trunk of the tree; the pipes poured out different drinks – rice wine, clear mare's milk and a kind of red wine which visitors likened to the highly esteemed La Rochelle wine of France.[69] In the grounds of the palace Ogodei liked to stage musical shows with jugglers, jesters, actors and dancers and to watch his favourite spectator sport: wrestling.[70] Visitors described an atmosphere of hedonism, revelry and drunkenness, with the khan well to the fore when he was in residence.

But as a true nomad Ogodei liked to be constantly on the move. A twelve-month study of his movements in 1235–36 reveals the following. He was in Karakorum until April 1235, then in the lakes and marshes of the River Orkhon until late May. He returned briefly to Karakorum only to depart for the mountains to the south-east. At the end of August he moved to his hunting lodge and winter residence on the Ongiin River to the south, where he stayed until returning to Karakorum in February 1236.[71] If in its juxtaposition of the modern and traditional perhaps Karakorum resembled most a city like Asunción, capital of modern Paraguay, as an artificial construct it was the Brasilia of its day, and the city had to be supplied daily with five hundred camel loads of food and merchandise; it was said that Ogodei had limited tolerance for the hustle and bustle of Karakorum.[72]

Ogodei once told his confidants that, of all his achievements, the thing he was most proud of was his fast courier service or yam.[73] Although Genghis had inaugurated the system of carrying intelligence by fast mounted couriers, it was Ogodei who perfected it, leaving his successors to improve the quantity rather than the quality. Most of the best data about the yam comes from the reign of Qubilai, as it was one of the things that most impressed Marco Polo. Each staging post held fresh horses and couriers as well as its own grain, cattle, other animals and wells. Ogodei considered he had done well by establishing thirty-seven posts between China just south of the Wall and Karakorum, but by the time of Qubilai this had expanded to

10,000 posts and 200,000 horses in his section of the empire alone; the yam was always a more important part of life in China, and therefore more efficiently run, than it ever was in Persia.[74]

Technically, the express courier system was divided into four segments, the *tayan* yam, relating to what we would nowadays call the diplomatic bag or pouch, the *narin* yam, for secret agents and military personnel, the *tergen* yam (stations with wagons) and the *morin* yam (simple horse stations).[75] Depending on the terrain, the distance between post stations varied: it could be as great as forty miles or as little as ten. By contrast, the Pony Express network, operated in the USA between April 1860 and October 1861 between St Joseph, Missouri and Sacramento, California until it was made obsolete by the telegraph, had its stations dotted at ten-mile intervals over 157 stations.[76] Famously the Pony Express advertised for riders as follows: 'Wanted. Young, skinny, wiry fellows not over eighteen. Must be expert riders willing to risk death daily. Orphans preferred.' But where even such prodigies of youth and endurance were expected to ride a maximum of one hundred miles a day, the Mongol equivalent – young men weighing no more than 125 pounds – had to be prepared for journeys of up to 250 miles a day. Each station had to have two hundred horses ready for use – hard riding limited each horse to about ten miles – and another two hundred grazing on a monthly rotational basis, and each station was inspected monthly.[77] As the couriers approached each post, they announced their arrival with bells, so that the locals could make all ready. If a journey had to be continued by night and there was no moon, runners went ahead of the mounted couriers with torches and flambeaux to show the way to the next post.[78]

The entire yam service was a testament to Mongol discipline and efficiency but, because the Mongols were so proud of it, they soon began to circulate tall tales about it. While it is possible to believe that some couriers possessed of great stamina could cover a distance of 1,300 miles with only brief rests, the claim that their torch-bearing runners could cover 160 miles in twenty-four hours strains credulity in the light of times clocked up by modern marathon runners.[79]

By the late 1230s Ogodei was linked by super-fast courier service with all important Mongol princes and oligarchs and could communicate with men like Chagatai and Batu in a matter of days. In theory, only people on official business and bearing a *paiza* or tablet were allowed to use the yam service. The tablet was an official pass of wood, silver and gold, engraved in the Uighur script. The Mongol army was in charge of the service, but the costs were largely dumped onto the peasantry, who had to bear the expense of accommodating couriers and providing forage for horses; only where the posts were too far from trunk roads did the khan 'graciously' consent to foot some part at least of the bill. A particular millstone for local inhabitants were the official messengers or couriers (*elchi*) who could requisition horses for themselves and their escorts and had carte blanche to behave in an arrogant and high-handed manner. Because these officials could also commandeer caravans, bandits often disguised themselves as *elchi*.[80]

The strain on the peasantry can be gauged by one simple fact: in China 750,000 households or 6 per cent of the population were in some way connected with the yam. The penalties for non-compliance with the requirements of the system, as indeed for failure to provide any kind of labour service or pay taxes, were severe. Non-payers had their wives and children taken away while serious offenders, including those whose families had fled to avoid abduction, were chained and tortured; if the absconding families were found, they were instantly executed.[81] But the draconian penalties did not stop the flight from the fields, which soon became an epidemic, and military campaigns were threatened because of the absence of taxpayers and, hence, funds.

Ambassadors and merchants were allowed to use the yam free under Genghis and Ogodei, and the system was widely abused, with the principals taking along their family, friends and in some cases escorts of 200–300 men on relatively trivial missions (or up to a thousand on important ones).[82] There was also a lot of covert grumbling that the peasantry had to pay for fripperies and indulgences, such as Ogodei's taste for fresh fruit, ordered by the khan from faraway parts but carried by the couriers at great speed. Because of this widespread corruption, in the 1250s Mongke introduced charges for all personnel. By this time the yam had become the focus for new settlements. Because horses, stock, water and food supplies provided the nucleus for colonisation, entire towns sprang up around what had once been lonely frontier posts.[83] Moreover since the yam had, right from the days of Genghis Khan, played a key part in Mongol intelligence and espionage, it became a multifaceted institution, satisfying more and increasingly complex demands as the empire expanded. Thus the yam fulfilled an important role in enabling what were originally primitive livestock breeders to maintain their sway for 150 years over the oldest and most populous civilisations of Asia.[84]

By the late 1230s the problems of the Mongol empire were becoming so complex and intricate that it would have needed a Philip II of Spain, working an 18-hour day, to cope with them. Ogodei did not even spend one hour a day on affairs of state, but increasingly retreated into a narcissistic round of dalliances, gambling and, especially, drinking. His consumption of alcohol, always great, became prodigious.[85] Chagatai warned him to cut down and seems to have brought maximum pressure to bear, for Ogodei agreed to cut his consumption in half and issued a decree that his servants should in future bring him only half his normal number of cups of wine; he then secretly ordered that the wine be served to him in vessels twice the size, so that he kept the letter of his promise to his brother but not the spirit.[86]

To say that alcohol contributed to the eventual decline of the Mongol empire risks making the historian sound like a temperance enthusiast or Edward Gibbon in one of his wilder moments, but it is a fact that once they gained access to the finer wines of the wider world, Mongol aristocrats tended to die young of obesity and cirrhosis and to suffer from gout – the khans Guyuk and Mongke were also notorious topers – and this was particularly marked among the women. Some even allege that alcoholism affected Mongol fertility in the period after Qubilai.[87]

While Ogodei was in his cups, a ferocious power struggle, with one eye on the succession, raged between various factions at court: between conservatives and progressives over the future governance of the empire (this was the draught in which Yelu Chu Cai was caught); between the descendants of Ogodei and the rival descendants of Tolui; among the princes, aristocrats and potentates, often with personal grievances which they aired at Karakorum; and even within Ogodei's own family.[88] Ogodei's first choice of successor was Kochu, his third son, but he died in 1236 on campaign in China. His next choice was his grandson Shiremun, Kochu's eldest son, but he was insufficiently assertive and Ogodei usually too intoxicated to impose his candidacy.

Koden, the second son, who had been Genghis's choice to succeed Ogodei, was generally considered too sickly to be a serious candidate.[89] Ogodei's wife Toregene meanwhile was lobbying and scheming hard to get her favourite son Guyuk promoted to the khanate, even though his health was not particularly robust.[90]

Meanwhile, there was even a faction of Nestorian Christians who wanted to make their religion the official ideology and were angered at Ogodei's partiality for Islam.[91] This was, as the saying goes, a ship that had already departed, for the empire was already showing clear signs of east–west bifurcation: Buddhism in the East and Islam in the West. Such was the predilection for Islam in the West that in Iran and elsewhere an informal deal was hammered out to allow the Yasa to coexist with sharia. And the great khan of the Ilkhans, Hulagu, actually sought and in 1258 obtained from the caliph a fatwa to state that his rule was legitimate.[92]

In these great struggles the clear winners were Toregene (over the successions) and the Mongol princes, who obtained their desired appanages in China.[93] But before any of the issues could be finally resolved, Ogodei suddenly died in December 1241. The received opinion is that he succumbed to alcoholic excess but there is much circumstantial evidence that he was poisoned, and this is the conclusion reached by Rashid al-Din. There were any number of possible motives for poisoning, but the closesness of the Ogodei and Chagatai clans suggests that the perpetrator was aiming at that particular power nexus.[94] Further circumstantial evidence comes from the death of Chagatai soon afterwards (in 1242) and the even more mysterious death of Koden sometime in 1246–48. The official line was that Chagatai was killed in a hunting accident when he was wounded by a recoiling arrow, but it is suggested that this is no more than wishful thinking by his Islamist enemies.[95]

Ogodei was buried in his personal appanage of Dzungaria, not at Genghis' (pretended) burial site on Burqan Qaldun. He left behind a grove to grow for his soul and ordered that anyone who so much as cut a twig from it was to be flogged mercilessly.[96] Thus departed a great figure in Mongol history. As part of his legacy he left what was probably the Mongols' greatest single exploit: the conquest of Russia and eastern Europe.

16

The Invasion of Eastern Europe

In 1235 Ogodei held a great quriltai on the slopes of Mount Dalan-Daba ('the seventy passes') in Mongolia.[1] The khan, who if he had known anything of the Romans would have approved of their motto *festina lente* ('make haste slowly') spent a leisurely month, alternating carousing with meetings of his grand council. Finally he announced that, with the wars against Jalal al-Din, Jin China and Korea all success-fully completed, the next target for the Mongols would be Russia and eastern Europe; on the list of those to be definitively subdued were the Cumans, the Volga Bulgars, the Russians, all the peoples of the Crimea, and the Hungarians.[2]

This decision has usually been considered to have been prompted either by mindless glory-hunting or the Mongols' sense of their 'manifest destiny' that impelled them to world conquest in accordance with the wishes of the great god Tengerri. In fact it was more prosaically based. As more and more Mongol princes, begotten as a result of Genghis's policy of intermarriage, reached adulthood, they demanded the wealth and privileges, the lands and appanages of the previous generation. These aspirations had to be satisfied or a dangerous pre-civil war situation would arise. Since Siberia was a frozen wasteland, and the subcontinent of India much too hot for Mongol tastes, that left just two possibilities: expansion south into Song China or expansion west to Russia.

Ogodei fully intended to press ahead with the conquest of southern China but he was aware of the difficulties – principally that the Mongols had not yet gained the necessary experience of riverine and maritime warfare[3] – and thought of it as a longer-term project. But in the West there was no obvious obstacle, as Jebe and Subedei's great raid of 1221–23 had demonstrated. It was time to put flesh on the bones of the famous boast about the westward boundary of Jochi's ulus – 'as far as our horses' hooves can travel' – and ascertain just how far that was.

Ogodei was aware that the conquest of Russia and Europe was the greatest and most ambitious the Mongols had ever undertaken. Relatively speaking, both the Jin realm and the empire of Khwarezmia were on Mongolia's doorstep, but in this case Ogodei's armies would be operating at least 8,000 miles from their home base, with all the massive logistical and commissariat problems such huge distances would engender.[4] Always circumspect, Ogodei planned for the great adventure painstakingly – it is possible that it was the administrative strain of working out the enterprise to the last detail that wore him out and made him determined on a life of pure pleasure thereafter.

The most basic thing was to ensure a steady supply of horses, beasts of burden and 'meat on the hoof'. Additional taxes were decreed. Because of an empire-wide shortage of horses by 1233, the previous levy of one horse in every hundred in private hands was raised to the very steep one in ten, and a new tax in cattle of one in every hundred was instituted.[5]

Between 120,000 and 130,000 troops were assembled; Ogodei ordered that every ulus, appanage, town and city had to contribute men. Batu, son of Jochi, was given supreme command of the expedition and assigned 4,000 elite Mongol troops – his 'Immortals' or Old Guard – as the core of his force. More Mongols joined him from the four corners of the realm but most of the rest of the soldiers were Turks, and questions were raised at the quriltai about their loyalty and reliability. However, they were well trained and disciplined and Ogodei, a shrewd judge, had confidence in them, rightly, as it turned out.[6]

Although Batu was titular commander, as the brains of the entire operation Ogodei relied on the 59-year-old Subedei, by 1235 a hardened veteran of dozens of campaigns. Both Genghis and Ogodei had had their doubts about Subedei on the grounds that he was a military prima donna who did not collaborate with other commanders but, until 1232, he had a powerful champion in Tolui, the one member of the Mongol royal family with a true appreciation of the older man's gifts. Instancing the very successful collaboration with Jebe in 1221–23, Tolui argued that the problem was not that Subedei was a prima donna but that he could not suffer military fools gladly; he esteemed and respected Jebe, another military genius, but had only contempt for Genghis's overpromoted favourites like Shigi Qutuqu. Ogodei, who adored his brother Tolui, listened to the eulogy and was eventually won round.[7]

The omens for a successful collaboration this time were perhaps not propitious. Batu seems to have been a divisive figure, not without ability but hardly a Jebe or a Muqali. The Franciscan Carpini, who observed him closely in 1245, recorded this verdict: 'Batu is kindly towards his own men, nevertheless he is greatly feared by them; in battle he is the most cruel of men, very shrewd and also extremely cunning in war, for he has now been fighting for many years.'[8] Sadly, we lack a proper physical description of the future khan of the Golden Horde, for Rubruck remarked only that Batu was 'about the height of my lord John of Beaumont' – which drew from a Russian historian the following sardonic comment: 'It is a pity we have not had the honour of knowing M. de Beaumont.'[9] Other notable Mongol grandees who joined the expedition were Berke, Shiban and Orda, Batu's brothers; Orda, as the eldest of Jochi's sons, should have had precedence over Batu but all the sources describe him as a military lightweight, lacking in personal gravitas.[10]

Also present were Mongke and Bujek (Tolui's son), Baidar and Buri (son and grandson of Chagatai), Ogodei's sons Guyuk and Qadan and his grandson Qaidu, and Subedei's son Uriankhadai. It was meant to be a glittering array of all the talents, emphasising that this conquest was a major effort by the entire empire and that all its resources were being harnessed;[11] it was certainly an impressive turnout, containing two future great khans and two future khans of the Golden Horde. Ogodei had originally wanted to command the host in person, but he was dissuaded by Mongke at the quriltai.[12]

It was typical of Ogodei – and it showed him to be a true son of Genghis – that he masked his ultimate intentions by sending a perfunctory raiding expedition to Sind in 1236, to keep potential targets of the mighty expeditionary host guessing as to his true intentions. It may have been as a result of this probe, which seemed to portend invasion, or the series of stiff notes Ogodei had sent the Delhi sultan about his indulgence of Jalal al-Din in the 1220s, that obliged the sultan to make a token submission to the Mongols.[13] At any rate, the last possible uncertainty on the Mongol flank had been removed, and Chormaqan had secured all strategic objectives south of the Caucasus.

Ogodei's first task was to eliminate the Volga Bulgars and the Cumans as a military factor. The Mongols were initially angry with the Cumans for two reasons: they had given shelter to the Merkit and sided with shah Muhammad.[14] War had dragged on between the Mongols and the Cumans from 1216 to 1229, most intensively during the great raid by Subedei and Jebe in 1221–23, but the Mongols had failed to deliver a knockout blow; it was the same story with the Volga Bulgars.[15]

In 1229 Ogodei sent out Subedei on a campaign against both these gadflies; he defeated their combined forces in the Urals north of the Caspian and sacked the town of Saqsin on the lower reaches of the Volga but did not follow up his victory; as this was most untypical of him, one must presume it was because he had received orders summoning him back to the front in China.[16] The best he was able to achieve was to enrol some of the defeated Cumans into the Mongol army, though the majority fled west. Even while he dealt the Jin a mortal blow, Ogodei continued to send forces into the steppe (three tumens under Batu in 1232) to harry both Bulgars and Cumans, but although the Mongols laid waste vast swathes of territory and did massive damage to landscape and property, they ran into unexpectedly stiff opposition on the battlefield, and little was achieved.

Ogodei was irritated by the lack of progress made in this theatre but he underrated the difficulties of pacifying such a numerous people; only when he committed huge forces to the task in 1235 did it become feasible.[17] After the quriltai Ogodei took Subedei aside and made him personally responsible for the final subjugation or extermination of both Cumans and Bulgars.

The Mongol army moved out westwards, Batu and his brothers forming the vanguard and departing in late 1235; Subedei and the main force followed in February–March 1236.[18] The entire force rendezvoused on the borders of the Volga Bulgars' territory; at last Subedei had the numbers to deal decisively with this arrogant foe who had singed his beard in 1222. His revenge was terrible. Commanding perhaps 40,000 men against an enemy force of 50,000, he caught the Bulgars at Bolgar on the Volga (south of its confluence with the Kama) in autumn 1236 and routed them; the slaughter was terrific.[19] Then he destroyed the Bulgar capital, thus ending the Bulgars' role as middlemen in the trade between northern Europe and Central Asia. Some of the Bulgars fled west for refuge with the Russian principalities. Two important Bulgar chiefs initially submitted, then rebelled, calling down massive retaliation.[20] The Mongols systematically destroyed any possible rallying point in their rear, sacking the Bulgar towns of Bilyar, Bolgar, Kenek, Zhukotin and Suvar. All tribes from the Urals to the Volga – Chermisi, Bashkirs, Mordvinians, Burtasi, Saksinians, Ossetians were conquered or submitted.[21] All these tribes became vassals of the Golden Horde.

Subedei obediently followed Genghis's original instructions and handed over the territory to Jochi's sons; Orda received the land between the Irtysh and the Urals while Batu got the greater prize of the western steppe and the (as yet unconquered) Russian principalities.[22] There was little left of the Volga Bulgars: four-fifths of them were said to have perished in the devastating Mongol campaign.[23]

As soon as he had defeated the Bulgars at Bolgar, Subedei detached part of his army and assigned it to the younger commanders, with orders to search out and destroy the Cumans while he mopped up in Volga Bulgar country. He considered it important to 'blood' all his charges (Batu and his brothers, Mongke, Buri, Qadan and so on) before the invasion of Russia; each was given a separate assignment against different sub-tribes of the Cumans.[24] The Cumans, just as formidable as the Bulgars, were shamanists whereas the Volga Bulgars were Muslims.[25]

Although the Mongols devastated their territory, they were massively inconvenienced by the guerrilla warfare waged by the most intelligent Cuman chief, Bachman. Mongke, the future Great Khan, directed operations against him, making spectacularly effective use of the battue tactics on which he had been weaned. Mongke, with Bujek as his deputy, used a flotilla of two hundred huge river boats, said to contain one hundred men each. This armada cruised the Volga, inspecting the forests on both banks and gradually tightening the ring on Bachman.[26]

An advanced detachment combing overland found evidence of a recently abandoned camp. The Mongols met an old woman who told them that Bachman was holed up on a nearby island. The detachment had no boats with which to cross to the island but, seemingly miraculously, a high wind suddenly arose and lowered the level of the river, allowing the Mongols to ford across.[27] Once landed on the island, they achieved complete surprise and butchered the Cumans where they stood guard; one of them managed to raise the alarm but in the scramble to escape most of those in the encampment drowned in the Volga. The Mongols captured Bachman and bore him in triumph to Mongke, who was jubilant when he heard about the 'wind miracle': 'Heaven has opened my way,' he exclaimed. Mongke then ordered Bachman to kneel before him, but the Cuman chief refused. 'I have myself been a king and do not fear death,' he said. 'I am not a camel that I should kneel.'[28] He also taunted the Mongols by saying that their men left on his island would be trapped there when the waters rose. The enraged Mongke ordered Bujek to cut him in two with a giant sword.[29]

With the Cumans brought to heel, by autumn 1237 there were no potential enemies left east of Russia. The Cumans, though, had not quite been finished off, and it would take another campaign in 1239 before the Mongols finally gave them the *coup de grâce*. Once again the Mongols' greater discipline and the disunity of their foes had handed them the advantage. One estimate is that there were 600,000 Cumans on the steppes. If we assume one-tenth of that figure as warriors – and this is a very conservative figure given the crossover between pastoralists and warriors – the Cumans could have fielded an army of at least 60,000; such a host, if united, could even have conquered Russia. But, fatally for them, the various clans and factions among the Cumans could never make common cause.[30]

Batu and Subedei now began their invasion of Russia, first targeting the eastern and northern principalities. Although the Russians had had at least a year's warning of grave danger on their eastern borders, they had done nothing, perhaps thinking the Mongol–Cuman clash was some kind of civil war within the domains of their old enemy the Polovtsians. In many ways the prelude to the great Russian invasion of 1237–40 was uncannily like the run-up to Subedei and Jebe's great raid fifteen years earlier, with the period 1223–37 a carbon copy of 1200–22. The same petty factionalism, complacency and lack of interest in the interlopers' identity on display in the earlier period was repeated.[32]

If there was any beneficiary in the Russian power struggles of 1223–37 it was Suzdalia which, significantly, had taken no part in the great defeat at Kalka. Novgorod was the cockpit for conflict in northern Russia, and the key puppet-master was Yuri of Suzdalia, Grand Prince of Vladimir.[33] Novgorod was the scene both of princely faction and of acute conflicts within the boyar class. Meanwhile in southern Russia Daniel Romanovich of Galicia and Volhynia, the princes of Smolensk and Michael of Chernigov were locked in a struggle for control of Kiev. Finally, in 1235, the turmoil in the south erupted in a great civil war; between 1235 and

1240 the city of Kiev changed hands seven times. The upshot was that southern Russia was exhausted, with Suzdalia and Novgorod emerging as the most powerful states in the land of Rus, though Novgorod was beginning to be threatened from the west, both from predatory German merchants and Catholic missionaries wanting to convert the Livonian tribes to the western form of Christianity.[34]

Quite why the princes of Smolensk, Chernigov and Galicia acted like this despite a terrible threat looming from the east is a moot point: it has been variously explained as greed, mindless ambition and just plain stupidity. It was certainly self-destructive folly, as it is estimated that a united Russia could have fielded at least 100,000 troops, if all major cities and the Polovtsians contributed to the levy.[35] But it meant that any chance of a united Russian front against the Mongols was vain. Batu and Subedei could pick off the principalities at their leisure, even enjoying the (for the Mongols) unusual pleasure of local superiority in numbers. The Russians had no central command, no liaison between cities and, crucially, no credible system of intelligence and espionage and thus no knowedge of the Mongols' advanced siege techniques; their clash with the Mongols was a classic of amateur versus professional.

Meanwhile Batu and Subedei decided, rightly, to strike at the most powerful opponent first. Displaying his usual improvisatory genius, Subedei elected to strike in the depth of winter, when frozen rivers meant that horses could cross on the ice and supplies and materiel could be conveyed easily by sledge.[36] Catching the Russians completely off balance by his winter campaign, Subedei was about to succeed where Napoleon and Hitler would later fail.

The Mongols' first target was Ryazan, about 200 miles south-east of Moscow. This was held by the princes of Ryazan, Roman and his brother Yuri. The princes foolishly rejected Subedei's 'surrender or die' demand (the surrender to be accompanied by a tithe of the city's wealth) and sent frantically for help to Yuri of Vladimir. Subedei opened the siege on 16 December 1237 and methodically surrounded the town with a palisade. After five days Ryazan fell, and the usual massacre ensued. Roman by now had walled himself in Kolomna, halfway to Moscow, but Yuri of Vladimir, along with his wife and family, was taken and executed.[37] Yuri did send reinforcements but they had barely started their journey when they learned that Ryazan had fallen. One of the medieval Russian chroniclers lamented its downfall:

They burned this holy city with all its beauty and wealth . . . And
churches of God were destroyed and much blood was spilled on the
holy altars. And not one man remained alive in the city. All were dead
. . . And there was not even anyone to mourn the dead.[38]

Reinforcements were sent to Roman too, and again they arrived too
late, for Kolomna was taken and gutted, the Mongols' fury being
accentuated by the death of Genghis's son Kolgen (by his favourite
wife Qulan) during the siege. Roman himself was killed in the fighting,
and Kolomna remained a ruin for decades.[39]

The Mongols next advanced on Moscow, then an insignificant town,
defeated Vladimir, one of Grand Duke Yuri's sons, sacked Moscow and
then proceeded to take another fourteen towns in a lightning campaign.[40]
One or two towns held out for a few days at most. Finally it was the
turn of the capital, Vladimir, which had been left in charge of Yuri's
sons Vsevolod and Mstislav; this succumbed after an eight-day assault.
Batu erected a palisade around the town before bringing up scaling
ladders and catapults. On the morning of 7 February he launched a
massive attack, the defences were broken into in four places and by
noon most of the serious fighting was over. The garrison in the citadel
held out for another twenty-four hours. The rest of the resistance,
including refugees and all female members of Prince Yuri's family, took
refuge in the Cathedral of the Assumption, which they foolishly thought
of as sanctuary (as if the Mongols understood the customs of European
Christianity) and where they perished in the flames as it was burnt
down around them, or were butchered when trying to escape the
inferno. The surrender of the garrison led to its inevitable massacre.[41]

Finally the Mongols ran Grand Prince Yuri himself to earth at the
River Sit' (a tributary of the Mologa) on 4 March 1238. The lacklustre
Yuri was trying to make contact with his brother's army, had prepared
no contingency plans in the event of being intercepted by the Mongols
and, not surprisingly, was heavily defeated; he himself joined the
growing roster of royal Russian casualties and perhaps he was glad
to die, given that his entire family had perished, most of them in the
conflagration at Vladimir. The Mongols claimed they had executed
him, but the truth was that the Russians panicked and Yuri's generals
callously beheaded him in the hopes that this sacrificial victim would
delay the inevitable Mongol pursuit. Yuri's title of Grand Duke was

taken over by his brother Yaroslav, who left his ruling position in Kiev and ceded the city to Michael of Chernigov.[42]

At this stage the Mongols divided their forces to effect a huge sweep through northern Russia and crush any remaining pockets of defiance. Batu took a north-easterly track while Subedei headed north-west, into the territory of Novgorod. The city of Novgorod itself was an obvious magnet for the Mongols because of its plethora of artisans: shoemakers, silversmiths, leather workers, tanners, coppersmiths, steel smelters, ironworkers, woodworkers, carpenters, lathe turners, coopers, engravers, spoon makers, joiners, bone carvers, icon painters, spinners, weavers, bakers, brewers and fishmongers.[43] If the Mongols had followed their usual practice of transporting all skilled workers in a city, they would have had to transfer two-thirds of the city to Mongolia. Novgorod boasted a modern drainage system and three cathedrals but was a constricted and overcrowded city, with a farrago of courtiers, boyars, merchants, craftsmen, free men, serfs and slaves, not to mention visiting traders, all crammed into a relatively tiny space. Quite apart from the extreme political factionalism that disfigured it, it was a place of tragedy, notorious for the high rate of epidemics, even with all the care taken over hygiene. It was also a firetrap, where conflagrations were frequent: 4,300 houses were destroyed in one fire in 1211 and a similar number in another inferno in 1231.[44] Novgorodians had a reputation for callous selfishness; they had been conspicuously absent at Kalka in 1222 and never displayed solidarity with the other Russian princes.

It was not entirely surprising, then, that when Subedei laid siege to the city of Torzhok, the most south-easterly town in the principality of Novgorod, and the inhabitants sent frantic pleas for help to the capital, they were ignored.[45] Even unaided, Torzhok put up a furious resistance and fell only on 23 March after a two-week siege. The next obvious target was Novgorod itself, but Subedei suddenly turned back when only fifty-five miles from the city. It was said that a spring thaw made the ground too muddy for effective use of horses, but this was Novgorodian propaganda put out years after the event. In fact the thaw was at least a month away. What happened was that Novgorod sent a massive bribe and pledged to pay tribute in future as a Mongol vassal.[46] This satisfied the usual 'surrender or die' requirement, so the Mongols turned south.

On the way back to base, Subedei showed himself once again a man of unusual intelligence: he avoided all areas he had devastated on the way north, bypassed the surviving towns so as not to get bogged down in irrelevancies and posed as a champion of ordinary people by pointedly raiding boyars' estates only. His colleague Batu, however, did miscalculate when the town of Kozelsk in Kaluga province proved too tempting. Thinking he had easy pickings, Batu found himself held up by a seven-week siege. Despite the loss of face, he had to send to Subedei for significant reinforcements before he could reduce it. In his fury at this defiance, he made a point of slaughtering every human being when the town finally fell.[47]

Subedei and Batu reunited and called a long halt for rest and recreation, spending the remainder of 1238 and most of 1239 on the steppes west of the River Don and calling for fresh mounts from Mongolia. They also recruited large numbers of steppe horses uplifted from the Cumans and other tribes – breeds such as Kazakh, Altai, Trans-Baikal, Yakut and Kirgiz, all, like their own ponies, capable of working in very cold weather and with very strong hooves.[48] The Mongol leaders rested their men in rotation, using some for garrison duties in the key conquered towns and others for campaigning; probably about half the total force would be campaigning and the other half on furlough at any given time.

Eager to increase the experience of his young commanders, Batu assigned each one a separate task, directed against the tribes of northern Caucasia and the Cumans of the south Russian steppes. Berke was sent east to extirpate the Cumans, who had revived since their defeats in 1237; Shiban and Buri waged war in the Crimea against Polovtsians, Circassians and Ossetians; Mongke and Qadan hounded the Alans in Caucasia. There was yet another defeat for the Georgians, who from 1222 to 1238 were beaten in six major battles, against either the Mongols or Jalal al-Din.[49]

These campaigns were all spectacularly successful. Shiban and Buri made an example of the town of Sudaq in the Crimea; sacked by Jebe and Subedei in 1222, it now received a second dose of Mongol mercy.[50] Mongke completed the conquest of the southern steppe area in 1239 when he took the Alan capital of Maghas.[51] Berke's triumph against the Cumans was even more resounding. Routed over and over again, the principal Qangli chieftain Koten finally took 40,000 survivors west in a large-scale migration; a local ruler on the Danube was obliged to allow them passage across the river and through Bulgaria in a southerly direction. Proceeding through Thrace, which they systematically laid waste, Koten and his myrmidons then changed direction until they finally reached the borders of Hungary, where a message was sent to King Bela promising massive conversion to Christianity if Koten and his men were allowed to settle peacefully on Hungarian soil. In an evil hour Bela agreed; the concession was to lead to huge repercussions.[52]

In twelve months the Mongols had achieved wonders of pacification on the steppes by proceeding patiently and securing their rear; lesser commanders might have been tempted to achieve the conquest of southern Russia prematurely, but Subedei bided his time. The year 1239 was one of those when, it seemed, the Mongols could do no wrong. One party of outriders even penetrated as far north as Karelia on the borders of Russia and Finland.[53] The Mongols also learnt of the Arctic Ocean from discussing it with Finns and others; hearing of polar winters, they dubbed it the Sea of Darkness.[54]

With the army thoroughly rested, reorganised and brought up to strength by reinforcements from Mongolia, Batu and Subedei waited until late summer 1240 before striking south into Ukraine. For reasons not entirely clear, Subedei seems to have left this campaign almost entirely to Batu. He began by taking and sacking the city of Pereyaslav and sweeping through the southern half of the principality of Chernigov, adding Glukhov, Sosnitsa, Khorobor and Snovsk to the lengthening tally of pillaged towns. Batu ranged up and down the Desna River (a left-hand tributary of the Dnieper) and its tributary, the River Seym, before closing in on the city of Chernigov. The Mongols next followed their usual procedure of surrounding a major city and then bringing giant catapults and trebuchets to bear. One of these had a range of three hundred yards and could hurl stones so heavy that it took four men to lift each one. The senior Russian prince led a sortie but this ended in a disastrous defeat, after which the city surrendered (18 October 1240).[55]

There was even less question than before of the Rus princes making common cause in face of the deadly peril that threatened them. Yaroslav of Vladimir, who controlled Novgorod, was locked in deadly rivalry with Michael of Chernigov for the putative title of greatest prince in Russia. Michael seems to have intrigued with the Lithuanians to attack Smolensk, but Yaroslav defeated the alien intruders in 1239. It is certain that he and his eldest son Alexander had already made a definitive submission to the Mongols.

Alexander, who had been left in charge of Novgorod since 1236 at the age of 16, won himself the title of Nevsky when he defeated a small force of Swedes on the River Neva in 1240.[56] Both this, and the battle he won two years later against the Teutonic Knights, have been inflated out of all proportion by Russian state propaganda from the thirteenth century to the present day. It is quite clear that the Swedish battle, fought on 15 July 1240, was little more than a skirmish, for the total of Novgorod casualties was just twenty.[57] (Historians cannot agree what the conflict between Sweden and Novgorod was about, with some opting for a secret campaign of Catholic conversion masterminded by the Pope and spearheaded by troops from Germany, Sweden and Denmark, and others concluding that it was an outward overspill of ancient Russo-Swedish conflicts over Finland and Karelia.)[58]

Worsted by his deadly enemy Yaroslav of Vladimir, Michael was in no mood to fight the mighty Mongols, so he fled westwards in great haste and, like Koten and the Cumans, found sanctuary in Hungary. But he left behind a legacy that doomed Kiev. After the surrender of Chernigov, Mongke and his retinue rode to the outskirts of Kiev, whose beauty amazed Tolui's son. Hearing that there was a strong peace party in Kiev, he sent envoys to the city proposing very generous terms if the burghers surrendered. The useless Michael killed the envoys to prevent any chance of surrender, then rode off to safety, leaving the hapless citizens to reap the whirlwind. Everyone knew that the killing of Mongol emissaries was the *ne plus ultra* and that no quarter would subsequently be given.[59]

Accordingly Batu advanced on Kiev from the south, swatting aside the Turkic tribe, the Karakalpaks, who were supposedly the southern buffer between Kiev and any invader, and invested the city. Even without Michael's desertion, morale was hardly sky-high in the city. For the previous five years disputes about the succession to the principality and the constant intervention of other princes had weakened it spiritually and morally. In seventy years it had been sacked four times: by Suzdalia, Galicia-Volynia, Chernigov and Smolensk, and economically it had declined in comparison with all four of these scourges. Its location so close to the power bases of the Polovtsians scarcely helped. As one historian has commented, 'the rapid changes of rulers in Kiev over the past five years can hardly have inspired the inhabitants of the capital with confidence.'[60]

Nevertheless, Kiev was far from negligible, and the inhabitants put up a surprisingly strenuous defence, led by a senior officer or *voivode* named Dmitri, who had been left behind when every last prince followed Michael's example and bolted westward. Kiev, with a population of at least 40,000 and probably closer to 100,000, was well defended, on a hilly position, by a ring of forts along the River Dnieper and on the northern and western approaches on the right bank; Kiev did not expand onto the left bank until the twentieth century. Its citadel was on high ground, surrounded by palaces and churches in an inner ring and, in an outer, by a suburban area by the river where the merchants and artisans lived, proudly surveying the wharves and the Dnieper River that linked Kiev to all major cities in Rus; the poorer townspeople cultivated plots of land beyond the city walls.[61]

Batu directed the siege with Mongke and Orda as his chief aides, making sure to terrify the Kievans with a dreadful cacophony, in which mingled the bellowing of camels, the neighing of horses and the whooping of Mongols singing out their war cries; it was said that the din was so bad that conversation inside the city was impossible.[62] The Mongols were present in force, as indicated by their ability to surround and circumvallate the entire city. They located their siege artillery near the most south-easterly of the four great gates of Kiev ('the Polish Gate') on a wooded slope that gave good cover. It was said to have taken the Mongols ten days to blast through the city's four sets of fortifications, but once the walls crumbled and they were inside the city, the end came quickly.[63] The garrison attempted a last stand in and around the Church of Tithes in the centre of the city, but there were so many refugees and defenders, most of whom had also brought their goods and chattels, that they caused the upper floors of the great church to give way under the combined weight.[64] Both the citadel and the church collapsed almost simultaneously. All was over by the feast of St Nicholas (patron saint of Rus) on 6 December 1240. The siege had lasted nine days.

Batu gave the city over to sack and plunder but spared the life of Dmitri, who had impressed him with his exceptional courage – and also to show Mongol contempt for all the runaway princes.[65] Even though Kiev had often fallen to its enemies, the ease with which Batu had overcome it created a sensation in western Europe for, despite its decline, the splendid city was still regarded as the showpiece of Rus and the spiritual mother of the Russians. Now it lay in ruins, laid waste and reduced to rubble, the devastation so great and the pile of skulls and bones so high that it depressed the Franciscan Carpini when he passed by five years later.[66] It was the end of the Old Russia and the dawning of the dominance of the Golden Horde. Predictably, the divines of the Orthodox Church concluded that the downfall of Rus was a consequence of Russian sinfulness. Bishop Serapion of Vladimir claimed that God had allowed the Mongols to conquer the land of Rus because of the evil and lawlessness that ran from top to bottom in the social hierarchy.[67]

After Kiev Batu pressed on into Galicia-Volynia, but his campaign there was something of a walkover, with the exception of brief defiance shown by the town of Kolodyazhin on the River Sluch. The cities of Vladimir-Volynski and Halych fell after brief sieges, and Ladyzhyn and Kamenets in Podolia joined the inventory of sacked towns. Daniel of Galicia became the final prince to flee, making his way to Poland and Hungary. The boyar Dmitri of Kiev proved a valuable adviser to Batu, but his champions go too far when they claim that it was he who directed the Mongols' attention to eastern Europe; Hungary was already in Batu's sights once the Cumans had fled there.[68]

In any case, the conquest of Russia was now complete. Yet there had been casualties, not from Russian valour or force of arms but because of the factionalism among the Mongols themselves which Genghis had been able to contain but which now threatened to overwhelm Ogodei and his empire. At one of the many victory banquets held by Batu during his non-stop string of victories, a drunken wrangle developed when Batu pledged his troops in wine and took the first swig from a ceremonial goblet. Guyuk, who hated Batu, protested that Batu was in no way superior to the other princes and should not have arrogated such a privilege.[69] He was egged on by Buri, the grandson of Chagatai and son of Mogetugen who had perished at the siege of Bamiyan in 1221.[70] While Chagatai had shown no particular feeling for Mogetugen, he adored Buri, even though his grandson was both a hothead and a notorious drunkard. Mongke, who respected

Batu and knew that Ogodei had worked hard to reconcile the house of Jochi to the other princely dynasties, got on his feet to defend Batu. At this Guyuk raised the temperature with two egregious insults. Batu, he said, was just an old woman with a quiver; he was thus an inferior and, like all women risen above their station, should be kicked and trodden on.[71] Even while the assembled company was reeling, not quite believing what they had heard, Guyuk ratcheted up the tension another notch by saying that people like Batu should be whipped or hit with burning sticks – the traditional Mongol punishment for female criminals – implying that Batu was both evil and unnatural.[72] As if this was not enough to stupefy the audience in the ger, yet another dissident arose to lash Batu with his tongue. This time the reprobate was Harqasun, a minor crony in the Guyuk entourage. He proposed that a tail be attached to Batu – to attach a tail to someone was the Mongol way of bringing someone into hatred, ridicule and contempt.[73]

The banquet broke up in universal hubbub and uproar. Batu had the three offenders arrested and, given a free hand, would have executed them on the spot. But he knew that Ogodei was governed by *raison d'état* and would think this an overreaction, almost certain to plunge the empire into civil war. He sent the three of them back to Mongolia under heavy guard, together with a written statement of what had occurred, signed and verified by witnesses of the most impeccable standing. When Ogodei read the report, he was said to have fallen into the most towering rage courtiers had ever experienced from a khan, even in Genghis's day. At first he contemplated executing the trio and refused to see Guyuk, even though he was his son. He exclaimed angrily to his entourage: 'May he and he alone rot like an egg.'[74]

After keeping him in suspense for a few days while he mulled things over, Ogodei summoned Guyuk for the most devastating tongue-lashing. He had since learned that Guyuk was deeply unpopular with his troops because he was a by-the-book martinet. 'Do you think that the Russians surrendered because you were mean to your men?' he began with heavy sarcasm. 'Or because you captured two or three warriors, you imagine you won the war? From what I learn, you didn't even capture a single goat.'[75] He ordered the punishment: Guyuk was to return to Batu and make a public apology in front of the entire army or he would be put to death. As for Buri, Ogodei hesitated to offend Chagatai, so he sent him his grandson and left the punishment to him; Chagatai sent Buri back to Europe on identical terms. Interestingly, it has been pointed out that both decisions were against the code of the Yasa.[76] Maddeningly, the sources do not tell us what happened to Harqasun, except that he survived; the entire episode is cloudy, and the authorities cannot even agree whether Harqasun was the son of Eljigidei or a mere commoner.

The upshot was interesting.[77] Ogodei died before Guyuk began his journey westward, so Guyuk was released from the necessity of apologising to the detested Batu. Buri did return, made his peace with the commander-in-chief and served with distinction in Wallachia. But Batu and his ally Mongke never forgot the insult. Guyuk died young in 1248 after two years as Great Khan, so was always beyond their reach, but both Buri and Harqasun were executed during the great purges of 1251–52; Buri was beheaded and Harqasun run through with a sword by a Horde commander who had always detested him.[78]

The Mongols were now on the eastern frontiers of Poland, and in Europe their advent caused a panic among the common people that spread as far as Spain and the Netherlands.[79] The 'Mongol storm' was already sending winds and waves as far as the Atlantic. The invasion of Russia was known about in Scotland in 1238. In England in the same year there was a glut of herrings on the market (first reported in Lowestoft), because Novgorod, preoccupied with the Mongol threat, had for once failed to send its fishing fleet out into the North Sea to compete with English fishermen.[80]

Typical of the complacent attitude evinced in England was this effusion from Peter des Roches, bishop of Winchester, in a letter to Henry III: 'Let these dogs devour one another and be utterly exterminated and then we shall see the universal Catholic Church founded on their ruins and there will be one fold and one shepherd.'[81] That was also the attitude of the three popes who reigned during the chaotic period 1238–1243. One reason was the increasing tendency of peripheral European states to acknowledge the primacy of the Roman church in return for military aid from western Europe; the Rus princes had already appealed to the papacy for help, and the hope in the Vatican was that they might be prepared to abandon the 'heresies' of the Greek and Russian Orthodox churches in return for a military umbrella.[82] Indeed the more one examines the attitudes of the western kingdoms to the Mongols, the more one sees the short-termism of selfishness and pride. Defenders – and they are few – of the West at this juncture allege that kings, princes and pontiffs perceived the Mongols as putative allies because of their devastating attacks on Islamic powers, and that they saw them as the legendary Prester John, the fabled king from the East who would finally unite the world in Christendom.

There is no doubting that the Prester John legend was very strong for a while, but such ignorance did not really survive the 1220s.[83] By the mid-1230s the nature and identity of the Mongols was fairly clear. Queen Rusudan of Georgia was in frequent touch with the Vatican and her accounts of the storm from the East would have lost nothing in the telling, while Bela IV of Hungary had reported in detail about the Mongols' near-annihilation of the Cumans.[84] And a host of other evidence reached western Europe in the 1230s, leaving statesmen and decision-makers in no doubt about what they were up against.[85] Moreover, the Mongols in 1237 sent out multiple demands for submission to the western kingdoms. Bela was told as early as 1237 what to expect if he did not reverse his policy on sheltering the Cumans; even the papacy received an order to submit.[86]

Essentially, though, western European inertia and passivity in face of this unprecedented menace boiled down to a single factor: each of the principal actors, the Holy Roman Emperor Frederick II, King Louis IX of France, and the popes, all had agendas and priorities in terms of which the Mongols were a mere footnote. Louis IX (St Louis) was obsessed with organising a crusade against the Mamelukes of Egypt and paid little attention to the Mongols.[87] The record of the papacy was even more dismal. In the first half of the thirteenth century pontiffs had preoccupations very far from the Mongol empire. Pope Innocent III (1198–1216) had preached a great crusade against the Albigensians (Cathar heretics) in southern France; this bloody conflict was at white heat until 1233 and the Albigensians were not finally suppressed until 1255.[88] The sack of Byzantium by the men of the Fourth Crusade in 1204 also showed Christendom hopelessly divided.

But above all it was the campaign waged by successive popes against Frederick II that weakened the West's ability to show a united front to the Mongols. Honorius III (reigned 1216–1227) may have

been a close friend of Francis of Assissi but his record was not
otherwise distinguished. Even more myopic was Gregory IX (reigned
1227–1241), who went so far as to excommunicate Frederick in 1239.
In retaliation Frederick marched on Rome but was forced to retire.
The energies of the Pope in the crucial period 1240–41 were also
entirely directed against Frederick. In May 1241 Gregory convened a
council to depose Frederick as Emperor, but he (Frederick) intercepted the ships carrying the French and Italian prelates to the
council; he then threw them into prison and made sure they were
ill-used.[89]

Even before this high drama, pope Gregory had foolishly discounted
the threat from the Mongols. When the queen of Georgia begged
him for help against the Mongols, he replied airily that her kingdom
was too far away for help to be sent; in any case, he added, his priority
was the Islamic threat in Spain and the Near East. He turned down
a proposal from the Assassins in 1238 for a grand alliance of Christendom
and Islam against the Mongols. In the same year he showed where
his true priorities lay by preaching a crusade against the Russians
because they had opposed his previous crusade in the Balkans.[90]
Amazingly, there were five papacy-inspired crusades going on in the
1240s, and only one of them, and the least considerable, was against
the Mongols. The last of the Cathars were still holding out; Richard
of Cornwall was heading an attack on Muslims in the Holy Land; St
Louis was bending all his energies against Constantinople, ostensibly
crusading for the union of Greek and Latin churches; and the Swedes,
Danes and Teutonic Knights were moving against Novgorod where
the young Alexander Nevsky occupied a precarious perch.[91]

A small crusade was launched against Batu in 1241, though principally by the German church rather than the Pope. The army actually
set out from Nuremburg in July 1241 but stopped after marching fifty
miles, possibly because the Mongols were no longer reported on the
German border. Ludicrously chauvinistic German annalists later
claimed that Batu and Subedei had been frightened off by this 'host'.[92]
This is preposterous on two counts. In September 1241 Germany
descended into chaos as a result of the revolt of the barons against
Frederick's son Conrad, and the nation remained on the brink of civil
war for a decade; the money raised for the crusade against the Mongols
was spent instead on a crusade against the Hohenstaufen dynasty.

Secondly, there is clear evidence that the 'crusade' was a mere self-defence force and there was never any question of its entering Hungary.[93]

In any case, all ideas of general anti-Mongol crusades went into abeyance when Pope Gregory died in August 1241. He at least had promised Bela IV a crusade 'in principle' but now all was subsumed in the maelstrom of Vatican politics as the conclave was held to elect a new pontiff. Celestine IV emerged in October 1241 but lasted a mere three weeks (25 October–10 November 1241). The luckless Bela sent an embassy to Rome to lobby the new pope but the envoys' ship was caught in a storm on the Adriatic and they all drowned. When Bela tried again in June 1243, he was fobbed off by the cardinals.[94]

Yet the most culpable ostrich of all the western European leaders was the Holy Roman Emperor Frederick II, sometimes absurdly hailed as the greatest man of the thirteenth century – absurd if only because true greatness is measured by achievement, not natural talents or abilities. Known as 'the wonder of the world (*Stupor Mundi*)', Frederick was a man of extraordinary energy and ability who spoke six languages (German, French, Latin, Greek, Sicilian and Arabic), a patron of science, literature and the arts but also a religious sceptic who denounced Moses, Jesus and Muhammad as frauds and liked to mock organised religion and utter deliberate blasphemies.[95] Nietzsche hailed him as the first European and some historians have glossed this as first modern ruler. Dante, on the other hand, consigned him to the sixth region of his Inferno for crusading while excommunicate and recruiting Saracens into his army. Red-haired, bald, myopic, with green eyes like a serpent, Frederick was fascinated by astrology, besotted with exotic animals but contemptuous of human beings, to the point where he conducted Nazi-style 'scientific' experiments on them.[96] He was also an expert falconer and world authority on the birds. When Batu sent him the order to submit, Frederick laughed it off and said that he would do well as a Mongol subject, since both he and Ogodei were top-class falconers.[97] He disdained his native Germany but adored his kingdom in Sicily. After his coronation in 1220 at the age of 26, he stayed just one year (1236–37) in Germany, with the remainder spent either in Sicily or on the Sixth Crusade; he was criticised for this much as Richard the Lionheart was for his almost total absence from England.

He spent most of his reign locked in combat with the papacy in a wide-ranging conflict that disfigured Western Christendom, initially because the papal dominions blocked the route between his domains in north Italy and his realm in Sicily, which he turned into a showpiece of efficient bureaucracy.[98] This struggle reached its apogee during the pontificate of Gregory IX; the ultimate point of absurdity was in mid-February 1241 when, with the Mongols already deep inside Poland and Hungary, the Pope wrote a pastoral letter to the Hungarians calling for prayer, not against the invaders from the east but against Frederick the infidel.[99] Frederick was excommunicated four times and dubbed the Antichrist by Gregory IX. It was hoped that the election of a new pope in 1243 would change things but Innocent IV, on stepping into the shoes of the Fisherman in June, immediately confirmed the excommunication.[100]

Both Frederick and the papacy were far more interested in their own internecine conflict than the looming external threat from the Mongols, and both sides claimed they could do nothing against Batu and Subedei unless the other party bowed the head and made peace. It is true that Frederick wrote to both St Louis of France and Henry III of England to propose joint action against the Mongols,[101] but the proposal was a mere diplomatic ploy to gain propaganda advantage and show the papacy as incompetent – which it was, but so was Frederick *as regards* the Mongols. So limp was his response to the 'centaurs of the steppes' that a rumour arose that he had deliberately invited the Mongols to invade Europe.[102]

A united Europe would have been an impossible obstacle for Batu and Subedei to overcome but at the very moment of its supreme peril the West could not have been more hopelessly divided; this time the Mongols had not even had to foment any internal discontent among their enemies. Accordingly the two leaders planned their next move with confidence. Batu and Subedei planned to take the main army of 30,000, reinforced now with prisoners from Russia forced to serve in the front ranks, into Hungary. But they had to reckon with the possibility that Poland, Bohemia and even Frederick II might lend a hand to Bela IV of Hungary when they attacked. Their strategy therefore encompassed a simultaneous attack on Poland, to be led by Qadan, Ogodei's second son, and Baidar, son of Chagatai, commanding a force of about 20,000.[103]

This was of course classic Mongol strategy: protect a threatened flank by attacking the potential enemy on that flank. Qadan and Baidar had instructions not to press deeper into Moravia if they overran Poland but, once the threat to the flank was neutralised, to swing south and join Batu and Subedei in Hungary. Moving out from Volynia, the two up-and-coming Mongol princes crossed the frozen Vistula on an icy causeway on 13 February 1241 and immediately routed the Polish force waiting for them on the far side at Tursk.

Their intelligence was first-class and they knew all the Polish weaknesses, principally that the land was riven with factionalism. The Poland of the thirteenth century comprised roughly the southern half of modern Poland; the Baltic coast had been occupied by Teutonic Knights and Lithuanians, forcing the Poles inland. The rump that was left was itself divided into four mini-states.[104] There was the domain of Bolesław IV, titular king of Poland, the provinces of Cracow and Sandomir under Conrad of Masovia, Mieczysław (Mieszko) II, Duke of Oppeln-Ratibor (modern Opole and Raciborz) and Duke Henry II of Silesia; of these Henry of Silesia was easily the most powerful even though the mercurial Bolesław insisted that the other three had to bend the knee to him, with the inevitable result of ongoing civil war.[105]

The Poles were almost ludicrously mismatched against the Mongols. Discipline was poor in the Christian armies which had only the most rudimentary organisation and staff work. Aside from the four-way struggle for power, there were other internal jealousies, and commands were given out on the basis of birth, not merit. The primary weapons of the Poles were the lance and the broadsword, whose effectiveness depended on being able to get to close quarters; the Mongols by contrast had long-distance archery and even primitive explosives, and they depended on speed, not heavy armour. Finally there was the difference between a lumbering Christian commander, in the thick of battle where his standard could be easily identified, and a Mongol general who was highly mobile and communicated by flags.[106] There is evidence, too, that the Poles might already have been psychologically overawed by their opponents. By this time westerners routinely referred to the Mongols as 'Tartars' – using the name of one of the minor tribes of Mongolia but conscious of the pun on 'Tartarus', the hell of classical mythology.[107]

Advancing westward towards Lublin, the Mongols appear to have split up temporarily, with Baidar and Qadan each taking one of the two tumens Subedei had assigned to them. It is quite clear that there were two tumens operating in Poland, though the 'downsizing' school of historians likes to insist there was just one – in which case it would have been madness to divide the force.[108] While it is accepted that tumens, like Roman legions, were rarely at full strength, the extra fighters recruited from the conquered Rus states have to be taken into account.[109]

Baidar's group ran into Bolesław IV and a large army on 18 March at Chmielnik and routed him utterly. It was a devastating defeat: the best modern historian of Poland in the English-speaking world says simply that the assembled nobility of Little Poland (the south-eastern sector of the modern nation) perished all at once.[110] Bolesław fled and took no further part in the campaign, though he did allow his Moravians leave to fight on against the Mongols if they so chose. The two Mongol forces reunited soon afterwards and marched on Cracow. They found it deserted, entered it in silence on Palm Sunday and burnt it to the ground.

The Poles had meanwhile broken down the bridges over the River Oder but the Mongols were undeterred and crossed the river at Ratibor on an improvised fleet of boats. Their next target was Breslau (modern Wrocław), capital of Silesia. They took the main city with ease – some say Henry of Silesia deliberately left it as bait to slow the enemy down – but the citadel remained defiant and would have been costly to capture, so Baidar elected to bypass it.[111] He had received intelligence that Henry of Silesia was at Liegnitz (Legnica) with a large force, marking time until his brother-in-law Wenceslas I of Bohemia could join forces with him with another army. Baidar and Qadan decided not to waste time on lengthy and strategically pointless sieges of strongly fortified citadels, but to strike at Henry before he could be reinforced.[112]

And so, ten miles from Liegnitz, near Wahlstatt, on 9 April 1241, there occurred one of the most traumatic events in Polish history. The Mongols were represented by three sons of Ogodei and his brothers: Baidar, Qadan and Orda. On the Polish side, commanded by Henry of Silesia, were four main groups: Henry himself with a picked force of Silesian knights, Moravian volunteers and elite units from the military orders, the Templars and Hospitallers; Bavarians released by Bolesław; Mieczysław and the army of Oppeln/Opole;

and Sulisław, the brother of the Palatine (*voivode*) of Cracow (who had been slain at Chmielnik) with his levies, including conscripts from Greater Poland. It was, on paper, a formidable array.[113]

Henry rode to the battlefield, reasonably confident that the Mongols would find no answer to his heavily armoured knights. It was said that as he passed the church of the Blessed Virgin in Liegnitz town, a stone fell from the roof and narrowly missed his head; it was interpreted as a bad omen.[114] Henry opted to attack the Mongol centre in relays, sending successive waves against the enemy vanguard, hoping to crack it so that disarray and confusion would follow, with ranks of Mongol horsemen trampling each other. The first assault was made by his own Silesian knights and the second by Sulisław and his contingent, but both were were beaten off with a fusillade of Mongol arrows.[115] Next he sent forward the Bavarian troops previously under Bolesław's command. At this the Mongols appeared to falter and began retreating but as they did so, they set up a smokescreen on the flanks, using smoke-bombs which they had perfected in China against the Jin, gradually drawing the Polish cavalry away from their infantry and meanwhile working round their flanks unseen with their own light cavalry. Knowing nothing of such weapons, the Silesians later concocted a story that the Mongols had unfurled a huge banner from which they released a cloud of 'miasmata' with a dreadful foetor, allegedly the cause of mass vomiting in their ranks.[116]

That was a later rationalisation, for at the time the Poles were euphoric. Seeing the Mongols fleeing and a gap opening up between the Bavarian pursuers and his main force, Henry sent up the cavalry under Mieczysław in support. At this point the Mongols added subterfuge to their initial feigned retreat. They increased the smokescreen and from within the gloom made anyone in their army who could speak Polish shout out, 'Run, run!' Mieczysław was confused and suspected that the Bavarians had been ambushed, but could see nothing clearly. He decided to retreat to safety.[117] By this time the Polish quartet had become split up and confused. With perfect timing the Mongol leaders ordered the counter-attack on the strung-out Poles. Their heavy cavalry wheeled about and charged while the light cavalry deluged the Poles with arrows.

Bewilderment being first cousin to panic, it was not long before the Poles became suffused with the spirit of *sauve qui peut*, but it was too late. The Mongols picked their units off piecemeal and slaughtered them at will, using their deadly arrows to turn what started as a battle into a virtual turkey-shoot.[118] Hardly a man escaped. One who did was Mieczysław, who fled back to the security of the citadel at Liegnitz. Henry, finding himself and his knights surrounded, made several attempts to cut his way out of the ever tightening Mongol cordon but in vain; the only result for his efforts was that he had two horses shot from under him.

There are two accounts of his death. One was that he was run through by a lance under the armpit, expired and had his head cut off after death. The other, more likely, account is that the Mongols captured him and forced him to kneel beside the corpse of a beloved Mongol general killed at Sandomir before they decapitated him. His headless and naked body was later recognised by his wife Anne, allegedly because he had six toes on his left foot.[119] He was buried in the Franciscan church of St Vincent at Breslau.

Liegnitz was a catastrophe for Poland. Almost all the 20–25,000 men in their army were massacred in a disaster as complete in its own way as Hannibal's victory over the Romans at Cannae in 216 BC. The Mongols were said to have cut the ears from the fallen and filled nine gigantic sacks with them.[120] Many myths arose from the debacle at Liegnitz. One was that a large number of Teutonic Knights had died, including their Grand Master Poppo von Osterna, but the order was not represented by a single cavalryman at the battle, and Poppo himself died in 1257. Evidently there was confusion with the Templars, who did suffer grievously. Their Grand Master Ponce d'Aubon reported to St Louis that he had lost five hundred dead, including nine brothers, three senior knights and two sergeants.[121]

The two principal Polish survivors, Mieczysław and Bolesław, seemed to have learned nothing from their experience and continued feuding until the former's death in 1246. Superficially, the Mongol victory in Poland scarcely affected the course of that nation's history at all, though some historians claim that the loss of Silesia delayed Polish unification for a century. Chistendom in general reacted to the defeat with a kind of collective denial, most clearly seen in Carpini's reports in 1245 when he claimed that the Mongols were forced to withdraw after taking heavy losses at Liegnitz. Almost inevitably, given the medieval mindset on one hand and a bizarre logical alchemy on the other, the Jews were accused of having colluded with the Mongols to incite the invasion.[122]

The propagandist nonsense continued when Baidar and Qadan turned south into Moravia (the eastern part of the modern Czech Republic), hoping to locate Wenceslas I and bring him to battle. They camped for two weeks near Otmuchow, between Opole and Klodzko, resting their victorious troops. Advancing on Klodzko (on the borders of present-day Poland and the Czech Republic), they found, as at Breslau and Liegnitz earlier, that the citadel was too strong to take unless they were prepared to spend months investing it – but the orders from Batu and Subedei expressly stated that they should not be diverted from their sole concern, which was to disable the Poles so that they could not intervene in Hungary.[123] Nevertheless, in May they cut a swathe of destruction through Moravia, sacking several towns and monasteries, even raiding the border towns of Austria on the left bank of the Danube.[124]

They approached Olmutz (Olomouc) but found the castle too well defended by Jaroslav of Sternberg, a *voivode* of Wenceslas I, who was far too terrified to face the Mongols himself and skulked in the mountains of Bohemia; from this arose the absurd canard that the Mongols had suffered a serious reverse at Olmutz – one more item in the inventory of European nonsense about the invasion of 1240–42.[125] From afar Wenceslas sent out a number of small forces to try to lure the Mongols into ambush, but their intelligence was far too good to be caught in that way.[126] The common people of Moravia largely deserted the towns and hid in the woods and in caves. A few hardier souls actually tried to sell produce to the invaders and were astonished to find that the Mongols ate neither bread nor vegetables.[127] There were the usual atrocities common to victorious warriors in all eras, who consider the civilian population, and especially the women, to be fair game. Finally Baidar and Qadan received a courier from Subedei telling them of great success in Hungary and requesting their presence on garrison duties. The Mongols turned south-east, crossed the Carpathians and rejoined the main army in the land of the Magyars.[128]

17

Hungary and the Adriatic

Batu and Subedei meanwhile had closed in on Hungary, then a nation of around two million people and a little larger than the modern country in area, ranging from the Carpathians and the Transylvanian Alps to the Adriatic, including much of modern Croatia. The Mongols had correctly identified the Alfold region of the Pannonian plain as the gateway to western Europe, and an ideal base for their operations, as the puszta – a flat, treeless, savannah-like area ideal for horses and horse-breeding – most closely resembled the steppes of Central Asia and Mongolia. It was a perfect launchpad from which the rest of Europe could be invaded and conquered.[1] It was therefore a key area which should have been heavily defended by the nations of western Europe, who instead fiddled while Hungary burned.

Since Hungary was reportedly the premier military nation in Europe, with its knights the flower of medieval chivalry, it would have been in a strong position even unaided if only it had been homogeneous and united. But ever since the foundation of the nation at the beginning of the eleventh century, there had been constant disputes about the royal succession, which allowed both Byzantium and the German emperor to intervene. The reign of Bela III (1172/3–1196) has often been seen as a golden age, but the next leading member of the Arpad dynasty, the frivolous and unprincipled Andrew II (1205–1235) was a disaster.[2] For the first seven years after his father's death, Andrew conspired continuously against his brother king Emeric of Hungary, who had made him governor of Croatia and Dalmatia. These intrigues culminated with the battle of Rad in 1199 when Emeric defeated his turbulent brother and Andrew was forced into exile in Austria. The papacy patched up a peace between the warring siblings in 1200 but matters went sour again when Andrew married Gertrude of Merania, a bad influence who encouraged him to hatch further plots. Emeric died in 1204 and passed the succession to his infant son Ladislaus, who did not survive long.[3]

On his death in May 1205, Andrew succeeded. He had already proved himself amoral, unscrupulous and treacherous. When Bela III had died, he had left Andrew a huge sum of money on the strict condition that he went on crusade. Vain, lightheaded, unprincipled, Andrew used the money instead to buy himself a personal following of syco- phants and refused to go to the Holy Land, even when threatened with excommunication by Pope Innocent III.[4] His irresponsibility and selective financial generosity – that is, only to his followers – alienated the great barons who staged an attempted coup in 1213, in the course of which Gertrude was assassinated. Andrew weakly executed only the ringleader of the coup and pardoned all the other participants. Gertrude left behind two noteworthy children, Bela (later Bela IV), who became the great political survivor of Hungary (reigned 1235–1270) and Elizabeth (1207–1231), a remarkable woman who followed the tenets of Francis of Assisi and gave away all her wealth to the poor; she was later canonised by the Catholic Church.[5]

The young Bela always hated his father, and the rancour increased when in 1215 Andrew married Yolanda, niece of Henry, the Latin emperor of Constantinople, hoping (in vain) to inherit that throne also. In 1217 Andrew embarked from Split for the Fifth Crusade but had barely arrived in the Holy Land before he was homeward bound again. The conflict with the barons produced anarchy until 1222. Andrew, wildly ambitious but spendthrift, waged no fewer than four- teen wars of aggression in the first fifteen years of his reign, at the very time he was spending madly on a luxurious royal household. When he tried to increase taxation, the barons rebelled and issued the so-called Golden Bull, Hungary's version of the Magna Carta.[6] This absolved the nobility from all taxation and from the necessity of waging war outside Hungary's frontiers. But Andrew, having signed the document, showed scant respect for the Bull. Eventually the papacy was sucked into the conflict when Robert, archbishop of Esztergom put the country under interdict in 1231 because Andrew had not fulfilled the clauses of the Bull. Andrew got round this by going over the bishop's head and appealing to the Vatican. The concordat he signed with the pope in 1233 at Bereg was a shameful document, on paper generating huge revenues for the Church; the problem was that Andrew did not abide by the document and continued in his old ways.[7]

It was to general relief that he died in 1235 but young Bela, succeeding as Bela IV, opened a fresh can of worms. Anarchy prevailed throughout the kingdom, there had been a botched attempt to devalue the currency, and the great landowners had become a law unto themselves. Bela was a narrow-minded, pedantic, humourless, deeply conservative figure, whose first instinct was to annul the Golden Bull and put the clock back to the time of his namesake, the great Bela III.[8] While not able to rescind the Golden Bull without an open breach with the papacy, Bela struck out viciously at its authors and at all barons who had supported his hated father. The former he put in jail or exiled; the latter he treated more harshly and even blinded one of them. As part of his general persecution of the nobility, he denied them the right to sit in the royal presence.[9] He also reduced the power of the barons by switching the source of royal income away from land and agriculture to coinage, mining and customs duties.[10] And whereas in the past kings of Hungary had rewarded nobles who fought for them with estates and properties, Bela not only failed to continue this tradition but also expropriated such estates granted to previous generations.[11] Bela considered himself much too grand to deal with the resulting lawsuits from the nobles; he insisted that they had to deal with his chancellors and hear decisions from them. These lawsuits, in the manner of Jarndyce v Jarndyce in *Bleak House*, were deliberately designed to drag on forever, thus financially ruining those who stayed to await the outcome – which would usually turn on an irrational whim by a chancellor anyway.[12] As if all this was not enough, Bela decided to squabble with the Vatican because Gregory IX forbade him to employ Jews and Muslims in the royal household; the upshot was the excommunication of many of the king's closest supporters. The result of all this was that Bela came to be more cordially detested by the aristocracy of Hungary than even his father Andrew had ever been.[13]

Yet perhaps an even more important reason for Bela IV's deep unpopularity by the late 1230s related to his controversial policy towards the Cumans. Koten, their leader, a veteran of the battle of Kalka in 1222, had taken one beating too many from the Mongols, and in 1238, after further costly defeats by them, had ordered a great migration westward to escape his tormentors. Around 40,000 warriors accompanied him. The Latin emperor in Constantinople allowed 10,000 of them to settle in Thrace (Bulgaria) in 1241, where they played an important role in the development of Bulgaria as a state; one of Koten's daughters married the French nobleman Narjot de Toucy, who was Regent of the Latin empire in 1228–31 and 1238–39.[14] Meanwhile the other 30,000, under Koten, arrived on the borders of Hungary in 1239 and asked permission to settle within Bela's realm, hinting broadly that if they were denied access they would enter anyway. Bela saw a golden chance to form his own praetorian guard as a bulwark against the hostile barons. He agreed to admit them provided they accepted mass conversion to Catholicism and swore an oath of personal loyalty to him; significantly, he made this offer without any reference to his nobility but with the enthusiastic backing of the Dominican order.[15]

He sent a deputation of Dominican friars as his envoys to Koten, who agreed the terms, and the two leaders later met in Transylvania to ratify the deal.[16] There was cynicism on both sides, each trying to use the other for maximum advantage. No documents were kept relating to the deal struck between Koten and Bela, which deepened the suspicion among the barons that Bela had acquired a private army on the cheap in return for a bogus 'conversion'. It was also said that he was trying to solve the problem of troublesome nomads on his frontier by absorbing them and hoping for credit from the Vatican by posing as a champion of the Faith.[17]

Bela professed himself enthusiastic about his new allies, all the more prized because of the looming Mongol threat, but Koten and his horde requited this with cattle-rustling, looting, rape and mass destruction of orchards, vineyards and crops. The foolish Bela had taken no thought for how nomads, used to a life of casual plunder, were supposed to coexist with a settled peasantry.[18] Aristocracy and peasantry made common cause in detesting the new arrivals, and their relish for rape raised sexual tensions to boiling point, whereby each side made it almost a point of honour to mistreat and abuse the other's women.

There have always been two views about which side was the more culpable. A contemporary witness spoke of Cuman resentment that 'their women were bedded by the Hungarians as if they were worthless.'[19] But in the words of a modern historian of Hungary, 'Complaints were voiced that the Cuman men were paying too much attention to Hungarian women, whereas it seemed that the ugliness of the Cuman women debarred the Hungarians from seeking compensation in kind.'[20] Hungarian hatred of the Cumans poured out in a deluge of anger. There were two especial complaints. Whereas Bela sought to dampen down native anxieties about the newcomers by announcing that he would disperse the Cumans throughout various provinces, he never dared put his plan into operation for fear of provoking Koten and his myrmidons to revolt.[21] Hungarian peasants were exhorted to take all their grievances before local tribunals for judgement, but they found that Bela had stacked the deck against them by blatant favouritism. If a Cuman complained about a Hungarian, he was given full justice, but if a Hungarian brought charges against a Cuman, he was told to go away and cease being a troublemaker; if he persisted, he was treated to the lash. When challenged about all this, Bela simply expounded a ludicrous doctrine that the 'favouritism' shown to the Cumans was simply the special consideration anyone would show to a guest.[22]

Disgusted and disillusioned with Bela, more and more aristocrats looked for salvation to the emperor, Frederick II. Frederick was bitter that Bela had remained neutral during his own struggles with the papacy. When anti-Bela oligarchs offered him the crown of Hungary in 1236–37, with the proviso that he would invade and expel Bela, Frederick did not turn the offer down but, claiming that he needed more time to consider it, kept it on ice.[23] He also encouraged his quarrelsome and aggressive vassal prince Frederick II of Austria and Styria (reigned 1230–1246) to foment trouble in Hungary. This Duke Frederick also increased his pressure on Bela by making him a huge loan on usurious terms.[24]

When Bela appealed to 'Stupor Mundi' to aid him against a Mongol invasion, Frederick said he was unable to help because the papacy was making war on him; when he approached the papacy, he was told that the emperor was at fault, and it was Frederick's belligerence that prevented the Vatican from helping.[25] The emperor was widely suspected of being content to see Bela so weakened that either he lost his throne or he would be forced to accept vassal status under him.[26]

Despite all his setbacks, Bela remained absurdly confident of being able to hold his own against Batu and Subedei if it came to a showdown. In part this was smug complacency: Hungary had been at peace externally for a very long time (since the days of Andrew) and Bela was confident of his military strength, especially with the Cumans as a light cavalry arm. There was also something of a condescending mentality of innate superiority to 'mere' nomadic barbarians who, it was thought, could not stand up to the finest knights in Christendom.[27]

Partly his aplomb was rational for, as a modern historian has remarked, 'the Hungarian army was an imposing force, and it is certain it would have been able to oppose with success any of the contemporary European powers.'[28] Yet the same stupidity that induced him to admit the Cumans into his realm manifested itself in Bela's dealings with the Mongols. Batu sent an embassy to him, demanding that he expel the Cumans forthwith, as they were the Mongols' traditional enemies. The principal emissary was said to have been an Englishman who entered the service of the Mongols after being banished from his homeland for life. Not only did Bela reply defiantly and insultingly, but he killed the envoys, thus making it certain that he would be marked down for destruction.[29]

For a week or two Batu and Subedei played cat-and-mouse with Bela, advancing to the frontier, pulling their forces back to lull the Hungarians, then advancing again, this time in earnest. Bela hurriedly sent troops to the Verecke pass in the north-eastern Carpathians, the enemy's most likely entry point. He also called out a general levy but the reponse was disappointing; it was a case of 'crying wolf' – the peasants had heard 'The Mongols are coming' once too often.[30]

Given that Bela had thought to snuggle up to the Vatican by his mass 'conversion' of the Cumans, what happened next was ironical, for it was priestcraft that awoke the nomadic kraken. Ugolin, Archbishop of Kalocsa (and royal chancellor 1230–35) was a long-standing confidant of Bela and had been commissioned by him to go to Venice for an archiepiscopal conclave to discuss opposition to Emperor Frederick. Ugolin and his fellow prelates were just on the point of setting out when Bela abruptly cancelled the trip, citing the imminent threat of Mongol invasion. Irritated and exasperated at the thought they now had to face danger instead of lolling in comfort in Venice, the divines vindictively stirred up resentment against the Cumans, preaching that the Cumans were the Mongols' fifth column and foolish Bela had been duped.[31]

Seriously rattled, Koten asked Bela for an armed escort to the royal presence. Bela responded by arresting him and his guards while he pondered what to do. An angry mob stormed down to the palace where Koten was being held. Bela and his men held off the baying crowd for a while with expert archery, but in the end sheer weight of numbers told. The mob burst in, lynched Koten and then beheaded him, and massacred all the guards, ending by throwing the severed heads out of the windows to the savage crowd below.[32] In the atmosphere of duplicity and double-crossing that was Hungary in the 1240s it was easily believed that the entire murder raid had been a set-up operation by Bela himself or Frederick of Austria.

At news of their leader's death, Koten's people rose up in fury and laid waste the whole of Hungary west of the Danube. In retaliation the Hungarians struck back savagely, forcing the surviving Cumans south and out of the country. It was an episode of mass murder, where the Hungarians took the line that the only good Cuman was a dead one, and the Cumans responded in kind.[33] At least one pitched battle was fought, between the levies of Bishop Bulcsu of Csanad and other nobles when these worthies, fleeing to upper Hungary, collided with the Cumans and were forced to hack their way through them. It was hardly a propitious start to a life-and-death struggle against the Mongols. And Bela's much-cosseted 'praetorians' were no longer available to do battle with the Mongols.

Bela himself was being rapidly overtaken by events. On 17 February he convened a well-attended assembly in Buda, in those days a separate city from Pest on the other side of the Danube and notable for a vast foreign population, including Germans, Slavs and Muslims.[34] Unaware of the most recent developments, the barons cried out for the imprisonment of Koten, alleging that the Cumans were really Mongols masquerading as another tribe. They also imposed very stiff conditions for their support, which Bela seems to have conceded, doubtless intending to break his word once he had defeated the Mongols. But even as the nobles were debating, word came in that the Mongols were through the Carpathians. Bela dismissed the assembly and got his army on the march, sending his queen and the elderly clergy to safety in Austria.[35]

The Mongol strategy for the invasion of Hungary was masterly and bears all the hallmarks of Subedei, especially his genius at coordinating widely separated armies. Whereas when making systematic conquests the Mongols proceeded slowly to allow their herds to keep pace, speed was to be the essence of this attack and they planned to live entirely off the land.[36] Subedei's objective was to bring Bela to battle as soon as possible and defeat him, before the West could mount a rescue operation. But it was important that while driving for Buda and Pest on the Danube, eastern Hungary should be thoroughly subjugated. He therefore devised an advance in three columns, perfectly planned and coordinated so that the three separate forces would unite at the Danube. Anticipating Napoleon's methods and using fast couriers, Subedei made sure that the three armies were constantly in touch and could come together at great speed. The two flank columns would trace the circumference of an elongated circle while the central force, under Batu, would move along the diameter.[37]

Batu's brother Shiban would cover the northern sector between Poland and Moravia. With its flank covered by the Vistula, this column moved west to the north of the Carpathians, crossed the nine-hundred-mile-long ridge of mountains through the easy Jablonica pass, and then proceeded south-west down the Morava and Vah Rivers. Sweeping round in a curved trajectory, it protected the main force from any flank attack from Austria. The left wing under Qadan swept in a south-easterly direction via the Borgo or Tihuta pass through Moldavia (between the eastern Carpathians and the Dniester River), with detachments thrown out into Wallachia, land of bears, wolves and lynxes, and then through the pass into Transylvania before following the course of the Tisza River towards Pest.[38]

The main army under Batu went through the Verecke pass and debouched into the upper Tisza valley. This force encountered the army of the Count Palatine of Hungary on the other side of the mountains and routed it in short order on 12 March, allowing the hapless Palatine to return to Bela with news of his own defeat.[39] The progress made by Batu was remarkable, for roads in Hungary were then virtually non-existent and Bela had prepared a labyrinth of obstacles for any invader approaching Hungary through the Verecke pass – ditches, trenches, felled trees – all designed to funnel invaders into well-guarded 'gates'. It was said that by 1241 Hungary's few roads were so overgrown with weeds and thorns that travellers had to navigate from village to village by ascending high ground and plotting a route from one church steeple to the next. Batu circumvented the system of obstacles and booby-traps by sending his pioneer corps ahead to remove obstacles, cut new paths through forests and even lay new roads.[40] Subedei was at some distance from Batu. He started after him, soon caught up, and went ahead to form the vanguard.[41]

Easily the most action-packed and devastating journey of the three was that achieved by the southern column under Qadan. In northern Transylvania, at the town of Rodna in the heart of silver-mining country, his men were confronted by a large party of armed Saxon miners, who had made the town into a German enclave. The Mongols simply turned tail and fled. The foolish miners, exulting in their 'victory' held a celebratory banquet and were hopelessly drunk when the Mongols returned at night and slaughtered them. Hearing of this debacle, another six hundred Germans in another mining town sent in their surrender, and were at once pressed into service in Qadan's front line.[42] Qadan's forces ranged far and wide, reaching modern Timisoara to the south-west. Their progress was notable for slaughter and devastation.[43]

Using the German miners as guides, the Mongols arrived at the city of Oradea (today just inside the Romanian border), a populous centre with a citadel. They gutted the entire town except for the citadel then massacred all the inhabitants as revenge for the defiance of the citadel's garrison. The women were gang-raped and there were mass beheadings outside the city; some unfortunates were burned alive inside the cathedral. The Mongols then used a variant of the feigned retreat, left the town, camped five miles away and waited. The garrison finally emerged, thinking it was safe, whereupon the Mongols made a lightning raid at dawn and butchered them, reserving a few for torture. A handful managed to scramble back into the citadel, but the Mongols then demolished it with trebuchets. The stench from the dead soon became intolerable, and Qadan ordered evacuation, but he was still not convinced he had accounted for all the Hungarians. He lay in wait and, when survivors began to creep back to town out of the woods, sprang out and slaughtered them.[44]

Bishop Benedict of Oradea had been collecting a great army on Bela's orders and was about to march west with a large force to join him at Pest; instead, on hearing of the sack of his city he turned towards the invaders, but fell victim to another of the Mongols' favourite ploys. Fearing themselves outnumbered, the Mongols had hundreds of dummies mounted on spare horses, with orders that they would be brought to the skyline at precisely the right moment. When the Hungarians appeared, the Mongol army fled in feigned panic, drawing them towards the hills where the phantom army was hidden. Suddenly a new 'host' (the dummies) appeared on the horizon. Fearing that they had been lured into an ambush, Bishop Benedict's men wheeled around in a panic; the Mongols then turned, pursued and slaughtered them.[45]

The list of towns and villages taken by Qadan's column went on and on: the episcopal city of Csanad (also called Urbs Morisena, the heart of the original realm founded by the Arpads in 1000) was sacked and Szeged was afflicted 'with every sort of atrocity'[46] – although this time the inhabitants found safety in nearby marshes – as were others whose locations are no longer identifiable, such as Voivoden and Emmata.

The sack of Szeged was notable for featuring a race between the forces of Bujek, who had been sent on raids to the far south, and Qadan's 's main detachment coming from the north-east. It is unclear why Qadan was allowed so much leeway to loot and sack while Shiban had express orders never to halt on his march, and some say only part of Qadan's force linked up with Batu and Subedei on the Danube, with Qadan absent from the subsequent battle, having stayed behind to complete his progamme of gutting and pillaging.[47] This would explain the many puzzling references to the Mongols at Oradea and elsewhere being outnumbered. It also explains why Shiban's column linked up with Batu on 17 March but Qadan's left wing not until 2 April.[48] Only when Shiban was almost within hailing distance of Batu did the leader let him off the leash and allow him to sack Vac, a city twenty-two miles north of modern Budapest on the eastern bank of the Danube, below the bend where the river changes course and flows south.

Shiban's men enjoyed a thorough sacking and moved into a position slightly north-west of Batu. Shiban had performed brilliantly, averaging fifty miles a day over very difficult country.[49] Yet even that paled alongside Subedei's achievement. He covered 180 miles in three days, riding through deep snow and barely stopping for food. Once at the Danube, and about ten miles ahead of Batu, Subedei took his men straight into battle. Archbishop Ugolin of Kalocsa thought he saw a chance to isolate Subedei's vanguard from the main Mongol force but once again fell for the feigned retreat stratagem. Subedei lured his force into a marsh where they got bogged down and ended up as sitting ducks for Mongol arrows; miraculously Ugolin and a handful of retainers escaped.[50]

When Bela heard of this rash adventure, he was enraged at the archbishop's folly. He had ordered all barons and churchmen to assemble at Pest to form a huge army for a decisive trial of strength with the Mongols, and it was implicit in his orders that there were to be no sideshows or individual forays. Duke Frederick of Austria was another who disobeyed these orders. He attacked a Mongol foraging party, claimed a great victory, proclaimed Bela a coward and promptly went home. Bela was held responsible for these pointless diversions as much as for his other genuine mistakes – his failure to build forts on the Polish–Hungarian border, his sluggish response to the invasion, and his killing the Mongol envoys in the first place. Emperor Frederick II, who had never liked Bela and despised him, never tired of pointing to these three areas as special proof of Bela's military incompetence.[51]

The hosts of Batu and Bela were now in sight of each other, on either side of the Danube. Batu tried to tempt the king onto the eastern bank but Bela, though no great military talent, knew enough not to cross a mighty river with formidable conquerors waiting for him on the far side. Realising that Bela was never going to take the bait, Batu and Subedei began to retreat eastwards, and there followed six days of forced marches with a jubilant Bela on their tail. Near where the River Hernad flows into the River Sajo (a tributary of the Tisza), the Mongols drew up their forces; Bela halted on the other side of the Sajo, on the plains of Mohi, south-west of Batu's force, near the vine-clad slopes of Tokaj.

Beyond the plain were extensive marshes, deeply flooded as both rivers had recently been in spate.[52] There Bela built a fortified camp, intended to be a ring of steel, with large wagons laagered in a circle. This would certainly keep most enemies out, but of course in the event of a reverse it could also keep his own men in. As always with medieval battles, and especially those involving the Mongols, the numbers in the armies are disputed. The older authorities used to give statistics of 70,000 Hungarians ranged against 40,000 Mongols but it seems likely that these numbers are too high; modern historians tend to opt for about 20,000 Mongols versus 25,000 Hungarians, but certainty is impossible.[53]

There was a 200-yard-long bridge across the Sajo hard by Bela's camp, surrounded by swamps. Once again Batu tried to lure Bela across a river by exhibiting tiny forces, and once again the king declined, possibly because the Mongols were not entirely visible on the tree-lined shores.[54] It seems likely that morale was not particularly high on either side. Bela's exhortation to his troops was reported to have fallen flat, while Batu seems to have had so little confidence in the outcome that he went up a hillside to pray to Tengerri and asked the Islamic troops in the army to direct their prayers for success to Allah.[55] Batu had all his best commanders with him, including the brilliant Subedei, who may already have learned of the triumph at Liegnitz only the day before, via his super-fast mounted couriers. Bela had the support of most of the bishops of Hungary, including the martial Ugolin, who had always supported the barons. Bela's brother Coloman, at 33 two years his junior, was also present, and he was generally considered a much better captain than Bela.[56]

It is difficult to imagine what might have broken the stalemate, but on the evening of 10 April a deserter from the Mongols arrived in the Hungarian camp. Some say it was a press-ganged Russian who had managed to escape his intended role as arrow fodder; others that it was a disgruntled Ruthenian slave. In any case, the man brought vital news. It was well known that the Mongols liked to avoid fighting at night and even broke off battles at dusk in order to resume them in the morning. Subedei knew that the Hungarians knew this and planned to turn the knowledge to his advantage by launching a surprise night attack across the bridge, commanded by Batu, preparatory to a dawn assault on Bela's camp. He meanwhile intended to find a way across the river lower down and come on the Hungarians from the rear. It was therefore essential that Batu did not attack prematurely.[57]

Coloman, Ugolin and the master of the Templars, Rembald de Voczon, at once set out with a large force of infantry and marched five miles in the darkness, reaching the bridge at midnight. They found that the Mongols were already well launched on their surprise and were halfway across the bridge. Taken by surprise, the Mongols were driven back and took a lot of casualties from the enemy crossbowmen who at close range were effective in a way they could never have been on an open battlefield.[58] Thinking they had repelled the main assault, by 2 a.m. the Hungarians began celebrating their victory. But the force assaulting the bridge was just one of three. Shiban had been sent north to find a ford, cross the river and attack the bridge from the other side. Subedei meanwhile had, as promised, set off south with a third force, hoping to loop round behind Bela's camp. At 4 a.m., just as dawn was breaking, Batu attacked the bridge again, this time using giant stone-throwing catapults to clear away the crossbowmen.

After some more hard fighting, the Hungarians withdrew to their camp at news that Shiban was attempting to take them in the rear.[59] Shiban pressed on to the camp, where the trio of Coloman, Ugolin and Rembald once more sallied forth with their men to give battle. By now it was about 8 a.m. and Batu had got across the bridge with the main army and was hurrying to support Shiban. Coloman's contingent now found itself in danger of being taken between two fires and retreated to the camp, where most of the Hungarian troops had lingered, somehow imagining that Coloman and his comrades would be able to see off any Mongol incursions.[60] Back at the fortified encampment Ugolin got into a furious slanging match with Bela, accusing him of incompetence: he had made no contingency plans in case the Hungarians had not been able to hold the Mongols at the bridge.

For the third time Batu found himself in a slugging match with the Hungarians on terrain where the Mongols could not deploy in their usual formation. In this phase of the battle he took more heavy casualties and lost thirty of his elite guards. Meanwhile Subedei had found a suitable crossing lower down the river and crossed his forces on an improvised pontoon bridge.[61] Just when the battle with Batu was raging indecisively, Subedei's forces suddenly appeared in the Hungarian rear. At sight of this third Mongol division, the Hungarians' nerve cracked and panic ensued. Now attacking from three directions, using flaming arrows and a range of new weapons, including gunpowder, primitive firearms and naphtha bombs,[62] the Mongols began to eat up their opponents. They overwhelmed the laager with showers of arrows, described as being like swarms of locusts or grasshoppers. Bela could not draw up his troops properly because of the restricted space and soon his men became exhausted from the heat of so many sweating bodies packed around them. The fusillade lasted from early morning until noon, with Coloman and his contingent holding up best; Bela's brother made three unsuccessful sorties before getting away on a swift horse.[63] The general slaughter was tremendous.

The Mongols then deliberately left a gap in their ranks through which the broken and demoralised Hungarians streamed. Batu, who was dismayed by his casualties, at first did not want to pursue, but Subedei insisted and took charge.[64] More slaughter followed as the Mongols, freed from the constraints of space, could now ride the enemy down and massacre at will. To make matters worse for the refugees, heavy rainfall impeded their progress, turning the ground into a quagmire, and often leaving them trapped in mud and at the mercy of their pursuers. Many others drowned when they were caught at the Danube ferry, plunged into the river only to be swept away by the swift currents and drowned.[65]

The flower of Hungarian chivalry perished that day. Altogether, in the battle and the pursuit the Mongols were said to have slain 30,000, for they massacred non-combatants and camp followers as well. Coloman, though badly wounded, rode to the Danube ferry at Pest, announced *sauve qui peut*, got across and reached Szeged in southeastern Hungary. In May he joined Bela, who had also escaped, in Zagreb, but never recovered from the wounds sustained at Mohi and died there soon afterwards.[66] Among the notable Hungarian fatalities were Archbishop Ugolin, Archbishop Matthias of Esztergom, Bela's close friend Bishop Gregory of Gyor, Bishop Raynauld of Transylvania, Bishop James of Nitra, Eradius Archdeacon of Vac, Albert Archdeacon of Esztergom and Nicholas of Sibiu, Bela's vice-chancellor.[67] Bishop Bartholomew of Pecs got away and joined Bela later in Dalmatia.[68]

The battlefield at Mohi was a gruesome and piteous sight. More than ten thousand bodies lay there, dismembered by sabres, burned to a cinder, beheaded, some picked clean by corvids and other birds of prey, or by foxes, wolves and hogs. The ground was red with blood, and one could walk for two days through the canyons of the dead, 'nothing but corpses, fallen warriors lying around like stones in a quarry'.[69] The quarry simile was widely popular. In another description, 'Corpses lay around as common as flocks of cattle or sheep or pigs standing on open ground to pasture or like stones cut for a building in a quarry.'[70] Those who drowned in rivers or marshland were eaten by fish, worms and even waterfowl or distorted by water. Others were burnt to a crisp by bombs and gunpowder, and the fat from burning corpses was so profuse that when peasants tried to incinerate the corpses they put out the fire. Since animals and birds of prey did not like to eat charred corpses, they tended to lie around unconsumed, filling the air with a noisome foetor; the spontaneous necropolis thus engendered diseases which finished off most of the wounded and many of the uninjured.

Wounded and terrified horses wandering distraught across the battlefield added to the impression of hell on earth, and many such valiant steeds had to be finished off by peasants just so that the hideous screeching and neighing would stop.[71] Piles of Bela's gold, silver and other treasures were left on the field. The Mongols, euphoric in victory, were uninterested in looting on the day but came back a few days later, piled up the valuables and then shared it out according to the usual strict formula – always weighted towards the grandees – used by the Mongols when apportioning loot.[72]

Mohi was a classic victory achieved by encirclement – always the great strategist's dream outcome. There have not been that many perfect examples of this almost Platonic idea of triumph on the battle-field – Hannibal at Cannae, Napoleon at Austerlitz and Slim on the Irrawaddy in 1945 being the best known of the handful of instances, but Mohi belongs in that class. Simply put, the Mongols outclassed the Christian armies at every level: discipline, organisation, speed, mobility, disinformation, deception, even weaponry.[73] From China they had brought the gunpowder technology that so startled the Hungarians. Their superiority in archery was such that their arrows penetrated all western armour while their own repelled all western shafts except the crossbow quarrels fired at very close range.[74] They had all kinds of heavy bows, including a giant one that took two strong men to draw, complete with silver-beaded arrows full of holes that made a whistling sound like pipes when shot.[75]

Subedei in his hour of glory also refuted the notion that cavalry could not function without a stable infantry base. The armies of medieval Christendom relied on the mass charge and shock tactics; the Mongols, anticipating Napoleon, on deadly fire. Mohi proved two things: that lightly armed cavalry could always beat heavy cavalry if their mobility was far superior; and that the Mongols, by using deadly fire systematic-ally to pave the way for the final assault, were original, for this was the first time in military history that devastating artillery fire was so used.[76]

When the Mongols later withdrew to Central Asia, all the vanquished nations absurdly competed with each other for the honour of having 'repelled' the Mongols. The Hungarians claimed that they lost Mohi by the slimmest of margins and only through ill luck; the Poles, equally risibly, contended that they had exhausted Mongol strength at Liegnitz and this was the long-term reason for their failure to invade western Europe; the Germans fatuously maintained that when it came time for the Mongols to face 'real' (i.e. German) warriors they turned tail and fled; the Russians even tried to get in on the act by claiming that the Mongols had lost too many men during the conquest of Mother Russia. This after-the-event vainglory is more redolent of boasting in the pub by a loudmouth than serious historical analysis.[77]

The chief culprit in spreading these nonsensical ideas was Carpini, who convinced himself that he had evolved a formula for defeating the nomads, of which the key element was their alleged fear of crossbows.[78] Naturally they feared them at close range, as in the exceptional circumstances on the Mohi bridge, but crossbows were considered a bagatelle on an open battlefield where they lacked the range to trouble fast, mobile mounted archers. Mongols, conscious of their exiguous numbers, hated taking battle casualties, which was why they liked to line their front ranks with captives forced to fight. Two senior commanders killed in the campaigns in Poland and Hungary hardly constitutes a winnowing.

It is true that Batu found a few hundred fatalities at Mohi too many, but he had only his own blundering to blame.[79] The root cause of the setback at the bridge was Batu's deep jealousy of Subedei. Whereas Subedei and Jebe had worked brilliantly together in 1221–23, the collaboration between Batu and Subedei was not a happy one. One of the jibes made in the drunken outburst by Guyuk and Buri at the infamous banquet was that Batu was a mere glory-hunter, a nonentity and opportunist who hitched himself to Subedei's coat-tails so that he could claim credit for the veteran general's successes.[80]

Certainly there was bad blood between the two commanders. Subedei was irked by Batu's defeatism, his low morale and his reluctance to engage Bela. After the battle Batu, enraged by his casualties, tried to pin the blame on Subedei, saying he had taken too long over his diversionary attack. Calmly and restrainedly Subedei pointed out that whereas Batu had crossed on the bridge at the shallowest point of the river, he had had to build a bridge downstream where the water was much deeper.[81] Piqued by this, Batu announced that, having won a victory he had done enough and intended to withdraw from Poland and Hungary. Implicitly shaming him in front of the other Mongol aristocrats, Subedei replied: 'You may do as you wish. But I intend to cross the Danube.'[82]

Everybody knew that the victory was really Subedei's and a tribute to his genius, in particular that he knew the courier and yam system inside out so that he could coordinate large forces over huge distances.[83] Mohi was his 65th battle (one for each year of his age) and he had won at least sixty of them.[84] The judgement of a modern scholar is judicious:

> [He) understood the limits and fragility of steppe power; for that reason, his campaigns were always conducted with the greatest economy of force and minimal loss. This he achieved primarily through a remarkable imagination, a thorough understanding of his enemies, and a willingness to take carefully calculated risks.[85]

While the Mongol commanders quarrelled, Bela managed to make a clean getaway. His first port of call was Bratislava on the left bank of the Danube, where Duke Frederick of Austria invited him to be his guest in his domains. The upshot was disastrous: 'Alas the poor king was like a fish who, trying to escape from the icebox, jumps into the fire to be roasted.'[86] Once Frederick had him in his power, he evinced his hatred in two ways. First he unleashed his army on defenceless west Hungary and sent a force to sack the fortress of Gyor on the right bank of the Danube. The locals resisted, penned the Germans up in the castle and burned them alive inside. Frederick sent another army and ordered the fortress burnt to the ground. Enraged by this 'contumacity', Frederick announced that all Hungarian oligarchs would be stripped of everything of value they possessed to compensate for the 'extra cost' of policing west Hungary; he also mulcted any rich Germans who had fled from eastern Hungary.[87]

Then he put in a peremptory demand to Bela for the repayment of an outstanding loan – but which was, in fact, reparation payments imposed by Bela's father Andrew on Frederick after the Austrian–Hungarian war of 1235; Frederick was actually demanding that what he had paid as an indemnity should now be repaid with interest. Bela had no choice: he had to pay the sum or remain Frederick's prisoner. Since he paid mainly in gold, silver, jewellery, goblets and other effects, Frederick was able to cheat him. He put a ludicrously low valuation on Bela's treasures against the mark; whereas the true value of the items was around 6,000 marks, Frederick valued them at 2,000, then presented an account tricked out with compound interest which brought the total ransom to 7–10,000 marks.[88] Somehow Bela scraped up the sums demanded and departed, leaving his wife behind.

He would have his revenge in 1246 when he defeated Frederick at the battle of the Leitha River and killed him; the 35-year-old Frederick was struck through the jaw by a lance.[89] In May 1241 it was as much as he could do to flee south to Zagreb in Croatia, whence he wrote to the pope and Emperor Frederick pleading for an anti-Mongol crusade; so desperate was he that he offered to become the emperor's vassal if he would only help him regain Hungary. Frederick promised help and laboriously assembled an army to be commanded by his son Conrad. But by the time this host was ready to march, the Mongols had already quit Hungary of their own volition.[90] Pope Gregory died on 22 August 1241, making all hope from the Vatican vain. Learning that Bela was in Zagreb, Batu sent Qadan and a large force of picked cavalry after him, hoping to duplicate the successful pursuit and death of shah Muhammad, rather than the embarrassing failure to catch up with the king of Korea.[91]

During the summer and autumn of 1241 the Mongols consolidated their hold on Hungary east of the Danube by a systematic programme of atrocities and extermination: 'like hounds tracking rabbits and boars [they] rushed through the thick of the thorn bushes, the shadows of the groves, the depths of the water and the heart of the wasteland.'[92] It is tempting to see the hand of Subedei in this for, military genius that he was, he was also an old-school, unreconstructed devotee of massacre. Ogodei's veto had prevented him from similar measures at Kaifeng in 1233, but now Subedei was far from 'meddlers' like Yelu Chu Cai and could indulge his natural instincts.

Two things impressed and depressed observers of the Mongols in Hungary. One was their relish for mass rape, with a particular liking for ravishing women before the eyes of their fathers or husbands, though in some cases Hungarian males simply handed over their women to the Mongols in return for being allowed to keep their cattle, sheep and horses.[93] Another was the way they combined honeyed words with arrant treachery. As they ranged far and wide over the puszta, the Mongols liked to sack towns and watch the inhabitants flee. They would then lie in wait in concealment until the citizens returned to rebuild their shattered homes, thinking the Mongols were far away. The Mongols would then rise up from their ambush and massacre them. Another nasty trick was to announce a general amnesty and even send some of their prisoners into the woods with word that it was safe to surrender; the unfortunates who trusted them would then emerge from the copses and forests only to be slaughtered.[94]

In this way the Mongols soon put a halt to the incipient movement towards guerrilla warfare. Guerrillas can survive only with the coop- eration of peasant populations, and who would support guerrillas knowing the terrible and inevitable retribution that would follow? In any case, the Mongols had other forms of control. Many quislings – the most hated people in the ocean of hatred that was Hungary in 1241 – came forward to act as civilian bureaucrats in a puppet admin- istration.[95] After Mohi the Mongols had found the royal seal on the body of the chancellor and cynically used it to issue bogus decrees purporting to come from Bela, ordering people not to flee but to remain in their houses.[96]

In this way the Mongols cut a swathe of destruction right through eastern Hungary in 1241, using their mangonels and catapults against any town that dared to resist them, particularly targeting monasteries as the rallying point of dissidents. The task was relatively simple when compared with China, for there were no cities or fortresses with the strong walls the Jin had possessed.[97] The Mongol armies of destruc- tion fanned out in all directions, as far as the borders of Austria, Bohemia, Moravia, Silesia and Poland. In July one raiding party reached Wiener Neustadt in north-east Austria, south of Vienna.[98]

The winter of 1241–42 was exceptionally severe, and the Danube itself froze. Subedei suggested to Batu that they cross on the ice and carry the destruction into western Hungary. Batu was dubious, fearful lest the frozen surface collapse under the weight of thousands of mounted warriors. Mongol ingenuity, as ever, found a solution. Their wranglers took a herd of horses out into the middle of the frozen river and left them there while scouts watched from the eastern bank.

Sure enough, Hungarians from the west bank, sensing serendipity, came to the middle of the river and took the horses back with them. Knowing it was safe to proceed, the Mongols crossed the river with great speed.[99]

It seems that on the other side they made contact with Qadan, who lamented his failure to find Bela and the paucity of his forces, which made him circumspect about proceeding to the Dalmatian coast where the Mongols would be opposed in strength. Batu divided his forces, gave half to Qadan, and with the other half targeted Esztergom, a wealthy city with a population of some 12,000.[100] The inhabitants resisted, so Batu brought up thirty siege engines, with which he subjected the defenders to a non-stop battering from stones and arrows. Finally, the Esztergomians realised resistance was hopeless, and set fire to all the wooden houses in the suburbs, leaving only the stone palaces unscathed. They buried all their gold and silver, burned all their holdings of precious cloth and killed all their horses so that the Mongols could not have them.

It was this last item that infuriated Batu and led him to issue a 'no quarter' order.[101] The ever-tightening circle soon had the defenders penned up in the palaces. At this point it is related that the three hundred wealthiest and most aristocratic women sought an audience with Batu and begged for their lives. But he was so angry at the stories of the buried loot that he ordered the women beheaded on the spot, then swept in to Esztergom centre and massacred all they could lay hands on, except for a handful who still held out in the citadel under the resourceful Spanish commander, Burgrave Simeon.[102] Batu decided to ignore this and press on to the castle of St Martin of Pannonia where the loot was said to be plentiful. Western Hungary, however, was largely saved from the devastation visited on the eastern part, for three reasons. First, there were few attractive targets left, since the Cumans had laid waste the country when they rose in rebellion after the murder of Koten.[103] Secondly, Batu lacked the resources he had in the east because he had had to detach significant numbers to allow Qadan to pursue Bela to the Adriatic. And, most important of all, within a week of Ogodei's death on 11 December 1241, Batu knew of it. This meant that everything in the Mongol empire was now in the melting pot.[104]

Suitably reinforced, Qadan began the hot pursuit of Bela along the

Adriatic coast. His route after parting from Batu was along the shores of Lake Balaton and then south into Croatia. Bela, aware that Zagreb was not safe from the Mongols, fled south too, always a few steps ahead of his pursuers. At first he made a stopover on Rab, a fourteen-mile-long island off the northern coast of Croatia, supposedly unreachable from the mainland except by specially constructed flyboats.[105] But he never entirely trusted the local ruler and, hearing of the Mongol approach, moved down to Trogir in southern Croatia, a small island city seventeen miles west of Split. Qadan got on his trail, stormed down the coast and sacked Split but was delayed by a false rumour that Bela was holed up in the fortress of Klis overlooking Split, a rocky eminence inaccessible on three sides.[106]

The Mongols laid siege to this fortress in March 1242. Their usual arrow shower made no impression on the defenders, and as Qadan's force was a fast, highly mobile search-and-destroy force, he had no siege engines with him. He ordered his men to make a sneak attack by crawling up the one approach to the fortress on their bellies, but the defenders spotted them and killed a number of them by rolling huge rocks down on them. Infuriated by this, as they always were by casualties, the Mongols unusually came to close quarters with the enemy, so that ferocious fighting took place around, and sometimes on, the walls. The Mongols finally broke in, looted all the houses and uplifted a huge weight of plunder, but the garrison retreated into the even more impregnable citadel.[107]

By now Qadan had received intelligence that Bela had duped them into a sideshow and was nowhere near the fortress. He divided his men in two, one to finish ransacking Split, the other to investigate the approaches to Trogir. The Trogir party issued a formal demand for the surrender of Bela, which the citizens ignored. Construing this as another piece of disinformation like the experience at Klis, Qadan pressed on down the coast and sacked and gutted Kotor (in modern Montenegro).[108] He reached his farthest south at Shkoder (Scutari) in northern Albania but, on reporting to Batu that he had still not found the elusive Bela, he was ordered to cut across country and rejoin the main army in Wallachia, lest he be cut off in Dalmatia by a hostile coalition when Batu was too far east to help him.[109]

In April 1242, accordingly, Qadan marched across Bosnia and Serbia to the rendezvous point. Batu proceeded along the south bank of the

Danube to Wallachia, while Orda struck south-east through Transylvania, burning settlements and doling out particularly cruel punishment en route. There was resistance all the way from local tribes, particularly in the northern Balkans.[110] The three armies reunited in Wallachia. As a parting shot the Mongols 'magnanimously' released all their prisoners and told them they were free to go home; they then cynically massacred them under the rubric 'shot while trying to escape'. When they reached Bulgaria, they sacked Tarnovo and mauled the troops of Baldwin II of Constantinople, reminding him that this was punishment for having sheltered the Cumans.[111] Baldwin called for reinforcements from Constantinople.

There followed two battles: the first, a relatively trivial affair, Baldwin won, but then Batu hit back with all his might and routed him in a far more serious encounter.[112] Batu never forgot this 'insolence' and, when khan of the Golden Horde in the 1250s, made a point of exacting tribute from Bulgaria. Finally the Mongols withdrew eastwards through Moldavia and spent the winter of 1242–43 on the lower Volga, where Batu had decided to base himself as heir to his father Jochi's ulus.[113]

The Mongols could feel justly proud of themselves in military terms. During the campaign of 1236–42 they had marched at least 16,000 miles from Karakorum, if we bear in mind the variations in route which meant that they almost never travelled 'as the crow flies', the zigzags to the north and south of Russia and the passages through mountain passes and other difficult terrain, not to mention diversions and sidetrips to 'mop up' recalcitrant foes.

The devastation they had wrought in Hungary was stunning. After 1242 there was widespread famine and heavy mortality among the peasants, who had been unable to sow crops or reap a harvest for twelve months; some said the death toll from pestilence and disease was even greater than the losses inflicted by the Mongols.[114] Abandoned villages, ruined churches and despoiled monasteries were a long-term reminder of the Mongol invasion. The events of 1241–42 in Hungary were deeply traumatic and 'in the time of the Tartars' became for people in the 1260s and 1270s much like 'during the war' for Britons who lived through the Second World War.[115] Some said Hungary had been ruined for centuries. Transylvania and the regions east of the Danube had been hit hardest; the only place west of the river to sustain serious damage was Esztergom, but we should remember that this region had previously been laid waste by the Cumans (later historians tended to forget this and to lay all the misery at the door of the Mongols).[116] The death toll in 1241–42 is impossible to ascertain accurately – for one thing we are at the mercy of medieval chroniclers – but if we aggregate statistics reported from the various sacked towns (4,000 at Rodna, 6,040 at Bistrita, etc) and add them to the roster of fatalities at Mohi, and then add in the losses from disease and famine, it is easy to get a figure of 25 per cent of the population or 500,000 dead. This is particularly the case if we consider that few of the prisoners taken by the Mongols would have survived; apart from the mass killing in Wallachia before Batu left for Russia, large numbers of them, pressed into service in the front rank, would have been counted among Mongol casualties. Those who survived the battle would not have lasted long on the diet permitted by their captors – largely the intestines, feet and heads of butchered animals.[117] Most modern historians opt for a lower figure, but none goes lower than 15 per cent or 300,000.[118]

Additionally, there was huge displacement of population and large numbers of skilled artisans were transported to Mongolia.[119] Rubruck found that Buri in particular had made slaves of skilled workers, including Germans used in mining silver and manufacturing weapons in remote parts of central Asia. Other captives of note in Batu's camp on the Volga included a Parisian goldsmith, the woman from Metz previously mentioned, the son of an English noble and the nephew of a bishop of Normandy – all people who had the bad luck to be in the wrong place at the wrong time.[120]

The one clear long-term beneficiary of the Mongol invasion was Bela himself, who despite the devastation in his country, could still rally enough resources when he returned to make war on Duke Frederick of Austria and defeat him.[121] Bela had learned a hard lesson from the Mongols, but he did absorb it, even if no one else did: as Denis Sinor remarked, 'For the first time she (Hungary) received a lesson which she was never to learn, namely that it was vain for her to expect any help from the West.'[122] Bela built stone castles and walled fortresses all over his realm and in his obsession with 'the Tartars' became something of an expert on them and was frequently consulted on them after 1242 by Pope Innocent IV.[123] Despite the treachery of the Cumans in 1241, he let them back into his realm in 1245 and began to fuse them with the Knights Hospitaller as the country's military backbone.[124] Bela also abandoned his 'put the clock back' policy towards his barons and made generous land grants to keep them on his side and lessen the former antagonisms. His one bad mistake was to assign the government of Transylvania to his son Stephen and exercise a dual kingship with him – a disastrous experiment that led to civil war in 1264–65. The great survivor died in 1270, aged 64, after a 35-year reign, having lived long enough to be regarded with high esteem as 'the second founder of the country'.[125]

The Mongol devastation of Hungary alerted western Europe to what might be in store for it: but suddenly Batu and his hordes were gone, the danger was over and Europe could breathe again. From that day to this the question of why they turned back has exercised historians. The most commonly accepted 'explanation' is that after Ogodei's death every Mongol was bound in duty to return to Mongolia to elect his successor. Accepting the (likely) cause of the khan's death as poisoning by his aunt, as against the convenient notion that it was alcoholism, a leading Russian historian has commented: 'This woman, whoever she was, must be considered the saviour of Western Europe.'[126]

But this idea is not convincing, for a number of reasons. In the first place, the quriltai that elected Guyuk as khaghan did not take place until 1246, four and a half years after Ogodei's death. Secondly, Batu did not return to Mongolia (lingering, as we have seen, in the Volga region), for he was very well informed about all the intrigues that flickered through Karakorum after Ogodei's death and thought (rightly) that his life would be in danger.

Thirdly, senior commanders and Mongol notables were not in any case automatically recalled to Mongolia after Ogodei's death. The most salient example is that of Baiju, Mongol commander in Iraq and western Iran, whom Ogodei had appointed as Chormaqan's successor. On 26 June 1243 Baiju won a shattering victory over the Seljuk Turks under Kaykhusraw II at Kose Dag against the odds. (Allegedly he dismissed the numerical superiority of the Seljuks with a typical Mongol comment: 'The more they are, the more glorious it is to win and the more plunder we will secure.') As a result of this triumph, which made the years 1241–43 rival 1220–22 for non-stop Mongol victories, the empire of Trebizond in Anatolia submitted to Baiju and his armies were able to advance into Syria.[127] But there was no question of his having to return to Mongolia for a quriltai.

Another possible explanation is that the Mongols abandoned the idea of an invasion of western Europe because the terrain, largely forested and with no great plains, would not have provided the forage and pasture needed for their horses and other animals. It is alleged that even in Hungary the Mongols were operating to the limit of their capacity, for the puszta, the Great Hungarian Plain, was the only area of grassland west of the Black Sea capable of supporting horses on any scale; here they were limited to 40,000 square miles, as against the 300,000 square miles in the great steppes of their homeland. To feed 100,000 horses one would need 4,200 tonnes of grain in winter or summer, and where would this come from unless, implausibly, it was transported 8,000 miles from Mongolia? Additionally, warhorses needed a lot of care from grooms and wranglers, increasing the numbers the Mongols would have to deploy, and were susceptible to precisely the diseases and parasites that the cold and damp of northern Europe would engender.[128]

Against this theory one can cite factors which might be considered 'circumstantial evidence'. The Mongols were capable of adapting their military methods, as they demonstrated in the long war with Song China and particularly under Qubilai when they attempted conquests in Burma, Vietnam, Indonesia and Japan – though, with the exception of the conquest of Song China, it is notable that none of these campaigns was successful. Napoleon operated with huge numbers of horses in his conquests and as late as the Second World War the Germans were able to utilise millions of horses even with the depleted grazing grounds in industrial Europe. One can, however, argue that such comparisons are anachronistic: by the time of Napoleon much more of Europe had been converted to pasture, and in the case of the Second World War one has to factor in railways, superior veterinary corps and mobile horse transports, none of which was available to the Mongols. Tellingly, though, the Huns under Attila, also entirely dependent on horses for their military superiority, fought campaigns in Italy and France, where it was not problems of pasture that halted them. A judicious conclusion would be that horses and pasturage certainly played *some* part in the Mongol decision to withdraw.[129]

Another popular theory is that the entire question is misplaced, since the Mongols never intended to conquer western Europe. According to this version the Mongols invaded Hungary purely to punish Bela for having harboured the Cumans and to ensure that there could be no threat to Batu's ulus in Rus – the Golden Horde.[130] This idea has the merit of simplicity – for the Mongol withdrawal would then need no explanation – but is in conflict with a mass of inconvenient evidence, not least that the Mongols were hopelessly divided. In short, while this was almost certainly Batu's aim, it was not Subedei's, as he stated that his dream was to behold the Atlantic. There is no documentary evidence as to what exactly Ogodei's instructions to his two commanders were, but it is likely that they were issued on a contingency basis – that if the conquest of the Rus states and eastern Europe went well, he would provide the necessary resources for the conquest of western Europe.

What is certain is that Batu's decision to return to the Volga caused a major rift with Subedei. He cut all his links with Batu, rode back to Mongolia with his retainers and openly supported Guyuk and the houses of Ogodei and Tolui against Batu and the house of Jochi. He avoided all involvement in the murderous intrigues of 1242–46 but was present in 1246 at the quriltai that elected Guyuk. He then retired to the homeland of his Uriangqai tribe east of Lake Baikal, where he died in 1248 aged 72.[131] His son Uriankhadai went on to great things under Mongke in the war against the Song.

It is fairly clear from all the evidence that Subedei, Ogodei and Guyuk all wanted to conquer western Europe. Carpini in 1245 reported that Guyuk had a threefold project: election as khaghan, defeat of Batu in the civil war that had by then broken out between them, and then a fresh invasion of Poland and Hungary as a launch-pad for the conquest of Germany and Italy.[132] Guyuk claimed he wanted to attack Germany first, and proved that he had very good intelligence about the emperor Frederick's military capability, but Carpini told his colleague Salimbene di Adam he was convinced that Guyuk's real objective was Italy, both because of its wealth and because that was where 'Stupor Mundi' (not to mention the Pope) had his power base. Despite Carpini's boasting about German military might, which implied that the choice of Italy was the softer option, the likelihood is that the Mongols, knowing of the emperor's predilection for Italy, had simply decided to go for the jugular.[133]

Carpini noted that Guyuk was supremely realistic and was planning for a campaign that was expected to last eighteen years before victory was assured. As to the chances of success, the consensus of historians then and since was that the Mongols would have reached the Atlantic, but only provided their empire was united in a concerted, monolithic endeavour. Nor would Byzantium have been spared, as a Byzantine expert has pointed out: 'The successors of Genghis Khan . . . could doubtless have swept the Byzantine as well as the Latin and Bulgarian empires out of existence had the mood taken them.'[134] This was all the more so since, whereas the Mongols knew every last nuance of European politics, the West was still mired in ignorance about them, variously identifying them as the Ishmaelites or the Antichrist, the forces of Satan, the chaos world, the allies of heterodoxy, anarchy and disorder, fomenters of Islam, Cathars, Lombardy separatists or even the shock troops of an international Jewish conspiracy.

The West, in short, was long on emotion but short on reason and intelligence.[135] Carpini claimed to have discovered the secret of how the West could defeat the Mongols in battle, but this was no more than propaganda to keep Western spirits up.[136] While he whistled in the dark, more sober observers were stupefied by the Mongol with- drawal and suspected it might be like the Greeks' abandonment of Troy when they left behind the wooden horse. Matthew Paris thought the 'Tartars' would come again and that nothing could stop them reaching the Atlantic.[137] The Council of Lyons in 1245 heard an estimate from one bishop that the war with the Mongols might well last thirty- nine years – it is not clear where this exactitude came from.[138]

The sober truth was that by 1242 the Mongol empire was hopelessly divided by faction fighting, that civil war loomed and that anything so momentous as an invasion of Western Europe was not remotely conceivable. Batu, in short, withdrew from Europe because of manpower shortages and the looming conflict with Guyuk, and retreated to the upper Volga to prepare for the trial of strength which he knew would come.

His main problem was an acute lack of men. Once it was known that Ogodei was dead, the levies formerly loyal to Guyuk and Buri demanded to be allowed to return home, and there was nothing Batu could do to stop them unless he wanted a mini-civil war in his own empire; Mongke went with them, taking back to Karakorum his own anti-Batu version of the infamous banquet and the subsequent feud.[139] It was then that Batu showed his calibre as a politician. He may have been mediocre as a battlefield commander but he excelled in diplomacy and intrigue. Even before Ogodei died, while Batu planned the future of what would become the Golden Horde, he decided to shore up his position by seeking allies among the Rus princes, and he proved a shrewd picker.

Deeply unpopular with Novgorod's boyars, Alexander Nevsky had left the city for two years after his victory over the Swedes at the Neva but was then hurriedly recalled when the Teutonic Knights invaded Russia and took the city of Pskov to the west of Novgorod.[140] Purging the pro-German clique in Novgorod, Nevsky engaged the knights and their allies in a minor battle on the ice of Lake Peipus on 5 April 1242. The numbers involved on both sides were not large; only about one hundred Teutonic knights took part, with the rest of their army being Swedish and Lithuanian volunteers. Nevsky won a complete victory, though the Suzdalian chronicle attributes the real merit in this success to Alexander's brother Andrei.[141] Only about twenty knights were killed ('hardly indicative of a major encounter' as a sceptical historian notes), and there was no mass destruction when the German army plunged through the ice after it gave way under their weight.[142] Russian nationalists such as the Metropolitan Kirill in his *Life of Nevsky* elevated what was not much more than a skirmish to one of the great battles of the ages; Soviet propagandists reinforced this bogus view and this is the perception that has stuck.[143] Nevsky, meanwhile, was acclaimed as one of the very greatest Russian heroes, and canonised by the Orthodox Church both for his staunch opposition to overtures from an ecumenical Vatican and for his stoical and self-denying submission to Mongol rule.

The historical Nevsky, as opposed to the legendary creature so beloved in Russian mythology, was a slippery and serpentine character. The most significant thing about the battle of Lake Peipus is that Batu's envoys were present at Nevsky's side as military advisers; certainly the threat from the Teutonic Knights was the most important factor leading him to throw in his lot with the Mongols.[144] In fact Nevsky's relations with the Mongols were a tale of ambivalence and duplicity, with the hero self-servingly and ruthlessly focusing on his ambitious political goals; it was this that dictated his unswerving loyalty to Batu and his successors.[145]

Batu rewarded him by supporting him against his brother Andrei, who favoured religious rapprochement with Rome. The Mongols were very hard on Russians who tried to entangle the Vatican, thought to be the 'nerve centre' and real seat of power in the West. When Alexander's father Grand Prince Yaroslav seemed likely to renounce Russian Orthodoxy and submit to the papacy, the Mongols had him poisoned, though authorities differ on whether the 'contract' on his life was ordered by Batu or Ogodei's widow Toregene.[146] After Batu's death Nevsky enjoyed particularly good relations with the next khan of the Golden Horde, Sartaq (he was said to have entered into an *anda* relationship with him) who became a Christian. Even though Sartaq was probably poisoned by his uncle Berke, who succeeded him and converted to Islam, Nevsky continued on amicable terms with the new khan. As he had shown in the case of his father, and now his blood brother, Nevsky was not the kind of person to allow emotion and sentiment to get in the way of realpolitik.[147]

Ogodei's death really signalled the end of the Mongol empire that Genghis had striven so hard to found, though the formal structure continued in existence until the end of the 1250s. Guyuk was not elected as khaghan until 1246, a delay which had a fourfold explanation. It took that long for his mother, the Regent Toregene, to muster the necessary support; there was uncertainty about Batu's intentions, with Subedei vainly trying to act the honest broker and reconcile him and Guyuk; there was a general moral crisis in Mongolia because of the widespread rumour that Ogodei had been poisoned; and the shamans all declared that an early election would be inauspicious.[148]

During the four-and-a-half-year regency, Toregene and her close friend from Khorasan (originally her maid), Fatima, presided over bloody purges, including the arrest of Genghis's brother Temuge and the execution of all leading members of his faction. But she still faced the seemingly insuperable obstacle that both Koden, Ogodei's second son and Genghis's personal choice to succeed Ogodei, and Shiremun, Ogodei's grandson and his *own* personal choice, had better claims than Guyuk.

Koden did not trust himself to Toregene's mercies and formed a rival court in the former Qara Khitai, to which fled all Ogodei's former ministers dismissed by the Regent, especially Chinqai and the two Yalavachs. Toregene announced that both these candidatures were invalid: Shiremun was too young and Koden too sickly – a prize piece of humbug, given that her beloved Guyuk enjoyed even worse health.[149]

She did not long survive her triumph in seeing Guyuk elected in 1246, and on her death Guyuk put her policies into reverse. He restored the disgraced ministers and executed his mother's favourite Abd al-Rahman, to whom she had given the tax-farming concession in China. When Koden died mysteriously and in suspicious circumstances, Guyuk put Fatima on trial for having compassed his death by witchcraft and had her killed too, apparently by throwing her into a fast-moving river, knowing she could not swim. He also had Temuge executed.[150]

Guyuk made clear his contempt for all previous Mongol history by declaring that Ogodei had been not tough enough as khan and far too lax in all key areas. His authoritarian turn of mind was well illustrated by the peremptory demand he sent to all European rulers in 1245, ordering them to submit; surprisingly, he has nonetheless found scholarly defenders.[151] Batu declared his election illegal on the grounds that, as senior Mongol, he had to be present at a quriltai for its decisions to be binding. Guyuk tried to hamstring him by declaring a crusade against the West, but his sister-in-law Sorqoqtani, Tolui's widow, kept him informed of all that happened at Karakorum and this ploy came to nothing.[152] Civil war was imminent when Batu and Guyuk began advancing towards each other in 1248. With Batu having crossed the River Ili and Guyuk as far west as Beshbaliq, Guyuk suddenly died; his poor health (he suffered acutely from colic) and alcoholism were blamed but many suspected poisoning, with Sorqoqtani as the mastermind.[153]

There followed another three-year female regency, with Guyuk's widow Oghul Qaimish, a notably foolish woman, on the throne. Meanwhile Sorqoqtani, described by Rashid al-Din as the most intelligent woman in the world, worked behind the scenes to secure the elevation of Mongke, her son (and Tolui's eldest), to the khanate. She and Batu were on very good terms as a result of her services to him during Guyuk's reign and also because she shared the creed of Nestorian Christianity with his son Sartaq.[154]

In 1251, with the support of Batu, Mongke was elected khaghan. He was an intensely serious ruler, the first non-alcoholic khan since Genghis, and under him foreign conquest once more became a priority.

He had no interest in western Europe, probably because that would have meant treading on Batu's toes, and devoted most of his energies to a renewed war with the Song. He did, however, have one of the abiding faults of the Mongols: blood-letting. He executed the ex-regent Oghul Qaimish and also Buri, to please Batu, who had never forgotten the insult at the banquet in 1240. Oghul Qaimish had joined a plot to murder Mongke and place Shiremun on the throne, in which a number of Mongol princesses were involved. These women were beaten with burning sticks to make them confess, and Mongke and his supporters milked the conspiracy for all it was worth.[155]

Shiremun himself was found to have been involved in the intrigue but Mongke did not kill him at once, and instead sent him to the front in China where the khaghan's brother Qubilai commanded the army. This turned out to be a reprieve only, for Shiremun, having failed to die fighting in China, was finally put to death in spring 1258 when Mongke went south to take personal charge of the campaign against the Song. All three hundred or so of Shiremun's closest supporters perished in a bloody purge immediately after the attempted coup.[156]

In 1259 Mongke died, either of cholera or dysentery, the first Mongol khan to die while actually campaigning.[157] This was the point at which the unified empire definitively broke up, though the Golden Horde had been independent in all but name since 1242. Two separate and simultaneous quriltais elected different great khans. Qubilai emerged the victor in this struggle and went on to found the Yuan dynasty in a united China in 1279.

The empire shivered into four parts. Apart from Qubilai's China and the Golden Horde, which dominated Russia for another two hundred years, there was the Chagatai Khanate in central Asia (covering parts of the modern nations of Mongolia, Russia, India, China, Pakistan, Afghanistan, Turkmenistan, Uzbekistan, Tajikistan and Kazakhstan)[158] and the Ilkhanate, founded by Mongke's brother Hulagu in 1256 and including eastern Turkey, Iran, Iraq, Azerbaijan, Georgia, Armenia, western Afghanistan, south-western Pakistan and parts of modern Turkmenistan.[159] Just thirty years after Genghis's death his mighty empire had crumbled into four realms with different destinies. It is a measure of his genius, and of the talent of his son Ogodei, that the entire mighty edifice had lasted so long.

Conclusion

Genghis Khan was the greatest conqueror the world has ever known. He and his sons vanquished peoples from the Adriatic to the Pacific. The Mongols eventually reached Austria, Finland, Croatia, Hungary, Poland, Vietnam, Burma, Japan and Indonesia. His empire stretched from the Persian Gulf to the Arctic Ocean. Mongol influence extended as far as Mali in Africa. The Mongol empire covered twelve million contiguous square miles – an area as large as Africa and bigger than North America; by contrast the extent of the Roman empire was about half that of the continental U.S.A. By 1240 Mongol conquests covered most of the 'known' world and, even at Genghis's death in 1227, embraced more than half this world.[1] The modern population of the countries ruled by the empire at its greatest extent contain three billion of the world's seven billion population.

All this was achieved by a man who seemed to come from nowhere; the only similar feat, though in a very different sphere, was that of Jesus of Nazareth. Genghis had no tradition to build on, for although there had been powerful steppe kingdoms and nations before him, he was unaware of them.[2] Alexander the Great had a powerful military machine constructed by his father Philip of Macedonia; Julius Caesar had three hundred years of Roman military superiority to build on; Napoleon could rely both on the ancient French tradition of Condé and Turenne as well as the élan of the French Revolution and the mass mobilisation it unleashed.

In a real sense Genghis had to invent his own tradition and solve a plethora of political and social problems as he went along. Besides his military and administrative genius and his uncanny ability to read men, Genghis was truly original in that he saw how it was possible for nomads, employing the quantum leap in military technology afforded by his mounted archers, to dominate civilised societies and extract tribute from them. All this he did while being illiterate and having no access through books to the wisdom of the ages.[3] By contrast, Alexander was taught by Aristotle, one of the great minds of the ages, Caesar had the best education Roman wealth could buy and Napoleon was heir to both the Enlightenment and the Romantic movement, deeply influenced as he was by both Rousseau and Voltaire.

On paper a primitive nomad, Genghis was not disfigured by racial or religious prejudice, and was fascinated by written scripts, literate culture and the teachings of sages. It is not a mere trope that in Buddhist historiography Genghis and Qubilai are regarded as the successors of Ashoka.[4] He soon realised what he could gain from collaboration with alien cultures. He transcended the limitations of such as Subedei by appreciating the advantages that could accrue from learning from China and Islam, even if this irritated the more purblind Mongol princes, and thus revealed himself as the supreme pragmatist.[5]

But there was nothing one-dimensional about him. His attitudes reveal deep ambivalence and complexity: between conservatism and innovation, between ancient and traditional modes of thought and the fresh and original, between visions of world empire and a sentimental, nostalgic hankering after old nomadic ways, and even between the quasi-Pauline notion of 'one nation' of Mongols and his instinctive preference for 'divide and rule', as conveyed in one of his sayings: 'People conquered on different sides of the lake should be ruled on different sides of the lake.'[6]

If ever the phrase 'great man' applied in history, it applied to Genghis. He may also be the man with the greatest number of descendants in history. Geneticists have recently established that about 0.8 per cent of the population of Asia has an identical Y-chromosome, indicating the likelihood of a common ancestor, possibly some time around 1000 AD. This would imply that about 0.5 per cent of the world's population has this common ancestor and that he has 16–17 million descendants.[7] Another study, by entirely different geneticists, shows clear evidence of Mongol DNA entering the Hazara people of Pakistan around 1300. Furthermore, six other populations, as far west as Turkey, show similar evidence of genetic mixing with Mongols as conquering soldiers begat offspring on women in conquered areas. The Uighurs have 50 per cent Mongol genetic input, the Uzbheks 39 per cent but the Turks only 8 per cent, showing the kind of progressive westward decrease in Mongol ancestry that one might expect.[8] The easy availability of huge numbers of women to Genghis and his sons, as to no other identifiable Asian personality, makes it likely that Genghis might be this mysterious philoprogenitor. It is argued that if Genghis had thirty-two children (a reasonable assumption) and each of those had another sixteen, even if the numbers of offspring decreased steadily and arithmetically over the generations, as the Mongols ceased to have such automatic access to women when the empire declined, it would take only about three hundred years to reach sixteen million inhabitants. That would take us to the mid-sixteenth century. If we then factored in childhood deaths, mortality from war and disease, this would explain why that number was not in fact reached in the sixteenth century but only in the late twentieth century.[9]

Nevertheless the theory has not been generally accepted. The difference of a couple of centuries between the dates of Genghis's life and the timing of this putative ancestor could no doubt be explained away, but there are simply too many imponderables to allow such a neat calculation, and even on the best-case scenario, the most we would have, without a tissue sample from Genghis himself, is probability. The 'Genghis as father of us all' school probably represents the extreme end (and some might say the *reductio ad absurdum*) of the 'great man' approach to history.

Of course to historians of a certain kind any elevation of the individual is unpalatable and misleading. Engels famously stated that great men appear when a given socio-economic situation requires them, but the argument is circular because the only sign that social circumstances require them is the fact that they actually do appear.[10] This proposition first made its full-blooded appearance in the writings of Montesquieu in the eighteenth century. He wrote:

> It is not chance that rules the world. Ask the Romans, who had a continuous sequence of success when they were guided by a certain plan, and an uninterrupted sequence of reverses when they followed another. There are general causes, moral and physical, which act in every monarchy, elevating it, maintaining it or hurling it to the ground. All accidents are controlled by these causes. And if the chance

of one battle – that is, a particular cause – has brought a state to ruin, some general cause made it necessary for that state to perish from a particular battle. In a word, the main trend draws with it all particular accidents.[11]

Pace Montesquieu, this is a mere assertion and is not borne out by Genghis's career, where chance and contingency played so great a part. It was chance that in his youth the old Mongol confederacy had degenerated into a shambles, so that his followers were more closely tied to him as a charismatic leader and not a mere contestant for the khanship with other chiefs or his own brothers. Moreover, not being a member of the senior Mongol lineage, he could create his own dynasty and his own despotism without being hedged in by tradition. Also, the early death of his father meant he did not have to wait in the wings as, say, Marcus Aurelius had to for twenty-two years as deputy to Emperor Antoninus Pius. It was chance that he was not killed in battle or by disease. The accumulation of contingent circumstances goes on and on.[12]

In their reluctance to concede that great individuals really can and do make history, and in the absence of any socio-economic 'requirement' in Mongolia in the late twelfth century, some historians have fastened on climate as the key factor explaining the rise of Genghis Khan. Climatic determinism is a very old idea, going back to Montesquieu and, beyond him, to Ibn Khaldun in the fourteenth century.[13] Montesquieu's case is particularly relevant, as he loathed the Mongols, thought that Asia was irremediably wedded to despotism and slavery, and that climate was the root cause.[14] Theories on the Mongols and climatology essentially cluster into five groups, apart from Montesquieu's strict determinism.

The first is that in some general way, not particularly defined, the climate and environment on the steppe produced a particular kind of hardy people. This idea is particularly associated with the Russian theorist Lev Gumilev. Annual vacillations in solar radiation determine the amount of grassland that can be used for grazing livestock. A critical column of air – what Gumilev calls a 'transtropic maximum' – responsible for cyclones and rainfall, may have moved away from the steppes because of solar activity, engorging the Caspian but desiccating the Aral Sea.[15] In some unexplained way this connects with 'passionarity' – the level of activity a people needs for expansion. According to Gumilev, all ethnic groups pass through phases of birth, development, climax, inertia, convolution and memorial. National 'passionarity' at the 'acmatic' (i.e. climactic) phase leads to great conquest; according to Gumilev it was the Arab world that was in this phase in his lifetime but it was the Mongols who were at this level in the late twelfth century.[16]

Some may feel these ideas are metaphysical and even mystical. The other notions are more comprehensible. The second climatic theory is that aridity on the steppes forced the Mongols outwards on their course of world expansion, and that drought favoured the nomads more than settled communities, who could not simply load their effects onto carts and trek on.[17] An ingenious variant of this is that it may simply have been a decrease in winds and sandstorms that released the Mongols from a cycle of subsistence.[18] Drought and desiccation are of huge importance on the steppe, for if desert increases at the expense of pastureland (as has happened in Mongolia in the past half century), the consequences are serious.[19]

The third idea is that cold weather and polar winds are the key factor. Some claim that Jin China during the crucial years 1211–34 was the victim of unusually cold weather, and that such conditions in northern Eurasia in the 1220s generally weakened resistance to Mongol expansion. But the theorists espousing this interpretation have been accused of neglecting subtleties and nuances, for example extrapolating from conditions in Alaska and Switzerland to those in Mongolia and China and not factoring in longitudinal differences; for example, it is pointed out that whereas Greenland was colder than usual in the period 1180–1210, northern Scandinavia was hotter in 1160–90.[20] The fourth idea is that it was wetter conditions that aided the rise of the Mongols, since high grassland productivity caused by this meant that more horses could be raised and therefore the potential for foreign adventures increased. According to an influential coterie of tree-ring scientists, in 1211–30 Mongolia experienced one of its coolest and wettest periods ever, precipitating a boom in grass production, livestock and human population.[21]

Most promising of the climatic arguments are those that make climate one of a network of causal factors and differentiate clearly between necessary and sufficient conditions. The leading Mongolist

Owen Lattimore, for example, amalgamated a 'neoclassical' view that nomads moved out of Mongolia because of ecological and climatic factors coming from outside with a 'semiclassical' view that overcultivation or a switch from hunting to grazing will in itself bring about desertification and climate change.[22] Following the example of the American climatologist Ellsworth Huntington, Lattimore fused climate with a cyclical view of history. This is interesting on two counts. Lattimore was famously identified by Senator McCarthy as a leading 'Red' in the 1950s but his views were at a considerable distance from orthodox Soviet Marxism, which pushed hard the idea of a linear development in history, from primitive communal societies to slavery to feudalism and finally to capitalism. Cyclical views of history, associated with Machiavelli, Vico, Gibbon, Nietzsche, Herder, Spengler and Arnold Toynbee, are usually considered the prerogative of the political Right.

Lattimore's spirals were complex. He claimed that to say Genghis Khan appeared like a thunderbolt, as it were from nowhere, seriously distorted the history of the steppes. On the other hand, the Mongols were not just a rerun of the Hsiung-nu and earlier nomads; there was a sense in which Genghis was 'emergent' and represented an advance.[23] Lattimore's borrowings from Marxism, in short, were idiosyncratic and eclectic. A similar 'pick-and-mix' attitude to orthodox Marxism is evident in the work of Gumilev who tells us that 'the unification of the steppe was a historical necessity'[24] ('why?' one asks) but adds that it was not historical necessity that it was Genghis who should prevail; it could have been Jamuga, or the Kereit or the Naiman, and it is in this area that chance and contingency take over. Gumilev is multicausal also in pointing out that, under pressure from climate, the Mongols hunted out both wild ungulates and natural predators – even wolves were under threat from their ferocious dogs and trained eagles.[25]

Finally, there are those who adumbrate a theory of psychological types derived from climate, again a development of Montesquieu. For example, 'Such a climate [the steppes] forms a type of man who is incredibly tough, of an almost superhuman endurance, adaptable, alert in mind but not devoted to metaphysical speculation.'[26]

Two things are very clear. First, there is a widespread resistance to the idea that Genghis as a genius might have been causally responsible for almost the entirety of his achievement. Secondly, arguments about the Mongols derived from climatology tend to end in a cul-de-sac through lack of evidence, self-contradiction or being cancelled out by rival theories starting from the same initial premise. Simple correlations between Mongol expansion and climate change are not tenable, as some additional factor is always needed to make the argument cogent.[27]

But the story of climate and the Mongols does have one interesting twist. The Mongol invasions resulted in vast tracts of formerly cultivated land, devastated by the invaders, being reclaimed by forests, while the culling of the population by the wars themselves and the resulting plagues and diseases accelerated this process. It has been estimated that in this way 700 million tons of carbon were eliminated from the atmosphere – enough to offset an entire year of pollution from petrol (gasoline) in the modern world.[28] Genghis and his sons, it seems, were not just red with blood but, unknowingly, environmentally green.

The hottest topic involving Genghis Khan and the Mongols is their responsibility for worldwide fatalities in the forty years or so after 1206. There is the wildest divergence here and although balance is necessary, it is hard to attain. There is a tendency for writers on Genghis to bifurcate into extremism of one kind or the other, either accusing or rehabilitating. One school of thought would make the Mongols culpable for just about every military atrocity that has ever occurred; the other would make them harbingers of world peace and security, beset by a few regrettable excesses. One historian makes Genghis responsible for the ferocity not only of the Spanish *Reconquista* against the Moors in the late fifteenth century but also their massacre of the Aztecs and Incas. The Mongols are supposed to have imported ruthless ferocity to Islam, which in turn transmitted it to the Crusaders, and thence back to Spain and, after Columbus's voyages of discovery, the New World: 'the awful fate of the Incas and Aztecs . . . ultimately washed back to Genghis Khan himself.'[29] A better historian has riposted that 'ruthless ferocity' was actually introduced to Islam by the Crusaders.[30]

On the other hand are the writers who soft-pedal the casualties caused by the Mongols and stress instead their enlightened attitude to women, their avoidance (mostly) of torture, their transmission of culture and the arts and, even, their role as fount and origin of the

Renaissance.[31] Of course in a quasi-Hegelian sense in which everything ultimately links with everything else, such connections can be made, but this one seems fanciful and far-fetched. These divergent modern views are a projection across the centuries of the diametrically opposed views of the Mongols entertained in thirteenth-century England. For Matthew Paris the Mongols were Gog and Magog aroused from their slumber, they were the demons of Tartarus, the myrmidons of Satan himself. For the great Franciscan thinker Bacon the Mongols represented the triumph of science and philosophy over ignorance.[32]

There can be no denying that Genghis and the Mongols were responsible for millions and millions of deaths. Different reasons have been adduced: the Mongols spread terror and cruelty because they had a small-scale steppe mentality transposed onto a global stage; because in terms of the Mongols' divine mission resistance was blasphemy;[33] because they feared and hated walled cities and expended their fury on them once taken; because it was the most efficient way to warn already conquered peoples not to attempt 'stab in the back' revolts as the Mongols pressed ever onwards. The simplest explanation for the chilling policy of 'surrender or die' was that the Mongols, as a far from numerous people, were always obsessed with casualties, so that the best-case scenario was a walkover surrender in which none of their troops died. This explains why nearly all the cities that surrendered without even token resistance received relatively good treatment.[34]

Since one version of Genghis is that of a cruel despot who raised mountains of human skulls, we should first ask: how many died as a result of his wars and conquests? This is a peculiarly difficult question to answer, for a number of reasons. Ancient and medieval chroniclers routinely multiplied numbers, sometimes tenfold, so we have to discount their figures; on the other hand, modern historians in general have an almost equal and opposite tendency to 'downsize' to evince their scholarly scepticism. Estimates of fatalities can be made only when we have accurate population statistics, but medieval census figures are unreliable. Finally, calculating war losses is a notorious minefield; scholars cannot even agree on figures for deaths in the Second World War.

The obvious starting point is the twenty-three-year war Genghis waged in Jin China, for this was his toughest campaign, the longest and most calamitous in terms of loss of human life. What was the population of Jin China in 1211 and what was it in 1234 when Genghis's successor Ogodei emerged triumphant? The census conducted in China in 1236 by Yelu Chu Cai reported 1,730,000 households and eight and a half million people, whereas the last Jin census (1207–08) produced 7,684,438 households and 45,816,079 people.[35] The one before that, in 1195, recorded 58,834,711.[36]

That would indicate a catastrophic decline in population, but the huge crevasse between the two figures alerts us that there is something very wrong here. Various explanations have been adduced, and it is likely that all are valid. Many census evaders hid in woods or mountains; the Mongols themselves took away tens of thousands of craftsmen; many Chinese emigrated to south-east Asia or at least to Song China to escape the Mongol invasion.[37] Even more potently, many Chinese went unreported in areas where Mongol lords had enslaved them, causing them to disappear from the records. Children were left off the census returns on the grounds that they might not survive the high rate of infant mortality. But most of all there was bureaucratic corruption and incompetence. Officials hated the chore of periodic censuses and simply guessed or made up the figures; in some cases they under-reported so as not to incur a higher tax quota.[38] There are so many variables to be considered in assessing the population of medieval China that any conclusion is bound to be impressionistic.

The problem did not end in the Mongol era. A distinguished Sinologist has concluded that, depending on which model one uses, the population of China in 1600 could have been 66 million, 150 million or 230 million.[39] An 'educated guess' as to the total numbers in China, after the Mongol conquest of the Song in 1279, puts the numbers somewhere between 110 and 150 million, with perhaps 80–100 million in the former Song south, sustained by Champa rice.[40]

The population decline in northern China as a result of the Mongol conquests may have been exaggerated in the past but it was still substantial. Was it huge? One of the problems is that different experts have given different answers to different questions. Some assess the death toll over the entire Mongol period of hegemony in the Far East, from 1206 to 1368. Others group together the fatalities from the wars of Genghis, Qubilai and Tamerlane. With little help from scientific demography, we can only infer from other great Chinese military catastrophes, involving devastation similar to the Mongol invasions, bearing in mind that the fatalities in those conflicts are also disputed. The two obvious analogies for the Mongol invasion of 1211–34 are the An Lu-shan revolt under the Tang dynasty in 755–63 and the great Taiping rebellion of 1850–64. Figures of 36 million dead have been claimed for the An Lu-shan convulsion, although sinologists describe this statistic as absurd.[41] The generally accepted figure is 26 million and, even if we halve that for reasons of caution and scepticism, we are still left with the huge figure of 13 million for seven years of warfare.[42] As for Taiping, incredible figures as high as 100 million have been claimed but again, no reputable scholar is prepared to go below a figure of twenty million dead, and this is regarded as a conservative minimum.[43] Twenty to thirty million dead in the Taiping rising, lasting fourteen years, and 26 million in the An-Lushan, lasting seven, can be convincingly correlated with the twenty-three years of Mongol-Jin conflict. As a kind of footnote one could add that 27 million were killed in the Sino-Japanese conflict of 1937–45.

In short, sustained warfare in China always produces massive casualties. And there are natural disasters to be taken into account also, which thirteenth-century chroniclers would be unlikely to treat in detail. The Yellow River, scene of so many battles between Genghis's captains and the Jin, carried off between one and two million people in 1887 and another 500–700,000 in 1938 after terrifying flooding, and in 1931 China lost between 2,500,000 and 3,700,000 to floods.[44] Many casualties even in modern warfare are not listed in official statistics. A recent view is that the Japanese in 1941–45 killed 30 million Filipinos, Malays, Vietnamese, Cambodians and Burmese, which, if true, would take the fatality roster for the Second World War, currently anywhere between 75–82 million, well over the hundred million mark.[45] Even the Thirty Years War (1618–48), fought in supposedly civilised Europe, reduced the population of Germany from 21 million to 13 million and accounted for eleven and a half million deaths (the birth rate partly compensating for the huge death rate).[46] The mortality in King Leopold's Congo in 1885–1908 was at least ten million and possibly as high as 22 million.[47] (Incidentally, it should be noted that children born during wars are often not recorded on the grounds that they might not survive, and in medieval times there was very high child mortality.)

All of this is circumstantial evidence for the terrifying figure of deaths in China in 1211–34 – thirty million – which is widely accepted: perhaps 7.5 per cent of the total population of the world at that time.[48] To the probable 30 million deaths in China we can add at least another seven and a half million from the campaigns against Khwarezmia in 1220–22 and those in Europe in 1222–23 and 1237–42. In the case of Khwarezmia we are at sea, for there is no reliable information whatever about the population of medieval Iran.[49] We have only the chroniclers and the later reports of the great traveller Ibn Battuta in the early fourteenth century to go on.[50] Some authors are prepared to accept their ludicrous figures for deaths at Merv (1,300,000), Herat (1,600,000) and Nishapur (1,750,000), although it is obvious that the chroniclers have added a nought in each case, magnifying the casualties tenfold. Such writers claim that Genghis killed 15 million people in Khwarezmia (possibly three times greater than the entire population) and that Iran did not regain its pre-Mongol demographic level until the mid-twentieth century.[51]

From all the best scholarship on casualties in this war, it is more likely that the losses, though huge, were not at such stratospheric levels. Possibly the population of Iran declined from five million to 3.5 million, and that of Afghanistan from 2.5 million to 1.75 million. If we also discount the hyperbole of the chroniclers to the effect that Russia lost half its population, a more sober estimate would see the Russian population declining from 7.5 million to seven million.[52] The death toll due to the Mongols in Russia and eastern Europe would therefore be around the million mark. If we add Russia, eastern Europe, the Khwarezmian empire to China and Genghis's minor wars, we end up with the convincing total of 37.5 million.[53]

This enormous toll is partly attributable to the 'surrender or die' policy and the stiff-necked opposition of populations who had been beguiled by their own rulers' propaganda and did not know what they were getting into. The murderous quality of Genghis was overdone by Islamic historians, who regarded the Mongols as 'The Great Satan', and ignored the atrocities and massacres committed by their own side, especially Jalal al-Din. The distortion was further increased when the Mongols colluded in exaggerated stories about their brutality, hoping to scare the enemy into giving up without a fight, out of sheer terror. There are no signs in Genghis of a mindless or psychopathic cruelty;

everything was done for a purpose.[54] And that purpose was not savage, blind ferocity or conquest simply for plunder, as with previous nomads, but with the purpose of conquering the world in the name of Tengerri and establishing an empire out of which the Mongols could suck tribute, enjoying the fruits of conquest without having to relinquish the traditional way of life that Genghis held so dear.[55]

Since Genghis considered his role as world conqueror self-evident, there was no need to work up hatred against the conquered or make out that his enemies were subhuman. He was admirably free of both racial prejudice and religious intolerance. Many of the contemporary attacks on him were propaganda attempts to encourage native resistance against the invader, eruptions of emotion in response to the deep trauma of defeat or simply ignorant attempts to explain the inexplicable phenomenon that had appeared from the East.[56]

To an extent the Mongols had themselves to blame for their bad press, for they were notorious for not keeping their word. They would have approved of Hobbes's dictum (previously quoted) that covenants without the sword are but words, and one of Genghis's sayings was a cynical gloss on this: 'Game killed by mouth cannot be loaded onto a horse. Game slaughtered by words cannot be skinned.'[57] The stories that each Mongol killed one hundred people in Khwarezmia in five years lost nothing in the telling, even though it seems a far from impossible target in theory. In the realm of absurdity, however, is the story that 50,000 Mongols had to kill twenty-four people each in a single day. As a modern commentator has remarked,

> Who would have maintained order as the victims awaited their turn for execution? How could knives and swords have been kept sharp for such an arduous task? Where would the mounting piles of bodies and their possessions have been stored? Would the executioners have worked shifts and continued through the night? Would food and drink have been served to executioners and victims as the job proceeded?[58]

Another consideration is that it was often the Mongols' local recruits who were more enthusiastic at slaughter than the Mongols themselves; the behaviour of the Georgians at the siege of Baghdad in 1258 is a case in point.[59] It is important not to judge Genghis by twenty-first century standards but to see him in the context of general behaviour in the thirteenth century. He exceeded in degree but not in kind the other killers of the age. One could give any number of instances: the slaughter of the Song by the Jin in Kaifeng in 1127; the massacre of the Albigensians by fellow-Christians at Béziers and Carcassonne in 1209; Edward I's butchery of 8,000 Scots at Berwick in 1296; the 30,000 Hindus killed at Chittor in 1303 by the troops of Ala al-Din Khilji; the Byzantine blinding of the Bulgars in 1014; the behaviour of Christians at Antioch and Jerusalem during the First Crusade – one could go on and on. It is wisest to accept the judgement of a notable historian of Russia: 'Chingis was no more cruel, and no less, than empire builders before and since. Moral judgments are of little help in understanding his importance.'[60]

Another crime laid at the door of Genghis and the Mongols is their alleged enslavement of Russia. From this, it is alleged, comes the Russian propensity for autocracy and the long line of despots stretching from Ivan the Terrible to Putin with Peter the Great, Catherine the Great, Lenin and Stalin being only the most notable. Echoing the psychologist C. G. Jung, who saw Hitler as an introjection of Wotan and the German forest gods, some Russian specialists have speculated that two and a half centuries under the 'Mongol yoke' left a permanent scar and that Russia absorbed tyranny into its collective unconscious, thus retarding the nation by three whole centuries.[61]

The best Russian scholars reject the idea and claim that the impact of the Mongols on Russian life was superficial. Donald Ostrowski says that sixteenth-century Russian Orthodox divines played up the 'Mongol yoke' to disguise the failings of the nation and especially those of their own church.[62] George Vernadsky considers that the long-term Mongol impact was largely beneficial, as it absorbed Russia into the international network of long-distance trade, and through the *Pax Mongolica* co-opted the Rus states into the medieval world's 'globalisation'; in this view he is endorsed by Charles Halperin.[63] Particularly in the north-east, the principalities had not only recovered from the Mongol invasions by the 1280s but received a major fillip from the expansion of the Mongol-driven 'world system'.[64]

In the nineteenth century, when imperial propaganda made a point of attributing any and every problem to the pent-up consequences of the 'Mongol yoke', the seclusion of women, said to be a consequence of the mass Islamic conversion of the Golden Horde, was also laid at the door of Genghis and his successors.[65] Unfortunately for this perception, the Mongols did not seclude women. Carpini, Rubruck, Marco Polo and all other travellers to the Mongol courts testified to the prominent position of women in Mongol life, often using the fact as an excuse for a rant on this 'unnatural' approach to gender relations.[66] Halperin, indeed, goes further and argues that seclusion was an indigenous *Muscovite* tradition, beginning in the sixteenth century.[67] The most one can say about Russia is that it borrowed many things from the administrative practices of the Mongols – they would have been foolish not to – and that the Yasa in particular influenced Russian law and culture.[68] The 'Mongol yoke' argument was sometimes used in the Soviet era, but by then most efforts were concentrated on proving that the rise of Genghis represented the triumph of feudalism over the clan principle, thus neatly slotting him into the paradigm of historical materialism as required by orthodox Marxism. It was ironical that the early Soviet scholars used Marxism to interpret Genghis and the Mongols, for nomadism was probably the most implausible sociological category to be explained by class analysis.[69]

Just as there is every reason to rehabilitate the Mongols against unjust accusations of extreme cruelty and barbarism, which plunged the nations they conquered into darkness, so one has to be careful in assessing the great benefits to the world often ascribed to Genghis and his successors. There are two main views. One credits the Mongols with introducing a long era of peace in Eurasia, allowing a kind of early globalisation to flourish, while the other is sceptical and claims that, if there really was a *Pax Mongolica*, it was a very short-lived affair.

The pro-Genghis camp asserts that it was as a result of his activities that China was brought into contact with the Islamic world and thus with the West, since the West had already made its presence felt in the Muslim world during the Crusades. Trade and the Yasa were the main pillars of the Mongol peace, aided by the yam. The Mongol propensity for trade rather than war gradually increased, particularly when Genghis himself was won over to the idea that agriculture generated more wealth than nomadism.[70] It was said that you could travel from Palestine to Mongolia with a gold plate on your head and not be molested, but the journey was still an arduous one because of primitive transport. Even in the glory days of the *Pax Mongolica*, it took a traveller 295 days to get from Turkey to Peking.[71]

Yet the Mongols undoubtedly opened up the world. Until 1250 there was in the West a narrow European viewpoint which saw the world virtually end at Jerusalem. The journeys of Carpini, Rubruck and Marco Polo (and the Chinese traveller Rabban Bar Sauma in the opposite direction) cleared the way for new vistas. Learned people finally got a sense of the size of the world and its population.[72] The globe shrank as Venetian traders appeared in Peking, Mongolian envoys in Bordeaux and Northampton, and Genoese consuls in Tabriz. There were Arab tax officials in China, Mongolian lawyers in Egypt, French craftsmen in Karakorum. The art of Iran was influenced by Uighur and Chinese motifs.[73] From China to the Islamic world and Europe came the knowledge of firearms, silk cultivation, ceramics and woodblock printing.

The Mongol empire, in short, served as a transmission belt for trade, technology, science and culture, particularly but not solely between Iran and China, and the Mongol conquests were the rivet that held the 'world system' together for a hundred years after 1250.[74] The southern route of the Silk Road, which had fallen into disuse in favour of the northern and middle routes, was revived and linked the Aral and Caspian Seas with Byzantium.[75] The beginnings of a Mongol aesthetic culture were discernible, even though most Mongol literature dates from the fourteenth century. There was, however, a poem written in 1225 about an archery contest held to commemorate Genghis's return that year from his triumph in Khwarezmia. Mongol sculptures, dealing with death, natural life, warfare and mythology and generally carved on rock faces – petroglyphs – grew ever more sophisticated, as did their frescoes and paintings on Buddhist themes, foreshadowing the eventual conversion of Mongolia in the sixteenth century to Lamaistic Buddhism.[76] Finally, some writers trace a causal line from the *Pax Mongolica* to the discovery of the New World by Columbus.[77]

That the Mongol conquests resulted in greater global knowledge, that culture and technology was transmitted from western Europe to China and vice versa via the Middle East, that religious conversions in faraway lands became possible, all this cannot seriously be doubted. But did this constitute a genuine *Pax Mongolica*? Carpini's statement that there was no significant theft or robbery in the Mongol empire in the mid-1240s has been much commented on[78] but was he present at an untypical moment? Some historians claim that, if there was a

Pax Mongolica, it was short-lived, possibly enduring only the twenty years from 1242–61.[79] After that the empire splintered into four fragments – some of which were hostile to others, as the Ilkhans to the Chagatai realm and the Golden Horde to Qubilai's China. There was no comparison with the *Pax Romana* which lasted two centuries.[80]

Others say that it was largely one-way traffic, as there were no Chinese equivalents of Rubruck, Marco Polo or John of Montecorvino.[81] The diplomatic contacts between the Mongol world and the West were nugatory and largely petered out.[82] The importance of journeys across Asia from the West has in any case been exaggerated; it bears no comparison to the breakthrough achieved in the Age of Discovery from the late fifteenth century on. The collapse of Genghis's unified empire was one of the key factors allowing Europe to pull ahead of the Orient by the sixteenth century, and this process began as early as 1260.[83] A true world system is possible only if maritime trade is brought into the picture, but the Mongols feared the sea (rightly, as it turned out from their later abortive invasion of Japan) and preferred a gruelling journey overland of possibly eighteen months to the terrors of the ocean, with the Indian Ocean being the main barrier.[84] The security offered to international traders was supposed to be predicated on the early partnership between Genghis and his successors with merchants, but this was no ideological affair whereby the Mongols uniquely favoured mercantile endeavours. Mongols did not regard the mercantile interest as a thing apart and, if merchants were found on enemy territory, they too were regarded as hostile and could be slaughtered or their goods confiscated as the local commander saw fit.[85]

Finally, there were unintended consequences deriving from the role of the empire as a hinge for the 'world system'. Rinderpest or steppe murrain, a disease in ungulate animals similar to measles in humans, devastated cattle herds in Asia from the 1240s on, spread by the Mongols' great conquests of 1236–42. Even worse, the Mongols may have been responsible for the spread of the Black Death. Even though there are many conflicting views on the origin of this pandemic, it seems clear that central Asia was a major vector of the disease, in particular the new avenues of the Silk Route opened up by Mongol conquest which had their terminus at the Crimea.[86]

The empires of Alexander the Great, Tamerlane and Napoleon crumbled as soon as they died. It was the genius of Genghis to construct an empire that lasted longer, and it says much for the talent of Ogodei that he took his father's legacy and expanded it to its greatest extent. The house that Genghis built was unique, a one-off, *sui generis*. It is not amenable to any general explanation and presents a stubborn and irreducible mass standing in the way of any smooth, linear conception of history. Devotees of such linearity are hugely tempted to make Genghis's 'nomadism-plus' society into a subgroup of feudalism, but all the usual definitions of the term, involving inter-mittent labour and military service to a liege-lord, do not cover the Mongol experience.

The temptation is clear, for the formation of a retinue system (the *nokor*, the keshig) usually marks a decisive step in the transition from a tribal to a feudal order, as it cuts across kinship relations, substituting conventional for biological bonds of loyalty.[87] The Russian historians spoke of 'nomadic feudalism' and even the great Mongol scholar Rachewiltz refers to 'a kind of feudalism'.[88] But feudalism was primarily an economic affair, whereas the key to the Mongol empire was always personal relations and personal policies, as we can see in the differen-tial policies of Genghis and Ogodei. Always mindful of the Mongols' small numbers and the consequent impact of casualties, Genghis used slave labour at home and foreign troops abroad, and transported artisans, craftsmen and experts to Mongolia. Ogodei then shifted towards the exploitation of the settled population, concentrating on duties on trade, taxes and *corvée*.[89]

But the Mongol system was always inherently unstable, as they neither traded nor produced so depended entirely on the toil of the conquered. Like the shark or Lewis Carroll's Red Queen, the Mongols could not stand still and had to move constantly forward. Nomadic pastoralism was a more highly specialised and skilled exploitation of the natural world than pre-feudal agriculture, but increases in produc-tivity were impossible, unlike in agriculture, as the ratio of humans to livestock was fixed. Soil can be improved but herds require land which must remain the same; agriculture, in a word, can change qualitatively but pastoralism only quantitatively.[90] Pastoralism as a mode of production was incompatible with a political structure of state-directed extraction of tribute. The 'contradiction' between a world empire and a nomadic base was marked.

Moreover, the Mongols could not go on conquering indefinitely, which their system required if tribute was to be distributed to an ever-increasing number of oligarchs with 'entitlement'. Even if they had reached the Atlantic, sooner or later the bubble would have burst, and as soon as this happened the contraction would be exponential.[91] The Mongol empire was thus doomed to two different species of impossibilism. Its inner dynamic would in the end bring it crashing down. And in any case the leaders faced a dilemma. If they remained as nomads, they would have to impose semi-pastoralism on the conquered, but the demographic increase of the 'natives' would eventually lead them to rebel and overcome the oppressors. It must be remembered that the ratio of Mongols to tribute-bearing people was about one to one hundred.[92]

On the other hand, to abandon pastoralism and horses – the engine of conquest – would be to throw their best card away. If they merged with the conquered through processes of denomadisation, acculturation, sinicisation and so on, they would lose their military superiority spontaneously, again inviting their subjects to rebel and displace them.[93] The great civil war between Qubilai and his younger brother Ariq Boke in 1260–62 was essentially about the collision between the approaches of acculturation and defiant nomadism respectively.[94] With hindsight, one can see the entire Mongol experiment as ultimately doomed from the outset, though of course contemporaries could not construe it thus.[95]

By a curious historical irony, it was nomadism itself, requiring a high degree of cooperation and thus preventing a strict division of labour and hence the emergence of an intellectual or literate elite, always nudging the leaders towards meritocracy, that won Genghis his current reputation in Mongolia as the father of democracy and an ethnic hero.[96] It is altogether just that Genghis should be partially rehabilitated. Alexander the Great, Napoleon and Julius Caesar slaughtered and massacred (Caesar is alleged to have killed one million Gauls between 59 and 49 BC) but it is their achievements that are usually celebrated, not the blood-letting. But it would be a mistake to go too far in the direction of the modern trend for hagiography. While the Mongols' military achievements were stupendous, they were otherwise totally parasitic. They were unoriginal, founded no new religions, produced no worthwhile cultural artefacts, developed no new crops or new technologies (though they transmitted existing ones), created no worthwhile painting, pottery, architecture or literature and did not even bake bread; they essentially relied on the captive craftsmen and experts for everything. Their motto could almost have been the infamous one by the French symbolist writer Villiers de l'Isle-Adam: 'As for living, our servants will do that for us.'[97] Their fabled skill in building bridges scarcely compensated.

The Mongols were an unbalanced people. They had achieved a quantum leap in military technology putting them far ahead of western Europe, but the Europeans meanwhile were producing Roger Bacon, Dante, Anthony of Padua, Thomas Aquinas and even Frederick, *Stupor Mundi*, and St Louis. The Mongols ratcheted up hecatombs of slaughter and, while western Europe was also guilty of horrific atrocities, especially against the Albigensians, it was at least producing the *Divine Comedy*, the *Carmina Burana*, the *Roman de la Rose* and the amazing series of cathedrals either completed or begun in the thirteenth century: at Chartres, Amiens, Reims, Beauvais, Toledo, Burgos, Cologne, York, Lichfield and Salisbury.

Genghis was the greatest conqueror of the ages but alongside a man who was an exact contemporary, Francis of Assisi (he died in 1226) he seems a moral pygmy. The parallels between the two are fascinating. Twelve hundred and six, the year of the great quriltai that turned Temujin into Genghis Khan, saw Francis's breakthrough trial before Bishop Guido. Genghis's ascent of Mount Burqan Qaldun is paralleled by Francis's descent into the caves of Subiaco.[98] There are other convergences. Francis was in Egypt when Subedei and Jebe on their great raid were (relatively) close by. In Jungian terms Genghis can be seen as the overdevelopment of the animus or masculine principle, with St Francis overdoing the anima or feminine principle. There are further curiosities. The Franciscans were particularly badly treated in Hungary, so Subedei's devastation of the country could almost be seen as a kind of divine revenge. And it was the Franciscans who first made contact with the Mongols and brought back an amazing story that will endure as long as mankind itself: the career of Genghis Khan.

Appendix 1
Mongol Religion

The religion of the Mongols was extraordinarily complex, as it compre-
hended a threefold view of the world, corresponding roughly to the
transcendental, the mystical and the practical; one might call it a triply
intersecting cosmology. At the transcendental level the Mongols
believed in a Supreme Being, Koke Mongke Tengerri, who presided
over the Eternal Blue Heaven. Yet even here there was ambiguity, as
the Mongols never clearly differentiated between Tengerri as a personal
god on one hand, and as the representation of cosmic order on the
other. Were God and Heaven synonymous, with Tengerri as the proper
name for the cosmos, or did he precede the Eternal Blue Heaven and
create it? Philosophers would say that at this level there was an unresolved confusion between the concepts of God and Heaven. If God
and Heaven were identical, that would justify the oft-repeated assertion
that the Mongol religion was monotheistic, which does receive some
support from the *Secret History*.[1]

Yet there is far more compelling evidence that the nomads' belief-
system was polytheistic. Tengerri, as well as personifying the principles
of cosmic order, existed as a personal deity who created all things,
especially the sun and moon, which were sacred to him. You could
pray to him to get fortune and happiness for yourself, your sons and
your daughters.[2] Under him in the heavenly hierarchy there were
supposed to be ninety-nine lesser gods, all with distinctive natures and
attributes, with forty-four assigned to the eastern side of the world,
fifty-five to the western; four more were sometimes assigned to the
north (Tengerri took care of the south himself). The number ninety-
nine was chosen because of the Mongols' belief in the mystical significance of the number nine, but inevitably such a neat cosmology soon
became muddled with the addition of extra gods.[3]

Tengerri in Heaven was especially complemented by the goddess Itugen, an earth or fertility deity. There was a god of the hearth, named Natigai, mentioned by Marco Polo, to whom one prayed for health, wives, children and livestock. Then there was a separate sun-god, in whose honour a great festival – 'the Day of the Red Disc' – was held on the sixteenth day of the first month of summer. The constellation of the Great Bear was venerated as the god of Fate and Destiny. A fertility deity named 'the White Old Man' was also worshipped. He was supposed to be a white-clothed, white-haired old man who leaned on a dragon-headed staff. He particularly fascinated the Buddhists who later incorporated him into their own religion, to the point where there were stories about meetings between Lord Buddha and the White Old Man.[4] Then there was a fire god, who seemed to be able to answer every prayer, since one could beseech him for all of the following: blessings at birth, including long life, fame, power and riches; protection from heat, frost and all noxious qualities of wood and iron and (paradoxically) from fire; warding off illnesses; protection from wolves, thieves and cattle murrain; provision of good health for cattle, horses, camels, bulls, geldings, mares, stallions, dogs, and so on; and similar protection for slaves and their precious labour.[5] Finally, and very importantly, the Mongols believed in a version of 'guardian angels': protective deities in the form of armed horsemen known as *sulde*, whose particular task was to protect the great khans and aristocrats so that they could fulfil the destiny preordained by Tengerri.[6]

If the world of Tengerri and the lesser gods defines what we have called the transcendental element in Mongol religion, the mystical is represented most of all by animism: roughly speaking, the belief that not only animals but plants, rivers, mountains, lakes and even the wind and rain are imbued with spirits. Particularly important were the cults of natural phenomena such as mountains, trees and animals (where the wolf held pride of place with the Turks, with the Mongols it was, naturally, the horse). Since animism implied that spirits were everywhere, it followed that they had to be placated and appeased when any significant event was due to take place – birth, marriage, death, hunting, war. Mongols believed that the soul resided in blood, so that if you shed blood you also emptied out the soul. This was why they never liked to shed the blood of high-ranking enemies but found other ways to execute them, usually by strangulation with a bowstring, breaking a man's back or violently dragging the condemned around wrapped up in a carpet.[7] There were special cults of mountain tops and river springs, since the Mongols believed that water was symbolic of a higher power. Sun worship was important and, for reasons not entirely clear, the Mongols associated the sun with the South and, in paying tribute to solar power, genuflected towards the south.[8]

Quite distinctly from the gods and goddesses associated with particular phenomena, animist beliefs impelled the nomads to informal tribute to the elements, and this was performed by laymen (and women). For example, in worshipping the earth as a deity, they liked to make a household god of him out of felt. Incense offerings accompanied by prayer, perhaps led by a 'lay preacher', were the most common forms of appreciation of the winds and the mountains. The normal ritual of worship was to kneel nine times (the reliable magic number) with the head uncovered and a belt hanging round one's neck.[9]

Fire worship tended to be accompanied by more substantial offerings, such as the breastbone of a sheep covered with melted butter. In parts of Mongolia the fire offering was the exclusive preserve of women, carried out on the twenty-ninth day of the last month of the year.[10] Yet another objection to the notion of Mongol religion as simple monotheism is that, as Carpini ruefully noted, on some indices the nomads could be regarded as idolaters, since they had the custom, once an animal was killed, of offering its heart in a cup to an idol.[11] These idols could be of many kinds, whether representations of animals or humans – what anthropologists call zoomorphic or anthropomorphic images. Cult sites in the charge of laymen were often marked by a cairn of stones with a vertical pole sticking out of them. The lay preachers – sometimes carelessly referred to as 'clan shamans' (though the term causes more problems than it is worth, as we shall see) – simply conducted prayers and sacrifices without attempting the feats of the true shaman; there was no pretence that they could travel to the sky or shape-shift into animals.[12]

Animism as the mystical aspect of religion provided the bridge, so to speak, between the transcendentalism of the Mongol folk religion of the Eternal Blue Heaven and the down-to-earth functions of shamanism. There is much scholarly debate about all aspects of shamans – those figures often loosely referred to in other cultures as medicine men or witch doctors. Some say the very notion of shamanism is imprecise – a mere conflation of different elements found in very variegated and diverse cultures – and that to be exact, we should refer only to Mongol shamans, African shamans, North American varieties, and so on. Some radical empiricists go even further and say that, even within Mongolian culture, there have always been several different types of shamans *as well as* other non-shamanic magico-religious specialists.[13] In some writings there is a distinction between 'black' shamans who go into trances, assume the shape of animals and ascend into the sky, and 'white' shamans who do none of these things but, rather like Western priests, act as intermediaries between the everyday world and that of the supernatural, limiting themselves to invoking blessings for humans and livestock from the spirits and gods of the 'upper world'.[14]

These technical debates need not detain us here. As a generalisation it is clear that the function of shamans in Mongolia was to protect a man, his family, property and flocks against illness and other manifestations of evil or evil spirits; one might say that shamanism and demonology are in a co-dependent relationship.

The demons feared by the Mongols were of different kinds: sky demons, bird demons and wandering lights as well as traditional ghosts and phantoms. The 'black' shamans claimed to be especially able to deal with these, which they did by conversing with the spirits of the human departed; the idea was that it made sense to address yourself to forebears who had 'conquered' death. Immediately one can see that there was a conceptual problem about shamanism, as its devotees claimed to be dealing both with the spirits of the dead and with the spirits of nature, and in any given case it was unclear which it was. A further problem arises because there was in Mongol cosmology no distinct kingdom of the dead and no conception of an afterworld such as Hades or the Elysian Fields or Heaven and Hell. The Mongol view of the afterlife was as a continuation of that on earth, and this alerts us to another key aspect of shamanism, that it was relentlessly practical; the Mongols were always interested in religion primarily for what it could give them in this life. This is why the term 'witch doctor' expresses an essential truth; it was the role of shamans as healers and doctors rather than priests that most attracted their adherents. Part ancestor worship, part animism, part totemism, shamanism was a classic instance of the mystifying and obfuscating role of religion.[15]

Shamans occupied an important place in Mongol life; in the early days of nomadic society chieftains were themselves often shamans, and it is not surprising that they came to see themselves as the centre of the universe. Their elite position was much coveted, and for this reason evolved into a hereditary role. Their primacy and privilege they justified by the alleged dangers of their calling – danger not just from demons but because during their work the soul had to leave the body and was therefore unprotected.[16] In order to acquire power over the weather and disease and to be able to predict the future the shaman had to go into a trance, from which an early awakening was potentially lethal. Moreover, there was a complex initiation ceremony in which the shaman had to undergo tortures such as being dismembered by spirits or eaten by a wild animal before being restored to his original shape – a symbolic death and resurrection.[17]

To prepare for his professional ordeals the shaman wore a special uniform and armed himself with magical and talismanic objects; only if equipped with these, it was thought, could he gain access to the spirits of the dead. He wore a headdress of feathers and a kaftan ornamented with various metallic items and a bell. Some shamans wore clothes that made them look like an eagle, but others wore strips of leather or cloth on the kaftan to indicate the similarity to serpents; others again wore uniforms with markings simulating a tiger's stripes. In all cases the idea was to harness the power of fearsome animals. Shamans also wore an apron to which were attached a number of mirrors – usually nine (that number again!); the mirrors were supposed to frighten evil spirits, to reflect their secret thoughts and to protect the shaman from any invisible weapons the demons might hurl at them. Some Mongolian shamans wore coronets of leather and had an imitation horn on the head representing a totemic animal.[18] Other accoutrements were red headcloths, a staff and a drum. The drum and the drumstick were very important elements in the shaman's kit, as the noise was said to enable the shaman to summon spirits to help him in his work. Often, too, he would have a human helper to beat the drum for him.[19] Additionally, the shaman bore a sceptre or beating-stick, rather like the magic wand in Western fairy-tales, which was supposed to enable him to journey to a place where he would battle demons.

Thus attired, he would go into a state of trance or ecstasy. Unlike the case of Western spiritualism, where the spirits dominate the medium, in this trance the shaman was the sovereign and master.[20] Once in the trance it was time for the journey through the heavens, for only thus could illnesses and other evils be averted. Deep in his trance the shaman would journey to the sky on a magic horse, flying through the air like witches on a broom in Western folkore and superstition. Shamanism was primarily a male preserve. There were female shamans, and daughters of chiefs in particular were sometimes admitted into the 'priesthood', but in general women were discouraged and, if admitted, restricted to divination or healing, on the ground that battling demons was simply too dangerous.[21]

The complexity of Mongol religion is evident. It was clearly more of a broad syncretism of various beliefs than a homogeneous worldview, and some of the 'contradictions' are obvious. In particular a divorce between the overarching religion of the Eternal Blue Sky and the practice of shamanism is evident. Even if we could resolve the conundrum about the coexistence of spirits of the dead, demons and spirits of nature – partly reflected in the division between 'black' and 'white' shamans and that between shamans properly so-called and other maguses and prophets – there seems to be no connection between the universe of Tengerri and that in which the shamans operated. We are entitled to ask, surely, why the shamans never bend their energies towards worship of the Eternal Blue Heaven. Shamanism is sometimes said to be 'autochthonous' – that is, it springs naturally and spontaneously from the soil of Mongolia – but in that case how can we connect it with the very different principle of fire gods and fire worship which seems equally 'autochthonous' and links with the Zoroastrianism of Persia?[22] In any case, one can plausibly argue that the religion of Tengerri and the Eternal Blue Heaven is far more 'autochthonous' than shamanism, since it is very likely that the 'big sky' terrain of the steppes would naturally engender a belief in a supreme sky god.[23]

Two very different theories have been advanced for the potency of shamanism among the Mongols. One derives from the work of the great sociologist Émile Durkheim, the first to point out that in some sense religion projects the structures of human society onto the wider cosmos. According to this view, small-scale communities such as that of the nomads imagine a spirit world close to their own where contacts are direct and face-to-face. Steep hierarchies of status and gender, on the other hand, are characteristic of 'universal' religions, and on this view the Mongols were more 'organic' in their beliefs than their neighbours. Against this other scholars argue that shamanism is the result of the impact of the wider world of sedentary societies on 'hunter-gatherer' and other primitive social organisations.[24]

What is clear is that Mongol religion was utterly different from the universal religions of their neighbours (Christianity, Buddhism, Islam, Confuciansim) but that there was an unresolved conflict between the official religion of Tengerri and shamanism. As we have seen, Genghis Khan progressively jettisoned elements of shamanism in an aggressive campaign to promote the cult of Tengerri, in part because shamanism was inappropriate for a world empire. Shamanism related to the world of Temujin, the poor Mongol boy, but the empire of Genghis required a universal religion. The cosmology of sky and earth fulfilled this need for a while but, after his death, the cult of Tengerri was progressively abandoned for the more functional universal religions like Islam, Buddhism and Christianity.[25] Yet shamanism was a tough practice to dislodge, and it continued potent in Mongolia into the late fourteenth century and beyond, being especially vibrant among the Buriyat tribe, even when the rest of the empire outside Mongolia had gone over to other faiths.[26]

Appendix 2
The Fall of Qara Khitai

Yelu Dashi, founder of Qara Khitai, was perhaps the most impressive steppe leader before Genghis himself. Yelu's remarkable aplomb was evinced while still in Mongolia when he had himself declared king of the free Khitans, but in 1132 he devised a new title of gur-khan for himself and was publicly acclaimed as such by his troops.[1] Already he had proved himself an opportunist and master politician. When the ruler of the city of Balasaqun, a capital of the Qara-Khanids (in modern Kyrgyzstan), asked for his help in 1128 against rebellious Qanglis, Yelu promptly arrived with his army and seized the throne; as the Persian historian Juvaini put it, 'he ascended a throne that had cost him nothing'.[2] One immediate result was an accession of a further 16,000 Khitan warriors, who had been serving the Qara-Khanids as mercenaries. The numbers in his army grew exponentially, and in 1132–34 he conquered three more important cities or towns: Kashgar, an oasis settlement (on the three-way border between modern China, Tajikistan and Kyrgyzstan), Khotan and Beshbaliq (both in the modern Chinese province of Xinjiang).[3] Buoyed by these successes, in 1134 he attempted an invasion of China, which ended in fiasco.

He then decided to move farther west and in 1137 arrived in the Ferghana valley (today this lies at the intersection of Kyrgyzstan, Tajikistan and Uzbekistan), a fertile area on the northern Silk Road and at various points in history, the main artery for trade between China and Persia.[4] That same year he defeated the Qara-Khanids under their ruler Mahmud II in a pitched battle at Khujand (in modern Tajikistan). This marked a definite ascent in his career. The Qara-Khanids had once been the most powerful people in this area but, defeated by the Seljuk Turks, became their vassals and paid tribute while retaining day-to-day independence. Mahmud appealed for help

to the Seljuks, who had to respond to retain credibility, especially as
Kashgar, Khotan and Beshbaliq were also Seljuk vassals.[5]

It is worth emphasising what a powerful enemy Yelu had made by
his conquests. At this stage the mighty Seljuks, scourge of the first
two Crusades and the dominant power in western Asia since 1037,
controlled an immense empire from the Hindu Kush to western
Turkey and from the Aral Sea in the north to the Persian Gulf.[6] It was
perhaps fortunate for Yelu that the Seljuks were already past their
prime, but in 1141 few would have given the Khitans much of a chance
against these Turkish masters. Nonetheless, the supremely confident
Yelu went out to meet them on the battlefield of Qatwan, north of
Samarkand, on 9 September 1141, even though outnumbered three to
one.

Led by the Seljuk sultan himself, Ahmad Sanjar, the Seljuks soon
showed they had declined seriously since their glory days in the First
Crusade. Their army was cut to pieces, with massive loss of life, of
which the Persian historians spared nothing in the telling. The numbers
engaged were perhaps 20,000 Khitans against 60,000 Seljuks, but the
chroniclers managed to produce a casualty list exceeding 100,000.
Nevertheless, the defeat was serious. Although Sanjar himself was
lucky to escape, his wife and family fared less well and were led into
captivity.[7]

Victory made Yelu the dominant power in western Central Asia.
Some scholars say the Seljuks went into a decline from which they
never recovered (their empire met its final demise in 1194). Yelu now
had an ever-victorious army of at least 25,000 – some say as large as
70–100,000.[8] His defeat of the Turks caused a sensation worldwide
and is thought to be the origin of the Prester John legend, wherein
a Christian king in the East takes the Islamic enemies of Christendom
in the rear and helps to promote the cause of the Cross against the
Crescent.[9]

At any rate, Qatwan marked the definite foundation of the state
of Qara Khitai. The subsequent conquest of Transoxiana proceeded
very quickly. Very soon Qara Khitai covered a wide stretch of territory, from the Uighur domains in the east to Transoxiana in the west
and from Lake Balkhash in the north to Balkh in Afghanistan in the
south.[10] Unfortunately for Yelu, he did not live to enjoy his triumph
very long and died in 1143. The state he established was at its apogee

for less than two years, for after his death it immediately began on the downward slope.[11]

Nevertheless the kingdom he bequeathed to his young son Yelu Yilie (with his widow Xiao Tabuyan initially ruling as regent) was an impressive creation. The Qarluqs of Almaliq, Uighurs and Muslim Turks of Khwarezmia were all their vassals but enjoyed considerable autonomy; the Qara Khitans were content with nominal overlordship and annual tribute.[12] The economy was more diversified than the Mongols', as it encompassed pastoralism, agriculture and manufacturing. It is interesting to note the spectrum of pastoralism as one goes farther west. Whereas with the Mongols the horse was sovereign, with the Tangut horses and camels had equal value, while in Qara Khitai sheep and oxen were the most important animals (one estimate of domesticated animals says that 41 per cent were sheep, 26 per cent oxen and only 19 per cent horses).[13] The flourishing agricultural sector of Qara Khitai generated melons, grapes, peaches, plums, almonds, apples, pears, pomegranate, wheat, rice and other grains; cotton was another major product. Manufacturing and craftsmanship were well represented by ceramics, glassware, metalwork, tools, utensils, weapons, carriages, boats, jewellery, jade, lacquer, clothes, textiles, leather, weaving, paper and wine-making.[14]

But Qara Khitai was always peculiar in being China away from China, so to speak, with the Liao identity carefully preserved. Although Yelu Dashi ruled a multi-ethnic state of Chinese, Khitans, Turks and Naiman, the elite was strongly Chinese and retained their consciousness of medieval China as the defining symbol of power, wealth and status; this was the tradition they sought to perpetuate.[15] Elite Qara Khitans kept their Chinese identity and never converted to Islam, even though this was the majority religion of their subjects. In this and other areas, notably administration and officers like the later Mongol daruqachi, they both took over the system of the Liao empire (with Chinese titles, calendars, coins, and so on) and anticipated the empire of Genghis Khan, and scholars have predictably indulged their favourite hobby of assimilating all Genghis's innovations to earlier Khitan models.[16] There was always a determined effort to maintain all the old Chinese customs and traditional dress, against that mythical day when the Qara Khitans might return to rule China. Highly literate, they had their own script, which they used when issuing orders to officials which they sealed with an official stamp in the ancient Chinese way. They even paid their troops regular wages.[17]

Although Buddhist themselves, they had no official state religion and practised religious tolerance, with a particular partiality for Nestorian Christianity (a factor in the genesis of the Prester John legend), although, curiously, they were always regarded in the world of Islam as the unregenerate enemies of Allah. Within Qara Khitai were sizeable Buddhist and Nestorian communities, a Manichean sect and even a Jewish ghetto. Some say that the Buddhism of Qara Khitai had been diluted so as to make room for ideas like fire-worship and the bizarre ritual of sacrificing a grey ox with a white horse.[18]

A notable feature of the culture of Qara Khitai was endogamy. Marriages were tightly controlled, and the traditional marriage between the Yelu 'king' clan and the Xiao 'queen' clan continued; any form of 'marrying out' was severely discouraged. Women had a high status in Qara Khitai, and indeed two of their five gur-khans were women – the importance of empresses was another Liao tradition.[19]

Sadly for Qara Khitai, none of this rich variety addressed the deep problems with which the state was beset after the death of Yelu Dashi. His son Yilie was a minor when he succeeded in 1143 and the long period of regency by his mother Tabuyan was not politically successful. In 1163 Yilie died and was succeeded by his sister Yelu Pusuwan, whose main contribution was to send her husband out on unfocused military raids and expeditions. She finally caused scandal by falling in love with his younger brother; to avert further damage to the reputation of the state her father-in-law had them both executed in 1177.[20]

Under Yelu Zhilugu, who succeded in 1178 and was generally conceded to be a weak ruler, Qara Khitai's strength and reputation plummeted still further. There was always an unresolved tension in the state between the Buddhist elite and the Muslim majority. Whereas the Liao had been a minority elite in China but had for a long period been accepted as a legitimate regime, this never really happened in Qara Khitai where there was always 'a limited imperial domain surrounded by a vast agglomeration of vassal peoples, sedentary as well as nomadic'.[21] The vassal peoples bided their time, awaiting their chance to throw off the Liao yoke, which meant that in order to survive Qara Khitai had to be both strong and continuously successful. Yet on the contrary from the 1170s on, the weakness of central power became more and more obvious. The ruling elite never struck back hard or decisively enough at their aggressors, thus exposing their vulnerability and encouraging other discontented nations to try their luck.[22]

Corruption by civil servants and officialdom became a major problem. The regional commissions or political commisars in the vassal territories became bywords for injustice, and this encouraged the oppressed to look outside the realm for their salvation; the *idiqut* Barchuq's joining Genghis in 1211 was only the most spectacular example of this process.[23] Eventually, the siphoning off of wealth on a huge scale by Qara Khitan officials caused a financial crisis in what should have been a prosperous economy; the nadir was reached when the state had to withdraw its proud boast and admit it could no longer pay its troops wages.[24] This led to a situation where the financial tail wagged the political dog. Where wise rulers would have been paying serious attention to the spectacular rise of the Mongols in the east, instead they spent their time raiding and plundering in the rich regions of Khorasan, Transoxiana and Khwarezmia, thus diminishing their popularity locally still further. By the time Genghis was acclaimed at the 1206 quriltai Qara Khitai was already in serious trouble.[25]

If Qara Khitai was the *Titanic*, the iceberg was the kingdom of Khwarezm, which would eventually become the empire of Khwarezmia. The first ruler of this area, later acknowledged as the first 'shah' was Qutb ad-Din Muhammad (1097–1127), who was appointed governor of the province (then in the Seljuk empire) by the Seljuk sultan and granted de facto independence in return for his loyalty. The second shah Atsiz (1127–1156) had grander ambitions and rebelled against the Seljuks but was defeated and had his independent powers trimmed. When Yelu Dashi defeated the Seljuks at Qatwan in 1141, Atsiz saw his chance and occupied the cities of Merv and Nishapur. But it turned out he had merely replaced one master with another; the Qara Khitans ordered him out and obliged him to pay tribute to them.[26]

The third shah Il-Arslan (1156–1172) was ambitious and managed to expand the boundaries of Khwarezmia into Khorasan and Transoxiana. He tried to inveigle the Seljuks into a campaign against Qara Khitai, hoping that his reward in the event of success would be Samarkand. When this plan came to nothing, Il-Arslan tried refusing tribute to Qara Khitai but was defeated in battle and died soon after.[27] His successor Tekish (the fourth shah, 1172–1200) had vaulting ambitions but these were constrained by rivalry with his brother, who broke away to rule a rival principality in Khorasan.[28] Tekish's chance came in 1193 when his brother died and he inherited Khorasan.

His rise to united power coincided with a significant development in the Islamic world. The Abbasid caliphs of Baghdad had been merely the spiritual leaders of Mohammedanism, with actual political power in the hands of the Seljuk sultans. But things changed during the reign of the caliph al-Nasir li-Din Allah (1180–1225), for he aspired to temporal power and proposed an alliance with Tekish against the Seljuks. Tekish jumped at the chance, and the combined armies defeated the Seljuks near Rayy in 1194, after which Tekish beheaded the sultan Toghrul III.[29] Al-Nasir was delighted, thinking he would now inherit the space left vacant by the Seljuks, but Tekish doublecrossed him and declared that *he* would be the new sultan. Thereafter there was always bad blood between the caliphate and the rulers of Khwarezmia. War between the caliph and Tekish seemed certain until Al-Nasir, in an act of statesmanship, agreed in 1198 to accept Tekish as ruler of Iraq, Khorasan and Turkestan.[30]

But Tekish had also introduced a problem that would bedevil his son and successor. He had built up the Turkish element in his army, but the Turks regarded themselves as an elite, above the law and subject only to the whim of the shah; they behaved badly, committed shocking atrocities including mass rape and pillage, and alienated the very population a belligerent shah would need to depend on.[31] Apart from the Turkish guard, there were few mourners when Tekish died of a peritonsillar abscess in 1200.[32]

Before his death the turbulent Tekish had introduced still another complication into the politics of the area by intriguing with the Islamic Ghurids of Afghanistan. The Ghurids, based in Bamiyan and Ghor in central Afghanistan, had been defeated by the Seljuks and their sultan Sanjar in 1152 and were then regarded as a back number, but enjoyed a spectacular revival under Muhammad of Ghor (1173–1206), who at his death ruled a realm stretching from north-eastern Iran to Bengal.[33] Muhammad's brother Ghiyath al-Din, ruler of Bamiyan, always had designs on Khorasan and was backed by his brother. In 1198 he seized Balkh, a possession of the Qara Khitans. Shah Tekish urged Qara Khitai not to take this affront lying down and warned that Ghiyath's ambitions did not rest there. Qara Khitai sent a huge army against the Ghurids but was badly defeated. The gur-khan Yelu Zhilugu rounded furiously on Tekish, blamed him for the disaster and demanded compensation for the 12,000 Qara Khitans slain in the battle. Tekish turned back to the Ghurids to rescue him, and they agreed to do so, provided he submitted to the caliph of Baghdad and restored any Ghurid territory the Qara Khitans might seize in compensation. Agreeing to this was almost the last thing Tekish did before his death.[34]

The real winner from the ferocious clash between Qara Khitai and the Ghurids was Tekish's son Muhammad II, who succeeded in 1200. His father's mortal enemy the caliph al-Nasir warned Yelu Zhilugu that it was Muhammad who was his real adversary and suggested an alliance between Qara Khitai and the Ghurids to fight him. This proposal came to nothing, as both sides were girding themselves for another round of warfare; had al-Nasir continued with his meddling, the outcome might have been an alliance between the new shah and the Ghurids, as Muhammad always identified Qara Khitai as the real enemy he needed to vanquish if he was to found an empire. In the short term he continued to make overtures to Qara Khitai hoping to use Zhilugu for his own purposes, as the Ghurids had taken advantage of Tekish's death to seize parts of Khorasan.[35] In any case, Zhilugu rebuffed the overture from the caliph on the grounds that the shah had acted four-square and he could not simply play turncoat with a loyal ally.[36]

For two years Muhammad was at war with the Ghurids, aided greatly by Ghiyath al-Din's death in 1203 and his brother Muhammad of Ghor's preoccupation with India.[37] At first things went badly for the shah, he was defeated and had to seek assistance from Qara Khitai. Zhilugu responded well and sent a huge army across the Oxus in pursuit of the Ghurids. Muhammad and his Qara Khitan allies caught up with the Ghurids and, with the help of numerical superiority and a strong wind blowing in the enemy's faces, defeated them. Quite how decisive the victory really was is disputed, for the Ghurids managed to hang on to Balkh even after Muhammad claimed he had 'routed' them.[38]

Then Muhammad of Ghor returned from India, thirsting for revenge. First, though, he had to suppress a mutiny in his army and then a rebellion of the Khokhars, a tribe in the mountains between

Lahore and Multan. In February 1205 he was triumphant and finally returned to Lahore laden with booty. He then announced a major war to destroy Qara Khitai. Next year he moved from Lahore to Ghazni in Afghanistan and ordered his viceroy in Bamiyan to prepare pontoon bridges so that he could cross the Oxus during an invasion of Transoxiana. Suddenly, in March 1206 near Jhelum (Pakistan) he fell to an assassin's knife, murdered either by a Khokhan or one of the new cult of Assassins.[39] All plans for an invasion of Transoxiana were laid aside.

Muhammad, ever the opportunist, moved into the gap left by the death of the Ghor potentate and occupied Balkh himself.[40] Zhilugu made the ultra-diplomatic gesture of recognising the shah's suzerainty over Khorasan, but Muhammad construed statesmanship as weakness. Stung by taunts that he enjoyed an altogether too cosy relationship with an infidel, and encouraged by friendly contacts with the sultan of Samarkand, he finally decided to show his true colours and attack Qara Khitai.[41] He chose the confused local politics of Bukhara, riven by strife between oriental versions of the Montagus and Capulets, as his *casus belli*. The two sides appealed, respectively, to Zhilugu and Muhammad, and the shah, defiant and uncompromising, made it clear he would not back down.[42] He crossed the Oxus in 1207, entered Bukhara and installed his own candidate.

For a while there was inconclusive warfare between Qara Khitai and Khwarezmia. In one skirmish the shah himself was captured but showed ingenuity by disguising himself as a servant and then concocting a story that he served a great lord who would pay a large ransom for his release. After somehow gulling his captors that he would return with the money, he made his escape.[43]

By this time both sides were reeling from internal troubles. While he was fighting Zhilugu, his brother Ali-Shah and his military governor in Nishapur had both usurped the title of shah. Muhammad's return put them both to flight; the Nishapur governor and his son were killed the following year. In 1209 Muhammad executed both his rebellious brother and the Ghurid sultan, thus ending the Ghurid dynasty. By the end of 1209 he had not only restored his situation in Khorasan but added Herat to his conquests while retaining Bukhara.[44]

Zhilugu meanwhile had had to deal with fresh rebellions in Khotan and Kashgar in 1204 and was increasingly conscious of being under threat from two directions, from the shah in the west and the Mongols in the east – for 1209 was the year when the *idiqut* of the Uighurs deserted him for Genghis.[45] He could deal militarily with the shah but not if he had to take the Mongols into consideration at the same time. In 1205 the rebellions became more serious when Arslan, khan of the Qarluqs, joined Khotan and Kashgar in revolt. Zhilugu put down the risings but once more did not treat his rebels harshly, hoping his forbearance would appease his Muslim subjects and that the virus of insurrection would not spread to other Islamic provinces. It was a forlorn hope, for the wars with the shah had given the Muslims the chance they had been looking for ever since the defeats at Khujand and Qatwan.[46]

In 1207 an even more formidable rebellion took place under the most powerful of the gur-khan's vassals, Othman of Samarkand, who allied himself with the shah. They consolidated their hold on Bukhara but Zhilugu did at least manage to hang on to Ferghana. Qara Khitai gained a respite for a whole year in 1208 when Muhammad was himself hit by an internal revolt which took the pressure off.[47] The normally feckless Zhilugu at last revealed some tenacity when negotiating with Muhammad. He told him he was prepared to allow him to have de facto control of Bukhara and Khorasan, but could not permit non-payment of tribute which by now (1210) was three years in arrears. The shah decided that the time was not yet right for an all-out war with Qara Khitai. To save face he departed on a campaign against the troublesome Cuman nomads on his northern frontier, leaving his mother Terken Qatun to behave deferentially when the Qara Khitan envoys arrived and to pay them the full tribute.[48]

In 1210 Zhilugu could still console himself that, though his borders had shrunk with the loss of Balkh and Khotan, he still controlled territory eastwards as far as the land of the Naiman and north to the Yenisey and upper Irtysh, with the River Oxus as his western limit.[49] And, as always with those imbued with Chinese culture – and both the Liao and Jin shared this characteristic – he took an odd and irrational comfort from having multiple capital cities in his realm. It was at this stage that Ququluq of the Naiman entered the scene (see above, Chapter 9).

Bibliography

This does not purport to be a complete bibliography of Genghis Khan and the Mongols but simply lists the books consulted during the writing.

Primary Documents and Collections of Primary Sources

Abel-Rémusat, Jean-Pierre, *Nouveaux mélanges asiatiques*, 2 vols (1829)

Abramowski, L. & A. E. Goodman, *A Nestorian Collection of Christological Texts* (1972)

Armstrong, Regis, J. Wayne Hellmann & William J. Short, eds, *Francis of Asissi: Early Documents*, 4 vols (1999–2002)

Bacon, Roger, trans. R. B. Burke, *Opus Majus*, 2 vols (1928)

Bawden, Charles R., ed. and trans., *The Mongol Chronicle Altan Tobči* (1955)

Beazley, C. R., ed., *The Texts and Versions of John de Piano Carpini and William de Rubruquis* (1900)

Bedrosian, Robert, ed. & trans., *Kirakos Gandzakets'i's History of the Armenians* (1986)

Benedetto, L. F., ed., *The Travels of Marco Polo* (1931)

Blake, Robert P. & Richard N. Frye, ed. and trans., *The History of the Nation of Archers . . . by Grigor of Akanc* (1954)

Bouquet, Martin, *Recueil des historiens des Gaules et de la France*, 19–20 (1880)

Boyle, J. A., ed. & trans., *Genghis Khan: The History of the World Conqueror by Ata-Malik Juvaini*, 2 vols (1997)

Boyle, J. A., ed. & trans., *The Successors of Genghis Khan* (1971)

Bregel, Yuri, ed. & trans., *Firdaws al-Iqbal: History of Khorezm by Shir Muhammad Mirab Munis and Muhammad Riza Mirab Agahi* (1999)

Bretschneider, Emil, *Mediaeval Researches from Eastern Asiatic Sources*, 2 vols (1888; repr. 2002)

Broadhurst, Roland C., ed. & trans., *The Travels of Ibn Jubayr . . .* (1952)

Browne, Edward Granville, ed. & trans., Chahar Maqala *('Four Discourses')* of Nizam-i-'Arudi of Samarqand (1921)

Browne, Edward Granville, ed. & trans., *The Lubabu 'l-Albáb of Muhammad Awfi*, 2 vols (1906)

Brundage, James A., ed & trans., *The Chronicle of Henry of Livonia* (1961)

Budge, E. A. Wallis, trans. & ed., The *Chronography of Gregory Abu'l Faraj* . . . *Commonly Known as Bar Hebraeus*, 2 vols (1932, repr. 2003)

Budge, E. A. Wallis, *The Monks of Kublai Khan, Emperor of China* (1928)

Chan, Hok-lam, trans., *The Fall of the Jurchen Chin: Wang E's Memoir on Ts'ai-chou under the Mongol Siege, 1233–1234* (1993)

Cleaves, F. W., ed. & trans., *The Secret History of the Mongols* (1982)

Cross, Samuel H., & Olgerd P. Sherbowitz-Wetzor, *The Russian Primary Chronicle: Laurentian Text* (1953)

Dankoff, Robert, trans., *Wisdom of Royal Glory: A Turko-Islamic Mirror for Princes by Yusuf Khass Hajib* (1983)

Davis, Dick, trans., Abolqasem Ferdowsi, *Shahnameh: The Persian Book of Kings* (2006)

Dawson, Christopher, ed., *The Mongol Mission: Narratives and Letters of the Franciscan Missionaries in Mongolia and China in the Thirteenth and Fourteenth Centuries, Translated by a Nun of Stanbrook Abbey* (1955)

Dmytryshyn, Basil, *Medieval Russia: A Source Book 900–1700* (1973)

Dörrie, Heinrich, ed., *Drei Texte zur Geschichte der Ungarn und Mongolen* (1956)

Fennell, John & Dimitri Obolensky, eds., *A Historical Russian Reader: A Selection of Texts from the XIth to the XVth Century* (1969)

Frye, Richard N., ed. & trans., *al-Narshakhi's The History of Bukhara* (1957)

Gibb, H. A. R, trans., *The Travels of Ibn Battuta*, 4 vols (1971–94)

Haenisch, Erich, trans., *Die Geheime Geschichte der Mongolen* (1948)

Haenisch, Erich, trans., *Zum Untergang zweier Reiche: Berichte von Augenzeugen aus den Jahren 1232–1233 und 1368–1370* (1969)

Hambis, Louis, trans., *Le chapitre CVII du Yuan Che* (1945)

Hambis, Louis, ed. & trans., *Marco Polo: La description du monde* (1955)

Hammer-Purgstall, Josef von, ed. & trans., *Geschichte Wassafs* (1856)

Harcourt, E. S., & Humphrey ap Evans, eds, *Said Gah-I-Shaukati, An Urdu Treatise on Falconry in the East* (1968)

Hildinger, Erik, trans., *The Story of the Mongols whom we call Tartars by Friar Giovanni DiPiano Carpini* (1996)

Jackson, Peter, & David O. Morgan, eds & trans., *The Mission of Friar William of Rubruck: His Journey to the Court of the Great Khan Mongke, 1253–1255* (1990)

Joinville, Jean de, trans. R. Hague, *Life of St Louis* (1955)

Kahn, Paul, *The Secret History of the Mongols: The Origins of Chingis Khan, An*

Adaptation of the Yüan Ch'ao Pi Shih, *Based Primarily on the English Translation by Francis Woodman Cleaves* (1988)

Krause, F. E. A., ed. & trans., *Cingis Han. Die Geschichte seines Lebens nach den chinesischen Reichsannalen* (1922)

Kurucz, György, ed., *Guide to Documents and Manuscripts in Great Britain Relating to the Kingdom of Hungary from the Earliest Times to 1800* (1992)

Latham, Ronald E., ed., *The Travels of Marco Polo* (1958)

Lunde, Paul & Caroline Stone, eds & trans., *The Meadows of Gold: The Abbasids by Mas'udi* (1989)

Marsden, William, trans., *The Travels of Marco Polo* (1818, repr. 1987)

Matthew Paris, ed. & trans. H. R. Luard, *Chronica Majora*, 7 vols (1880)

Michael, Maurice, ed. & trans., *The Annals of Jan Długosz: A History of Eastern Europe from* AD 965 *to* AD 1480 (1997)

Michel, Francisque, ed., *Mémoires de Jean, sire de Joinville ou Histoire et chronique du très-chrétien roi Saint Louis* (1858)

Minorsky, V., *Sharaf al Zaman Tahir Marvazi on China, the Turks and India* (1942)

Mitchell, Robert & Neville Forbes, trans., *The Chronicle of Novgorod* (1914)

Moule, Arthur C. & Paul Pelliot, trans., *Marco Polo: The Description of the World*, 2 vols (1938)

Nabokov, Vladimir, trans., *The Song of Igor's Campaign: An Epic of the Twelfth Century* (1960)

Nesawi, Mohammed en- [Shihab al-Din Muhammad al-Nasawi], trans. O. Houdas, *Histoire du Sultan Djelal ed-Din Mankobirti* (1895)

Olbricht, Peter & Elisabeth Pinks, eds and trans., *Meng-Ta pei-lu und Hei-Ta shih-lüeh: chinesische Gesandtenberichte über die frühen Mongolen 1221 und 1237* (1980)

Onon, Urgunge, ed. & trans., *The Secret History of the Mongols: The Life and Times of Chinggis Khan* (2001)

Pegolotti, Francesco Balducci, ed. Allan Evans, *La pratica della Mercatura* (1936)

Pelliot, Paul & Louis Hambis, eds & trans., *Histoire des campagnes de Genghis Khan* (1951)

Perfecky, George A., ed, *The Galician–Volynian Chronicle* (1973)

Perić, Olga et al, eds & trans, *Thomae Archidiaconis Palatensis Historia Salonitanorum atque Spalatinorum Pontificum: Archdeacon Thomas of Split, History of the Bishops of Salona and Split* (2006)

Pertz, G. H. et al, eds, *Monumenta Germaniae Historica, Scriptores* 38 vols (2000)

Phillot, D. C., ed. & trans., *The Baz-nama-yi Nasiri: A Persian Treatise on Falconry* (1908)

Quatremère, Etienne Marc, trans., *Histoire des sultans mamlouks d'Égypte, écrite en arabe par Taki-Eddin-Ahmed-Makrizi [Ahmad ibn 'Ali Maqrizi]* (1845)

Rachewiltz, Igor de, *The Secret History of the Mongols, Translated with a Historical and Philological Commentary* (2nd ed., 2006)

Rady, Martyn & László Veszprémy / János M. Bak & Martyn Rady, eds & trans., *Anonymi Bele Regis Notarii Gesta Hungarorum: Anonymus, Notary of King Béla, The Deeds of the Hungarians / Magistri Rogerii Epistola in Miserabile Carmen . . . : Master Roger's Epistle . . .* (2010)

Ratchnevsky, Paul & Françoise Aubin, eds & trans., *Un code des Yuan*, 3 vols (1977)

Raverty, H. G., ed. & trans., *[Minhaj Siraj Juzjani,] Tabakat-i-Nasiri: A General History of the Muhammadan Dynasties of Asia*, 2 vols (1881)

Reich, Emil, *Selected Documents Illustrating Mediaeval and Modern History* (2004)

Ricci, A., ed., *The Travels of Marco Polo* (1931)

Richard, Jean, ed., *Simon de St Quentin, Histoire des Tartares* (1965)

Richards, D. S., ed. & trans., *The Chronicle of Ibn al-Athir for the Crusading Period from Al-Kamil fi'l-Ta'rikh, Part 3: The Years 589–629/1193–1231: The Ayyubids after Saladin and the Mongol Menace* (2008)

Risch, Friedrich, trans., *Johann de Piano Carpini: Geschichte der Mongolen und Reisebericht 1245–1247* (1930)

Rockhill, William Woodville, ed. & trans., *The Journey of William Rubruck to the Eastern Part of the World, 1253–1255, as Related by Himself, with Two Accounts of the Earlier Journey of John of Pian de Carpine* (1900)

Rodenberg, Karl, ed., *Epistolae Saeculi XIII e Regestis Pontificorum Romanorum Selectae*, 3 vols (1883-94)

Salimbene de Adam, ed. Giuseppe Scalia, *Cronica*, 2 vols (1998–9)

Silvestre de Sacy, Antoine Isaac, Baron, *Chrestomathie arabe* (1806–26)

Skelton, R. A., T. E. Marston & George D. Painter, *The Vinland Map and the Tartar Relation* (1995)

Société de Géographie, *Recueil de Voyages et de Mémoires* (1839)

Stevenson, J., ed, *The Chronicle of Melrose* (1835)

Szentpétery, Imre, et al, eds, *Scriptores Rerum Hungaricum Tempore Ducum Regumque Stirpis Arpadianae Gestarum*, 2 vols (1938)

Thackston, W. H., ed. & trans., *Habibu's-siyar [by] Khwandamir*, 2 vols (1994)

Thackston, W. H., ed. & trans., *Rashiduddin Fazlullah's Jami'u't-Tawarikh: Compendium of Chronicles. A History of the Mongols*, 3 vols (1998)

Theiner, Augustin, ed., *Vetera Monumenta Historica Hungariam Sacram Illustrantia* (1861)

Thomson, Robert W., ed. & trans., *Rewriting Caucasian History: The Medieval Armenian Adaptation of the Georgian Chronicles* (1996)

Veszprémy, László & Frank Shaer, with a study by Jenő Szűcs, *Simonis de Kéza Gesta Hungarorum: Simon of Kéza, the Deeds of the Hungarians* (1999)

Waley, Arthur, *The Secret History of the Mongols and Other Pieces* (1963)

Waley, Arthur, *The Travels of an Alchemist . . .* (1931)

Waugh, T., ed. & trans., *The Travels of Marco Polo* (1984)

Wiener, Leon, *Anthology of Russian Literature: From the Earliest Period to the Present Time* (1902)

Wood, Casey A. & F. Marjorie Fyfe, eds & trans., *The Art of Falconry: Being the De Arte Venandi cum Avibus of Frederick II of Hohenstaufen* (2004)

Yule, Henry & Henri Cordier, *The Book of Ser Marco Polo the Venetian Concerning the Kingdoms and Marvels of the East*, 2 vols (1903)

Yule, Henry & Henri Cordier, *Cathay and the Way Thither*, 2 vols (1866); revised ed., with Henri Cordier, 4 vols (1926)

Yusuf Khass Hajib, trans. Robert Dankoff, *Wisdom of Royal Glory: A Turko-Islamic Mirror for Princes* (1983)

Zenkovsky, Serge A., ed. and trans., *Medieval Russia's Epics, Chronicles and Tales* (1974)

Zenkovsky, Serge A. & B. J., eds and trans., *The Nikonian Chronicle* (1984)

Secondary Sources

Abazov, Rafis, *Palgrave Concise Historical Atlas of Central Asia* (2008)

Aberle, David F., *The Kinship System of the Kalmuk Mongols* (1953)

Abramzon, S. M., *The Kirgiz and their Ethnogenetical, Historical and Cultural Connections* (1971)

Abulafia, David, *Frederick II: A Medieval Emperor* (1988)

Abulafia, David, *The New Cambridge Medieval History*, 5: *c. 1198–1300* (1999)

Abulafia, David & Nora Berend, eds, *Medieval Frontiers: Concepts and Practices* (2002)

Abu-Lughod, Janet L., *Before European Hegemony: the World System, AD 1250–1350* (1989)

Adle, Charyar & Irfan Habib, *History of Civilizations of Central Asia*, 5 *(2004)*

Adshead, S. A. M., *Central Asia in World History* (1993)

Aigle, Denise, ed. *L'Iran face à la domination mongole, études* (1997)

Albrecht, Thorsten & Rainer Atzbach, *Elisabeth von Thüringen: Leben und Wirken in Kunst und Kulturgeschichte* (2007)

Alexander, Bevin, *How Wars Are Won: The Thirteen Rules of War from Ancient Greece to the War on Terror* (2003)

Alinge, Curt, *Mongolische Gesetze* (1934)

Al-Khalili, Jim, *The House of Wisdom. How Arabic Science Saved Ancient Knowledge and Gave Us the Renaissance* (2010)

Allen, W. E. D., *A History of the Georgian People* (1932)

Allsen, Thomas T., *Commodity and Exchange in the Mongol Empire: A Cultural History of Islamic Textiles* (1997)

Allsen, Thomas T., *Culture and Conquest in Mongol Eurasia* (2001)

Allsen, Thomas T., *Mongol Imperialism: The Policies of the Great Khan Mongke in China, Russia and the Islamic Lands* (1987)

Allsen, Thomas T., *The Royal Hunt in Eurasian History* (2007)

Altunian, G., *Die Mongolen und ihre Eroberungen in kaukasischen und kleinasiatischen Ländern im XIII. Jahrhundert* (1911)

Amitai-Preiss, Reuven, *The Mongols in the Islamic Lands: Studies in the History of the Ilkhanate* (Aldershot 2007)

Amitai-Preiss, Reuven & D. O. Morgan, eds, *The Mongol Empire and its Legacy* (1999)

Amitai[-Preiss], Reuven & Michal Biran, *Mongols, Turks and Others: Eurasian Nomads and the Sedentary World* (2005)

Anderson, Perry, *Passages from Antiquity to Feudalism* (1974)

Angold, Michael, ed., *The Cambridge History of Christianity, 5: The East* (2006)

Anthony, David W., *The Horse, the Wheel and Language: How Bronze-Age Riders from the Eurasian Steppes Shaped the Modern World* (2007)

Arbel, Benjamin, et al, eds, *Latins and Greeks in the Eastern Mediterranean after 1204* (1989)

Argue, Derry, ed. & trans., *George Turberville: The Book of Falconry or Hawking* (2006)

Arnold, Udo, *Die Hochmeister des Deutschen Ordens 1190–1994* (1998)

Asimov, M. S. & C. E. Bosworth, *History of Civilizations of Central Asia, 4, 2 parts* (1998-2003)

Atwood, C. P., *Encyclopedia of Mongolia and the Mongol Empire* (2004)

Aubin, Françoise, ed., *Études Song: In Memoriam Étienne Balars* (1967)

Ayalon, David, *Outsiders in the Lands of Islam: Mamluks, Mongols and Eunuchs* (1988)

Babcock, Michael A., *The Night Attila Died* (2005)

Bacon, Elizabeth E., *Obok: A Study of Social Structure in Eurasia* (1958)

Badger, G. P., *The Nestorians and their Rituals, 2 vols* (1852)

Bahadur, Abu'l Ghazi, *History of the Turks, Mongols and Tartars, 2 vols* (1730)

Bahn, Paul G., *The Atlas of World Archaeology* (2003)

Baker, E. C. Stuart, *The Game Birds of India, Burma and Ceylon* (1921)

Baldick, Julian, *Animal and Shaman: Ancient Religions of Central Asia* (2000)

Balzer, Marjorie Mandelstam, ed., *Shamanic Worlds: Rituals and Lore of Siberia and Central Asia* (1997)

Bamana, Gaby, ed., *Christianity and Mongolia: Past and Present* (2006)

Barber, Malcolm, ed., *The Military Orders: Fighting for the Faith and Caring for the Sick* (1994)

Barclay, Harold, *The Role of the Horse in Man's Culture* (1980)

Barfield, Thomas J., *Perilous Frontier: Nomadic Empires and China 221 BC to AD 1757* (1989)

Barfield, Thomas J., *The Nomadic Alternative* (1993)

Barnes, Ian and Robert Hudson, with a foreword by Bhikhu Parekh, *The History Atlas of Asia* (1998)

Barthel, H., *Mongolei: Land zwischen Taiga und Wüste* (1990)

Barthold, Wilhelm, *Four Studies on the History of Central Asia*, 3 vols (1962)

Barthold, Wilhelm, *Histoire des turcs d'Asie centrale* (1945)

Barthold, Wilhelm, *An Historical Geography of Iran* (1984)

Barthold, Wilhelm, *Turkestan down to the Mongol Invasion* (1928)

Bartold, V. V. [Wilhelm Barthold], *The Kyrgyz: A Historical Essay* (1927)

Bauer, W., ed., *Studia Sino-Mongolica* (1979)

Baumer, Christopher, *Southern Silk Road: In the Footsteps of Sir Aurel Stein and Sven Hedin* (2000)

Bayarsaikhan, Bekhjargal, *Travelling by Mongolian Horse* (2005)

Beazley, C. R., *The Dawn of Modern Geography*, 3 vols (1906)

Becker, Jasper, *The Lost Country: Mongolia Revisited* (1992)

Beckingham, Charles F., *Between Islam and Christendom* (1983)

Beckingham, Charles F. & Bernard Hamilton, eds, *Prester John, the Mongols and the Ten Lost Tribes* (1996)

Beckwith, Christopher, *Empires of the Silk Road: A History of Central Eurasia from the Bronze Age to the Present* (2009)

Beckwith, Christopher, *Warriors of the Cloisters: Central Asian Origins of Science in the Medieval World* (2012)

Bell, James S., *Journal of a Residence in Circassia during the Years 1837, 1838 and 1839* (1840)

Bell-Fialkoff, Andrew, ed., *The Role of Migration in the History of the Eurasian Steppe: Sedentary Civilization versus 'Barbarian' and Nomad* (2000)

Bemmann, J., et al, eds, *Current Archaeological Research in Mongolia* (2009)

Bemmann, J., et al, *Mongolian–German Karakorum Expedition, 1: Excavations in the Craftsmen-Quarter at the Main Road* (2010)

Berend, Nora, *At the Gate of Christendom: Jews, Muslims and 'Pagans' in Mediterranean Hungary c. 1000–c. 1300* (2001)

Bernard, Henri, *La découverte des nestoriens mongols aux Ordos et l'histoire ancienne du christianisme en Extrême-Orient* (1935)

Berta, Árpád, ed., *Historical and Linguistic Interaction between Inner Asia and Europe* (1997)

Bezzola, G., *Die Mongolen in abendländischer Sicht, 1200–1270* (1974)

Bigalli, D., *I Tartari e l'Apocalisse: ricerche sull'escatologia in Adamo Marsh e Ruggero Bacone* (1971)

Binbaş, Ilker Evrim & Nurten Kiliç-Schubel, eds, *The Horizons of the World: Festschrift for İsenbike Togan* (2011)

Biran, Michal, *The Empire of the Qara Khitai in Eurasian History: Between China and the Islamic World* (2005)

Biran, Michal, *Qaidu and the Rise of the Mongol State in Central Asia* (1997)

Birge, Bettine, *Women, Property and Confucian Reaction in Sung and Yüan China (960–1368)* (2002)

Blair, Sheila S., *A Compendium of Chronicles: Rashid al-Din's Illustrated History of the World* (1995)

Blench, Roger, *Pastoralism in the New Millennium* (2001)

Bloom, Jonathan M. & Sheila S. Blair, eds, *The Grove Encyclopedia of Islamic Art and Architecture*, 3 vols (2009)

Blume, F. H., *Annotated Justinian Code* (1943), revised T. Kearley (2009)

Blunden, Caroline & Mark Elvin, *Cultural Atlas of China* (1991)

Bodio, Stephen J., *Eagle Dreams: Searching for Legends in Wild Mongolia* (2004)

Boeschoten, Hendrik & Julian Rentzsch, eds, *Turcology in Mainz* (2010)

Boland-Crewe, Tara & David Lea, eds, *The Territories of the People's Republic of China* (2002)

Bold, Bat-Ochir, *Mongolian Nomadic Society: A Reconstruction of the 'Medieval' History of Mongolia* (2001)

Boikova, Elena Vladimirovna & Giovanni Stary, eds, *Florilegia Altaistica: Studies in Honour of Denis Sinor* (2006)

Bond, Brian, *Basil Liddell Hart: A Study of his Military Thought* (1977)

Bonnefoy, Yves, ed., *Asian Mythologies* (1993)

Bosworth, C. E., *Historic Cities of the Islamic World* (2007)

Bosworth, C. E., ed., *Iran and Islam: In Memory of the late Vladimir Minorsky* (1971)

Bosworth, C. E. et al, eds, *The Islamic World from Classical to Modern Times* (1989)

Bougard, Fr & M. Sot, eds, *Liber, Gesta, histoire: Écrire l'histoire des évêques et des papes* . . . (2009)

Bouillane de Lacoste, Henry de, *Au pays sacré des anciens Turcs et des Mongols* (1911)

Bourre, Jean-Paul, *Villiers de L'Isle-Adam: Splendeur et Misère* (2002)

Bowles, Gordon T., *The People of Asia* (1977)

Boyd, Lee & Katherine A. Houpt, *Przewalski's Horse: The History and Biology of an Endangered Species* (1994)

Boyle, J. A., *The Mongol World Empire* (1977)

Boyle, J. A., ed., *The Cambridge History of Iran, 5: The Saljuq and Mongol Periods* (1968)

Bradbury, Jim, *The Medieval Siege* (1992)

Brandes, Wolfram & Felicitas Schmieder, eds, *Endzeiten: Eschatologie in den monotheistischen Weltreligionen* (2008)

Brătianu, George Ioan, *Recherches sur le commerce génois dans la mer Noire au XIIIe siècle* (1929)

Bregel, Yuri, *An Historical Atlas of Central Asia* (2003)

Brisbane, Mark, Nikolaj Makarov & Evgenij Nosov, eds, *The Archaeology of Medieval Novgorod in Context* (2012)

Broadbridge, A. F., *Kingship and Ideology in the Islamic and Mongol Worlds* (2008)

Brook, Timothy, *The Confusions of Pleasure: Commerce and Culture in Ming China* (1998)

Brook, Timothy, *The Troubled Empire: China in the Yuan and Ming Dynasties* (2010)

Brose, Michael C., *Subjects and Masters: Uyghurs in the Mongol Empire* (2007)

Brosset, M.-F., *Histoire de la Géorgie depuis l'antiquité jusqu'au XIXe siècle*, 7 vols (1858)

Brown, Neville, *The Geography of Human Conflict: Approaches to Survival* (2009)

Brown, Neville, *History and Climate Change: A Eurocentric Perspective* (2005)

Browne, Edward Granville, *A Literary History of Persia*, 2 vols (1915)

Bryer, Anthony A. M., ed., *The Empire of Trebizond and the Pontos* (1980)

Buchanan, Brenda J., ed., *Gunpowder: The History of an International Technology* (1996)

Buell, Paul D., *The A–Z of the Mongol Empire* (2010)

Buell, Paul D., *Historical Dictionary of the Mongol World Empire* (2003)

Bulag, Uradyn E., *Collaborative Nationalism: The Politics of Friendship on China's Mongolian Frontier* (2010)

Bull, Bartle, *Around the Sacred Sea: Mongolia and Lake Baikal on Horseback* (1999)

Bulliet, Richard, *The Camel and the Wheel* (1975)

Bulliet, Richard, *The Patricians of Nishapur: A Study in Medieval Islamic Social History* (1972)

Bulliet, Richard et al, eds., *The Earth and Its Peoples: A Global History* (2000)

Burbank, J. & F. Cooper, *Empires in World History: Power and the Politics of Difference* (2010)

Burnaby, Frederick, *A Ride to Khiva* (1876)

Cable, Mildred & Francesca French, *The Gobi Desert* (1943)

Cable, Roger, *Nomads in Archaeology* (1991)

Cahen, Claude, *Pre-Ottoman Turkey: A General Survey of the Natural and Spiritual Culture and History* (1968)

Cahen, Claude, trans. P. M. Holt, *The Formation of Turkey: The Seljukid Sultanate of Rum, 11th to 14th Century* (2001)

Canfield, R. L., ed., *Turco–Persia in Historical Perspective* (1991)

Carey, Brian Todd, *Warfare in the Medieval World* (2007)

Carruthers, Douglas, *Unknown Mongolia*, 2 vols (1913)

Cassady, Richard F., *The Emperor and the Saint: Frederick II of Hohenstaufen, Francis of Assisi and Journeys to Medieval Places* (2011)

Chakin, Mark, *The Kingdom of Armenia* (2001)

Chaliand, Gérard, *Nomadic Empires* (2005)

Chambers, James, *The Devil's Horsemen* (1979)

Chan, Hok-lam, *China and the Mongols* (1999)

Chan, Hok-lam, *Legitimation in Imperial China: Discussions under the Jurchen–Chin Dynasty, 1115–1234* (1984)

Chandler, Tertius, *Four Thousand Years of Urban Growth: An Historical Census* (1987)

Chandra, Satish, *Medieval India: From Sultanate to the Mughals, 1: The Delhi Sultanate, 1206–1526* (1997)

Chapin, David, *Long Lines: Ten of the World's Longest Continuous Family Lineages* (2012)

Chase, Kenneth Warren, *Firearms: A Global History to 1700* (2003)

Chavannes, Édouard & Paul Pelliot, *Un traité manichéen retrouvé en Chine* (1913)

Ch'en, Paul Heng-Chao, *Chinese Legal Tradition under the Mongols: The Code of 1291 as Reconstructed* (1979)

Chi, Ch'ao-ting, *Key Economic Areas in Chinese History* (1936)

Chou, Chin-Seng, trans. Edward Kaplan, *An Economic History of China* (1974)

Christian, David, *A History of Russia, Central Asia and Mongolia, 1: Inner Eurasia from Prehistory to the Mongol Empire* (1998)

Christiansen, Eric, *The Northern Crusades: The Baltic and the Catholic Frontier 1100–1525* (1980)

Ciocîltan, Virgil, trans. Samuel Willcocks, *The Mongols and the Black Sea Trade in the Thirteenth and Fourteenth Centuries* (2012)

Cipolla, Carlo M., ed., *The Fontana Economic History of Europe, 1: The Middle Ages* (1972)

Claessen, Henri J. M., ed., *The Early State* (1978)

Claessen, Henri J. M. & J. G. Oosten, eds, *Ideology and the Formation of Early States* (1996)

Clark, Larry V. & Paul A. Draghi, *Aspects of Altaic Civilization*, 2 vols (1978)

Clarke, Edward Daniel, *Travels in Russia, Tartary and Turkey* (1839)

Clausewitz, Carl von, trans O. J. Matthijs Jolles, *On War* (1943)

Clot, André, *Harun al-Rashid and the World of The Thousand and One Nights* (1990)

Coene, Frederick, *The Caucasus: An Introduction* (2009)

Conermann, Stephan & Jan Kusber, *Die Mongolen in Asien und Europa* (1997)

Constant, Antoine, *L'Azerbaidjan* (2002)

Cooper, Alan D., *The Geography of Genocide* (2009)

Cordier, Henri, *Histoire générale de la Chine*, 2 vols (1920)

Cotterell, Arthur, *The Imperial Capitals of China: An Inside View of the Celestial Empire* (2008)

Cribb, Roger, *Nomads in Archaeology* (1991)

Crosby, Alfred W., *Throwing Fire: Projectile Technology through History* (2002)

Crossley, Pamela Kyle, Helen F. Siu & Donald S. Sutton, eds, *Empire at the Margins: Culture, Ethnicity and Frontier in Early Modern China* (2006)

Crowdy, Terry, *The Enemy Within* (2006)

Crummey, R. O., *The Formation of Muscovy 1304–1613* (1987)

Cummins, J. G., *The Hound and the Hawk: The Art of Medieval Hunting* (1988)

Curta, Florin, *South-East Europe in the Middle Ages 500–1250* (2006)

Curtin, Jeremiah, *A Journey in Southern Siberia: The Mongols, their Religion and their Myths* (1909)

Curtin, Jeremiah, *The Mongols: A History* (1907)

Daftary, Farhad, *The Ismailis: Their History and Doctrines* (1990)

Danchev, Alex, *Alchemist of War: The Life of Basil Liddell Hart* (1998)

Daniel, Elton L., *The History of Iran* (2001)

Daniels, P. T. & W. Bright, eds, *The World's Writing Systems* (1996)

Darling, Linda T., *A History of Social Justice and Political Power in the Middle East* (2012)

Daryaee, Touraj, *The Oxford Handbook of Iranian History* (2012)

Dashdondog, Bayarsaikhan, *The Mongols and the Armenians 1220–1235* (2010)

David, F. N., *Games, Gods and Gambling: A History of Probability and Statistical Ideas* (1998)

Davies, Norman, *God's Playground: A History of Poland*, I: *The Origins to 1795* (1979)

Davis, R. L., *Wind against the Mountain: The Crisis of Politics and Culture in Thirteenth-Century China* (1996)

Despeux, Catherine & Livia Kohn, *Women in Daoism* (2003)

Detwiler, Donald S., *Germany: A Short History* (1999)

DeVries, Kelly and Robert Douglas Smith, *Medieval Military Technology* (2nd ed., 2012)

De Waal, Thomas, *The Caucasus: An Introduction* (2010)

DeWeese, Devin, *Islamization and Native Religion in the Golden Horde* (1975)

De Windt, Harry, *From Pekin to Calais by Land* (1892)

Di Cosmo, Nicola, *Ancient China and its Enemies: The Rise of Nomadic Power in East Asian History* (2002)

Di Cosmo, Nicola, *Military Culture in Imperial China* (2009)

Di Cosmo, Nicola, *Warfare in Inner Asian History* (2002)

Di Cosmo, Nicola, Allen J. Frank & Peter B. Golden, *The Cambridge History of Inner Asia*, I: *The Chinggisid Age* (2009)

Di Cosmo, Nicola & D. J. Wyatt, *Political Frontiers, Ethnic Boundaries and Human Geographies in Chinese History* (2003)

Dienst, Heide, *Die Schlacht an der Leitha 1246* (1971)

Dimnik, Martin, *The Dynasty of Chernigov 1146–1246* (2003)

Doerfer, Gerhard, *Türkische und mongolische Elemente im Neupersischen*, 4 vols (1975)

d'Ohsson, Abraham Constantin, Baron, *Histoire des Mongols depuis Tchinguiz Khan jusqu'à Timour Bey*, 4 vols (1835)

Donner, Kai, *La Sibérie* (1946)

Drews, Robert, *Early Riders: The Beginnings of Mounted Warfare in Asia and Europe* (2004)

Driver, G. R. & John C. Miles, eds & trans., *The Babylonian Laws* (2007)

Drompp, Michael R., *Tang China and the Collapse of the Uighur Empire: A Documentary History* (2005)

Du Halde, Jean-Baptiste, *Description géographique, historique, chronique et physique de l'empire de la Chine et de la Tartarie Chinoise*, 4 vols (1735)

Dumper, Michael R. T. & Bruce E. Stanley, eds, *Cities of the Middle East and North Africa: A Historical Encyclopedia* (2008)

Dunn, Ross E., *The Adventures of Ibn Battuta* (1986)

Dunnell, Ruth W., *Chinggis Khan: World Conqueror* (2010)

Dunnell, Ruth W., *The Great State of White and High* (1996)

Dunnell, Ruth W., 'Tanguts and the Tangut State of Ta Hsia' (Ph.D. diss., Princeton 1983)

Dupuy, R. Ernest & Trevor N., eds, *The Harper Encyclopedia of Military History* (1993)

Durand-Guedy, David, ed., *Turko-Mongol Rulers, Cities and City Life* (2013)

Dvornik, Francis, *Origins of Intelligence Services* (1974)

Eberhard, Wolfram, *Conquerors and Rulers: Social Forces in Medieval China* (1952)

Ebrey, Patricia Buckley, *The Cambridge Illustrated History of China* (2010)

Ebrey, Patricia Buckley, *East Asia: A Cultural and Political History* (2012)

Edbury, P. W., *Crusade and Settlement* (1985)

Edmonds, Richard Louis, *Northern Frontiers of Qing China and Togukawa Japan: A Comparative Study of Frontier Policy* (1985)

Eikemeier, Dieter & Herbert Franke, *State and Law in East Asia* (1981)

Eisma, Doeke, *Chinggis Khan and the Conquest of Eurasia* (2006)

Eisma, Doeke, *Mongol Rule: Reflections on Mongol Sociopolitics* (2003)

Elisseeff, Vadim, *The Silk Roads: Highways of Culture and Commerce* (2000)

Ellis, John, *Cavalry: The History of Mounted Warfare* (2004)

Elman, Benjamin A., *A Cultural History of Civil Examinations in Late Imperial China* (2003)

Elverskog, J., *The Jewel Translucent Sutra: Altan Khan and the Mongols in the Sixteenth-Century* (2003)

Elvin, Mark & Liu Cuirong, eds, *Sediments of Time: Environment and Society in Chinese History* (1998)

Elvin, Mark & G. W. Skinner, *The Chinese City between Two Worlds* (1974)

Encyclopaedia Of Islam (1st ed., 1913–38 (repr. as *E. J. Brill's First Encyclopaedia of Islam*, 9 vols, 1993), 2nd ed., 1960–2005, 3rd ed., 2007–)

Endicott-West, Elizabeth, *Mongolian Rule in China: Local Administration in the Yuan Dynasty* (1989)

Engel, Pál, *The Realm of St Stephen: A History of Medieval Hungary, 895–1526* (2001)

Engels, Friedrich, *Socialism: Utopian and Scientific* (1880)

Enkhtuvshin, B. & S. Tsolmon, *Chinggis Khan and the Contemporary Era* (2003)

Équipe Écologie, L', *Pastoral Production and Society* (1979)

Erdmann, F. von, *Temudschin* (1862)

Eskildsen, Stephen, *The Teachings and Practices of the Early Quanzhen Taoist Masters* (2006)

Fabrycky, Wolter J. & Paul E. Torgesen, *Operations Economy: Industrial Applications of Operations Research* (1966)

Faegre, Torvald, *Tents: Architecture of the Nomads* (1979)

Fairbank, John K., ed., *The Cambridge History of China*, 10: *Late Ch'ing 1800–1911, Part 1* (1978)

Fairbank, John K. & Albert Feuerwerker, eds, *The Cambridge History of China*, 13: *Republican China 1912–1949* (1987)

Fairbank, John King & Merle Goldman, *China: A New History* (2006)

Farquhar, David M., *The Government of China under Mongolian Rule: A Reference Guide* (1990)

Fehrenbach, T. R., *Comanches: The History of a People* (2007)

Fennell, John, *The Crisis of Medieval Russia 1200–1304* (1983)

Fennell, John & Antony Stokes, *Early Russian Literature* (1974)

Ferdinandy, Miguel de, *Tschingis Khan: Der Einbruch des Steppenmenschen* (1958)

Ferguson, R. Brian & Neil L. Whitehead, eds, *War in the Tribal Zone: Expanding States and Indigenous Warfare* (1992)

Findley, Carter Vaughn, *The Turks in World History* (2005)

Fine, John van Antwerp, *The Early Medieval Balkans: A Critical Survey from the Sixth to the Late Twelfth Century* (1991)

Fine, John van Antwerp, *The Late Medieval Balkans: A Critical Survey from the Late Twelfth Century to the Ottoman Conquest* (1994)

Fitzgerald, C. P., *China: A Short Cultural History* (1961)

Fitzhugh, William, Morris Rossabi and William Honeychurch, eds, *Genghis Khan and the Mongol Empire* (Washington 2009)

Fletcher, Joseph F., *Studies on Chinese and Islamic Inner Asia* (1995)

Foltz, Richard C., *Religions of the Silk Road: Overland Trade and Cultural Exchange from Antiquity to the Fifteenth Century* (2000)

Fonnesberg-Schmidt, Iben, *The Popes and the Baltic Crusades* (2007)

Forde, C. Daryll, *Habitat, Economy and Society: A Geographical Introduction to Ethnology* (1934)

Forrest, W. G., *The Emergence of Greek Democracy 800–400 BC* (1966)

Forsyth, James, *The Caucasus: A History* (2013)

Fragner, B. G. et al, eds, *Pferde in Asien: Geschichte, Handel, und Kultur* (2009)

Franke, Herbert, *From Tribal Chieftain to Universal Emperor and God: The Legitimation of the Yuan Dynasty* (1978)

Franke, Herbert, *Sung Biographies*, 3 vols (2006)

Franke, Herbert & Denis Twitchett, eds, *The Cambridge History of China, 6: Alien Regimes and Border States 907–1368* (1994)

Franke, Otto, *Geschichte des chinesischen Reiches*, 5 vols (1948)

Franklin, Simon & Jonathan Shepard, *The Emergence of Rus 750–1200* (1996)

Friedland, Paul, 'A Reconstruction of Early Tangut History' (Ph.D. diss., University of Washington 1969)

Friedman, John Block & Kristen Mossler Figg, *Trade, Travel and Exploration in the Middle Ages: An Encyclopedia* (2000)

Fromherz, Allen James, *Ibn Khaldun: Life and Times* (2010)

Frye, Richard N., *Bukhara: The Medieval Achievement* (1977)

Frye, Richard N., *The Golden Age of Persia: The Arabs in the East* (1975)

Fügedi, Erik, trans. J. M. Bak, *Castle and Society in Medieval Hungary* (1986)

Gabriel, Richard A., *The Great Armies of Antiquity* (2002)

Gabriel, Richard A., *Subotai the Valiant: Genghis Khan's Greatest General* (2004)

Gabriel, Richard A. & Donald W. Boose, Jr, *The Great Battles of Antiquity* (1994)

Gaubil, Antoine, *Histoire de Gentchiscan et de toute la dinastie des Mongous ses successeurs conquérans de la Chine* (1731, repr. 2011)

Gellner, Ernest, *Soviet and Western Anthropology* (1980)

Gerhartl, Gertrud, *Wiener Neustadt: Geschichte, Kunst, Kultur, Wirtschaft* (1993)

Gernet, Jacques, *Daily Life in China on the Eve of the Mongol Invasion, 1250–1276* (1962)

Gernet, Jacques, *A History of Chinese Civilization* (1996)

Gervers, Michael & Wayne Schlepp, eds, *Nomadic Diplomacy, Destruction and Religion from the Pacific to the Adriatic* (1994)

Gettleman, Marvin E. & Stuart Schaar, eds., *The Middle East and Islamic World Reader* (2003)

Gibert, Lucien, *Dictionnaire historique et géographique de la Mandchourie* (1934)

Giles, Herbert A., *A Chinese Biographical Dictionary* (1898)

Glazebrook, Philip, *Journey to Khiva* (1992)

Gleason, Abbott, ed., *A Companion to Russian History* (2009)

Göckenjan, Hansgerd & James R. Sweeney, *Der Mongolensturm: Berichte von Augenzeugen und Zeitgenossen, 1235–1250* (1985)

Godbey, Allen Howard, *The Lost Tribes a Myth: Suggestions towards Rewriting Hebrew History* (1974)

Goff, Jacques, *Saint Louis* (1996)

Golden, Peter B., *An Introduction to the History of the Turkic Peoples* (1992)

Golden, Peter B., *Nomads and their Neighbours in the Russian Steppes: Turks, Khazars and Qipchaqs* (2003)

Golden, Peter B., ed., *The King's Dictionary: the Rasulid Hexaglot, Fourteenth-Century Vocabularies in Arabic, Persian, Turkic, Greek, Armenian and Mongol* (2000)

Goodrich, L. Carrington, *A Short History of the Chinese People* (2002)

Gordon, Stewart, ed., *Robes and Honor: The Medieval World of Investiture* (2001)

Gottschalk, H. L., *Al-Malik al-Kamil von Ägypten und seine Zeit* (1958)

Graff, David A., *Medieval Chinese Warfare 300–900* (2002)

Graff, David A. & Robin Higham, eds, *A Military History of China* (2002)

Grant, R. G., *Battle: A Visual Journey through 5,000 Years of Combat* (2009)

Grekov, B. & A. Yakoubovski, *La Horde d'Or* (1939)

Grenard, Fernand, *Genghis Khan* (1935)

Grothusen, Klaus-Detlev & Klaus Zernack, eds, *Europa Slavica – Europa Orientalis* (1980)

Grousset, René, *Le conquérant du monde* (1944); trans. Marian McKellar & Denis Sinor as *Conqueror of the World: The Life of Chingis-Khan* (1967)

Grousset, René, *L'empire mongol* (1941)

Grousset, René, *The Empire of the Steppes* (1970)

Grousset, René, *The Rise and Splendour of the Chinese Empire* (1959)

Gumilev, Lev, trans R. E. Smith, *Searches for an Imaginary Kingdom: The Legend of the Kingdom of Prester John* (1987)

Haeger, John W., ed., *Crisis and Prosperity in Sung China* (1975)

Halbertsma, Tjalling H. F., *Early Christian Remains of Inner Mongolia* (2008)

Halperin, Charles J., *Russia and the Golden Horde: The Mongol Impact on Medieval Russian History* (1985)

Halperin, Charles J., *The Tatar Yoke: The Image of the Mongols in Medieval Russia* (1986)

Halperin, Charles J., ed., Victor Spinei & George Bilavschi, *Russia and the Mongols: Slavs and the Steppe in Medieval and Early Russia* (2007)

Hambis, Louis, *Gengis-Khan* (1973)

Hambis, Louis, *La Haute Asie* (1953)

Hamby, Gavin, *Central Asia* (1967)

Hamdun, Said & Noel King, *Ibn Battuta in Black Africa* (1994)

Hamilton, James R., *Les Ouighours à l'époque des cinq dynasties d'après les documents chinois* (1955)

Han, Guanghui, *History of the Population and Geography of Beijing* (1996)

Hana, Corinna, *Bericht über die Verteidigung der Stadt Té-an während der Periode K'ai-Hsi 1205–8* (1970)

Hanne, Eric J., *Putting the Caliph in his Place: Power, Authority and the Late Abbasid Caliphate* (2007)

Hardund, H., *Mongolian Journey* (1949)

Hare, John, *Mysteries of the Gobi: Searching for Wild Camels and Lost Cities in the Heart of Asia* (2009)

Harlez, C. de, *Histoire de l'Empire de Kin* (1887)

Harrell, S., ed., *Cultural Encounters on China's Ethnic Frontiers* (1995)

Hartl, Daniel L. & Elizabeth W. Jones, *Genetics: Analysis of Genes and Genomes* (2008)

Hartmann, Angelika, *An-Nasir li-Din Allah (1180–1225): Politik, Religion, Kultur in der späten 'Abbasidenzeit* (1975)

Hartog, Leo de, *Genghis Khan: Conqueror of the World* (1989)

Hartog, Leo de, *Russia and the Mongol Yoke: The History of the Russian Principalities and the Golden Horde 1221–1502* (1996)

Haslund, Henning, *Mongol Journey* (1949)

Hatton, Ronald, *Shamans, Siberial Spirituality and the Western Imagination* (2001)

Haw, Stephen G., *Marco Polo's China: A Venetian in the Realm of Khubilai Khan* (2006)

Hawting, G. R., ed., *Muslims, Mongols and Crusaders* (2005)

Haxthausen, A. von, *The Russian Empire; Its Peoples, Institutions and Resources*, 2 vols (1856)

Hazai, G. & P. Zieme, eds, *Sprache, Geschichte und Kultur der altaischen Volker* (1974)

Hazard, B. H., *Japanese Marauders and Medieval Korea: A Study of the Genesis of the Wako* (1958)

Hedin, Sven, *My Life as an Explorer* (1925)

Hedley, John, *Tramps in Dark Mongolia* (1910)

Heirman, Ann & Stephan Peter Bumbacher, eds., *The Spread of Buddhism* (2007)

Heissig, Walther, trans. Geoffrey Samuel, *The Religions of Mongolia* (1980)

Heissig, Walther, ed., *Altaica Collecta* (1976)

Heissig, Walther, ed., *Synkretismus in den Religionen Zentralasiens* (1987)

Heissig, Walther & Klaus Sagaster, eds, *Gedanke und Wirkung: Festschrift zum 90. Geburtstag von Nikolaus Poppe* (1989)

Heissig, Walther & Claudius C. Müller, eds, *Die Mongolen* (1989)

Heissig, Walther, et al, eds, *Tractata Altaica: Denis Sinor Sexagenario Optime de Rebus Altaicis Merito Dedicata* (1976)

Helland, J., *Five Essays on the Study of Pastoralists and the Development of Pastoralism* (1980)

Hendricks, Bonnie L., *International Encyclopedia of Horse Breeds* (2007)

Henthorn, William E., *Korea: The Mongol Invasions* (1963)

Hercus, L. A. et al, eds, *Indological and Buddhist Studies* (1982)

Herrin, Judith & Guillaume Saint-Guillain, *Identities and Allegiances in the Eastern Mediterranean after 1204* (2011)

Herrmann, Albert, *A Historical Atlas of China* (1966)

Hildinger, Erik, *Warriors of the Steppe: A Military History of Central Asia 500 BC to 1700 AD* (1977)

Hill, John E., *Through the Jade Gate to Rome: A Study of the Silk Routes during the Later Han Dynasty, First to Second Centuries CE* (2009)

Hirmer Verlag, *Dschingis Khan und seine Erben: Das Weltreich der Mongolen* (2005)

Ho, Ping-ti, *Studies in the Population of China, 1368–1953* (1959)

Hochschild, Adam, *King Leopold's Ghost* (1999)

Hodgson, Marshall G. S., *The Secret Order of Assassins: The Struggle of the Early Nizârî Ismâ'îlîs against the Islamic World* (2005)

Holmes, Richard, ed., *The Oxford Companion to Military History* (2001)

Holtman, Robert B., *The Napoleonic Revolution* (1981)

Hong, Wontack, *East Asian History: A Tripolar Approach* (2012)

Hook, Sidney, *The Hero in History: A Study in Limitation and Possibility* (1955)

Hourani, Albert, *A History of the Arab Peoples* (1991)

Hovannisian, Richard G., ed., *The Armenian People from Ancient to Modern Times, 1: The Dynastic Periods from Antiquity to the Fourteenth Century* (1997)

Hsiao, Ch'i-Ch'ing, *The Military Establishment of the Yuan Dynasty* (1978)

Hsiao, Kung-chuan, trans. F. W. Mote, *A History of Chinese Political Thought* (1978)

Huc, Abbé, ed. Julie Bedier, *High Road in Tartary* (1948)

Hucker, Charles O., *China's Imperial Past: An Introduction to Chinese History and Culture* (1975)

Humphrey, Caroline & Urgunge Onon, *Shamans and Elders: Experience, Knowledge and Power among the Daur Mongols* (1996)

Hunyadi, Zsolt & József Laszlovsky, eds, *The Crusades and the Military Orders: Expanding the Frontiers of Medieval Latin Christianity* (2001)

Hutton, Ronald, *Shamans: Siberian Spirituality and the Western Imagination* (2001)

Hyland, Ann, *The Medieval Warhorse from Byzantium to the Crusades* (1994)

Ikram, S. M., *Muslim Civilization in India* (1964)

Irwin, Robert, *Camel* (2010)

Isoaho, Mari, *The Image of Aleksandr Nevskiy in Medieval Russia: Warrior and Saint* (2006)

Jackson, Peter, *The Delhi Sultanate: A Political and Military History* (1999)

Jackson, Peter, *The Mongols and the West* (2005)

Jackson, Peter, *Studies on the Mongol Empire and Early Muslim India* (2009)

Jagchid, Sechin, *Essays in Mongolian Studies* (1988)

Jagchid, Sechin & P. Hyer, *Mongolia's Culture and Society* (1979)

Jagchid, Sechin & Van Jay Symons, *Peace, War and Trade along the Great Wall: Nomadic–Chinese Interaction through Two Millennia* (1989)

Jaimoukha, Amjad, *The Circassians: A Handbook* (2001)

Janhunen, Juha, *Manchuria: An Ethnic History* (1996)

Janhunen, Juha, ed., *The Mongolic Languages* (2003)

Janhunen, Juha, ed., *Writing in the Altaic World* (1999)

Jankovich, Miklos, *They Rode into Europe* (1971)

Jaques, Tony, *Dictionary of Battles and Sieges*, 3 vols (2007)

Jarring, G. & S. Rosen, eds, *Altaic Papers* (1985)

Jay, Jennifer W., *A Change in Dynasties: Loyalism in Thirteenth Century China* (1991)

Johnson, Douglas L., *The Nature of Nomadism: A Comparative Study of Pastoral Migration in Southwestern Asia and Northern Africa* (1969)

Johnson, Linda Cooke, *Women of the Conquest Dynasties: Gender and Identity in Liao and Jin China* (2011)

Jones, David E., *Poison Arrows* (2007)

Juntunen, Mirja & Birgit N. Schlyter, eds, *Return to the Silk Routes: Current Scandinavian Research on Central Asia* (2009)

Kadoi, Yuko, *Islamic Chinoiserie: The Art of Mongol Iran* (2009)

Kantorowicz, Ernst, *Frederick the Second, 1194–1250* (1957)

Kaplan, Edward H. & Donald W. Whisenhunt, *Opuscula Altaica: Essays Presented in Honor of Henry Schwarz* (1994)

Kaplonski, Christopher, *Truth, History and Politics in Mongolia: The Memory of Heroes* (2004)

Kauz, Ralph, ed., *Aspects of the Silk Road: From the Persian Gulf to the East China Sea* (2010)

Keegan, John, *A History of Warfare* (1994)

Keen, Maurice, *Medieval Warfare: A History* (1999)

Kellner-Heinkele, Barbara, ed., *Altaica Berolinensia: The Concept of Sovereignty in the Altaic World* (1993)

Kelly, Christopher, *Attila the Hun* (2008)

Kelly, Jack, *Gunpowder: Alchemy, Bombards and Pyrotechnics: The History of the Explosive that Changed the World* (2005)

Kennedy, Hugh, *The Court of the Caliphs* (2004)

Kennedy, Hugh, ed., *The Historiography of Islamic Egypt c. 950-1800* (2001)

Kennedy, Hugh, *When Baghdad Ruled the Muslim World: The Rise and Fall of Islam's Greatest Dynasty* (2006)

Kepping, Ksenia, *Recent Articles and Documents* (2003)

Kerner, R. J., *The Urge to the Sea: The Course of Russian History* (1942)

Kessler, Adam T., *Empires Beyond the Great Wall: The Heritage of Genghis Khan* (1993)

Khalikov, A. H., *The Mongols, the Tatars, the Golden Horde and Bulgaria* (1994) (in Russian)

Khan, Iqtidar Alam, *Gunpowder and Firearms: Warfare in Medieval India* (2004)

Khazanov, A. M., trans. Julia Crookenden, *Nomads and the Outside World,* (1994)

Khazanov, A. M. & André Wink, eds, *Nomads and the Sedentary World* (2001)

Kiernan, F. A. & J. K. Fairbank, eds, *Chinese Ways in Warfare* (1974)

Klopprogge, Axel, *Ursprung und Ausprägung des abendländischen Mongolenbildes im 13. Jahrhundert: Ein Versuch zur Ideengeschichte des Mittelalters* (1993)

Knapp, R. G., *China's Walled Cities* (2000)

Kohlberg, Etan, *A Medieval Muslim Scholar at Work: Ibn Tawus and his Library* (1992)

Kohn, George C., *Dictionary of Wars* (2006)

Kohn, Livia, ed., *Daoism Handbook* (2000)

Kolbas, Judith G., *The Mongols in Iran: Chingiz Khan to Uljaytu, 1220–1309* (2006)

Komaroff, Linda, *Beyond the Legacy of Genghis Khan* (2006)

Komaroff, Linda & S. Carboni, eds, *The Legacy of Genghis Khan* (2002)

Komjathy, Louis, *Cultivating Perfection: Mysticism and Self-Transformation in Early Quanzhen Daoism* (2007)

Kontler, László, *A History of Hungary* (2002)

Köpeczi, Béla, *History of Transylvania, 1: From the Beginnings to 1606* (2001)

Kosztolnyik, Z. J., *Hungary in the Thirteenth Century* (1996)

Kozlow, P. K., *Die Mongolei, Amdo und die tote Stadt Chara-choto* (1955)

Krader, Lawrence, *Social Organization of the Mongol–Turkic Pastoral Nomads* (1963)

Kradin, Nikolay, et al, eds, *Nomadic Pathways in Social Evolution* (2003)

Krämer, F., K. Schmidt & J. Singer, *Historicizing the Beyond: The Mongolian Invasion as a New Dimension of Violence* (2011)

Krause, F. E. A., *Cingis Han: Die Geschichte seines Lebens nach den chinesischen Reichsannalen* (1922)

Krause, F. E. A., *Die Epoche der Mongolen* (1924)

Kröger, Jens, *Nishapur: Glass of the Early Islamic Period* (1995)

Krueger, John R., *Poetical Passages in the Erdeni-yin Tobči* (1961)

Krueger, John R., *Tuvan Manual* (1977)

Krumeich, Gerd & Susanne Brandt, eds, *Schlachtenmythen: Ereignis–Erzählung–Erinnerung* (2007)

Kubinyi, András, *Die Anfänge Ofens* (1972)

Kuhn, Dieter, *The Age of Confucian Rule: The Song Transformation of China*

Kuno, Y. S., *Japanese Expansion on the Asiatic Mainland*, 2 vols (1940)

Kürsat-Ahlers, Elçin, *Zur frühen Staatenbildung von Steppenvölkern* (1994)

Kwanten, Luc, *Imperial Nomads: A History of Central Asia, 500–1500* (1979)

Kwanten, Luc & Susan Hesse, *Tangut (Hsi Hsia) Studies: A Bibliography* (1980)

Lamb, Harold, *Genghis Khan: The Emperor of All Men* (1927)

Lamb, Harold, *The March of the Barbarians* (1940)

Lamb, H. H., *Climate, History and the Modern World*, (2nd ed., 1995)

Lamb, H. H., *Climate, Present, Past and Future* (1977)

Lambert, S. D., *The Phratries of Attica* (1998)

Lambton, Ann K. S., *Continuity and Change in Medieval Persia: Aspects of Administrative, Economic and Social History 11th–14th Century* (1988)

Lane, Frederic Chapin, *Venice: A Maritime Republic* (1973)

Lane, George E., *Daily Life in the Mongol Empire* (2006)

Lane, George E., *Early Mongol Rule in Thirteenth-Century Iran: A Persian Renaissance* (2003)

Lane, George E., *Genghis Khan and Mongol Rule* (2004)

Lang, Jieming, *Chinese Siege Warfare: Mechanical Artillery and Siege Weapons of Antiquity* (2006)

Langer, Lawrence N., *Historical Dictionary of Medieval Russia* (2001)

Langlois, John D., ed., *China under Mongol Rule* (1981)

Larner, John, *Marco Polo and the Discovery of the World* (1999)

Lary, Diana, *Chinese Migrations: The Movement of People, Goods and Ideas over Four Millennia* (2012)

Lattimore, Owen, *Inner Asian Frontiers of China* (1940)

Lattimore, Owen, *Mongol Journeys* (1941)

Lattimore, Owen, *The Mongols of Manchuria* (1934)

Lattimore, Owen, *Studies in Frontier History* (1962)

Lawson, Todd, ed., *Reason and Inspiration in Islam* (2005)

Lazarev, Victor Nikitich et al, eds, *The Russian Icon: From Its Origins to the Sixteenth Century* (1997)

Lech, Klaus, *Das mongolische Weltreich* (1968)

Ledyard, Gari, *Early Koryo–Mongol Relations with Particular Reference to the Diplomatic Documents* (1963)

Lee, Hyun-hee, et al, eds, *A New History of Korea* (2005)

Lee, Keekok, *Warp and Weft: Chinese Language and Culture* (2008)

Lee, Mabel Ping-hua, *The Economic History of China* (1921)

Lee, Peter H., ed., *Sourcebook of Korean Civilization*, 1: *From Early Times to the Sixteenth Century* (1993)

Leigh Fermor, Patrick, *Between the Woods and the Water* (1986)

Lerski, Jerzy Jan, *Historical Dictionary of Poland, 966–1945* (1996)

Lessing, F. D., *Mongolian–English Dictionary* (1973)

Le Strange, Guy, *Baghdad during the Abbasid Caliphate* (1900)

Le Strange, Guy, *The Lands of the Eastern Caliphate* (1905–2011)

Lev, Y., ed., *War and Society in the Eastern Mediterranean, 7th–15th Centuries* (1997)

Lévêque, Pierre, *Cleisthenes the Athenian* (1996)

Lewis, Bernard, *The Assassins: A Radical Sect in Islam* (1967)

Lewis, Bernard, ed., *Islam from the Prophet Muhammad to the Capture of Constantinople*, 2 vols (1973)

Lewis, Mark Edward, *China's Cosmopolitan Empire: The Tang Dynasty* (2009)

Li, Lillian M., Alison J. Dray-Novey & Haili Kong, eds, *Beijing: From Imperial Capital to Olympic City* (2007)

Li, Xiaobing, *China at War: An Encyclopedia* (2012)

Liddell Hart, Basil, *Great Captains Unveiled* (1927)

Liddell Hart, Basil, *Strategy: The Indirect Approach* (1954)

Lieberman, Victor, *Strange Parallels*, 2 vols (2009)

Lieu, S. N. C., *Manichaeism in Central Asia and China* (1998)

Lieu, S. N. C., *Manichaeism in the Later Roman Empire and Medieval China: A Historical Survey* (1985)

Ligeti, Louis, ed., *Mongolian Studies* (1970)

Ligeti, Louis, ed., *Tibetan and Buddhist Studies*, 2 vols (1984)

Lincoln, W. Bruce, *The Conquest of a Continent: Siberia and the Russians* (2007)

Lissner, Ivan, *The Living Past* (1957)

Liu, Xinru, *The Silk Road in World History* (2011)

Lo, Winston Wan, *The Life and Thought of Yeh Shih* (1974)

Löb, Ladislaus et al, eds, *Forms of Identity: Definitions and Changes* (1994)

Lorge, Peter Allan, *War, Politics and Society in Early Modern China, 900–1795* (2006)

Lovell, Julia, *The Great Wall: China against the World, 1000 BC–2000 AD* (2006)

Luniya, Bhanwarlal Nathuram, *Life and Culture in Medieval India* (1978)

Maalouf, Amin, trans. J. Rothschild, *The Crusades through Arab Eyes* (2006)

Macdonald, Helen, *Falcon* (2006)

McEvedy, Colin & Richard Jones, *Atlas of World Population History* (1978)

Macfarlane, Alan, *The Savage Wars of Peace: England, Japan and the Malthusian Trap* (2003)

McGovern, William M., *Early Empires of Central Asia* (1939)

McGrew, Robert E., *Encyclopedia of Medical History* (1985)

McKay, Alex, *The History of Tibet*, 1 (2003)

Mackerras, Colin, ed.,*The Uighur Empire According to the Tang Dynastic Histories: A Study in Sino-Uighur Relations, 744–840* (1972)

McLeod, John, *The History of India* (2002)

MacLeod, Roy, *The Library of Alexandria: Centre of Learning in the Ancient World* (2004)

McLynn, Frank, *1066: The Year of the Three Battles* (1998)

McLynn, Frank, *Fitzroy Maclean* (1992)

McNeill, William, *In Pursuit of Power: Technology, Armed Force and Society since AD 1000* (1982)

McNeill, William, *Plagues And Peoples* (1976)

Magocsi, Paul Robert, *Historical Atlas of Central Europe* (2002)

Magocsi, Paul Robert, *A History of Ukraine* (1996)

Magocsi, Paul Robert and Ivan Pop, *Encyclopedia of Rusyn History and Culture* (2002)

Malek, Roman & Peter Hofrichter, eds, *Jingjiao: The Church of the East in China and Central Asia* (2006)

Man, John, *Gobi: Tracking the Desert* (1997)

Man, John, *The Great Wall* (2008)

Man, John, *The Mongol Empire: Genghis Khan, his Heirs and the Founding of Modern China* (2014)

Mann, Robert, *The Igor Tales and their Folkloric Background* (2005)

Manz, Beatrice F., ed., *Central Asia in Historical Perspective* (1994)

Maroń, Jerzy, *Legnica 1241* (1996)

Marston, Sallie, Paul L. Knox, Diana M. Liverman et al, eds, *World Regions in Global Context: Peoples, Places and Environments* (2002)

Martels, Zweder von, ed., *Travel Fact and Travel Fiction: Studies on Fiction, Literary Tradition, Scholarly Discovery and Observation on Travel Writing* (1994)

Martin, Geoffrey J., *Ellsworth Huntington* (1973)

Martin, H. Desmond, *The Rise of Chingis Khan and His Conquest of North China* (1950)

Martin, Janet, *Medieval Russia 980–1584* (1995)

Mason, Ian L., ed., *The Evolution of Domesticated Animals* (1984)

Matthiessen, Peter, *Baikal: Sacred Sea of Siberia* (1992)

May, Timothy, *Culture and Customs of Mongolia* (2009)

May, Timothy, *The Mongol Art of War* (2007)

May, Timothy, *The Mongol Conquests in World History* (2012)

Mayor, Adrienne, *Greek Fire, Poison Arrows and Scorpion Bombs: Biological and Chemical Warfare in the Ancient World* (2003)

Mehta, J. L., *Advanced Study in the History of Medieval India*, 2 vols (1986)

Meignan, Victor, *From Paris to Pekin over Siberian Snows* (1885)

Mellor, Philip, Mathew Baylis and Peter Mertens, eds, *Bluetongue* (2008)

Melville, Charles Peter, *The Fall of Amir Chupan and the Decline of the Ilkhanate, 1327-1337* (1999)

Meri, Josef W., *Medieval Islamic Civilization: An Encyclopedia*, 2 vols (2006)

Michell, George, ed., *Architecture of the Islamic World: Its History and Social Meaning* (1978)

Miller, Peter N., ed., *The Sea: Thalassography and Historiography* (2013)

Miller, W., *Trebizond: The Last Greek Empire of the Byzantine Era, 1204–1461* (1926)

Millward, James A., *Beyond the Pass: Economy, Ethnicity and Empire in Qing Central Asia* (1998)

Millward, James A., *A History of Xinjiang* (2007)

Minorsky, V., *Iranica* (Teheran 1964)

Minorsky, V., *Studies in Caucasian History* (1953)

Mohr, Erna, *The Asiatic Wild Horse* (1971)

Molnar, Adam, *Weather Magic in Inner Asia* (1994)

Montesquieu, Charles de Secondat, Baron de, *Considerations on the Causes of the Greatness of the Romans* (1734)

Montesquieu, Charles de Secondat, Baron de, trans. Thomas Nugent, *The Spirit of the Laws* (1949)

Moorcroft, William & George Trebeck, *Travels in the Himalayan Provinces of Hindustan* (1841, repr. 1971)

Morgan, David O., *Medieval Persia 1040–1797* (1988)

Morgan, David O., *The Mongols*, 2nd ed. (2007)

Morgan, David O. & Anthony Reid, eds, *The New Cambridge History of Islam, 3: The Eastern Islamic World, Eleventh to Eighteenth Centuries* (2010)

Morris, Neil, *North-East Asia* (2007)

Moser, Henri, *À travers l'Asie centrale* (1886)

Moses, Larry W., *The Political Role of Mongol Buddhism* (1977)

Moses, Larry W. & Stephen A. Halkovic, Jr, *Introduction to Mongolian History and Culture* (1997)

Moss, Walter G., *A History of Russia*, 1: *To 1917* (2003)

Mostaert, Antoine, *Dictionnaire Ordos*, 3 vols (1944)

Mostaert, Antoine, *Sur quelques passages de l'Histoire Secrète des Mongols* (1953)

Mote, Frederick W., *Imperial China 900–1800* (1999)

Moule, Arthur C., *The Rulers of China* (1957)

Mu, Wang, trans. Fabrizio Pregadio, *Foundations of Internal Alchemy: the Taoist Practice of Neidan* (2011)

Muldoon, J., *Popes, Lawyers and Infidels* (1979)

Münkler, Herfried, trans. Patrick Camiller, *Empires: The Logic of World Domination from Ancient Rome to the United States* (2007)

Munro, Hector Hugh, *The Rise of the Russian Empire* (1900)

Nairne, W. P., *Gilmour of the Mongols* (1924)

Namkhainyambuu, Tserendash, trans. Mary Rossabi, *Bounty from the Sheep: Autobiography of a Herdsman*, (2000)

Naquin, Susan, *Peking: Temples and City Life, 1400–1900* (2000)

Nashriyoti, Davr, *Khiva: The City and the Legends* (2012)

Nauman, Igor V., *The History of Siberia* (2006)

Needham, Joseph, ed., *Science and Civilization in China*, 7 vols (1954–)

Neville, Peter, *A Traveller's History of Russia* (2006)

Nicol, Donald M., *The Last Centuries of Byzantium, 1261–1453* (1993)

Nicolle, David, *Armies of Medieval Russia 750–1250* (1999)

Nicolle, David, *Kalka River 1223* (2001)

Nicolle, David, *Lake Peipus 1242* (1996)

O'Connell, Robert L., *Of Arms and Men: A History of War, Weapons and Aggression* (1989)

Ohler, Norbert, *Elisabeth von Thüringen: Fürstin im Dienst der Niedrigsten* (2006)

Olbricht, Peter, *Das Postwesen in China unter der Mongolenherrschaft im 13. und 14. Jahrhundert* (1954)

Olderogge, Dmitrii Alekseevich, ed., *The Countries and Peoples of the East* (1974)

Olschki, Leonardo, *Guillaume Boucher: A French Artist at the Court of the Khans* (1946)

Oman, Charles, *A History of the Art of War in the Middle Ages*, 2 vols (1924)

Ostrowski, Donald, *Muscovy and the Mongols: Cross-Cultural Influences on the Steppe Frontier, 1304–1589* (1998)

Pacey, Arnold, *Technology in World Civilization: A Thousand-Year History* (1991)

Paludan, Ann, *Chronicle of the Chinese Emperors* (1998)

Pan, Lynn, *China's Sorrow: Journeys around the Yellow River* (1985)

Parker, E. H., *A Thousand Years of the Tartars* (1895)

Parker, Sybil P., ed., *Grzimek's Encyclopedia of Mammals*, vol. 5 (1990)

Parson, John C., *Medieval Queenship* (1997)

Partington, James Riddick, *A History of Greek Fire and Gunpowder* (1960)

Payne-Gallwey, Ralph, *The Crossbow: Medieval and Modern* (2007)

Peacock, Andrew G. S., *Early Seljuq History: A New Interpretation* (2010)

Peers, C. J., *Imperial Chinese Armies 590–1260 AD* (1996)

Peers, C. J., *Medieval Chinese Armies 1260–1520* (1992)

Pelenski, Jaroslaw, *The Contest for the Legacy of Kievan Rus'* (1996)

Pelliot, Paul, *Notes critiques d'histoire Kalmouke* (1960)

Pelliot, Paul, *Notes sur l'histoire de la Horde d'Or* (1950)

Pelliot, Paul, *Notes sur Marco Polo*, 3 vols (1973)

Pelliot, Paul, *Recherches sur les chrétiens d'Asie centrale et d'Extrême-Orient* (1973)

Percheron, M., *Dieux et démons, lamas et sorciers de Mongolie* (1953)

Perdue, Peter C., *China Marches West: the Qing Conquest of Central Eurasia* (2005)

Peregrine, Peter N. & Melvin Ember, eds, *Encyclopedia of Prehistory, 3: East Asia and Oceania* (2001)

Perrie, Maureen, ed., *The Cambridge History of Russia, 1: From Early Rus' to 1689* (2006)

Pertusi, Agostino, ed., *Venezia e il Levante fino al secolo XV*, 2 vols (1973)

Peters, Edward, ed., *Christian Society and the Crusades, 1198–1229* (1971)

Pfeiffer, Judith & Sholeh A. Quinn, eds, *History and Historiography of Post-Mongol Central Asia and the Middle East* (2006)

Philby, Harry St John Bridger, *Harun al Rashid* (1933)

Phillips, E. D., *The Mongols* (1969)

Phillips, J. R. S., *The Medieval Expansion of Europe* (1998)

Pinker, Steven, *The Better Angels of Our Nature: Why Violence Has Declined* (2011)

Pipes, Richard, ed., *Karamzin's Memoir on Ancient and Modern Russia* (1966)

Pittard, Dana J. H., 'Thirteenth Century Mongol Warfare: Classical Military Strategy or Operational Art?' (monograph, School of Advanced Military Studies, Fort Leavenworth, Kansas, 1994)

Pletcher, Kenneth, *The Geography of China: Sacred and Historic Places* (2010)

Pletcher, Kenneth, ed., *The History of China* (2011)

Poppe, N., ed., *American Studies in Altaic Linguistics* (1962)

Porter, Patrick, *Military Orientalism: Eastern War through Western Eyes* (2009)

Poucha, P., *Die Geheime Geschichte der Mongolen als Geschichtsquelle und Literaturdenkmal* (1956)

Pregadio, Fabrizio, *Awakening to Reality: A Taoist Classic of Internal Alchemy* (2009)

Pregadio, Fabrizio, *Chinese Alchemy: An Annotated Bibliography of Works in Western Languages* (2011)

Pregadio, Fabrizio, ed., *The Encyclopedia of Taoism*, 2 vols (2008)

Provence, Université de, *Histoire et société: Mélanges offerts à Georges Duby, textes réunis par les médiévistes de l'Université de Provence* (1992)

Purton, Peter Fraser, *A History of the Late Medieval Siege 1200–1500* (2010)

Qureshi, I. H.., *The Administration of the Sultanate of Delhi* (1958)

Raaflaub, K. et al, eds, *Origins of Democracy in Ancient Greece* (2007)

Rachewiltz, Igor de, *Papal Envoys to the Great Khan* (1971)

Rachewiltz, Igor de et al, eds, *In The Service of the Khan: Eminent Personalities of the Early Mongol-Yuan Period (1200–1300)* (1993)

Rady, Martyn C., *Nobility, Land and Service in Medieval Hungary* (2000)

Ramsey, S. Robert, *The Languages of China* (1987)

Raphael, Kate, *Muslim Fortresses in the Levant: Between Crusaders and Mongols* (2011)

Rashid, Ahmed, *Jihad: The Rise of Militant Islam in Central Asia* (2002)

Ratchnevsky, Paul, *Genghis Khan: His Life and Legacy* (1991)

Rayfield, Donald, *Edge of Empires: A History of Georgia* (2012)

Reber, Ortrud, *Elizabeth von Thüringen: Landgräfin und Heilige* (2006)

Reichert, Folker E., *Begegnungen mit China: Die Entdeckung Ostasiens im Mittelalter* (1992)

Reid, Daniel P., *The Tao of Health, Sex and Longevity: A Modern Practical Guide to the Ancient Way* (1989)

Reyna, S. P. & R. E. Downs, eds, *Studying War: Anthropological Perspectives* (1994)

Riasanovsky, Nicholas, *A History of Russia* (1993)

Riasanovsky, Nicholas & Mark D. Steinberg, *A History of Russia* (new ed., 1999)

Riasanovsky, V. A., *Fundamental Principles of Mongol Law* (1937)

Rice, G. W., ed., *Muslims and Mongols: Essays on Medieval Asia* (1977)

Richard, Jean, *La papauté et les missions d'Orient au moyen age* (1977)

Richard, Jean, *Saint Louis: Roi d'une France féodale, soutien de la Terre Sainte* (1983)

Robertson, A., *Handbook of Animal Diseases in the Tropics* (1976)

Robinson, David M., *Empire's Twilight: North-East Asia under the Mongols* (2009)

Robinson, H. Russell, *Oriental Armour* (1967)

Rockhill, William Woodville, *The Land of the Lamas* (1891)

Roemer, Hans Robert, et al, eds, *History of the Turkic Peoples in the Pre-Islamic Period* (2000)

Rogers, Clifford J., ed., *The Oxford Encyclopedia of Medieval Warfare and Military Technology* (2010)

Rojas, Carlos, *The Great Wall: A Cultural History* (2010)

Roman, Eric, *Austria–Hungary and the Successor States: A Reference Guide from the Renaissance to the Present* (2003)

Ronan, Colin A., *The Shorter Science and Civilization in China*, 5 vols (1995)

Ropp, Paul S., *China in World History* (2010)

Rossabi, Morris, *The Mongols: A Very Short Introduction* (2012)

Rossabi, Morris, *The Mongols and Global History: A Norton Documentary Reader* (2011)

Rossabi, Morris, *Voyager from Xanadu: Rabbas Sauma and the First Journey from China to the West* (2010)

Rossabi, Moris, ed., *China among Equals: The Middle Kingdom and its Neighbors 10th–14th Centuries* (1983)

Roux, Jean-Paul, *L'Asie Centrale* (1997)

Roux, Jean-Paul, *La mort chez les peuples altaïques anciens médiévaux d'après les documents écrits* (1963)

Rummel, R. J., *Death by Government* (1994)

Rummel, R. J., *Statistics of Democide* (1997)

Ruotsala, Antti, *Europeans and Mongols in the Middle of the Thirteenth Century: Encountering the Other* (2001)

Rybatzki, V. et al, eds, *The Early Mongols: Language, Culture and History* (2009)

Sabloff, P. L. W., ed., *Modern Mongolia: Reclaiming Genghis Khan* (2005)

Saeki, P. Y., *Nestorian Documents and Relics in China* (1951)

Sagaster, Klaus, ed., *Religious and Lay Symbolism in the Altaic World* (1989)

Salisbury, Harrison E., *The Coming War Between Russia and China* (1969)

Salzman, Philip Carl, *Pastoralists: Equality, Hierarchy and the State* (2004)

Sandquist, T. A. & M.R. Powicke, eds, *Essays in Medieval History presented to Bertie Wilkinson* (1969)

Saunders, J. J., *The History of the Mongol Conquests* (1971)

Sawyer, Ralph D., *Ancient Chinese Warfare* (2011)

Schafer, Edward H., *The Golden Peaches of Samarkand* (1985)

Schäfer, Peter & Mark R. Cohen, *Toward the Millennium: Messianic Expectations from the Bible to Waco* (1998)

Schmidt, S., K. Tarnovsky & I. Berkhin, *A Short History of the USSR* (1984)

Schmilewski, Ulrich, *Wahlstatt 1241: Beiträge zur Mongolenschlacht bei Liegnitz und zu ihren Nachwirkungen* (1991)

Schneider, J., *La ville de Metz au XIIIe et XIVe siècles* (1950)

Schottenhammer, Angela, *The East Asian 'Mediterranean': Maritime Crossroads of Culture, Commerce and Human Migration* (2008)

Schram, S. R, ed., *Foundations and Limits of State Power in China* (1987)

Schubert, J. & U. Schneider, eds, *Asiatica, Festschrift für Friedrich Weller* (1954)

Schurmann, H. F., *Economic Structure of the Yuan Dynasty* (1956)

Schuyler, Eugene, *Turkistan: Notes of a Journey in Russian Turkistan, Kokand, Bukhara and Kuldja* (1966)

Schwartz, Stuart B., ed., *Implicit Understandings; Observing, Reporting and Reflecting on the Encounters between Europeans and Other Peoples in the Early Modern Era* (1994)

Schwarz, Henry G., ed., *Studies on Mongolia* (1979)

Seaman, Gary, ed., *Ecology and Empire: Nomads in the Cultural Evolution of the Old World* (1989)

Seaman, Gary, ed., *Foundations of Empire: Archaeology and Art of the Eurasian Steppe* (1992)

Seaman, Gary & Daniel Marks, *Rulers from the Steppe: State Formation on the European Periphery* (1991)

Sedlar, Jean W., *East Central Europe in the Middle Ages, 1000–1500* (1994)

Semenow, G. L., *Studien zur sogdischen Kultur an der Seidenstrasse* (1996)

Seth, Michael J., *A Concise History of Korea: From the Neolithic Period through the Nineteenth Century* (2006)

Seth, Vikram, *From Heaven Lake: Travels through Sinkiang and Tibet* (1983)

Settle, Raymond W. & Mary Lund, *Saddles and Spurs: The Pony Express Saga* (1972)

Setton, Kenneth M., gen. ed., *A History of the Crusades*, 6 vols (1969–89)

Severin, Tim, *In Search of Genghis Khan* (1991)

Sha'bani, Reza, *The Book of Iran* (2005)

Sharma, R. C., et al, *Mongolia: Culture, Economy and Politics (Indian–Mongolian Assessment)* (1992)

Shifu, Wang, trans. Stephen H. West & Wilt L. Idema, *The Story of the Western Wing* (1991)

Shoolbraid, G. M. H., *The Oral Epic of Siberia and Central Asia* (1975)

Shultz, Edward J., *Generals and Scholars: Military Rule in Medieval Korea* (2000)

Sicker, Martin, *The Islamic World in Ascendancy: From the Arab Conquest to the Siege of Vienna* (2000)

Silverberg, Robert, *The Realm of Prester John* (1996)

Silvers, Brock, *The Taoist Manual: An Illustrated Guide Applying Taoism to Daily Life* (2005)

Silverstein, Adam J., *Postal Systems in the Pre-Modern Islamic World* (2007)

Singh, Nagendra K., ed., *Encyclopaedic Historiography of the Islamic World*, 3 vols (2004)

Sinor, Denis, *History of Hungary* (1959)

Sinor, Denis, *Inner Asia and its Contacts with Medieval Europe* (1977)

Sinor, Denis, *Orientalism and History* (1954)

Sinor, Denis, *Studies in Medieval Inner Asia* (1997)

Sinor, Denis, ed., *Aspects of Altaic Civilization* (1962–1990)

Sinor, Denis, ed., *The Cambridge History of Early Inner Asia* (1990)

Skinner, George W., *The City in Late Imperial China* (1977)

Skrine, Francis Henry Bennett & Edward Denison Ross, *The Heart of Asia: A History of Russian Turkestan and the Central Asian Khanates from the Earliest Times* (1899)

Smith, P. J. & R. von Glahn, eds, *The Song–Yuan–Ming Transition* (2003)

Sneath, David, *The Headless State: Aristocratic Orders, Kinship Society and Misrepresentations of Nomadic Inner Asia* (2007)

Sneath, David, ed., *Imperial Statecraft: Political Forms and Techniques of Governance in Inner Asia, 6th–20th Centuries* (2006)

Solonin, K. J., *Tangut Chan Buddhism and Guifeng Zong-mi* (2005)

Soloviev, Sergei M., ed. & trans. Helen Y. Prochazka, *The Shift Northward: Kievan Rus 1154–1228* (2000)

Soucek, Svat, *A History of Inner Asia* (2000)

Spencer, Edmund, *Travels in the Western Caucasus* (1836)

Spengen, Wim van, *Tibetan Border Worlds: A Geohistorical Analysis of Trade and Traders* (2010)

Spinei, Victor, *The Romanians and the Turkic Nomads North of the Danube Delta from the Tenth to the Mid-Thirteenth Century* (2009)

Spuler, Bertold, *Die Goldene Horde* (1965)

Spuler, Bertold, *The History of the Mongols* (1972)

Spuler, Bertold, *Die Mongolen in Iran* (1985)

Spuler, Bertold, *The Muslim World, 2: The Mongol Period* (1960)

Standen, N. & D. Powers, eds., *Frontiers in Question: Eurasian Borderlands 700–1700* (1999)

Stein, M. Aurel, *Ancient Khotan: Detailed Reports of Archaeological Explorations in Chinese Turkestan* (1907)

Stein, M. Aurel, *Ruins of Desert Cathay*, 2 vols (1987)

Stein, R. A., *Tibetan Civilization* (1972)

Stephan, John J., *Sakhalin: A History* (1971)

Stephenson, Paul, *Byzantium's Balkan Frontier: A Political Study of the Northern Balkans, 900–1204* (2000)

Stewart, John, *Nestorian Missionary Enterprise: The Story of a Church on Fire* (1928)

Stewart, Stanley, *In the Empire of Genghis Khan: A Journey among Nomads* (2001)

Strakosch-Grassmann, Gustav, *Der Einfall der Mongolen in Mitteleuropa in den Jahren 1241 und 1242* (1893)

Street, J. C., *The Language of the Secret History of the Mongols* (1957)

Stürner, Wolfgang, *Friedrich II*, 2 vols (2000)

Sumption, Jonathan, *The Albigensian Crusade* (1978)

Sunquist, Mel & Fiona, *Wild Cats of the World* (2002)

Suny, Ronald Grigor, *The Making of the Georgian Nation* (1994)

Świętosławski, Witold, *Arms and Armour of the Nomads of the Great Steppe in the Times of the Mongol Expansion, 12th–14th Centuries* (1999)

Sykes, Percy, *A History of Persia* (1921)

Tanner, Harold Miles, *China: A History, 1: From Neolithic Cultures through the Great Qing Empire, 10,000 BCE–1799 CE* (2010)

Tao, Jing-Shen, *The Jurchen in Twelfth-Century China: A Study of Sinicization* (1976)

Tao, Jing-Shen, *Two Sons of Heaven* (1988)

Telfer, J. Buchan, *The Bondage and Travels of Johann Schiltberger* (1879)

Temple, Robert, *The Genius of China: 3,000 Years of Science, Discovery and Invention* (2007)

Tetley, G. E., *The Ghaznavid and Seljuk Turks: Poetry as a Source for Iranian History* (2008)

Thayer, Helen, *Walking the Gobi* (2007)

Thiébaud, Jean-Marie, *Personnages marquants d'Asie Centrale, du Turkestan et de l'Ouzbékistan* (2004)

Thomas, Nicholas & Caroline Humphrey, eds, *Shamanism, History and the State* (1999)

Tillman, Hoyt C. & Stephen H. West, *China under Jurchen Rule: Essays on Chin Intellectual and Cultural History* (1995)

Togan, İsenbike, *Flexibility and Limitation in Steppe Formations: The Kerait Khanate and Chinggis Khan* (1998)

Tolstoy, Leo, trans. Rosemary Edmonds, *War and Peace* (1957)

Torday, Laszlo, *Mounted Archers: The Beginning of Central Asian History* (1997)

Toynbee, Arnold J., *Between Oxus and Jumma* (1961)

Toynbee, Arnold J., *A Study of History*, 12 vols (1934–61)

Tregear, T. R., *A Geography of China* (1965)

Tumler, P. M., *Der deutsche Orden im Werden, Wachsen und Wirken bis 1400* (1955)

Turnbull, Stephen, *Chinese Walled Cities 221 BC–AD 1644* (2009)

Turnbull, Stephen, *Genghis Khan and the Mongol Conquests, 1190–1400* (2003)

Turnbull, Stephen, *The Great Wall of China* (2007)

Turnbull, Stephen, illustr. Angus McBride, *The Mongols* (1980)

Turnbull, Stephen, *Siege Weapons of the Far East AD 960–1644* (2002)

Turner, Samuel, *Siberia: A Record of Travel, Climbing and Exploration* (2008)

Twitchett, Denis C., ed., *The Cambridge History of China, 3: Sui and T'ang China 589–906* (1979)

Twitchett, Denis C., *Printing and Publishing in Medieval China* (1983)

Tyerman, Christopher, *God's War: A New History of the Crusades* (2006)

Unlu, Resat Baris, *The Genealogy of a World Empire: The Ottomans in World History* (2008)

Upton, Roger, *Falconry: Principles and Practice* (1991)

Urban, William, *The Teutonic Knights: A Military History* (2003)

Urbańczyk, Przemysław, ed., *Europe around the Year 1000* (1973)

Vámbéry, Arminius, *The History of Bokhara* (1873)

Vámbéry, Arminius, *The Story of Hungary* (1887)

Van de Ven, Hans, *Warfare in Chinese History* (2000)

Van Oost, P., *Au pays des Ortos* (1932)

Van Seters, John, *The Pentateuch: A Social-Science Commentary* (2004)

Vásáry, István, *Cumans and Tatars: Oriental Military in the Pre-Ottoman Balkans, 1183–1365* (2005)

Vernadsky, G., *Ancient Russia* (1943)

Vernadksy, G., *Kievan Russia* (1948)

Vernadsky, G., *The Mongols and Russia* (1953)

Vernadsky, G., ed., *A Source Book for Russian History from Early Times to 1917*, 3 vols (1972)

Verschuer, Charlotte von, *Across the Perilous Sea: Japanese Trade with China and Korea from the Seventh to the Sixteenth Centuries* (2006)

Vitebsky, Piers, *The Reindeer People: Living with Animals and Spirits in Siberia* (2005)

Vitebsky, Piers, *The Shaman* (2001)

Vladimirtsov, Boris, *The Life Of Genghis Khan* (1948)

Vladimirtsov, Boris, *Le régime social des Mongols: le féodalisme nomade* (1948)

Wagner, Donald B., *Iron and Steel in Ancient China* (1993)

Wagner, Palmer J., *American Appaloosa Anthology* (2000)

Waldron, Arthur, *The Great Wall of China: From History to Myth* (1990)

Walker, Harlan, ed., *Food on the Move* (1997)

Wallace, Robert, *The Rise of Russia* (1967)

Wang, Helen & John Perkins, eds, *Handbook to the Collections of Sir Aurel Stein in the British Museum* (2008)

Ward, Steven R., *Immortal: A Military History of Iran and its Armed Forces* (2009)

Watson, Rubie S. & Patricia Buckley Ebrey, eds, *Marriage and Inequality in Chinese Society* (1991)

Weatherford, Jack, *Genghis Khan and the Making of the Modern World* (2004)

Weatherford, Jack, *The Secret History of the Mongol Queens: How the Daughters of Genghis Khan Rescued his Empire* (2010)

Wedgwood, C. V., *The Thirty Years War* (1938)

Weiers, Michael, *Geschichte der Mongolen* (2004)

Weiler, Björn K. V., *Henry III of England and the Staufen Empire: 1216–1270* (2006)

Weiss, Roberto, *The Renaissance Discovery of Classical Antiquity* (1973)

Welch, Holmes, *Taoism: The Parting of the Way* (1966)

Wells, Spencer, *The Journey of Man: A Genetic Odyssey* (2002)

Welsford, Thomas, *Four Types of Loyalty in Early Modern Asia* (2012)

West, Barbara A., *Encyclopedia of the Peoples of Asia and Oceania* (2009)

Westrem, Scott D., ed., *Discovering New Worlds: Essays on Medieval Exploration and Imagination* (1991)

White, Lynn, *Medieval Technology and Social Change* (1962)

White, Matthew, *Atrocities: The One Hundred Deadliest Episodes in Human History* (2013)

Whiting, Marvin C., *Imperial Chinese Military History 8000 BC–1912 AD* (2002)

Wiet, Gaston, trans. Seymour Feiler, *Baghdad: Metropolis of the Abbasid Caliphate* (1971)

Wilkinson, Charles K., *Nishapur: Pottery of the Early Islamic Period* (1973)

Wilkinson, Endymion, *Chinese History: A Manual* (2000)

Williams T., ed., *Merv, the Medieval City of Sultan Kala: Development and Infrastructure from the Seventh to the Thirteenth Centuries* (2010)

Willey, P., *Eagle's Nest: Ismaili Castles in Iran and Syria* (2005)

Wilson, Don & Dee Ann Reeder, eds, *Mammal Species of the Wild: A Taxonomic and Geographic Reference*, 2 vols (2005)

Winchester, Simon, *The Man Who Loved China* (2008)

Wink, André, *Al-Hind: The Making of the Indo-Islamic World*, 2: *The Slave Kings and the Islamic Conquest, 11th–13th Centuries* (1997)

Wittfogel, Karl, *Oriental Despotism: A Comparative Study of Total Power* (1981)

Wittfogel, Karl & Feng Chia-Sheng, *History of Chinese Society: Liao, 907–1125* (1949)

Wolf, Gunther, ed., *Stupor Mundi: Zur Geschichte Friedrichs II von Hohenstaufen* (1982)

Wolff, O., *Geschichte der Mongolen oder Tataren* (1872)

Woods, John E. et al, eds, *History and Historiography of Post-Mongol Central Asia and the Middle East* (2006)

Wright, Arthur F. & Denis Twitchett, *Confucian Personalities* (1962)

Wyatt, Don J., ed., *Battlefields Real and Imagined: War, Border, and Identity in the Chinese Middle Period* (2008)

Xu, Elina-Qian, *Historical Development of the Pre-Dynastic Khitan* (2005)

Yang, Lien-Sheng, *Studies in Chinese Institutional History* (1961)

Yarshater, E., ed., *The Cambridge History of Iran*, 3: *The Seleucid, Parthian and Sassanian Periods*, 2 vols (1983)

Yarshater, E., ed., *Encyclopedia Iranica*, 15 vols (2009)

Yate, C. E., *Khurasan and Sistan* (1900)

Younghusband, Francis, *The Heart of a Continent* (1904)

Zhao, George Qingzhi, *Marriage as Political Strategy and Cultural Expression: Mongolian Royal Marriages from World Empire to Yuan Dynasty* (2008)

Zippert, Christian & Gerhard Jost, *Hingabe und Heiterkeit: Vom Leben und Wirken der heilige Elisabeth* (2007)

Žygas, Egle Victoria & Peter Voorhies, eds, *Folklorica: Festschrift for Felix J. Oinas* (1982)

Notes

For reasons of space, titles of books are given in short form, and the reader is referred to the bibliography for further information

Abbreviations of principal primary sources used in the notes:

IAA: Richards, D. S., ed. & trans., *The Chronicle of Ibn al-Athir for the Crusading Period from Al-Kamil fi'l-Ta'rikh, Part 3: The Years 589–629/1193–1231: The Ayyubids after Saladin and the Mongol Menace* (2008)

JB: Boyle, J. A., ed. & trans., *Genghis Khan: The History of the World Conqueror by Ata-Malik Juvaini*, 2 vols (1997)

JR: Raverty, H. G., ed. & trans., *[Minhaj Siraj Juzjani,] Tabakat-i-Nasiri: A General History of the Muhammadan Dynasties of Asia*, 2 vols (1881)

Rachewiltz, *Commentary*: Rachewiltz, Igor de, *The Secret History of the Mongols, Translated with a Historical and Philological Commentary* (2nd ed, 2006), ii (commentary)

RT: Thackston, W. H., ed. & trans., *Rashiduddin Fazlullah's Jami'u't-Tawarikh: Compendium of Chronicles. A History of the Mongols*, 3 vols (1998)

SHC: Cleaves, F. W. ed. & trans., *The Secret History of the Mongols* (1982)

SHO: Onon, Urgunge, ed. & trans., *The Secret History of the Mongols: The Life and Times of Chinggis Khan* (2001)

SHR: Rachewiltz, Igor de, *The Secret History of the Mongols, Translated with a Historical and Philological Commentary* (2nd ed., 2006), i (translation)

SHW: Waley, Arthur, *The Secret History of the Mongols and other pieces* (1963)

Introduction

1. Le Strange, *Baghdad* pp. 264-283 • 2. Wiet, *Baghdad* pp. 118-119 • 3. Broadhurst, *Travels of Ibn Jumayr* p. 234 • 4. Wiet, *Baghdad* pp. 122-127 • 5. JB ii pp. 618-640 • 6. Morgan, *Mongols* pp. 129-135 • 7. For the Ismailis see Lewis, *Assassins*; Daftary, *Ismailis*; Hodgson, *Secret Order of Assassins* • 8. RT ii pp. 487-490 • 9. RT ii pp. 491-493 • 10. Spuler, *History of the Mongols* pp. 115-119 • 11. Sicker, *Islamic World in Asendancy* p. 111; Meri, *Medieval Islamic Civilization* p. 510 • 12. Hammer-Purgstall, *Geschichte Wassafs* pp. 68-71; Le Strange, *Baghdad* • 13. Spuler, *History of the Mongols* pp. 120-121 • 14. RT ii pp. 494-499 • 15. MacLeod, *Library of Alexandria* p. 71 • 16. Hammer-Purgstall, *Geschichte Wassafs* pp. 72-75. • 17. Wiet, *Baghdad* pp. 164-165 • 18. Somogyi, Joseph de, 'A Qasida on the Destruction of Baghdad by the Mongols,' *Bulletin of the School of Oriental and African Studies* 7 (1933) pp. 41-48 • 19. Spuler, *History of the Mongols* pp. 125-164. There is an interesting article, comparing Hulagu's sack of Baghdad with the U.S. destruction of the city some 750 years later, by Ian Frazier, 'Annals of History: Invaders: Destroying Baghdad,' in the *New Yorker*, 25 April 2005.

Chapter 1

1. For the 'world island' and the 'heartland' theory see H. J. Mackinder, 'The Geographical Pivot of History,' *The Geographical Journal* 23 (1904) pp. 421-437; Pascal Venier, 'The Geographical Pivot of History and Early Twentieth-Century Geopolitical Culture,' *The Geographical Journal* 170 (2004) pp. 330-336 • 2. Lattimore, *Studies in Frontier History* pp. 241-258 • 3. Robert N. Taafe, 'The Geographical Setting,' in Sinor, *Cambridge History* pp. 19-40 • 4. A good introduction to the 'stans' is Rashid, *Jihad*. • 5. For this view see Cable & French, *The Gobi Desert* • 6. René Grousset, *The Empire of the Steppes* p. xxii had a theory that along the south–north axis trade went south and migration went north. • 7. For the Altai and Tarbaghatai see Taafe, 'The Geographical Setting' in Sinor, *Cambridge History* pp. 24-25, 40. Cf also Jackson & Morgan, *Rubruck* p. 166 • 8. Stewart, *In the Empire* p. 132: 'Sometimes the forest cuts deeply into the steppe as, for example, does the famous Utken forest on the slopes of the Kangai; sometimes the steppe penetrates northward, as do the Khakass steppes in the upper reaches of the Yenisei or the broad trans-Baikal steppe'; Gumilev, *Imaginary Kingdom* p. 18 • 9. Mount Burqan Qaldun has been tentatively identified as Mount Khenti Khan in the Great Khenti range in north-eastern Mongolia (48° 50' N, 109° E): Rachewiltz, *Commentary* p. 229; Huc, *High Road in Tartary* pp. 123-127 • 10. Stewart, *In The Empire* p. 159. Cf also Bull, *Around the Sacred Sea* • 11. Owen Lattimore, 'Return to China's Northern Frontier,' *The Geographical Journal* 139

(June 1973) pp. 233-242 • **12.** For various accounts see Cable & French, *Gobi Desert*; Man, *Gobi*; Younghusband, *Heart of a Continent*; Thayer, *Walking the Gobi* • **13.** Stewart, *In The Empire* p. 153 • **14.** Nairne, *Gilmour* p. 74 • **15.** De Windt, *From Pekin to Calais* p. 107 • **16.** ibid. p. 103 • **17.** ibid. pp. 134-35 • **18.** Lattimore, *Inner Asian Frontiers* p. 12 • **19.** Severin, *In Search of Genghis Khan* p. 18 • **20.** Dawson, *Mongol Mission* pp. 5-6 • **21.** Barfield, *Perilous Frontier* pp. 22-23 • **22.** Asimov & Bosworth, *History of Civilizations*, iv part 2 pp. 275-276 • **23.** Gumilev, *Imaginary Kingdom* pp. 62-63 • **24.** For the Amur river see Du Halde, *Description géographique*; M. A. Peschurof, 'Description of the Amur River in Eastern Asia,' *Proceedings of the Royal Geographical Society* 2 (1857-58) • **25.** For the Amur as the traditional boundary between Russia and China see Kerner, *The Urge to the Sea*; Stephan, *Sakhalin* • **26.** Gumilev, *Imaginary Kingdom* p. 87; Asimov & Bosworth, *History of Civilizations*, iv part 2 p. 280 • **27.** Joseph F. Fletcher, 'The Mongols: Ecological and Social Perspectives,' in *Harvard Journal of Asiatic Studies* 46 (1986) pp. 11-50 (at p. 13), repr. in Fletcher, *Studies on Chinese and Islamic Inner Asia* • **28.** For all these distinctions see (amid a vast literature) Cribb, *Nomads* esp. pp. 19-20, 84-112; Forde, *Habitat* p. 396; Johnson, *Nature of Nomadism* pp. 18-19; Blench, *Pastoralism* pp. 11-12; Helland, *Five Essays* • **29.** R. & N. Dyson-Hudson 'Nomadic Pastoralism,' *Annual Review of Anthropology* 9 (1980) pp. 15-61 • **30.** Krader, *Social Organisation* pp. 282-283 • **31.** Barfield, *Perilous Frontier* pp. 22-23 • **32.** Jagchid & Hyer, *Mongolia's Culture* pp. 20-26 • **33.** Barfield, *Perilous Frontier* pp. 23-24 • **34.** Elizabeth Bacon, 'Types of Pastoral Nomadism in Central and South-West Asia,' *Southwestern Journal of Anthropology* 10 (1954) pp. 44-68 • **35.** Lawrence Krader, 'The Ecology of Central Asian Pastoralism,' *Southwestern Journal of Anthropology* 11 (1955) pp. 301-326 • **36.** To say nothing of permafrost. Owen Lattimore established that near Yakutsk the permafrost penetrated the soil to a depth of 446 feet (Lattimore, *Studies in Frontier History* p. 459). • **37.** Barfield, *Perilous Frontier* p. 20 • **38.** D. L. Coppock, D. M. Swift and J. E. Ello, 'Livestock Feeding Ecology and Resource Utilisation in a Nomadic Pastoral Ecosystem,' *Journal of Applied Ecology* 23 (1986) pp. 573-583 • **39.** Lattimore, *Mongol Journeys* p. 165 • **40.** Rachewiltz, *Commentary* p. 711 • **41.** V. A. Riasanovsky, *Fundamental Principles* p. 20; Hyland, *Medieval Warhorse* p. 126 • **42.** Buell, *Historical Dictionary* p. 242 • **43.** Barfield, *Perilous Frontier* p. 21 • **44.** Dawson, *The Mongol Mission* pp. 98-100 • **45.** Richard, *Simon de St Quentin* pp. 40-41 • **46.** Buell, *Historical Dictionary* p. 156 • **47.** Lattimore, *Inner Asian Frontiers* p. 168; *Mongol Journeys* p. 198 • **48.** C. Buchholtz, 'True Cattle (Genus Bos),' in Parker, *Grzimek's Encyclopedia*, v pp. 386-397; Mason, *Evolution* pp. 39-45; D. M. Leslie & G. M. Schaller, 'Bos Grunniens and Bos Mutus,' *Mammalian Species* 36 (2009) pp. 1-17 • **49.** Seth, *From Heaven Lake* p. 107 • **50.** Jackson & Morgan, *Rubruck* p. 158; Yule & Cordier, *The Book of Ser Marco Polo* i pp. 277-279 • **51.** Burnaby, *Ride*; the tradition continues to this day. The noted traveller Tim Severin described a 400-strong herd as 'a constantly bawling, groaning, squealing, defecating troop' (Severin, *In Search of Genghis Khan* p. 22). • **52**. Bulliet, *Camel* p. 30 • **53**. Peter Grubb, 'Order Artiodactyla,' in Wilson & Reeder, *Mammal Species* (2005) i pp. 637-722; Irwin, *Camel* pp. 101, 143, 161; Bulliet, *Camel* pp. 143, 227 • **54**. Irwin, *Camel* pp. 142-143; E. H. Schafer, 'The Camel in China down to the Mongol Dynasty,' *Sinologica* 2 (1950) pp. 165-194, 263-290 • **55**. Wilson & Reeder, *Animal Species* p. 645; Lattimore, *Mongol Journeys* pp. 147-163; Gavin Hanby, *Central Asia* p. 7; De Windt, *From Pekin to Calais* pp. 128-129; Bretschneider, *Mediaeval Researches* i pp. 150-151 • **56**. Irwin, *Camel* pp. 53, 176-177; De Windt, *From Pekin* pp. 109, 128; Huc, *High Road in Tartary* pp. 132-133 • **57**. Boyd & Houpt, *Przewalski's Horse*. Whereas most wild horses are feral (previously domesticated), the Przewalski's horse is truly wild (Tatjana Kavar & Peter Dovc, 'Domestication of the Horse; Genetic Relationships between Domestic and Wild Horses,' *Livestock Science* 116 (2008) pp. 1-14; James Downs, 'The Origin and Spread of Riding in the Near East and Central Asia,' *American Anthropologist* 63 (1961) pp. 1193-1230). • **58**. Lattimore, *Inner Asian Frontiers* p. 168; White, *Medieval Technology* pp. 15-17 • **59**. Hendrick, *Horse Breeds* p. 287; Neville, *Traveller's History* p. 14; Severin, *In Search of Genghis Khan* p. 50 • **60**. S. Jagchid & C. R. Bawden, 'Some Notes on the Horse Policy of the Yuan Dynasty,' *Central Asiatic Journal* 10 (1965) pp. 246-265 (at pp. 248-250) • **61**. Carruthers, *Unknown Mongolia* ii p. 133 • **62**. Gumilev, *Imaginary Kingdom* p. 120 • **63**. Lattimore, *Mongol Journeys* p. 193: Jagchid & Bawden, 'Horse Policy,' pp. 248-250 • **64**. H. Desmond Martin, 'The Mongol Army,' *Journal of the Royal Asiatic Society* 1 (1943) pp. 46-85 • **65**. Hyland, *Medieval Warhorse* p. 129 • **66**. ibid. p. 131 • **67**. De Windt, *From Pekin* p. 112 • **68**. Hyland, *Medieval Warhorse* pp. 133-134 • **69**. Waugh, *Marco Polo* p. 57 • **70**. Hyland, *Medieval Warhorse* p. 130. In any case, 'Keeping all males entire would have led to absolute chaos in the droves of horses that travelled as back-up mounts in a Mongol army' (ibid. p. 129). • **71**. ibid. p. 130 • **72**. Jagchid & Bawden, 'Horse Policy,' p. 249-250 • **73**. Asimov & Bosworth, *History of Civilizations* iv part 2 p. 282. There are 153 species of mammals, 105 species of fish and 79 of reptiles. The number of bird species is disputed, depending on technical arguments over taxonomy, but is usually assessed as between 459 and 469. • **74**. Lattimore, *Mongol Journeys* p. 165 • **75**. For the many Mongol encounters with lions see Bretschneider, *Mediaeval Researches* i pp. 31, 148-149; ii pp. 134, 265-266, 270, 293, 295. The Mongols sometimes hunted lions (Lane, *Daily Life* p. 17). Bretschneider (i p. 116) mentions a Mongol lion hunt in which ten lions were killed. • **76**. JB ii p. 613 • **77**. Wilson & Reeder, *Mammal Species* p. 548; Helmut Henner, 'Uncia uncia,' *Mammalian Species* 20 (1972) pp. 1-5; Sunquist, *Wild Cats* pp. 377-394; Buell, *Historical Dictionary* p. 119 • **78**. Jackson & Morgan, *Rubruck* p. 142; Pelliot, *Recherches sur les chrétiens* pp. 91-92; Rockhill, *Land of the Lamas* pp. 157-158. The quote is from De Windt, *From Pekin* p. 114 • **79**. Wilson & Reeder, *Mammal Species* pp. 754-818; Lattimore, *Mongol Journeys* pp. 256-258; Severin, *In*

Search pp. 219-220 • **80**. Asimov & Bosworth, *History of Civilizations* iv part 2 p. 286; Bretschneider, *Mediaeval Researches* i pp. 98, 130; Lattimore, *Mongol Journeys* p. 170 • **81**. Bretschneider, *Mediaeval Researches*, i pp. 31, 128, 143-145; ii p. 250 • **82**. De Windt, *From Pekin* p. 146, 220; Bretschneider, *Mediaeval Researches* ii p. 192; Huc, *High Road* pp. 43-44; Lattimore, *Mongol Journeys* p. 166 • **83**. Skelton, Marston & Painter, *Vinland Map* p. 86 • **84**. Jackson & Morgan, *Rubruck* p. 89 • **85**. Dawson, *Mongol Mission* pp. 6-7 • **86**. Blake & Frye, *Grigor of Akanc* p. 295 • **87**. Lane, *Daily Life* • **88**. Dawson, *Mongol Mission* p. 18; Jackson & Morgan, *Rubruck* p. 89 • **89**. Schuyler Cammann, 'Mongol Costume, Historical and Recent,' in Sinor, *Aspects* pp. 157-166 • **90**. Dawson, *Mongol Mission* pp. 7-8; Jackson & Morgan, *Rubruck* p. 89; Bretschneider, *Mediaeval Researches* i pp. 52-53; Yule, *Cathay and the Way Thither* (1866 ed.) ii p. 222; Arthur Waley, *Travels of an Alchemist* p. 67 • **91**. Jackson & Morgan, *Rubruck* pp. 72-73; Waley, *Travels* op. cit. p. 66; Schuyler Cammann, 'Mongol dwellings, with special reference to Inner Mongolia,' in Sinor, *Aspects* pp. 17-22; Jagchid & Hyer, *Mongolia's Culture* pp. 62-67; cf also Torvald Faegne, *Tents* • **92**. Dawson, *Mongol Mission* p. 17 • **93**. Jackson & Morgan, *Rubruck* pp. 79, 84; JB i p. 21; J. A. Boyle, 'Kirakos of Ganjak on the Mongols,' *Central Asiatic Journal* 8 (1963); Matthew Paris, *Chronica Majora* iv. pp. 76-77, 388; vi p. 77; d'Ohsson, *Histoire* • **94**. Gregory G. Guzman, 'Reports of Mongol Cannibalism in the 13th Century in Latin Sources: Oriental Fact or Western Fiction?' in Westrem, *Discovering New Worlds* pp. 31-68; L. Hambis, 'L'histoire des Mongols avant Genghis-khan d'après les sources chinoises et mongoles, et la documentation conservée par Rasid-al-Din,' *Central Asiatic Journal* 14 (1970) pp. 125-133 (at p. 129) • **95**. Jackson & Morgan, *Rubruck* pp. 76, 80-83, 175; Dawson, *Mongol Mission* pp. 16-17; Pelliot, *Notes sur Marco Polo* i p. 240; Yule & Cordier, *Ser Marco Polo* i pp. 259-260; Hildinger, *Story of the Mongols* (1966) p. 17 • **96**. Boyle, 'Kirakos of Ganjak,' p. 21; Hildinger, *Story* p. 17; d'Ohsson, *Histoire* ii pp. 59, 86, 107, 204 • **97**. Jackson & Morgan, *Rubruck* p. 108 • **98**. Joseph F. Fletcher, 'The Mongols: Ecological and Social Perspectives,' p. 14 • **99**. Walter Goldschmidt, 'A General Model for Pastoral Social Systems,' in Équipe Écologie, *Pastoral Production and Society* pp. 15-27 • **100**. Joseph F. Fletcher, 'The Mongols: Ecological and Social Perspectives,' pp. 39-42 • **101**. Christian, *History of Russia* i pp. 81-85 • **102**. For Carpini's allegations see Dawson, *Mongol Mission* pp. 17-18 • **103**. ibid. p. 103; Jackson & Morgan, *Rubruck* p. 91 • **104**. Vladimirtsov, *Le régime social* p. 35 • **105**. Cribb, *Nomads* (1991) p. 18

Chapter 2

1. RT i pp. 113-120; SHC pp. 1-10 • **2**. Gumilev, *Imaginary Kingdom* p. 89 • **3**. SHC p. 11; Louis Hambis, 'L'Histoire des Mongols avant Genghis-khan' *Central Asiatic Journal* 14 (1970) pp. 125-133; Franke & Twitchett, *Cambridge History* p. 330;

Vladimirtsov, *Life of Genghis* p. 11 • **4**. Lattimore, 'The Geographical Factor,' *The Geographical Journal* 91 (1938) pp. 14-15; Lattimore, *Studies in Frontier History* (1962) pp. 241-258. For the Uighurs see Mackerras, *Uighur Empire* • **5**. RT i pp. 120-123; SHC p. 11; Rachewiltz, *Commentary* pp. 296, 316; Buell, *Dictionary* pp. 105, 218, 229 • **6**. Gumilev, *Imaginary Kingdom* pp. 94-95. For a lucid overall survey see Fletcher, *Studies* pp. 12-13 • **7**. For the Naiman see RT i pp. 67-70; Hambis, *Gengis-Khan* pp. 7-22; Wittfogel & Feng, *Liao* p. 50; S. Murayama, 'Sind die Naiman Turken oder Mongolen?' *Central Asiatic Journal* 4 (1959) pp. 188-198; Pelliot & Hambis, *Campagnes* pp. 215-221, 299-311; Roemer et al, *History of the Turkic Peoples*; W. Barthold, '12 Vorlesungen über die Geschichte der Türken Mittelasiens,' in *Die Welt des Islams* 17 (1935) p. 151 • **8**. The Kereit have attracted a lot of attention. RT i pp. 61-67; Togan, *Flexibility and Limitation*, esp. pp. 60-67; D. M. Dunlop, 'The Kerait of Eastern Asia,' *Bulletin of the School of Oriental and African Studies* 11 (1944) pp. 276-289; Pelliot & Hambis, *Campagnes* pp. 207-209; Erica D. Hunter, 'The conversion of the Keraits to Chrstianity in AD 1007,' *Zentralasiatische Studien* 22 (1991) pp. 142-163 • **9**. RT i pp. 43-55; Wittfogel & Feng, *Liao* pp. 101-102, 528, 573-598; Togan, *Flexibility* pp. 66-68; Louis Hambis, 'Survivances de toponymes de l'époque mongole en Haute Asie,' in *Mélanges de sinologie offerts a Monsieur Paul Demiéville, Bibliothèque de l'Institut des Hautes Études Chinoises*, 20 (1974) pp. 19-41 (at pp. 26-29); S. G. Kljastornys, 'Das Reich der Tartaren in der Zeit von Cinggis Khan,' *Central Asiatic Journal* 36 (1992) pp. 72-83; Pelliot & Hambis, *Campagnes* pp. 2-9 • **10**. RT i pp. 52-54; JB i p. 63; Pelliot & Hambis *Campagnes* pp. 227-228, 271-278. • **11**. RT i pp. 125-129; SHC p. 11; Ratchnevsky, *Genghis Khan* pp. 9-10. But some sceptics say the insults allegedly offered by Qabul on these occasions should not be taken literally but read allegorically as indicating the generally poor state of Mongol–Jin relations (see Grousset, *Empire of the Steppes* p. 197). • **12**. Barfield, *Perilous Frontier* p. 183 • **13**. Asimov & Bosworth, *History of Civilizations* iv part 1 p. 246. But see the contrary case argued in N. Iszamc, 'L'état féodal mongol et les conditions de sa formation,' *Études Mongoles* 5 (1974) pp. 127-130 • **14**. Louis Hambis, 'Un épisode mal connu de l'histoire de Gengis-khan,' *Journal des Savants* (January–March 1975) pp. 3-46 • **15**. Tamura Jitsuzo, 'The Legend of the Origin of the Mongols and Problems Concerning their Migration,' *Acta Asiatica* 24 (1973) pp. 9-13; Barthold, *Turkestan* (1928) p. 381; Paul Pelliot, 'Notes sur le "Turkestan" de W. Barthold,' *T'oung Pao* 27 (1930) pp. 12-56 (at p. 24) • **16**. RT i p. 130; Pelliot & Hambis, *Campagnes* pp. 132-133; Grousset, *Empire* p. 198. Ambaghai was taking his daughter to marry into the Ayiru'ut Buiru'ut sept, one of the subtribes of the Tartars. It is interesting that the practice of exogamy was so deeply ingrained with the Mongols that the Tayichiud would consider a match with the Tartars, their greatest enemies (Vladimirtsov, *Le régime social* pp. 58-59). Another version of the ambush is that it was not the intended bridegroom and family who betrayed him, but Tartar mercenaries (*juyin*) employed as gendarmes by the Jin who set the ambuscade (Rachewiltz, *Commentary* pp. 300-301). • **17**. Grousset, *Empire* pp. 194, 200 • **18**. Erdmann, *Temudschin* (1862) pp. 194-230 • **19**. Vladimirtsov, *Le régime social* pp.89-92 • **20**. d'Ohsson, *Histoire* i p. 33 • **21**. RT i pp. 130-131 • **22**. Ratchnevsky, *Genghis Khan* p. 12; Barfield, *Perilous Frontier* p. 184 • **23**. RT i p. 132; SHC pp. 11-13 • **24**. Rachewiltz, *Commentary* p. 320 • **25**. Gumilev, *Imaginary Kingdom* p. 140 • **26**. Vladimirtsov, *Life of Genghis* p. 12; Ratchnevsky, *Genghis Khan* pp. 15-16; Olbricht & Pinks, *Meng-ta pei-lu* p. 3 • **27**. SHO pp. 127-128; SHR pp. 74-75; Togan, *Flexibility* pp. 68-69 • **28**. ibid. pp. 69-70 • **29**. The Tanguts had an unfortunate habit of supporting all the losers on the steppes (Khazanov, *Nomads* pp. 234-236). • **30**. Togan, *Flexibility* pp. 70-72 • **31**. K. Uray-Kohalmi, 'Siberische Parallelen zur Ethnographie der geheimen Geschichte der Mongolen,' in Ligeti, *Mongolian Studies* pp. 247-264 (at pp. 262-263) • **32**. L. V. Clark, 'The Theme of Revenge in the *Secret History of the Mongols*,' in Clark & Draghi, *Aspects of Altaic Civilization* pp. 33-57; Clark, 'From the Legendary Cycle of Cinggis-gayan: The Story of an Encounter with 300 Yayichiud from the *Altan Tobci*,' *Mongolian Studies* 5 (1979) pp. 5-39 (at pp. 37-38) • **33**. RT i p. 134; SHC pp. 11-13 • **34**. Rachewiltz says that the name of this earlier wife 'cannot be determined despite many scholarly efforts' (Rachewiltz, *Commentary* p. 313). Ratchnevsky, however, (*Genghis Khan* pp. 15-16, 224) is adamant that her name was Suchigu or Suchikel, sometimes referred to as Ko'agchin. • **35**. For the Ongirrad subclan as Hoelun's home see Pelliot & Hambis, *Campagnes* pp. 402-409; Vladimirtsov, *Le régime social* pp. 58-59. The Buriyat have generated a considerable literature. See Lattimore, *Mongols of Manchuria* p. 61; Atwood, *Encyclopedia* p. 61; Eric Haenisch, *Die Geheime Geschichte* p. 112; Elena Skubuik, 'Buryat,' in Hahnunen, *Mongolian Languages* pp. 102-128; Lincoln, *Conquest* pp. 51-52; West, *Encyclopedia* (2009) pp. 132-133. Travellers' tales on the Buriyat include Sharon Hudgins, 'Feasting with the Buriats of Southern Siberia,' in Walker, *Food on the Move* pp. 136-156; Curtin, *A Journey*; Matthiessen, *Baikal* • **36**. Rashid's date of 1155 was followed by the early twentieth-century Russian historians Vladimirtsov and Barthold. Pelliot, always a contrarian, proposes the impossibly late date of 1167 (Pelliot, *Notes sur Marco Polo* i pp. 281-288). But the best authorities such as Rachewiltz and Ratchnevsky plump for 1162. See the detailed argumentation in Ratchnevsky, *Genghis Khan* pp. 17-19; Rachewiltz, *Commentary* pp. 320-321. • **37**. Rachewiltz, *Commentary* pp. 269, 272, 322-324 • **38**. SHC p. 14; Pelliot, *Notes sur Marco Polo* i pp. 288-289; Dunnell, *Chinggis Khan* p. 21 remarks that this was apt for a child of destiny. • **39**. Rachewiltz, *Commentary* p. 322 • **40**. RT i p. 135; Pelliot & Hambis, *Campagnes* pp. 171-175 • **41**. RT i p. 106; Gumilev, *Imaginary Kingdom* p. 142. For the game of knucklebones they played see Jean-Paul Roux, 'À propos des osselets de Gengis Khan,' in Heissig et al, *Tractata Altaica* pp. 557-568. Cf also F. N. David, *Games, Gods and Gambling* p. 2 • **42**. Vladimirtsov, *Le régime social* op. cit. p. 76; Pelliot

& Hambis, *Campagnes* p. 232; Wittfogel & Feng, *Liao* p. 239 • **43**. Ratchnevsky, 'La condition de la femme mongole au 12/13e siècle,' in Heissig et al, *Tractata Altaica* pp. 509-530 • **44**. Togan, 'The Qongrat in History,' in Pfeiffer & Quinn, *History and Historiography* pp. 61-83; Pelliot & Hambis, *Campagnes* pp. 393, 402-405; Wittfogel & Feng, *Liao* pp. 92, 634 • **45**. SHC p. 15; SHW p. 243; Pelliot & Hambis, *Campagnes* pp. 423-429 • **46**. Togan, 'The Qongrat in History,' p. 74 • **47**. Henry Serruys, 'Two Remarkable Women in Mongolia,' *Asia Major* 19 (1957) pp. 191-245 • **48**. Mostaert, *Sur quelques passages* pp. 10-12 • **49**. SHC p. 17 • **50**. Riasanovsky, *Fundamental Principles* p. 239 • **51**. Zhao, *Marriage as Political Strategy* p. 4 • **52**. SHR p. 14; Ratchnevsky, *Genghis Khan* p. 14. Dai Sechen's dream was full of symbolism, especially as regards shading, since white was regarded as a lucky colour by the Mongols (Rachewiltz, *Commentary* p. 328). • **53**. Togan, *Flexibility* pp. 121-125 • **54**. L. V. Clark, 'The Theme of Revenge,' pp. 33-57 • **55**. SHC p. 18 • **56**. Silvestre de Sacy, *Chrestomathie arabe* ii p. 162 • **57**. Ratchnevsky, *Genghis Khan* p. 22. • **58**. Rachewiltz, *Commentary* p. 344 • **59**. RT i p. 133 • **60**. Ratchnevsky, *Genghis Khan* p. 22 • **61**. May, *Mongol Conquests* p. 266 • **62**. SHC p. 22; Ratchnevsky, *Genghis Khan* pp. 20, 24 • **63**. Rachewiltz, *Commentary* pp. 346-347 • **64**. RT i p. 138 • **65**. Pelliot & Hambis, *Campagnes* pp. 185-187 • **66**. Roux, *La mort* pp. 92-96 • **67**. SHC pp. 23-24 • **68**. SHC p. 25; SHR pp. 23-24 • **69**. Ratchnevsky, *Genghis Khan* pp. 25-26 • **70**. RT i pp. 93-94; SHC pp. 25-26 • **71**. SHC pp. 27-28; SHO pp. 70-71 • **72**. Ratchnevsky, *Genghis Khan* p. 26 • **73**. SHC p. 29; SHO p. 73 • **74**. SHO pp. 73-74; SHR pp. 26-27 • **75**. SHO p. 75; SHW p. 252 • **76**. SHC pp. 30-31 • **77**. SHO pp. 75-76. For the subsequent career of Bo'orchu, who seems to have died in 1227, roughly the same time as Genghis himself, see Pelliot & Hambis, *Campagnes* pp. 342-360 • **78**. Riasanovsky, *Fundamental Principles* p. 90 • **79**. Pelliot & Hambis, *Campagnes* pp. 411-414; Vladimirtsov, *Le régime social* pp. 58-59 • **80**. RT i pp. 80-89 • **81**. Krader, *Social Organization* pp. 39, 89 is the source for this. In the kind of language beloved of academic anthropologists he tells us that Temujin's marriage was an example of matrilateral cross-cousin marriage (ibid. p. 344). • **82**. Rachewiltz, *Commentary* pp. 391-392 • **83**. RT i p. 93 • **84**. SHO pp. 79-81; SHR pp. 31-32; SHW p. 256. • **85**. Ratchnevsky, *Genghis Khan* p. 34 • **86**. JB i pp. 187-188; Boyle, *Successors* p. 31 • **87**. SHC pp. 34-38 • **88**. Gumilev, *Imaginary Kingdom* p. 143. On the other hand, it has been argued strongly that the Merkit raid is not historical but a folkloric trope, a perennial motif in epic poetry about the theft of women, whether of Europa by Zeus, Helen by Paris or the Princess Sita's seizure in the Hindu epic *Ramayana*. The raid is one of the prime exhibits in H. Okada, 'The *Secret History of the Mongols*, a Pseudo-historical Novel,' *Journal of Asian and African Studies* 5 (1972) pp. 61-67 (at p. 63). But the theory is unconvincing if only because it makes Chagatai's later violent hostility to Jochi on the grounds of his illegitimacy impossible to fathom. • **89**. Togan, *Flexibility* p. 73; Pelliot & Hambis, *Campagnes* pp. 250, 401 • **90**. Mostaert, *Sur quelques passages*

p. 32 • **91**. Pelliot & Hambis, *Campagnes* pp. 279-281; Rachewiltz, *Commentary* p. 421 • **92**. SHC pp. 38-39 • **93**. SHO pp. 91-92; SHR p. 41; Rachewiltz, *Commentary* p. 428 • **94**. SHC pp. 43-47. As Ratchnevsky tersely comments: 'Rashid's version is implausible' (*Genghis Khan* p. 35). • **95**. SHC pp. 39-42 • **96**. RT i p. 107 • **97**. RT i pp. 107-108 • **98**. Ratchnevsky, *Genghis Khan* p. 36 • **99**. SHO pp. 85-87; SHR pp. 35-36 • **100**. SHO pp. 87-90; SHR pp. 37-39; Rachewiltz, *Commentary* p. 417 • **101**. Rachewiltz, *Commentary* p. 435 • **102**. SHC pp. 52-53; SHO pp. 95-96; SHR pp. 44-45; SHW p. 262 • **103**. V. V. Bartold, 'Chingis-Khan,' in *Encyclopaedia of Islam* (1st ed., repr. 1968 v pp. 615-628 (at p. 617)); Vladimirtsov, *Le régime social* pp. 107-108; Vladimirtsov, *Genghis Khan* p. 130 • **104**. Grousset, *Conqueror of the World* p. 67 • **105**. SHO pp. 96-97; SHR pp. 44-46 • **106**. Vladimirtsov, *Le régime social* pp. 105-107 • **107**. As Rachewiltz sagely remarks, 'If neither Temujin nor his wife could understand Jamuga's poetic riddle, what hope have we, who are so far removed from that culture, to understand what was the *real* meaning of those words?' (Rachewiltz, *Commentary* p. 442) • **108**. Owen Lattimore, 'Chingis Khan and the Mongol Conquests,' *Scientific American* 209 (1963) pp. 55-68 (at p. 62); Lattimore, 'Honor and Loyalty: the case of Temujin and Jamukha,' in Clark & Draghi, *Aspects* pp. 127-138 (at p. 133) • **109**. Grousset, *Empire* pp. 201-202; Gumilev, *Imaginary Kingdom* pp. 143-145 • **110**. The numbers mentioned in the *Secret History* are unreliable for a number of reasons: 1) the author embellished with poetic licence and routinely inflated the size of armies; 2) the author anachronistically projected back into the twelfth century names, titles, technologies and modalities that belonged to an era fifty years in the future; 3) numbers in Mongol histories have a mystical or symbolic significance and therefore cannot be taken seriously for historical research. See Larry Moses, 'Legends by Numbers: the symbolism of numbers in the *Secret History of the Mongols*,' *Asian Folklore Studies* 55 (1996) pp. 73-97 and Moses, 'Triplicated Triplets: the Number Nine in the *Secret History of the Mongols*,' *Asian Folklore Studies* 45 (1986) pp. 287-294 • **111**. For exhaustive detail on the Thirteen see Pelliot & Hambis, *Campagnes* pp. 35-37, 53-135. See also Louis Ligeti, 'Une ancienne interpolation dans l'*Altan Tobci*,' *Acta Orientalia Academiae Scientiarum Hungaricae* 26 (1972) pp. 1-10 • **112**. SHO p. 104; SHR p. 152; Buell, *Dictionary* p. 159 • **113**. SHO pp. 127-128, 150-154, 177; SHR pp. 74-75, 96-100, 123-124 • **114**. SHO p. 90; SHW p. 263 • **115**. Grousset, *Empire*; Vladimirtsov, *Le régime social* p. 101 • **116**. SHO pp. 99-100; SHR p. 48. When he conquered the Tumed later, Temujin actually made good on this promise (SHO pp. 195-196; SHR p. 138). • **117**. SHO p. 78; SHR p. 30; Atwood, *Encyclopedia* p. 9; Pelliot & Hambis, *Campagnes* pp. 155, 164, 340-341 • **118**. Martin, *Rise of Chingis Khan* p. 66 • **119**. Grousset described the Uriangqai's skates as follows: 'Small, well-polished bones tied to their feet with which they speed so swiftly over the ice that they catch animals in the night' (*Empire* pp. 579, 582). • **120**. For Subedei's early life see Abel-Rémusat, *Nouveaux mélanges* ii

p. 97; Hildinger, *Story of the Mongols* p. 65; Gabriel, *Subotai* pp. 1-5 • **121**. SHO p. 76; SHR p. 28 • **122**. Vladimirtsov, *Genghis Khan* p. 33 • **123**. SHC p. 58 • **124**. Barfield, *Perilous Frontier* pp. 187-188

Chapter 3

1. SHO p. 106; SHR p. 53; SHW p. 266 • **2**. ibid.; Rachewiltz, *Commentary* pp. 475-476 • **3**. Pelliot & Hambis, *Campagnes* pp. 135-137 • **4**. Denis Sinor, 'The Legendary Origin of the Turks,' in Zygas & Voorheis, eds, *Folklorica* pp. 223-257 (at pp. 243-246) • **5**. Buell, *Dictionary* pp. 9-11 • **6**. Ratchnevsky, *Genghis Khan* pp. 49-50, 235. • **7**. It was not just Temujin who had to endure hostility from brothers and uncles. • **8**. Wittfogel & Feng, *Liao* p. 648 • **9**. Gabriel, *Subotai* p. 9 • **10**. SHO p. 103; SHR pp. 50-51 • **11**. Pelliot & Hambis, *Campagnes* pp. 196-207 • **12**. For the planning of the campaign see Pelliot, 'L'édition collective des oeuvres de Wang Kono-wei,' *T'oung Pao* 26 (1929) pp. 113-182 (at pp. 126-128). For the military aspects see Pelliot & Hambis, *Campagnes* pp. 192-200 • **13**. Pelliot & Hambis, *Campagnes* pp. 202-203 • **14**. Ratchnevsky, *Genghis Khan* p. 235 claims this location was at 43° N 109° E. • **15**. SHO pp. 108-110; SHR pp. 57-58; Hambis, *Genghis Khan* pp. 47, 57; Pelliot & Hambis, *Campagnes* pp. 195-199 • **16**. Pelliot, *Notes sur Marco Polo* i pp. 291-295 • **17**. Ratchnevsky, *Genghis Khan* pp. 52-53 • **18**. Abel-Rémusat, *Mélanges* p. 90 • **19**. Ratchnevsky, *Genghis Khan* p. 56 • **20**. SHO pp. 113-114; SHR p. 61 • **21**. RT i pp. 163-164; SHO pp. 107-108, SHR p. 55 • **22**. SHW pp. 267-268 • **23**. Rachewiltz, *Commentary* pp. 511-512 • **24**. Ratchnevsky, *Genghis Khan* p. 43 • **25**. Gumilev, *Imaginary Kingdom* p. 138 • **26**. SHO pp. 110-111; SHR pp. 58-59; Ratchnevsky, *Genghis Khan* p. 54 • **27**. SHW p. 270; SHC pp. 64-65; Pelliot, *Notes sur Marco Polo* i p. 322; Pelliot & Hambis, *Campagnes* p. 223 • **28**. SHO p. 114; SHR pp. 61-62 • **29**. Grousset, *Empire* p. 204 • **30**. Ratchnevsky, *Genghis Khan* pp. 54-55 • **31**. Krause, *Cingis Han* p. 15; d'Ohsson, *Histoire* i pp. 53-54, 74 • **32**. Ratchnevsky, *Genghis Khan* p. 57 • **33**. Pelliot & Hambis, *Campagnes* p. 309 • **34**. Hambis, *Genghis Khan* pp. 61-62 • **35**. RT i pp. 177-178; SHO pp. 132-133; SHR pp. 80-81 • **36**. RT i p. 64; Barthold, *Turkestan* p. 362; Pelliot & Hambis, *Campagnes* pp. 333-334 • **37**. SHO p. 134; SHR p. 82 • **38**. RT i pp. 178-179; Krause, *Cingis Han* p. 17 • **39**. RT i pp. 179-180; SHC pp. 76-78; Mostaert, *Sur quelques passages* p. 69; d'Ohsson, *Histoire* i p. 60 • **40**. RT i pp. 165, 175, 180-181; SHO pp. 126-128; SHR pp. 73-75; SHC pp. 80-81 • **41**. RT i p. 182; SHC p. 68; Pelliot, *Notes sur Marco Polo* i pp. 225-226; Pelliot & Hambis, *Campagnes* pp. 248-249 • **42**. Gumilev, *Imaginary Kingdom* p. 150 • **43**. Ratchnevsky, *Genghis Khan* pp. 38-39 • **44**. RT i p. 182; SHO p. 115; SHR pp. 62-63. As Lattimore says about Sorqan Shira's similar circumspection: 'It required nerve and good timing to elude the obligations of collective responsibility imposd by the institution of the subordinate tribe' (Lattimore, 'Chingis Khan and the Mongol Conquests,' *Scientific American* 209 (1963) pp. 55-68 (at p. 60)). • **45**. SHC pp. 73-74; SHO pp. 120-121; SHR pp. 67-68. One version of this explanation has it that the Ongirrad had originally decided to submit to Temujin but that, on their way to him, they were mistaken for the enemy and attacked by Kereit under Jochi Qasar. Enraged by their treatment, they joined Jamuga instead. (Martin, *Rise of Chingis Khan* pp. 72-73) • **46**. Rachewiltz, *Commentary* locates the site of the battle at 48° N 11° E, between the Onon and Kerulen. • **47**. Pelliot, *Notes sur Marco Polo* i pp. 424-425; Pelliot in *T'oung Pao* 13 (1912) pp. 436-438 • **48**. For descriptions of the battle see RT i pp. 85, 183; ii p. 43; SHO p. 117; SHR p. 64; Grousset, *Empire* p. 201; Gumilev, *Imaginary Kingdom* pp. 155-156; Whiting, *Military History* p. 367 • **49**. For Jamuga's use of these arrows see SHO pp. 87-88; SHR pp. 37-38 • **50**. SHO pp. 118-119; SHR pp. 65-67; d'Ohsson, *Histoire* i p. 63 • **51**. SHC pp. 69-70 • **52**. SHC p. 81 • **53**. Grousset, *Empire* p. 207; see also Melville, *Amir Chupan* • **54**. See the first-rate analysis in Rachewiltz, *Commentary* pp. 528-531 • **55**. SHO pp. 118-119; SHR pp. 65-67 • **56**. SHC pp. 74-75; SHW p. 275; lSHO pp. 121-122; SHR p. 69. It is only fair to point out that some scholars are sceptical about the historicity of the Jebe incident, viewing it as a standard motif or *topos* in epic poetry. For a nuanced discussion of the pros and cons of this argument see Rachewiltz, *Commentary* pp. 533-534, 536-538. • **57**. Some scholars dispute that the policy was genocide and claim that Temujin intended to execute only all such males in the tribal confederacy. To act otherwise would be a waste of potential slave labour and 'arrow fodder'. (Rachewiltz, *Commentary* p. 571) • **58**. SHW p. 278; SHO p. 129; SHR p. 176; Grousset, *Empire* p. 208. For a complete list of the Tartar clans and septs at Dalan Nemurges see Pelliot & Hambis, *Campagnes* pp. 240-245 • **59**. SHW p. 279 • **60**. Hambis, *Genghis Khan* pp. 72-73; Rachewiltz, *Commentary* pp. 572-573 • **61**. RT i pp. 182-183; Krause, *Cingis Han* p. 19 • **62**. SHW pp. 279-280; SHO pp. 130-131; SHE p. 79 • **63**. Ratchnevsky, *Genghis Khan* p. 99; Pelliot & Hambis, *Campagnes* p. 172 • **64**. Grousset, *Empire* p. 208 • **65**. SHO p. 135; SHR p. 84; Vladimirtsov, *Le régime social* p. 76. Ilkha's title was 'Senggum'. Some historians have mistaken the title for the man and refer to the Kereit prince as 'Senggum' as if this were a proper name. • **66**. Rachewiltz (*Commentary* p. 594) points out that in his contemptuous references to Ilkha, Toghril implies that the Senggum is his only son. Now it is known that Toghril had at least two sons, so either he was being distinctly unpaternal to the other one(s) or they had already died. • **67**. RT i p. 183 • **68**. SHO pp. 136-137. Others say the quid pro quo was to be marriage between Temujin's daughter Qojin and Ilkha's son Tusaqa (Ratchnevsky, *Genghis Khan* pp. 84-86). • **69**. RT i p. 184 • **70**. Ratchnevsky, *Genghis Khan* p. 68 • **71**. SHC pp. 88-90 • **72**. SHW p. 281: SHO pp. 136-139; SHR pp. 58-61 • **73**. This is the translation provided by Waley (SHW p. 281). Onon endorses this translation except for changing the two key descriptions to 'the lark that stays with you' as opposed to 'a distant lark'. Onon claims this is the difference between the species *melanocorypha mongolica* and *alauda* (usually known as *eremophila*) *alpestris* (SHO p. 133). Grousset has a much looser translation: 'I am the lark living ever in the same place in the good season and the bad – Temujin is the wild goose [sic] which flies away in winter.' (Grousset, *Empire* p. 209) Gumilev, *Imaginary Kingdom,* has 'I am a permanently present gull [sic] but my *anda* is a migratory bird, a lark.' • **74**. SHO p. 156; SHR pp. 102-103; Gumilev, *Imaginary Kingdom* p. 252 • **75**. SHO p. 158; SHR p. 104 • **76**. SHC p. 93; Ratchnevsky, *Genghis Khan* pp. 84-86 • **77**. SHW p. 285 • **78**. For full details see RT i p. 185. For Temujin's reward of the two herdsmen at the quriltai of 1206 see SHO pp. 191, 209; SHR pp. 133-134, 149-150; Rachewiltz, *Commentary* pp. 607-609 • **79**. RT i p. 191 • **80**. Vladimirtsov, *Genghis Khan* p. 51 • **81**. SHO pp. 143-145; SHR pp. 91-92 • **82**. RT i p. 186 • **83**. SHC pp. 148-149 • **84**. SHO pp. 145-146, 197-199; SHR pp. 91-92, 139-141; SHC pp. 96-98 • **85**. Rachewiltz, *Commentary* pp. 623-624. For other accounts of Qalqaljid Sands see JB i p. 37; Pelliot & Hambis, *Campagnes* pp. 45-47; Grousset, *Empire* pp. 157-160 • **86**. SHO pp. 148-149; SHR p. 95 • **87**. SHO p. 147; SHR pp. 92-93 • **88**. SHC pp. 98-99; SHO p. 147; SHR p. 94 • **89**. Ratchnevsky, *Genghis Khan* pp. 70-71 • **90**. JB i p. 38; SHO pp. 149-150, SHR p. 95; Pelliot & Hambis, *Campagnes* pp. 406-407 • **91**. Ratchnevsky, *Genghis Khan* p. 77 • **92**. RT i pp. 187-190; Mostaert, *Sur quelques passages* pp. 96-97; SHO pp. 150-157; SHR pp. 96-104; SHC pp. 102-109. Temujin listed the following as his principal grievances: 1) he had brought back Jaqa Gambu from China to help Toghril; 2) he had executed Sacha Beki and Taichen at the Ong Khan's request; 3) he gave to Toghril booty from his raid on the Merkit in 1196 but when the Ong Khan raided them in 1198, he gave Temujin nothing; 4) he had sent his four best generals – the 'four hounds' – to rescue Toghril when sorely beset by the Naiman. • **93**. Ratchnevsky, *Genghis Khan* p. 78 • **94**. Pelliot & Hambis, *Campagnes* pp. 71-72 • **95**. d'Ohsson, *Histoire* i p. 45; Pelliot & Hambis, *Campagnes* pp. 42-46. The exact location of the famous Lake Baljuna is unknown. It may be a tributary of the Ingoda River or it may be another name for Lake Balzino, source of the River Tura, south of modern Chita. • **96**. Grousset, *Conqueror of the World* pp. 134-135 • **97**. Pelliot, always a contrarian, maintained that the Baljuna covenant was legendary (Pelliot, 'Une ville musulmane dans la Chine du Nord sous les Mongols,' *Journal Asiatique* 211 (1927) pp. 261-279). But Cleaves, in a superb display of scholarship, has proved beyond doubt that the oath was a genuine historical event (Cleaves, 'The Historicity of the Baljuna Covenant,' *Harvard Journal of Asiatic Studies* 18 (1955) pp. 357-421). See also Krause, *Cingis Han* p. 23; Grenard, *Genghis Khan* (1935) p. 246 • **98**. Krause, *Cingis Han* p. 94 • **99**. Rachewiltz, *Commentary* p. 664 • **100**. SHO pp. 158-159; SHR pp. 104-105 • **101**. d'Ohsson, *Histoire* i p. 81; SHO pp. 159-160; SHR pp. 105-106 • **102**. Rachewiltz, *Commentary* p. 664 • **103**. Krause, *Cingis Han* p. 24; Herrmann, *Atlas of China* p. 49. • **104**. For Muqali see SHC p. 147; Rachewiltz, 'Muqali, Bol, Tas and An-t'ung,' *Papers on Far Eastern History*

15 (1977) pp. 45-62 • **105**. RT i pp. 65, 191; SHR pp. 109-110; SHO p. 164; SHC pp. 113-115; d'Ohsson, *Histoire* i p. 82 • **106**. Pelliot, 'À propos des Comans', *Journal Asiatique* 15 (1920) pp. 125-185 (at pp. 180-185) • **107**. Rachewiltz, *Commentary* p. 677 • **108**. SHO p. 165; SHR pp. 110-112 • **109**. Ratchnevsky, *Genghis Khan* p. 180 • **110**. Pelliot & Hambis, *Campagnes* pp. 416-417 • **111**. ibid pp. 36, 56, 123-124, 127, 245-247, 398 • **112**. RT i pp. 94-95 • **113**. RT i p. 192 • **114**. For the Naiman see RT i pp. 67-70; Roemer et al, *History of the Turkic Peoples* • **115**. Pelliot, 'Chrétiens d'Asie centrale et d'Extrême-Orient,' *T'oung Pao* (1914) pp. 630-631; Rachewiltz, *Commentary* p. 685 • **116**. RT i pp. 70, 201; Pelliot & Hambis, *Campagnes* p. 364 • **117**. Mostaert, *Sur quelques passages* p. 110; Pelliot & Hambis, *Campagnes* pp. 308-309; Rachewiltz, *Commentary* p. 679 • **118**. ibid. p. 689 • **119**. SHC pp. 119-120; Mostaert, *Sur quelques passages* p. 252 • **120**. Larry Moses, 'A theoretical approach to the process of Inner Asian confederation,' *Études Mongoles* 5 (1974) pp. 113-122 (at pp. 115-117) • **121**. SHR pp. 111-112 • **122**. RT i p. 202 • **123**. ibid. p. 201 • **124**. For example, the decisive battle of Chakirmaut was fought at the foot of Mount Naqu. Some of the sources, aware that *two* battles were fought against the Naiman, identify Chakirmaut and Naqu Cliffs as two separate and distinct battles. Grousset amalgamates aspects of both battles in his account (*Empire Mongol* pp. 163-168). • **125**. SHC pp. 125-127; Vladimirtsov, *Genghis Khan* p. 60 • **126**. SHW p. 297; SHO pp. 169-170; SHR pp. 115-116 • **127**. Rachewiltz regards this as the first order issued under Temujin's new legal code, the Yasa (Rachewiltz, *Commentary* p. 697). • **128**. SHO pp. 171-172; SHR pp. 116-117 • **129**. Rachewiltz thinks some of these locations are implausible (*Commentary* pp. 695-696). • **130**. Rachewiltz locates Mt Naqu at 47° N 104° E *(Commentary* p. 703). • **131**. Krause, *Cingis Han* p. 26 • **132**. SHO pp. 172-176; SHR pp. 118-121 • **133**. d'Ohsson, *Histoire* i p. 87; Ratchnevsky, *Genghis Khan* p. 85 • **134**. RT i p. 204 • **135**. SHO p. 177; SHR p. 122 • **136**. RT i p. 202 • **137**. For Tayang's death see d'Ohsson, *Histoire* i pp. 87-88; Rachewiltz, *Commentary* p. 720 • **138**. Grousset, *Conqueror of the World* pp. 152-161 • **139**. SHO p. 177; SHR p. 122 • **140**. ibid. • **141**. SHO p. 185 • **142**. SHR pp. 128-130 • **143**. Mostaert, *Sur quelques passages* 126-127 • **144**. See the outstanding analysis in Gumilev, *Imaginary Kingdom* pp. 244-260 • **145**. For two different assessments see Timothy May, 'Jamugka and the Education of Chinggis Khan,' *Acta Mongolica* 6 (2006) pp. 273-286 and Owen Lattimore, 'Honor and Loyalty: the case of Temukin and Jamukha,' in Clark & Draghi, *Aspects of Altaic Civilization* pp. 127-138 • **146**. 'Cat out of the bag' occurs in Gumilev, *Imaginary Kingdom* p. 257. Cf Rachewiltz: 'As we would expect, in all these sources Jamuga appears directly or indirectly as the villain but occasionally *the cat is out of the bag* [my italics], as it were, and we catch a glimpse of what may have been the true state of affairs' (*Commentary* p. 472). As for the quasi-Gnostic writing about Jamuga, Gumilev has a good description: 'a political cypher which has been deliberately served up as a riddle' (Gumilev, *Imaginary*

Kingdom p. 144). • **147**. Conan Doyle, *The Sign of Four*, Chapter Six • **148**. SHO pp. 187-189; SHR pp. 130-133 • **149**. This is a variant on the subject-predicate mistake famously analysed by Ludwig Feuerbach. 'God made Man' says the Christian catechism, whereas for Feuerbach and all atheists the reality is that man made God (see Feuerbach, *Lectures on the Essence of Religion* (1849)). • **150**. SHO pp. 187-189; SHR pp. 130-132 • **151**. SHC pp. 137-141 • **152**. For Eljigidei see JB i pp. 184, 249, 271-274; SHO pp. 215-219, 271-274; SHR pp. 157-158, 209-213; Hambis, *Genghis Khan* pp. 29-30 • **153**. Rachewiltz, *Commentary* p. 757; Ratchnevsky, *Genghis Khan* p. 88; Gumilev, *Imaginary Kingdom* p. 235 • **154**. For the contrast with Daritai see Ratchnevsky, 'Die Rechtsverhältnisse bei den Mongolen im 12–13 Jahrhundert,' *Central Asiatic Journal* 31 (1987) pp. 64-110 (at pp. 102-103). For the implications of Temujin's atrocity in terms of Mongol attitudes to oath taking see F. Isono, 'A Few Reflections on the *Anda* Relationship,' in Clark & Draghi, *Aspects of Altaic Civilization* pp. 81-87; Isono, 'More about the *Anda* Relationship,' *Journal of the Anglo-Mongolian Society* 8 (1983) pp. 36-47; Henry Serruys, 'A Note on Arrows and Oaths among the Mongols,' *Journal of the American Oriental Society* 78 (1958) pp. 279-294. • **155**. Gumilev, *Imaginary Kingdom* p. 259

Chapter 4

1. RT i pp. 72-74; Krause, *Cingis Han* pp. 27, 65 • **2**. SHO p. 182; SHR pp. 125-126 • **3**. RT i pp. 204-205; Rachewiltz, *Commentary* pp. 724-725, 730-732. Some say Toqto'a was not killed until 1208, but I follow Rachewiltz in thinking 1205 overwhelmingly likely (ibid. pp. 734-735). • **4**. SHO p. 181; SHW p. 304; SHR pp. 126-128; SHC pp. 133 • **5**. Gabriel, *Subotai* p. 20 • **6**. Rachewiltz, *Commentary* pp. 735-736; Krause, *Cingis Han* p. 11 • **7**. RT i p. 204; SHC p. 141; SHO pp. 190-191; SHR pp. 133-134 • **8**. Rachewiltz, 'The Title Chinggis Qan/Qaghan Re-examined,' in Heissig & Sagaster, *Gedanke und Wirken* pp. 281-298 (esp. pp. 282-288). For the earlier interpretations see Pelliot, 'Notes sur le "Turkestan",' loc. cit. p. 25; Ratchnevsky, *Genghis Khan*, pp. 89, 246-247; Pelliot, *Notes sur Marco Polo* i pp. 296-303; Vladimirtsov, *Genghis* pp. 37-38 • **9**. Telfer, *Johann Schiltberger* • **10**. Moule & Pelliot, *Marco Polo* i pp. 222-223. For the cult that developed around Genghis's banner see Pelliot, 'Notes sur le "Turkestan",' loc. cit. p. 32 • **11**. For the formation of the Mongol state in 1206 and some of the implications see Lane, *Daily Life* pp. 4, 12; A. M. Khazanov, 'The Origin of Genghis Khan's State: An Anthropological Approach,' *Ethnografia Polska* 24 (1980) pp. 29-39; A. Sarkozi, 'The Mandate of Heaven. Heavenly Support of the Mongol Ruler,' in Kellner-Heinkele, *Altaica Berolinensia* pp. 215-221 • **12**. SHO pp. 194-195, 205-207; SHR pp. 137-138, 145-148; SHC p. 146 • **13**. RT i pp. 91-93 • **14**. SHO pp. 195-196; SHR p. 138; SHC p. 147; Pelliot, *Campagnes* p. 138 • **15**. SHO pp. 191-192, SHR pp. 134-136 • **16**. Mostaert, *Sur quelques passages* p. 74; SHC pp. 148-149; SHO pp. 177-179. For some

interesting reflections on Jurchedei see Rachewiltz, *Commentary* pp. 787-788 • **17.** SHC p. 153; SHO pp. 202-203; SHR p. 143; Pelliot, *Campagnes* pp. 155, 164, 340-341 • **18.** SHO pp. 209-210; SHR p. 151 • **19.** SHO pp. 208-209; SHR pp. 149-150 • **20.** SHO pp. 202, 207, 225; SHR pp. 143, 148, 167 • **21.** SHO p. 201; SHR p. 142; SHC pp. 129, 153; Mostaert, *Sur quelques passages* p. 129; Grousset, *Conqueror of the World.* For the higher seating of the paladins see Dawson, *Mongol Mission* p. 57 • **22.** For the nine paladins see Elisabetta Chiodo, 'History and Legend: The Nine Paladins of Cinggis (Yisün örlüg) according to the "Great Prayer" (Yeke öčig),' *Ural-Altaischer Jahrbücher* 131 (1994) pp. 175-225 (esp. pp. 207-210). For the peculiarity of Qubilai's position see Rachewiltz, *Commentary* pp. 793-794 • **23.** Galatians 3: 18 • **24.** Vladimirtsov, *Le régime social* pp. 110-118 • **25.** Buell, *Dictionary* p. 287 • **26.** 'The genealogies of the medieval Mongols . . . were ideological statements designed to enhance political unity, not authentic descriptions of biological relationships' (Franke & Twitchett, *Cambridge History* p. 325). Bodonchar stories usually involved the 'holy fool' or halfwit, who got the better of his supposed intellectual superiors (Rachewiltz, *Commentary* p. 260). Bodonchar's mother was Ah-lan Qo'a, previously married to Dobun-Mergen, said to be a Cyclopean figure with one eye (Buell, *Dictionary* p. 103, 122-123, 149). • **27.** Bacon, *Obok* pp. 47-65; Vladimirtsov, *Le régime social* pp. 56-74 • **28.** For a complete reassemblage of this jigsaw puzzle see Bold, *Mongolian Nomadic Society* • **29.** Neil L. Whitehead, 'The Violent Edge of Empire,' in Ferguson & Whitehead, *War in the Tribal Zone* pp. 1-30 • **30.** Rudi Paul Lindner, 'What was a Nomadic Tribe?' *Comparative Studies in Society and History* 24 (1982) pp. 689-711. Unbelievably, there is yet another problem, as Rachewiltz notes: 'Unfortunately many of the problems concerning Cinggis's own lineage and the origin of the Mongol clans cannot be solved because the traditions in the Persian and Chinese sources and in the *Secret History* cannot be reconciled with each other' (Rachewiltz, *Commentary* p. 236). • **31.** Vladimirtsov, *Le régime social* pp. 110-112; Jagchid & Hyer, *Mongolia's Culture* pp. 19-72, 245-296; Lattimore, 'Honor and Loyalty: the case of Temujin and Jamukha,' in Clark & Draghi, *Aspects* pp. 127-138 (at pp. 130-132) • **32.** Fletcher, *Studies* pp. 17-19 • **33.** Bold, *Mongolian Nomadic Society* p. 110 • **34.** Lattimore, *Studies in Frontier History* pp. 510-513 (at p. 507) • **35.** Buell, *Dictionary* pp. 245-246 • **36.** SHC pp. 161-167 • **37.** JB i p. 37 • **38.** Asimov & Bosworth, *History of Civilizations* iv part 1 pp. 250-251 • **39.** For Bujir see Rachewiltz, *In the Service* pp. 131-135 • **40.** SHO p. 210; SHR p. 151 • **41.** Rachewiltz, *Commentary* pp. 763-765 • **42.** JB i p. 32; Barthold, *Turkestan* p. 386 Spuler, *The Muslim World* ii p. 36 • **43.** Michael C. Brose, 'Central Asians in Mongol China: Experiencing the "other" from two perspectives,' *Medieval History Journal* 5 (2002) pp. 267-289 • **44.** Josiah Ober, '"I Besieged That Man"; Democracy's Revolutionary Start,' in Raaflaub et al, *Origins of Democracy* pp. 83-104; Lambert, *Phratries*; Leveque, *Cleisthenes*; Forrest, *Emergence of Greek Democracy* • **45.** For these earlier manifestations see Jean-Philippe Geley, 'L'ethnonyme mongol à l'époque pré-činggisquanide (XIIe siècle),' *Études Mongoles* 10 (1979) pp. 59-89 (esp. pp. 65-83); P. B. Golden, 'Imperial Ideology and the Sources of Political Unity amongst Pre-Cinggisid Nomads of Western Eurasia,' *Archivum Eurasiae Medii Aevi* 2 (1982) pp. 37-76; Thomas T. Allsen, 'Spiritual Geography and Political Legitimacy in the Eastern Steppe,' in Claessen & Oosten, *Ideology* pp. 116-135 (esp pp. 124-127); Rachewiltz, *Commentary* p. 296 • **46.** Lane, *Daily Life* p. 15 • **47.** Rachewiltz, *Commentary* pp. 817-842 • **48.** M. Biran, 'The Mongol Transformation from the Steppe to Eurasian Empire,' *Medieval Encounters* 10 (2004) pp. 338-361. Almost every writer on Genghis emphasises his supposed debt to the Khitans (see Krader, *Social Organisation* p. 201). But as Biran underlines, the points of similarity were wholly artificial. The Mongols were much more destructive; they favoured direct, the Khitans indirect, rule; the Mongols depended on continuous expansion and paid their troops with booty, not wages; and the Khitans never mastered mass mobilisation for vast conquests (Biran, *Qara Khitai* pp. 202-206). • **49.** Slavery under the Mongols is much misunderstood. Usually they had bond slaves, and nothing similar to the system pre-1861 in the Southern States of the USA existed. • **50.** Vladimirtsov, *Le régime social* pp. 80-82 • **51.** For the Nirun/Durlukin distinction see Erdmann, *Temudschin* pp. 194-230 • **52.** For a survey of the vast change see Khazanov, *Nomads* pp. 128, 132-133, 148-152; Cribb, *Nomads in Archaeology* pp. 45-49 • **53.** Asimov & Bosworth, *History of Civilizations* iv part 1 pp. 243-259 • **54.** Barfield, *Perilous Frontier* p. 192 • **55.** SHO pp. 212-213; SHR pp. 152-154; SHC pp. 162-166 • **56.** Pelliot, 'Notes sur le "Turkestan",'pp. 27-31; F. W. Cleaves, 'A Chancellery Practice and the Mongols in the Thirteenth and Fourteenth Centuries,' *Harvard Journal of Asiatic Studies* 14 (1951) pp. 493-526 (esp. pp. 517-521); E. Haenisch, 'Weiterer Beitrag zum Text der Geheimen Geschichte der Mongolen,' *Zeitschrift der deutschen Morgenländischen Gesellschaft* 111 (1961) pp. 139-149 (at pp. 144-149) • **57.** Atwood, *Encyclopedia* p. 298 • **58.** SHO pp. 213-219; SHR pp. 155-161; SHC pp. 166-171 • **59.** Pelliot, 'Notes sur le "Turkestan",' pp. 28-31; Mostaert, *Sur quelques passages* pp. 244-249, Édouard Chavannes, 'Inscriptions et pièces de la chancellerie chinoise de l'époque mongole,' *T'oung Pao* 5 (1904) pp. 357-447 (at pp. 429-432); Yule & Cordier, *Ser Marco Polo* pp. 379-381 • **60.** JB i p. 31; Dawson, *Mongol Mission* pp. 26, 32-33; Jackson & Morgan, *Rubruck* p. 31 • **61.** SHO pp. 203, 214; SHR p. 157 • **62.** Hsiao, *The Military Establishment of the Yuan Dynasty* (Harvard 1978) pp. 33-35; T. Allsen, 'Guard and Government in the Reign of Grand Khan Mongke, 1251–59,' *Harvard Journal of Asiatic Studies* 46 (1986) pp. 495-521; Charles Melville, 'The *keshig* in Iran,' in Komaroff, *Beyond the Legacy* pp. 135-165 • **63.** JB i p. 40 • **64.** Rachewiltz, *Commentary* pp. 877-878 • **65.** Lech, *Mongolische Weltreich* p. 98 • **66.** SHC p. 175; SHO p. 225; SHR pp. 166-167 • **67.** JB i pp. 42-43; Barthold, *Turkestan* pp. 392-393. For the Korean land settlement see Henthorn, *Korea* p. 195 • **68.** F. Schurman,

'Mongolian Tributary Practices in the Thirteenth Century,' *Harvard Journal of Asiatic Studies* 19 (1956) pp. 304-389. A possible defence of Genghis is his oft-declared tenet that leaving the succession to the one who emerged as most able would inevitably result in civil war, and this was best avoided by fixed inheritances (JB i p. 186). • **69.** Peter Jackson, 'From *Ulus* to Khanate: The Making of the Mongol States,' in Amitai-Preiss & Morgan, *Mongol Empire* pp. 12-38 (at pp. 35-36); Jagchid & Hyer, *Mongolia's Culture* p. 355 • **70.** The director of the bureau of political commissars was Belgutei (Buell, *Dictionary* pp. 15-16, 123-124, 166, 170, 224-225, 254, 279). • **71.** John Masson Smith, 'Mongol and Nomadic Taxation,' *Harvard Journal of Asiatic Studies* 33 (1970) pp. 46-85; D. O. Morgan, 'Who Ran the Mongol Empire?' *Journal of the Royal Asiatic Society* 10 (1982) pp. 124-136; F. W. Cleaves, 'Daruya and Gerege,' *Harvard Journal of Asiatic Studies* 16 (1953) pp. 235-279 • **72.** For some of these problems see Biran, *Qaidu* pp. 69-77; Barthold, *Four Studies* i pp. 128-131 • **73.** JB ii pp. 579-583; RT ii pp. 406-409 • **74.** Christopher Atwood, '*Ulus*, Emirs, Keshig, Elders, Signatures and Marriage Partners,' in Sneath, *Imperial Statecraft* pp. 141-173 • **75.** SHC p. 175. Eljigidei received 3,000 (up 1,000 from the 1206 figure), Temuge got 5,000 and Kolgen 4,000. • **76.** JB i p. 39; F. W. Cleaves, 'Teb Tengerri,' in *Ural-Altaische Jahrbücher* 39 (1967) pp. 248-260; Rachewiltz, *Commentary* pp. 869-873 • **77.** Grousset, *Empire* pp. 229-232 • **78.** SHO p. 226; SHR p. 168 • **79.** Pelliot, *Campagnes* p. 172; Ratchnevsky, *Genghis Khan* p. 99 • **80.** RT ii p. 289; Grousset, *Empire* pp. 217, 585 • **81.** SHO p. 227; SHR pp. 169-170; SHC pp. 177-178 • **82.** ibid. • **83.** Grenard, *Genghis* p. 631; Rachewiltz, *Commentary* p. 877 • **84.** JB i p. 39; Barfield, *Perilous Frontier* p. 194 • **85.** SHO pp. 228-229; SHR p. 170 • **86.** All of this is dealt with in great detail in SWC pp. 176-182. See also Rachewiltz, *Commentary* pp. 878-885 • **87.** SHO p. 231; SHR pp. 173-174; SHC pp. 179-181 • **88.** ibid. • **89.** Fletcher, *Studies* pp. 34-35 • **90.** RT i p. 431 • **91.** For the increasing importance of beki see Vladimirtsov, *Le régime social* pp. 60-62; Pelliot, 'Notes sur le "Turkestan",' loc. cit pp. 49-51; Doefer, *Elemente* pp. 235-236 • **92.** JR ii pp. 1077-1078; V. N. Basilov, 'The Scythian Harp and the Kazakh Kobyz: In Search of Historical Connections,' in Seaman, *Foundations of Empire* pp. 74-100 (at p. 94) • **93.** J. J. Saunders, 'The Nomad as Empire Builder: A Comparison of the Arab and Mongol Conquests,' in Rice, *Muslims and Mongols* pp. 36-66; Jean Paul Roux, 'Tangri: Essai sur le ciel-dieu des peuples altaïques,' *Revue de l'histoire des religions* 149 (1956) pp. 49-82, 197-230; 150 (1956) pp. 27-54, 173-212; N. Palliser, 'Die Alte Religion der Mongolen und der Kultur Tschingis-Chans,' *Numen* 3 (1956) pp. 178-229; Osman Uran, 'The Ideal of World Domination among the Medieval Turks,' *Studia Islamica* 4 (1955) pp. 77-90 • **94.** Gumilev, *Imaginary Kingdom* p. 260 • **95.** Paul Meyvaert, 'An Unknown Letter of Hulagu II, Il-Khan of Persia to King Louis XI of France,' *Viator* 11 (1980) pp. 245-259 (at p. 252) • **96.** SHC p. 182 • **97.** L. Hambis, 'Un épisode mal connu de l'histoire de Gengis-Khan,' *Journal des Savants*, Jan-March 1975 pp. 3-46 • **98.** Pelliot, *Notes* *sur Marco Polo* i pp. 77-78; Allsen, *Culture and Conquest* pp. 128-129; Meignan, *Paris to Pekin* (1885) pp. 354-355 • **99**. Amitai-Preiss & Morgan, *Mongol Empire* pp. 200-222 • **100**. Ratchnevsky, 'Die Rechtsverhältnisse bei den Mongolen im 12–13 Jahrundert,' *Central Asiatic Journal* 31 (1987) pp. 64-110 (at pp. 78-80) • **101**. Dawson, *Mongol Mission* p. 12 • **102**. JB i pp. 204-205; Jackson & Morgan, *Rubruck* p. 90; Dawson *Mongol Mission* p. 17 • **103**. Alinge, *Mongolische Gesetze* p. 43; Lech, *Mongolische Weltreich* p. 96; Silvestre de Sacy, *Chrestomathie arabe* ii pp. 161-162; d'Ohsson, *Histoire* ii p. 618. For the lightning dragon see RT i p. 82 • **104**. Dawson, *Mongol Mission* p. 11 • **105**. ibid. pp. 54-56, 63, 194, 196; Jackson & Morgan, *Rubruck* p. 117; Heinrich Dörrie, 'Drei Texte der Geschichte der Ungarn und der Mongolen,' *Nachtrichten der Akademie der Wissenschaften in Göttingen* 6 (1956) pp. 125-202 (at p. 175); Skelton, Marston & Painter, *Vinland Map* pp. 90-91 • **106**. Yule & Cordier, *Ser Marco Polo* i pp. 385-386; Yule, *Cathay and the Way Thither* ii p. 224 • **107**. Darling, *Social Justice* pp. 103-106 • **108**. See especially the four-part article by David Ayalon, 'The Great Yasa of Chingiz Khan: A Re-examination,' *Studia Islamica* 33 (1970) pp. 97-140; 34 (1971) pp. 151-180; 36 (1972) pp. 117-158; 38 (1973) pp. 107-156. He writes that there are 'possibly insuperable difficulties in establishing the nature and contents of the Mongol *yasa*, its association with Chingiz Khan himself, or even whether it existed as a written coherent, enforceable code of laws' (34 (1971) p. 172). • **109**. D. O. Morgan, 'The "Great Yasa" of Chingiz Khan and Mongol Law in the Ilkhanate,' *Bulletin of the School of Oriental and African Studies* 49 (1986) pp. 163-176 (at pp. 169-170) • **110**. Gibb, *Ibn Battuta* pp. 560-561; cf also Robert Irwin, 'What the Partridge Told the Eagle: A Neglected Arabic Source on Chinggis Khan and the Early History of the Mongols,' in Amitai-Preiss & Morgan, *Mongol Empire* pp. 5-11 • **111**. Riasanovsky, *Fundamental Principles* p. 25 • **112**. Morgan, 'Great Yasa' p. 169 • **113**. Which is essentially what the arch-sceptic Ayalon does (Ayalon, 'The Great Yasa' (1971) p. 134; (1972) pp. 152-154). Even Morgan, who accepts part of Ayalon's argument, decisively parts company from him at this point (Morgan, 'Great Yasa' p. 166). • **114**. Driver & Miles, *Babylonian Laws*; Darling, *Social Justice* pp. 15-32 (esp pp. 21-22) • **115**. Van Seters, *Pentateuch*, esp. pp. 190-210 • **116**. Exodus 12 • **117**. Blume, *Justinian Code* (2009) • **118**. Holtman, *Napoleonic Revolution* • **119**. Lech, *Mongolische Weltreich* p. 96 • **120**. Riasanovsky, *Fundamental Principles* pp. 84-85 • **121**. ibid. p. 86 • **122**. G. Vernadsky, 'The Scope and Content of Chingis Khan's Yasa,' *Harvard Journal of Asiatic Studies* (1938) pp. 337-360 (at pp. 350-351) • **123**. ibid. p. 350; Lech, *Mongolische Weltreich* p. 125 • **124**. Silvestre de Sacy, *Chrestomathie arabe* ii p. 161 • **125**. Riasanovsky, *Fundamental Principles* pp. 83-85 • **126**. Ayalon argues that the exemption for religious leaders was not in the original Yasa – with the implication that Genghis's meeting with Chang Chun (see Chapter 13) may have been a crucial influence (Ayalon, 'Great Yasa'(1971) p. 121). • **127**. Alinge, *Mongolische Gesetze* p. 67; Dawson, *Mongol Mission* p. 15

• **128.** Spuler, *Goldene Horde* p. 362; Spuler, *Mongolen in Iran* p. 373; Vladimirtsov, *Genghis Khan* p. 63 • **129.** Riasanovsky, *Fundamental Principles* pp. 184-185 • **130.** JR ii p. 1079; Vernadsky, 'Scope and Content,' loc. cit. p. 352; J. A. Boyle, 'Kirakos of Gandrak on the Mongols,' *Central Asiatic Journal* (1963) pp. 199-214 (at pp. 201-202) • **131.** Ayalon, 'Great Yasa' (1971) pp. 107, 118-119 • **132.** Vladimirtsov, *Genghis Khan* pp. 65-66 • **133.** Bouillane de Lacoste, *Pays sacré* pp. 80-81 • **134.** Vernadsky, 'Scope and Content' loc. cit. p. 358 • **135.** Ratchnevsky, *Genghis Khan* p. 195 • **136.** JR ii p. 953 • **137.** Rachewiltz, 'Some Reflections on Cinggis Qan's Jasa,' *East Asian History* 6 (1993) pp. 91-104 • **138.** Riasanovsky, *Fundamental Principles* p. 86 • **139.** ibid. p. 35 • **140.** Dawson, *Mongol Mission* p. 17; Jackson & Morgan, *Rubruck* pp. 93-94; Matthew Paris, *Chronica Majora* iv. p. 388; Boyle, 'Kirakos of Kanjak,' loc. cit. p. 202; Jagchid & Hyer, *Mongolia's Culture* pp. 95-96; Vernadsky, *Mongols and Russia* p. 102 • **141.** Riasanovsky, *Fundamental Principles* p. 36; Vernadsky, 'Scope and Content,' loc. cit. p. 356 • **142.** JR ii pp. 1080-1081; SHO pp. 159-160, 192, 269-270; SHR pp. 105-106, 134-136, 207-208 • **143.** JR ii p. 953; JB i p. 53; Pelliot, *Recherches* p. 98; Yule & Cordier, *Ser Marco Polo* pp. 266-268; Latham, *Travels of Marco Polo* p. 101 • **144.** Vernadsky, 'Scope and Content,' loc. cit. p. 356 • **145.** RT ii pp. 510-511 • **146.** Ostrowski, *Muscovy and the Mongols* p. 72 • **147.** Vernadsky, 'Scope and Content,' loc. cit. p. 342 • **148.** Ratchnevsky, *Genghis Khan* p. 194 • **149.** ibid. • **150.** Pelliot, 'Les Mongols et la papauté,' *Revue de l'Orient chrétien* 23 (1923) pp. 16, 128; E. Voegelin, 'The Mongol orders of submission to European powers, 1245–1255,' *Byzantion* 15 (1942) pp. 378-413 (esp. pp. 404-409) • **151.** Riasanovsky, *Fundamental Principles* pp. 146, 158; Vernadsky, *The Mongols and Russia* pp. 99-110 • **152.** Riasanovsky, *Fundamental Principles* p. 149 • **153.** ibid. pp. 151-152; Lech, *Mongolische Weltreich* pp. 96-97; Sylvestre de Sacy, *Chrestomatie arabe* ii p. 161 • **154.** Dawson, *Mongol Mission* p. 17; Vernadsky, 'Scope and Content' loc. cit. pp. 352-353 • **155.** JR ii pp. 1080-1081 • **156.** Lewis, *Islam* i pp. 89-96 • **157.** Riasanovsky, *Fundamental Principles* p. 159 • **158.** Dawson, *Mongol Mission* pp. 14-15; Ratchnevsky, 'Die Yasa (Jasaq) Cinggis Khans und ihre Problematik,' in G. Hazai & P. Zieme, *Sprache, Geschichte und Kultur* pp. 471-487 • **159.** E. Endicott-West, 'Aspects of Khitan Liao and Mongolian Yuan Rule: A Comparative Perspective,' in Seaman & Marks, *Rulers from the Steppe* pp. 199-222 • **160.** Riasanovsky, *Fundamental Principles* pp. 173-189 (esp. pp. 182-183) • **161.** ibid. pp. 183-184 • **162.** D. Aigle, 'Le grand *jasaq* de Gengis-Khan, l'empire, la culture Mongole et la shari'a,' *Journal of the Economic and Social History of the Orient* 47 (2004) pp. 31-79 • **163.** Ayalon, 'Great Yasa,' loc. cit. (1971) p. 164 • **164.** ibid. pp. 137-138 • **165.** Ostrowski, *Muscovy* p. 71 • **166.** Vernadsky, 'Scope and Content,' loc. cit. p. 360; Riasanovsky, *Fundamental Principles* pp. 278-297; Ch'en, *Chinese Legal Tradition* • **167.** Darling, *Social Justice* pp. 105-125 (esp. pp. 103-105, 111); Ayalon, 'Great Yasa,' loc. cit. (1973) p. 141 • **168.** Riasanovsky, *Fundamental Principles* p. 88

Chapter 5

1. Rachewiltz, 'Muqali, Bol, Tas and An-t'ung,' *Papers on Far Eastern History* 15 (1977) pp. 45-62 (at p. 47); Pelliot, 'Notes sur le "Turkestan",' loc. cit. pp. 12-56 (at p. 33); Rachewiltz, *Commentary* p. 815 • **2.** RT ii pp. 272-275; Vladimirtsov, *Genghis* p. 58; d'Ohsson, *Histoire* ii pp. 3-5 • **3.** Barthold, *Turkestan* pp. 383-385; Vladimirtsov, *Genghis* pp. 67-68 • **4.** Pelliot, *Notes sur Marco Polo* ii pp. 858-859; Ratchnevsky, *Genghis Khan*, p. 224 • **5.** Dawson, *Mongol Mission* p. 33; Barthold, *Turkestan* pp. 383-385 • **6.** Buell, *Dictionary* pp. 261-262 • **7.** Hartog, *Genghis Khan* p. 45; Lane, *Daily Life* pp. 97-98 • **8.** Michael Edwards & James C. Stanfield, 'Lord of the Mongols: Genghis Khan,' *National Geographic* 190 (December 1996) pp. 14-23 • **9.** JB i p. 32 • **10.** JB i p. 30; Jagchid & Hyer, *Mongolia's Culture* pp. 370-372 • **11.** JB i p. 33; Benedetto, *Marco Polo* pp. 114-116; Beazley, *John de Piano Carpini* p. 121 • **12.** JB i p. 40; Vernadsky, 'Scope and Content,' loc. cit. p. 351; Riasanovsky, *Fundamental Principles* p. 164 • **13.** JB i pp. 27-28; Dawson, *Mongol Mission* pp. 100-101 • **14.** JB i pp. 28-29 • **15.** Yule, *Cathay* ii pp. 234-240 • **16.** Jagchid & Hyer, *Mongolia's Culture* pp. 27-37 • **17.** Jackson & Morgan, *Rubruck* p. 85 • **18.** N. T. Munkuyer, 'A Mongolian Hunting Practice of the Thirteenth Century,' in Heissig et al, *Tractata Altaica* pp. 417-435 (esp. pp. 421-423) • **19.** Risch, *Johann de Piano Carpini* pp. 161-169 • **20.** H. D. Martin, 'The Mongol Army,' *Journal of the Royal Asiatic Society* 75 (1943) pp. 46-85 (at p. 70); Robinson, *Oriental Armour* p. 138 • **21.** Hildinger, *Story of the Mongols* p. 72 • **22.** Barthold, *Turkestan* p. 421; Denis Sinor, 'The Inner Asian Warrior,' *Journal of the American Oriental Society* 101 (1981) pp. 133-144 (at p. 137) • **23.** Martin, *Rise of Chinggis Khan* p. 19; Świętosławski, *Arms and Armour* • **24.** E. G. Pulleyblank, 'Why Tockosian?' *Journal of Indo-European Studies* 23 (1995) pp. 415-430; Edward McEwan, Robert L. Miller & A. Bergman, 'Early Bow Designs and Construction,' *Scientific American* 264 (June 1991) pp. 50-56; Jagchid & Hyer, *Mongolia's Culture* p. 367 • **25.** Rachewiltz, *Commentary* pp. 714-715; Hok-Lam Chan, 'Siting by Bowshot: A Mongolian Custom and its Sociopolitical and Cultural Implications,' *Asia Major*, 3rd series 4 (1991) pp. 53-78 • **26.** Buell, *Dictionary* pp. 112-114; Turnbull & McBride, *The Mongols* pp. 13-22; Gabriel & Boose, *Great Battles of Antiquity* pp. 539-541 • **27.** Parker, *Tartars* p. 258 • **28.** For this subject in general see Mayor, *Greek Fire*. For a study of poisoned arrows in a specific area (the American West) see Jones, *Poison Arrows* • **29.** Marsden, *Marco Polo*, p. 214; Vernadsky, *Mongols and Russia* pp. 126-128; Hyland, *Medieval Warhorse* p. 131; S. Jagchid & C. R. Bawden, 'Some Notes on the Horse Policy of the Yuan Dynasty,' *Central Asiatic Journal* 10 (1965) pp. 246-265 • **30.** Lane, *Genghis Khan* p. 31. Mounted archery was made obsolete in great warfare by the invention of firearms but still survived in 'little wars' like those of the American West. The Comanches were particularly skilled exponents (Fehrenbach, *Comanches* pp. 124-125). • **31.** Denis Sinor, 'On Mongol

Strategy,' *Proceedings of the Fourth East Asian Altaistic Conference* (Taipei 1971) pp. 238-249 • **32.** T. Allsen, 'Mongolian Princes and Their Merchant Partners, 1200–1260,' *Asia Major* 2 (1989) pp. 83-126 • **33.** Dvornik, *Intelligence Services* p. 274 • **34.** JB i p. 373; Dawson, *Mongol Mission* p. 36; May, *Art of War* pp. 69-70 • **35.** Yule & Cordier, *Ser Marco Polo* pp. 121-131 • **36.** Hollyn Conant, 'Genghis Khan's Communications Network,' *Military Review* 94 (August 1994) pp. 65-77 • **37.** F. Isono, 'Kuriyen Reconsidered,' *Journal of the Anglo-Mongolian Society* 12 (1989) pp. 3-25 • **38.** Riasanovsky, *Fundamental Principles* p. 83 • **39.** Moule & Pelliot, *Marco Polo* i p. 173 • **40.** Martin, *Rise of Chingis Khan* p. 17; Jagchid & Hyer, *Mongolia's Culture* pp. 370-372; T. Allsen, *Mongol Imperialism* p. 25. For the river crossing see Risch, *Carpini* p. 17 • **41.** Dawson, *Mongol Mission* pp. 33-34 • **42.** Leo de Hartog, 'The Army of Genghis Khan,' *Army Defence Journal* 109 (1979) pp. 476-485 (at p. 480) • **43.** SHO p. 282 • **44.** Liddell Hart, *Great Captains Unveiled* p. 28 • **45.** Dawson, *Mongol Mission* p. 36 • **46.** Skelton, Marston & Painter, *Vinland Map* pp. 88-89 • **47.** SHO p. 285 • **48.** Martin, 'Mongol Army,' loc. cit.; Gabriel & Boose, *Great Battles of Antiquity* pp. 545-547 • **49.** SHO pp. 118-125; SHR pp. 65-72 • **50.** Skelton, Marston & Painter, *Vinland Map* pp. 98-99; Risch, *Carpini* p. 175 • **51.** Hartog, 'Army of Genghis Khan,' loc. cit. p. 482 • **52.** SHO p. 286 • **53.** The feigned retreat is of course as old as warfare itself. It was used by the Spartans at Thermopylae in 480 BC to lure Xerxes' Immortals into a trap (Herodotus 8. 24) and by William the Conqueror at the Battle of Hastings in 1066 (see McLynn, *1066* p. 224). As late as 1866 the Sioux chief Red Cloud used it to inflict defeat on the US cavalry in the 'Fetterman Massacre'. For its use in warfare in general see Alexander, *How Wars are Won* pp. 94-95 • **54.** For the huge superiority of the Mongol horses see Denis Sinor, 'What is Inner Asia?' in Heissig, *Altaica Collecta* pp. 245-258 (at p. 251); Sinor, 'Inner Asian Warriors,' *Journal of the American Oriental Society* 101 (1981) pp. 133-144 (at p. 137). For the special circumstances surrounding the emergence of the Mongol heavy cavalry see V. P. Alekseev, 'Some Aspects of the Study of Productive Factors in the Empire of Chingiz Khan,' in Seaman & Marks, *Rulers from the Steppe* pp. 186-198 (at p. 192) • **55.** Dawson, *Mongol Mission* p. 37 • **56.** As in the relentless pursuit of Shah Muhammad II in 1220–1221 and Bela IV of Hungary in 1241 (see below). Cf also Vernadsky, *Mongols and Russia* pp. 110-120 • **57.** RT i p. 204; Vladimirtsov, *Genghis* p. 65 • **58.** RT i pp. 204-205; Barthold, *Turkestan* pp. 361-362; d'Ohsson, *Histoire* i pp. 104-105 • **59.** Rachewiltz, *In the Service* p. 18 • **60.** RT i pp. 226-227 • **61.** Barthold, *Turkestan* pp. 401-402 • **62.** For a general survey of the Forest Peoples see Rachewiltz, *Commentary* pp. 852-854. For the Buriyat see West, *Encyclopedia* pp. 132-133 and Matthiessen, *Baikal*. For the Oyirad see RT i pp. 54-57; Rachewiltz, *Commentary* p. 852. For the Tumed see RT i p. 58. For the Tuvans see Krueger, *Tuvan Manual*; M. N. Mongush, 'Tuvans of Mongolia and China,' *International Journal of Central Asian Studies* 1 (1996) pp. 225-243; Lattimore,

Mongols of Manchuria p. 165; Bowles, The People of Asia pp. 278-279 • 63. Vladimirtsov, Le régime social op. cit. pp. 41, 61 • 64. RT i p. 59 • 65. SHC p. 7 • 66. SHO pp. 115-117; SHR pp. 62-65 • 67. RT i p. 204; Martin, Rise of Chingis Khan p. 102 • 68. Rachewiltz, Commentary p. 852 • 69. SHC p. 173; Pelliot, Notes sur l'histoire de la Horde d'Or pp. 141-142 • 70. Rachewiltz, Commentary p. 854. For the Mongol mania for gyrfalcons see Hambis, Marco Polo p. 426 • 71. Rachewiltz, Commentary p. 851. For Qorchi's appointment to this position at the 1206 quriltai see SHO pp. 196-197; SHR pp. 138-139 • 72. SHO p. 224; SHR p. 166 • 73. Ratchnevsky, Genghis Khan pp. 117-118, 254-255 • 74. RT i p. 227 • 75. SHW p. 311; SHO p. 223; SHR p. 165 • 76. For this ride see Carruthers, Unknown Mongolia i pp. 114-115 • 77. Donner, Sibérie p. 132 • 78. d'Ohsson, Histoire i p. 157 • 79. SHO p. 224; SHR pp. 165-166 • 80. SHW p. 312 • 81. Pelliot, Notes critiques d'histoire Kalmouke i pp. 55-64; P. D. Buell, 'Early Mongol Expansion in Western Siberia and Turkestan (1207–1219): A Reconstruction,' Central Asiatic Journal 36 (1992) pp. 1-32 opts for a different chronology for these events. • 82. Colin Mackerras, Uighur Empire • 83. Golden, Turkic Peoples pp. 176-183; Barfield, Perilous Frontier pp. 165-169 • 84. Beshbaliq (Jimsar) is located at 43° 59' N, 89° 4' E; Asimov & Bosworth, History of Civilizations iv part 2 p. 578; Beckwith, Empires of the Silk Road pp. 148, 159; Pelliot & Hambis, Campagnes pp. 82-95 • 85. Barthold, Turkestan pp. 48-52; B. Spuler, History of the Mongols (1972) pp. 31, 176; Colin Mackerras, 'The Uighurs,' in Sinor, Cambridge History pp. 317-342 • 86. Brose, Subjects and Masters pp. 88-89 • 87. JB i pp. 53-61; Yule, Cathay and the Way Thither i p. 209; d'Ohsson, Histoire i pp. 429-435 • 88. Bretschneider, Mediaeval Researches i p. 260 • 89. Brose, Subjects and Masters pp. 86-87 • 90. JB i pp. 44-47; SHO pp. 221-222; SHR p. 163; Thomas T. Allsen, 'The Yuan Dynasty and the Uighurs of Turfan in the Thirteenth Century,' in Rossabi, China among Equals pp. 248-280 (at pp. 246-248); d'Ohsson, Histoire i p. 419 • 91. JB i pp. 46-47; Allsen, 'The Yuan Dynasty,' loc. cit. p. 247 • 92. JB i p. 140 • 93. Rachewiltz, Commentary pp. 848-849; Jackson & Morgan, Rubruck pp. 283-284; Pelliot, Recherches pp. 667-67. Bretschneider ties himself in knots on this issue, absurdly claiming that Altalun died before she could marry the idiqut, that Genghis substituted another daughter but that Barchuq then died before he could marry her (Bretschneider, Mediaeval Researches i p. 261); JB i p.175; Weatherford, Secret History of the Mongol Queens pp. 47, 51, 57, 69-72, 79-80, 91, 97, 102 • 94. Brose, Subjects and Masters pp. 50-54 • 95. ibid. pp. 259, 264-265. For the Uighur script see J. Richard, 'La limite occidentale de l'expansion de l'alphabet Ouighour,' Journal Asiatique 239 (1951) pp. 71-75. For their culture in general see Hamilton, Les Ouighurs • 96. SHO p. 221; SHR p. 162; Rachewiltz, Commentary p. 843; Biran, Qara Khitai p. 75 • 97. The fundamental work on the Tanguts is Dunnell, Great State of White and High, but there is also much valuable work in learned articles and theses: Mary Ferenczy, 'The Foundation of Tangut Statehood as seen by Chinese Historiographers,' in Ligeti,

Tibetan and Buddhist Studies i pp. 241-249; Dunnell, 'Who are the Tanguts? Remarks on Tangut Ethnogenesis and the Ethnonym Tangut,' *Journal of Asian History* 18 (1984) pp. 778-789; Paul Friedland, 'A Reconstruction of Early Tangut History,' Ph.D. thesis, University of Washington 1969. See also Kwanten & Hesse, *Tangut . . . Studies*; Asimov & Bosworth, *History of Civilizations*, iv part I pp. 206-214 • **98.** Mote, *Imperial China* pp. 257-259 • **99.** Franke & Twitchett, *Cambridge History* pp. 155-157, 162, 165, 168-170, 196 • **100.** Ksenia Kepping, 'The Name of the Tangut Empire,' *T'oung Pao* 80 (1994) pp. 357-376; Beckwith, *Silk Road* p. 31; Gerard Clauson, 'The Future of Tangut (Hsi Hsia) Studies,' *Asia Major* 11 (1964) pp. 54-77 • **101.** Franke & Twitchett, *Cambridge History* pp. 123-153; Mote, *Imperial China* pp. 257-259; Gumilev, *Imaginary Kingdom* pp. 98-100, 593 • **102.** Mote, *Imperial China* pp. 261-264; Solonin, *Tangut Chan Buddhism* • **103.** Biran, *Qara Khitai* p. 64; Franke & Twitchett, *Cambridge History* pp. 155, 197 • **104.** H. D. Martin, 'The Mongol Wars with Hsi Hsia, 1205–1227,' *Journal of the Royal Asiatic Society* (1942) pp. 195-228 (at pp. 198-199) • **105.** RT i p. 204 • **106.** For details of the Tangut army see Stein, *Tibetan Civilization* pp. 70-77 • **107.** G. Jenkins, 'A Note on Climatic Cycles and the Rise of Genghis Khan,' *Central Asiatic Journal* (1974) pp. 217-226 • **108.** Togan, *Flexibility* p. 70; Franke & Twitchett, *Cambridge History* pp. 164, 206; Asimov & Bosworth, *History of Civilizations* iv part I p. 213 • **109.** Mote, *Imperial China* p. 254; Franke & Twitchett, *Cambridge History* p. 157 • **110.** ibid. p. 183 • **111.** RT i p. 204 • **112.** Franke & Twitchett, *Cambridge History* p. 205 • **113.** Atwood, *Encyclopedia* p. 590; Ruth W. Dunnell, 'The Fall of the Xia Empire: Sino-Steppe Relations in the Late Twelfth to Early Thirteenth Centuries,' in Seaman & Marks, *Rulers from the Steppe* pp. 158-183 • **114.** Martin, *Rise* p. 116. Dabsun Nor (Lake Dabuxun) is at approx. 37° N, 95° E. • **115.** Hambis, *Genghis* pp. 98-99 • **116.** Krause, *Cingis Han* p. 29 • **117.** Martin, *Rise* p. 117 • **118.** Krause, *Cingis Han* p. 29 • **119.** Martin, *Genghis Khan* p. 118 • **120.** ibid. • **121.** There is some suggestion in the sources that the Tanguts were regarded as inferior by the Jin and possibly even the Mongols. Rubruck, in his asides about the Tanguts, can find nothing good to say about them except that they were 'swarthy'. (Jackson & Morgan *Rubruck* p. 159). • **122.** Martin, *Rise* p. 118 • **123.** RT ii pp. 289-290; SHR pp. 177-178 • **124.** Martin, *Rise* pp. 119-120

Chapter 6

1. Vernadsky, *Mongols and Russia* pp. 43-44 • **2.** SHR p. 18 • **3.** SHO pp. 81-82; SHR p. 33 • **4.** SHO pp. 73-74; SHR pp. 26-27 • **5.** SHR p. 20-21 • **6.** SHR p. 15; Ratchnevsky, *Genghis Khan* p. 153 • **7.** Lattimore, *Mongol Journeys* p. 182 • **8.** Hedley, *Tramps* p. 245 • **9.** De Windt, *From Pekin* p. 117. De Windt reported that one of the key Mongolian phrases to learn was 'tie up your dogs'. (ibid. p. 118) • **10.** This is certainly one war hero's view. See McLynn, *Fitzroy Maclean*

p. 101. On spur-of-the-moment impulses the words of Conrad's Lord Jim (in the film of that name) are worth bearing in mind: 'I've been a so-called coward and a so-called hero, and there's not the thickness of a sheet of paper between them.' • **11**. SHO pp. 118-119; SHR pp. 65-67. The ingratitude was noticed in Dunnell, *Chinggis Khan* p. 40 • **12**. SHO pp. 226-227; SHR pp. 168-170 • **13**. SHO pp. 107-108; SHR pp. 54-56 • **14**. SHO pp. 178-180; SHR pp. 123-124 • **15**. SHO pp. 90, 105, 186; SHR pp. 39, 53, 130-132 • **16**. JR ii pp. 1041-1042; d'Ohsson, *Histoire* i pp. 413-414. Barthold, however, amazingly says he had unusual self-control and ability to curb his temper (*Turkestan* p. 459). • **17**. Vladimirtsov, *Genghis* pp. 162-163 • **18**. Gumilev, *Imaginary Kingdom* p. 234 • **19**. SHO pp. 71-72, 74-76, 184, 252, 260; SHR pp. 25-29, 126-128, 192-193, 198-199 • **20**. SHO pp. 207-208; SHR pp. 148-149 • **21**. Ratchnevsky, *Genghis Khan* p. 164 • **22**. Jackson, *Mongols and the West* p. 47; Ratchnevsky, *Genghis Khan* pp. 158-159. 'Genghis was not someone who shared' (L. Hambis, 'Un épisode mal connu,' loc. cit. p. 7). • **23**. Vernadsky, *Mongols and Russia* p. 6; Grousset, *Empire* p. 248 • **24**. Ratchnevsky, *Genghis Khan* p. 161 • **25**. JR ii p. 990 • **26**. John Masson Smith, 'The Mongols and World Conquest,' *Mongolica* 5 (1994) pp. 206-214 • **27**. Vladimirtsov, *Genghis* pp. 168-169 • **28**. JR ii p. 1077; Antoine Mostaert, 'À propos de quelques portraits d'empereurs mongols,' *Asia Major* (1927) pp. 19-156; Pelliot, 'L'édition collective des oeuvres de Wang Kouo-Wei,' *T'oung Pao* 26 (1929) pp. 113-182 (at p. 166); Pelliot, 'Notes sur le "Turkestan",' *T'oung Pao* 27 (1930) pp. 12-56 (at p. 13) • **29**. RT ii p. 295 • **30**. Riasanovsky, *Fundamental Principles* p. 88 • **31**. RT ii p. 295; Riasanovsky, *Fundamental Principles* p. 87 • **32**. ibid. He also saw no great distinction between the arts of war and peace. He said that if you can manage your own house, you can manage an estate, and if you can keep ten men in military order, you can discipline 10,000. • **33**. RT ii p. 295 • **34**. RT ii p. 296 • **35**. RT ii pp. 294-295; SHO p. 15 • **36**. Needham, *Science and Civilization* v part 4 pp. 103-106, 141-150 • **37**. Riasanovsky, *Fundamental Principles* p. 88; d'Ohsson, *Histoire* i p. 412. Genghis himself liked a drink, though in moderation, and liked to have guitars playing and minstrels singing while he drank, as did Batu and many of his other descendants (Dawson, *Mongol Mission* p. 57; Jackson & Morgan, *Rubruck* p. 175). • **38**. Riasanovsky, *Fundamental Principles* p. 89 • **39**. ibid. p. 91; Ratchnevsky, *Genghis Khan* p. 153 • **40**. JR ii pp. 1077-1078 • **41**. Foltz, *Religions of the Silk Road* p. 113; Anatoly M. Khazanov, 'Muhammad and Jenghiz Khan Compared: The Religious Factor in World Empire Building,' *Comparative Studies in History and Society* 35 (1993) pp. 461-479 • **42**. Ratchnevsky, *Genghis Khan* p. 197 • **43**. DeWeese, *Islamization* pp. 100-101 • **44**. Gumilev, *Imaginary Kingdom* pp. 169-218 • **45**. Nikolai N. Seleznyov, 'Nestorius of Constantinople: Condemnation, Suppression, Veneration,' *Journal of Eastern Christian Studies* 62 (2010) pp. 165-190 • **46**. Françoise Michaud, 'Eastern Christianities,' in Angold,

Cambridge History of Christianity v pp. 373-403 • **47**. Pelliot, *Recherches* pp. 623-644 • **48**. Henri Bernard, *La découverte des nestoriens*; John Stewart, *Nestorian Missionary Enterprise*; Morris Rossabi, *Voyager from Xanadu* • **49**. Pelliot, *Recherches* op. cit. • **50**. Wittfogel & Feng, *Liao* p. 308; Asimov & Bosworth, *History of Civilizations* iv part 1 pp. 74-76; Pelliot, *Recherches* p. 626 • **51**. JB i p. 259; Boyle, *Successors* p. 188; Pelliot, *Recherches* pp. 242-248 • **52**. Dawson, *Mongol Mission* pp. 144-145, 177-179; Jackson & Morgan, *Rubruck* pp. 163-164, 211-214 • **53**. SHO pp. 173-176; SHR pp. 118-121 • **54**. JB ii p. 549; Pelliot & Hambis, *Campagnes* pp. 175-177; Vladimirtsov, *Le régime social* pp. 66-67 • **55**. However, Rashid states categorically that Temuge was Genghis's favourite brother (RT i p. 137). • **56**. For the complex sibling rivalries among Genghis's four sons see Pelliot, *Notes sur l'histoire* pp. 10-27. Jochi was not his eldest child, as his sister Fujin was older (Boyle, *Successors* p. 97). • **57**. SHO pp. 136-137, 202; SHR pp. 84, 143 • **58**. Larry Moses, 'The Quarrelling Sons in the *Secret History of the Mongols*,' *Journal of Asian Folklore Studies* 100 (1987) pp. 63-68 • **59**. JR ii p. 1096. See also P. Golden, 'Tusi, the Turkic Name of Joci,' *Acta Orientalia Academiae Scientiarum Hungaricae* 55 (2002) pp. 143-151 • **60**. RT i p. 227 • **61**. Boyle, *Successors* pp. 97-116 (esp. pp. 97-100) • **62**. For general surveys of his character and personality see Pelliot, *Notes sur Marco Polo* i pp. 250-254; Hambis, *Yuan Che* pp. 57-64 • **63**. Abel-Rémusat, *Nouveaux mélanges* pp. 61-63; Pelliot & Hambis, *Campagnes* p. 298 • **64**. JB i p. 40; Boyle, *Successors* pp. 154-155; Ratchnevsky, *Genghis Khan* p. 164 • **65**. JB i p. 41; Grousset, *Empire* pp. 67-71, 228-230, 236-238 • **66**. JR ii pp. 1106-1107, 1110-1111, 1144-1148; RT i p. 44 • **67**. Boyle, *Successors* p. 138 • **68**. RT i p. 77 • **69**. For a complete account of the lineage of the house of Chagatai see Boyle, *Successors* pp. 135-144. For Yesulun, Togen and Mogetugen, ibid. pp. 135-137 • **70**. Grousset, *Empire* p. 256 • **71**. JR ii pp. 1141-1142 • **72**. For Ogodei see, initially, Pelliot, *Notes sur Marco Polo* i pp. 125, 253, 287; Pelliot & Hambis, *Campagnes* pp. 266, 375 and, in much greater detail, Chapter Fourteen below. • **73**. JB ii pp. 552-553; Ratchnevsky, 'La condition de la femme mongole,' loc. cit. pp. 517-518 • **74**. RT i p. • **75**. SHO pp. 205-207; SHR pp. 145-148 • **76**. Rachewiltz, *Commentary* pp. 805-806; Rachewiltz, *In the Service* pp. 76-78 • **77**. RT i p. 147; Boyle, *Successors* p. 98. Ayalon 'Great Yasa' (1971) pp. 152-154) claims that Juvaini overestimated Tolui's importance. • **78**. For Tolui's lineage see Boyle, *Successors*, pp. 159-162 • **79**. ibid. p. 164 • **80**. JR ii p. 1093; Thomas Allsen, 'The Yuan Dynasty and the Uighurs of Turfan,' loc. cit. p. 271 • **81**. For Shigi see Ratchnevsky, 'Sigi-qutuqu, ein mongolischer Gefolgsmann im 12–13 Jahrhundert,' *Central Asiatic Journal* 10 (1965) pp. 87-120; Rachewiltz, *In the Service* pp. 75-94. The foundling story is in JR ii p. 1093 and in F. Aubin, 'Le statut de l'enfant dans la société mongole,' *L'Enfant* 35 (1975) pp. 459-599 (at pp. 471-472) but is adequately rebutted in Rachewiltz, *Commentary* p. 497. • **82**. Harcourt & Evans, *Said Gah-I-Shaukati*; Philott, *Baz-nama-yi Nasiri*;

Argue, *George Turberville*; Latham, *Travels of Marco Polo* p. 144 • **83**. Macdonald, *Falcon* pp. 52-56, 90 • **84**. ibid. p. 59 • **85**. For an exact description and analysis of the swans Genghis's falcons might have killed see Baker, *Game Birds* pp. 20-27; cf also Upton, *Falconry* • **86**. RT i p. 147 • **87**. Rachewiltz, *Commentary* p. 726 • **88**. RT i p. 148; JR ii pp. 1091-1092 • **89**. JR ii p. 1092 • **90**. RT i p. 149 • **91**. JR ii p. 1007; Lech, *Mongolische Weltreich* pp. 98, 201-203; Waley, *Travels of an Alchemist* p. 54 • **92**. The judgement is that of Ratchnevsky, *Genghis Khan* p. 165. For the all-girl orchestra see Vladimirtsov, *Genghis* p. 124 • **93**. Rachewiltz, *Commentary* pp. 726-727 • **94**. SHO pp. 130-131; SHR p. 79 • **95**. Rachewiltz, *Commentary* p. 577 • **96**. RT i pp. 148-149; d'Ohsson, *Histoire* i pp. 418-419 • **97**. See the opposing views in Pelliot & Hambis, *Campagnes* p. 375 and F. Aubin, 'Le statut de l'enfant,' loc. cit. pp. 471-475 • **98**. Pelliot, *Notes critiques d'histoire Kalmouke*, i pp. 61-62; Boyle, *Successors* p. 164; Rachewiltz, *Commentary* pp. 854-856, 914-915 • **99**. Quoted in Zhao, *Marriage* p. 37 • **100**. ibid. pp. 28-29 • **101**. RT i pp. 25-26 • **102**. Zhao, *Marriage* pp. 93-118 (Ongirrad); pp. 119-126 (Ikires); pp. 127-146 (Oyirad); pp. 163-178 (Uighurs). See also Jennifer Holmgren, 'Observations on Marriage and Inheritance Practices in Early Mongol and Yuan Society with Particular Reference to the Levirate,' *Journal of Asian History* 20 (1986) pp. 127-192 • **103**. May, *Culture and Customs* pp. 37-39, 103-115 • **104**. 'A Mongol woman does many things that in other Asiatic socities would be men's work. She does them responsibly and without being told, because in the normal life the men are frequently away from home' (Lattimore, *Mongol Journeys* p. 186). • **105**. Riasanovsky, *Fundamental Principles* p. 242 • **106**. Lane, *Daily Life* pp. 228-229 • **107**. Jackson & Morgan, *Rubruck* p. 74 • **108**. For a full analysis of Borte in this period see Rachewiltz, *Commentary* pp. 350-357 • **109**. d'Ohsson, *Histoire* i p. 329 • **110**. Marsden, *Travels of Marco Polo* pp. 417-419 • **111**. Jennifer Holmgren, 'Observations on Marriage,' loc. cit.; Riasanovsky, *Fundamental Principles* pp. 234-238 • **112**. RT i p. 89 • **113**. Zhao, *Marriage* pp. 18-19 • **114**. Skelton, Marston & Painter, *Vinland Map* • **115**. Riasanovsky, *Fundamental Principles* pp. 241-242 • **116**. Schuyler Cammann, 'Mongol Costume: Historical and Recent,' in Sinor, *Aspects* pp. 157-166; Dawson, *Mongol Mission* pp. 7-8; Jackson & Morgan, *Rubruck* p. 89; Bretschneider, *Mediaeval Researches* i pp. 52-53; Yule, *Cathay* ii p. 222; Waley, *Travels of an Alchemist* p. 67 • **117**. Ratchnevsky, 'La condition de la femme mongole,' loc. cit p. 516 • **118**. Gibb, *Ibn Battuta* ii p. 480; Dunn, *Adventures* pp. 299-300; Hamdun & King, *Ibn Battuta* pp. 38-39. For Christian disapproval see Lisa Balabanlilar, 'The Begims of the Mystic Feast. Turco-Mongol Tradition in the Mughal Harem,' *Journal of Asian Studies* 69 (2010) pp. 123-147 • **119**. Ostrowski, *Muscovy and the Mongols* pp. 73, 81 • **120**. JB ii p. 52; Boyle, *Successors* pp. 159, 168, 197, 199-200; Budge, *Chronography* p. 412; Morris Rossabi, 'Kublai Khan and the Women in his Family,' in Bauer, *Studia Sino-Mongolica* pp. 153-180 (at pp. 158-166); Dawson, *Mongol Mission* p. 26; Jackson & Morgan, *Rubruck* p. 125; Pelliot, 'Le vrai nom de "Seroctan",' *T'oung Pao* 29 (1932) pp. 43-54 • **121**. Ratchnevsky, 'La condition de la femme mongole,' loc. cit. pp. 517-518, 522 • **122**. Zhao, *Marriage* p. 29; Barthold, *Turkestan* pp. 487-491 • **123**. JR ii p. 1144; JB i pp. 245-246; Boyle, *Successors* pp. 176, 242; Budge, *Chronography* p. 412 • **124**. See Lane, *Daily Life* pp. 239-254 for all details on these. Cf also Rossabi, 'Kublai Khan and the Women,' loc. cit; George Qingzhi Zhao & Richard W. L. Grisso, 'Female Anxiety and Female Power: Political Intervention by Mongol Empresses during the Thirteenth and Fourteenth Centuries,' *Toronto Studies in Central Asia* 7 (2005) pp. 17-46; Weatherford, *Secret History of the Mongol Queens*

Chapter 7

1. Rachewiltz, *Commentary* p. 491. For the 1196 campaign see Pelliot & Hambis, *Campagnes* pp. 199-203 • **2**. See Lewis, *China's Cosmopolitan Empire* • **3**. Brook, *Troubled Empire* pp. 26, 65, 80, 82, 260 • **4**. 'The conquest of China was not a primary goal of the Mongols but, ironically, simply a consequence of their having completely destroyed the Jurchen Chin regime which they had planned to extort' (Barfield, *Perilous Frontier* p. 197). • **5**. Lattimore, 'The Geography of Chingis Khan,' *Geographical Journal* 129 (1963) pp. 1-7; S. Bira, 'The Mongolian Conception of Chinggis Khan: Historic and Mythical Hero,' *Mongolica* 3 (1992) pp. 32-47 • **6**. Barfield, *Perilous Frontier* pp. 49-51, 91-94, 150-151 • **7**. Larry V. Clark, 'The Theme of Revenge,' in Clark & Draghi, *Aspects* ii pp. 37-57; Lien-sheng Yang, 'Hostages in Chinese History,' in Yang, *Studies* pp. 43-57 • **8**. SHC p. 186 • **9**. Joseph Fletcher, 'The Mongols: Ecological and Social Perspectives,' *Harvard Journal of Asiatic Studies* 46 (1986) pp. 11-50 (at pp. 32-33); Grenard, *Genghis* pp. 111-112; H. Franke, *From Tribal Chieftain* pp. 17-18; Sechin Jachid, 'Traditional Mongol Attitudes and Values as Seen in the *Secret History of the Mongols* and the *Altan Tobchi*,' in Jagchid, *Essays* pp. 51-66 • **10**. Barthold, *Turkestan* pp. 393-396; Vladimirtsov, *Genghis* pp. 76-77 • **11**. Fletcher, 'The Mongols,' loc. cit. pp. 32-33; Barfield, 'Inner Asia and the Cycles of Power in China's Imperial History,' in Seaman and Marks, *Rulers from the Steppe* pp. 21-62 (at p. 25) • **12**. J. P. Marques, 'Sur la nature du nomadisme des steppes eurasiatiques,' *L'Homme* 108 (1988) pp. 84-98 • **13**. Denis Sinor, 'The Greed of the Northern Barbarians,' in Clark & Draghi, *Aspects* pp. 171-182 • **14**. Gumilev, *Imaginary Kingdom* p. 177 • **15**. Khazanov, *Nomads and the Outside World* pp. 235-236; Khazanov, 'Ecological Limitations of Nomadism in the Eurasian Steppes and their Social and Cultural Implications,' *Asian and African Studies* 24 (1990) pp. 1-15 • **16**. Fletcher, 'The Mongols,' loc. cit. p. 15 • **17**. Barfield, *Perilous Frontier* pp. 164-186 • **18**. Using the famous bifurcation suggested by

Claude Lévi-Strauss, one scholar has differentiated between the 'raw' barbarians of Outer Mongolia and the 'cooked' tribes within the shadow of the Great Wall (Magnus Fiskesjo, 'On the "Raw" and "Cooked" Barbarians of Imperial China,' *Inner Asia* 1 (1999) pp. 139-168). • **19.** Paul D. Buell, 'The Role of the Sino-Mongolian Frontier Zone in the Rise of Chingis Qan,' in Schwarz, *Studies on Mongolia* pp. 63-76 (esp. pp. 63-68) • **20.** For the pre-Liao history of the Khitans see Xu, *Historical Development*, esp. pp. 237-258; Herbert Franke, 'The Forest Peoples of Manchuria: Khitans and Jurchens,' in Sinor, *Cambridge History* pp. 400-423; Barfield, *Perilous Frontier* pp. 168-173 • **21.** For the emperors who succeeded A-Pao-Chi, of whom the most distinguished and long-lived was Sheng-Tsun (982–1031) see Franke & Twitchett, *Cambridge History* pp. 56-123; Moule, *Rulers of China* pp. 91-95 • **22.** For the foundation of the Tangut state see Dunnell, *Great State* p. 3 • **23.** Pelliot, *Notes sur Marco Polo* i pp. 216-229; Barfield, *Perilous Frontier* p. 174 • **24.** Tao, *Two Sons* passim; Di Cosmo & Wyatt, *Political Frontiers* pp. 192-219; Standen & Powers, *Frontiers in Question* • **25.** Wittfogel & Feng, *Liao* p. 554 • **26.** Gernet, *Chinese Civilization* p. 354 • **27.** Mote, *Imperial China* pp. 200-202 • **28.** Pelliot, *Notes sur Marco Polo* i pp. 376-390; P. Huang, 'New Light on the Origin of the Manchus,' *Harvard Journal of Asiatic Studies* 50 (1990) pp. 239-282 • **29.** Tao, *Jurchen* pp. 21-22 • **30.** Barfield, *Perilous Frontier* p. 179 • **31.** ibid. • **32.** Respectively, Barfield, ibid. p. 179 and Mote, *Imperial China* p. 211. Nevertheless, one can argue that the Liao must have ignored many warning signs. Their armies had been heavily defeated by the Jurchens in 1026 when they had provoked the tribes of Manchuria by a plundering raid (Wittfogel & Feng, *Liao* p. 588). • **33.** Mote, *Imperial China* pp. 195-197 • **34.** ibid. pp. 203-214; Grousset, *Empire* p. 137 • **35.** Franke & Twitchett, *Cambridge History* p. 279; Mote, *Imperial China* pp. 223-224 • **36.** Sechin Jagchid, 'Khitan Struggles against Jurchen Oppression: Nomadization versus Sinicization,' *Zentralasiatische Studien* 16 (1982) pp. 165-185 • **37.** Wittfogel & Feng, *Liao* p. 634 • **38.** The zigzag course in and out of sinicisation pursued by the Jin is traced in Mote, *Imperial China* pp. 226-243; Hok Lam Chan, *Legitimation in Imperial China. Discussions under the Jurchen-Chin dynasty, 1115-1234* (1984) pp. 55-72, 116. See also Jung-Chen Tao, *Jurchen in Twelfth-Century China* • **39.** Franke & Twitchett, *Cambridge History* pp. 315-319; Tao, *Jurchen* pp. 41-44 • **40.** Mote, *Imperial China* p. 237 • **41.** Franke & Twitchett, *Cambridge History* pp. 205-206 • **42.** Sechin Jagchid, 'Patterns of Trade and Conflict between China and the Nomads of Mongolia,' in Jagchid, *Essays* pp. 3-20; Jagchid & Symons, *Peace, War and Trade* • **43.** Sechin Jagchid, 'The Historical Interaction between Nomadic People in Mongolia and the Sedentary Chinese,' in Seaman & Marks, *Rulers from the Steppe* pp. 63-91 • **44.** For the Jin–Song wars see Lorge, *War, Politics and Society* pp. 53-56; Mote, *Imperial China* pp. 207-209, 299-304; Franke & Twitchett, *Cambridge History* pp. 235-249

• **45**. Mote, *Imperial China* pp. 287, 394 • **46**. Chou, *Economic History* pp. 102-104. For the world systems approach see McNeill, *In Pursuit of Power* • **47**. Tao, *Jurchen* pp. 108-109 • **48**. Mote, *Imperial China* p. 266. The entire subject of the population of medieval China is, not surprisingly, disputed territory. Martin, *Rise of Chingis Khan* p. 125 gives a a figure of 48,490,000 for the Jin but argues that the population must have been much larger, as the census figures do not include the very poor or the many tax evaders. • **49**. Franke & Twitchett, *Cambridge History* pp. 302, 313-315 • **50**. ibid. p. 302 • **51**. Tao, *Jurchen* pp. 90-91 • **52**. Wittfogel & Feng, *Liao* pp. 553, 669 • **53**. Franke & Twitchett, *Cambridge History* pp. 294-298 • **54**. Needham, *Science and Civilization* i p. 68 • **55**. Tregear, *Geography of China* pp. 218-219 • **56**. Elvin & Cuirong, *Sediments of Time* pp. 554-560; Lorge, *War, Politics and Society* p. 147 • **57**. Grousset, *Rise and Splendour* p. 303; Martin, *Rise of Chingis* pp. 125-126 • **58**. Franke & Twitchett, *Cambridge History* pp. 245-249 • **59**. Brook, *Troubled Empire* pp. 26, 65, 80, 82, 260 • **60**. Franke & Twitchett, *Cambridge History* pp. 245-249 • **61**. Buell, *Dictionary* pp. 24, 172-175 • **62**. Rachewiltz, *In the Service* p. 113 • **63**. Ratchnevsky, *Genghis Khan* pp. 106, 250-251 • **64**. Rachewiltz, 'Personnel and Personalities in North China in the Early Mongol Period,' *Journal of the Economic and Social History of the Orient* 9 (1966) pp. 88-144 (at p. 98) • **65**. Lattimore, *Mongol Journeys* pp. 128-129 • **66**. Pelliot, 'Chrétiens d'Asie centrale et d'Extrême-Orient,' *T'oung Pao* 15 (1914) pp. 623-644 (at p. 631); Halbertsma, *Early Christian Remains* pp. 150-157 • **67**. Pelliot & Hambis, *Campagnes* pp. 181-182 • **68**. Martin, *Rise of Chingis* pp. 114-115 • **69**. d'Ohsson, *Histoire* i p. 122 • **70**. Martin, *Rise* pp. 120-121 • **71**. Lattimore, 'The Geography of Genghis Khan,' *Geographical Journal* 129 (1963) pp. 1-7 • **72**. Mote, *Imperial China* pp. 284-288 • **73**. Bartold, *Turkestan* pp. 393-396; Vladimirtsov, *Genghis* pp. 76-77 • **74**. Thomas Allsen, 'The Yuan Dynasty and the Uighurs of Turfan,' loc. cit. pp. 243-280 • **75**. H. D. Martin, 'Chingis Khan's First Invasion of the Chin Empire,' *Journal of the Royal Asiatic Society* (1943) pp. 182-216 (esp. pp. 190-192) • **76**. Lattimore, *Mongol Journeys* p. 126 • **77**. ibid. • **78**. On this point Genghis has at least one modern supporter. Gumilev, *Imaginary Kingdom* (p. 175) compares the genocide attempted by the Jin in those years to the slaughter of Indians by the Puritans of New England in the seventeenth century and of the Patagonian Indians by the Argentine government in the late nineteenth. • **79**. Martin, *Rise* pp. 101, 149 • **80**. d'Ohsson, *Histoire* i p. 128 • **81**. JR ii p. 954 • **82**. Gaubil, *Gentchiscan* p. 16 • **83**. Mongol numbers are always disputed. The population of medieval Mongolia has been estimated as anything from 700,000 to two million (I incline to the latter figure). If we assume a rough-and-ready one-in-ten figure for military mobilisation that would provide purely Mongol armies of between 70,000 and 200,000. • **84**. For a modern analysis of the resources of the Gobi see Hedley, *Tramps* pp. 92, 239 • **85**.

Rachewiltz, *In the Service* pp. 3-4 • **86**. Pelliot, 'Chrétiens d'Asie centrale,' loc. cit. pp. 623-624; Saeki, *Nestorian Documents* pp. 423-427; d'Ohsson, *Histoire* i p. 129 • **87**. Martin, *Rise* p. 133 • **88**. For the geography of this area see Lattimore, *Inner Asian Frontiers* pp. 21-25 • **89**. Van Oost, *Au pays des Ortos* • **90**. Arthur Waldron, 'The Problem of the Great Wall of China,' *Harvard Journal of Asiatic Studies* 43 (1983) pp. 643-663; Buell, *Dictionary* p. 171; Herrmann, *Historical Atlas* p. 39; Haw, *Marco Polo's China* pp. 52-54; Pletcher, *Geography of China* p. 95; Waldron, *Great Wall*; Lovell, *Great Wall*; Rojas, *Great Wall*; Man, *Great Wall* • **91**. Martin, *Rise* p. 134 • **92**. Lattimore, *Inner Asian Frontiers* pp. 543-546 • **93**. Martin, *Rise* pp. 133-134 • **94**. ibid. pp. 135-136 • **95**. Rachewiltz, *Commentary* p. 890 • **96**. Wittfogel & Feng, *Liao* p. 521 • **97**. RT i pp. 216-217 • **98**. Rachewiltz, *In the Service* p. 4 • **99**. JR ii pp. 956-957 • **100**. Krause, *Cingis Han* p. 30 • **101**. Martin, *Rise* pp. 141-142, 336-337 • **102**. Waley, *Travels of an Alchemist* pp. 62-63 • **103**. RT i p. 217 • **104**. Martin, *Rise* pp. 142-143; d'Ohsson, *Histoire* i p. 131 • **105**. Rachewiltz, *Commentary* p. 891 • **106**. SHO p. 234; SHR p. 175; Martin, *Rise* p. 143 • **107**. May, *Mongol Conquests* p. 225. For the similarity (but not identity) of these Chinese horses to the Mongol ones see Hyland, *Medieval Warhorse* pp. 126-127; Herrlee G. Creel, 'The Role of the Horse in Chinese History,' *American Historical Review* 70 (1965) pp. 647-662; S. Jagchid & C. R. Bawden, 'Some Notes on the Horse Policy of the Yuan Dynasty,' *Central Asiatic Journal* 10 (1965) pp. 246-268 • **108**. Martin, *Rise* p. 144 • **109**. Harlez, *Histoire de l'empire de Kin* pp. 208-209 • **110**. Olbricht & Pinks, *Meng-ta pei-lu* p. 61 • **111**. ibid. pp. 58, 187 • **112**. For Subedei's exploits in 1211-12 see Gabriel, *Subotai* p. 17 • **113**. Grousset, *Empire* pp. 228-229 • **114**. RT i pp. 215-216 • **115**. Krause, *Cingis Han* p. 74 • **116**. SHO p. 234; SHR p. 175 • **117**. Martin, *Rise* pp. 146-147 • **118**. There are good descriptions of the geography of Shaanxi in Millward, *Beyond the Pass*. • **119**. Martin, *Rise* pp. 149-150 • **120**. ibid. p. 150 • **121**. Buell, *Dictionary* pp. 28-29, 289 • **122**. Mark C. Elliott, 'The Limits of Tartary: Manchuria in Imperial and National Geographies,' *Journal of Asian Studies* 59 (2000) pp. 603-646; Parker, *A Thousand Years* pp. 249-250 • **123**. Carl Sverdrup, 'Numbers in Mongol Warfare,' *Journal of Medieval History* 8 (2010) pp. 109-117 (at pp. 115-116) • **124**. Lattimore, *Inner Asian Frontiers* p. 113 • **125**. Krause, *Cingis Han* pp. 30-31; Martin, *Rise* pp. 197-198 • **126**. JR ii p. 958: Bretschneider, *Mediaeval Researches*, i p. 125; Gaubil, *Gentchiscan* p. 37 • **127**. JR ii p. 958 • **128**. d'Ohsson, *Histoire*, i p. 133 • **129**. Krause, *Cingis Han* pp. 30-31 • **130**. Martin, *Rise* p. 157 • **131**. JR ii p. 958; Martin, *Rise* p. 159 • **132**. Martin, *Rise* p. 160 • **133**. d'Ohsson, *Histoire* i p. 140 • **134**. Françoise Aubin, 'The Rebirth of Chinese Rule in Times of Trouble,' in Schram, *Foundations and Limitations* pp. 113-146 (at p. 134) • **135**. Mote, *Imperial China* p. 244 • **136**. Martin, *Rise* pp. 160-161 • **137**. d'Ohsson, *Histoire* i p. 137 • **138**. Martin, *Rise* pp. 162-163 • **139**. ibid. • **140**. Krause, *Cingis Han* pp. 30-32; Boyle, *Successors* pp. 145-146, 165 • **141**. d'Ohsson, *Histoire* i pp. 140-141 • **142**. Du Halde, *Description* iv pp. 15-16; Edmonds, *Northern Frontiers* pp. 115-117 • **143**. Krause, *Cingis Han* pp. 32, 78 • **144**. Pelliot, *Notes sur Marco Polo* i pp. 8-9; Boyle, *Successors* p. 65 • **145**. Gibert, *Dictionnaire historique* pp. 668-669 • **146**. Judges 15: 4 • **147**. Gibert, *Dictionnaire historique* p. 481 • **148**. Krause, *Cingis Han* pp. 32, 78 • **149**. Cheng-Ching no longer exists as a city but seems to have been in the vicinity of modern Jinan – for which see Elvin & Skinner, *Chinese City* pp. 171-172. • **150**. RT i p. 219; Pelliot, *Notes sur Marco Polo* i p. 7. For more detailed studies of the campaign of the princes see ibid. i pp. 803, 842; ii p. 736; Boyle, *Successors* pp. 145-146 • **151**. Krause, *Cingis Han* p. 72 • **152**. Martin, *Rise* p. 165 • **153**. d'Ohsson, *Histoire* i pp. 140-141 • **154**. Ramsey, *Languages of China* pp. 19-26; Lee, *Warp and Weft* pp. 39-40 • **155**. Herbert Franke, 'Siege and Defense of Towns in Medieval China,' in Kiernan & Fairbank, *Chinese Ways in Warfare* pp. 159-195; Sen Dou Chang, 'The Morphology of Walled Capitals,' in Skinner, *City in Late Imperial China* pp. 75-100 • **156**. Pelliot, *Notes sur Marco Polo* ii pp. 802, 842 • **157**. Martin, *Rise* p. 166 • **158**. For fuller details of Genghis's great sweep see RT i pp. 218-219; Krause, *Cingis Han* pp. 31, 35, 71, 74, 75; Pelliot, *Notes sur Marco Polo* ii p. 736; d'Ohsson, *Histoire* i pp. 141-142 • **159**. Hildinger, *Warriors of the Steppe* p. 124. See also Giles, *Chinese Biographical Dictionary* • **160**. Janhunen, *Manchuria* pp. 3-8; Edmonds, *Northern Frontiers of Qing China* op. cit. pp. 138-140 • **161**. Lattimore, *Mongols of Manchuria* pp. 44-46 • **162**. d'Ohsson, *Histoire* i p. 159 • **163**. Gibert, *Dictionnaire historique* p. 481; Lattimore, *Mongols of Manchuria* p. 193 • **164**. Abel-Rémusat, *Nouveaux mélanges* ii p. 64 • **165**. d'Ohsson, *Histoire* i p. 142 • **166**. Martin, *Rise* p. 169 • **167**. ibid p. 170 • **168**. Franke, *Geschichte* iv p. 272; Franke & Twitchett, *Cambridge History* pp. 250-267 • **169**. SHO p. 236; SHR pp. 176-177; Krause, *Cingis Han* pp. 32-33 • **170**. Elisabetta Chiodo, 'Praising Činggis Qayan and His Campaigns,' *Ural-Altaische Jahrbücher* 17 (2002) pp. 189-233

Chapter 8

1. Pelliot, *Notes sur Marco Polo* ii p. 789 • **2**. RT ii p. 222 • **3**. d'Ohsson, *Histoire* i pp. 143-144 • **4**. Needham, *Science and Civilization* op. cit. i p. 68 • **5**. Krause, *Cingis Han* p. 33 • **6**. Rachewiltz, 'Muqali, Bol, Tas and An-t'ung,' *Papers in Far Eastern History* 15 (1977) pp. 45-62 (at p. 49) • **7**. Franke & Twitchett, *Cambridge History* p. 258 • **8**. Martin, *Rise* p. 169 • **9**. Ratchnevsky, *Genghis Khan* pp. 113-115; Susan Naquin, *Peking* • **10**. Li, Dray-Novey & Kong, *Beijing* p. 13; Phillips, *Mongols* p. 56. Han, *Population and Geography of Beijing* scales these figures down considerably. • **11**. Gabriel, *Great Armies* p. 38; McGraw, *Encyclopedia* pp. 103-104 • **12**. Bethan V. Purse et al, 'Climate Change and the Recent Emergence of Bluetongue in Europe,' *Nature Reviews Microbiology* 3

(2005) pp. 171-181; Mellor et al, *Bluetongue*; Robertson, *Handbook of Animal Diseases* • **13**. Anastasius van den Wyngaert, 'Itinera et Relationes Fratrum Minorum saeculi XIII et XIV,' *Sinica Franciscana* i (1929) pp. 47-48, 56; Rockhill, *William of Rubruck* p. 64; Matthew Paris, *Chronica Majora* iv p. 386; Robert des Rotours, 'Quelques notes sur l'anthropophagie en Chine,' *T'oung Pao* 1963 pp. 386-427; Risch, *Geschichte der Mongolen*; Wittfogel & Feng, *Liao* p. 425 • **14**. RT i p. 223 • **15**. Krause, *Cingis Han* p. 33 • **16**. d'Ohsson, *Histoire* i pp. 146-147 • **17**. Martin, *Rise* p. 177 • **18**. Krause, *Cingis Han* p. 34; Hambis, *Genghis* p. 103 • **19**. Chase, *Firearms* p. 58; Jaques, *Battles and Sieges* i p. 123; Walter J. Fabrychy & Paul E. Jorgesen, *Operations Economy* p. 254; Lissner, *Living Past* p. 193 • **20**. Martin, *Rise* p. 178 • **21**. JR ii p. 965 • **22**. Barthold, *Turkestan* pp. 393-394. See also Boyle, *Cambridge History of Iran* v pp. 303-304 • **23**. Ping-ti Ho, 'An Estimate of the Total Population of Sung-Chin China,' *Études Song* i (1970) pp. 32-53; Franke & Twitchett, *Cambridge History* p. 622; Koln, *Dictionary of Wars* p. 206 • **24**. Needham, *Science and Civilization* i p. 139 • **25**. ibid. iv part 3 pp. 269-272, 307-309, 313, 350-352 • **26**. Gernet, *Daily Life* p. 15; Abu-Lughod, *Before European Hegemony* p. 337 • **27**. Temple, *Genius of China* pp. 218-219 • **28**. Brook, *Confusions of Pleasure* pp. 46-49 • **29**. Krause, *Cingis Han* pp. 34-35 • **30**. Waley, *Travels of an Alchemist* pp. 33-34 • **31**. JR ii p. 954 • **32**. Abel-Rémusat, *Nouveaux mélanges* ii p. 64 • **33**. RT i p. 224; SHO pp. 239-240; SHR pp. 179-180; d'Ohsson, *Histoire* i p. 148; Rachewiltz, *In the Service* pp. 80-82; Ratchnevsky, 'Sigi Qutuqu, ein mongolischer Gefolgsmann im 12–13 Jahrhundert,' *Central Asiatic Journal* 10 (1965) pp. 87-120 (at pp. 98-103); Buell, *Dictionary* pp. 243-244 • **34**. Lee, *Economic History* pp. 325-326 • **35**. This became the jacquerie of the Red Coats or Red Jackets, sometimes hailed as primitive rebels or the first of the peasant revolutionaries – though most sober historians think this anachronistic and assert that the Red Coats were simply bands of *condottieri*. Françoise Aubin, 'The Rebirth of Chinese Rule in Times of Trouble: China in the Early Thirteenth Century,' in Schram, *Foundations and Limits* pp. 113-146 • **36**. Martin, *Rise* p. 181. The *Secret History* becomes very confused at this point, as it has 'Red Caps' fighting *for* the Jin (SHO p. 238; SHR pp. 178-179). The Jin actually used a force known as the 'Multicoloured Caps' as an anti-Red Cap force (Rachewiltz, *Commentary* pp. 912-913). • **37**. Vernadsky, *Mongols and Russia* pp. 33-34 • **38**. Martin, *Rise* p. 182 • **39**. ibid. p. 187 • **40**. ibid p. 184 • **41**. This was an almost exact repeat of the rout they had suffered here under the Prince of Hailing in 1161 (Ruth Mostern, 'From Battlefields to Counties: War, Border and State Power in Southern Song Huainan,' in Wyatt, *Battlefields* pp. 227-252 (at p. 241); Needham, *Science and Civilization* i p. 134; Tilman & West, *China under Jurchen Rule* p. 29). • **42**. Martin, *Rise* p. 185 • **43**. ibid. • **44**. Lary, *Chinese Migration* p. 49 • **45**. Henthorn, *Korea* p. 5 • **46**. Gaubil, *Gentchiscan* p. 26 • **47**. Martin, *Rise* p. 202 • **48**. ibid. • **49**. ibid. p. 203 • **50**.

Parker, *Thousand Years* pp. 249-250 • **51**. Ratchnevsky, *Genghis Khan* pp. 114-115 • **52**. For Muqali's intelligence see Buell, *Dictionary* pp. 199, 261; Grousset, *Empire* p. 206 • **53**. Martin, *Rise* p. 211 • **54**. ibid. pp. 211-213 • **55**. Krause, *Cingis Han* pp. 34-35 • **56**. RT i p. 246 • **57**. Martin, *Rise* p. 214 • **58**. ibid. p. 215 • **59**. Henthorne, *Korea* p. 6 • **60**. His relationship with the Mongols was singular. In 1217, when Muqali was elsewhere, he revolted again and fled to an island when the Mongols invaded the Liao valley and Liaodong. He then moved to the Tumen River basin to avoid both Jin and Mongols and set himself up as a petty princeling of a domain he called Dongxia. Once established, he resubmitted to the Mongols, and provided them with invaluable information about the internal affairs of Korea (Franke & Twitchett, *Cambridge History* pp. 258-259). • **61**. RT i pp. 98-99; SHO p. 239; SHR pp. 178-179 • **62**. Hartog, *Genghis* p. 71 • **63**. Lattimore, *Inner Asian Frontiers* pp. 21-25 • **64**. Erdmann, *Temudschin* p. 328; Buell, *Dictionary* p. 236 • **65**. Krause, *Cingis Han* p. 86 • **66**. RT i p. 225 • **67**. Olbricht & Pinks, *Meng-ta pei-lu* p. 187 • **68**. Martin, *Rise* p. 189 • **69**. ibid. p. 190 • **70**. ibid. p. 191 • **71**. ibid. • **72**. Franke, *Geschichte* iv pp. 266-274 • **73**. d'Ohsson, *Histoire* i pp. 161-162 • **74**. Vladimirtsov, *Genghis* pp. 78-83 • **75**. Rachewiltz, *In the Service* pp. 116-117 • **76**. Dunnell, *Great State* p. xxv; Asimov & Bosworth, *History of Civilizations* iv part i pp. 191-214 • **77**. Rachewiltz, *In the Service* p. 6 • **78**. Rachewiltz, 'Muqali, Bol, Tas and An-t'ung,' loc. cit. p. 50 • **79**. Martin, *Rise* p. 244 • **80**. Robinson, *Empire's Twilight* p. 302; d'Ohsson, *Histoire* i p. 357; Franke & Twitchett, *Cambridge History* p. 358 • **81**. d'Ohsson, *Histoire* i pp. 358-359; Rachewiltz, *In the Service* p. 47; Lien-Sheng Yang, 'Hostages in Chinese History,' *Harvard Journal of Asiatic Studies* 15 (1952) pp. 507-521 • **82**. Rachewiltz, *In the Service* pp. 48-49. The duel recalls that between the Prince de Condé and the Vicomte de Turenne in the seventeenth century. • **83**. Franke & Twitchett, *Cambridge History* p. 358 • **84**. Martin, *Rise* pp. 250-251 • **85**. RT i p. 227 • **86**. Allsen, *Commodity and Exchange* pp. 76-78 • **87**. Robinson, *Empire's Twilight* pp. 308-309 • **88**. Rachewiltz, 'Personnel and Personalities in North China in the Early Mongol Period,' *Journal of the Economic and Social History of the Orient* 9 (1996) pp. 88-144 (esp. pp. 128-132) • **89**. Tao-chung Yao, 'Chi'u Ch'u-chi and Chinggis Khan,' *Harvard Journal of Asiatic Studies* 46 (1986) pp. 201-219 • **90**. Franke & Twichett, *Cambridge History* p. 362; Pelliot & Hambis, *Campagnes* pp. 360-372 • **91**. Henthorn, *Korea* pp. 5-6, 22; Michael C. Rogers, 'Koryo's Military Dictatorship and its relationship with Kin,' *T'oung Pao* 47 (1949) pp. 43-62 • **92**. Michael C. Rogers, 'Factionalism and Koryo Policy under the Northern Song,' *Journal of the American Oriental Society* 79 pp. 16-25 • **93**. Lee, *New History* pp. 343-350 • **94**. Henthorn, *Korea* pp. 18-22 • **95**. Robinson, *Empire's Twilight* pp. 7-9, 57 • **96**. ibid. pp. 53, 265 • **97**. Pelliot, *Notes sur Marco Polo* i p. 307; Gari Ledyard, 'Yin and Yang in the China-Manchuria-Korea Triangle,' in Rossabi, *China among*

Equals pp. 313-353; Ledyard, *Early Koryo–Mongol Relations* • **98**. Henthorn, *Korea* pp. 27-29; Gari Ledyard, 'The Mongol Campaigns in Korea and the Dating of the *Secret History of the Mongols*,' *Central Asiatic Journal* 9 (1964) pp. 1-22; Atwood, *Encyclopedia* p. 319 • **99**. Charles A. Peterson, 'Old Illusions and New Realities: Sung Foreign Policy, 1217–1234,' in Rossabi, *China among Equals* pp. 204-239 • **100**. ibid. p. 205. For the disasters of 1206–1208 and the Sung war with the Jin see Hana, *Der Stadt Té-an* pp. 21-65 • **101**. Needham, *Science and Civilization* i pp. 134-139; Gernet, *Daily Life* pp. 17-18; Twitchett, *Printing and Publishing* • **102**. Yuan-kang Wang, 'Explaining the Tribute System: Power, Confucianism and War in Medieval East Asia,' *Journal of East Asian Studies* 13 (2013) pp. 207-232 • **103**. Françoise Aubin, 'Li Chi'an,' in Franke, *Sung Biographies* ii pp. 542-546 • **104**. Waley, *Travels of an Alchemist* p. 48; Franke & Twitchett, *Cambridge History* p. 359 • **105**. Martin, *Rise* pp. 258-259 • **106**. d'Ohsson, *Histoire* i p. 363 • **107**. Krause, *Cingis Han* pp. 35-36 • **108**. Rachewiltz, *In the Service* pp. 62-64 • **109**. d'Ohsson, *Histoire* i pp. 360-361 • **110**. Rachewiltz, 'Muqali, Bol,' loc. cit. pp. 51-52 • **111**. Bretschneider, *Mediaeval Researches* i pp. 25-34; Krause, *Cingis Han* p. 37 • **112**. Riasanovsky, *Fundamental Principles* p. 89 • **113**. ibid. pp. 89-90 • **114**. Franke & Twitchett, *Cambridge History* p. 359; Martin, *Rise* pp. 264-265 • **115**. Pelliot, 'Notes sur le "Turkestan",' loc. cit. pp. 13-14 • **116**. Grousset, *Conquérant* p. 348 • **117**. Peterson, 'Old Illusions,' loc. cit. pp. 208, 210 • **118**. For Chao Fang see Franke, *Geschichte* iv p. 273; Franke, *Sung Biographies* i pp. 54-56 • **119**. Charles A. Peterson, 'First Sung Reactions to the Mongol Invasions of the North, 1211–1217,' in Haeger, *Crisis and Prosperity* pp. 215-252 (at pp. 247-248) • **120**. Peterson, 'Old Illusions,' loc. cit. pp. 213-214, 219-220 • **121**. Lo, *Yeh Shih* pp. 105-107; Peterson, 'Old Illusions,' pp. 215-217 • **122**. Herbert Franke, 'Sung Embassies: Some General Observations,' in Rossabi, *China among Equals* pp. 116-137 (at p. 136) • **123**. ibid. • **124**. Rachewiltz, 'Muqali, Bol,' loc. cit. pp. 52-53 • **125**. Martin, *Rise* pp. 264-265 • **126**. ibid. pp. 265-266 • **127**. d'Ohsson, *Histoire* i p. 365 • **128**. Martin, *Rise* p. 267 • **129**. ibid p. 269 • **130**. RT ii p. 299 • **131**. Krause, *Cingis Han* p. 38; d'Ohsson, *Histoire* i p. 366 • **132**. Martin, *Rise* p. 270 • **133**. ibid. p. 271 • **134**. Franke & Twitchett, *Cambridge History* p. 360 • **135**. Martin, *Rise* p. 272 • **136**. Krause, *Cingis Han* p. 38 • **137**. Rachewiltz, 'Muqali, Bol,' loc. cit. p. 54; Pelliot & Hambis, *Campagnes* p. 371 • **138**. Peterson, 'Old Illusions,' loc. cit. p. 209 • **139**. Goodrich, *Short History* p. 173 • **140**. Luc Kwanten, 'The Career of Muqali: A Reassessment,' *Bulletin of Sung and Yuan Studies* 14 (1973) pp. 31-38. The only distant comparison – though they do not rate so highly – are the American Civil War trio of Grant, Sherman and Sheridan. • **141**. Henthorn, *Korea* pp. ix, 27-29, 195 • **142**. Martin, *Rise* p. 276 • **143**. Rachewiltz, *In the Service* p. 64 • **144**. ibid. • **145**. Franke & Twitchett, *Cambridge History* p. 360 • **146**. Rachewiltz, *In the Service* p. 64 • **147**. ibid p. 29 • **148**. Martin, *Rise* p. 277 • **149**. ibid. pp. 278-279 • **150**.

ibid. p. 280 • **151**. ibid. pp. 280-281 • **152**. Chi, *Key Economic Areas* pp. 106-107, 140 • **153**. Franke, *Geschichte* iv p. 285 • **154**. Peterson, 'Old Illusions,' loc. cit. p. 221 • **155**. Saunders, *Mongol Conquests* pp. 196-202 • **156**. Pletcher, *History of China* pp. 172-173 • **157**. Needham, *Science and Civilization* v part 6 p. 135. For a detailed discussion see Payne-Gallwey, *Crossbow* • **158**. For the Khitan influence see P. Buell, 'Sino-Khitan Administration in Mongol Bukhara,' *Journal of Asian History* 13 (1979) pp. 121-151; Silverstein, *Postal Systems* p. 142

Chapter 9

1. Hardy's poem of course refers to the fated collision of the *Titanic* and the iceberg. It was the collision of Khwarezmia and Qara Khitai that introduced Fate in the shape of Genghis and, as such, can be seen to have the same kind of inevitability. • **2**. Wittfogel & Feng, *Liao* • **3**. For a full account of the career of Yelu Dashi see Biran, *Qara Khitai* pp. 19-40 • **4**. Denis Sinor, 'The Khitans and the Kara Khitans,' in Asimov & Bosworth, *History of Civilizations* iv part 1 pp. 227-242 (at p. 235) • **5**. Biran, *Qara Khitai* pp. 103, 107-108 • **6**. RT i pp. 228-231; JB i pp. 62-64 • **7**. JB i p. 64; ii pp. 351, 394, 396 • **8**. JB ii pp. 360-361 • **9**. Barthold, *Turkestan* p. 367 • **10**. Wittfogel & Feng, *Liao* p. 668 • **11**. ibid. p. 652; Barthold, *Turkestan* pp. 358, 362, 367 • **12**. JB i pp. 346, 349, 359-360 • **13**. Biran, *Qara Khitai* p. 78 • **14**. JB i pp. 361, 395; Barthold, *Turkestan* pp. 365-366; Barthold, *Histoire des turcs* pp. 109-111 • **15**. Sinor, 'Western Information on the Khitans and Some Related Questions,' *Journal of the American Oriental Society* 115 (1995) pp. 262-269 • **16**. Waley, *Travels of an Alchemist* pp. 88-89 • **17**. Barthold, *Turkestan* pp. 382-384 • **18**. JB ii p. 395; Asimov & Bosworth, *History of Civilizations* iv part 1 pp. 134-136; Barthold, *Turkestan* pp. 365-366 • **19**. Christian, *History of Russia* i p. 379 • **20**. Barthold, *Four Studies* i p. 395; Barthold, *Turkestan* p. 364; Hartmann, *An-Nasir li-Din Allah* p. 80 • **21**. Herodotus (1.203) knew that the Caspian was an inland sea but the contrary views of Pliny the Elder, *Natural History* (6.15.36-37) and Strabo, *Geography* (2.5.14) proved tenacious. For the Caspian in the Mongol era see Pelliot, *Notes sur Marco Polo* i pp. 61-62; Pelliot, *Recherches* pp. 104-106 • **22**. JB i p. 65 • **23**. Wittfogel & Feng, *Liao* p. 653 • **24**. Barthold, *Turkestan* pp. 363, 366, 368 • **25**. JB i pp. 65-68, 70-73, 75; Biran, *Qara Khitai* pp. 180-191, 194-196 • **26**. JB i pp. 65, 75 • **27**. JB ii p. 396 • **28**. Biran, *Qara Khitai* pp. 81-82 • **29**. For this part of Muhammad's career see Barthold, *Turkestan* pp. 322-351; cf also Grousset, *Empire* p. 169 • **30**. Biran, *Qara Khitai* p. 65 • **31**. Barthold, *Turkestan* p. 401 • **32**. JB i pp. 75-76 • **33**. Biran, *Qara Khitai* p. 83; *Turkestan* p. 402; Pelliot, 'Notes sur le "Turkestan",' loc. cit. p. 55 • **34**. Biran, *Qara Khitai* pp. 80-81 • **35**. Thomas T. Allsen, '"Ever Closer Encounters": The Appropriation of Culture and the Apportionment of Peoples in the Mongol Empire,' *Journal* *of Early Modern History* 1 (1997) pp. 2-25; Peter B. Golden, "'I Will Give the People Unto Thee": The Chingissid Conquests and their Aftermath in the Turkic World,' *Journal of the Royal Asiatic Society*, 3rd series 10 (2000) pp. 21-41; Bretschneider, *Mediaeval Researches* i p. 298 • **36.** JB i pp. 67-68 • **37.** Bretschneider, *Mediaeval Researches* i p. 233; d'Ohsson, *Histoire* i p. 172; Spuler, *Muslim World* ii p. 89 • **38.** Bretschneider, *Mediaeval Researches* i pp. 301-304; ii pp. 39-41, 68-73; Pelliot & Hambis, *Campagnes* pp. 109-116 • **39.** JB p. 67; Biran, *Qara Khitai* pp. 195-196 • **40.** SHO p. 221; SHR p. 163; Rachewiltz, *Commentary* p. 845. Other locations through which Jebe passed, according to Chinese sources, were T'ien Shan, Issyk Kul, the Bebel Pass, Uch-Turfan and Aksu (Martin, *Rise* p. 231). • **41.** JB i pp. 69-70; ii pp. 370-383 • **42.** JB i p. 68; Barthold, *Turkestan* p. 403 • **43.** JB ii pp. 347, 357; Biran, *Qara Khitai* p. 171 • **44.** There is a very good account of the Irghiz River in Schuyler, *Turkistan* p. 16. • **45.** JB ii p. 371 • **46.** RT i pp. 235-236; JR i pp. 269-270 • **47.** JB ii pp. 371-373; Barthold, *Turkestan* pp. 369-372 • **48.** Nesawi [Nasawi], *Djelal ed-Din Mankobirti* pp. 19-20; Grenard, *Genghis* p. 140 • **49.** JB i pp. 303-304; Barthold, *Turkestan* pp. 393-394 • **50.** JR ii p. 966 • **51.** d'Ohsson, *Histoire* i p. 205 • **52.** JB i p. 304 • **53.** Barthold, *Turkestan* pp. 396-397 • **54.** ibid. • **55.** JR i p. 270 • **56.** JB ii pp. 390-391; Hartmann, *An-Nasir* pp. 83-84; Spuler, *Muslim World* ii p. 8 • **57.** Hartmann, *An-Nasir* p. 82; Barthold, *Four Studies* i p. 88 • **58.** Thomas T. Allsen, 'Mongolian Princes and their Merchant Partners, 1200–1260, *Asia Minor*, 3rd series 2 (1989) pp. 83-126 (at p. 91) • **59.** Minorsky, *Sharaf al Zaman Tahir Marzavi* (1942) pp. 14-15; Hourani, *Arab Peoples* p. 112 • **60.** JB i pp. 77-78; Lech, *Mongolische Weltreich* p. 19; Barthold, *Four Studies* i p. 71; Vladimirtsov, *Genghis* p. 93 • **61.** Biran, *Qara Khitai* p. 138 • **62.** Eisma, *Chinggis Qan* pp. 78-79; d'Ohsson, *Histoire* i pp. 205-206 • **63.** Togan, *Flexibility and Limitation* p. 57 • **64.** Vernadsky, *Mongols and Russia* p. 117 • **65.** JR ii p. 967 • **66.** The Otrar incident is well documented and comprehensively commented on in RT i p. 234; JB i pp. 79-80, 304-305, 367; IAA iii pp. 204-205; JR i p. 271; Barthold, *Turkestan* pp. 398-399; Pelliot, 'Notes sur le "Turkestan",' loc. cit. pp. 52-53 • **67.** JR ii p. 967; Bretschneider, *Mediaeval Researches* i p. 277; Barthold, *Turkestan* pp. 397-399 • **68.** JR ii p. 1141 • **69.** IAA iii pp. 205-206 • **70.** ibid. p. 206 • **71.** ibid. • **72.** These issues relate to the classic theories of strategy set out in Liddell Hart, *Strategy*. See also Bond, *Basil Liddell Hart*; Alex Danchev, 'Liddell Hart and the Indirect Approach,' *Journal of Military History* 63 (1999) pp. 313-337 • **73.** Clausewitz, *On War* • **74.** Ratchnevsky, *Genghis Khan* p. 124 • **75.** Bregel, *Firdaws al-Iqbal*; D. N. Mackenzie, 'Khwarezmian Language and Literature,' in Yarshater, ed., *Cambridge History of Iran* (1983) iii part 2 pp. 1244-1249 • **76.** Christian, *History of Russia* i p. 379; Barthold, *Turkestan* p. 377 • **77.** JR i p. 240; Wittfogel & Feng, *Liao* p. 431; Pelliot & Hambis, *Campagnes* pp. 89-91 • **78.** JB ii p. 466; Spuler, *History of the Mongols* p. 32 • **79.** Eisma, *Chinggis Khan* p. 84 • **80.**

Ratchnevsky, *Genghis Khan* pp. 124, 129-130 • **81.** Bahn, *World Archaeology* pp. 134-135; Gunnar Jarring, 'The Toponym Takla-makan,' *Turkic Languages* I (1997) pp. 227-240 • **82.** Barthold, 'Tarim,' in *Encyclopaedia of Islam* (1st ed., repr. 1993) i p. 673; Hedin, *Explorer* pp. 219, 233; Stein, *Ancient Khotan*; John E. Hill, *Through the Jade Gate* pp. 13, 121, 160-161; Baumer, *Southern Silk Road* • **83.** Toynbee, *Between Oxus and Jumma* • **84.** Le Strange, *Eastern Caliphate* pp. 437-439; Cordier, *Histoire générale* ii pp. 207-211 • **85.** Asimov & Bosworth, *History of Civilizations* iv part I pp. 130-172 • **86.** Vámbéry, *Bokhara* p. III • **87.** d'Ohsson, *Histoire* i pp. 212-213

Chapter 10

1. JR i p. 272 • **2.** This is the area associated with the later famous travellers Aurel Stein, Sven Hedin, Albert von Le Coq and Paul Pelliot (see Christopher Baumer, *Southern Silk Road*). For the Tarim basin see W. Barthold, 'Tarim,' loc. cit. i p. 673. For the Taklamakan Desert see Gunnar Jarring, 'The Toponym Taklamakan,' loc. cit. pp. 227-240; Bahn, *World Archaeology* pp. 134-135. The Taklamakan desert was also important in eighteenth-century Chinese history (see Perdue, *China Marches West*). • **3.** Yule, *Cathay* i p. 192. The pass is located at 39° 56' N 73° 41' E. • **4.** Bretschneider, *Mediaeval Researches* i pp. 13-15 • **5.** Le Strange, *Eastern Caliphate* pp. 497-488 • **6.** JR ii pp. 963-966; JB ii p. 376; Ratchnevsky, *Genghis Khan* p. 120 • **7.** Bira Shagdar, 'The Mongol Empire in the Thirteenth and Fourteenth Centuries,' in Elisseeff, *Silk Roads* pp. 127-144 (at p. 133) • **8.** For different accounts of this battle see Lamb, *March of the Barbarians* pp. 124-125, 133-134; Chambers, *Devil's Horsemen* pp. 9-10; Gabriel, *Subotai* pp. 78-79 • **9.** Pittard, 'Mongol Warfare' pp. 12-13 • **10.** Grenard, *Genghis* p. 139; Hartog, *Genghis* p. 96 • **11.** Barthel, *Mongolei* pp. 34-36 • **12.** Bretschneider, *Mediaeval Researches* i p. 14. The Dabistan-Daban pass is at roughly 46° N 92° E. • **13.** The Ob–Irtysh River, 3,360 miles long, is the seventh longest in the world. Scholars dispute whether the Ob or the Irtysh should be given primacy (as in the Mississippi–Missouri case), but the conventional view is to see the Irtysh as a tributary of the Ob rather than vice versa. For the importance of the Irtysh in history see Di Cosmo, *Military Culture* pp. 181-185; Millward, *Xinjiang* p. 33 • **14.** The ancient mentions are Herodotus 4.13.1 and Ptolemy 6.16.7. The classic description of the Dzungaria Gate is in Carruthers, *Unknown Mongolia* pp. 415-418. • **15.** Vernadsky, *Mongols and Russia* pp. 57-60 • **16.** Lane, *Daily Life* p. 116 • **17.** Leo de Hartog, 'Army of Genghis Khan,' loc. cit. p. 484; Hartog, *Genghis* pp. 52-53 • **18.** Barthold (*Turkestan* p. 404) estimates 250,000 in total, 150–200,000 on the Khwarezmia campaign and another 50,000 in China. • **19.** Martin, *Rise* p. 237 • **20.** Franke & Twitchett, *Cambridge History* p. 210 • **21.** Eisma, *Chinggis Khan* pp. 81-82 • **22.** Asa Gambu's reply seems an uncanny pre-echo of the famous Rob Roy MacGregor's declaration when asked by his putative Jacobite allies to join in the battle of Sheriffmuir in 1715: 'No! No! If they canna do it wi'out me, they canna do it wi'me.' • **23.** Bretschneider, *Mediaeval Researches* i p. 277; Barthold, *Four Studies* pp. 92-108; Barthold, *Turkestan* pp. 403-404 • **24.** Gaubil, *Gentchiscan* p. 34 • **25.** Waley, *Travels of an Alchemist* p. 85 • **26.** For a description of Almaliq, its cotton fields, canals and fruit orchards see ibid. pp. 85-86; cf also Pelliot, 'L'édition collective des oeuvres de Wang Kouo-Wei,' *T'oung Pao* 26 (1929) p. 174 • **27.** SHO p. 249; SHR pp. 189-191 • **28.** JR ii pp. 968-969 • **29.** For Banakat see Le Strange, *Eastern Caliphate* pp. 474, 488 • **30.** There is an outstanding analysis of all this in C. C. Walker, 'Genghis Khan's Invasion of South-West Asia,' *Canadian Defence Quarterly* (1932–1933) pp. 23-39, 156-173 (reprinted as a monograph in 1940). • **31.** JB i pp. 79-80, 82-86, 347-348; JR ii pp. 968-970; Barthold, *Turkestan* pp. 356, 364, 397-398, 406-407 • **32.** Walker, 'Genghis Khan's Invasion,' loc. cit. • **33.** Barthold, *Histoire des turcs* pp. 123-124; Le Strange, *Eastern Caliphate* pp. 484-485; Skrine & Ross, *Heart of Asia* pp. 157-159 • **34.** JB i pp. 82-84 • **35.** Spuler, *Mongolen in Iran* pp. 24-26 • **36.** JR ii p. 1048 • **37.** d'Ohsson, *Histoire* i pp. 219-221 • **38.** JR ii p. 910 • **39.** RT ii pp. 241-242; JR ii pp. 970-971; JB i pp. 84-85 • **40.** Bretschneider, *Mediaeval Researches* i p. 278; Ratchnevsky, *Genghis Khan* p. 130 • **41.** Wolff, *Mongolen* pp. 60-71 • **42.** JB i pp. 96-97 • **43.** JB i p. 87; Barthold, *Turkestan* p. 179 • **44.** JB i p. 92; d'Ohsson, *Histoire* i pp. 221-224 • **45.** Barthold, *Turkestan* pp. 417-419 • **46.** RT ii pp. 243-245; JR ii pp. 972-973 • **47.** JB i pp. 92-95 • **48.** Gabriel, *Subotai* p. 81 • **49.** JB i pp. 98-102; Barthold, *Turkestan* pp. 407-409; d'Ohsson, *Histoire* i pp. 227-228 • **50.** Liddell Hart (*Great Captains Unveiled* pp. 11-15) regards it as possibly *the* strategic masterpiece in all history. • **51.** See Alex Danchev, 'Liddell Hart and the Indirect Approach,' loc. cit. pp. 313-337; Danchev, *Alchemist of War* • **52.** Vámbéry, *Bokhara* p. 28; Wolff, *Mongolen* p. 69 • **53.** Le Strange, *Eastern Caliphate* pp. 461-462 • **54.** Asimov & Bosworth, *History of Civilizations* iv part 1 p. 265; Barthold, *Turkestan* p. 88 • **55.** Frye, *Bukhara* p. 93; Frye, *al-Narshakhi*; Barthold, *Turkestan* pp. 103-104, 112 • **56.** Eisma, *Chinggis Khan* p. 86 • **57.** Barthold, *Turkestan* p. 424 • **58.** Togan, *Flexibility and Limitation* pp. 54-55; Barthold, *Turkestan* pp. 354-355 • **59.** JB i pp. 102-107; Barthold, *Turkestan* p. 409 • **60.** Ibn al-Athir says 11 February (IAA iii p. 308) while Juzjani says 15 February (JR ii pp. 978-979). Rashid, while giving full details of the siege, mentions no exact date (RT ii pp. 245-247). • **61.** JR ii pp. 976-977; Togan, *Flexibility* p. 55; Dankoff, *Wisdom* p. 221 • **62.** IAA iii p. 209 • **63.** Barthold, *Turkestan* pp. 409-410 • **64.** Ratchnevsky, *Genghis Khan* p. 131. • **65.** Eisma, *Chinggis Khan* p. 87 • **66.** JB i p. 107; d'Ohsson, *Histoire* i pp. 231-234 • **67.** Spuler, *Mongolen in Iran* p. 22; Barthold, *Turkestan* p. 410 • **68.** Le Strange, *Eastern Caliphate* p. 463 • **69.** Bloom & Blair, *Grove Encyclopedia of Islamic Art* iii pp. 170-177; Asimov & Bosworth, *History of Civilizations* iv part 1 p. 265 • **70.** Le

Strange, *Eastern Caliphate* pp. 463-471 • **71**. JB ii pp. 376-377 • **72**. Part of this weakness was the Shah's own fault. Two years after the final conquest of his empire he still had not replaced the governors he had mindlessly killed (Barthold, *Four Studies* i p. 71). • **73**. ibid. i p. 39; Barthold, *Turkestan* p. 405 • **74**. ibid. p. 419 • **75**. JR ii p. 971 • **76**. IAA iii p. 210; JB ii p. 378; Barthold, *Turkestan* p. 419 • **77**. IAA iii p. 209; JB i pp. 117-119 • **78**. RT ii pp. 247-249; JR ii p. 990; JB i pp. 117-119 • **79**. d'Ohsson, *Histoire* i pp. 235-239 • **80**. Barthold, *Turkestan* p. 480 • **81**. IAA iii pp. 209-210 • **82**. JB i pp. 121-122; JR ii p. 980 • **83**. JB i p. 122; Barthold, *Turkestan* p. 413 • **84**. d'Ohsson, *Histoire* i p. 240 • **85**. In 1221, on his way to visit Genghis, the Chinese sage Chang Chun and his large party of monks did a meticulous count that established that only a quarter of the pre-1219 population had survived (Waley, *Travels of an Alchemist* p. 93). • **86**. Le Strange, *Eastern Caliphate* p. 465 • **87**. Eisma, *Chinggis Khan* p. 89 • **88**. IAA iii p. 210 • **89**. Waley, *Travels* p. 110 • **90**. Le Strange, *Eastern Caliphate* pp. 433-436, 441-444, 457-458 • **91**. Wolff, *Mongolen* p. 77 • **92**. Eisma, *Chinggis Khan* pp. 90-96 • **93**. ibid. • **94**. RT ii p. 255; JB i p. 129 • **95**. d'Ohsson, *Histoire* i p. 241 • **96**. ibid. pp. 241-242 • **97**. JR i p. 275 • **98**. JR i p. 276 • **99**. d'Ohsson, *Histoire* i pp. 242-243 • **100**. Barthold, *Turkestan* pp. 428, 446 • **101**. JR i p. 274 • **102**. SHC pp. 199-200 • **103**. IAA iii p. 210 • **104**. JB i p. 143 • **105**. d'Ohsson, *Histoire* i p. 244 • **106**. Barthold, *Turkestan* pp. 378-379 • **107**. d'Ohsson, *Histoire* i p. 244 • **108**. RT ii pp. 250-251 • **109**. JB i p. 144 • **110**. JB i p. 145 • **111**. For Ferdowsi see Frye, *Golden Age* p. 200; Davis, *Shahnameh*. For Tus in general see Kennedy, *Court of the Caliphs* • **112**. Eisma, *Chinggis Khan* p. 92 • **113**. JB i p. 307; Barthold, *Turkestan* pp. 420-422. For Damghan see Bloom & Blair, *Grove Encyclopedia* i p. 291; Sha'bani, *Book of Iran* p. 221 • **114**. IAA iii pp. 212-213; JR i p. 277 • **115**. JB ii pp. 466-468; d'Ohsson, *Histoire* i pp. 259-260 • **116**. JR ii p. 1082. For Eljigidei see JB i pp. 184, 249 • **117**. Eisma, *Chinggis Khan* p. 93 • **118**. IAA iii p. 213 • **119**. JR i p. 277; JB ii p. 384; Barthold, *Turkestan* pp. 422-425; d'Ohsson, *Histoire* i p. 254 • **120**. Spuler, *Mongolen in Iran* p. 22; Barthold, *Turkestan* p. 160; d'Ohsson, *Histoire* i pp. 250-251 • **121**. JB ii p. 384; Barthold, *Turkestan* pp. 422-425; • **122**. d'Ohsson, *Histoire* i pp. 254-255 • **123**. JB ii p. 385; JR ii pp. 993-994 • **124**. d'Ohsson, *Histoire* i p. 254 • **125**. JR i p. 279 • **126**. Bretschneider, *Mediaeval Researches* i p. 280; Wolff, *Mongolen* p. 80 • **127**. d'Ohsson, *Histoire* i p. 278 • **128**. IAA iii pp. 211-212 • **129**. JB i pp. 142-149

Chapter 11

1. For the history and culture of Khwarezm see Yuri Bregel, 'The Sarts in the Khanate of Khiva,' *Journal of Asian History* 12 (1978) pp. 121-151; Bregel, *Firdaws al-Iqbal*; D. N. MacKenzie, 'Khwarazmian Language and Literature,' in E. Yarshater, ed., *Cambridge History of Iran* iii part 2 pp. 1244-1249 • **2**. JB i pp. 174-175 • 3. d'Ohsson, *Histoire* i p. 265. For Khiva see Burnaby, *Ride to Khiva*; Philip Glazebrook, *Journey to Khiva*; Moser, *Asie centrale*; Nashriyoti, *Khiva* • 4. JR ii p. 1097 • 5. d'Ohsson, *Histoire* i p. 266 • 6. Le Strange, *Eastern Caliphate* pp. 458-459; Sykes, *Persia* p. 64; Daniel, *Iran* p. 28 • 7. Le Strange, *Eastern Caliphate* pp. 457-458 • 8. Barthold, *Turkestan* pp. 433-434 • 9. JR ii pp. 1100-1101; Barthold, *Turkestan* p. 432 • 10. JB iii pp. 399-402; Bretschneider, *Mediaeval Researches* i p. 280 • 11. d'Ohsson, *Histoire* i p. 267 • 12. JB i pp. 123-125 • 13. JR i p. 280 • 14. SHO p. 250; SHR p. 191; Barthold, *Turkestan* pp. 433, 437 • 15. JB i pp. 123-125 • 16. JR ii pp. 1098-1099 • 17. JB ii pp. 126-127 • 18. IAA iii pp. 227-228; d'Ohsson, *Histoire* i pp. 268-269 • 19. Barthold, *Turkestan* pp. 435-437 • 20. d'Ohsson, *Histoire* i p. 270 • 21. JB i p. 96; Bretschneider, *Mediaeval Researches* i p. 131; Allsen, *Mongol Imperialism* p. 89 • 22. IAA iii p. 228; *Encyclopaedia of Islam* (2nd ed.) ii pp. 41-44 • 23. JB ii pp. 402-404 • 24. JB i pp. 174-175; Barthold, *Turkestan* pp. 424-426 • 25. SHO p. 251; SHR p. 194 • 26. SHO p. 252; SHR p. 194 • 27. IAA iii p. 225 • 28. JB i p. 130; Bloom & Blair, *Islamic Art and Architecture* i pp. 258-259; Le Strange, *Eastern Caliphate* pp. 420-421 • 29. JB i p. 131; Boyle, *Cambridge History of Iran* v pp. 303-421 (at p. 312); Barthold, *Turkestan* pp. 427-455 • 30. d'Ohsson, *Histoire* i p. 272 • 31. J. A. Boyle, 'On the Titles given in Juvaini to certain Mongolian Princes,' *Harvard Journal of Asiatic Studies* 19 (1956) pp. 146-154 (at pp. 146-148); Boyle, 'Iru and Maru in the Secret History of the Mongols,' *Harvard Journal of Asiatic Studies* 17 (1954) pp. 403-410 • 32. For the comparison with Bukhara see Dumper & Stanley, *Cities of the Middle East* pp. 95-99; cf Frye, *al-Narshakhi*. The entire vexed question of the size of medieval cities is discussed in Chandler, *Urban Growth*. • 33. Bloom & Blair, *Islamic Art and Architecture* ii pp. 476-479 • 34. For Tolui on the road to Merv see JR ii p. 1028. For the mausoleums of the great Iranian cities – Bukhara, Urgench, Merv and Herat – see Asimov & Bosworth, *History of Civilizations*, iv part 2 pp. 516-531, 545-549 • 35. ibid. p. 265 • 36. ibid. p. 297 • 37. The Merv system was a classic example of what one scholar has called 'oriental despotism', known to Marxists as the 'oriental mode of production' (see Wittfogel, *Oriental Despotism*). • 38. Asimov & Bosworth, *History of Civilizations* iv part 2 p. 266; Williams, *Merv* • 39. d'Ohsson, *Histoire* i pp. 279-282 • 40. ibid. pp. 283-284 • 41. JB i pp. 153-158 • 42. IAA iii pp. 226-227 • 43. JR ii pp. 1031-1033 • 44. JB i pp. 158-162; Boyle, 'Dynastic and Political History of the Il-Khans,' in Boyle, *Cambridge History of Iran* v pp. 303-421 (at pp. 313-314) • 45. d'Ohsson, *Histoire* i pp. 287-288 • 46. Grousset, *L'Empire* pp. 240-241 • 47. Eisma, *Chinggis Khan* pp. 98-99 • 48. d'Ohsson, *Histoire* i pp. 275-276 • 49. JR ii p. 1033 • 50. JB i p. 145 • 51. There is a considerable literature on medieval Nishapur. Asimov & Bosworth, *History of Civilizations* iv part 2 pp. 412-422, 440-443; Bosworth, *Historic Cities* pp. 421-439; Bloom & Blair, *Islamic Art* iii pp. 59-60; Bulliet, *Patricians*;

Wilkinson, *Pottery*; R. W. Bulliet, 'Medieval Nishapur: A Topographical and Demographic Reconstruction,' *Studia Iranica* 5 (1976) pp. 67-89; Meri, *Medieval Islamic Civilization* ii; Kröger, *Glass*; C. Melville, 'Earthquakes in the History of Nishapur,' *Iran* 18 (1980) pp. 103-120. For the population of Nishapur see Bulliet, 'Medieval Nishapur,' loc. cit. p. 88. For Sufism see Margaret Malamud, 'Sufi Organisations and Structures of Authority in Medieval Nishapur,' *International Journal of Middle East Studies* 26 (1994) pp. 427-442. Naturally no attempt will be made here to refer to the many books on Omar Khayyam. • **52**. JB i pp. 169-178 • **53**. d'Ohsson, *Histoire* i pp. 289-291. The ballista was a magnified crossbow which propelled javelins, unlike the mangonel, which hurled stones (Oman, *Art of War* i pp. 137-138). • **54**. JR ii p. 1035 • **55**. IAA iii p. 27 • **56**. JB i pp. 169-178 • **57**. JB i p. 152; Bretschneider, *Mediaeval Researches* i p. 281; Boyle, *Successors* p. 165 • **58**. JR ii p. 997 • **59**. Le Strange, *Eastern Caliphate* pp. 407-410; Bloom & Blair, *Islamic Art* ii pp. 146-150; Asimov & Bosworth, *History of Civilizations* iv part 2 p. 272 • **60**. IAA iii p. 27 • **61**. JR ii p. 1036 • **62**. JR ii pp. 1037-1039 • **63**. ibid. • **64**. JB ii p. 403 • **65**. d'Ohsson, *Histoire* i pp. 286-287 • **66**. JB ii pp. 404, 460 • **67**. JR ii p. 1083 • **68**. ibid. • **69**. d'Ohsson, *Histoire* i p. 273 • **70**. IAA iii p. 225 • **71**. JB i pp. 132-133; Boyle, *Successors* p. 137 • **72**. d'Ohsson, *Histoire* i p. 296 • **73**. Pelliot, *Horde d'Or* pp. 86-87 • **74**. JR i p. 289; JB i p. 405; Barthold, *Turkestan* p. 442 • **75**. Yule, *Cathay* iv pp. 209, 257; Dupuy, *Harper Encyclopedia* p. 366 • **76**. JR i p. 289 • **77**. JB ii pp. 406-407 • **78**. d'Ohsson, *Histoire* i p. 302; Barthold, *Turkestan* p. 441 • **79**. Barthold pp. 441-443 • **80**. JR i p. 290 • **81**. JR ii p. 1003; Barthold, *Turkestan* p. 443 • **82**. RT ii p. 256 • **83**. Eisma, *Chinggis Khan* p. 102 • **84**. ibid. • **85**. Barthold, *Turkestan* pp. 445-446 • **86**. JB i p. 174; ii p. 411 • **87**. JR i p. 291 • **88**. IAA iii p. 229 • **89**. d'Ohsson, *Histoire* i p. 306 • **90**. Nesawi [Nasawi], *Djelal ed-Din Mankobirti* pp. 138-141 • **91**. JB ii pp. 410-411. That this quote is authentic seems confirmed by the similar wording used by Rashid: 'From that father that such a son should come! In all the world no one has ever seen or heard of such a man among the renowned ancients. After saving himself on the shore from such a battle, he will perform many valiant feats' (RT ii p. 256). • **92**. JR i p. 291 • **93**. d'Ohsson, *Histoire* i pp. 307-308 • **94**. JB ii pp. 411-413; JR i p. 537 • **95**. JB ii p. 391 • **96**. The story of Jalal's two-year sojourn in India is a saga in itself, though irrelevant to the history of Genghis Khan. There were frequent battles with local tribesmen, in one of which Jalal was wounded in the arm, and even an inchoate alliance with a Khokhar chieftain, whose daughter he is said to have married. Jalal tried to mould an alliance of the Khilji, Turkoman and Ghori tribes, but this foundered (predictably) on the issue of booty. Jalal spent much time with his Khokar allies in the Salt Range. He penetrated deep into Sind and tried to persuade governor Qabacha to help him, but the governor was too terrified of the Mongols. Jalal's army went on to sack a number of cities (JB ii pp. 411-421; JR i pp. 294-295). • **97**. JB ii pp. 415-421; Eisma, *Chinggis Khan* p. 103; Chandra, *Delhi Sultanate* p. 40 • **98**. RT ii p. 257; JB i pp. 141-142; JR i pp. 534-539; Boyle, 'Iru and Maru,' loc. cit.; d'Ohsson, *Histoire* i pp. 309-310; Barthold, *Turkestan* p. 446 • **99**. JB i, p. 37; JR ii pp. 1046, 1081. For the absurd claims by Indian nationalists see Qureshi, *Administration* pp. 136, 140; Ikram, *Muslim Civilization* pp. 44-45, 59, 63 • **100**. McLeod, *History of India* p. 35 • **101**. Jackson, *Delhi Sultanate*; Wink, *Slave Kings*; Mehta, *Medieval India* i • **102**. Gibb, *Ibn Battuta* ii p. 478 • **103**. ibid. ii p. 479 • **104**. J. M. Smith, 'Mongol Manpower and Persian Population,' *Journal of the Economic and Social History of the Orient* 18 (1975) pp. 271-299 • **105**. JB i p. 137; Barthold, *Turkestan* p. 454 • **106**. Ratchnevsky, *Genghis Khan* p. 134 • **107**. JR ii pp. 1045-1047, 1081-1084; JB i p. 139 • **108**. Rockhill, *Rubruck* pp. 187-188; Bretschneider, *Mediaeval Researches* i p. 289; Krause, *Cingis Han* p. 39; Chun-chiang Yen, 'The Chüeh-tuana as Word, Art Motif and Legend,' *Journal of the American Oriental Society* 89 (1969) pp. 578-599 (at pp. 589-591) • **109**. JR ii p. 1073; JB i pp. 135-138 • **110**. JR ii p. 1072 • **111**. Eisma, *Chinggis Khan* p. 102 • **112**. JB i p. 135; JR ii pp. 1007, 1043, 1057, 1073, 1126; Bretschneider, *Mediaeval Researches* i p. 282 • **113**. JR ii p. 1047; Bretschneider, *Mediaeval Researches* i p. 293; d'Ohsson, *Histoire* i p. 317; Vladimirtsov, *Genghis* p. 106; Yate, *Khurasan* • **114**. Browne, *Literary History of Persia* ii pp. 427-431; Grousset, *Empire* p. 243 • **115**. JR ii p. 1048; cf also Dumper & Stanley, *Cities of the Middle East* p. 169 – quoting the four-teenth-century historian Saif bin Muhammad bin Yaqub Saifi • **116**. JR ii p. 1050 • **117**. d'Ohsson, *Histoire* i p. 315; Barthold, *Turkestan* p. 449 • **118**. JB i p. 131; JR ii pp. 1023-1026 • **119**. d'Ohsson, *Histoire* i pp. 312-313 • **120**. JR ii p. 1050 • **121**. Le Strange, *Eastern Caliphate* pp. 408-409; d'Ohsson, *Histoire* i p. 314. A meticulous account of the siege of Herat is in Bretschneider, *Mediaeval Researches* ii pp. 278-290 • **122**. JR ii pp. 1051-1055 • **123**. JR ii p. 1055 • **124**. ibid. pp. 1062-1066 • **125**. ibid. pp. 1066-1070 • **126**. J. T. Wylie, 'The First Mongol Conquest of Tibet Reinterpreted,' *Harvard Journal of Asiatic Studies* 37 (1977) pp. 103-133 (at pp. 104-107) • **127**. Chase, *Firearms* p. 58; Adle & Habib, *History of Civilizations* v p. 58 • **128**. Kim Stubbs, 'Facing the Wrath of Genghis Khan,' *Military History* (May 2006) pp. 30-37 • **129**. Jurgen Paul, 'L'invasion mongole comme révélateur de la société irannienne,' in Aigle, *L'Iran* pp. 37-53 (esp. p. 41) • **130**. As is argued in Nesawi [Nasawi], *Djelal ed-Din Mankobirti*, passim

Chapter 12

1. For these qualities of the Mongol horse see Bayarsaikhan, *Mongol Horse* • **2**. Lamb, *Genghis*, p. 45 • **3**. Thackston, *Habibu's-siyar* i p. 118 • **4**. Kolbas, *Mongols in Iran* pp. 76-77; Boyle, *Cambridge History of Iran* v p. 308-311 • **5**. IAA iii p. 214; RT ii p. 259; C. E. Bosworth, 'Zanran,' in *Encyclopedia of Islam* (2nd ed.) xi p. 447 • **6.** Buell, *Dictionary* p. 235 • **7.** d'Ohsson, *Histoire* i p. 325 • **8.** IAA iii p. 214 • **9.** Altunian, *Mongolen und ihre Eroberungen* p. 21 • **10.** For exhaustive detail see Constant, *L'Azerbaidjan* • **11.** Morgan, *Mongols* p. 142 • **12.** P. Halfter, 'Die militärischen Triumphe der Georgier und ein wenig beachtetes Erdbeben an der Grenze Armenisch-Kilikiens (c. Ende August 1213),' *Le Muséon* 122 (2009) pp. 423-427 • **13.** Strabo 11.13.5; 11.14.5; Ptolemy 5.12; Pliny the Elder 6.39 • **14.** IAA iii p. 215; RT ii p. 259; E. Schütz, 'Tatarenstürme in Gebirgsgelande,' *Central Asiatic Journal* 17 (1973) pp. 253-273 (at p. 256) • **15.** Pierre-Vincent Claverie, 'L'apparition des Mongols sur la scène politique occidentale, 1220–1223,' *Le Moyen Age* 105 (1999) pp. 601-613 (at pp. 608-609); M.-F. Brosset, *Histoire de la Géorgie* i pp. 440, 442, 459 • **16.** IAA iii pp. 216-217 • **17.** ibid. p. 217; Tyerman, *God's War* pp. 641-649 • **18.** Peters, *Christian Society* pp. 90-91, 123-124 • **19.** IAA iii pp. 218-219 • **20.** ibid. iii p. 219 • **21.** d'Ohsson, *Histoire* i pp. 332-333 • **22.** IAA iii p. 220 • **23.** ibid.; d'Ohsson i pp. 333-334 • **24.** Altunian, *Die Mongolen* p. 21; Schütz, 'Tatarenstürme,' loc. cit. p. 258 • **25.** d'Ohsson, *Histoire* i pp. 334-336 • **26.** Utik, then a province of Armenia, is today in Azerbaijan. (Mark Chakin, *Armenia* p. 181) • **27.** Bedrosian, *Kirakos Gandzakets'i* pp. 234-235 • **28.** IAA iii p. 221 • **29.** Bedrosian, *Kirakos* pp. 201-203. For other accounts of the Mongols in Armenia see Bedrosian, 'Armenia during the Seljuk and Mongol Periods,' in Hovannisian, *Armenian People* i pp. 241-291 (esp. p. 256); Thomson, *Rewriting Caucasian History*; Dashdondog, *Mongols and Armenians* p. 43; Herrin & Saint-Guillain, *Identities and Allegiances* • **30.** This is the modern Shamkir, now in Azerbaijan, scene of a Georgian victory over the Azerbaijanis in 1195 (Allen, *Georgian People* p. 104). • **31.** IAA iii pp. 221-222 • **32.** Gabriel, *Subotai* p. 93 • **33.** RT ii p. 259; IAA iii p. 221; Schütz, 'Tatarenstürme,' loc. cit. p. 257; Suny, *Making of the Georgian Nation* pp. 39-44; Rayfield, *Edge of Empires* • **34.** Rodenberg, *Epistolae* i pp. 178-179 • **35.** d'Ohsson, *Histoire* i p. 335; RT ii p. 260; IAA iii p. 222. For the Caucasus see de Waal, *Caucasus*; Coene, *Caucasus* • **36.** I. Nasidze et al, 'Genetic Evidence Concerning the Origin of the South and North Ossetians,' *Annals of Human Genetics* (2004) pp. 588-589. For the Alans see Jackson & Morgan, *Rubruck* op. cit. pp. 102-103, 259; Dawson, *Mongol Mission*, p. 41. They had been converted to Greek Orthodox Christianity in the tenth century (Jean Dauvillier, 'Byzantins d'Asie centrale et d'Extrême-Orient au moyen age,' *Revue des Études Byzantines* 11 (1953) pp. 73-80). • **37.** For the Circassians see Spencer, *Western Caucasus* p. 6; cf also Bell, *Journal*; Jaimoukha, *Circassians* • **38.** Pelliot, 'À propos des Comans,' *Journal Asiatique* 11 (1920) pp. 133-150 (esp. p. 149); A. Bruce Boswell, 'The Kipchak Turks,' *Slavonic Review* 6 (1928) pp. 68-85; Vernadsky, *Kievan Russia* pp. 86-90, 222-225, 235-238 • **39.** d'Ohsson, *Histoire* i p. 337 • **40.** RT ii p. 260; IAA iii p. 222 • **41.** Bretschneider, *Mediaeval Researches* i pp. 295-298 • **42.** Wallace, *Rise of Russia* p. 38 • **43.** Marie

Nystazopoulou-Pélékidis, 'Venise et la Mer Noire du XIe au XVe siècle,' in A. Pertusi, ed., *Venezia* i pp. 541-582; Phillips, *Medieval Expansion* pp. 96-114; Lane, *Venice* • **44.** L. Petachi, 'Les marchands italiens dans l'empire mongol,' *Journal Asiatique* 250 (1962) pp. 549-574; Crowdy, *Enemy Within* p. 49; Brătianu, *Commerce génois*. The Mongols always favoured the Venetians and protected their merchants on the Silk Road (Peter Jackson, *Delhi Sultanate* pp. 252-253). • **45.** Ciocîltan, *Black Sea Trade*, esp. pp. 141-157. See also the extensive work by Nicola di Cosmo, 'Mongols and Merchants on the Black Sea Frontier in the 13th and 14th Centuries: Convergences and Conflicts,' in Amitai & Biran, *Mongols, Turks* pp. 391-424; di Cosmo, 'Black Sea Empire and the Mongol Empire: A Reassessment of the Pax Mongolica,' *Journal of the Economic and Social History of the Orient* 53 (2010) pp. 83-108 • **46.** JB i p. 107; Chambers, *Devil's Horsemen* p. 24 • **47.** Magocsi, *Ukraine* p. 76 • **48.** Pipes, *Karamzin* pp. 105, 110 • **49.** Volodymyr Mezentsev, 'The Territorial and Demographic Development of Medieval Kiev and Other Major Cities of Rus: A Comparative Analysis Based on Recent Archaeological Research,' *The Russian Review* 48 (1989) pp. 145-170 • **50.** Martin, *Medieval Russia* p. 61; Franklin & Shepard, *Emergence of Rus* pp. 2, 13, 279, 282, 287 • **51.** ibid., pp. 337-339. See also the articles in Perrie, *Cambridge History of Russia*, viz: Jonathan Shepard, 'The Origins of Rus c. 900–1015,' pp. 45-72; Simon Franklin, 'Kievan Rus, 1015–1125,' pp. 73-97; Martin Dimnick, 'The Rus Principalities, 1125–1246,' pp. 98-126 • **52.** Fennell, *Crisis* pp. 6-9, 12-15, 23; Pelenski, *Contest for the Legacy* • **53.** Moss, *History of Russia* i pp. 55-59 • **54.** Thomas S. Noonan, 'Suzdalia's eastern trade in the century before the Mongol Conquest,' *Cahiers du monde russe et soviétique* 19 (1978) pp. 371-384; Martin, *Medieval Russia* pp. 70, 98-101, 112, 121; Langer, *Medieval Russia* pp. 245-248; Soloviev, *Shift Northward* • **55.** Moss, *History of Russia* p. 60 • **56.** Fennell, *Crisis* pp. 45-51 • **57.** ibid. pp. 17-19; Martin, *Medieval Russia* pp. 66-70, 81-88, 101-103, 106-107, 121-122, 126, 128 • **58.** Lazarev, *Russian Icon* pp. 47-48, 53-56, 67; Valentin L. Ianin, 'Medieval Russia,' in Persie, *Cambridge History of Russia* i pp. 188-210; Riasanovsky & Steinberg, *History of Russia* pp. 75-76; Martin, *Medieval Russia* p. 126 • **59.** Mitchell & Forbes, *Chronicle of Novgorod*, p. 25; Martin, *Medieval Russia* pp. 114-115 • **60.** Paul Bushkovitch, 'Urban Ideology in Medieval Novgorod: An Iconographic Approach,' *Cahiers du monde russe et soviétique* 16 (1975) pp. 19-26 • **61.** Martin, *Medieval Russia* p. 123 • **62.** Christian, *History of Russia* i p. 364 • **63.** Riasanovsky, *History of Russia* (1993 ed.) p. 42 • **64.** Bretschneider, *Mediaeval Researches* i p. 297; ii p. 71 • **65.** Barthold, *Histoire des turcs* pp. 88-91; Golden, *Nomads and their Neighbours*; Golden, *Turkic Peoples* • **66.** Robert L. Wolff, 'The Second Bulgarian Empire: Its Origins and History to 1204,' *Speculum* 24 (1949) pp. 167-206; Paul Stephenson, *Byzantium's Balkan Frontier: A Political Study of the Northern Balkans, 900-1204* (Cambridge 2000); Spinei, *Romanians* • **67.** *Monumenta*

Germaniae Historiae, Scriptores 21 (1869) p. 216; A. Bruce Boswell, 'The Kipchak Turks,' *Slavonic Review* 6 (1928) pp. 68-85 • **68**. Vásáry, *Cumans and Tatars* pp. 4-7, 13-56; Christian, *History of Russia* i p. 361; Pelliot & Hambis, *Campagnes* pp. 43-114 • **69**. Chaliand, *Nomadic Empires* p. 52 • **70**. Christian, *History of Russia* i p. 358 • **71**. Vernadsky, *Source Book for Russian History* i p. 31 • **72**. Jackson & Morgan, *Rubruck* p. 70 • **73**. Peter B. Golden, 'The Qipchaqs of Medieval Russia,' in Seaman & Marks, *Rulers from the Steppe* pp. 186-204 (at pp. 197-198) • **74**. For a good summary of the Polovtsian raids and the counter-campaigns see Vernadsky, *Kievan Russia* pp. 86-90, 222-225, 235-238 • **75**. For the complex politics of Chernigov and Igor's role see Dimnik, *Dynasty of Chernigov* pp. 108-240 • **76**. Nabokov, *Song of Igor's Campaign* ll. 93-112 • **77**. ibid. ll. 153-171 • **78**. These events are described in a number of sources: Mitchell & Forbes, *Chronicle of Novgorod* p. 32; Cross & Sherbowitz-Wetzor, *Russian Primary Chronicle*; S. A. Zenkovsky, *Medieval Russian Epics* pp. 137-138; 'The Lay of Igor's Campaign,' in Fennell & Obolensky, *A Historical Russian Reader* pp. 63-72; Martin, *Medieval Russia* p. 131 • **79**. Nabokov, *Song* ll. 733-834 • **80**. Halperin, *Russia and the Golden Horde* p. 15 • **81**. T. S. Noonan, 'Rus, Pechenegs and Polovtsy: Economic Interactions along the Steppe Frontier in the Pre-Mongol Era,' *Russian History* 19 (1992) pp. 301-327 • **82**. Mitchell & Forbes, *Chronicle of Novgorod* p. 65 • **83**. ibid. p. 64. For more on Russian ignorance of the Mongols see Grekov & Iakoubovski, *Horde d'Or* pp. 54, 1901-91; Bretschneider, *Mediaeval Researches* i p. 296; Bezzola, *Mongolen in abendländischer Sicht* p. 41 • **84**. J. Fennell, 'The Tatar Invasion of 1223,' *Forschungen zur osteuropäischen Geschichte* 27 (1980) pp. 18-31. Fennell, like many other writers, places the Battle of Kalka in the year 1222, which the best scholarship has now established as the true date. If the battle of Kalka was indeed fought in 1223, there is an entire twelve-month black hole to be accounted for, as our detailed narrative has made clear. • **85**. Fennell, *Crisis* p. 65 • **86**. Grekov & Iakoubovski, *Horde d'Or* p. 193 • **87**. Fennell, *Crisis* p. 66 • **88**. Chambers, *Devil's Horsemen* pp. 17-30 • **89**. Gabriel, *Subotai* p. 99. Vernadsky (*Kievan Russia* p. 237) says that Mtsislav the Bold 'succeeded in defeating a detachment of Mongol troops' but does not mention that they had been left behind as a suicide squad (*suggestio falsi?*). • **90**. Munro, *Rise of the Russian Empire* p. 81 • **91**. For the entire Kalka campaign the best guide is Nicolle, *Kalka* • **92**. Rachewiltz, *In the Service* p. 132 • **93**. Mitchell & Forbes, *Chronicle of Novgorod* pp. 65-66; Fennell, *Crisis* p. 91 • **94**. Gabriel, *Subotai* p. 100 • **95**. Nicolle, *Kalka* p. 74; Martin, *Medieval Russia* p. 132 • **96**. Grekov & Iakoubovski, *Horde d'Or* p. 194; Bretschneider, *Mediaeval Researches* i p. 297 • **97**. Nicolle, *Kalka* pp. 76-82 • **98**. ibid. p. 75 • **99**. IAA iii p. 224 • **100**. Nicolle, *Kalka* p. 74 • **101**. Jackson, *Mongols and the West* p. 49 • **102**. Mitchell & Forbes, *Chronicle of Novgorod* p. 66; Zenkovsky, *Medieval Russian Epics* p. 195 • **103**. For a good summary of the campaign and its consequence see Grousset, *L'empire mongol* pp. 517-520 • **104**. For a description of the lands the Mongols traversed on the way to Samara see Dawson, *Mongol Mission* p. 131; Haxthausen, *Russian Empire* ii pp. 70, 223; Clarke, *Travels* p. 47 • **105**. I. Zimonyi, 'The First Mongol Raid against the Volga Bulgars,' in Jarring & Rosen, *Altaic Papers* pp. 197-204 (at pp. 197-199); A. M. Khalikov, *Mongols, Tatars* p. 24 (I am grateful to Dr Malcolm Chapman for translations of the relevant sections of this source.) • **106**. The correct version (in my view) is in d'Ohsson, *Histoire*, i p. 346 and Grousset, *Empire of the Steppes* p. 247. Ibn al-Athir implies that the Mongol defeat at Samara Bend was serious (IAA iii p. 224) and is backed by Jackson, *Mongols and the West* p. 39. For other views see Barthold, *Four Studies* i p. 41 and de Hartog, *Mongol Yoke* p. 25. Chambers, *Devil's Horseman* p. 31 is adamant that the story of a serious Mongol reverse is lying Bulgar propaganda. • **107**. *Encyclopedia of Islam* (2nd ed.) viii pp. 895-898 • **108**. Rachewiltz, *In the Service* p. 19 • **109**. JR ii pp. 1102-1103; Chambers, *Devil's Horsemen* p. 31; Rachewiltz, *In the Service* pp. 19-20; Hartog, *Genghis* p. 123. For a judicious analysis of Jebe see Rachewiltz, *Commentary* pp. 533-538 • **110**. Liddell Hart, *Great Captains Unveiled* • **111**. George Lane, 'The Mongols in Iran,' in Daryaee, *Iranian History* pp. 243-70 (at p. 248); d'Ohsson, *Histoire* i p. 323 • **112**. IAA iii p. 215

Chapter 13

1. Rachewiltz, *In the Service* pp. 95-96 • **2**. Asimov & Bosworth, *History of Civilizations* iv part 2 pp. 510-512 • **3**. Devin DeWeese, 'Stuck in the Throat of Chingiz Khan: Envisioning Mongol Conquest in some Sufi Accounts of the Fourteenth to the Seventeenth Centuries,' in Pfeiffer & Quinn, *Post-Mongol Central Asia* pp. 23-60 (at pp. 32-33, 52) • **4**. ibid. pp. 46-49 • **5**. Hamid Algar, 'Some Observations on religion in Safavid Persia,' *Iranian Studies* 7 (1974) pp. 287-293; Devin DeWeese, 'The Eclipse of the Kubraviyah in Central Asia,' *Iranian Studies* 21 (1988) pp. 45-83; Lawson, *Reason and Inspiration* p. 303. • **6**. DeWeese, 'Stuck in the Throat,' loc. cit. pp. 42-43, 46-47 • **7**. Kohn, *Daoism*; Silvers, *Taoist Manual* • **8**. Vincent Goosaert, 'Quanzhen,' in Pregadio, *Encyclopedia of Taoism* ii pp. 814-820; Komjathy, *Cultivating Perfection* • **9**. Despaux & Kohn, *Women in Daoism* pp. 142-148 • **10**. Eskildsen, *Early Quanzhen Taoist Masters* pp. 10. 12, 18 • **11**. For a full suvey of Chang Chun's career see Rachewiltz, *In the Service* pp. 208-223 • **12**. Tao, *Jurchen* pp. 106-107 • **13**. For these arguments see Komjathy, *Cultivating Perfection* • **14**. There is a huge literature on alchemy and Quanzhen. Representative titles include Pregadio, *Awakening to Reality*; Pregadio, *Chinese Alchemy*; Mu, *Neidan* • **15**. Rachewiltz, *In the Service* p. 143 • **16**. Arthur Waley, *Travels of an Alchemist* pp. 44-45 • **17**. Édouard Chavannes, 'Inscriptions et pièces de chancellerie chinoises de l'époque mongole,' *T'oung Pao* 9 (1908) pp. 297-428 (at p. 399). Another version can be found in Bretschneider, *Mediaeval Researches* i pp. 37-39 • **18**. Chung to Genghis, April 1220, in Chavannes, 'Inscriptions,' loc. cit. p. 303 • **19**. Waley, *Travels of an Alchemist*; Bretschneider, *Mediaeval Researches* i pp. 43-44 • **20**. Chavannes, 'Inscriptions,' p. 305 • **21**. Waley, *Travels of an Alchemist* pp. 59-64 • **22**. ibid. pp. 64-65; Bretschneider, *Mediaeval Researches* i pp. 50-51 • **23**. We are not told who the queen was. The inference was that it must have been the ordo of Yesugei or Yesui (and possibly both). It cannot have been Borte's, and Qulan's *ordo* was in the Khenti Mountains of eastern Mongolia (Weatherford, *Secret History of the Mongol Queens* p. 28). In any case Qulan was with Genghis in the Hindu Kush. • **24**. For the city of craftsmen see Allsen, *Commodity and Exchange* p. 35. For Chinqai see Rachewiltz, *In the Service* pp. 95-110; Dawson, *Mongol Mission* pp. 66-67; Pelliot, *Notes sur Marco Polo* ii p. 825 • **25**. Waley, *Travels of an Alchemist* pp. 72-75; Bretschneider, *Mediaeval Researches* i p. 61 • **26**. Waley, *Travels of an Alchemist* pp. 75-77 • **27**. ibid. p. 78; Bretschneider, *Mediaeval Researches* i pp. 64-67 • **28**. Pelliot, 'Des artisans chinois à la capitale Abbasid,' *T'oung Pao* 26 (1928) pp. 1-762 • **29**. Waley, *Travels of an Alchemist* p. 85; Bretschneider, *Mediaeval Researches* i p. 69 • **30**. Waley, *Travels of an Alchemist* pp. 86-92; Bretschneider, *Mediaeval Researches* i pp. 73-77 • **31**. Waley, *Travels of an Alchemist* p. 93 • **32**. For Yelu Ahai see JB i p. 97; Rachewiltz, *In the Service* pp. 112-121 (esp. pp. 118-119); Pelliot, 'Notes sur le "Turkestan",' loc. cit. pp. 47-48 • **33**. For Yelu Chu Cai see Rachewiltz, *In the Service* pp. 136-175 • **34**. ibid. p. 144 • **35**. ibid. • **36**. Waley, *Travels of an Alchemist* pp. 94-98 • **37**. Bretschneider, *Mediaeval Researches* i pp. 82-86 • **38**. Waley, *Travels of an Alchemist* pp. 98-100 • **39**. As later revealed in the debates held at the Mongol court in the 1250s between Friar William of Rubruck and the priests of rival religions (Jackson & Morgan, *Rubruck* pp. 225-233). Cf Richard Fox Young, 'Deus Unus or Dei Plures Sunt? The Function of Inclusiveness in the Buddhist Defense of Mongol Folk Religion against William of Rubruck,' *Journal of Ecumenical Studies* 26 (1989) pp. 100-137 • **40**. Waley, *Travels of an Alchemist* p. 102 • **41**. ibid. pp. 103-16; Bretschneider, *Mediaeval Researches* i pp. 87-93 • **42**. Waley, *Travels of an Alchemist* pp. 111-112; Bretschneider, *Mediaeval Researches* i pp. 94-96 • **43**. Tao-chung Yao, 'Chi'u Ch'u-chi and Chinggis Khan,' *Harvard Journal of Asiatic Studies* 46 (1986) pp. 201-219; Ratchnevsky, *Genghis Khan*, pp. 134-135, 149-150, 238 • **44**. This might be described as an ur-Kantian notion, as Kant described his *noumenon* as an object of thought but not of knowledge. • **45**. See Chavannes & Pelliot, *Un traité manichéen* p. 289 • **46**. Reid, *The Tao of Health* p. 26; Welch, *Taoism* p. 154 • **47**. Waley, *Travels of an Alchemist* pp. 24, 118. As for the precious gift of 'life', scholars are divided about whether Chang meant Genghis's or, as a Buddhist, all life including the boar's. An educated guess might be that he was being deliberately ambiguous. • **48**. JB ii p. 613 • **49**. Waley, *Travels of an Alchemist* p. 115 • **50**. ibid. pp. 115-116 • **51**. Bretschneider, *Mediaeval Researches* i pp. 97-108 • **52**. Chavannes, 'Inscriptions et pièces,' loc. cit. p. 372 • **53**. Waley, *Travels of an Alchemist* pp. 119-133 • **54**. ibid. pp. 135-136 • **55**. ibid. p. 150. • **56**. Rachewiltz, *In the Service* p. 145 • **57**. ibid. p. 198 • **58**. Paul Demieville, 'La situation religieuse en Chine au temps de Marco Polo,' *Oriente Poliano* (Rome 1957) pp. 193-236 (at pp. 200-201); Rachewiltz, 'The *Hsi-Yu-lu* by Yeh-Lü Ch'u Ts'ai,' *Monumenta Serica* 21 (1962) pp. 1-128 (at pp. 25-37) • **59**. RT ii p. 258; Barthold, *Four Studies* i pp. 41, 64; Grousset, *Empire* p. 244 • **60**. JR ii pp. 1083-1084 • **61**. Martin, *Rise* pp. 283-284 • **62**. JR ii p. 1084 • **63**. d'Ohsson, *Histoire* i pp. 322-323 • **64**. SHO p. 251; SHR pp. 192-193; Barthold, *Turkestan* p. 455; d'Ohsson, *Histoire* i p. 233 • **65**. SHO p. 260; SHR p. 198 • **66**. A. P. Martinez, 'The Use of Mint-Output Data in Historical Research on the Western Appanages,' in Sinor, *Aspects* pp. 87-126; Atwood, *Encyclopedia* p. 362 • **67**. Of the many examples of this see, Eleanor Sims, 'Trade and Travel: Markets and Caravanserais,' in Michell, *Architecture* pp. 80-111; Verschuer, *Across the Perilous Sea* • **68**. JB i p. 96; Yule, *Cathay* ii pp. 287-288; Bretschneider, *Mediaeval Researches* i p. 283; Barthold, *Turkestan* pp. 456-457 • **69**. Riasanovsky, *Fundamental Principles* p. 88; Fletcher, 'The Mongols,' loc. cit. p. 50 • **70**. For the improved Mongol diet see Paul D. Buell, 'Pleasing the palate of the Qan: changing foodways of the imperial Mongols,' *Mongolian Studies* 13 (1990) pp. 69-73; Buell, 'Mongol Empire and Turkicisation: the evidence of food and foodways,' in Amitai-Preiss & Morgan, eds, *Mongol Empire* op. cit. pp. 200-223; Lane, *Daily Life* pp. 173-178 • **71**. Hildinger, *Story of the Mongols* pp. 17, 51 • **72**. Lane, *Daily Life* pp. 152-153 • **73**. John Smith, 'Dietary Decadence and Dynastic Decline in the Mongol Empire,' *Journal of Asian Studies* 34 (2000) pp. 35-52 • **74**. W. Barthold, 'The Burial Rites of the Turks and Mongols,' *Central Asiatic Journal* 12 (1968) pp. 195-227; Boyle, 'Kirakos,' p. 207; J. A. Boyle, 'A Form of Horse Sacrifice among the Thirteenth and Fourteenth-Century Mongols,' *Central Asiatic Journal* 10 (1965) pp. 145-150; Pelliot, *Recherches* p. 99 • **75**. Skelton, Marston & Painter, *Vinland Map* pp. 92-93 • **76**. de Windt, *From Pekin to Calais* • **77**. H. Haslund, *Mongol Journey* pp. 172-173. According to experts, the word *kodagalaku* in Mongolian means the depositing of a corpse on the steppes (Lessing, *Mongolian–English Dictionary* p. 477). For the connections of this practice with Mongol religion in general see Bonnefoy, *Asian Mythologies* pp. 314-339; Heissig, *Synkretismus* • **78**. JR ii p. 1102; d'Ohsson, *Histoire* i p. 447 • **79**. Barthold, *Turkestan* p. 458 • **80**. JB i p. 118 • **81**. Gumilev, *Imaginary Kingdom* p. 323; Pelliot, *Horde d'Or* pp. 10-27 • **82**. JR ii p. 1103 • **83**. The words are by Thomas Hobbes, *Leviathan* Part 1, Chapter 17 • **84**. JR ii p. 1103; Barthold, *Turkestan* p. 495 • **85**. Morgan, *The Mongols* pp. 64-65 • **86**. As has been well said, 'Asha Gambu's definite refusal to negotiate or compromise provoked the Mongols' devastatingly thorough obliteration of the Tangut state' (Franke & Twitchett, *Cambridge History* p. 211). • **87.** Martin, *Rise* • **88.** ibid. p. 285 • **89.** Franke & Twitchett, *Cambridge History* pp. 210-211 • **90.** Martin, *Rise* p. 286 • **91.** Pelliot, *Notes sur Marco Polo* i pp. 304-330 • **92.** JB i p. 147 • **93.** SHC p. 205; SHO pp. 257-258; SHR pp. 196-198 • **94.** Krause, *Cingis Han* p. 39 • **95.** Martin, *Rise* pp. 289-290 • **96.** Ksenia Kepping, 'The Name of the Tangut Empire,' *T'oung Pao* 80 (1994) pp. 357-376; Kepping, 'Chinggis Khan's Last Campaign as seen by the Tanguts,' in Kepping, *Recent Articles* pp. 172-195 • **97.** Vladimirtsov, *Genghis* p. 185 • **98.** Mote, *Imperial China* p. 257 • **99.** JR ii pp. 1085-1086 • **100.** Meignan, *Paris to Pekin* pp. 356-357 • **101.** For Qara Qoto see Wang & Perkins, *Collections of Sir Aurel Stein* pp. 42-44; Kozlow, *Charachoto* p. 383; John Carswell, 'A Month in Mongolia: Khara-Khoto revisited,' *Asian Affairs* 29 (1998) pp. 287-298 • **102.** RT ii p. 261; Franke & Twitchett, *Cambridge History* p. 211 • **103.** ibid. • **104.** Ebrey, *East Asia* p. 199; Kohn, *Dictionary of Wars* p. 205; Li, *China at War* p. 139. There are also some pointers to the devastation in A. P. Terentyev-Katansky, 'The Appearance, Clothes and Utensils of the Tanguts,' in Olderogge, ed., *Countries and Peoples* pp. 215-244. • **105.** Pelliot, *Notes sur Marco Polo* i p. 315; Yule & Cordier, *Ser Marco Polo* i Chapter 45 • **106.** R. W. Dunnell, 'Locating the Tangut Military Estabishment: Uraqai (Wulahai) and the Heishui Zhenyan army,' *Monumenta Serica* 40 (1992) pp. 219-234 (at pp. 223-228) • **107.** Franke & Twitchett, *Cambridge History* p. 211 • **108.** Martin, *Rise* p. 300 • **109.** ibid. pp. 293-294 • **110.** It is surprising that there is no mention of Subedei's important campaign in Gabriel, *Subotai.* • **111.** For the Nan Shan or Qilian mountains see Winchester, *Man Who Loved China* p. 126. For the Alashan desert see Lattimore, 'Return to China's Northern Frontiers,' *Geographical Journal* 139 (1973) pp. 233-242 • **112.** Martin, *Rise* p. 293. For the historical importance of Wuwei see Hill, *Through the Jade Gate* p. 45. • **113.** The Nine Fords of the Yellow River feature in what has been described as the most famous love story in Chinese literature, by Wang Shifu: *The Story of the Western Wing,* p. 118. See also the book review by David L. Rolston, 'The Story of the Western Wing,' *The China Quarterly* 145 (1996) pp. 231-232 • **114.** Pelliot, *Notes sur Marco Polo* iii p. 296; Martin, *Rise* p. 295 • **115.** Pelliot, *Notes sur Marco Polo* i pp. 315-317; Rachewiltz, *Commentary* pp. 973-975; Martin, *Rise* p. 294 • **116.** d'Ohsson, *Histoire* i p. 273 • **117.** RT ii pp. 261-262; Pelliot, *Notes sur Marco Polo* i p. 315; ii pp. 641-643; Krause, *Cingis Han* pp. 39-40 • **118.** Martin, *Rise* p. 299 • **119.** Herrmann, *Atlas of China* pp. 42, 44, 47; Yule & Cordier, *Ser Marco Polo* i pp. 282-283 • **120.** SHC p. 207; SHO p. 261; SHR pp. 199-200 • **121.** RT ii p. 263 • **122.** RT ii p. 263; Pelliot, *Notes sur Marco Polo* i pp. 310-315; ii pp. 641-642 • **123.** Ruth W. Dunnell, 'The Fall of the Xia Empire: Sino-Steppe Relations in the Late Twelfth and Thirteenth Centuries,' in Seaman & Marks, *Rulers from the Steppe* pp. 158-183 (at pp. 178-179) • **124**. Mote, *Imperial China* pp. 256-257; Franke & Twitchett, *Cambridge History* p. 214 • **125**. For an assessment of the population losses see Boland-Crewe & Lea, *People's Republic of China* p. 215 • **126**. Martin, *Rise* p. 296 • **127**. ibid. • **128**. For the myriad problems engendered by this division of the empire see, in greater detail, RT ii pp. 349-350. 535, 583, 649, 654 • **129**. JB i p. 119; T. Allsen, 'The Princes of the Left Hand: An Introduction to the History of the *Ulus* of Ordu in the Thirteenth and Early Fourteenth Centuries,' *Archivum Eurasiae Medii Aevi* 5 (1987) pp. 5-40 • **130**. P. Jackson, 'The Dissolution of the Mongol Empire,' *Central Asiatic Journal* 22 (1978) pp. 186-244 (esp. p. 193); Fletcher, 'The Mongols,' loc. cit. p. 50 • **131**. JR ii pp. 1086-1087 • **132**. Wittfogel & Feng, *Liao* pp. 398-400; Ratchnevsky & Aubin, *Un code des Yuan* iii p. lxvi; Ayalon, 'The Great Yasa,' loc. cit. (1971) pp. 151-180; Peter Turchin, Jonathan M. Adams & Thomas D. Hall, 'East-West Orientation of Historical Empires,' *Journal of World-Systems Research* 12 (2006) pp. 219-229 • **133**. Barfield, *Perilous Frontier* pp. 210-212 • **134**. RT ii p. 262; SHO p. 15 • **135**. Rachewiltz, 'Some Remarks on the Ideological Foundations of Chingis Khan's Empire,' *Papers on Far Eastern History* 7 (1993) pp. 21-36; Eric Voegelin, 'The Mongol Orders of Submission to the European Powers, 1245–1255,' *Byzantion* 15 (1941) pp. 378-413 • **136**. SHC p. 209; SHO p. 261; SHR pp. 199-200 • **137**. Krause, *Cingis Han* p. 40; Vladimirtsov, *Genghis* p. 115 • **138**. Rachewiltz, *Commentary* pp. 975-977 • **139**. Mostaert, *Sur quelques passages* pp. 220-225 • **140**. Rachewiltz, *Commentary* p. 995 • **141**. JR ii p. 1096; JB i p. 180 • **142**. Pelliot, *Notes sur Marco Polo* i p. 328 • **143**. For this story see the study by Babcock, *The Night Attila Died* • **144**. Buell, *Dictionary* pp. 240-241. Rachewiltz refers to 'colourful folklore motifs such as unusual sexual injury caused by the Tangut queen' (*Commentary* p. 980). • **145**. ibid. For an investigation of the possible causes of death see D. C. Wright, 'The Death of Chinggis Khan in Mongolian, Chinese, Persian and European Sources,' in Berta, *Historic and Linguistic Interaction* pp. 425-433; E. Haenisch, 'Die letzte Feldzüge Cinggis Hans und sein Tod nach der ostasiatischen Überlieferung,' *Asia Minor* 9 (1933) pp. 503-551. See also the review of same by Pelliot in *T'oung Pao* 31 (1934) pp. 157-167 • **146**. RT ii pp. 263-264; JR ii p. 1088; JB i p. 183; Krause, *Cingis Han* pp. 40-41; Pelliot, *Notes sur Marco Polo* i pp. 305-309, 327 • **147**. RT ii p. 264 • **148**. Krueger, *Erdeni-yin Tobči*; Bawden, *Altan Tobči* pp. 144-145 • **149**. Ratchnevsky, *Genghis Khan* pp. 142-144 • **150**. JR ii p. 1089 • **151**. Ratchnevsky, *Genghis Khan* p. 144

Chapter 14

1. JB i p. 163; Barfield, *Perilous Frontier* pp. 207-209 • **2**. JB ii p. 549 • **3**. Mostaert, *Sur quelques passages* pp. 100-185; Françoise Aubin, 'Le statut de l'enfant sans la societé mongole,' *L'Enfant* 35 (1975) pp. 459-599 (at pp. 551-553); d'Ohsson,

Histoire ii p. 9; • **4**. Krause, *Cingis Han* p. 41; Boyle, *Successors* pp. 186-187 • **5**. Rachewiltz, *Commentary* p. 936 • **6**. JB i pp. 183-190; Boyle, *Successors* pp. 30-31, 181-182; Rachewiltz, *Commentary* p. 936 • **7**. SHC pp. 190-195; SHR pp. 181-186 • **8**. Mostaert pp. 200-207 • **9**. Boyle, *Successors* p. 190; d'Ohsson, *Histoire* ii p. 13 • **10**. JB ii p. 549; Bretschneider, *Mediaeval Researches* i p. 160; Pelliot & Hambis, *Campagnes* pp. 175-177; Vladimirtsov, *Le régime social* pp. 66-67 • **11**. Boyle, *Successors* p. 43. • **12**. Pelliot, *Horde d'Or* pp. 24, 28-29 • **13**. Peter Jackson, 'From *Ulus* to Khanate: The Making of the Mongol States c. 1220–1290,' in Amitai-Preiss & Morgan, *Mongol Empire* pp. 12-38 • **14**. For Toregene see JB i pp. 239-244 • **15**. JR ii p. 1104 • **16**. Boyle, *Successors* p, 228; Pelliot, *Notes sur Marco Polo* i p. 253 • **17**. SHO p. 277; SHR pp. 207-208 • **18**. Boyle, *Successors* pp. 93-94; JB i pp. 235-236 • **19**. Boyle, *Successors* p. 80 • **20**. JB i pp. 201-202; Boyle, *Successors* pp. 76, 81-82 • **21**. JB i pp. 208-235 provides many stories of Ogodei's generosity, making it appear almost pathological or mythical, as if he were a hero in a Frank Capra movie. • **22**. Boyle, *Successors* pp. 83-89, 92-93 • **23**. SHO p. 262; SHR pp. 201-202 • **24**. Boyle, *Successors* pp. 147-148 • **25**. ibid. pp. 155-156 • **26**. Barthold, *Four Studies* i pp. 114-115 • **27**. Boyle, *Successors* pp. 155-156 • **28**. JR ii pp. 1144-1148 • **29**. RT i p. 44; JR ii pp. 1106-1107 • **30**. JB i pp. 205-206 • **31**. ibid. pp. 206-207 • **32**. ibid. p. 207 • **33**. JR ii pp. 1110-1115 • **34**. Barthold, *Four Studies* i pp. 35-37. There was another similar incident when a Muslim was unable to repay a loan to an Uighur moneylender. The man was then told he had to convert to Buddhism or accept the local punishment of a beating. He appealed to Ogodei, who quashed the judgement, ordered the Uighur usurer beaten instead, confiscated his house and wife and gave them to the Muslim debtor. • **35**. Fletcher, 'Mongols', p. 37 • **36**. JB ii pp. 411-426; d'Ohsson, *Histoire* iv pp. 64-68 • **37**. JB ii pp. 421-423 • **38**. ibid. p. 424 • **39**. IAA iii pp. 237-240 • **40**. ibid. iii pp. 244-245 • **41**. ibid. iii pp. 242-243, 254-256 • **42**. ibid. iii pp. 252-253, 256-259 • **43**. J. A. Boyle, *Cambridge History of Iran* v p. 327 • **44**. A large amount of material on Jalal's 1225–28 campaign against the Georgians is available: IAA iii pp. 269-70, 276-277; JB ii pp. 426-438; Spuler, *Mongolen in Iran* p. 30; Minorsky, *Caucasian History* pp. 149-156. • **45**. IAA iii pp. 272-273 • **46**. JR i p. 296 • **47**. IAA iii p. 288 • **48**. JR i p. 297 • **49**. JB ii pp. 438-439 • **50**. IAA iii p. 289 • **51**. Lewis, *Assassins*; Hodgson, *Secret Order*; Daftary, *Ismailis* • **52**. Minorsky, *Caucasian History* p. 156 • **53**. JB ii pp. 441-443 • **54**. IAA iii pp. 258-259; Minorsky, *Caucasian History* pp. 102-103; Grousset, *Empire* pp. 260-261 • **55**. IAA iii pp. 297-298 • **56**. ibid. p. 298 • **57**. ibid. pp. 260, 277-278; George Lane, 'The Mongols in Iran,' in Daryaee, *Iranian History* pp. 243-70; Lane, *Early Mongol Rule* • **58**. JB ii p. 438; IAA iii p. 279; Hartmann, *An-Nasir li-Din Allah* pp. 85-86; Minorsky, *Caucasian History* p. 154 • **59**. Boyle, *Successors* p. 43 • **60**. ibid. p. 47 • **61**. IAA iii p. 304 • **62**. ibid. iii p. 303 • **63**. JR i p. 297; JB ii p. 451; IAA iii pp. 299-300; Hans Gottschalk, 'Der

Bericht des Ibn Nazif al-Hamawi über die Schlacht von Yasyčimen (15–28 Ramadan 622/7–10 August 1230),' in *Wiener Zeitschrift für die Kunde des Morgenlandes* 56 (1960) pp. 55-67; A. C. S. Peacock, 'The Saljuq campaign against the Crimea and the Expansionist Policy of the early reign of Ala al-Din Kayqubad,' *Journal of the Royal Asiatic Society* 16 (2006) pp. 143-149; Cahen, *Pre-Ottoman Turkey* pp. 120-121, 1301-33; Grousset, *Empire* p. 261 • **64**. IAA iii p. 303 • **65**. d'Ohsson, *Histoire* iii pp. 47-48 • **66**. JB ii pp. 453-457 • **67**. IAA iii pp. 305-307 • **68**. JR i p. 298; Boyle, *Successors* p. 48 • **69**. JB ii p. 459; Boyle, *Successors* p. 48 • **70**. JB ii pp. 459-460; Spuler, *Mongolen in Iran* p. 31 • **71**. Nesawi [Nasawi], *Djelal ed-Din Mankobirti* p. 230 • **72**. Spuler, *Mongolen in Iran* pp. 35-38 • **73**. IAA iii p. 304 • **74**. ibid. iii pp. 308-310; d'Ohsson, *Histoire* iii pp. 47-74; Allsen, *Culture and Conquest* p. 84 • **75**. The entire subject of the Mongol attitude to Christianity is reviewed in Pelliot, 'Les Mongols et la papauté,' *Revue de l'Orient chrétien* 23 (1923) pp. 3-30; 24 (1924) pp. 225-235; 28 (1932) pp. 3-84. The particular references to Chormaqan are at 28 (1932) pp. 236-246. • **76**. Richard Foltz, 'Ecumenical Mischief under the Mongols,' *Central Asiatic Journal* 43 (1999) pp. 42-69 • **77**. d'Ohsson, *Histoire* iii pp. 75-76 • **78**. Suny, *Making of the Georgian Nation* pp. 39-44 • **79**. A. G. Galstyan, trans. R. Bedrosian, 'The Conquest of Armenia by the Mongol Armies,' *The Armenian Review* 27 (1985) pp. 4-108; Altunian, *Die Mongolen* pp. 35-37; Robert Bedrosian, 'Armenia during the Seljuk and Mongol periods,' in Hovannisian, *Armenian People* i pp. 241-271 (esp. p. 256); Dashdondog, *Mongols and the Armenians* p. 43 • **80**. JB ii pp. 489-500; Spuler, *Die Mongolen in Iran* p. 34; d'Ohsson, *Histoire* iii pp. 78-84 • **81**. JR ii p. 1137 • **82**. Franke & Twitchett, *Cambridge History* p. 263. It was bad luck for another Jin envoy that this happened while he was at the Mongol court. In retaliation Ogodei ordered humiliation and a slow death instead of instant execution. The envoy had his beard cut off and was then sent to the front as one of the 'arrow fodder' unfortunates in the van of the Mongol army (d'Ohsson, *Histoire* ii p. 19). • **83**. d'Ohsson, *Histoire* ii pp. 16-18 • **84**. One estimate is that in the years 1230–35, if we include the simultaneous campaigns against Jalal, the Jin, Korea and the steppe Bulgars, Ogodei had forces 400,000 strong at his disposal (Martin, *Rise* p. 15). • **85**. d'Ohsson, *Histoire* ii pp. 19-20 • **86**. Whiting, *Military History* p. 355 • **87**. d'Ohsson, *Histoire* ii p. 20 • **88**. Vladimirtsov, *Genghis* pp. 112-113 • **89**. SHO p. 264; SHR p. 202 • **90**. Charles A. Peterson, 'Old Illusions and New Realities: Sung Foreign Policy, 1217–1234,' in Rossabi, *China among Equals* pp. 204-239 (at p. 221) • **91**. Franke, *Geschichte* iv pp. 286-287 • **92**. JR i p. 286 • **93**. JR i p. 287 • **94**. d'Ohsson, *Histoire* ii pp. 22-24 • **95**. Abel-Rémusat, *Nouveaux mélanges* p. 93 • **96**. d'Ohsson, *Histoire* ii pp. 24-25 • **97**. Gabriel, *Subotai* p. 63 • **98**. Although scholars are usually sceptical about tales of Mongol cannibalism, the outbreak of anthropophagy by desperate men in Tolui's army in 1231–32 can hardly be gainsaid (Gregory G. Guzman, 'Reports of Mongol Cannibalism in the Thirteenth-Century Latin Sources: Oriental Fact or Western Fiction?' in Westrem, ed., *Discovering New Worlds* pp. 31-68). See also Rachewiltz, *Commentary* p. 915 • **99.** Boyle, *Successors* p. 35 • **100.** ibid. p. 36 • **101.** JR ii pp. 1137-1138 • **102.** Boyle, *Successors* p. 37 • **103.** ibid. p. 38 • **104.** JR ii p. 1138 • **105.** Tao, *Jurchen* p. 23 • **106.** d'Ohsson, *Histoire* ii pp. 25-26 • **107.** ibid. • **108.** Boyle, *Successors* p. 39 • **109.** Rachewiltz, *In the Service* p. 20 • **110.** ibid. p. 61 • **111.** Franke, *Geschichte* iv pp. 285-286 • **112.** Abel-Rémusat, *Nouveaux mélanges* p. 95 • **113.** C. Sverdrup, 'Numbers in Mongol Warfare,' *Journal of Medieval Military History* 8 (2010) pp. 109-117 (at p. 116) • **114.** Paul J. Smith, 'Family, *Landsmann* and Status-Group Affinity in Refugee Mobility Strategeies: the Mongol Invasions and the Diaspora of Sichuanese Elites, 1230–1300,' *Harvard Journal of Asiatic Studies* 52 (1992) pp. 665-708 • **115.** Peterson, 'Old Illusions,' loc. cit. p. 224; Jagchid & Symons, *Peace, War and Trade* pp. 134-135 • **116.** Buell, *Dictionary* p. 138 • **117.** This manifested itself particularly in the battles between Jin and Song in the twelfth century, when the aetiology of disease was thought to be connected with marmots (Perdue, *China Marches West* p. 47). • **118.** Mote, *Imperial China* p. 447 • **119.** SHO pp. 265-266; SHR pp. 203-205; SHC pp. 211-214 • **120.** JB i pp. 38-39, 167-168; ii p. 549 • **121.** Fletcher, 'The Mongols,' p. 36; Rachewiltz, *Commentary* pp. 999-1001. See also JR ii p. 1138; Boyle, *Successors* pp. 38-39, 167-168 • **122.** Gumilev, *Imaginary Kingdom* pp. 297-298 • **123.** JB ii pp. 550-553; Boyle, *Successors* pp. 168-171 • **124.** Haenisch, *Zum Untergang zweier Reiche* pp. 7-26 • **125.** d'Ohsson *Histoire*, ii pp. 34-35 • **126.** W. Abramowski, 'Die chinesischen Annalen von Ögödei und Güyük – Übersetzung des 2. Kapitels des Yüan Shih,' *Zentralasiatische Studien* 10 (1976) pp. 117-167 (at pp. 124-130) • **127.** d'Ohsson, *Histoire* ii p. 29 • **128.** Jixing Pan, 'On the origin of rockets,' *T'oung Pao* 73 (1987) pp. 2-15 • **129.** Feng Chia-Sheng, 'The Discovery and Diffusion of Gunpowder', *Historical Journal* 5 (1947) pp. 29-84 • **130.** G. Schlegel, 'On the Invention of Firearms and Gunpowder in China', *T'oung Pao* 3 (1902) pp. 1-11 • **131.** RT ii p. 450; Franke, *Geschichte* iv pp. 287-288; Paul E. Chevedden, 'The Invention of the Counterweight Trebuchet: A Study in Cultural Diffusion,' *Dumbarton Oaks Papers* 54 (2000) pp. 71-116. It appears that the counterweight trebuchet was first used methodically at a siege by the Byzantines in 1165. They were famously used by Richard the Lionheart at the siege of Acre in 1189–91. Double counterweight trebuchets were later used by Emperor Frederick II ('*Stupor Mundi*') and by Louis IX on crusade. It seems a fair inference that the Mongols, who totally outclassed Europeans in the warfare of 1237–42, would have used them by the early 1230s. • **132.** d'Ohsson, *Histoire* ii p. 32. • **133.** As graphically portrayed in Chan, *Fall of the Jurchen Chin* • **134.** Waley, *Travels of an Alchemist*, p. 34 • **135.** d'Ohsson, *Histoire* ii p. 40 • **136.** ibid. p. 41

• **137**. JR ii p. 1139 • **138**. Franke, *Geschichte* iv pp. 288-289 • **139**. d'Ohsson, *Histoire* ii pp. 43-44 • **140**. ibid. pp. 45-46 • **141**. Franke, *Geschichte* iv p. 290 • **142**. See below, Chapter 15 • **143**. Franke & Twitchett, *Cambridge History* p. 264 • **144**. Peterson, 'Old Illusions,' loc. cit. p. 224 • **145**. Franke, *Geschichte* iv p. 290 • **146**. ibid. v p. 137; JR ii p. 1139 • **147**. Barfield, *Perilous Frontier* p. 198 • **148**. Grousset, *Empire* p. 259 • **149**. Peterson, 'Old Illusions,' loc. cit. pp. 226-230 • **150**. Franke, *Geschichte* iv pp. 291-303, 350; d'Ohsson, *Histoire* ii pp. 78-84 • **151**. Henthorn, *Korea*, p. 53; Kuno, *Japanese Expansion* ii. pp. 387-393; Hazard, *Japanese Marauders* • **152**. Henthorn, *Korea*, pp. 61-68, 93-94; G. Ledyard, 'The Mongol Campaign in Korea and the dating of the *Secret History of the Mongols*,' *Central Asiatic Journal* 9 (1964) pp.1-22 • **153**. Yule & Cordier, *Marco Polo*, ii. pp. 180-181 • **154**. Henthorn, *Korea* pp. 68-75, 93-99; Louis Hambis, 'Notes sur l'histoire de Corée à l'époque mongole,' *T'oung Pao* 45 (1957) pp. 151-218 • **155**. Hans Sagaster, 'The History of Buddhism among the Mongols,' in Heirman & Bumbacher, *Spread of Buddhism* pp. 379-432; Paul Ratchnevsky, 'Die Mongolische Grosskhane und die buddhistische Kirche,' *Asiatica: Festchrift F. Weller* (1954) pp. 489-504 • **156**. Allsen, *Royal Hunt* p. 23 • **157**. Henthorn, *Korea* pp. 92-101 • **158**. Allsen, *Culture and Conquest* p. 53; Atwood, *Encyclopedia* p. 319 • **159**. Turrel J. Wylie, 'The First Mongol Conquest of Tibet Reinterpreted,' *Harvard Journal of Asiatic Studies* 37 (1977) pp. 103-133 (at pp. 103-106) • **160**. ibid. p. 112

Chapter 15

1. SHR pp. 209-213; W. Abramowski, 'Die chinesischen Annalen von Ögödei und Güyük,' loc. cit. pp. 117-167 (at p. 152); Jackson & Morgan, *Rubruck* pp. 33-39. According to Yarshater, *Encyclopedia Iranica* viii pp. 366-367, the Eljigidei employed by Ogodei is not the same as the one employed by Genghis to execute Jamuga and the one who destroyed Herat in 1222, but this theory of 'two Eljigideis' does not command universal assent. • **2**. Buell, *Dictionary* p. 202 • **3**. Rachewiltz, *In the Service* pp. 95-112. • **4**. Paul D. Buell, 'Chinqai (1169–1252), Architect of Mongolian Empire,' in Kaplan & Whisenhunt, *Opuscula Altaica* pp. 168-186 • **5**. Franke & Twitchett, *Cambridge History* p. 373; Waley, *Travels of an Alchemist* p. 92; Bretschneider, *Mediaeval Researches* i p. 70 • **6**. Francis Woodman Cleaves, 'A Chancellery Practice of the Mongols in the Thirteenth and Fourteenth Centuries,' *Harvard Journal of Asiatic Studies* 14 (1951) pp. 493-526; István Vásáry, 'The Origins of the Institution of *Basqaqs*,' *Acta Orientalia Academiae Scientiarum Hungaricae* 32 (1978) pp. 201-206; Vásáry, 'The Golden Horde Term *Daruga* and its Survival in Russia,' *Acta Orientalia Academiae Scientiarum Hungaricae* 30 (1976) pp. 187-196; Barthold, *Turkestan* pp. 468-469 • **7**. Introductory remarks are found at Ratchnevsky, *Genghis Khan*,

p. 138 and d'Ohsson, *Histoire* iv pp. 381-405. Deeper analysis is provided in Vásáry, 'The Origin of the Institution of *Basqaqs*,' loc. cit. p. 323; Spuler, *Mongolen in Iran* pp. 40-42; Spuler, *Goldene Horde* p. 338; Doerfer, *Türkische und mongolische Elemente* iv p. 242. The institution of daruqachi was one of Genghis's innovations that survived into the Yuan empire of China. For a detailed study see Endicott-West, *Mongolian Rule* • **8**. For Chinqai's huge importance into the reign of Guyuk in the mid-1240s see Dawson, *Mongol Mission* pp. 63-67 • **9**. Paul D. Buell, 'Sino-Khitan administration in Mongol Bukhara,' *Journal of Asian History* 13 (1979) pp. 121-151 • **10**. Rachewiltz, *In the Service* pp. 122-128 (esp. p. 123) • **11**. SHO p. 254; SHR p. 195; Spuler, *Mongolen in Iran* pp. 40-42; Lane, *Daily Life* p. 62; Christian, *History of Russia* i p. 415 • **12**. Rachewiltz, *In the Service* pp. 124-125 • **13**. Two studies of Yelu by Rachewiltz are fundamental: 'Yeh-lü Ch'u-ts'ai (1189–1243): Buddhist Idealist and Confucian Statesman,' in Wright & Twitchett, *Confucian Personalities* pp. 189-216 and the entry in *In the Service*, op. cit. pp. 136-175 • **14**. Rachewiltz, 'Yeh-lu . . . Buddhist Idealist,' loc. cit. pp. 192-193; Rachewiltz, *In the Service* pp. 139-140 • **15**. Rachewiltz, 'The *Hsi-Yu-lu* by Yeh-Lü Ch'u Ts'ai,' *Monumenta Serica* 21 (1962) pp. 1-128 (esp. pp. 17-37) • **16**. Wittfogel & Feng, *Liao* pp. 749-751 • **17**. Bretschneider, *Mediaeval Researches* i pp. 9-10 • **18**. Rachewiltz, 'Yeh-lu . . . Buddhist Idealist,' loc. cit. pp. 194-195 • **19**. Gumilev, *Imaginary Kingdom* p. 238. Some scholars have gone the other way and claim that Yelu has been vastly overrated (Buell, *Dictionary* pp. 287-289). • **20**. Allsen, *Culture and Conquest* pp. 177-179; Buell, *Dictionary* pp. 133-134 • **21**. Grousset, *Empire* p. 321. The 'horseback' quote is notoriously migratory, having been attributed to a number of sages during Chinese history • **22**. H. F. Schurmann, 'Mongolian tributary practices of the thirteenth century,' *Harvard Journal of Asiatic Studies* 19 (1956) pp. 304-389 • **23**. Rachewiltz, 'Yeh-lu . . . Buddhist Idealist,' loc. cit. p. 202; Rachewiltz, *In the Service* pp. 151-152 • **24**. Allsen, *Imperialism* pp. 144-148 • **25**. Rachewiltz, 'Yeh-lu . . . Buddhist Idealist,' loc. cit. pp. 212-213 • **26**. Rachewiltz, *In the Service* p. 159; P. Ratchnevsky, 'Sigi-qutuqu,' *Central Asiatic Journal* 10 (1965) pp. 87-110 (at p. 87) • **27**. Rachewiltz, 'Yeh-lu . . . Buddhist Idealist,' loc. cit. p. 202 • **28**. Franke & Twitchett, *Cambridge History* p. 378 • **29**. J. Masson Smith, 'Mongol and nomadic taxation,' *Harvard Journal of Asiatic Studies* 30 (1970) pp. 46-85. For the unsystematic fiscal approach of the Mongols see A. K. S. Lambton, 'Mongol fiscal administration in Persia,' *Studia Islamica* 44 (1986) pp. 79-99; 45 (1987) pp. 97-123 • **30**. Morgan, *Mongols* pp. 100-103 • **31**. Kwanten, *Imperial Nomads* pp. 128-129 • **32**. d'Ohsson, *Histoire* ii p. 63 • **33**. Some of the administrative implications of this are teased out in F. W. Cleaves, 'A Chancellery Practice of the Mongols in the Thirteenth and Fourteenth Centuries,' loc. cit. pp. 493-526 • **34**. Rachewiltz, 'Yeh-lu . . . Buddhist Idealist,' loc. cit. p. 205 • **35**. Rachewiltz, *In the Service* pp. 60-69 •

36. Farquhar, *Government of China* p. 45; Gernet, *Daily Life* p. 65; Fairbank & Goldman, *China* pp. 95-107; Elman, *Civil Examinations* • **37**. Makino Shuji, 'Transformation of the Shih-jen in the late Chin and early Yuan,' *Acta Asiatica* 45 (1983) pp. 1-26 • **38**. Ch'i-ch'ing Hsiao, 'Yen Shih, 1182–1240,' *Papers on Far Eastern History* 33 (1986) pp. 113-128 (at pp. 119-122) • **39**. Rachewiltz, 'Yeh-lu . . . Buddhist Idealist,' loc. cit. p. 202; Rachewiltz, *In the Service* p. 151 • **40**. ibid. p. 165 • **41**. Franke & Twichett, *Cambridge History* p. 377 • **42**. On this subject in general and its implications see Nikolay N. Kradin, 'Nomadic Empires: Origin, Rise and Decline,' in Kradin et al, *Nomadic Pathways* pp. 73-87; Kradin, 'Nomadism, Evolution and World Systems: Pastoral Societies and Theories of Historical Development,' *Journal of World-Systems Research* 8 (2002) pp. 363-388 • **43**. Franke & Twitchett, *Cambridge History* p. 377 • **44**. Thomas T. Allsen, 'Sharing out the Empire: Apportioning Lands under the Empire,' in Khazanov & Wink, *Nomads and the Sedentary World* pp. 172-190 • **45**. Jackson, *Mongols and the West* p. 291 • **46**. JB i pp. 209-210, 213-215 • **47**. Rachewiltz *In the Service* p. 160 • **48**. ibid. • **49**. Franke & Twitchett, *Cambridge History* p. 377 • **50**. Abel-Rémusat, *Nouveaux mélanges* ii pp. 64-68 • **51**. For Shih-mo Hsien-te-pu see Rachewiltz, *In the Service* pp. 147-148, 160; Waley, *Travels of an Alchemist* p. 53. For Buyruq Qaya (1197–1265) see *In the Service* pp. 480-481; Buell, *Dictionary* p. 128; Buell, *A–Z of the Mongol Empire* p. 40 • **52**. Rachewiltz, *In the Service* p. 165 • **53**. For the latter phase of Yelu's relationship with Ogodei see Bretschneider, *Mediaeval Researches* i pp. 12-24; Tanner, *China: A History* i pp. 239-280 • **54**. Franke & Twitchett, *Cambridge History* p. 378 • **55**. ibid. p. 380 • **56**. Rachewiltz, 'Yeh-lu . . . Buddhist Idealist,' loc. cit. p. 208 • **57**. ibid. • **58**. ibid. 215; Rachewiltz, *In the Service* pp. 105-106, 125 • **59**. Michael Weiers, *Geschichte der Mongolen* p. 76 • **60**. Gregory G. Guzman, 'European Captives and Craftsmen among the Mongols, 1231–1255,' *The Historian* 72 (2010) pp. 122-150 • **61**. Jackson & Morgan, *Rubruck* pp. 182-183; Pelliot, *Recherches* pp. 161-164; J. Schneider, *Metz* pp. 191-192 • **62**. For Beshbaliq see JB i pp. 271-272; Barthold, *Four Studies* i pp. 114-115. For Kemkemjek see Asimov & Bosworth, *History of Civilizations* iv part 2 p. 584 • **63**. Jackson & Morgan, *Rubruck* pp. 144-145 • **64**. Bretschneider, *Mediaeval Researches* ii p. 331 • **65**. JB i pp. 236-239; JR ii pp. 1140-1141; Boyle, *Successors* pp. 61-62; Bretschneider, *Mediaeval Researches* i p. 123; Pelliot, *Notes sur Marco Polo* i pp. 166-167; Jackson & Morgan, *Rubruck* pp. 209-213, 221; Dawson, *Mongol Mission* pp. 156, 183-184. See also Phillips, *Mongols* pp. 96-103 • **66**. Asimov & Bosworth, *History of Civilizations* iv part 2 pp. 582-583 • **67**. Jackson & Morgan, *Rubruck* pp. 209-210 • **68**. See the essays by Hans-Georg Hüttel in Hirmer Verlag, *Dschingis Khan* pp. 133-137, 140-146 • **69**. Morgan & Jackson, *Rubruck* pp. 178-179; Pelliot, *Recherches* pp. 161-164; Durand-Guedy, *Turko-Mongol Rulers* p. 232; Shiraishi Noriyuki, 'Avraga Sita: the "Great Ordû" of Genghis Khan,' in Komaroff,

Beyond the Legacy pp. 83-93 (at pp. 89-90) • **70**. Thomas T. Allsen, 'Command Performances: Entertainers in the Mongolian Empire,' *Russian History* 28 (2001) pp. 37-46 • **71**. J. A. Boyle, 'The Seasonal Residences of the Great Khan Ogodei,' *Central Asiatic Journal* 16 (1972) pp. 125-131, reproduced in Hazai & Zieme, *Sprache, Geschichte und Kultur* pp. 145-151. • **72**. Eva Becker, 'Karakorum – Bukinič vs. Kiselev,' *Zentralasiatische Studien* 37 (2008) pp. 9-32 • **73**. SHC pp. 227-228; SHR pp. 217-218 • **74**. Latham, *Travels of Marco Polo* pp. 150-155 • **75**. Boyle, *Successors* pp. 62-64 • **76**. For the Pony Express see Settle, *Saddles and Spurs*. See also Alberto E. Minetti, 'Efficiency of Equine Express Postal Systems', *Nature* 426 (2003) pp. 785-786 • **77**. As with the tumens, these notional figures were not always attained. One study finds the sources providing figures ranging anywhere between fifteen and five hundred horses at the ready, depending on the nature and location of the posts (Lane, *Daily Life* p. 121). • **78**. Olbricht, *Postwesen in China* pp. 36-41, 66, 87 • **79**. Ricci, *Marco Polo* pp. 152-157 • **80**. Ratchnevsky, *Genghis Khan* pp. 180-181: Silverstein, *Postal Systems* • **81**. Ratchnevsky, *Genghis Khan* pp. 181-183 • **82**. Doerfer, *Türkische und mongolische Elemente* i pp. 102-107; Boyle, *Successors* p. 219 • **83**. Spuler, *Mongolen in Iran* pp. 349-350, 422-425 • **84**. Ratchnevsky, *Genghis Khan* p. 186 • **85**. JB i pp. 197-200; Boyle, *Successors* pp. 65-66; d'Ohsson, *Histoire* ii pp. 84-86 • **86**. ibid. ii pp. 86-87 • **87**. Thomas T. Allsen, 'Ögedei and Alcohol,' *Mongolian Studies* 29 (2007) pp. 3-12; Boyle, *Successors* p. 188; Lane, *Daily Life* p. 163 • **88**. Rachewiltz, *In the Service* pp. 102-104 • **89**. Boyle, *Successors* pp. 19, 180-181, 201; Fletcher, 'The Mongols,' pp. 37-38 • **90**. JB i pp. 239-244; Boyle, *Successors* p. 180; Hambis, *Le chapitre CVII du Yuan Che* pp. 3-4. For more on Koden and Shiremun see Buell, *Dictionary* pp. 184, 243 • **91**. Devin DeWeese, 'Islamization in the Mongol Empire,' in Di Cosmo, Frank & Golden, *Chinggisid Age* pp. 120-134 • **92**. Kohlberg, *Ibn Tawus* p. 10; Lambton, *Continuity and Change* p. 249 • **93**. Schurmann, *Economic Structure* pp. 66-67 • **94**. RT ii p. 330; Boyle, *Successors* pp. 65, 120; Franke, *Geschichte* iv p. 305; d'Ohsson, *Histoire* ii p. 87 • **95**. JR ii p. 1148 • **96**. Dawson, *Mongol Mission* p. 13; J. A. Boyle, 'The Burial Place of the Great Khan Ögedei,' *Acta Orientalia* 32 (1970) pp. 45-50

Chapter 16

1. Pelliot & Hambis, *Campagnes* p. 244 • **2**. Boyle, *Successors* pp. 54-55 • **3**. For Song expertise on this see Needham, *Science and Civilization* iv part 3 pp. 678-687; Atwood, *Encyclopedia* p. 509 • **4**. Denis Sinor, 'The Mongols in the West,' *Journal of Asian History* 33 (1999) pp. 1-44 • **5**. Hyland, *Medieval Warhorse* p. 131; Doerfer, *Türkische und mongolische Elemente* i pp. 387-391 • **6**. Vernadsky, *The Mongols in Russia* p. 49; Moss, *History of Russia* p. 69 • **7**. Buell, *Dictionary* pp. 255-258 • **8**. Dawson, *Mongol Mission* p. 57 • **9**. Moss, *History of Russia* p.

71. The waspish Russian historian was Nikolai Karamzin, who wrote a twelve-volume history of Russia in the early nineteenth century. For an analysis of Batu see Spuler, *Goldene Horde* pp. 10-32. See also Pelliot, *Notes sur Marco Polo* i pp. 88-89; Boyle, *Successors* p. 107; T. Allsen, 'The Princes of the Left Hand,' *Archivum Eurasiae Medii Aevi* 5 (1987) pp. 5-40 (esp. p. 10) • **10**. JR ii p. 1164 • **11**. Bretschneider, *Mediaeval Researches* i pp. 308-309, d'Ohsson; *Histoire*, ii p. 111; Rachewiltz, *In the Service* p. 22 • **12**. Spuler, *Goldene Horde* p. 16 • **13**. JR ii pp. 809-813; Peter Jackson, *Delhi Sultanate* pp. 39, 104 • **14**. Thomas T. Allsen, 'Prelude to the Western Campaign: Mongol Military Operations in the Volga–Ural region, 1217–1237,' *Archivum Eurasiae Medii Aevi* 3 (1983) pp. 5-24 (at pp. 10-13); Vernadsky, *Ancient Russia* pp. 222-228 • **15**. István Zimonyi, 'The Volga Bulghars between Wind and Water, 1220-1236,' *Acta Orientalia Academiae Scientiarum Hungaricae* 46 (1993) pp. 347-355 • **16**. Spuler, *Goldene Horde* p. 15 • **17**. Bretschneider, *Mediaeval Researches* i pp. 306-308; Allsen, 'Prelude,' loc. cit. pp. 14-18; d'Ohsson, *Histoire* ii p. 15 • **18**. Bretschneider, *Mediaeval Researches* i p. 309 • **19**. Göckenjan & Sweeney, *Mongolensturm* p. 104 • **20**. Bretschneider, *Mediaeval Researches* i p. 310 • **21**. Detailed linguistic analysis of some of the place-names mentioned in the sources can be found in Donald Ostrowski, 'City Names of the Western Steppes at the Time of the Mongol Invasion,' *Bulletin of the School of Oriental and African Studies* 61 (1998) pp. 465-475. • **22**. Allsen, 'Prelude,' loc. cit. pp. 19-24 • **23**. Gerald Mako, 'The Islamization of the Volga Bulghars: A Question Reconsidered,' *Archivum Eurasiae Medii Aevi* 18 (2011) pp. 199-223 • **24**. Bretschneider, *Mediaeval Researches* i p. 311 • **25**. Pelliot, 'À propos des Comans,' *Journal Asiatique* 208 (1920) pp., 125-185; Barthold, *Histoire des turcs* pp. 89-91; Peter B. Golden, 'Cumanica IV: The Tribes of the Cuman–Qipchags,' *Archivum Eurasiae Medii Aevi* 9 (1997) pp. 99-122; Golden, 'Religion among the Qipchags of Medieval Eurasia,' *Central Asiatic Journal* 42 (1998) pp. 180-237; Golden, 'War and Warfare in the pre-Chinggisid Steppes of Eurasia,' in Di Cosmo, *Warfare* pp. 105-172; Standen & Powers, *Frontiers in Question* • **26**. JB ii pp. 553-554; Boyle, *Successors* pp. 58-59 • **27**. Bretschneider, *Mediaeval Researches* i p. 311 • **28**. ibid. p. 312 • **29**. Pelliot, 'À propos des Comans,' loc. cit. pp. 166-167. For Bujek see JB ii p. 269 • **30**. Christian, *History* i p. 361 • **31**. Mitchell & Forbes, *Chronicle of Novgorod* p. 81 • **32**. Fennell, *Crisis* pp. 69-70 • **33**. 'Vladimir–Suzdalia,' in Langer, *Medieval Russia* pp. 245-248 • **34**. Fennell, *Crisis* p. 71-75; Martin, *Medieval Russia* p. 126 • **35**. Fennell, *Crisis* p. 85, using a figure arrived at by the Russian historian S. M. Soloviev • **36**. Grekov & Yakubovski, *Horde d'Or* p. 200 • **37**. Spuler, *Goldene Horde* p. 17; Vernadsky, *Source Book* i p. 45; d'Ohsson, *Histoire* ii pp. 113-115 • **38**. Zenkovsky, *Epics, Chronicles and Tales* p. 202 • **39**. RT ii p. 327; Boyle, *Successors* p. 59; Bretschneider, *Mediaeval Researches* i p. 313 • **40**. The sources mention Yaroslavl, Volzhsky, Gorodets, Kostroma, Galich, Pereslavl,

Rostov, Yuryev-Polsky, Dmitrov, Tver, Kashin, Volok, Torzhok and Ksnyatin. (Mitchell & Forbes, *Chronicle of Novgorod* p. 83; d'Ohsson, *Histoire* ii pp. 116-117). • **41**. Mitchell & Forbes, *Chronicle of Novgorod* pp. 82-83; Bretschneider, *Mediaeval Researches* i p. 315; Fennell, *Crisis* p. 80 • **42**. Spuler, *Goldene Horde* p. 18; Bretschneider, *Mediaeval Researches* i pp. 313-314, 317; Fennell, *Crisis* pp. 80-81; Vernadsky, *Mongols and Russia* p. 51 • **43**. Vernadsky, *Kievan Russia* p. 199. See also (for an approach via archaeology) Brisbane et al, *Medieval Novgorod* (2012) • **44**. Vernadsky, *Kievan Russia* p. 311 • **45**. Bretschneider, *Mediaeval Researches* i p. 313 • **46**. Mitchell & Forbes, *Chronicle of Novgorod* pp. 83-84; d'Ohsson, *Histoire* ii p. 117; Fennell, *Crisis* p. 81 • **47**. Boyle, *Successors* p. 60; Grekov & Yakubovski, *Horde d'Or* p. 202; Moss, *History of Russia* p. 69 • **48**. Hyland, *Medieval Warhorse* p. 127 • **49**. Boyle, *Successors* pp. 60-61; Bretschneider, *Mediaeval Researches* i pp. 316-317. For the Georgian defeat see Altunian, *Mongolen und ihre Eroberungen* pp. 33-41; Spuler, *Mongolen in Iran* pp. 34-35, 41-42; Dawson, *Mongol Mission* p. 41 • **50**. Rachewiltz, *In the Service* p. 24 • **51**. Pelliot, 'À propos des Comans,' loc. cit. p. 169 • **52**. Bretschneider, *Mediaeval Researches* i p. 322; Vásáry, *Cumans and Tatars* p. 81 • **53**. Pentti Aalto, 'Swells of the Mongol Storm around the Baltic,' *Acta Orientalia Academiae Scientiarum Hungaricae* 36 (1982) pp. 5-15 • **54**. JR ii pp. 1170-1171. Another expedition, under Batu's brother Shinqor in 1242–43, was said to have penetrated so far north that they met people with fair hair and there was just one hour of night (Wolff, *Mongolen oder Tartaren* pp. 148, 383). • **55**. Bretschneider, *Mediaeval Researches* i p. 317; Fennell, *Crisis* pp. 81-82 • **56**. Mitchell & Forbes, *Chronicle of Novgorod* pp. 84-85 • **57**. Fennell, *Crisis* p. 104 • **58**. ibid. • **59**. Bretschneider, *Mediaeval Researches* i pp. 307, 317-318; Grekov & Yakubovski, *Horde d'Or* pp. 204, 305; Fennell, *Crisis* p. 82; Vernadsky, *Mongols and Russia* p. 52 • **60**. David B. Miller, 'The Kievan Principality on the Eve of the Mongol Invasion: An Inquiry into Current Historical Research and Interpretation,' *Harvard Ukranian Studies* 10 (1986) pp. 215-240; Pelenski, *Contest for the Legacy*; Soloviev, *Shift Northward*. The quote is from Fennell, *Crisis* p. 82. • **61**. Franklin & Shepard, *Emergence of Rus* pp. 2, 13, 279, 282, 287 • **62**. Bretschneider, *Mediaeval Researches* i p. 318 • **63**. Fennell, *Crisis* p. 83 • **64**. Vernadsky, *Mongols and Russia* p. 52 • **65**. Boyle, *Successors* p. 69 • **66**. Dawson, *Mongol Mission* pp. 29-30 • **67**. Wiener, *Anthology of Russian Literature* i pp. 105-106 • **68**. Bretschneider, *Mediaeval Researches* i pp. 319-323; Spuler, *Goldene Horde* pp. 20-25; Vernadsky, *Mongols and Russia* pp. 52-58; d'Ohsson, *Histoire* ii p. 122; Dimnik, *Dynasty of Chernigov* pp. 331-358 • **69**. SHR pp. 206-207 • **70**. Skelton, Marston & Painter, *Vinland Map* pp. 76-77 • **71**. Christian, *History* i p. 412 • **72**. SHR pp. 206-207; SHC pp. 215-216; Boyle, *Successors* p. 138 • **73**. Rachewiltz, *Commentary* pp. 1012-1013 • **74**. ibid. pp. 1015-1016 • **75**. ibid. pp. 1017-1019 • **76**. P. Ratchnevsky, 'Die Rechtsverhältnisse bei den Mongolen im

12.–13. Jahrhundert,' *Central Asiatic Journal* 31 (1987) pp. 64-110 (at pp. 89-90) •
77. Rachewiltz, *Commentary* pp. 1012-1013, 1015-1016; d'Ohsson, *Histoire* ii p.
627 • **78.** JB ii p. 587; Boyle, *Successors* pp. 138, 204, 212; Jackson & Morgan,
Rubruck pp. 144-145; Dawson, *Mongol Mission* p. 59 • **79.** Stevenson, *Chronicle
of Melrose*, p. 86; Jackson, *Mongols and the West* p. 65 • **80.** Matthew Paris,
Chronica Majora iii pp. 488-489; Buell, *Dictionary* p. 161 • **81.** Matthew Paris,
Chronica Majora iii pp. 488-489; iv pp. 76-78, 112-119 • **82.** Jackson, *Mongols and
the West* p. 61. • **83.** For Prester John and the Mongols see Yule, *Cathay* i pp.
173-182; Yule & Cordier, *Ser Marco Polo* i pp. 226-245; David Morgan, 'Prester
John and the Mongols,' in Beckingham & Hamilton, *Prester John* pp. 159-170.
Marco Polo identified Prester John not with Genghis but with Toghril (Ong
Khan) (ibid. pp. 165-166). Other accounts seem to have conflated Genghis
and his deadly enemy Ququluq. There were many variants on the Prester
John theme. One idea was that the turmoil in Russia was because 'Prester
John's' armies had revolted against him (Aubrey de Trois-Fontaines, *Chronica*
in *Monumenta Germaniae Historica, Scriptores* 23 p. 942). Another was that the
Mongols were the legendary giants Gog and Magog and that the Muslims
should fear them even more than the Christians did. See David Cook,
'Apocalyptic Incidents during the Mongol Invasion,' in Brandes & Schmieder,
Endzeiten pp. 293-312; C. Burnett, 'An Apocryphal Letter from the Arabic
Philosopher al-Kindi to Theodore, Frederick II's Astrologer concerning Gog
and Magog, the Enclosed Nations and the Scourge of the Mongols,' *Viator*
15 (1984) pp. 151-167 • **84.** Rodenberg, *Epistolae* i pp. 178-179; Denis Sinor, 'Les
relations entre les Mongols et l'Europe jusqu'à la mort d'Arghoun et de Béla
IV,' *Journal of World History* 3 (1956) pp. 39-62 (at p. 40) • **85.** C. W. Connell,
'Western Views on the Origin of the "Tartars": An Example of the Influence
of Myth in the Second Half of the Thirteenth Century,' *Journal of Medieval
and Renaissance Studies* 3 (1973) pp. 115-137 (at pp. 117-118); Axel Klopprogge,
'Das Mongolenbild im Abendland,' in Conermann & Kusber, *Mongolen im
Asien* pp. 8-101; Kloprogge, *Ursprung und Ausprägung* pp. 155-159; Aubrey de
Trois-Fontaines, *Chronica* in *Monumenta Germaniae Historica, Scriptores* 23 p.
911 • **86.** *Monumenta Germaniae Historica, Scriptores* 32 p. 208; Dörrie, *Drei
Texte zur Geschichte der Ungarn und Mongolen*, pp. 125-202 (at pp. 165-182); Denis
Sinor, 'Les relations entre les Mongols et l'Europe,' loc. cit pp. 39-62 (at p.
43); Antoine Mostaert & F. W. Cleaves, 'Trois documents mongols des archives
secrètes vaticanes,' *Harvard Journal of Asiatic Studies* 15 (1952) pp. 419-506 • **87.**
Louis Hambis, 'Saint Louis et les Mongols,' *Journal Asiatique* 258 (1970) pp.
25-33; Richard, *Saint Louis* pp. 160-180; Goff, *Saint Louis* pp. 552-555; Peter
Jackson, 'The Crusades of 1239–1241 and their aftermath,' *Bulletin of the School
of Oriental and African Studies* 50 (1987) pp. 32-60. Nevertheless Louis did later
send out spies and envoys who made contact with the Mongols and brought

back much important intelligence. See Matthew Paris, *Chronica Majora* v pp. 37-38; vi pp. 113-116; Richard, *Simon de St Quentin* pp. 94-117; G. C. Guzman, 'Simon of St Quentin and the Dominican Mission to the Mongol Baiju: A Reappraisal,' *Speculum* 46 (1971) pp. 232-249 • **88**. For full details see Sumption, *Albigensian Crusade* • **89**. Abulafia, *Frederick II* pp. 346-347 • **90**. Christiansen, *Northern Crusades* pp. 126-130; Fonnesberg-Schmidt, *Popes and the Baltic Crusades* • **91**. Richard Spence, 'Gregory IX and the Attempted Expeditions to the Latin Empire of Constantinople: The Crusade for the Union of the Latin and Greek Churches,' *Journal of Medieval History* 5 (1979) pp. 163-176; Christiansen, *Northern Crusades* pp. 133-134 • **92**. *Monumenta Germaniae Historica, Scriptores* 10 p. 59; 17 p. 294; Peter Jackson, 'The Crusade against the Mongols, 1241,' *Journal of Ecclesiastical History* 42 (1991) pp. 1-18 • **93**. Jackson, *Mongols and the West* p. 67 • **94**. Theiner, *Vetera Monumenta* i pp. 184-185; Göckenjan & Sweeney, *Mongolensturm* p. 169; Jackson, *Mongols and the West* p. 66 • **95**. For biographies of Frederick see Abulafia, *Frederick II*; Kantorowicz, *Frederick the Second*; Wolf, *Stupor Mundi*; Stürner, *Friedrich II* • **96**. Maalouf, *Crusades through Arab Eyes* p. 230 • **97**. Aubrey de Trois-Fontaines, *Chronica* in *Monumenta Germaniae Historica, Scriptores* 23 p. 943 • **98**. Detwiler, *Germany* p. 43 • **99**. Bezzola, *Mongolen in abendländischer Sicht* p. 76 • **100**. Björn K. U. Weiler, *Henry III* pp. 86-94 • **101**. *Monumenta Germaniae Historica, Scriptores* 1 pp. 765, 796, 821-823, 826; 2 pp. 2, 102, 105 • **102**. Matthew Paris, *Chronica Majora* iv pp. 115-118; Göckenjan & Sweeney, *Mongolensturm* p. 253 • **103**. Nothing is more controversial than the issue of numbers during the Mongol invasion of Europe. Modern historians seem to compensate for the medieval chroniclers' habit of multiplying numbers tenfold by a compensating 'downsizing'. The truth is probably somewhere between the two extremes, but at the lower end. Estimates for the Mongol army in Poland range from the absurdly high 100,000 (far greater than the entire army in Russia and Eastern Europe) to an absurdly low 8,000 operating in Poland. Some Polish historians, doubtless wishing to minimise a national humiliation, have only 2,000 (!) Poles at the battle of Liegnitz. Others have the nmbers at Liegnitz approximately equal at 8,000 each. The most likely figure is somewhere around 20,000 (or slightly fewer) Mongols and 25,000 (or slightly fewer) Poles; see Eric Hildinger, 'The Battle of Liegnitz,' *Military History*, June 1997. For a convincing argument on Mongol numbers (and the 20,000 mark at Liegnitz) see John Masson Smith, 'Mongol Manpower and the Persian Population,' *Journal of the Economic and Social History of the Orient* 18 (1975) pp. 271-299 (at p. 272). Denis Sinor, 'The Mongols in the West,' loc. cit. accepts even higher numbers. The 'downsizers' are best represented by David Morgan (*Mongols* p. 88) and Carl Sverdrup, 'Numbers in Mongol Warfare', *Journal of Medieval Military History* 8 (2010) pp. 109-117. • **104**. Lerski, *Historical Dictionary* *of Poland* pp. 309-310 • **105.** Iwamura Shinobu, 'Mongol Invasion of Poland in the Thirteenth Century,' *Memoirs of the Research Department of the Toyo Bunko* 10 (1938) pp. 103-157 • **106.** Schmilewski, *Wahlstatt 1241* 35-75 • **107.** C. W. Connell, 'Western views of the origin of the "Tartars",' loc. cit. pp. 115-137 (esp. pp. 117-118); Matthew Paris, *Chronica Majora* iv pp. 111-112, 118; J. J. Saunders, 'Matthew Paris and the Mongols,' in Sandquist & Powicke, *Essays* pp. 116-132; Anna Rutkowska-Plachcinska, 'L'image du danger tatar dans les sources polonaises des XIIIe-XIVe siècles,' in Université de Provence, *Histoire et société* pp. 14-32 • **108.** Strakosch-Grassman, *Mongolen in Mitteleuropa* p. 42; Spuler, *Goldene Horde* p. 22. Some sources insist on one, despite much better evidence to the contrary. See Skelton, Marston & Painter, *Vinland Map* p. 80; Maroń, *Legnica 1241* pp. 123-131 • **109.** RT ii p. 411 • **110.** Davies, *God's Playground* i p. 71 • **111.** Strakosch-Grassmann, *Mongolen in Mitteleuropa* p. 39 • **112.** Denis Sinor, 'On Mongol Strategy,' *Proceedings of the Fourth East Asian Affairs Conference* (1971) pp. 238-249 (at p. 245) • **113.** Strakosch-Grassmann, *Mongolen in Mitteleuropa* p. 43 • **114.** This story and many others, which belong more to the realm of the historical novel than sober history, is recounted by the fifteenth-century Polish monk Jan Długosz. Michael, *Jan Długosz* • **115.** JB i pp. 225-226; RT ii pp. 325-326; Boyle, *Successors* pp. 56-57 • **116.** Hildinger, 'The Battle of Liegnitz,' loc. cit.; Michael, *Jan Długosz* • **117.** Strakosch-Grassmann, *Mongolen in Mitteleuropa* pp. 37-52; Oman, *Art of War* pp. 328-330 • **118.** d'Ohsson, *Histoire* ii pp. 124-126 • **119.** Skelton, Marston & Painter, *Vinland Map* pp. 80-81; Wolff, *Geschichte* p. 189 • **120.** Schmilewski, *Wahlstatt 1241* pp. 87-108 • **121.** Arnold, *Hochmeister* p. 27; Jürgen Sarnowsky, 'The Teutonic Order Confronts Mongols and Turks,' in Barber, *Military Orders* pp. 253-262; Urban, *Teutonic Knights* • **122.** Sophia Menache, 'Tartars, Jews, Saracens and the Jewish–Mongol "plot" of 1241,' *History* 81 (1996) pp. 319-342; Israel Jacob Yuval, 'Jewish Messianic Expectations towards 1240 and Christian Reactions,' in Shäfer & Cohen, *Toward the Millennium* pp. 105-121, esp. pp. 119-120 • **123.** Bretschneider, *Mediaeval Researches* i pp. 320-322 • **124.** *Monumenta Germaniae Historica, Scriptores* 9 p. 597; Strakosch-Grassmann, *Mongolen in Mitteleuropa* pp. 143, 189 • **125.** Vernadsky, *Mongols and Russia* p. 56 • **126.** Liddell Hart, *Great Captains Unveiled* p. 24 • **127.** Brundage, *Henry of Livonia* p. 205; Göckenjan & Sweeney, *Mongolensturm* p. 252; Dawson, *Mongol Mission* p. 16 • **128.** Strakosch-Grassmann, *Mongolen in Mitteleuropa* pp. 50-67; d'Ohsson, *Histoire* ii pp. 127-129

Chapter 17

1. A. N. J. Hollander, 'The Great Hungarian Plain: A European Frontier Area,' *Comparative Studies in Society and History* 3 (1961) pp. 74-88, 155-169 • **2.** Sinor, *Hungary* pp. 48-64 • **3.** Kontler, *Hungary* pp. 40-49 • **4.** Sinor, *Hungary* pp. 58-59

• **5.** The 800th anniversary of her birth produced a plethora of biographies: Albrecht & Atzbach, *Elisabeth von Thüringen*; Ohler, *Elisabeth von Thüringen*; Zippert & Jost, *Hingabe und Heiterkeit*; Reber, *Elizabeth von Thüringen* • **6.** Reich, *Select Documents* pp. 637-642; Roman, *Austria–Hungary* p. 480 • **7.** Sinor, *Hungary* pp. 57-60; James Ross Sweeney, 'The Decretal Intellecto and the Hungarian Golden Bull of 1222,' in *Album Elemér Mályusz* (1976) pp. 89-96 • **8.** Rady et al, *Gesta Hungarorum / Epistola in Miserabile Carmen* pp. 142-143; Szentpétery, *Scriptores rerum Hungaricarum* ii. p.555 • **9.** Engel, *Realm of St Stephen* pp. 91-93 • **10.** Rady et al, *Gesta Hungarorum / Epistola in Miserabile Carmen* pp. 144-145; Martyn C. Rady, *Nobility, Land and Service* pp. 179-182 • **11.** Rady et al, *Gesta Hungarorum / Epistola in Miserabile Carmen* pp. 144-147 • **12.** Engel, *Realm of St Stephen* p. 98 • **13.** Nora Berend, *At the Gate of Christendom* pp. 68-73; Robert C.Wolff, 'The "Second Bulgarian Empire": Its Origin and History to 1204,' *Speculum* 24 (1949) pp. 167-206; A. Lognon, 'Les Toucy en Orient et en Italie au XIIIe siècle,' *Bulletin de la Société des sciences historiques et naturelles de l'Yonne* 96 (1957) pp. 33-43 • **14.** *Monumenta Germaniae Historica, Scriptores* 9 p. 640; Göckenjam & Sweeney, *Mongolensturm* pp. 142-145, 238 • **15.** Rady et al, *Gesta Hungarorum / Epistola in Miserabile Carmen* pp. 138-139 • **16.** Berend, *At the Gate* pp. 85-95 • **17.** Ferdinandy, *Tschingis Khan* pp. 139-144 • **18.** Rady et al, *Gesta Hungarorum / Epistola in Miserabile Carmen* p. 141 • **19.** ibid. • **20.** Sinor, *Hungary* p. 69 • **21.** Veszprémy & Schaer, *Simon of Kéza*, p. 157 • **22.** Rady et al, *Gesta Hungarorum / Epistola in Miserabile Carmen* pp. 140-141, 154-155 • **23.** Sinor, *Hungary* p. 70 • **24.** Veszprémy & Schaer, *Simon of Kéza* pp. 145-147 • **25.** Kosztolnyik, *Hungary* pp. 151-216; Bezzola, *Mongolen in abendländischer Sicht* pp. 76-81 • **26.** Matthew Paris, *Chronica Majora* iv pp. 119-120 • **27.** Göckenjan & Sweeney, *Mongolensturm* pp. 150, 237 • **28.** Sinor, *Hungary* p. 70 • **29.** Strakosch-Grassmann, *Mongolen in Mitteleuropa*, pp. 9, 42; Bezzola, *Mongolen in abendländischer Sicht* p. 52; Matthew Paris, *Chronica Majora* iv pp. 270-277 (esp. p. 274) • **30.** Rady et al, *Gesta Hungarorum / Epistola in Miserabile Carmen* pp. 156-157, 164-165 • **31.** ibid. pp. 156-159; Matthew Paris, *Chronica Majora* iv pp. 112-119 • **32.** Rady et al, *Gesta Hungarorum / Epistola in Miserabile Carmen* pp. 172-175 • **33.** Thomas T. Allsen, 'Cumanica IV: The Cumano–Qipčaq Clans and Tribes,' *Archivum Eurasiae Medii Aevi* 9 (1997) pp. 97-122 (at pp. 102-105); Göckenjan & Sweeney, *Mongolensturm* pp. 150-159, 176-179 • **34.** Kubinyi, *Anfänge Ofens* pp. 16-17 • **35.** Sinor, *Hungary* pp. 70-71 • **36.** D. O. Morgan, 'The Mongol Armies in Persia,' *Der Islam* 56 (1976) pp. 81-96; Chambers, *Devil's Horsemen* p. 93 • **37.** Liddell Hart, *Great Captains Unveiled* p. 25 • **38.** Some idea of the terrain can be gathered from Florin Curta, 'Transylvania around AD 1000,' in Urbańczyk, *Europe around the Year* 1000 pp. 141-165. Because of the confusing chronology used in many of the primary sources, it is not clear if the sack of Alba Iulia ('the white city') in Transylvania happened at this point, or whether it was bypassed and the Mongols then doubled back to raze it in the period of total destruction after Mohi. For more on the role of Transylvania during the Mongol invasion see László Makkai, 'Transylvania in the Medieval Hungarian Kingdom (896–1526),' in Köpeczi, *Transylvania i* pp. 331-524. For a more modern description of Alba Iulia see Leigh Fermor, *Betweeen the Woods and the Water* p. 138 • **39**. Rady et al, *Gesta Hungarorum / Epistola in Miserabile Carmen* pp. 161-162 • **40**. Perić et al, *Thomas of Split, History* p. 259; J. R. Sweeney, '"Spurred on by the Fear of Death": Refugees and Displaced Persons during the Mongol Invasion of Hungary,' in Gervers & Schlepp, *Nomadic Diplomacy* pp. 34-62 (at p. 42) • **41**. Rachewiltz, *In the Service* p. 24 • **42**. Rady et al, *Gesta Hungarorum / Epistola in Miserabile Carmen* pp. 166-167 • **43**. Strakosch-Grassmann, *Mongolen in Mitteleuropa*, pp. 91-98, 153-158; Sedlar, *East Central Europe* pp. 210-221 • **44**. Rady et al, *Gesta Hungarorum / Epistola in Miserabile Carmen* pp. 200-201 • **45**. ibid. pp. 178-179; d'Ohsson, *Histoire* ii pp. 141-142 • **46**. Grousset, *Empire* p. 266 • **47**. ibid. pp. 594-595. On this point see also Strakosch-Grassmann, *Mongolen in Mitteleuropa* pp. 78-79 • **48**. ibid. pp. 99-101 • **49**. Rady et al, *Gesta Hungarorum / Epistola in Miserabile Carmen* pp. 168-169 • **50**. ibid. • **51**. Hristo Dimitrov, 'Über die bulgarisch-ungarischen Beziehungen, 1218–1255,' *Bulgarian Historical Review* 25 (1997) pp. 3-27 (at pp. 16-19); Matthew Paris, *Chronica Majora* iv pp. 113, 179; Göckenjan & Sweeney, *Mongolensturm* pp. 149-150; Strakosch-Grassmann, *Mongolen in Mitteleuropa* pp. 12-13, 91 • **52**. ibid. pp. 78-79 • **53**. Carey, *Warfare* pp. 124-128. But extreme caution is needed in this debate. Some of the very best sources are adamant that the Mongols were outnumbered two to one; see JB i p. 270; Göckenjan & Sweeney, *Mongolensturm* p. 251. • **54**. ibid. p. 240 • **55**. JB i. pp. 270-271; Rady et al, *Gesta Hungarorum / Epistola in Miserabile Carmen* pp. 180-181 • **56**. Andrew had four sons, one born posthumously. Apart from Bela (1206–1276), there was Coloman (1208–1241),who was ruler of Halych in 1214–1221 and, after 1226, governor of Slavonia; a short-lived namesake Andrew (1210–1234) and a fourth son, Stephen (1236–1272), born after King Andrew's death. • **57**. Skelton, Marston & Painter, *Vinland Map* pp. 80-81; Pelliot, *Horde d'Or* p. 153 • **58**. Skelton, Marston & Painter, *Vinland Map* pp. 82-83 • **59**. Perić et al, *Thomas of Split, History* pp. 261-273 • **60**. Rady et al, *Gesta Hungarorum / Epistola in Miserabile Carmen* pp. 182-183 • **61**. Bretschneider, *Mediaeval Researches* i. p. 331; d'Ohsson, *Histoire* ii p. 142 • **62**. For the use of firearms at Mohi see Chase, *Firearms* p. 58; Carey, *Warfare* pp. 124-128; James Riddick Partington, *Greek Fire* p. 250 • **63**. Strakosch-Grassmann, *Mongolen in Mitteleuropa* pp. 84-87; d'Ohsson, *Histoire* ii pp. 143-144 • **64**. Bretschneider, *Mediaeval Researches* i pp. 331-332 • **65**. Rady et al, *Gesta Hungarorum / Epistola in Miserabile Carmen* pp. 184-185 • **66**. ibid. • **67**. ibid. pp. 186-187 • **68**. Perić et al, *Thomas of Split, History* p. 293; László Koszta, 'Un prélat français en

Hongrie: Bertalan, évêque de Pécs, 1219–1251,' *Cahiers d'Etudes Hongroises* 8 (1996) pp. 71-96 • **69.** Vambéry, *Hungary* pp. 138-139 • **70.** Rady et al, *Gesta Hungarorum / Epistola in Miserabile Carmen* pp. 188-189 • **71.** ibid. pp. 189-191 • **72.** ibid. pp. 190-191 • **73.** Jean Richard, 'Les causes des victoires mongoles d'après les historiens orientaux du XIIIe siècle,' *Central Asiatic Journal* 23 (1979) pp. 104-117 • **74.** *Monumenta Germaniae Historica, Scriptores* 29 p. 262; Göckenjan & Sweeney, *Mongolensturm* p. 248; Richard, 'Les causes des victories,' loc.cit. pp. 109-110; Świętosławski, *Arms and Armour* pp. 21-41, 58-61 • **75.** Jackson & Morgan, *Rubruck* p. 185; Pelliot, *Recherches* p. 154; K. Uray-Köhalmi, 'Über die pfeifenden Pfeile der innerasiatischen Reiternomaden,' *Acta Orientalia Academiae Scientiarum Hungaricae* 3 (1953) pp. 45-71 • **76.** Liddell Hart, *Great Captains Unveiled* pp. 28-32 • **77.** My one criticism of the otherwise excellent *Mongols and the West* by Peter Jackson is that he takes all these assertions too seriously (see p. 73). • **78.** Dawson, *Mongol Mission* p. 46 • **79.** Buell, *Dictionary* p. 110 • **80.** Bretschneider, *Mediaeval Researches* i pp. 333-334; d'Ohsson, *Histoire* ii p. 69 • **81.** Bretschneider, *Mediaeval Researches* i p. 332; Buell, *Dictionary* pp. 235, 258 • **82.** Bretschneider, *Mediaeval Researches* i p. 331 • **83.** RT ii p. 519 • **84.** Liddell Hart, *Great Captains Unveiled* p. 30 • **85.** Rachewiltz, *In the Service* p. 25 • **86.** Sinor, *Hungary* p. 73 • **87.** Rady et al, *Gesta Hungarorum / Epistola in Miserabile Carmen* pp. 196-197 • **88.** ibid. pp. 192-195 • **89.** Matthew Paris, *Chronica Majora* iv p. 114; Veszprémy & Schaer, *Simon of Kéza* pp. 145-147; Dienst, *Leitha 1246* • **90.** Göckenjan & Sweeney, *Mongolensturm* pp. 164-165, 244; Sinor, *Hungary* p. 74 • **91.** Bretschneider, *Mediaeval Researches* i p. 325; Bezzola, *Mongolen in abendländischer Sicht* pp. 87-88 • **92.** Rady et al, *Gesta Hungarorum / Epistola in Miserabile Carmen* pp. 206-207 • **93.** ibid. pp. 208-209 • **94.** ibid. pp. 206-207; Dawson, *Mongol Mission* pp. 37-38 • **95.** Bezzola, *Mongolen in abendländischer Sicht* pp. 87-88 • **96.** Strakosch-Grassmann, *Mongolen in Mitteleuropa* pp. 20-31, 35 • **97.** Fügedi, *Castle and Society* pp. 45-48 • **98.** Gerhartl, *Wiener Neustadt* pp. 3-10 • **99.** Rady et al, *Gesta Hungarorum / Epistola in Miserabile Carmen* pp. 214-215 • **100.** d'Ohsson, *Histoire* ii pp. 146-155 • **101.** Rady et al, *Gesta Hungarorum / Epistola in Miserabile Carmen* pp. 216-217 • **102.** ibid. pp. 218-219 • **103.** Göckenjan & Sweeney, *Mongolensturm* pp. 159, 182-185 • **104.** Kahn, *Secret History* p.xxvi • **105.** Sinor, *Hungary* pp. 74-75 • **106.** Bretschneider, *Mediaeval Researches* i p. 325; Strakosch-Grassmann, *Mongolen in Mitteleuropa* pp. 166-167 • **107.** Perić et al, *Thomas of Split, History* p. 299 • **108.** Göckenjan & Sweeney, *Mongolensturm* p. 180 • **109.** ibid. pp. 181, 257-260. See also Fine, *Early Medieval Balkans* pp. 283-284; Fine, *Late Medieval Balkans* pp. 143-152 • **110.** Bretschneider, *Mediaeval Researches* i p. 326; Strakosch-Grassmann, *Mongolen in Mitteleuropa* pp. 168-173 • **111.** Budge, *Chronography* i p. 398 • **112.** *Monumenta Germaniae Historica, Scriptores* 9 p. 641 • **113.** Spuler, *Goldene Horde* pp. 124-126; Vásáry, *Cumans and Tatars* p. 70 • **114.** *Monumenta Germaniae*

Historica, Scriptores 20 p. 335; 22 p. 472; Göckenjan & Sweeney, *Mongolensturm* p. 266 • **115**. Berend, *At the Gate* pp. 37-38; Jackson, *Mongols and the West* p. 207 • **116**. *Monumenta Germaniae Historica, Scriptores* 17 p. 394; Göckenjan & Sweeney, *Mongolensturm* pp. 159, 182-185, 255 • **117**. Rady et al, *Gesta Hungarorum / Epistola in Miserabile Carmen* pp. 220-221 • **118**. Göckenjan & Sweeney, *Mongolensturm* pp. 182-185, 258; Rogers, *Medieval Warfare* iii p. 34 • **119**. Morris Rossabi, 'The Legacy of the Mongols,' in Manz, *Central Asia* pp. 27-44; John Masson Smith, 'Demographic Considerations in Mongol Siege Warfare,' *Archivum Ottomanicum* 13 (1994) pp. 323-394; James Ross Sweeney, '"Spurred on by Fear of Death",' loc. cit. pp. 34-62; Sweeney, 'Identifying the Medieval Refugee: Hungarians in Flight during the Mongol Invasions,' in Löb et al, *Forms of Identity* pp. 63-76 • **120**. Gregory G. Guzman, 'European Clerical Envoys to the Mongols: Reports of Western Merchants in Eastern Europe and Central Asia, 1231–1255,' *Journal of Medieval History* 22 (1996) pp. 53-67; cf also Olschki, *Guillaume Boucher* • **121**. Jackson, *Mongols in the West* p. 70 • **122**. Sinor, *Hungary* p. 76 • **123**. Bezzola, *Mongolen in abendländischer Sicht* pp. 110-113; Sinor, 'Les relations entre les Mongols et l'Europe jusqu'à la mort d'Arghoun et de Béla IV,' *Cahiers d'Histoire Mondiale* 3 (1956) pp. 39-62 (at p. 47); Sinor, 'John of Carpini's Return from Mongolia: New light from a Luxembourg Manuscript,' *Journal of the Royal Asiatic Society* (1957) pp. 193-206 (at pp. 203-205); A. Pálóczi-Horváth, 'L'immigration et l'établissement des Comans en Hongrie,' *Acta Orientalia Academiae Scientiarum Hungaricae* 29 (1975) pp. 313-333; Berend, *At the Gate* pp. 134-138; Anthony Luttrell, 'The Hospitallers in Hungary before 1418: Problems and Sources,' in Hunyadi & Laszlovsky, *Crusades and the Military Orders* pp. 269-281 (at pp. 271-272); J. Muldoon, *Popes, Lawyers and Infidels* pp. 59-60 • **124**. Berend, *At the Gate* pp. 68-73, 87-93, 97-100 • **125**. Sinor, *Hungary* pp. 77-78 • **126**. Vernadsky, *Mongols and Russia* p. 58 • **127**. Budge, *Chronography* i p. 409; Cahen, *Formation of Turkey* pp. 70-71; Cahen, *Pre-Ottoman Turkey* pp. 137-138; Miller, *Trebizond* pp. 24-26; Bryer, *Trebizond*; John Masson Smith, 'Mongol Nomadism and Middle Eastern Geography: Qishlaqs and Tumens,' in Amitai-Preiss & Morgan, *Mongol Empire and its Legacy* pp. 39-56; Atwood, *Encyclopedia* p. 555 • **128**. This theory is mainly associated with Denis Sinor. See Sinor, 'The Mongols in the West,' *Journal of Asian History* 33 (1999) pp. 1-44; Sinor, 'Horses and Pasture,' *Oriens Extremus* 19 (1972) pp. 171-183; Sinor, 'Horse and Pasturage in Inner Asian History,' in his *Inner Asia and its Contacts with Medieval Europe* pp. 171-184 (esp. pp. 181-183) • **129**. Greg S. Rogers, 'An Examination of Historians' Explanations for the Mongol Withdrawal from East Central Europe,' *East European Quarterly* 30 (1996) pp. 3-26 • **130**. Kosztolnyik, *Hungary* p. 182 • **131**. Rachewiltz, *In the Service* p. 25 • **132**. Dawson, *Mongol Mission* pp. 44-45 • **133**. *Monumenta Germanie Historica, Scriptores* 32 p. 210; Salimbene de Adam, *Cronica* i p. 317; Matthew Paris, *Chronica Majora* vi pp. 82; Dawson, *Mongol Mission* pp. 44-46 • **134.** Jackson, *Mongols and the West* p. 358; Nicol, *Last Centuries* p. 22 • **135.** Jackson, *Mongols and the West* pp. 143-147 • **136.** Dawson, *Mongol Mission* pp. 44-49 • **137.** *Monumenta Germaniae Historica, Scriptores* 17 p. 341; Matthew Paris, *Chronica Majora* vi p. 82 • **138.** ibid. iv p. 387 • **139.** JB i p. 240; ii p. 588 • **140.** Mitchell & Forbes, *Chronicle of Novgorod* pp. 86-87 • **141.** Fennell, *Crisis* p. 105; Tumler, *Deutsche Orden* pp. 266-267; Nicolle, *Peipus* • **142.** The quote is from Fennell, *Crisis* p. 106 • **143.** Donald Ostrowski, 'Alexander Nevskii's "Battle on the Ice": The Creation of a Legend,' *Russian History* 33 (2006) pp. 289-312; Dittmar Dahlmann, 'Der russische Sieg über die "teutonischen Ritter" auf dem Peipussee 1242,' in Krumeich & Brandt, *Schlachtenmythen* pp. 63-75; Fennell & Stokes, *Early Russian Literature* pp. 107-121. The extent to which Lake Peipus has been presented as a battle to rank with Gaugamela, Zama, Alesia or Waterloo is well-nigh incredible. In Eisenstein's 1938 film, which portrays Nevsky as a peerless hero, no historical context is given. The Mongols appear, meaninglessly, in the first ten minutes, as if they were spear-carriers or extras in the drama. A great film, certainly, with wonderful music by Prokofiev, but essentially historical nonsense. *Suppressio veri* and *suggestio falsi* are used to create the impression that Nevsky saved 'Russia' (which of course did not exist at that time) from threats both east and west – Stalin's way of saying that the USSR could withstand attacks from both Hitler's Germany and Japan. • **144.** Buell, *Dictionary* p. 266; Jürgen Sarnowsky, 'The Teutonic Order Confronts the Mongols and Turks,' in Barber, *Military Orders* pp. 253-262 • **145.** Isoaho, *Aleksandr Nevskiy* pp. 88-98 • **146.** Dawson, *Mongol Mission* pp. 62, 65, 70; Fennell, *Crisis* pp. 98-99, 107-108, 110-120 • **147.** For Sartaq see JR ii p. 1291; JB i p. 223; Jackson & Morgan, *Rubruck* pp. 117-119; Allsen, *Mongol Imperialism* pp. 136-138; Allsen, 'Mongol Census-Taking in Rus', 1245–1275,' *Harvard Ukrainian Studies* 5 (1981) pp. 32-53 (at p. 40); Dawson, *Mongol Mission* pp. 45, 65, 117-118; Jackson & Morgan, *Rubruck* pp. 114-122; Pelliot, *Horde d'Or* pp. 134-144; Spuler, *Goldene Horde* pp. 33-34. There was a brief interregnum in 1257 between the khanates of Sartaq and Berke when Sartaq's brother Ulaghchi reigned (Pelliot, *Notes sur Marco Polo* i pp. 92-95; Pelliot, *Horde d'Or* pp. 47-51). For Berke's conversion to Islam see Jean Richard, 'La conversion de Berke et les débuts de l'islamisation de la Horde d'Or,' *Revue des Études Islamiques* 35 (1967) pp. 173-184; István Vásáry, 'History and Legend in Berke Khan's conversion to Islam,' in Sinor, *Aspects* iii pp. 230-252 • **148.** JR ii p. 1149; JB i pp. 239-246 • **149.** JB i pp. 21,171,176; Hambis, *Le chapitre CVII*; Boyle, *Successors* p. 181. For Koden and Shiremun see Buell, *Dictionary* pp. 184, 243 • **150.** Bretschneider, *Mediaeval Researches* i p. 332; Boyle, *Successors* pp. 179, 183; David Ayalon, 'The Great Yasa,' *Studia Islamica* 34 (1971) pp. 151-180 (at pp. 157-159, 164-165; Spuler, *Mongolen in Iran* p. 39 • **151.** JB i pp. 255-257; Grousset,

Empire p. 271; Hodong Kim, 'A Reappraisal of Güyük Khan,' in Amitai & Biran, *Mongols, Turks and Others* pp. 309-338 • **152**. Allsen, *Mongol Imperialism* pp. 21-22, 54-63 • **153**. JR ii p.1151; Boyle, *Successors* pp. 99, 180-186; Jackson, 'The Dissolution of the Mongol Empire,' *Central Asiatic Journal* 22 (1978) pp. 186-244 (at pp. 200-201); Atwood, *Encyclopedia* p. 213 • **154**. Jackson & Morgan, *Rubruck* pp. 46-50, 163-164; Atwood, *Encyclopedia* p. 512 • **155**. Jackson & Morgan, *Rubruck* p. 169; Pelliot, 'Les Mongols et la papauté,' *Revue de l'Orient chrétien* 24 (1924) p. 203; Allsen, *Mongol Imperialism* pp. 30-37 • **156**. Boyle, *Successors* pp. 21-22, 216; W. Abramowski, 'Die chinesischen Annalen der Mongke,' *Zentralasiatische Studien* 13 (1979) pp. 7-71 (at pp. 20-21, 28); Morgan, *Mongols* pp. 103-104 • **157**. Lane, *Daily Life* p. 9 • **158**. Barnes & Hudson, *History Atlas of Asia* p. 87 • **159**. Morgan, *Medieval Persia* pp. 64-72

Conclusion

1. Krause, *Epoche der Mongolen* p. 6 • **2**. Khazanov, *Nomads and the Outside World*, pp. 238-239 • **3**. D. C. Wright, 'Was Chinggis Khan Literate?' in Janhunen, *Writing* pp. 305-312 • **4**. Unlu, *Genealogy of a World Empire* p. 88 • **5**. Sechin Jagchid, 'The Historical Interaction between the Nomadic People in Mongolia and the Sedentary Chinese,' in Seaman & Marks, *Rulers from the Steppe* pp. 63-91 (at p. 81) • **6**. Quoted in Weatherford, *Genghis Khan* p. 125 • **7**. T. Zerjal et al, 'The Genetic Legacy of the Mongols,' *American Journal of Human Genetics* 72 (2003) pp. 717-721. Not being a geneticist, I find the detailed argument difficult to follow, but it seems to hinge on the Haplogroup C-M217 and its subgroup C-M130. • **8**. Garrett Hellenthal, Simon Myers, Daniel Falush, et al, 'A Genetic Atlas of Human Admixture History,' *Science* 343 (14 February 2014) pp. 747-751 • **9**. S. Abilev et al, 'The Y-chromosome C3* Star Cluster Attributed to Genghis Khan's Descendants,' *Human Biology* 84 (2012) pp. 79-89. See also the discussion in Hartl & Jones, *Genetics* p. 309; Chapin, *Long Lines*; Cooper, *Geography of Genocide*; Wells, *Journey of Man* • **10**. The 'great man' theory and its critics form one of the most hotly contested battlegrounds in historiography, with luminaries such as Carlyle, Nietzsche and Kierkegaard promoting and Engels, Tolstoy and Herbert Spencer opposing. See Leonid Grinin, 'The Role of an Individual in History: A Reconsideration,' *Social Evolution and History* 9 (2010) pp. 95-136; Friedrich Engels, introduction to *Socialism*; Hook, *Hero* • **11**. Montesquieu, *Considerations on the Causes of the Greatness of the Romans* (1734) Chapter 18 • **12**. Fletcher, 'The Mongols,' loc. cit. pp. 35-36. *Pace* the strenuous objections in Tolstoy's *War and Peace*: 'The words *chance* and *genius* do not denote anything that actually exists, and therefore they cannot be defined. These two words merely indicate a certain degree of comprehension of phenomena. I do not know why a certain event occurs; I suppose that I cannot know; therefore I do not try to know, and I talk about *chance*. I see a force producing effects beyond the scope of ordinary human agencies; I do not understand why this occurs, and I cry *genius*' (*War and Peace*, Epilogue, part 1.2, translated by Rosemary Edmonds). The rhetoric is strong but the accompanying arguments are weak and amount to little more than Tolstoy's *ex cathedra* assertion that factors of inevitability *must* be at play. • **13**. For Ibn Khaldun and his views on climate see Warren E. Gates, 'The Spread of Ibn Khaldun's Ideas on Climate and Culture,' *Journal of the History of Ideas* 28 (1967) pp. 415-422; Fromherz, *Ibn Khaldun* • **14**. On climate see Montesquieu, *The Spirit of the Laws*, Chapter 14. On the Mongols see ibid. pp. 268-280 • **15**. Gumilev, *Imaginary Kingdom* pp. 21-24 • **16**. ibid. • **17**. Drought is emphasised in all the following studies: Lattimore, 'The Geographical Factor in Mongol History,' *Geographical Journal* 41 (1938) pp. 1-20, reproduced in *Studies in Frontier History* pp. 241-258; Ellsworth Huntington, 'Changes of Climate and History,' *American Historical Review* 18 (1913) pp. 213-232, and cf Martin, *Ellsworth Huntington* and G. F. Hudson's note in Toynbee, *Study of History* (1962) iii annex 2 p. 453; Brown, *History and Climate Change* pp. 211-221 • **18**. Brown, *Geography of Human Conflict* pp. 53-57 (esp. p. 54) • **19**. Yongkang Xue, 'The Impact of Desertification in Mongolia and the Inner Mongolian Grassland on the Regional Climate,' *Journal of Climate* 9 (1996) pp. 2173-2189 • **20**. Cold weather theorists include Gareth Jenkins, 'A Note on Climate Cycles and the Rise of Chinggis Khan,' *Central Asiatic Journal* 18 (1974) pp. 217-226 and William S. Atwell, 'Volcanism and Short-Term Climatic Change in East Asian and World History c. 1200–1699,' *Journal of World History* 12 (2001) pp. 29-98 (at pp. 42-45) • **21**. Mara Hvistendahl, 'Roots of Empire,' *Science* 337 (28 September 2012) pp. 1596-1599. Another 'wet conditions' advocate is H. H. Lamb, *Climate, History and the Modern World* pp. 184-185, 317. • **22**. Brown, *History and Climate Change* p. 217 • **23**. Lattimore, 'The Geographical Factor,' in *Studies in Frontier History* pp. 252-253; Lattimore, 'The Historical Setting of Inner Mongolian Nationalism,' ibid. pp. 440-455 • **24**. Gumilev, *Imaginary Kingdom* p. 259 • **25**. ibid. pp. 19-20 • **26**. Togan, *Flexibility and Limitation* p. 6 • **27**. Fletcher, 'The Mongols,' loc. cit. pp. 22-34. For further contributions to the climate debate see B. Beentjes, 'Nomadwanderungen und Klimaschwangen,' *Central Asiatic Journal* 30 (1986) pp. 7-17; A. W. B. Meyer, 'Climate and Migration,' in Bell-Fialkoff, *Role of Migration* pp. 287-294; V. G. Dirksen et al, 'Chronology of Holocene Climate and Vegetation Changes and their Connection to Cultural Dynamics in Southern Siberia,' *Radiocarbon* 49 (2007) pp. 1103-1121; B. van Geel, 'Climate Change and the Expansion of the Scythian Culture after 850 BC: A Hypothesis,' *Archaeological Science* 31 (2004) pp. 1735-1742; 33 (2006) pp. 143-148 • **28**. Julia Pongratz et al, 'Coupled Climate-Carbon Simulations Indicate Minor Global

Effects of Wars and Epidemics on Atmospheric CO_2,' *The Holocene* 21 (2011) pp. 848-851 • **29.** Keegan, *History of Warfare* (1994) p. 214. For the 'Mongols to blame' see also Salisbury, *Coming War* p. 31 • **30.** Ostrowski, *Muscovy and the Mongols* pp. 3-4 • **31.** Weatherford, *Genghis Khan* pp. xxiv, 237-238 • **32.** Martels, *Travel Fact* pp. 54-71. It is interesting that Weatherford, *Genghis* p. 236 has *Francis* Bacon in the late sixteenth century summing up the three break-through technologies that came to the West from the Mongols as printing, gunpowder and the compass, for Janet Abu-Lughod (*The World System* pp. 23-24) makes an explicit comparison between the two Bacons, having religion (Roger Bacon) contrast with politics (Francis Bacon) and the allegiance of the former to the Pope contrasted with that of the latter to the monarch. • **33.** Anatoly M. Khazanov, 'Muhammad and Jenghis Khan Compared: The Religious Factor in Empire Building,' *Comparative Studies in Society and History* 35 (1993) pp. 461-479 • **34.** J. J. Saunders, 'The Nomad as Empire-Builder: A Comparison of the Arab and Mongol Conquests,' in Rice, *Muslims and Mongols* pp. 36-66 • **35.** Schurmann, *Economic Structure* pp. 66-67; Thomas T. Allsen, 'Mongol Census-Taking in Rus', 1245–1275,' *Harvard Ukraine Studies* 5 (1981) pp. 32-53 (at pp. 33-36) • **36.** Hans Bielenstein, 'Chinese Historical Demography AD 2-1982,' *Bulletin of the Museum of Far Eastern Antiquities* 59 (1987) pp. 85-88; Ping-ti Ho, 'An Estimate of the Total Population of Sung–Chin China,' in Françoise Aubin, ed. *Études Song* pp. 3-53 • **37.** May, *Mongol Conquests* p. 224 • **38.** Brook, *Troubled Empire* pp. 42-44 • **39.** ibid. p. 45; Fitzgerald, *China* pp. 312-315 • **40.** Buell, *Dictionary* pp. 211-215; Brown, *History of Climate Change* p. 218; J. D. Durand, 'Population Statistics of China, AD 2–1953,' *Population Studies* 13 (1960) pp. 209-256. Morgan, *Mongols* p. 83 estimates the population of Jin China as 100 million before the Mongol conquest and 70 million after. For Champa rice see Ping-ti Ho, 'Early-Ripening Rice in Chinese History,' *Economic History Review* 18 (1956) pp. 200-218 • **41.** Pinker, *Better Angels* pp. 94, 707 cites the high figures. Fitzgerald, *China* pp. 314, 624 regards such high figures as risible. • **42.** Graff, *Medieval Chinese Warfare* p. 240; Twitchett, *Sui and T'ang China* • **43.** Fairbank, *Late Ch'ing* pp. 264-350 • **44.** Fairbank & Feuerwerker, *Republican China* • **45.** Chalmers Johnson, 'The Looting of Asia', *London Review of Books* 25 (20 November 2003) pp. 3-6 • **46.** Wedgwood, *Thirty Years War* • **47.** Hochschild, *King Leopold's Ghost* pp. 226-232 • **48.** Franke & Twitchett, *Cambridge History* p. 622. McEvedy & Jones, *World Population History* p. 172 accepts a decline in population from 115 million to 85 million as a result of the Mongol invasions. The nineteenth-century scholar Jeremiah Curtin thought that the death toll from the Mongols in China (including Hsi-Hsia) was 18,500,000 in 1211–23 alone (*Mongols* p. 141). • **49.** For the difficulty even of estimating the population of Samarkand see Schafer, *Golden Peaches* p. 280 • **50.** David O. Morgan, 'Ibn Battuta and the Mongols,' *Journal of the Royal*

Asiatic Society, 3rd series 11 (2001) pp. 1-11. See also Dunn, *Adventures of Ibn Battuta* • **51**. Authors prepared to accept a figure of 15 million fatalities in the defeat of the Khwarezmian empire and the 'mopping up' operations against Jalal al-Din include Ward, *Immortal* p. 39; Rummel, *Death by Government* pp. 48-51; Macfarlane, *Savage Wars* p. 50; Grant, *Battle* pp. 92-94 • **52**. Josiah C. Russell, 'Population in Europe,' in Cipolla, *Economic History* pp. 25-71 • **53**. Morgan, *Mongols* p. 83. Godbey, *Lost Tribes a Myth* p. 385 wants to downsize this to only 20 million. Pinker, *Better Angels* pp. 235-237 has been derided for his suggestion of 40 million deaths but, it seems, exaggerates only slightly. McEvedy & Jones *World Population History* pp. 170-173 steer a middle course and estimate 25 million; see also White, *Atrocities*. • **54**. Barthold, *Turkestan* p. 461 • **55**. Lattimore, 'Chingis Khan and the Mongol Conquests,' *Scientific American* 209 (1963) p. 62; Rachewiltz, *Papal Envoys* p. 65 • **56**. Noreen Giffney, 'Monstrous Mongols,' *Postmedieval* 3 (2012) pp. 227-245 • **57**. SHR pp. 181-186 • **58**. George Lane, 'The Mongols in Iran,' in Daryaee, *Iranian History* pp. 243-270 (at p. 249) • **59**. Bretschneider, *Mediaeval Researches* i p. 93 • **60**. Halperin, *Golden Horde* p. 22 • **61**. For this position see Schmidt, Tarnovsky & Berkhin, *USSR* pp. 29-30; Wittfogel, *Oriental Despotism* p. 225; Gleason, *Russian History* p. 78 • **62**. Ostrowski, *Muscovy and the Mongols* is a detailed, point-by-point (and convincing) refutation of the 'Mongol yoke' in every facet of Russian life. • **63**. Charles J. Halperin, 'George Vernadsky, Eurasianism, the Mongols and Russia,' *Slavic Review* 41 (1982) pp. 477-493; Halperin, *Golden Horde* • **64**. David B. Miller, 'Monumental Building as an Indicator of Economic Trends in Northern Rus' in the late Kievan and Mongol Periods 1138–1462,' *American Historical Review* 94 (1989) pp. 360-390 • **65**. Ostrowski, *Muscovy and the Mongols* pp. 64-68 • **66**. Dawson, *Mongol Mission* p. 18; Jackson & Morgan, *Rubruck* pp. 90-91; Latham, *Travels of Marco Polo* p. 98; Yule, *Ser Marco Polo* i p. 252 • **67**. Halperin, *Golden Horde* p. 116 • **68**. Ostrowski, *Muscovy and the Mongols* pp. 7, 63; Vernadsky, *Mongols and Russia* pp. 364-366 • **69**. Gumilev, *Imaginary Kingdom* pp. 222-223; Khazanov, *Nomads and the Outside World* pp. 152-164 • **70**. Barthold, *Four Studies* i p. 43 • **71**. Yule & Cordier, *Cathay* ii pp. 287-291; iii pp. 137-173 • **72**. Ciocîltan, *Black Sea Trade* pp. 2, 20-21 • **73**. Hamby, *Central Asia* p. 123 • **74**. Abu-Lughod, *Before European Hegemony* pp. 153-184; Adshead, *Central Asia* pp. 3-5, 26-27, 53; Gary Seaman, 'World Systems and State Formation on the Inner Eurasian Periphery,' in Seaman & Marks, *Rulers from the Steppe* pp. 1-20; Ruotsala, *Europeans and Mongols* • **75**. Asimov & Bosworth, *History of Civilizations*, iv part 2 pp. 221-226 • **76**. ibid. pp. 389-394, 451-453 • **77**. H. Franke, 'Sino-Western Contacts under the Mongol Empire,' *Journal of the Royal Asiatic Society* 6 (1966) pp. 59-71; Heissig & Müller, *Mongolen* pp. 54-57 • **78**. Pegolotti, *Pratica della mercatura* p. 22 • **79**. Larner, *Marco Polo* p. 28; Reichert, *Begegnungen mit China* pp. 83-84; Jackson, *Mongols in the West* pp. 309-310 • **80**. Hodong

Kim, 'The Unity of the Mongol Empire and Continental Exchanges over Eurasia,' *Journal of Central Eurasian Studies* 1 (2009) pp. 15-42 (at p. 16) • **81**. For John of Montecorvino see Yule, *Cathay* i pp. 165-173, 197-221; Beazley, *Dawn of Modern Geography* iii pp. 162-178, 206-210 • **82**. Denise Aigle, 'De la "non negotiation" à l'alliance aboutie: Réflexions sur la diplomatie entre les Mongols et l'Occident latin,' *Oriente Moderno* 88 (2008) pp. 395-434 • **83**. Abu-Lughod, *World System* p. 18 • **84**. RT iii pp. 565-566, 605-606; Ricci, *Marco Polo* pp. 16-17; Yule, *Cathay* iii p. 49; J. Richard, *Papauté et les missions* pp. 145-146; Abu-Lughod, *World System* pp. 185-211 • **85**. Thomas T. Allsen, 'Mongolian Princes and their Merchant Partners, 1200–1260,' *Asia Major*, 3rd series 2 (1989) pp. 83-126 • **86**. McNeill, *Plagues and Peoples* pp. 93, 102-120, 134, 140-147 • **87**. Owen Lattimore, 'Feudalism in History,' *Past and Present* 12 (1957) pp. 47-57 • **88**. Rachewiltz, *Papal Envoys* p. 65. For criticisms of 'nomadic feudalism' and indeed the Mongol system as in any way feudal see Bold, *Nomadic Society* pp. 21-24; Khazanov, *Nomads and the Outside World* pp. 132, 135, 139, 144, 159, 255 • **89**. Rachewiltz, *Papal Envoys* pp. 66-67; Vernadsky, *Mongols and Russia* pp. 118, 213, 339-341 • **90**. Lattimore, *Inner Asian Frontiers* pp. 61-65, 361-365 • **91**. Anderson, *Passages from Antiquity* p. 223 • **92**. Vernadsky, *Mongols and Russia* pp. 130-131 • **93**. Lattimore, *Inner Asian Frontiers* pp. 519-523 • **94**. Fletcher, 'The Mongols' p. 50 • **95**. See the outstanding analysis by Anderson, *Passages from Antiquity* pp. 218-225 • **96**. Almaz Khan, 'Chinggis Khan from Imperial Ancestor to Ethnic Hero,' in Harrell, *Cultural Encounters* pp. 248-277; P. L. W. Sabloff, 'Genghis Khan, Father of Mongolian Democracy,' in Sabloff, *Modern Mongolia* pp. 225-251 • **97**. In his play *Axël* (1890). See Bourre, *Villiers de L'Isle-Adam* • **98**. Armstrong et al, *Francis of Assisi: Early Documents*

Appendix 1

1. SHO pp. 93, 197-199; SHR pp. 43, 139-141 • **2**. A. Mostaert, 'À propos d'une prière au feu,' in Poppe, *American Studies in Altaic Linguistics* pp. 191-223; Heissig, *Religions of Mongolia* pp. 48-59 • **3**. E. Lot-Falck, 'À propos d'Atugan, déesse mongole de la terre,' *Revue de l'Histoire des Religions* 149 (1956) pp. 157-196; Yule & Cordier, *Marco Polo* i pp. 257-259; Heissig, *Religions* pp. 7, 76-84 • **4**. N. Poppe, 'Zum Feuerkultus bei den Mongolen,' *Asia Minor* 2 (1925) pp. 130-145 (at p. 141) • **5**. Rachewiltz, *Commentary* pp. 329-331; Heissig, *Religions* pp. 84-90 • **6**. Moule & Pelliot, *Marco Polo* i pp. 199-200; Baldick, *Animal and Shaman* pp. 95, 104, 108 • **7**. P. Pelliot, 'Notes sur le "Turkestan",' *T'oung Pao* 26 (1929) pp. 113-182 (at p. 133); Yule & Cordier, *Marco Polo* i p. 257; Moule & Pelliot, *Marco Polo* p. 257; Heissig, *Religions* pp. 102-110 • **8**. Moule & Pelliot, *Marco Polo* i p. 170 • **9**. Heissig, *Religions* pp. 6-7, 46 • **10**. Dawson, *Mongol Mission* p. 7 • **11**. Heissig, *Religions* p. 35 • **12**. Hutton, *Shamans* pp. 47-49;

Caroline Humphrey, 'Shamanic Practices and the State in Northern Asia,' in Thomas & Humphrey, *Shamanism* pp. 191-228 (at p. 208); Humphrey & Onon, *Shamans and Elders* p. 51 • **13**. Humphrey, 'Shamanic Practices,' loc. cit. pp. 199-200 • **14**. Dawson, *Mongol Mission* p. 12; Jackson & Morgan, *Rubruck* p. 72; Jean-Paul Roux, 'Tângri: Essai sur le ciel-dieu des peuples altaïques,' *Revue de l'Histoire des Religions* 149 (1956) pp. 49-82, 197-230; 150 (1956) pp. 27-54, 173-212 • **15**. Jean-Paul Roux, 'La tolérance réligieuse dans les empires turco-mongols,' *Revue de l'Histoire des Religions* 203 (1986) pp. 131-168 (at p. 164) • **16**. Caroline Humphrey, 'Theories of North Asian Shamanism,' in Gellner, *Soviet and Western Anthropology* pp. 242-252 • **17**. Vitebsky, *Shaman* p. 74 • **18**. ibid. pp. 56-73, 94-95 • **19**. Heissig, *Religions* pp. 17-19 • **20**. Vitebsky, *Shaman* pp. 25, 54-55, 81; Andrew Neher, 'A Physiological Explanation of Unusual Behavior in Ceremonies Involving Drums,' *Human Biology* 34 (1962) pp. 151-160 • **21**. Vitebsky, *Shaman* p. 22 • **22**. Hutton, *Shamans* p. 107; Heissig, *Religions* p. 20 • **23**. For the congruence of Mongol and Persian theology and theogony see Gumilev, *Imaginary Kingdom* pp. 267-269 • **24**. Jagchid & Hyer, *Mongolia's Culture* pp. 163-167 • **25**. Asimov & Bosworth, *History of Civilizations* iv part 2 pp. 65-66 • **26**. Heissig, *Religions* p. 7; Vitebsky, *Shaman* p. 135; Piers Vitebsky, 'Some Medieval European Views of Mongolian Shamanism,' *Journal of the Anglo-Mongolian Society* 1 (1974) pp. 24-42. See also Foltz, *Religions of the Silk Road*

Appendix 2

1. Denis Sinor claims that the title 'gur-khan' was much like Franco's 'Caudillo' and Hitler's 'Führer': 'The Khitans and the Kara Khitans,' in Asimov & Bosworth, *History of Civilizations* iv part 1 pp. 227-242 (at p. 235). • **2**. JB i pp. 354-361 • **3**. For the people who conquered the Qara-Khanids see E. A. Davidovich, 'The Karakhanids,' in Asimov & Bosworth, *History of Civilizations*, iv part 1 pp. 119-144; Peter B. Golden, 'The Karakhanids and Early Islam,' in Sinor, *Early Inner Asia* pp. 343-370 • **4**. Hill, *Jade Gate to Rome* • **5**. For the vassal status see Beckwith, *Empires of the Silk Road* pp. 148-159; Stein, *Ancient Khotan* pp. 123-133 • **6**. Grousset, *Empire* pp. 159-167; Golden, *Turkic Peoples*; Tetley, *Ghaznavid and Seljuk Turks* • **7**. Biran, *Qara Khitai* pp. 41-44 • **8**. ibid. pp. 146-160 for full details on all aspects of the Qara Khitai army • **9**. For Prester John see Beckingham & Hamilton, *Prester John*; Silverberg, *Realm of Prester John*; Hawting, *Muslims, Mongols and Crusaders*; Charles E. Nowell, 'The Historical Prester John,' *Speculum* 28 (1953) pp. 435-445 • **10**. Bretschneider, *Mediaeval Researches* i pp. 208-235 • **11**. For another view of Yelu see Thiebaud, *Personnages marquants* • **12**. For Almaliq see Yule, *Cathay and the Way Thither* ii pp. 288, 321, 388; Bretschneider, *Mediaeval Researches* i p. 224; ii p. 33 • **13**. Biran, *Qara*

Khitai pp. 133-135 • **14**. ibid. p. 136 • **15**. ibid. pp. 93-131, 146-147 • **16**. P. D. Buell, 'Sino-Khitan Administration in Mongol Bukhara,' *Journal of Asiatic History* 13 (1979) pp. 121-151; D. O. Morgan, 'Who Ran the Mongol Empire?' *Journal of the Royal Asiatic Society* (1982) pp. 124-136. • **17**. György Kara, 'On the Khitans' Writing System,' *Mongolian Studies* 10 (1987) pp. 19-24; Daniels & Bright, *Writing Systems* pp. 230-235 • **18**. Denis Sinor, 'Central Eurasia,' in Sinor, *Orientalism and History* pp. 82-103 (at p. 84); Hambis, *Haute Asie* p. 56; Spuler, *Goldene Horde* p. 346; C. E. Bosworth, 'The Political and Dynastic History of the Iranian World, AD 1000–1217,' in Boyle, *Cambridge History of Iran* v pp. 1-203 (at pp. 147-148); Lieu, *Manichaeism in Central Asia* pp. 126-176 • **19**. Jennifer Holmgren, 'Imperial Marriage in the Native Chinese and Non-Han State, Han to Ming,' in Watson & Ebrey, *Marriage and Inequality* pp. 58-96 (at pp. 81-82); Biran, *Qara Khitai*, pp. 160-168 • **20**. Pelliot, *Notes sur Marco Polo* i pp. 216-229; Barthold, *Four Studies* i pp. 27-29, 100-110 • **21**. Wittfogel & Feng, *Liao* p. 665 • **22**. Biran, *Qara Khitai* p. 84 • **23**. JB ii p. 360 • **24**. Biran, *Qara Khitai* pp. 84-85 • **25**. Soucek, *Inner Asia* pp. 99-100 • **26**. Bartold, *Turkestan* pp. 324-327; Barthold, *Four Studies* i p. 29; Herbert Franke, 'The Forest Peoples,' in Sinor, *Early Inner Asia* pp. 400-423 (at p. 410) • **27**. Grousset, *Empire* p. 160 • **28**. Barthold, *Turkestan* p. 339 • **29**. Hartmann, *An-Nasir li-Din Allah* pp. 70-78; Hanne, *Putting the Caliph* • **30**. Barthold, *Turkestan* pp. 348-349; Boyle, *Cambridge History of Iran* v p. 167 • **31**. C. E. Bosworth, 'The Political and Dynastic History of the Iranian World, AD 1000–1217,' in Boyle, *Cambridge History of Iran* v pp. 1-203 (at pp. 182-191) • **32**. JB i p. 314 • **33**. Bosworth, 'Ghurids' in Bernard Lewis, ed., *Encyclopedia of Islam* (1991) ii p. 100 • **34**. Biran, *Qara Khitai* pp. 65-66 • **35**. Budge, *Chronography* i p. 351 • **36**. Biran, *Qara Khitai* pp. 69-70 • **37**. For full details on Muhammad's early career see JR i pp. 254-267; JB i pp. 316-321 • **38**. JB ii pp. 325, 357, 390 • **39**. Luniya, *Life and Culture* p. 293; Biran, *Qara Khitai* p. 70 • **40**. JB i pp. 329-331; Bosworth in *Cambridge History of Iran* v. pp. 1-202 (at pp. 164-165) • **41**. JB ii pp. 341-352, 358-361; Barthold, *Turkestan* pp. 355-361 • **42**. Biran, *Qara Khitai* p. 72 • **43**. JB ii p. 352 • **44**. JB i pp. 336-339 • **45**. JB i pp. 65, 74 • **46**. Barthold, *Turkestan* p. 362 • **47**. Biran, *Qara Khitai* p. 73 • **48**. JB ii pp. 357-358 • **49**. RT i p. 68

Index